Databases
Illuminated

Catherine M. Ricardo
Iona College

JONES AND BARTLETT PUBLISHERS
Sudbury, Massachusetts
BOSTON   TORONTO   LONDON   SINGAPORE

World Headquarters

Jones and Bartlett Publishers
40 Tall Pine Drive
Sudbury, MA 01776
978-443-5000
info@jbpub.com
www.jbpub.com

Jones and Bartlett Publishers International
Barb House, Barb Mews
London W6 7PA
UK

Jones and Bartlett Publishers Canada
2406 Nikanna Road
Mississauga, ON L5C 2W6
CANADA

Library of Congress Cataloging-in-Publication Data
Ricardo, Catherine M.
Databases illuminated / Catherine M. Ricardo.
     p. cm.
ISBN 0-7637-3314-8 (Hardcover)
1. Database management. I. Title.
  QA76.9.D3R514 2004

                       2003023650

Production Credits
Acquisitions Editor: Stephen Solomon
Production Manager: Amy Rose
Senior Production Editor: Linda S. DeBruyn
Associate Production Editor: Karen C. Ferreira
Editorial Assistant: Caroline Senay
Marketing Manager: Matthew Bennett
Manufacturing Buyer: Therese Bräuer
Composition: Shepherd Incorporated
Cover Design: Anne Spencer
Illustration: George Nichols
Printing and Binding: Malloy, Inc.
Cover Printing: Malloy, Inc.

Printed in the United States of America
08 07 06 05 04   10 9 8 7 6 5 4 3 2 1

To my husband, Henry, and to Henry, Jr., Marta, Cathy, Christine, Tomás, and Nicholas.

Contents

4.   The Relational Model   168

7.   The Enhanced Entity-Relationship Model and the Object-Relational Model   373

8.   The Object-Oriented Model   431

14.   Social and Ethical Issues   673

15.   Data Warehouses and Data Mining   732

Preface

Purpose of This Book

The study of database systems, design, and management is an essential part of the education of computer science and information science students. A database course should provide a strong theoretical background, practice in database design, and the experience of creating and developing a working database. Having taught database courses for over twenty years, I have used many different textbooks and have found that some concentrate on theory and all but ignore implementation, while others present a wealth of detail about particular database management systems, but fall short on theory. This book is designed to help students integrate theoretical material with practical knowledge, using an approach that has a firm theoretical basis applied to practical database implementation.

Structure

Theoretical foundations are presented early and the concepts are used repeatedly throughout the book, including the chapters that deal with implementation. Logical database design is given full consideration. The entity-relationship model is introduced early and then mapped to the relational model. Relational normalization is studied in detail, and many examples of the normalization process are discussed. The enhanced entity-relationship model is presented, and mapped to both relational and object-relational models. The object-oriented model is presented using UML as a vehicle for logical design. XML and the semi-structured data model are introduced in Chapter 13. A continuing example of a university database is incorporated throughout the text, to illustrate concepts and techniques and to provide both continuity and contrast. Other examples are presented as needed. Purely relational, object-relational, and object-oriented database systems are described and used for implementation of the examples. Details of database management systems are described so that students can learn the specifics of these real-life systems, down to the physical implementation level. Microsoft Access™ is used initially in the examples, but Oracle™ is introduced as the material is developed. However, the examples are suitable for use with any relational or object-relational DBMS.

Purpose of the Sample Project and Student Projects

The various approaches are integrated in a sample project that is a unique feature of this book. Starting at the end of the first chapter, students see a sample project that is developed as the book progresses. This project is independent of the examples that are presented in the chapter text or in exercises. The design begins with a description of the application, a database needed by an art gallery. At the end of the first chapter, students see how the information needs are specified. After the students study planning techniques in Chapter 2, they see how to create a complete user-oriented data dictionary and how other planning tools could be used. When they learn about logical models, they see the step-by-step development of an E-R diagram at the end of Chapter 3. They see the steps involved in mapping the diagram to the relational model after Chapter 4, and normalizing the model after Chapter 5. Complete details of creating and manipulating a purely relational Oracle™ database using SQL are presented for the relational model after Chapter 6. The E-R diagram is expanded to a complete EE-R diagram and mapped to an object-relational database in Chapter 7, using the object-relational features of Oracle. The EE-R diagram is then transformed into a UML diagram in Chapter 8, which also includes the design and creation of an object-oriented database using ODL. The sample project is extended in Chapter 12 to show a distributed design that might be used in a client-server environment or a true distributed environment. Details of creating a simple website for the art gallery are provided in Chapter 13. Thus, every important technique of planning, design, and implementation is illustrated using real-life systems. The sample project section is always followed by continuing student projects, which require students to emulate the steps of the sample. From my experiences assigning similar projects while teaching database courses, I have found that students learn most effectively by creating a working database and developing their own continuing projects to incorporate new concepts, and that they benefit by seeing samples as they progress. Such realistic experiences provide insights that no amount of lecturing can produce. Later chapters deal with topics of database security, concurrency control, recovery techniques, query optimization, distributed databases, social and ethical issues, and data warehouses. Appendices cover physical data organization, the network model, and the hierarchical model, and can be found at: http://www.jbpub.com/catalog/9780763733148.

Learning Features

The writing style is conversational. Each chapter begins with a statement of learning objectives. Examples and applications are presented throughout the text. Illustrations are used both to clarify the material and to vary the presentation. Exercises, including lab exercises where appropriate, appear at the end of each chapter, with solutions provided in the Instructor's Guide. The sample project at the end of each chapter is an important part of the text, providing an application of the material just presented. The student projects that follow the sample are introduced in the first chapter, and students are expected to choose one, or have one assigned, and to develop that project to parallel the sample as they progress. Student projects may be done individually or in a group. Access™ and Oracle™ implementations of the example databases used in the text, and of the sample project, are available on the book's website; the student projects, since they are intended to be used as assignments, are not included. Resources for student laboratory exercises are also available on the website. Chapter summaries are included in the text to provide a rapid review or preview of the material and to help students understand the relative importance of the concepts presented. The Instructor's Guide contains PowerPoint™ presentations for each chapter, copies of figures, full statements of objectives for each chapter, alternative student projects, quizzes, chapter tests, comprehensive examinations for multiple chapters, and solutions to exercises.

Audience

The material is suitable for junior or senior computer science majors or information science majors with a good technical background. Students should have completed at least one year of programming, including data structures. The book could also be used as an introductory database text for graduate students or for self study.

Mapping to Curriculum Guidelines

Although this book was planned based on the author's experiences, it fits the ACM-IEEE curriculum guidelines well. CC2001 provides a model database course, CS270T, for the topic-based curriculum. The course includes three areas, Human-Computer Interaction (HCI), Information Management (IM), and Social and Professional Issues (SP). The units included in CS270T are listed below, along with the corresponding chapters in the book.

IM1 Information models and systems (3 core hours)—Chapters 1, 2

IM2 Database systems (3 core hours)—Chapter 2

IM3 Data modeling (4 core hours)—Sections 2.7, 13.4; Chapters 3, 4, 7, 8, Appendices B, C

IM4 Relational databases (5 hours)—Chapter 4

IM5 Database query languages (4 hours)—Sections 4.6, 7.7, 8.5; Chapters 6, 11, 13; Appendices B, C

IM6 Relational database design (4 hours)—Chapter 5

IM7 Transaction processing (3 hours)—Chapter 10

IM8 Distributed databases (3 hours)—Chapters 12, 13

IM9 Physical database design (3 hours)—Appendix A

HCI Foundations of human-computer interaction (2 core hours)—Chapter 14

SP6 Intellectual property (3 core hours)—Chapter 14

SP7 Privacy and civil liberties (2 core hours)—Chapters 9, 14

Elective topics (1 hour)—Chapter 15

The sample project and student projects also provide practice in data modeling, database design, human-computer interaction, relational databases, database query languages, distributed databases, and physical database design. Some aspects of privacy and civil liberties are discussed in the sample project, and similar issues will arise and should be treated in the student projects.

Acknowledgments

Many people have offered useful comments, advice, and encouragement during the writing of this book. Students and colleagues throughout the world who used my previous book, *Database Systems: Principles, Design, and Implementation,* have provided comments that have helped shape this book. Students in both undergraduate and graduate classes at Iona College have helped by providing feedback during class testing of the first draft of the manuscript. Ted Leibfried was instrumental in helping me get the project off the ground, and arranging for the class testing of the first draft at his institution, the University of Houston at Clearlake. I am very grateful for his insight and generous help. My colleagues at Iona, especially my chairperson, Bob Schiaffino, have been supportive throughout the process of developing this book. I am grateful to the college for awarding me a sabbatical leave last year so that I could work on this project.

I wish to thank Ayad Boudiab, Georgia Perimeter College; Jeffery Peden, Longwood University; Reggie Haseltine, University of Maryland; Jim Patus, Ivy Tech State College; and Marcus Schaefer, DePaul University, who reviewed the first draft and who made helpful suggestions that greatly improved the final manuscript. For his encouragement and support for this project, I am grateful to Michael Stranz, former Editor in Chief at Jones & Bartlett. I would like to thank the editorial and production staff at Jones and Bartlett, especially Caroline Senay and Karen Ferreira. I am very grateful to my editor, Stephen Solomon, for his guidance and support.

Finally I would like to thank my family, especially my husband, Henry, for his love, patience, and understanding and for his active help in critiquing and proofreading the manuscript.

CHAPTER 1

Introductory Database Concepts

Chapter Objectives

In this chapter you will learn:

- How databases are used in everyday life

- The major functions of a database management system

- Advantages of using an integrated database system

- Disadvantages of databases

- Roles in the integrated database environment

- The history of information systems

1.1   Databases in Everyday Life

Today, databases are so widely used that they can be found in organizations of all sizes, ranging from large corporations and government agencies to small businesses and even homes. Everyday activities often bring you into contact with databases, either directly or indirectly.

- When you visit a **consumer Web site** that allows online browsing and ordering of goods such as books or clothing, you are accessing a database. The information about available products and the data about your order are stored in a database. You may also be able to view stored data about previous orders you have placed. Some Web sites may use information about your orders, or even your browsing activities, to suggest products or services that are likely to interest you.

- When you visit an interactive **customer service** Web site, such as the home page of a utility company or a health insurer, you are able to access information about your own records of services or products provided. You may be able to update database entries with personal information such as your address or telephone number. Some customer service Web sites allow you to make changes to the services you subscribe to. For example, your telephone services provider or electric company may allow you to change plans online.

- If you use **online banking,** you can retrieve database records about deposits, withdrawals, bill payments, and other transactions for your accounts. You can transfer funds, order checks, and perform many other functions, all of which involve using a database.

- When you use a **credit card,** the salesperson usually waits for computer approval of your purchase before presenting you with a receipt for your signature. The approval process consults a database to verify that your card has not been lost or stolen and to find your credit limit, current balance, and amount of purchases already approved. The database is automatically updated to reflect the new approved amount. For a debit card, your bank's database is consulted to verify your account number, your PIN, your current balance, and your adjusted balance prior to approval of the purchase. The purchase amount is automatically deducted from your account as the transaction is completed.

- When you buy goods in a **supermarket** or **retail store,** scanners are used to read universal product codes or other identifiers of merchandise. Using the scanned code, the database system can identify the exact item and produce a receipt with the name of the item and its price, taking into account any special sale price. The system may also provide input for an **inventory control** system, so that the inventory record for each item can be updated to reflect the sale. If the inventory falls below a level called the reorder point, the computer can automatically place an order to replenish the stock.

- When you make travel plans, you can access an **airline reservations system** in which a database is used to keep track of scheduled flights and passenger reservations. Since several travelers may request reservations simultaneously, the system must be able to handle requests quickly, resolving conflicts and accepting requests until the maximum number of seats is reached. Many hotel chains and rental car companies also have centralized reservation systems to accept reservations for any of their locations, using an integrated database system.

- If you visit a doctor, you may find that your **medical records** and **billing data** are kept in a database. When you have a prescription filled, your pharmacist will probably use a database to record information about the prescription, check for interactions with drugs you are currently using, and print the label and receipt. Both the doctor and the pharmacist may use their databases to do third-party billing, automatically verifying your coverage and submitting insurance claims for covered expenditures, while you pay only your co-payment. All health providers in the United States are required to protect your privacy during these transactions, in accordance with the Health Insurance Portability Accountability Act (HIPAA) privacy legislation.

- Your **employment records** might be kept in a database that stores basic information such as your name, address, employee ID, job assignments, and performance evaluations. Your payroll is probably produced using a database that stores information about each pay period and data about the year's gross pay, tax deductions, and taxes withheld, among other things. Your pay stub reflects this data each payday.

- Your **school records** are probably kept in a database that is updated each term to record your registration in, completion of, and grade for each class.

- To do research, you can use a **bibliographic database** in which you enter keywords that describe the subject of interest. You may get back results that contain hypertext, allowing you to retrieve abstracts or entire articles of interest in your subject area.

As this short overview of activities demonstrates, databases are used to satisfy the information needs of many organizations and individuals in a variety of areas. However, a poorly designed database fails to provide the required information or provides outdated, flawed, or contradictory information. In order to maximize their potential benefits, it is important to understand the theoretical foundations, internal structure, design, and management of databases.

1.2　A Sample Database

Consider a simple database that records information about university students, the classes they take during one semester, and the professors who teach the classes. The information kept for each student includes the student's ID, name, major, and total number of credits earned. Using **Microsoft Access** for this example, we have a **table** for this data as shown in Figure 1.1(a). The `Student` table has five columns, named `stuId`, `lastName`, `firstName`, `major`, and `credits`. Each row of the table shows the student ID, last name, first name, major, and number of credits for one student. The values of these items for each student are placed in the columns with the corresponding names. The `Faculty` table has columns named `facId`, `name`, `department`, and `rank`, as shown in Figure 1.1(b). Each row of that table gives the faculty ID, last name, department, and rank of one faculty member. Class information kept for each class offered includes the class number, the faculty ID of the professor, the schedule, and the room, in appropriate columns as shown in the `Class` table in Figure 1.1(c). These three tables alone do not allow us to determine which classes a student is taking. To represent the fact that a student is enrolled in a particular class, we need another table, which we call `Enroll`, pictured in Figure 1.1(d). The columns of `Enroll` are `stuId`, `classNumber`, and `grade`. Notice that the Enroll table represents the **relationship** between `Student` and `Class`, telling us which rows of these tables are related (i.e., which students take which classes). For example, the first row, with values S1001, ART103A, tells us that the student whose ID is S1001 is enrolled in the class whose class number is ART103A. The last column of the row tells us the grade each student earned in each class. Since these represent current enrollments, we will assume that the grade is the mid-term grade. At the end of the semester, it can be changed to the final grade. Note that we did not put student names as well as the IDs in this table, because they are already in the

Student				
stuId	lastName	firstName	major	credits
S1001	Smith	Tom	History	90
S1002	Chin	Ann	Math	36
S1005	Lee	Perry	History	3
S1010	Burns	Edward	Art	63
S1013	McCarthy	Owen	Math	0
S1015	Jones	Mary	Math	42
S1020	Rivera	Jane	CSC	15

FIGURE 1.1(a)
The Student Table

Faculty			
facId	name	department	rank
F101	Adams	Art	Professor
F105	Tanaka	CSC	Instructor
F110	Byrne	Math	Assistant
F115	Smith	History	Associate
F221	Smith	CSC	Professor

FIGURE 1.1(b)
The Faculty Table

Class			
classNumber	facId	schedule	room
ART103A	F101	MWF9	H221
CSC201A	F105	TuThF10	M110
CSC203A	F105	MThF12	M110
HST205A	F115	MWF11	H221
MTH101B	F110	MTuTh9	H225
MTH103C	F110	MWF11	H225

FIGURE 1.1(c)
The Class Table

FIGURE 1.1(d)

The Enroll Table

	Enroll	
stuId	**classNumber**	**grade**
S1001	ART103A	A
S1001	HST205A	C
S1002	ART103A	D
S1002	CSC201A	F
S1002	MTH103C	B
S1010	ART103A	
S1010	MTH103C	
S1020	CSC201A	B
S1020	MTH101B	A

Student table, and we want to avoid the redundancy and possible inconsistency that storing the names twice would cause. The tables shown were created using Access, and we can use Access to update them, to ask questions (queries) about the data in them, to create reports about the data, and to do many other functions. As an example of a query, suppose we want the names of all students enrolled in ART103A. First, how do we find the answer to the question visually? Looking at the database, we see that the Enroll table tells us which students are enrolled in ART103A. However, it gives us the stuId of each student, not the name. Student names appear on the Student table. One plan for answering the question is to look at the Enroll table and find all the rows where the value of classNumber is ART103 and make note of the stuId values in those rows, namely, S1001, S1002, and S1010. Then we look at the Student table and find the rows containing those values in the stuId column. We find the answer to the question by listing the lastName and firstName values in those rows, giving us Smith Tom, Chin Ann, and Burns Edward. Access provides a **query tool** that allows us to check off which columns are included in a query and to specify conditions for the records in the results. Figure 1.2 shows the results of executing the preceding query using this tool. We can also use the **reporting tool** in Access to generate a variety of reports. Figure 1.3 shows a typical report called Class Lists that shows each class number, the ID and name of the faculty member teaching the class, and the IDs and names of all the students in that class.

Query1	
lastName	firstName
Smith	Tom
Chin	Ann
Burns	Edward

FIGURE 1.2

Results of the Query: "Find names of all students enrolled in ART103A"

Class Lists					
classNumber	facId	name	stuId	lastName	firstName
ART103A	F101	Adams	S1001	Smith	Tom
			S1002	Chin	Ann
			S1010	Burns	Edward
CSC201A	F105	Tanaka	S1002	Chin	Ann
			S1020	Rivera	Jane
HST205A	F115	Smith	S1001	Smith	Tom
MTH101B	F110	Byrne	S1020	Rivera	Jane
MTH103C	F110	Byrne	S1002	Chin	Ann
			S1010	Burns	Edward

FIGURE 1.3

Class Lists Report

1.3 The Integrated Database Environment

An **integrated database environment** has a single large repository of data, called the database, which is used simultaneously by many departments and users in an organization. All data needed by the organization for a specific group of applications or even for all of its applications is stored together, with as little repetition as possible. (Note: Although the word *data* is plural in standard English, it is customary to use it as both singular and plural in database literature, as in "data is" and "data are.") Several different types of records may appear in the database. The logical connections between the data items and records are also stored in the database, so that the system "knows," for example, which faculty record is connected to a particular class record. The database is not owned by a single department, but is a shared resource. In a large organization, the database is managed by a **database administrator** (DBA), who is responsible for creating and maintaining the database to satisfy the needs of users. All access to the database is controlled by a sophisticated software package called the **Database Management System** (DBMS). This package has programs that set up the original storage structures, load the data, accept data requests from programs and users, format retrieved data so that it appears in the form the program or user expects, hide data that a particular user should not have access to, accept and perform updates, allow concurrent use of the data without having users interfere with each other, and perform backup and recovery procedures automatically. These are just some of the many functions of the database management system.

Figure 1.4 illustrates an integrated database environment. Here, all the data about students, classes, faculty, and enrollments is stored in a single database. The data is integrated, so that the data items are stored in compatible formats and logical connections between them are also stored. The database contains a description of its own structure so the DBMS "knows" what data items exist and how they are structured or grouped. It is shared by many users, usually concurrently. All access to the data is through the DBMS. The applications programs, which might be written in different programming languages, go through the DBMS, which can present data in the form each program expects. Only the DBMS is aware of the storage structures used in the database. In addition to providing support for applications, the DBMS provides a user interface for interactive queries. Authorized users can question the database directly, using the query language of the particular DBMS.

1.4   Roles in the Integrated Database Environment

Many individuals or groups are involved in the operations of a database system. They play different roles, depending on the way they interact with the database, as depicted in Figure 1.5.

- End Users
  The database is designed, created, and maintained to serve the information needs of **end users,** people who use the data to perform their jobs. Regardless of the elegance of the database design or the sophistication of the hardware and software used, if the database does not provide adequate information to users, it is a failure. Ultimately, it is the users who judge the success of the system. Users can be categorized according to the way they access data. Sophisticated users (also called **casual users**) are trained in the use of the interactive query language, and access data by enter-

DATABASE   DBMS   APPLICATION   OUTPUT

FIGURE 1.4
**The Integrated Database
Environment**

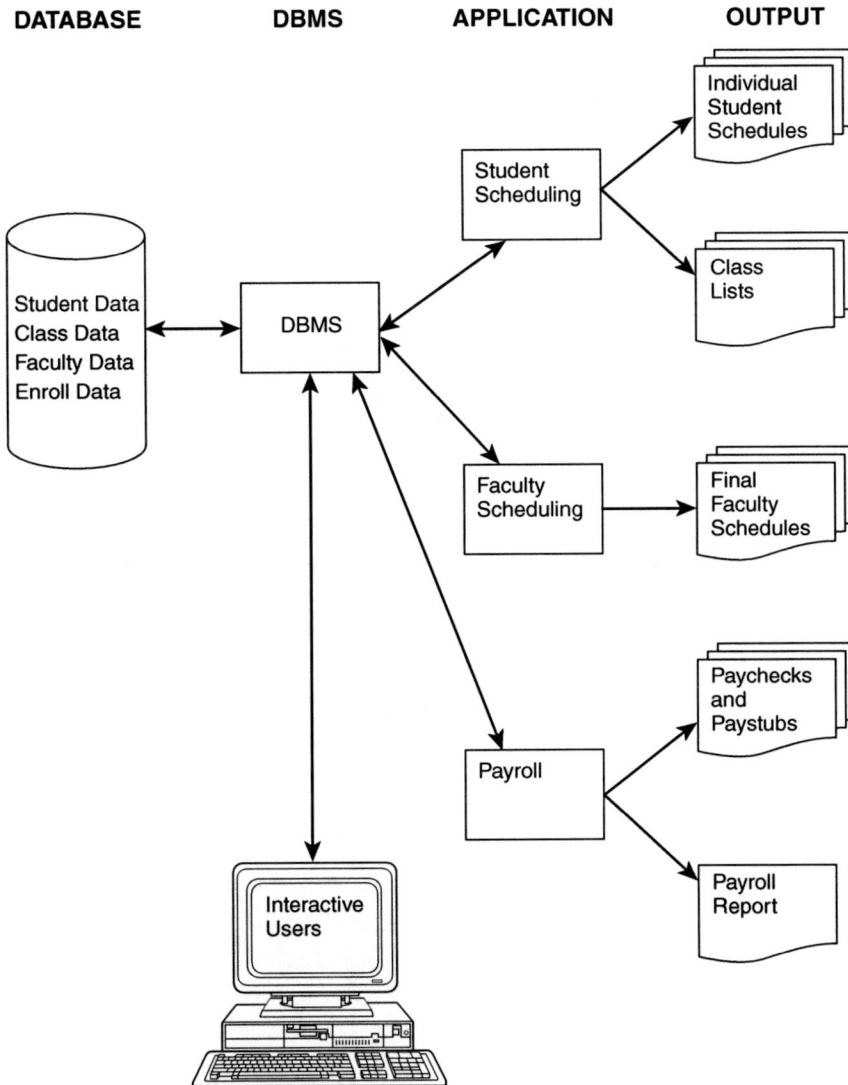

ing queries at workstations. The flexibility of the query language
allows them to perform many different operations on the database,
limited only by the view they have been assigned and their authorizations. Casual users may perform retrieval, insertion, deletion,
or update operations through the query language, provided they
are authorized to do so. **Naive users** do not use the interactive
query language, but access data through application programs that
have been written for them. They invoke the programs by entering
simple commands or choosing options from a menu. They do not

FIGURE 1.5

Roles in the Database Environment

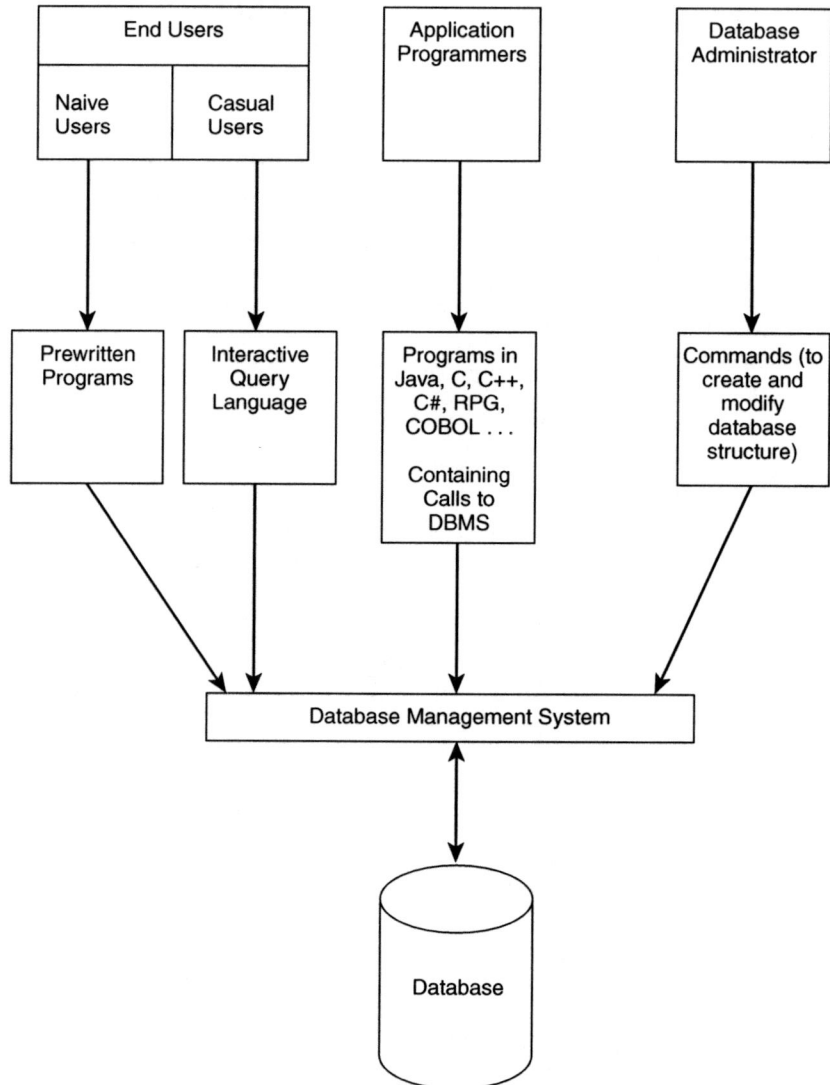

need to know any details of the structure or language of the database system. They interact with the system in a less sophisticated way, restricting their access to operations performed by the programs. The programs themselves may perform update or retrieval operations. An even larger group of **secondary users** may use the information in the database, without interacting directly with it, by receiving output that they use in their work.

For example, in a university Registrar's Office, clerks may be naive users, while the registrar may be a casual user. The clerks perform simple, repetitive tasks such as printing out student transcripts. They may enter the name of the transaction, TRANSCRIPT, or choose an option such as PRINT OUT TRANSCRIPT from a menu. The TRANSCRIPT program would prompt the clerk for the student ID or other identifying information, and complete its task without further instructions from the clerk. The registrar uses the query language to ask one-of-a-kind questions such as, "How many students are registered for six or more classes this semester?" If there is no pre-written program in the DBMS system to answer this question, the registrar writes statements in the query language of that particular database. The students who receive printed transcripts, and the professors who receive class rosters, are secondary users.

- Applications Programmers
  This group includes programmers who write batch, or interactive, applications for other users. Their application programs may be written in a variety of host programming languages such as Java, C, C++, C#, Visual BASIC, RPG, or COBOL. Each program that accesses the database contains statements that call the database management system to perform updates or retrievals on the database. Some sophisticated end users who have both the knowledge of the programming language, and who have permission to do so, are able to write applications for their own use.

- Database Administrator
  The database administrator is the individual or group responsible for designing, creating the structure of, and maintaining the database. In many cases the database is designed by a specialist, and the DBA takes over responsibility once the design is complete. The database designer begins the design process by interviewing users to determine their data needs. He or she examines the current system, analyzes the organization and its information needs, and develops a tentative model for the database. The model is refined and improved as the designer, in consultation with users, becomes more aware of their data needs and learns more about the functioning of the organization. When a satisfactory design is developed, the DBA implements it. Once again, users are consulted to determine whether the operational system is adequate. The design, refinement, and redesign of the system are all team efforts, with the designer, DBA, and users working together to develop the best data resource for the entire organization. The DBA interacts

with the operational database as a "superuser," one who controls and accesses information about the structure and use of the database itself, as opposed to end users, who access the data within the database. Chapter 2 contains a more detailed description of the functions of the database administrator.

1.5   Advantages of the Integrated Database Approach

Before integrated databases were created, **file processing** systems were used, and data used by an organization's application programs was stored in separate files. Typically, a department that needed an application program worked with the organization's data processing department to create specifications for both the program and the data needed for it. Often the same data was collected and stored independently by several departments within an organization, but not shared. Each application had its own data files that were created specifically for the application, and that belonged to the department for which the application was written. The integrated database approach has several advantages:

1. Sharing of Data

   The database belongs to the entire organization. The DBA manages the data, but the data does not belong to any individual or department. Thus the organization has control over the data it needs to conduct its business. Many users can be authorized to access the same piece of information. Authorization to access the data is given by the DBA, not by another department.

2. Control of Redundancy

   When stored in a database, information is integrated so that multiple copies of the same data are not stored unless necessary. Some limited redundancy is permitted to keep logical connections among data items or to improve performance. For example, in the university example discussed in Section 1.2, the student ID appeared in both the Student table and the Enroll table. The database management system "knows about" that repetition. A database ordinarily does not have multiple copies of entire records, unlike a file system, where different departments may have duplicates of entire files.

3. Data Consistency

   One effect of eliminating or controlling redundancy is that the data is consistent. If a data item appears only once, any update to its value needs to be performed only once, and all users will have access to the same new value. If the system has some controlled redundancy, when it receives an update to an item that appears more than once it can often do cascading updates. This means it will automatically update every occurrence of that item, keeping the database consistent. For example, if we change the ID of a student in the Student table, the Enroll records for that student will be updated to show the new ID automatically.

4. Improved Data Standards
    The DBA, who is responsible for designing and maintaining the database to serve the needs of all users, defines and enforces organization-wide standards for representation of data in the database. Included in this category are rules such as the format of all data items, conventions on data names, documentation standards, frequency of updates, update procedures, frequency of backups, backup procedures, and permitted usage of the database. For example, the DBA might make a rule for addresses to be stored in a particular format. In the United States, a convention might be that two-letter abbreviations are used for state names. The database can be set up so that any other representation is rejected. In other countries, postal zones might be defined to be a certain number of characters.

5. Better Data Security
    The data in an organization's database is a valuable corporate resource that should be protected from intentional or accidental misuse. Data security is the protection of the database from unauthorized access by persons or programs that might misuse or damage the data. A database system allows security restrictions to be defined and enforced on several levels. All authorized access to the database is through the DBMS, which can require that users go through security procedures or use passwords to gain access to the database. To preclude the possibility of having a user bypass the DBMS and gain access to data in an illegal manner, the DBMS can encrypt the data before storing it. Then, when an authorized user wishes to retrieve data, it will be decrypted automatically. Data retrieved in any other way will appear in its encrypted form. Authorized users may be unaware of data encryption. Each user is provided with a view of a predefined portion of the database. For

example, in a university the Registrar's Office may have access to some faculty information such as the Faculty Table in our earlier example, but not to such items as salary. Included in the view are descriptions of the data items the user is permitted to access, and the type of access allowed, whether retrieval only, update or deletion of existing records, or insertion of new records. If a user attempts to access an item that is not included in his or her view, or attempts an unauthorized operation, the DBMS automatically records the user ID in a security log that is available to the DBA.

6. Improved Data Integrity

    Some database management systems allow the DBA to define integrity constraints—consistency rules that the database must obey. These constraints apply to items within a record (intra-record constraints), or to records that are related to one another (inter-record constraints), or they might be general business constraints. For example, in class records, there may be a rule that the number of students enrolled in a class never exceeds some maximum allowed enrollment. Another rule may be that the faculty ID in a class record must correspond to an actual faculty ID in a faculty record. The DBMS is responsible for never allowing a record insertion, deletion, or update that violates an integrity constraint.

7. Balancing of Conflicting Requirements

    Each department or individual user has data needs that may be in conflict with those of other users. The DBA is aware of the needs of all users and can make decisions about the design, use, and maintenance of the database that provide the best solutions for the organization as a whole. These decisions usually favor the most important applications, possibly at the expense of the less vital ones.

8. Faster Development of New Applications

    A well-designed database provides an accurate model of the operations of the organization. When a new application is proposed, it is likely that the data required is already stored in the database. If so, the DBMS can provide data in the form required by the program. Development time is reduced because no file creation phase is needed for the new application, as it is when file processing systems were used.

9. Better Data Accessibility

   In addition to providing data for programs, most database management systems allow interactive access by users. They provide query languages that permit users to ask ad hoc questions and to obtain the desired information.

10. Economy of Scale

    When all of the organization's data requirements are satisfied by one database instead of many separate files, the size of the combined operation provides several advantages. The portion of the budget that would ordinarily be allocated to various departments for their data design, storage, and maintenance costs can be pooled, possibly resulting in a lower total cost. The pooled resources can be used to develop a more sophisticated and powerful system than any department could afford individually, providing features not available in a file processing environment. Programmer time that would ordinarily be devoted to designing files and writing programs to access them can be spent on improving the database. Any improvement to the database benefits many users.

11. More Control over Concurrency

    If two users are permitted to access data simultaneously, and at least one of them is updating data, it is possible that they will interfere with each other. For example, if both attempt to perform updates, one update may be lost, because the second might overwrite the value recorded by the first. If the updates are meant to be cumulative, this is a serious problem. Most integrated database management systems have subsystems to control concurrency so that transactions are not lost or performed incorrectly.

12. Better Backup and Recovery Procedures

    In a database environment, the database records are normally backed up (copied) on a regular basis, perhaps nightly. A tape or other medium is used to keep the backup secure. As transactions are performed, any updates are recorded to a log of changes. If the system fails, the tape and log are used to bring the database to the state it was in just prior to the failure. The system is therefore self-recovering.

1.6   Disadvantages of the Integrated Database Approach

There are also some disadvantages to an integrated database environment, compared to a file system:

1. High Cost of DBMS

   Because a complete database management system is a very large and sophisticated piece of software, it is expensive to purchase or lease.

2. Higher Hardware Costs

   Additional memory and processing power are required to run the DBMS, resulting in the need for upgrading hardware.

3. Higher Programming Costs

   Because a DBMS is a complex tool with many features, the organization's programmers need a thorough knowledge of the system in order to use it to best advantage. Whether the organization hires experienced database programmers or retrains its own programming personnel, it is paying for this expertise.

4. High Conversion Costs

   When an organization converts to a new database system, data has to be removed from existing files and loaded into the database. Because of the different formats used in files, this may be a difficult and time-consuming process. In addition, the applications programs, which contain details about the storage and structure of the old files, must be modified to work with the DBMS.

5. Slower Processing of Some Applications

   Although an integrated database is designed to provide better information more quickly than a traditional system using separate files, some applications are slower. For example, a typical payroll file is set up in a sequence that matches the payroll program, and contains only the data needed for this application. It is designed specifically to make that application as efficient as possible. In the database, the employee records may not be stored consecutively and the normal retrieval may not be in the sequence needed by the payroll program. Therefore, this program will take longer to execute.

6. Increased Vulnerability

   Whenever resources are centralized, there is an increased security risk. Since all applications depend on the database system, the failure of any system component can bring operations to a standstill. Failure of a single applications program can have an effect on other programs that may have used incorrect data created by the failed program.

7. More Difficult Recovery

   The recovery process after a database failure is complicated because many transactions could have been in progress when the system failed. As part of its recovery, the system must determine which transactions were completed and which were still in progress at the time of failure. If the database is damaged, it can be recovered by using the backup tape and the log. The fact that a database allows users to make updates concurrently further complicates the recovery process.

1.7   Historical Developments in Information Systems

The need to record data goes back to earliest recorded history. We see evidence of attempts to provide permanent records of transactions in Sumarian clay tables, in artifacts left by the Babylonians, in ancient Egyptian hieroglyphics, and even in cave paintings. Paper records or other written forms have been used for centuries to record information about family histories, treaties and other agreements, household or business inventories, school enrollment, employee records, payment for goods or services, census data, and many other facets of life.

The use of **punched cards** for data storage was introduced in 1890, when US census data was collected and stored on punched cards for the first time. The US Constitution requires that a complete census be conducted every 10 years. The 1880 census took seven years to complete because the country's population had increased so much that it was anticipated there would not be sufficient time to complete the census before 1900, when a new one would begin. The Census Bureau sponsored a competition to spur ideas about ways to make the census more efficient. Herman Hollerith, an employee at the bureau, proposed the use of punched cards to record census responses from each household and to facilitate processing of the responses. Such cards were already in use in the silk weaving industry in Lyon, France to control the Jacquard loom, which wove patterns in silk fabric. Hollerith designed a method of using the same technology to store the census data and to examine its patterns. He won the competition and because of his design the census was completed in record time—and a new technique for data processing was invented. After that success, mechanical punched-card equipment was used for many years for storing, sorting, analyzing, and reporting data, and punched cards served as an input medium for computers for both programs and data.

Punched paper tape was used to store both computer programs and data beginning in the early 1940s, when the earliest electro-mechanical and electronic computers were developed. Starting about 1950, **magnetic tape** was developed and used for input for early computers, including the UNIVAC 1, the first commercially available computer. Decks of punched cards, loops of punched paper tape, or reels of magnetic tape were all used in essentially the same way, both for storing programs and providing a method of storing and inputting data. Data on these mediums could be read only in the order in which it was stored. This type of **sequential file processing** was extremely efficient but not very flexible. Payroll was usually the first application that a business chose to automate, because of the complex calculations and reporting requirements that were tedious for human beings to perform.

Figure 1.6 provides an overview of a payroll application using sequential file processing. A **master file** containing relatively permanent payroll data for each employee was kept in order by a key field, perhaps Employee Number. The records in this file might also contain items such as the employee name, address, weekly salary, exemptions, tax deductions, year-to-date totals for gross pay, taxes, and take-home pay. Each week a **transaction file** containing new data such as the number of hours worked that week, any changes in salary, deductions or other data, and any other new information needed for this week's payroll would be prepared. Often magnetic tape was used for the master file, and punched cards for the transaction file. Both files had to be in the same order, by Employee Number. A program would read a master record, then read the transaction record for the same employee, and complete the payroll processing for that person. In the process, the information on the old master record would be changed to reflect new data, and a new record would be written to a new master tape. At the end of the program, the new tape would become the current master tape, and it would be used the following week. This is referred to as an **old master/new master** or a **father/son** system. The type of processing described here, where a set of records is submitted as a unit to a program that then operates on them without further human intervention, is referred to as **batch processing.**

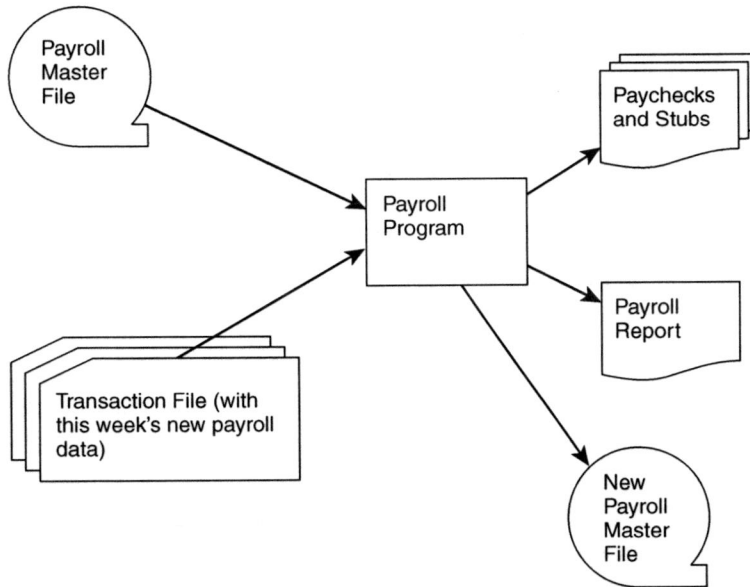

FIGURE 1.6
A Sequential File Process-ing System

Magnetic disk storage was available by the late 1950s, making **direct access** (nonsequential access) of records possible. Programs no longer required that the order of access match the physical order of the records. Updates could be made to the disk, without rewriting the entire file. Programming languages, including COBOL and PL/1, were developed during the 1960s for commercial data processing that used data stored on both tape and disk. Originally, simple file organizations were used to organize data on these secondary storage devices, but as applications became more complex more sophisticated methods of storing and retrieving data were needed. Two competing database models, the network and the hierarchical, were developed at this time. However, file systems continued to be used for many applications.

The **hierarchical model** for databases was developed during the 1960s as an ad hoc solution to immediate needs of real applications. The oldest hierarchical database management system, IBM's IMS, was developed to organize and store information needed by the space program for the Apollo moon landing project. North American Aviation, (which became Rockwell), and IBM worked jointly to produce the first version of IMS, which was released in 1968. Early versions of IMS were designed to be used with magnetic tape devices, but later magnetic disk became the standard. IMS soon became the dominant hierarchical database management system in the marketplace and was for many years the most widely used of all DBMSs, until it was replaced by relational systems. Several improvements were made to IMS after 1968, resulting in new releases to take advantage of hardware and software improvements, provide new features such as data communications, and maximize performance. The SABRE airline reservation system was based on IMS. IMS was known as a "workhorse," capable of processing large amounts of data efficiently. It used a tree structure familiar to programmers who are accustomed to working with files, and provided predictable performance.

One of the oldest database management systems, Integrated Data Store (IDS) was developed at General Electric by Charles Bachman during the early 1960s using the **network model.** This database management system influenced the development of the database area for many years. The Conference on Data Systems Languages (**CODASYL**), an organization consisting of representatives of major hardware and software vendors and users, was formed to try to standardize many aspects of data processing. It had successfully written standards for the COBOL language. In the late 1960s it formed a subgroup called the Database Task Group (**DBTG**) to address the question of standardization for database management systems. Influenced by IDS, the group proposed a network-based model and specifications for data definition and data manipulation languages. The draft report was published in 1969 and resulted in many suggestions for changes from its readers. The DBTG reconsidered its proposal and published its first official report in 1971. This landmark document was submitted to the American National Standards Institute (ANSI) in the hope that its specifications would be accepted as a standard for database management systems. However, ANSI refused to accept or reject the proposed standard. The 1971 report was succeeded by several newer versions, notably in 1973, 1978, 1981, and 1984, but it remains the principal document describing a network-based model generally referred to as the CODASYL model or the DBTG model, and several popular database management systems were based on it. In addition, it provided the vocabulary and framework for discussion of database issues, establishing for the first time the notion of a layered database architecture and common terminology. The DBTG evolved in 1972 into a permanent CODASYL committee, the DDLC, or Data Description Language Committee, which continued to operate and to publish its findings periodically in its *Journals of Development* until 1984, when its function was taken over by the ANSI X3H2 committee for standardization. Despite the fact that the DBTG and DDLC continued to make changes to the CODASYL model, the 1971 proposal was used by major vendors as the basis of their database management systems. The most widely used of these network-based systems was IDMS from Cullinet. Others included PRIME DBMS from PRIME Computer, IDS II from Honeywell, DMS 170 from Control Data Corporation, DC, DMSII and DMS1100 from UNISYS, and DBMS 10 and DBMS 11 from Digital Equipment Corporation.

Although the hierarchical and network models were powerful and efficient, they were complex, requiring users to understand data structures and access paths to data. They were designed for use with programs rather than for interactive access by users, so ad hoc queries were not supported. They were not based on a solid theoretical foundation, but were solutions built on existing file systems.

The **relational model** was first proposed by E. F. Codd in 1970, in a paper called "A Relational Model of Data for Large Shared Data Banks." It was the first model based on theoretical notions from mathematics, which provided a strong theoretical base. Research on the model was done by Codd and others at the IBM Research Laboratory in San Jose, California. **System R,** a prototype relational database management system, was developed by IBM researchers during the late 1970s. DB2, IBM's relational database management system, was based on System R. **SQL,** a language developed for System R, has become the standard data language for relational-model databases, with ANSI-approved standards published in 1986, 1989, 1992, and 1999. Other early relational model research projects were the **Peterlee Relational Test Vehicle,** developed at the IBM UK Scientific Laboratory and **INGRES,** developed at the University of California at Berkeley. The research led to a "university" version of INGRES, as well as a commercial product. **ORACLE** was developed and marketed using many of the System R results. The widespread use of microcomputers beginning in the 1980s led to the development of PC-based database management systems, which were all relational. Among early microcomputer-based relational database management systems were **dBase, R:Base, Foxpro,** and **Paradox.** Microsoft's Access, which uses the relational model, is now the most widely used microcomputer-based database management system. **Oracle, DB2, Informix, Sybase,** and Microsoft's **SQL Server,** all of which use the relational model, are currently the most popular enterprise database management systems.

The relational model uses simple tables to organize data. It does not allow database designers to express some important distinctions when they model an enterprise. In 1976, P. P. Chen developed a new type of model, the **entity-relationship** model. This is an example of a **semantic model,** one that attempts to capture the meaning of the data it represents. The entity-relationship model itself has been extended several times to make it semantically richer. Other semantic models for databases were developed to try to capture more of the meaning in data.

The need to store and manipulate complex data that is not easy to model using the simple tables of the relational model, as well as the development of programming languages using the object-oriented paradigm, led to the development of **object-oriented** databases in the 1990s. These databases were developed to handle the data required for advanced applications such as geographical information systems, multimedia, computer-aided design and computer-aided manufacturing (CAD/CAM), and other complex environments. Relational database management systems such as Oracle added some object-oriented capabilities to their products, resulting in hybrid **object-relational** databases.

Data warehouses were developed in the 1990s to provide a method of capturing data consolidated from many databases. A data warehouse usually stores historical data about an organization, for the purpose of **data mining,** a process of analyzing the data statistically to enable the organization to unearth the trends that may be present in its own records.

The widespread use of the Internet has had a tremendous impact on database development. The Internet connects users to a rich and constantly expanding network of databases, providing access to digital libraries, multimedia resources, educational resources, and much more. E-commerce Web sites provide access to databases of information about products and services to customers throughout the world. Wireless computing devices and thin clients such as PDAs are other developments that allow users to connect to database resources in new and flexible ways.

1.8   Chapter Summary

Databases are used in hundreds of thousands of organizations ranging from large government agencies to small businesses. The study of the theory, design, and management of databases enables us to maximize their potential benefits.

In a typical database, data is stored in a format that makes it is easy to access, either for individual queries or large reports. In an integrated database environment, all data is kept in a single repository called the database, and managed by the database administrator (DBA). All access to the database is through the database management system (DBMS), a software package that sets up storage structures, loads data, provides access for programs and interactive users, formats retrieved data, hides certain data, does updates, controls concurrency, and performs backup and recovery for the database. Data in a database is integrated, self-describing, and shared concurrently by many users. The DBMS provides a program interface and a user interface for interactive queries that are expressed in the query language of the particular DBMS. People in the integrated database environment include end users, application programmers, and the DBA, all of whom interact with the database in different ways.

Some of the advantages of the integrated database approach are sharing of data, control of redundancy, data consistency, improved data standards, better data security, improved data integrity, balancing of conflicting requirements, faster development of new applications, better data accessibility, economy of scale, more control over concurrency, and better backup and recovery procedures. Some of the disadvantages of the integrated database approach are the higher costs of DBMS, hardware, programming, and conversion, and the slower processing of some applications, increased vulnerability, and more difficult recovery.

The development of information systems depended on technological advances in hardware and software. Starting with punched cards, storage technology moved on to paper tape, magnetic tape, magnetic disk, and newer devices. Sequential file processing, required for tape, was replaced by direct file processing once direct-access devices such as disks were developed. The hierarchical database model was developed from file processing technology, and the first hierarchical database management system, IMS, was created by IBM and North American Aviation to handle the vast amount of data needed for the Apollo moon landing project. IDS, based on the network model, was developed by Charles Bachman at General Electric, and was the inspiration for the CODASYL DBTG standardization proposals. The relational model was proposed by E. F. Codd, and a prototype called System R, was developed, along with SQL, as the standard relational data language. Most current databases, especially PC-based ones, use the relational model. The entity-relationship model was developed by P. P. Chen to be a semantic model, capturing more of the meaning of data than the relational model. Object-oriented models were developed to allow representation of more complex data items needed for advanced database applications. Hybrid object-relational systems add some object features to relational databases. Data warehouses allow collection of data from many databases, providing an organization with a rich data resource for data mining. The widespread use of the Internet and the growth of e-commerce have made databases more accessible to the public.

Exercises

1.1   Give four examples of database systems other than those listed in Section 1.1.

1.2   Name five tasks performed by the DBMS.

1.3   List three functions that you can perform with a database that you cannot perform with a spreadsheet.

1.4   Distinguish between a database and a database management system.

1.5   List five advantages of a database system and give an example of each.

1.6   List five disadvantages of a database system and explain each.

1.7   List three responsibilities of the DBA.

1.8   Give an example of an end user and describe a typical task that a user can perform on a database.

1.9   Explain what is meant by a host programming language.

1.10 Provide an example of an application besides payroll that might use sequential batch processing and draw a diagram similar to Figure 1.6.

1.11 Briefly define each of the following terms used in database systems:

a. data integration

b. concurrency

c. query language

d. data consistency

e. integrity constraint

f. data encryption

g. economy of scale

h. recovery log

i. user view

j. security log

Lab Exercises

Lab Exercise 1.1: Exploring the Access Database for the University Example

This laboratory will provide practice in:

- Copying and using an existing database
- Examining existing tables, relationships, queries, and reports
- Designing and executing new queries
- Designing and running a new report
- Designing and using a form
- Updating tables

1. Download the UniversityDB database from the website for this book and save it in your own directory. Open it and use it for the following exercises.

Note: Access uses many of the same conventions as the rest of Microsoft Office, and provides several ways to perform tasks. There are many variations of the commands described in this section that work the same way. Feel free to explore those variations. If you close Access accidentally, just reopen it and continue the exercises. If you erase part of the database, delete your copy and begin again, making another copy from the CD.

2. Make sure the *Tables* object is chosen on the left panel of the University-DB window. Open the Student table by double clicking on its name in the right panel and look through the records of that table. Then close that table. Do the same for the remaining tables.

3. On the Access toolbar, find the icon for *Relationships*, which has three rectangles connected by lines. Click on the icon to see the relationships among the tables that Access "knows." Note that it "knows" that the facId in Class is related to the facId in Faculty, that the classNumber in Enroll matches the classNumber in Class, and that the stuId in Enroll matches the stuId in Student. Close the *Relationships* window.

4. Choose the *Queries* object on the left panel. Open *Query1* by double clicking on its name. Notice the query is executed immediately. Close the *Query1* results screen.

5. With the *Queries* object still chosen, from the UniversityDB database toolbar, choose *Design*. The design of *Query1* is displayed. The top window shows the tables that are used in the query, along with their relationships. The bottom window shows which fields are included in the query, along with any conditions (criteria). The designer can choose *Show* or not, to indicate whether the field is to be displayed in the result. From the design screen, press the ! icon on the Access toolbar to run the query. Close the results window.

6. Return to the design screen for *Query1*. Change the query: double click on the `major` field name in the `Student` table to add the major. Now add the condition `History` in the *Criteria* line for `major` and execute the query again, noticing the change in the results with this new condition. Close the results window without saving.

7. Choose the option *Create query in design view*. In the *Show Table* window, highlight `Class`, click on the *Add* button, highlight `Enroll`, and click on the *Add* button again. Click on the *Close* button. You are now back in the query design window. Choose `classNumber`, `schedule`, `room`, and `stuId` as the fields for the query, by double clicking on each one. Add the condition that `stuId` is `S1002` in the *Criteria* line for `stuId`. Execute the query to see the class schedule for student `S1002`. Close and save the query.

8. Create a query that you design yourself. You can vary your design by choosing different tables from the *Show Table* window, choosing different fields, putting multiple conditions on the same criteria line to indicate AND, or putting conditions on different lines to indicate OR. Explore the options and create several queries. Note that if you wish to compare strings, the case must match exactly, so be careful of capitalization.

9. Choose the *Reports* object on the left panel. Open the report *Class Lists* by double clicking on its name in the right panel. Enlarge the report window to read the report. Close the report. Choose the *Design* icon on the UniversityDB toolbar to see the design for that report. Close the *Design* screen.

10. Click on *Create report by using wizard*. Notice the drop-down window on the left that lists all the tables and queries. You could choose any combination of these objects for your report. Choose the Student table. From the field list just below, highlight lastName and press the right arrow button to select it for the report (or simply double click on the field name). Also choose firstName. If you accidentally choose an incorrect field, use the back arrow to deselect it. Change the table to Enroll. Choose classNumber and grade. Change the table to Class. Choose schedule and room. Now click on the *Next* button at the bottom of the *Report Wizard* window. You have the option to view your data by Student, Enroll, or Class. Choose Student and click on the *Next* button. Now you can choose grouping levels. Choose lastName, then click on *Next*. You can choose sorting on several fields. Choose Grade, *Ascending,* then click on *Next*. Choose the *Stepped* layout shown, then *Next*. Choose the default style, then *Next*. Make the title Classes by Student. Designed by <your name>, putting your own name in the brackets. Choose *Finish*. The report should execute. Examine it to see the effects of your choices.

11. Using the report wizard, design and run a second report of your own choosing. Save your report.

12. Choose *Forms* from the objects panel on the left. Choose *Create form by using wizard.* Choose the Student table, and click on the double arrow to select all its fields. Choose all the default specifications. Make the title StudentInput and click *Finish* to end the form design. The form should pop up, showing each student record. Use the form control arrow to step through the student records one at a time by pressing the right arrow. You can also enter data using the form. After the last record, you will see a blank form. Enter your own data—make up an ID (remember its value!), and enter your name, major, and credits. Close the *StudentInput* form.

13. Choose the *Tables* object again, and open the Student table. Notice that the record you entered using the form has been saved in the table. Close the Student table. Now open the Enroll table and add two records while in the normal (spreadsheet) view to show that you are enrolled in two classes. Be careful to use the same stuId you entered and to use existing classNumber values, or you will be unable to add the records. Delete the Enroll record of student S1010 in ART103A, by moving the cursor to the column before stuId to select the record and pressing the *Delete* key. Save your changes and close the table.

14. Choose the *Reports* object. Run the *ClassLists* report by double clicking on its name. Notice you and your new classes are listed, and the deleted record no longer appears.

15. Open the `Faculty` table. Change the rank of Professor Tanaka to `Assistant`, by typing in the new value directly in the cell. Save the change.

Lab Exercise 1.2: Creating and Using a New Access Database

This laboratory will provide practice in:

- Creating a new Access database
- Creating tables, specifying fields and keys
- Specifying relationships between tables
- Entering records
- Editing records
- Creating queries
- Creating simple reports
- Creating simple forms

For this lab, you will create a database that keeps track of your music collection and the friends who borrow music from you.

1. Open Access and choose *New, Blank Database* from the panel on the right of the opening screen. Choose your directory in the *Save in* window and change the filename from *db1* to `MyMusic`. Make sure the filetype is set to *Microsoft Access Databases,* and click on the *Create* button.

2. Make sure the *Tables* object is chosen on the left panel of the *MyMusic* window. Double click on *Create Table in Design View.* In the *Table1* window that pops up, enter the field names and data types for all the fields of your table. On the first line under *Field Name* type `title`. In the *Data Type* window on the same line, click on the down arrow to see the available data types. Choose *text.* Move down to the *Field Properties* window and type `35` as the field size. Move to the second line under *field name* and enter the field name `artist`, then data type *text*, size `20`. Make the third field `dateAcquired` and choose *date/time* as the data type. Make the fourth field `status` with data type of *text*, size `10`. Then from the Access menu, choose *File, Save As,* and type in the table name `Music`. You will get a message reminding you that you did not specify a primary key and asking if you would like Access to create one for you. Choose *yes.* Access will add an `ID` field with data type *AutoNumber.* Close the table.

3. Create a second table of friends who might borrow your music. The first field is `lastName`, data type *text* `20`. This time you will create your own key consisting of the `lastName`. To do so, move the cursor to the column just to the left of `lastName` and click on the *key* icon on the Access toolbar. Continue to create the rest of the fields

   ```
   firstName text 15
   areaCode text 3
   phone text 7
   ```

   Save this table as `Friend`.

4. Create a third table, `Borrow`, with fields

   ```
   ID Number Long Integer
   lastName text 20
   dateBorrowed date/time
   dateReturned date/time
   ```

   This table needs a composite key consisting of `ID` and `lastName`. To create the composite key, move the cursor to the first column to the left of `ID` and, holding the mouse button down, move the mouse down one line to select both the `ID` and the `lastName` line. With both highlighted, click the *key* icon. Save the table as `Borrow`.

5. To create relationships between the tables click on the *Relationships* icon on the Access toolbar. It consists of three rectangles connected by lines. In the *Show Table* window that pops up, highlight `Music`, click on the *Add* button, highlight `Borrow`, click on *Add,* highlight `Friend`, click on *Add,* then click on *Close.* The Relationship window opens, showing the three tables. Click on `lastName` in `Friend` and drag to `lastName` in `Borrow`. In the *Edit Relationship* window that pops up, you should see both fields listed. Check the box *Enforce referential integrity* and then click on the *Create* button. You will see a line connecting the two tables with 1.. ∞ on it. The 1 should be near the `Friend` table and the infinity symbol near the `Borrow` table. (If this is not the case, you made a mistake in designing the tables. You can click on the relationship line and press the *Delete* key to remove the relationship. Then you can return to the table design and correct any error.) Drag `ID` from `Music` to `Borrow` and create another relationship. Choose *Save* and close the relationship window.

6. Double click on the name of the `Music` table. Now you will enter data into that table. For the `Music` table, the system will enter an `ID` (1,2,3..) automatically (because you allowed it to create an *AutoNumber* key for you), but you should enter the names of albums you might have, the singer or artist, the date you got the album (in the United States, use the form mm/dd/yyyy; otherwise use the local convention for dates), and the status. You can leave the status blank or enter `borrowed`, `OK`, `scratched`, or any appropriate string value. When you have entered several albums, save the `Music` table and close it.

7. Enter data in your `Friend` table. This time `lastName` is the key. You must be careful not to enter two records with the same last name, and to remember the values you enter.

8. Now you can enter data in the `Borrow` table. Access will check to see that any ID you enter matches an ID in the `Music` table, and any `last-Name` matches one in the `Friend` table, so be sure the values are valid. The checking is done because you informed Access of the relationships and asked it to enforce referential integrity. Save this table.

9. Now you will create a query that you design yourself. Choose the *Query* object. Choose the option *Create query in design view*. In the *Show Table* window, highlight `Music`, click on the *Add* button, highlight `Borrow`, click on the *Add* button, highlight `Friend` and click on the *Add* button again. Click on the *Close* button. You are now in the query design window. Choose whatever fields you would like to include in your query. Remember you can choose any of the tables, choose different fields, put multiple conditions on the same criteria line to indicate AND, or put conditions on different lines to indicate OR. Explore the options and create several queries. Note that if you wish to compare strings the case must match exactly, so be careful of capitalization. Design and execute several queries, saving them under names you choose.

10. Now you should design a report. Choose the *Reports* object on the left panel. Click on *Create report by using Wizard*. Notice the drop-down window on the left that lists all the tables and queries. You could choose any combination of these objects for your report. Choose one table. From the field list just below, highlight any field you wish to include and press the right arrow button to select it for the report (or simply double click on the field name). Remember that if you accidentally choose an incorrect field, use the back arrow to deselect it.

After you have chosen the fields you wish from the tables and/or queries, click on the *Next* button at the bottom of the *Report Wizard* window. You have the option to view your data by various orders and grouping levels, and to choose a style for your report. Add a title that includes your name. Choose *Finish* to end the design and run the report.

11. Choose the *Forms* object from the objects panel on the left. Choose *Create form by using Wizard.* Choose one table, and click on the double arrow to select all its fields. Choose all the default specifications. The form should pop up, showing the table's records one at a time. Remember you can also enter data using the form. After the last record, you will see a blank form, on which you should enter your own data.

12. Save all your changes and exit Access.

Note: Once you have created a table, you can always add new records by simply opening the table and entering the data. You can update an existing record by moving the cursor to the field to be changed and typing in the new value. You can delete a record by highlighting it and pressing the *Delete* key or using the menu options. Practice each of these operations on any table you choose. You can print the table or any other object at any time from the Access menu by choosing *File, Print.*

SAMPLE PROJECT: THE ART GALLERY

Purpose of the Sample Project

The sample project sections included at the end of many of the chapters of this book provide the student with models for applying the concepts covered in the chapters. The project is a continuing example that illustrates a practical application of database design and implementation techniques. Following the sample project are several student projects. Students should choose at least one of the projects and work on its development as they progress through the book. The sample project shows how each step can be done. The student should read the sample and apply the steps to the chosen project.

General Description

The Art Gallery accepts original artworks by living contemporary artists to be sold on a commission basis. It currently offers work from about a hundred artists, and sells approximately a thousand pieces each year. The average selling price is several thousand dollars. There are about five thousand customers who have purchased pieces from the gallery. The sales staff consists of the gallery owner, Alan Hughes, and four sales associates. Their activities are supported by an office staff of two people.

Basic Operations

When an artist wishes to sell works, he or she contacts the gallery. Alan Hughes, the owner, visits the artist's studio and selects the works to be sold through the gallery. If the artist is well known to the gallery, this visit may be eliminated, and the works may be accepted automatically. An artist may submit one or several pieces for sale at a time. The artist, working with Alan, identifies an asking price for each work. The sales staff try to sell the work at that price, or as close to that price as possible. Customers may negotiate with salespeople, so that the actual selling price may be below the asking price. If it is below the asking price, the final selling price must be approved by the artist. The commission charged by the gallery is 10% of the selling price. The gallery splits the commission with the salesperson who makes the sale. Any salesperson can sell any work in the gallery. However, customers work with a single salesperson when they buy each piece, so that the salesperson's portion of the commission for a single piece goes to only one salesperson.

The gallery promotes the works by holding exhibits featuring various pieces. The exhibits are advertised in newspapers and other media, and potential customers are sent personal invitations. A showing is actually a reception that provides an opportunity for the public to see the pieces and to meet the artist or artists whose works are featured. A "one-man show" features works by a single artist, while a themed show features works by multiple artists centered on a single theme, such as "Mediterranean Seascapes." Works of art that have been featured at a showing remain on display until they are sold or returned to the artists. A piece may be purchased at the showing or at any time afterward. Occasionally, a work may be purchased from the gallery prior to the show and included in the exhibit, marked as "Sold," to provide the public with a better view of the artist's work. Not all works are promoted through showings. Some are simply displayed in the gallery. If a work has been at the gallery for six months without being sold, Alan contacts the artist and returns the work, unless both agree to continue displaying the work for an additional period of time.

At present, all data relating to artists, unsold works, shows, sales, and customers is kept in paper files. A description card is made up for each work currently on exhibit, and placed on the wall or floor stand next to the piece. A copy of the card is also placed in a file. The card lists the artist's name, title of the work, year created, type, medium, style, size, and asking price. Each work is an original, one-of-a-kind piece produced by a single artist. No two artists have the same name. The title of the work must be unique to the artist, but may not be totally unique to the gallery. For example, many artists may have works such as "Composition Number 5," but no artist has two works with that title. No prints or reproductions are sold at the gallery. An artist can produce several works in the same year. The type refers to the type of work, which may be painting, sculpture, collage, and so forth. The medium refers to the materials used in the work, such as oil, watercolor, acrylic, marble, or mixed. A piece using more than one medium is categorized as mixed. The style means the style of the work, which may be contemporary, impressionist, folk, or other. The size is expressed in units appropriate for the work; for example, for a painting, the size would be the number of inches in width and height, while a sculpture would have three dimensions.

When a purchase is made, a receipt is issued for the buyer, a payment check and stub are made out for the artist, the commission is allocated between the gallery and the salesperson, and all paper files are updated individually.

Information Needs

In addition to the data about artists, artworks, shows, sales, and customers currently kept in paper files, there are other information needs. For income tax purposes, the gallery is required to report the amount of sales for each artist each year, a task that is very time-consuming at present. Alan realizes that a database could provide more information than is available now from the paper files. He also wants to capture data not currently stored. He would like to keep track of customers who have made purchases and information about the amount of their purchases last year and so far this year. He would like to be able to send mailings to potential customers, and to record their preferences. In addition, he foresees that the gallery may begin to accept works owned by collectors as well as works directly from artists. The database design should include the possibility that the owner is not the artist.

Project Steps

- Step 1.1. Write out the format of every input document that provides information to be stored in the database.
- Step 1.2. Write out the format of every routine report to be produced using the database.
- Step 1.3. Sketch the input and output screens for every routine transaction to be performed against the database.
- Step 1.4. Write out an initial list of assumptions for the project.

Note: In real life, these steps would be preceded by meetings and interviews with the users of the present system and of the proposed system to determine the users' data needs and preferences. We will assume that these meetings have taken place and that the information that follows has been developed from them. Note that we are not making any assumptions about the internal structure of the database at this point. The reports and forms we design are based on user's needs, not on the database file structures.

- Step 1.1. Format of Input Documents

The following forms are used to provide information.

THE ART GALLERY

Artist Information Form

Date of Interview _____   Name of Interviewer _____

Artist Last Name _____   Artist First Name _____

Street _____

City_____   State ___   Zip _____

Telephone: Area Code ____ Number _____

Social Security Number _____

Usual Type _____

Usual Medium _____

Usual Style _____

FIGURE 1.7

Artist Information Form

1. **Artist Information Form.** When Alan interviews an artist, he collects contact information and data about the artist's usual works, as shown on the form in Figure 1.7. To allow for the possibility that in the future Alan's associates may do the interviews, the interviewer's name is listed.

2. **Collector Information Form.** When the gallery begins to offer works owned by people other than the artist, these collectors will also be interviewed. They may own one or many artworks, and their collections may or may not have works that are predominately by a single artist or of a single type, style, or medium. The form shown in Figure 1.8 will be filled out by the interviewer.

3. **Artwork Information Form.** For each artwork to be considered, the interviewer fills in the basic information needed for the description card, as shown in Figure 1.9. If the piece is chosen to be offered for sale by the gallery, the date listed and the asking price are filled in.

THE ART GALLERY

Collector Information Form

Date of Interview _____   Name of Interviewer _____

Collector Last Name _____   First Name _____

Street _____

City_____   State ___   Zip _____

Telephone: Area Code ____ Number _____

Social Security Number _____

If the collection is predominately by one artist, or has a distinguishing type, medium, or style, fill in this section.

Artist Last Name _____   Artist First Name _____

Collection Type _____

Collection Medium _____

Collection Style _____

FIGURE 1.8

Collector Information Form

THE ART GALLERY

Artwork Information Form

Artist Last Name _____   Artist First Name_____

Title _____

Year Completed _____

Type _____

Medium _____

Style _____

Size _____

If owned by someone other than the artist, please complete this section with the owner information.

    Owner Last Name _____   Owner First Name _____

    Street _____

    City_____   State ____   Zip _____

    Telephone: Area Code _____ Number _____

    Owner Social Security Number _____

If the piece is chosen to be offered by the gallery, please complete this section.

Date Listed _____

Asking Price _____

FIGURE 1.9

Artwork Information Form

4. **Sale Invoice.** When a work is sold, the sales associate fills out the form shown in Figure 1.10. Currently, a copy is given to the buyer, and the original is placed in the files. The unique invoice number is preprinted on the form. When the database is created, the invoice will be produced by the system.

5. **Mailing List Form.** The form shown in Figure 1.11 is left in various locations for potential customers to sign up for a mailing list.

   ▪ Step 1.2. Format of Routine Reports

The following reports are either currently produced or would be produced by the new system.

THE ART GALLERY

Sale Invoice

Invoice Number 99999

Title of Artwork _____

Artist: Last Name _____   First Name_____

Owner: Last Name _____   First Name_____

    Street _____

    City_____   State ___   Zip _____

    Telephone: Area Code ____ Number _____

    Owner Social Security Number _____

Buyer: Last Name _____   First Name_____

    Street _____

    City_____   State ___   Zip _____

    Telephone: Area Code ____ Number _____

Price _____

Tax _____

Total Paid _____

Salesperson Signature _____ Date _____

FIGURE 1.10

Sale Invoice

6. **Active Artists Summary Report.** The report shown in Figure 1.12 lists summary data about all active artists, including the total amount of each one's sales for last year and this year.

7. **Individual Artist Sales Report.** The report shown in Figure 1.13 would be generated for a period starting with whatever date is selected (e.g., January first of the current year) and ending with another selected date (e.g., today's date). It lists all the works of the artist that the gallery has received from the listing date specified to the date of the report. The status of the work can be sold, returned, or for sale. If the work was sold, the date sold and selling price are listed. If the work was returned, the return date is listed. If the work is for sale as of the date of the report, the asking price is listed. The total amount of sales of the artist's works during the period is displayed. The total value of asking prices of the artist's

THE ART GALLERY

Mailing List

Date _____

Last Name _____   First Name _____

Street _____

City_____   State ___   Zip _____

Telephone: Area Code ____ Number _____

Please indicate preferences (if any) below:

Preferred Artist _____

Preferred Style (e.g., contemporary, impressionist, folk) _____

Preferred Type (e.g., painting, sculpture, collage) _____

Preferred Medium (e.g., oil, watercolor, marble, mixed) _____

FIGURE 1.11
Mailing List Form

REPORT OF ACTIVE ARTISTS

Date of Report: mm/dd/yyyy

Name	Address	Phone	Type	Medium	Style	Sales Last Year	Sales YTD
XXXXX	XXXXX	XXX XXX XXXX	XXXXX	XXXXX	XXXXX	999999.99	999999.99
XXXXX	XXXXX	XXX XXX XXXX	XXXXX	XXXXX	XXXXX	999999.99	999999.99
...							
XXXXX	XXXXX	XXX XXX XXXX	XXXXX	XXXXX	XXXXX	999999.99	999999.99

FIGURE 1.12
Active Artists Summary Report

INDIVIDUAL ARTIST SALES REPORT

Date of Report: mm/dd/yyyy

Last Name_____ First Name_____

Address: Street _____

            City _____State _____ Zip_____

Telephone: Area Code_____   Number _____

Report for Works beginning with Date Listed of mm/dd/yyyy

Works Sold:

Title	Date Listed	Type	Medium	Style	Year	Asking Price	Sell Price	Date Sold
XXXXX	mm/dd/yyyy	XXXXX	XXXXX	XXXXX	yyyy	9999.99	9999.99	mm/dd/yyyy
XXXXX	mm/dd/yyyy	XXXXX	XXXXX	XXXXX	yyyy	9999.99	9999.99	mm/dd/yyyy
. . .								
XXXXX	mm/dd/yyyy	XXXXX	XXXXX	XXXXX	yyyy	9999.99	9999.99	mm/dd/yyyy

Total of Sales: 999999.99

Works Returned:

Title	Date Listed	Type	Medium	Style	Year	Asking Price	Date Returned
XXXXX	mm/dd/yyyy	XXXXX	XXXXX	XXXXX	9999	9999.99	mm/dd/yyyy
XXXXX	mm/dd/yyyy	XXXXX	XXXXX	XXXXX	9999	9999.99	mm/dd/yyyy
. . .							
XXXXX	mm/dd/yyyy	XXXXX	XXXXX	XXXXX	9999	9999.99	mm/dd/yyyy

Works for Sale:

Title	Date Listed	Type	Medium	Style	Year	Asking Price
XXXXX	99/99/9999	XXXXX	XXXXX	XXXXX	9999	9999.99
XXXXX	99/99/9999	XXXXX	XXXXX	XXXXX	9999	9999.99
. . .						
XXXXX	99/99/9999	XXXXX	XXXXX	XXXXX	9999	9999.99

Total of Asking Prices: 999999.99

FIGURE 1.13

Individual Artist Sales Report

			COLLECTORS SUMMARY REPORT					
Name	Address	Phone	Pref. Artist	Pref. Type	Pref. Medium	Pref. Style	Sales Last Year	Sales YTD
XXXXX	XXXXX	XXX XXX XXXX	XXXXX	XXXXX	XXXXX	XXXXX	999999.99	999999.99
XXXXX	XXXXX	XXX XXX XXXX	XXXXX	XXXXX	XXXXX	XXXXX	999999.99	999999.99
. . .								
XXXXX	XXXXX	XXX XXX XXXX	XXXXX	XXXXX	XXXXX	XXXXX	999999.99	999999.99

FIGURE 1.14

Collectors Summary Report

works currently for sale is also given. By choosing dates that cover the entire year, the total sales data on this report can also be used for the end-of-year tax reporting required by the government.

8. **Collectors Summary Report.** The Art Gallery plans to begin selling works owned by collectors, in addition to works owned by the artist who created them. When works owned by people other than the artist are made available, the report shown in Figure 1.14 will be needed.

9. **Individual Collector Sales Report.** This report, shown in Figure 1.15, is similar to the one for individual artists. It will be needed when the gallery begins to sell works owned by collectors. It gives information about works the collector has offered for sale through the gallery. It lists all works sold, works returned, and works for sale for that collector for the period specified. The total sales for each collector is sent to the government for tax reporting purposes at the end of the year.

10. **Works for Sale.** This report lists data about each work that is currently offered for sale in the gallery. The date of the showing to promote the work, if any, is given. The total of all asking prices is given. It is shown in Figure 1.16.

INDIVIDUAL COLLECTOR SALES REPORT

Date of Report: mm/dd/yyyy

Last Name_____ First Name_____

Address: Street _____

            City _____State _____ Zip_____

Telephone: Area Code_____ Number _____

Report for Works beginning with Date Listed of mm/dd/yyyy

Works Sold:

Title	Artist	Date Listed	Type	Medium	Style	Year	Asking Price	Sell Price	Date Sold
XXXXX	XXXXX	mm/dd/yyyy	XXXXX	XXXXX	XXXXX	yyyy	9999.99	9999.99	mm/dd/yyyy
XXXXX	XXXXX	mm/dd/yyyy	XXXXX	XXXXX	XXXXX	yyyy	9999.99	9999.99	mm/dd/yyyy
. . .									
XXXXX	XXXXX	mm/dd/yyyy	XXXXX	XXXXX	XXXXX	yyyy	9999.99	9999.99	mm/dd/yyyy

Total of Sales: 999999.99

Works Returned:

Title	Artist	Date Listed	Type	Medium	Style	Year	Asking Price	Date Returned
XXXXX	XXXXX	mm/dd/yyyy	XXXXX	XXXXX	XXXXX	9999	9999.99	mm/dd/yyyy
XXXXX	XXXXX	mm/dd/yyyy	XXXXX	XXXXX	XXXXX	9999	9999.99	mm/dd/yyyy
. . .								
XXXXX	XXXXX	mm/dd/yyyy	XXXXX	XXXXX	XXXXX	9999	9999.99	mm/dd/yyyy

Works for Sale:

Title	Artist	Date Listed	Type	Medium	Style	Year	Asking Price
XXXXX	XXXXX	99/99/9999	XXXXX	XXXXX	XXXXX	9999	9999.99
XXXXX	XXXXX	99/99/9999	XXXXX	XXXXX	XXXXX	9999	9999.99
. . .							
XXXXX	XXXXX	99/99/9999	XXXXX	XXXXX	XXXXX	9999	9999.99

Total of Asking Prices: 999999.99

FIGURE 1.15

Individual Collector Sales Report

WORKS FOR SALE

Date of Report: _____

Title	Artist	Type	Medium	Style	Owner's Name	Asking Price	Date Shown	Date Listed
XXXXX	XXXXX	XXXXX	XXXXX	XXXXX	XXXXX	9999.99	mm/dd/yyyy	mm/dd/yyyy
XXXXX	XXXXX	XXXXX	XXXXX	XXXXX	XXXXX	9999.99	mm/dd/yyyy	mm/dd/yyyy
. . .								
XXXXX	XXXXX	XXXXX	XXXXX	XXXXX	XXXXX	9999.99	mm/dd/yyyy	mm/dd/yyyy

Total Asking Prices: 999999.99

FIGURE 1.16
Works for Sale

11. **Sales This Week.** This report, shown in Figure 1.17, lists data about all sales of works during the current week. It is divided by salesperson, showing the works that each salesperson, sold this week, and his or her total sales. At the end, it gives the grand total of all sales for the week.

12. **Buyer Sales Report.** The buyer sales report is shown in Figure 1.18. Buyer data comes from invoices. The report shows buyers in alphabetical order by last name. Works they purchased this year are listed in order by date of purchase.

13. **Preferred Customer Report.** Alan would like to target potential customers, as well as current ones, by keeping information about all those who attend showings, or whose names are gathered from the potential customer information form. For each present and potential customer, he would like to keep identifying data and information about the customer's preferences, such as the name of a preferred artist, type, medium, and style for each customer. He hopes to increase sales and hold down costs by using this information to make up targeted invitation lists for showings of works that match customer preferences. For example, he would like to be able to get a report such as the one shown in Figure 1.19. This report could be run for the artist or artists being featured in a show. It lists potential customers whose stated preferences list the same artist, type, medium, or style as the works shown.

SALESPERSON	Artist	Title	Owner	Buyer	Sale Date	Selling Price	Comm
SALES FOR WEEK ENDING MM/DD/YYYY							
Salesperson	Artist	Title	Owner	Buyer	Sale Date	Selling Price	Comm
XXXX							
	XXX	XXX	XXX	XXX	mm/dd	9999.99	999.99
	XXX	XXX	XXX	XXX	mm/dd	9999.99	999.99
	. . .						
	XXX	XXX	XXX	XXX	mm/dd	9999.99	999.99
					Total:	9999.99	999.99
XXXX							
	XXX	XXX	XXX	XXX	mm/dd	9999.99	999.99
	XXX	XXX	XXX	XXX	mm/dd	9999.99	999.99
	. . .						
	XXX	XXX	XXX	XXX	mm/dd	9999.99	999.99
. . .					Total:	9999.99	999.99
XXXX							
	XXX	XXX	XXX	XXX	mm/dd	9999.99	999.99
	XXX	XXX	XXX	XXX	mm/dd	9999.99	999.99
	. . .						
	XXX	XXX	XXX	XXX	mm/dd	9999.99	999.99
					Total:	9999.99	999.99
Total of all Sales for Week: 99999.99							

FIGURE 1.17

Sales This Week

BUYERS SALES REPORT

Date mm/dd/yyyy

Last Name	First Name	Address	Phone	Total Purchases Last Year
XXXX	XXXX	XXXX	XXXX	9999.99

Purchases This Year:

Date Purchased	Artist	Title	Asking Price	Selling Price
mm/dd/yyyy	XXX	XXX	9999.99	9999.99
mm/dd/yyyy	XXX	XXX	9999.99	9999.99
. . .				
mm/dd/yyyy	XXX	XXX	9999.99	9999.99
Total Purchases This Year:			9999.99	9999.99

Last Name	First Name	Address	Phone	Total Purchases Last Year
XXXX	XXXX	XXXX	XXXX	9999.99

Purchases This Year:

Date Purchased	Artist	Title	Asking Price	Selling Price
mm/dd/yyyy	XXX	XXX	9999.99	9999.99
mm/dd/yyyy	XXX	XXX	9999.99	9999.99
. . .				
mm/dd/yyyy	XXX	XXX	9999.99	9999.99
Total Purchases This Year:			9999.99	9999.99

. . .
. . .
. . .

Last Name	First Name	Address	Phone	Total Purchases Last Year
XXXX	XXXX	XXXX	XXXX	9999.99

Purchases This Year:

Date Purchased	Artist	Title	Asking Price	Selling Price
mm/dd/yyyy	XXX	XXX	9999.99	9999.99
mm/dd/yyyy	XXX	XXX	9999.99	9999.99
. . .				
mm/dd/yyyy	XXX	XXX	9999.99	9999.99
Total Purchases This Year:			9999.99	9999.99

FIGURE 1.18

Buyers Sales Report

PREFERRED CUSTOMER REPORT

Artist	Title	Type	Medium	Style	Cust Name	Address	Pref Artist	Pref Type	Pref Medium	Pref Style
XXX	XXX	XXX	XXX	XXX	XXX	XXX	XXX	XXX	XXX	XXX
					XXX	XXX	XXX	XXX	XXX	XXX
					. . .					
					XXX	XXX	XXX	XXX	XXX	XXX
	XXX	XXX	XXX	XXX	XXX	XXX	XXX	XXX	XXX	XXX
					XXX	XXX	XXX	XXX	XXX	XXX
					. . .					
					XXX	XXX	XXX	XXX	XXX	XXX
. . .										
	XXX	XXX	XXX	XXX	XXX	XXX	XXX	XXX	XXX	XXX
					XXX	XXX	XXX	XXX	XXX	XXX
					. . .					
					XXX	XXX	XXX	XXX	XXX	XXX
. . .										
XXX	XXX	XXX	XXX	XXX	XXX	XXX	XXX	XXX	XXX	XXX
					XXX	XXX	XXX	XXX	XXX	XXX
					. . .					
					XXX	XXX	XXX	XXX	XXX	XXX
	XXX	XXX	XXX	XXX	XXX	XXX	XXX	XXX	XXX	XXX
					XXX	XXX	XXX	XXX	XXX	XXX
					. . .					
					XXX	XXX	XXX	XXX	XXX	XXX
	XXX	XXX	XXX	XXX	XXX	XXX	XXX	XXX	XXX	XXX
					XXX	XXX	XXX	XXX	XXX	XXX
					. . .					
					XXX	XXX	XXX	XXX	XXX	XXX

FIGURE 1.19

Preferred Customer Report

SALESPERSON PERFORMANCE REPORT							
Report Starting Date mm/dd/yyyy				**Report Ending Date mm/dd/yyyy**			
Salesperson Name	Add	SocSecNo	Artist	Title	Asking Price	Selling Price	Date Sold
XXX	XXX	999-99-9999	XXX	XXX	9999.99	9999.99	mm/dd/yyyy
				XXX	9999.99	9999.99	mm/dd/yyyy
			. . .				
			XXX	XXX	9999.99	9999.99	mm/dd/yyyy
				Total Sales for Period: 9999.99			
				Total Commission for Period: 9999.99			
XXX	XXX	999-99-9999	XXX	XXX	9999.99	9999.99	mm/dd/yyyy
				XXX	9999.99	9999.99	mm/dd/yyyy
			. . .				
			XXX	XXX	9999.99	9999.99	mm/dd/yyyy
				Total Sales for Period: 9999.99			
				Total Commission for Period: 9999.99			

FIGURE 1.20
Salesperson Performance Report

14. **Salesperson Performance Report.** The report shown in Figure 1.20 would be generated for a period starting with whatever date is selected (e.g., January first of the current year) and ending with another selected date (e.g., today's date). It provides an individual listing of each of the works sold by that person during the period, as well as his or her total sales for the period chosen. Typically, it would be run once a month, to allow Alan to evaluate each salesperson's performance.

15. **Aged Artworks Report.** This report shown in Figure 1.21, is generated at the end of each month. It lists the works of art that have been for sale in the gallery for six months or more. Alan uses it to contact the artist or collector to determine whether the works should be returned, or remain for sale for an additional period of time.

16. **Owner Payment Stub.** When an artwork is sold, a check is sent to the owner for 90% of the selling price. The stub that accompanies the check is shown in Figure 1.22.

ARTWORKS HELD OVER SIX MONTHS

Report Date mm/dd/yyyy

Owner Name	Owner Telephone	Artist Name	Title	Date Listed	Asking Price
XXX	XXX XXX XXXX	XXX	XXX	mm/dd/yyyy	9999.99
			XXX	mm/dd/yyyy	9999.99
		. . .			
		XXX	XXX	mm/dd/yyyy	9999.99
XXX	XXX XXX XXXX	XXX	XXX	mm/dd/yyyy	9999.99
		XXX	XXX	mm/dd/yyyy	9999.99
		. . .			
		XXX	XXX	mm/dd/yyyy	9999.99
. . .					
XXX	XXX XXX XXXX	XXX	XXX	mm/dd/yyyy	9999.99
			XXX	mm/dd/yyyy	9999.99
		. . .			
		XXX	XXX	mm/dd/yyyy	9999.99

FIGURE 1.21

Aged Artworks Report

THE ART GALLERY

Payment for Sale of Artwork

Owner Name _____

Owner Address _____

City_____   State ___   Zip _____

Telephone: Area Code ____ Number _____

Owner Social Security Number _____

Artist Name _____   Title _____

Type _____ Medium _____ Style _____ Size _____

Salesperson _____

Selling Price 9999.99   Tax 9999.99   Total Amount of Sale 9999.99

Amount Remitted to Owner 9999.99

FIGURE 1.22

Payment Stub

ART SHOW REPORT

Title of Show _____

Opening Date _____   Closing Date _____

Featured Artist _____ or Theme _____

Works Included:

Artist	Title	Asking Price	Status (*sold* or *for sale*)
XXX	XXX	9999.99	XXX
	XXX	9999.99	XXX
	. . .		
XXX	XXX	9999.99	XXX
	XXX	9999.99	XXX
	. . .		
. . .			
XXX	XXX	9999.99	XXX
	XXX	9999.99	XXX
	. . .		

FIGURE 1.23

Art Show Report

17. **Art Show Details.** For each show, this report provides information about the dates, featured artist or theme, and works shown. It
appears in Figure 1.23.

  ▪ Step 1.3. Sketch of Screens for Routine Transactions

For all transactions, the user is prompted to choose from a menu of possible
transactions, and is provided with instructions for filling in the information
needed. The screen displays the results, which may also be printed out.

18. **Adding a New Artist.** A member of the office staff enters the data
from the Artist Information Form. The screen has the same layout
as that form. The results screen informs the user that the artist has
been added, or that the artist is already in the database.

19. **Adding a New Collector.** Similarly, an office worker enters data
from the Collector information form, using a screen with the
same layout as the form. The results screen informs the user that
the person has been entered or is already in the database.

20. **Adding a New Work of Art.** Information about new artworks is taken directly from the information form and entered in a screen with the same layout as the form. The database is checked to ensure that the combination of artist name and title is unique, and then displays a screen saying the work has been added.

21. **Sale Transaction.** The data shown in the invoice, Figure 1.10, is entered on a sales transaction screen that has the same layout as the invoice. The receipt, which omits the owner's address and telephone number, is displayed as a response, and a clerk prints out the receipt.

22. **Adding a Potential Customer.** The data shown on the Mailing List form is entered for each potential customer. People who purchase an artwork, and collectors of artwork in the gallery are also automatically added to the customer file, using the information from sale invoices and information forms. The response screen confirms that the person was added, or that he or she was already in the database.

- Step 1.4. Initial List of Assumptions for The Art Gallery Project

1. Artist names are unique, but customer names and collector names are not.

2. For privacy reasons, only people who receive payments from the gallery are asked to provide their social security numbers, because these payments have to be reported for income tax purposes. Therefore, the gallery keeps social security numbers for salespersons, collectors, and artists, but not for buyers or potential customers.

3. An artist might have many works for sale in the gallery.

4. Each work is an original, one-of-a-kind piece. No prints or reproductions are sold.

5. Two works of art can have the same title, but the combination of title and artist name is unique.

6. A work of art can be owned either by the artist who created it or by another person, referred to here as a collector.

7. Even if the work of art is owned by a collector, it is important to keep information about the artist who created it, since that is a factor in determining its value.

8. A work of art is sold by the gallery only once. The gallery does not re-sell its own works.

9. A work of art might appear in more than one show. Some works do not appear in any show.

10. Payment for all sales is made immediately and in full at the time of purchase. Payment may be by credit, cash, or check. The owner is paid the balance and the salesperson is paid the commission at the end of the week.

11. The database does not include payroll information, except for the commission to be paid to salespeople for sales of artwork.

12. There are lists of valid values for type, style, and medium of artworks. Each has a value "other" for works that do not fit existing values.

13. Information about works not selected to be listed by the gallery is discarded.

14. Lists of artists, collectors, buyers, and potential customers are evaluated periodically to determine whether they should be dropped.

STUDENT PROJECTS: INTRODUCTION TO STUDENT PROJECTS

Several projects are described on the next few pages. You should study the project you will work on, read the preceding sample project, and use it as a model in carrying out the steps for your project. If you can do so, interview people who are familiar with the environment described in the project. Based on your interviews, the written description, and your own analysis of the project you have chosen, do the following steps. Remember that you should not make any assumptions about the internal structure of the database at this point. Your reports and forms should be based on user's needs, not on the database file structures.

- Step 1.1. Write out the format of every input document that provides information to be stored in the database.

- Step 1.2. Write out the format of every routine report to be produced using the database.

- Step 1.3. Sketch the input and output screens for every routine transaction to be performed against the database.

- Step 1.4. Write out an initial list of assumptions for the project.

Project One: Beta University Annual Fund

General Description

The Development Office of Beta University seeks to obtain donations for its Annual Fund from a variety of donors. The fund collects over $10 million each year. Donors include graduating seniors, alumni, parents, faculty, administrators, staff, corporations, or friends of the university. There are approximately 100,000 potential donors. The Annual Fund is directed by Suzanne Hayes, who is responsible for raising funds and keeping track of donations. Suzanne wishes to create a database to help with both of these major responsibilities.

Basic Operations

Suzanne tries to raise funds in several ways during each fiscal year, which extends from July 1 to June 30. Each fall, all potential donors to the Annual Fund receive personalized letters from her, emphasizing their close ties to Beta University. The letters contain reply envelopes and forms on which the donors can fill in the amount they are pledging to contribute that year, and the method of payment they choose. Payment can be sent as a single check in the envelope, donors can choose deferred payments over a period of a year, or they can provide their credit card numbers to pay in a single lump sum. Often, the employer of the donor or of the donor's spouse has a program to make a matching gift to the university, and the donor provides the contact information on the envelope. A letter acknowledging the gift and thanking the donor is sent as soon as the pledge is received. Suzanne is responsible for following up with the employer to collect the matching gift, which is paid in a single lump sum by the corporation.

Several fundraising events are held during the year. Suzanne solicits donations at a fall carnival, a holiday dinner dance, and a spring golf outing, among other events. Each class year has a class coordinator who helps by contacting members of his or her graduating class. An additional letter from the class coordinator is sent to ask for larger donations from reunion classes, those who are marking an important anniversary of graduation—whether five years, 10 years, or higher—prior to their reunion celebration weekend. Each spring there is a phonothon during which current students and volunteers call other potential donors and solicit pledges. All alumni who have not contributed by the end of May receive telephone calls from their class coordinator asking them for a donation. If the class coordinator is unable to contact his or her class-mates, Suzanne or a volunteer makes these calls instead.

The donations are categorized by the group they are from, by the year of the donor (if applicable) and by size. There are 10 "donor circles," which are categorized by the size of the gift—President's Circle for gifts over $50,000, Platinum Circle for gifts over $25,000, and so on. Gifts under $100 are not listed as belonging to a circle. An annual report listing all donors by category, year, and donor circle is published and mailed to all actual and potential donors during the summer. The report does not list the actual amount each person contributed.

Information Needs

At present, Suzanne has a mailing list on a word processor that is used to generate labels and letters to potential donors. She would like to be able to personalize each letter by adding a line about the amount of money the donor gave the previous year. A spreadsheet is used to keep track of pledges and donations. Large pledges from individual donors are ordinarily paid in monthly installments rather than in one payment, but currently there is no way to keep track of those payments. When a database is developed, Suzanne would like to be able to send reminders if payments are over a month late.

An Annual Fund Gift form is sent with all letters soliciting funds, with blanks for the donor to fill in the applicable information, as follows:

> **Beta University Annual Fund Gift.** Donor Name, Donor Address, Category (a check list specifying senior, alumnus/alumna, parent, administrator, etc.), Year of Graduation, Date of Pledge/Gift, Amount Pledged, Amount Enclosed, Payment Method, Number of Payments Chosen, Credit Card Number, Matching Corporation Name, Matching Corporation Address, Name of Spouse (if matching gift is from spouse's employer).

When pledges are received by class representatives or during the phonothon, the same information is collected on similar forms. Reports needed include:

1. **Annual Report to Donors.** This report was described previously. It lists names only, not amounts. However, the names have to be categorized as indicated. The report also has summaries, including the total amount raised from all sources, the total for each

class, the percent participation for each class, the total for each category, the grand total for each donor circle, and the class total for each donor circle. It is an important fundraising tool for the following year's drive, since it is mailed to each potential donor.

2. **Monthly Report.** This is an internal report that Suzanne uses to evaluate the progress of the fundraising for the year so far. It gives the totals and percentages of pledges and gifts received for the current month in all categories.

3. **Payments Due Report.** Suzanne would like a report each month listing the pledge payments that were due that month but were not received. It would list the donor's name and address, the amount due, the date due, the amount of the pledge, the amount received so far, and the date of the previous payment, if any.

4. **Event Report.** Suzanne would like to generate reports showing who attends each of the fundraising events, and what pledges and gifts were received from the attendees.

5. **Class Representative Contact List.** For each class representative, Suzanne would like a list of classmates to be contacted, including the name, address, telephone number, last year's donation information, and this year's donation information.

6. **Phonothon Volunteer Contact List.** Each volunteer caller is given a list with information about the potential donors he or she is expected to call, including the name, telephone number, address, category, year (if applicable), and last year's donation information.

In addition to the forms and reports listed here, there are several others that would be useful. Do Steps 1.1–1.4 based on the information provided and any additional applicable assumptions you need to make about the operations of the Annual Fund.

Project Two: Pleasantville Community Theater Group

General Description

The Pleasantville Community Theater Group is a nonprofit organization of about two hundred members, amateurs who enjoy producing and performing in plays. Members pay dues of $50 per year. The group produces two plays each year but not all members are active workers every year.

Basic Operations

The group produces plays in the fall and spring. Some members of the group have roles in the plays, while others work on scenery, costumes, publicity, programs, and other tasks. The group has two general meetings per year. Each fall they meet to elect officers—a president, vice president, secretary, treasurer, and house manager, who serve for the entire year. At the end of the spring season, the group meets again to evaluate the previous year's activities and to select the two plays and their producers for the following year. The producer of each play is then responsible for managing all aspects of that production, including recruiting volunteers, promotion, casting, and more. The group sometimes obtains sponsorship from local businesses for a production, and always prints a program with advertisements that help defray some of the production costs. The program also lists the cast, crew, and credits for the show. Most of the production work is done by the members, but skilled craftsmen are contracted as needed for specific tasks, such as electrical wiring. No professional actors are used. For a theater, the group uses the local high school auditorium, which has about a thousand seats.

Information Needs

The group wishes to have a database to keep track of members and productions. They also need to compile names and addresses of potential playgoers (patrons) so they can mail announcements about each production, to help sell tickets. In the past, open seating has been used, but they would now like to use assigned seats, since the auditorium identifies seats with row letters and seat numbers. There are 26 rows (A–Z) with 40 seats per row. This would allow the company to have subscriptions with assigned seating. The database should keep track of plays that are suitable for production by such a company. They also need to compile information about potential or past corporate sponsors. Some of the forms or reports that would be helpful are:

1. **Play Listing.** Plays that could be produced by the company are identified by title, author, type (drama, comedy, musical, and such), and number of acts.

2. **Program—Cast and Credits.** The program for each production should list the names of the actors and the jobs each member had for the production.

3. **Program—Sponsors.** The program should list all the corporations and individuals who donated money, goods, or services for each production.

4. **Report of Patrons.** This internal report lists mailing information for patrons, as well as a list of the productions they bought tickets for in the past.

5. **Ticket Sales Report.** This internal report should list the tickets, along with price and seat numbers, that patrons have ordered for productions.

6. **Admission Ticket.** The database should be able to print tickets when a patron orders them. The ticket should list the name of the play, the date, time, price, and seat.

7. **Member Dues Payment Report.** The treasurer needs a report that shows which members have paid dues and which members still owe them. Contact information for those who have not yet paid dues should be provided.

8. **Balance Sheet.** The treasurer is responsible for maintaining all information about income and expenditures for the year. Income comes from dues, sponsors, ticket sales, and other sources. Expenditures include costs for the productions, such as contractor's fees, equipment rental, auditorium rental fee, and other services. At the end of the year the sheet should show at most a modest profit, but never a loss. Therefore, the treasurer must be able to report on the current financial condition at any time, so that expenditures can be evaluated before funds are spent.

9. **Ticket Sales Transaction.** The ticket sales process requires an interactive transaction. The user should be able to input a request for one or more seats for a particular performance, and the return screen should display sufficient information to allow the user to determine whether the seats are available. If so, the transaction should be completed by reserving the seats and printing the tickets. If not, it should be possible to find alternate seats, if they exist.

In addition to the forms and reports listed here, there are several others that would be useful. Do Steps 1.1–1.4 based on the information provided here and any additional applicable assumptions you need to make about the operations of the Pleasantville Community Theater Group.

Project Three: Friendly Cars Dealership

General Description

Friendly Cars is a dealership that offers new cars from a single manufacturer. The dealership is located in a suburb of a large city. Its gross sales exceed $1 million per year. It has 10 employees—Jim Friendly (the owner/manager), eight salespeople, and an office manager. Most of its customers are from the surrounding area, and they learn about the dealership by word of mouth; from newspaper, radio, and television advertisements; via the Internet; or by referral from buying services.

Basic Operations

Potential customers usually come in person to the showroom to browse and test drive the cars. They comparison shop, visiting many dealerships of several manufacturers. They usually have a list of features they want, and some knowledge of the models the dealership offers. They are greeted by whichever salesperson is free when they walk into the showroom. In a few cases, they specify which salesperson they wish to deal with. They work with a single salesperson until the deal is completed, because all sales are done on a commission basis. There is a sticker price on each car, prominently displayed in the side window. Customers negotiate with the salesperson to get a better price. If the proposed price is significantly below the sticker price, the salesperson has to get Jim's approval before agreeing to the deal. Financing can be arranged with the manufacturer through the dealership, or the customer can get financing through his or her own bank. All taxes and license fees are paid through the dealership. The customer can have additional customization of the car, including special trim, alarm system, audio system, and other features done at the dealership before picking up the car. All the new cars come with a standard warranty, but customers can opt for an extended warranty at an additional cost. Trade-ins are accepted as partial payment for new cars. The dealership also sells these trade-ins as used cars, which can be models from a variety of manufacturers. No maintenance is done on the trade-ins; they are sold "as-is," with a limited 30-day warranty.

Information Needs

The dealership has a database management system that currently keeps track of the cars and sales information. However, Jim wishes to develop a new database that can provide more information more efficiently than the current system. The current system stores information about the cars, the customers, the salespeople, and the sales of cars. The following forms and reports are used:

1. **Price Sticker.** The price sticker that comes with the car when it is shipped from the manufacturer contains all the basic information about the car itself. It includes a vehicle ID that identifies the car uniquely, and is physically embedded in the car's body. The sticker also gives the list price, model, date of manufacture, place of manufacture, number of cylinders, number of doors, weight, capacity, options, color, and other specifications. The dealership adds the date the car was delivered and the mileage at the time of delivery.

2. **Customer Data.** Basic contact information about customers is obtained by salespeople when they greet them at the showroom. Additional customer information is gathered when a sale is made. Jim also seeks to gather names and addresses of potential customers using referrals, reply cards from newspapers and magazines, and other sources. These are used to mail promotional material to prospective customers.

3. **License, Tax, and Insurance Documents.** The dealership is required to submit information about each sale to the state prior to issuing a license plate for the car. They must also remit the state sales tax and license fee on each sale directly to the state. They are required to obtain and submit proof of insurance coverage to the state before releasing the car to the new owner.

4. **Bill of Sale.** When the car is delivered to the customer, a completed bill of sale—showing the customer information, salesperson name, vehicle ID, current mileage, and all specifications including any extra customization, financing, warrantee information, license and insurance information, price, and all other details—is provided to the customer, with a copy kept in the dealership. This bill of sale is the same whether the car is new or used.

5. **Salesperson Performance Report.** Jim would like a monthly report summarizing each salesperson's sales for the previous month. The amount of commission earned is also shown on the report.

6. **Customer Satisfaction Survey.** Within a month after each sale, the dealership sends a survey to the new owner, asking questions

about the customer's opinion of the car, the dealership, and the salesperson.

In addition to these forms and reports, there are several others that would be useful. Do Steps 1.1–1.4 based on the information provided here and any additional applicable assumptions you need to make about the operations of Friendly Cars.

Project Four: Images Photography Studio

General Description

Images Photography Studio is a small business that provides custom photography services to individual and corporate clients. The services include photographing weddings, graduations, awards ceremonies, business conferences, receptions, and other events. The studio also offers sittings for individual, family, or group portraits, which may be taken in the studio or at a location specified by the client. The studio photographs about two hundred events and takes about a thousand portraits per year. The staff consists of the manager/owner, Liz Davis, who is a professional photographer, five additional staff photographers, and an office manager.

Basic Operations

The client usually contacts the studio to make an appointment to meet with Liz or her representative. At the first meeting, the representative shows samples of the studio's work, and answers any questions the client might have. The client provides information including the services desired, location, date, time, and the name of the photographer requested, if any. Most events require two photographers, a primary one and an assistant, but portraits require only one. In addition to the six regular photographers, the studio maintains a list of freelance photographers to use for events when the staff photographers are booked or unavailable. The representative provides an estimate and makes a tentative booking. After the initial meeting, a contract is prepared and mailed to the client for a signature. The client returns the signed contract with a deposit, and the booking is finalized. The photographers cover the event or sitting, the film is developed, and proofs are produced. Each proof is assigned a unique identifying number, and a package of proofs is presented to the client. The client selects the pictures desired, and places the final order along with any special instructions, such as retouching, desired. The pictures or albums are produced and the final package is delivered to the client.

Payments are made for jobs at various times. Usually, a deposit is given at the time of the booking, and additional payments are made on the day of the event or sitting, on presentation of the proofs to the client, and when the final package is delivered. Many package options are available, including combinations of pictures of various sizes, several types of albums, and digital packages. The packages are described in a printed booklet, and are identified by number. The final package might differ from the original request, so the last payment needs to be adjusted accordingly. In the event the client is not pleased with the proofs, he or she has the option of refusing a final package, but the deposit and payments for the sitting are not refunded. Clients keep proofs, but the studio owns the copyright for the images and it keeps all negatives and digital files for six months, during which time the client may order additional photographs. At the end of six months, the negatives and files are discarded unless the client requests additional time.

Information Needs

The company currently keeps records by hand, but its business has grown enough so that a database is needed to help control its operations. The current manual system is unwieldy and inefficient, and the owner wishes to develop a database system that the office manager will be able to maintain. The system will be used to keep information about clients, jobs, and photographers. It will not include information about supplies, equipment, office expenses, or payroll. The forms used to provide information are:

1. **Inquiry Form.** This document is filled in when the client meets with the manager. It lists such items as contact information, services requested, and package chosen. During the interview, the manager checks to see what photographers are available at the requested time, and chooses one to put on the form. Entries are considered tentative and subject to change before a contract is drawn up.

2. **Contract.** The contract contains data from the inquiry form, as well as the name of the photographer(s) assigned to the job, planned payment data, and any additional requests from the client. Each contract form has a unique number, and it contains some pre-printed matter, such as the studio's name and address, and notices concerning cancellation, liability, and notice of copyright.

3. **Package Order Form.** The package order form is filled out when the client selects the proofs and decides on the final package. If the client orders additional pictures or albums during the six-month period following the final order, an additional order form is filled out. Each order form has a unique number.

The following reports are needed:

4. **Photographer Schedule.** A schedule is printed for any period desired, typically a week or a month, for each photographer. It provides basic information about the scheduled events or sittings, and refers to the contract number, which can be used by the photographer to get complete information about each scheduled event or sitting.

5. **Weekly Schedule.** The weekly schedule summarizes the scheduled activities for each day of the week, for all photographers. For each day, it lists the activities in order by time. The report can be run for any week desired, not only for the current week.

6. **Accounts Receivable.** This report summarizes payments that are due each month.

7. **Client Report.** This report can be run as desired to provide information about individual clients. It is typically run for corporate clients, to provide a summary of the services provided to them.

8. **Photographer Availability Transaction.** The database must be able to support a transaction in which the user enters the photographer's name and the date, and the output screen tells the hours he or she is available on that date.

In addition to the forms and reports listed here, there are several others that would be useful. Do Steps 1.1–1.4 based on the information provided here and any additional applicable assumptions you need to make about the operations of Images Photography Studio.

Project Five: Wellness Clinic—Medical Group

General Description

The Wellness Clinic is a facility providing medical care in a rural area of the country. Its professional staff consists of five medical doctors (physicians), two nurse-practitioners who provide non-acute care and can prescribe medication, two registered nurses, two midwives who provide pre-natal care and supervise delivery except in cases with complications, a pharmacist, and a medical technician. The non-professional staff members include an office administrator, a receptionist, and a bookkeeper who works part-time. The clinic serves several thousand patients, each of whom may visit the clinic any number of times per year, both for preventative care such as checkups or immunizations, and for treatment of illness. Its facilities consist of a waiting room with a reception desk, an administrative office, a nurses' station, 10 examining rooms with adjoining consultation rooms, a small operating room, a birthing room, a recovery room, a pharmacy, and a small laboratory.

Basic Operations

The clinic has regular hours of operation weekdays, Saturday mornings, and two evenings per week. Normally two physicians or one physician and one nurse practitioner, one registered nurse, and one midwife are in the clinic during regular hours. In addition, the professional staff members rotate responsibility for covering emergency calls 24 hours per day, seven days a week. At the end of each day, the administrator or receptionist sets up call forwarding so that emergency calls are automatically directed to the telephone number of the person providing emergency coverage. When the clinic opens in the morning, the call forwarding is halted. Two of the physicians are surgeons who perform routine surgery not requiring general anesthesia at the clinic one morning a week, assisted by a nurse. Others have specialties in pediatrics and internal medicine. However, all of the physicians can provide general and acute care for any of the patients. Patients who require major surgery or other hospital care must go to a hospital located outside the immediate area served by the clinic. The clinic staff members do not normally visit their patients who are in the hospital, instead leaving their care to the hospital staff with whom the clinic communicates during the hospitalization. However, the clinic provides both pre- and post-hospital care for the patients.

Hours of operation are divided into scheduled appointments and unscheduled hours that are open for walk-ins. Patients usually schedule checkups and immunizations well in advance. Patients suffering from chronic or acute illness can usually schedule appointments promptly, or they may come in during the unscheduled hours. The administrator is responsible for setting up all schedules, both for the staff and for patients, and for keeping records updated. Prior to the beginning of each month, the administrator makes up complete coverage schedules for all staff. The bookkeeper is responsible for doing all billing, and recording payments. The receptionist is responsible for making appointments, handling traffic, and making the patient's medical records available in a folder during the visit. The nurse prepares the patient, takes medical history, performs some medical routines or tests, takes samples for lab tests, updates the folder, and assists the practitioner (the physician, nurse practitioner, or midwife) during the visit. During the visit, the practitioner examines the patient, administers medical treatment, can perform some tests, can take samples for lab tests, and write prescriptions for medications or orders for additional lab tests. Each visit results in one or more diagnoses, which the practitioner adds to the patient's folder, along with any comments or observations. Prescriptions can be filled at the clinic's pharmacy at the patient's request. Some laboratory tests are performed at the clinic by the medical technician, using samples taken by one of the professionals. More specialized tests are performed at a medical laboratory at the hospital outside the region. Whenever possible, specimens such as blood samples are taken at the clinic and then sent to the hospital laboratory. If the lab test requires the presence of the patient and equipment that is not available at the clinic, the patient is sent to the hospital laboratory for the test, and results are sent back to the clinic.

Medical care is provided for all patients, regardless of their ability to pay. Bills are generated based on the services provided, not on the payment method. Private patients who can afford to pay out of pocket can do so at the time of service or be billed at the end of each month. Those who have medical insurance provide information about their insurance policies, and the insurance companies are billed. Usually in that case patients pay a small amount of co-insurance (co-pay), which is determined by the type of policy they hold, at the time of the visit. Those who cannot afford to pay normally have government-provided healthcare, for which they have a government-issued medical card. They pay nothing and the clinic is reimbursed by the government for the entire cost of the visit, including any lab tests performed and medications dispensed there. A small number of indigent patients who do not have health coverage are treated and the cost is absorbed by the clinic until the patient qualifies for government-provided coverage.

Information Needs

Currently all information about patients and their care is kept manually, and billing is done using a spreadsheet kept on a personal computer.

Physicians use standard mail, fax, or telephone communications to provide information to the hospital and receive information about patients who need hospital care. The clinic recently upgraded its computer and it will have access to hospital records for its patients, as well as on-line systems provided by insurance companies and the government for third-party billing. The clinic needs a database that keeps track of all the patient-related activities of the clinic, and to provide information about billing and payments. The database will not keep track of medical supplies, plant maintenance, or payroll information.

The following forms or reports are needed.

1. **Weekly Coverage Schedule.** This schedule needs to list the daily hours and the professional and non-professional staff who are scheduled to be in the clinic at specific times each day of the week. It also needs to list the name and telephone number of the person who is covering for emergencies during all hours each week. (Recall that the administrator provides the coverage information each month.)

2. **Daily Master Schedule.** This is a master schedule for all practitioners for each day. It should list each of the practitioners who are in that day, with all patient appointments scheduled. Most appointments are allocated 10 minutes, so each hour has six time slots. However, some appointments are given more than one time slot, depending on the nature of the care needed. Each professional has hours dedicated to walk-ins during which no pre-scheduled appointments are made. As walk-ins sign in for care, they are assigned to a practitioner and the patient's name is added to the schedule. The registered nurses do not have appointments scheduled, and are available to assist the practitioners with visits, or to administer tests or take samples on an unscheduled basis. The lab technician also does not have an appointment schedule.

3. **Individual Practitioner's Daily Schedule.** Each of the practitioners should receive an individualized printed copy of the schedule for any day he or she is in the clinic. Appointments list the patient's name and the reason given for the visit. The copy is updated manually by the nurse as visits for walk-ins are conducted.

4. **Physician's Statement for Insurance Forms.** This is a pre-printed form that is used as a receipt primarily for insurance purposes. It

lists the clinic name, address, and telephone number, along with the names and tax identification numbers of all the professionals on the staff. It also lists all the types of visits, the procedures that can be performed with a code for each, and some blank lines for "other," along with a line to enter the fee for each. It also has a list of the common diagnoses and codes, with a few blank lines for "other." At the bottom are lines for Total Charge, Amount Paid, and Balance Due. The provider uses this form during a visit to record visit type, procedures performed, and diagnosis. When the patient checks out after the visit, the receptionist fills in the fee for each service using a fee schedule, calculates the total, and writes in the amount paid, if any, and the Balance Due. One copy is kept by the clinic and another is given to the patient. At present, a third copy is mailed to the insurance company or government health agency, but in future the required information will be submitted electronically.

5. **Patient Monthly Statement.** Any patient who has an unpaid balance receives a statement that is compiled at the end of each month, listing all the services provided that month, any payments received, and the balance due.

6. **Precription Label and Receipt.** This form consists of two parts. The top part is gummed and used as a label for the container in which medication is dispensed. The label shows the Rx number, doctor name, patient name, patient address, directions, drug name, form, strength, quantity, pharmacist's name, date filled, original date, and number of refills remaining. The bottom part repeats the information on the label, and also lists the total price of the medication, the amount covered by insurance or the government, and the balance due from the patient, as well as more information about the drug, complete directions for use, and warnings about possible side effects and drug interactions. The receipt can be used for submitting claims for insurance coverage. In the future, this information will also be submitted electronically to insurance companies and the government medical care agency.

7. **Daily Laboratory Log.** This log is used to record all lab tests performed each day.

8. **Operating Room Schedule.** This schedule provides information about all scheduled surgeries for the day.

9. **Operating Room Log.** This records information about the surgeries actually performed on a given day, including identification of the patient, surgeon, and nurse, and notations and observations about the surgery.

10. **Daily Delivery Room Log.** This records information about all the deliveries performed each day.

11. **Recovery Room Log.** This report records information about the use of the recovery room, including the patient's name, attending practitioner, bed, date in, time in, date out, time out, and signature of the practitioner who signs the patient out. A nurse records the times and results of any medical checks performed while the patient is in recovery.

12. **Monthly Activity Report.** This is an internal report summarizing the clinic's activity each month. It shows such items as the number of visits conducted by each provider, the number of surgeries performed, the number of deliveries, the number of lab tests broken down by type, the number of prescriptions dispensed, the average time per visit, and so on.

These are just a few of many reports and forms that would be helpful to the staff of the clinic. In addition to the forms and reports listed here, there are several others that would be useful. Do Steps 1.1–1.4 based on the information provided here and any additional applicable assumptions you need to make about the operations of The Wellness Clinic.

2 CHAPTER

Database Planning and Database Architecture

Chapter Objectives

In this chapter you will learn the following:

- Why data is viewed as a corporate resource

- The distinction between data and information

- The four levels of discussion about data

- The meaning of the following terms: entity, entity set, attribute, relationship

- The meaning of the terms metadata, record type, data item type, data item, data aggregate, record, data dictionary, data instance, and file

2.7 Overview of Data Models

    2.7.1 Entity-Relationship Model

    2.7.2 Relational Model

    2.7.3 Object-Oriented Model

    2.7.4 Object-Relational Model

    2.7.5 Semistructured Data Model

2.8 Chapter Summary

Exercises

Lab Exercises

2.1 Exploring a Diagramming Tool

2.2 Exploring a Project Management Tool

2.3 Constructing a Simple Data Dictionary

SAMPLE PROJECT: Applying Planning Techniques to The Art Gallery Project

STUDENT PROJECTS: Applying Planning Techniques to the Student Project

- The steps in staged database design
- How a data dictionary is constructed and used
- The skills and functions of a database administrator
- The functions of a data sublanguage and a host language
- The distinction between data definition language (DDL) and data manipulation language (DML)
- The rationale for and contents of the three-level database architecture
- The meaning of logical and physical data independence
- Characteristics of various data models—entity-relationship, relational, object-oriented, object-relational, and semistructured

2.1   Data as a Resource

If you were asked to identify the resources of a typical business organization, you would probably include capital equipment, financial assets, and personnel, but you might not think of data as a resource. When a corporate database exists, the data it contains is a genuine corporate resource. Since the database contains data about the organization's operations (called **operational data**) that is used by many departments, and since it is professionally managed by a DBA, there is an increased appreciation of the value of the data itself, independent of the applications that use it. A **resource** is any asset that is of value to an organization and that incurs costs. An organization's operational data clearly fits this definition. To appreciate the value of an organization's data more fully, imagine what would happen if the data were lost or fell into the hands of a competitor. Many organizations, such as banks and brokerage houses, are heavily dependent on data, and would fail very quickly if their data were lost. Most businesses would suffer heavy losses if their operational data were unavailable. In fact, an organization depends on the availability of operational data in managing its other resources. For example, decisions about the purchase, lease, or use of equipment; financial investments and financial returns; and staffing needs should be made on the basis of information about the organization's operations. The recognition of data as a corporate resource is an important objective in developing a database environment. The database protects the data resource by providing data security, integrity, and reliability controls through the DBMS.

2.2   Characteristics of Data

In order to appreciate the importance of data as a corporate resource, we need to examine its characteristics more closely.

2.2.1   Data and Information

We often think of data as information, but these two terms have slightly different meanings. The term **data** refers to the bare facts recorded in the database. They may be items about people, places, events, or concepts. **Information** is processed data that is in a form that is useful for making decisions. Information is derived from the stored data by re-arranging, selecting, combining, summarizing, or performing other operations on the data. For example, if we simply print out all the stored items in the database shown in Figure 1.1, without identifying what they represent, we have data. However, if we print a formatted report such as like the one in Figure 1.3, showing the data in some order that helps us make a decision, we have information. In practice, most people use the two terms interchangeably.

2.2.2   Levels of Discussing Data

When we discuss data, it is important to distinguish between the real world, the small part of the real world that the database is concerned with, the structure of the database, and the data stored in the database. There are actually four levels of discussion or abstraction to be considered when we talk about databases.

We begin with the **real world,** or reality. On this level, we talk about the **enterprise,** the organization for which the database is designed. The enterprise might be a corporation, government agency, university, bank, brokerage house, school, hospital, or other organization that actually exists in the real world. As the organization functions in the real world, it is impossible to obtain information needed for decision making by direct observation of reality. There is too much detail involved to keep track of all the facts. Instead, we develop a model or a view of reality in which we represent those facets of the enterprise that we need to keep track of for decision making. The part of the real world that will be represented in the database is called a **miniworld** or a **universe of discourse.** For the miniworld, we begin to develop a **conceptual model,** which forms the second level of data discussion. We identify **entities** as representations of persons, places, events, objects, or concepts about which we collect data. For the organizations mentioned previously, we could choose entities such as customers, employees, students, bank accounts, investments, classes, or patients. We group similar entities into **entity sets.** For example, for the set of all customers we form the entity set we might call Customers. Similarly, we might have entity sets called Employees, Students, Accounts, Investments, Classes, and Patients—each consisting of all entity instances of the corresponding type. A conceptual model may have many entity sets. Each entity has certain **attributes,** which are characteristics or properties to describe the entity and that the organization considers important. Each entity set may have several attributes to describe its members. For the

Student entity set, attributes might include student ID, name, address, telephone number, major, credits passed, grade point average, and adviser. For the Bank Account entity set, attributes might include account number, date opened, owner name, co-owner name, and balance. Some entities may have **relationships** or associations with other entities. For example, in a university, students are related to classes by being enrolled in those classes, and faculty members are related to classes by teaching them. Students and faculty members may be related to one another by the teacher-student relationship or by the adviser-student relationship. Students may be related to one another by being roommates. The conceptual model will represent these relationships by relating the entity sets in some manner. The concepts of entity, attribute, and relationship will be discussed in more detail in Chapter 3. The database should be designed to be a useful model of the organization and its operations for the miniworld of interest. Every entity should be represented, along with its attributes and the relationships in which it participates. In the real world, changes are made to the objects represented by the entities, attributes, or relationships. For example, employees leave the organization, customers change their addresses, and students enroll in different classes. To keep track of the facts about these objects and such changes, we need to develop a conceptual model that allows not only the representation of the basic entities, attributes, and relationships, but also allows us to make changes that mirror the changes in reality.

The structure of the database, called the **logical model** of the database, is the third level of discussion. On this level, we talk about **metadata,** or data about data. For each entity set in the conceptual model, we have a **record type** in the logical model of the database. For example, for the Student entity set in the university, we would have a Student record type. A record type contains several **data item types,** each of which represents an attribute of an entity. For the Student record type, the data item types could be stuId, stuName, address, phone, major, credits, gpa, and adviser. A **data item** is the smallest named unit of stored data. Other words sometimes used for data item are data element, field, or attribute. Generally, a **field** means a set of adjacent bytes identified as the physical location for a data item, so it has a more physical meaning than the term data item. **Attribute** usually refers to a characteristic of an entity in the conceptual model, but since there is a correspondence between attributes and data items, the two words are often interchanged. Data items are sometimes grouped together to form **data aggregates,** which are named groups of data items within a record. For an `Employee` record, there may be a data aggregate called `empAdd`, which consists of the data items `street`, `city`, `state`, and `zip`. Data aggregates allow us to refer to the group of data items as a whole or to the individual items in the group. A **record** is a named collection of related data items and/or data aggregates. As previously mentioned, there is usually a record type for each entity set, and a data item type for each attribute. Relationships may also be represented by record types, but there are other ways to represent relationships.

Information about the logical structure of the database is stored in a **data dictionary,** also called a **data directory** or **system catalog.** This repository of information contains descriptions of the record types, data item types, and data aggregates in the database, as well as other information. For example, the data dictionary/directory might contain an entry for the `Employee` record type, stating that it consists of the data items `empId`, `jobTitle`, `salary`, `dept`, and `mgr`, and the data aggregates `empName` and `empAdd`. For each of the data items, there would be a descriptive entry showing the data item name (e.g., `empId`), its data type (e.g., `char(5)`), and any **synonyms,** which are other names used for the data item (e.g., `emp#`). For data aggregates, the dictionary/directory would list the components. For example, for `empAdd`, it would state that its components are the data items `street`, `city`, `state`, and `zip`, each of which would have been listed as a data item. The data dictionary/directory is actually a database about the database. However, data dictionaries usually do much more than simply store the description of the database structure. For some systems, they are actively involved in all database accesses.

The fourth level of discussion concerns actual data in the database itself. It consists of **data instances** or occurrences. For each object in the miniworld that we are representing as an entity, there will be an occurrence of a corresponding record in the database. For each student in the university, there is an occurrence of a student record. So, while there is only one `Student` record type, which is described in the data dictionary and corresponds to the Student entity set, there may be thousands of `Student` record occurrences, corresponding to individual student entities, in the database itself. Similarly, there will be many instances of each of the data item types that correspond to attributes. A **file** (sometimes called a data set) is a named collection of record occurrences. Usually a file contains all occurrences of one record type. For example, the `Student` file may contain

5000 `Student` records. Finally, the **database** may be thought of as a named collection of related files. Figure 2.1 summarizes the four levels of discussion of data.

Realm	Objects	Examples
Real World Containing Miniworld	Enterprise	Corporation, university, bank
	Some aspects of the enterprise	Human resources Student enrollment Customers and accounts
Conceptual Model	Entity Attribute Entity set Relationship	a student, a class name, schedule all students, all classes Student entity relates to Class entity by being enrolled in it

Logical Model Metadata:
   data definitions,
   stored in
   Data Dictionary
	Record type
	
	Data item type
	
	Data aggregate
		Student record type,
		Class record type
		
		stuId, classNumber
		
		address, consisting of
		street, city, state, ZIP

Data Ocurrences
   stored in the
   database
	Student record occurrence
	
	Data item occurrence
	
	File
	
	Database
		Record of student Tom Smith
		
		'S1001', Smith', 'Tom', 'History',90
		
		Student file with 5000 Student records
		
		University database containing Student file, Class file, Faculty file, . . .

FIGURE 2.1

Four Levels of Discussing Data

2.2.3   Data Sublanguages

The language that is used to describe a database to a DBMS is part of a **data sublanguage.** A data sublanguage consists of two parts: a **data definition language** (DDL) and a **data manipulation language** (DML). The DDL is used to describe the database, while the DML is used to process the database. These languages are called data sublanguages because general purpose programming languages were extended to provide database operations, so that the commands for definition and manipulation of database objects form a subset of the programming language itself, which is called the **host language.** There are standards for C, C++, C#, Java, COBOL, Fortran, and Ada as host languages for a standard data sublanguage called SQL. However, many database management systems have their own unique sublanguages that do not conform to any standard, and not all general purpose languages have database extensions. In many database systems, there is not a close connection between the host language and the data sublanguage, so commands in the data sublanguage are flagged, removed from the host language program, and replaced by subroutine calls before compilation of the program. They are then compiled by the DBMS, placed in an object module, and the object module is executed at the appropriate time. When data sublanguage commands occur as part of a program in a host language, the sublanguage is said to be **embedded** in the host language. In addition, most data sublanguages allow non-embedded or interactive commands for access from workstations.

2.3   Stages in Database Design

The process of analyzing the organization and its environment, developing a database model that accurately reflects the organization's functioning in the real world, and implementing that model by creating a database requires an appropriate methodology. Traditional systems analysis provides a possible approach, but a staged database design approach offers a better solution.

2.3.1   Systems Analysis Approach

A database design and implementation project could be viewed as a systems development project. Traditionally, software systems are developed using a systems analysis approach that identifies the steps in designing and

Stage	Activities
Preliminary Investigation	Interview users, study reports, transactions, procedures, software, documentation to identify problems in present system, and goals of new system.
Feasibility Study	Study alternatives, estimate costs, study schedules, benefits. Make recommendation.
Preliminary Design	Work with users to develop general system design. Choose best design. Develop system flowchart. Identify hardware, software, and personnel needs. Revise estimates.
Detailed Design	Do technical design. Plan program modules, algorithms, files, databases, I/O forms. Revise estimates.
System Implementation	Program modules, convert files, test system, write documentation, develop operational procedures, train personnel, do parallel operations, cut over to new system.
System Operation	Evaluate system. Monitor and modify system as needed.

FIGURE 2.2

Stages in Traditional Systems Analysis Lifecycle

implementing a system. There is an assumption that every system has a **lifecycle,** a period of time during which the system is designed, created, used, and then replaced by a new system. A typical lifecycle extends over several years, and consists of the stages shown in Figure 2.2. Using the traditional lifecycle approach, the system will eventually fail to meet users' needs, problems will be identified, and the cycle will begin again.

2.3.2   Staged Database Design Approach

A basic assumption behind the systems analysis lifecycle approach is that systems will eventually become obsolete and have to be replaced. In the database environment, there is reason to question this assumption. The database can be designed in such a way that it can evolve, changing to meet future information needs of the organization. This evolution is possible when the designer develops a true conceptual model of the organization with the following characteristics:

- The model faithfully mirrors the operations of the organization.
- It is flexible enough to allow changes as new information needs arise.
- It supports many different user views.
- It is independent of physical implementation.
- It does not depend on the data model used by a particular database management system.

A well-designed conceptual database model protects the data resource by allowing it to evolve so that it serves both today's and tomorrow's information needs. If the system is truly independent of its physical implementation, then it can be moved to new hardware to take advantage of technical developments. Even if the database management system chosen for implementation is replaced, the logical model may change, but the conceptual model of the enterprise can survive. The staged database design approach is a top-down method that begins with general statements of needs, and progresses to more and more detailed consideration of problems. Different problems are considered at different phases of the project. Each stage uses design tools that are appropriate to the problem at that level. Figure 2.3 shows the major design stages. They are

1. Analyze the user environment.
   The first step in designing a database is to determine the current user environment. The designer studies all present applications, determines their input and output, examines all reports generated by the present system, and interviews users to determine how they use the system. After the present system is thoroughly understood, the designer works closely with present users and potential users of the new system to identify their needs. The designer considers not only present needs but possible new applications or future uses of the database. The result of this analysis is a model of the user environment and requirements.

2. Develop a conceptual data model.
   Using the model of the user environment, the designer develops a detailed conceptual model of the database—identifying the entities,

FIGURE 2.3

Steps in Staged Database
Design

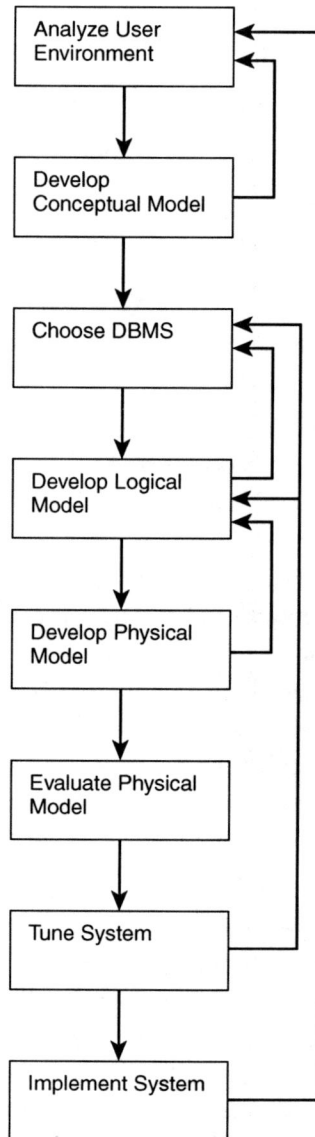

```
┌──────────────────┐
│ Analyze User     │◄────┐
│ Environment      │◄──┐ │
└──────────────────┘   │ │
        │              │ │
        ▼              │ │
┌──────────────────┐   │ │
│ Develop          │   │ │
│ Conceptual Model │───┘ │
└──────────────────┘     │
        │                │
        ▼                │
┌──────────────────┐     │
│ Choose DBMS      │◄──┐ │
└──────────────────┘◄┐ │ │
        │            │ │ │
        ▼            │ │ │
┌──────────────────┐ │ │ │
│ Develop Logical  │◄┘ │ │
│ Model            │◄──┘ │
└──────────────────┘     │
        │                │
        ▼                │
┌──────────────────┐     │
│ Develop Physical │     │
│ Model            │     │
└──────────────────┘     │
        │                │
        ▼                │
┌──────────────────┐     │
│ Evaluate Physical│     │
│ Model            │     │
└──────────────────┘     │
        │                │
        ▼                │
┌──────────────────┐     │
│ Tune System      │─────┘
└──────────────────┘
        │
        ▼
┌──────────────────┐
│ Implement System │
└──────────────────┘
```

FIGURE 2.3

Steps in Staged Database Design

attributes, and relationships that will be represented. In addition to the conceptual model, the designer has to consider how the database is to be used. The types of applications and transactions, the kinds of access, the volume of transactions, the volume of data, the frequency of access, and other quantitative data must be specified. Other constraints such as budgetary restrictions and performance requirements must also be identified. The result of this phase is a set of database specifications.

3. Choose a DBMS.
   The designer uses the specifications and his or her knowledge of available hardware and software resources to evaluate alternative database management systems. Each database management system imposes its own restrictions. The designer attempts to choose the system that best satisfies the specifications for the environment.

4. Develop the logical model.
   The designer maps the conceptual model to the data model used by the chosen DBMS, creating the logical model.

5. Develop the physical model.
   The designer plans the layout of data considering the structures supported by the chosen DBMS, and hardware and software resources available.

6. Evaluate the physical model.
   The designer then estimates the performance of all applications and transactions, considering the quantitative data previously identified and priorities given to applications and transactions. It can be helpful to develop a **prototype,** implementing a selected portion of the database so that user views can be validated and performance measured more accurately.

7. Perform tuning if indicated by the evaluation.
   Adjustments such as modifying physical structures or optimizing software can be done to improve performance.

8. Implement the physical model.
   If the evaluation is positive, the designer then implements the physical design and the database becomes operational.

The loops in Figure 2.3 provide opportunities for feedback and changes at various stages in the design process. For example, after developing the conceptual model, the designer communicates with user groups to make sure their data requirements are represented properly. If not, the conceptual model must be adjusted. If the conceptual model does not map well to a particular data model, another should be considered. For a particular DBMS, there might be several possible logical mappings that can be evaluated. If the physical model is not acceptable, a different mapping or a different DBMS can be considered. If the results of the performance evaluation are not satisfactory, additional tuning and evaluation may be performed. The physical model can be changed if tuning does not produce the required performance. If repeated tuning and optimization are not sufficient, it might be necessary to change the way the logical model is mapped to the DBMS or to consider a different database management system. Even after the system is implemented, changes might be needed to respond to changing user needs or a changing environment.

2.4   Design Tools

Many methodologies exist that can make the database design process easier for both designers and users. They vary from general techniques described in the literature to commercial products whose aim is to automate the design process. For example, **CASE** (Computer-Aided Software Engineering) packages that include various tools for system analysis, project management, design, and programming are available from many vendors. These packages provide tools that can be very useful in the database design process. The tools are usually categorized as upper-CASE, lower-CASE, or integrated. Upper-CASE tools are used in database planning for collecting and analyzing data, designing the data model, and designing applications. Lower-CASE tools are used for implementing the database, including prototyping, data conversion, generating application code, generating reports, and testing. Integrated CASE tools cover both levels. A user-oriented data dictionary is a tool that can be developed with or without a CASE package. **Project management software** is another type of tool that can be applied effectively to database development.

2.4.1   Data Dictionary

A data dictionary, as discussed in Section 2.2.2, is a repository of information that describes the logical structure of the database. It has entries for record types, data item types, and data aggregates, along with other information. The amount of information and the way the information is used varies with the system. Most vendors of DBMSs offer data dictionaries or data directories that store the database description and are used in creating and processing the database. The data dictionary contains **metadata,** or data about the data in the database. If the data dictionary is part of the DBMS, it is referred to as an **integrated** data dictionary or system catalog. An integrated data dictionary is always consistent with the actual database structure, because it is maintained automatically by the system. Integrated data dictionaries perform many functions throughout the life of the database, not only in the design phase. If the data dictionary is available without a particular DBMS, we refer to it as a **freestanding** data dictionary. A freestanding data dictionary can be a commercial product or a simple file developed and maintained by the designer. For example, CASE packages often include a data dictionary tool, and freestanding data dictionaries are available even for non-database environments. Both integrated and freestanding data dictionaries have advantages and disadvantages, but a freestanding dictionary may be preferable in the initial design stages, before the designer has chosen a particular DBMS. Since it is not tied to a DBMS, it allows the designer to enjoy the advantages of having this tool without committing to a particular implementation. A major disadvantage is that once the database is created, adjustments to its structure may not be entered into the freestanding data dictionary and, over time, the dictionary will not be an accurate reflection of the database structure.

A freestanding data dictionary is useful in the early design stages for collecting and organizing information about data. Each data item, its source(s), its name(s), its uses, its meaning, its relationship to other items, its format, and the identity of the person or group responsible for entering it, updating it, and maintaining its correctness must be determined. The data dictionary provides an effective tool for accomplishing these tasks. The database administrator (DBA) can begin development of the data dictionary by identifying data items, securing agreement from users on a definition of each item, and entering the item in the dictionary. Since users should not be aware of other users' data, the DBA should control access to the dictionary.

A data dictionary is useful for the following:

- Collecting and storing information about data in a central location. This helps management to gain control over data as a resource.

- Securing agreement from users and designers about the meanings of data items. An exact, agreed-upon definition of each item should be developed for storage in the data dictionary.

- Communicating with users. The data dictionary greatly facilitates communication, since exact meanings are stored. The dictionary also identifies the persons, departments, or groups having access to or interest in each item.

- Identifying redundancy and inconsistency in data item names. In the process of identifying and defining data items, the DBA may discover **synonyms,** which are different names for the same item. The database can accept synonyms, but the system must be aware of them. The DBA might also discover **homonyms,** which are identical names for different data items. These are never permitted in a database.

- Keeping track of changes to the database structure. Changes such as creation of new data items and record types or alterations to data item descriptions should be recorded in the data dictionary.

- Determining the impact of changes to the database structure. Since the data dictionary records each item, all its relationships, and all its users, the DBA can see what effects a change would have.

- Identifying the sources of and responsibility for the correctness of each item. A general rule for data entry is that data should be captured as near to its source as possible. The persons or departments that generate or capture values for each data item and those responsible for updating each item should be listed in the data dictionary.

- Recording the external, logical, and internal schemas and the mappings between them. This aspect will be discussed in Section 2.6.

- Recording access control information. A data dictionary can record the identities of all those who are permitted to access each item, along with the type of access-retrieval, insertion, update, or deletion.

- Providing audit information. The system data dictionary (i.e., the data directory or system catalog) can be used to record each access, allowing usage statistics to be collected for auditing the system and spotting attempted security violations.

Note that not all data dictionaries provide support for all of these functions, and some provide additional functions. Some just store the schema, some control documentation, and some system data directories are "metasystems" that control access to the database, generate system code, and keep statistics on database usage as well.

2.4.2   Project Management Software

This type of software provides a set of tools that can be used to plan and manage a project, especially when there are many people working on it. There are usually several types of graphs and charts available, such as **Gantt charts** as shown in Figure 2.12 and **PERT charts,** which are similar. The user specifies the objectives and scope of the project, identifies the major tasks and phases, indicates dependencies among the tasks, identifies the resources available, and sets a timeline for completion of the tasks and phases of the project. The software can be used to generate calendars, to produce graphs with many different views of the progress of the project, and to provide a means of communication among the project staff, using either intranet or Internet access. An example is Microsoft Project.

2.5   Database Administration

The database administrator is responsible for the design, operation, and management of the database. In many cases, the conceptual design is done by a database designer, and the DBA implements the design, develops the system, and manages it. The DBA must be technically competent, a good manager, a skilled communicator, and must have excellent interpersonal skills. Management skills are required to plan, coordinate, and carry out a multitude of tasks during all phases of the database project, and to supervise a staff. Technical skills are needed because the DBA has to be able to understand the complex hardware and software issues involved in order to design, develop, and manage the database, and to work with system and application experts in solving problems. Interpersonal skills are needed to communicate with users to determine their needs, to negotiate agreements on data definitions and database access rights, to secure agreements on changes to the database structure or operations that affect users, and to mediate between users with conflicting requirements. Excellent communications skills are required for all of these activities. The DBA has many functions that vary according to the stage of the database project. Since there are so many tasks to be performed, especially during the design and creation phases, the DBA may need to delegate some of these responsibilities. Major functions include planning, designing, developing and managing the database.

2.5.1   Planning and Design

- **Preliminary Database Planning.** If the DBA or database designer is chosen early enough in the project, he or she should participate in the preliminary investigation and feasibility study. If the DBA has not yet been chosen, one of the leaders of those studies may become a candidate for the position.

- **Identifying User Requirements.** The DBA or designer examines all reports generated by the present system and consults with users to determine whether the reports satisfy their information needs. He or she may work with present and potential users to design new reports they would like the proposed system to produce. Users are also asked what online transactions they would like to perform. The DBA studies all current applications, especially their input and output. The frequency of reports and transactions and the timeframe within which they must be produced are also recorded. The DBA uses his or her knowledge of the long-term and short-term objectives of the organization to prioritize user requirements.

- **Developing and Maintaining the Data Dictionary.** As he or she determines data needs of users, the DBA or designer stores data item names, sources, meanings, usage, and synonyms in the data dictionary. The DBA revises the data dictionary to include more information about the database as the project progresses.

- **Designing the Conceptual Model.** The DBA or designer identifies all entities, attributes, and relationships that are to be represented in the database, and develops a conceptual model that is an accurate reflection of the miniworld, capturing the operations of the organization in the real world that are of interest for the database.

- **Choosing a DBMS.** The DBA considers the conceptual model and other database specifications and the computer hardware and software available for the database, and chooses the DBMS that best fits the environment and meets the specifications.

- **Developing the Logical Model.** Once the DBMS is chosen, there may be several ways the conceptual model could be mapped to the data model used by the DBMS. The DBA chooses the one that appears to be most natural and appropriate, without considering the limitations of the DBMS.

- **Developing the Physical Model.** There may be several ways the logical model could be mapped to the data structures provided by the DBMS and to physical devices. The DBA evaluates each mapping by estimating performance of applications and transactions. The best mapping becomes the physical model.

2.5.2   Developing the Database

- **Creating and Loading the Database.** Once the physical model is developed, the DBA creates the structure of the database using the data definition language for the chosen DBMS. He or she establishes physical data sets, creates libraries, and loads the data into the database, usually using a DBMS utility program that accepts existing or converted files, places the data in the appropriate locations, and builds indexes and/or sets pointer values as records are loaded.

- **Developing User Views.** The DBA attempts to satisfy the data needs of all users. A user's view may be identical to the one requested in the initial design stages. Often, however, users' requests change as they begin to understand the system better. If the view does not coincide with the user's request, the DBA should present cogent reasons why the request has not been met and secure agreement on the actual view. Since user support is vital to the success of the database project, it is essential that users feel that the database serves them well.

- **Writing and Maintaining Documentation.** Ideally, the database documentation is written automatically by the data dictionary system as the project progresses. When the database is created, the DBA makes sure the documentation accurately reflects the structure of the database.

- **Developing and Enforcing Data Standards.** Since the database is shared by many users, it is important that standards be defined and enforced for the benefit of all. Users who are responsible for inserting and updating data must follow a standard format for entering data. The user interface should be designed to make it easy for users to follow the standards. For example, input screens should display default values, show acceptable ranges for items, and so on. Typical data standards include specifications for null values, abbreviations, codes, punctuation, and capitalization. The system can automatically check for errors and range restrictions. Other restrictions that can be checked by the DBMS before updates are accepted involve uniqueness of key values; and relationships between data values in a single record, between records in the same file, and between records in different files.

- **Developing and Enforcing Application Program Standards.** The DBA must develop standards for applications programs so that they obey database security and privacy restrictions, are subject to the auditability mechanism, make proper use of the high-level data manipulation language, and fit the application development facilities provided by the DBMS. These standards apply both to old applications that are converted for use with the database and to new applications.

- **Developing Operating Procedures.** The DBA is responsible for establishing procedures for daily startup of the DBMS (if necessary), smooth running of database operations, logging of transactions, periodic backups, security and authorization procedures, recording hardware and software failures, taking performance measurements, shutting down the database in an orderly fashion in case of failure, restarting and recovering after failure, and shutting down at the end of each day (if necessary). Since these procedures are performed by operators, the DBA must consult with the operations manager to ensure that operators are trained in all aspects of database operations.

- **Doing User Training.** End users, application programmers, and systems programmers who access the database should participate in training programs so that they can learn to use it most effectively. Sessions may be conducted by the DBA, the vendor of the DBMS, or other technical trainers, either onsite or in a training center.

2.5.3 Database Management

- **Monitoring Performance.** The DBA is responsible for collecting and analyzing statistics on database performance and responding to user complaints and suggestions regarding performance. The running time for applications and the response time for interactive queries should be measured, so that the DBA can spot problems in database use. Usually, the DBMS provides facilities for recording this information. The DBA continually compares performance to requirements and makes adjustments when necessary.

- **Tuning and Reorganizing.** If performance begins to degrade as changes are made to the stored data, the DBA can respond by adding or changing indexes, reorganizing files, using faster storage devices, or optimizing software. For serious performance problems, he or she may have to change the physical model and reload the entire database.

- **Keeping Current on Database Improvements.** The DBA should be aware of new features and new versions of the DBMS that become available. He or she should evaluate these new products and other hardware and software developments to determine whether they would provide substantial benefits to the organization.

2.6 The Three-Level Database Architecture

In Section 2.3, we presented a staged database design process that began with the development of a conceptual model and ended with a physical model. Now we are ready to examine these and related concepts more closely. When we discuss a database, we need some means of describing different aspects of its structure. An early proposal for a standardized vocabulary and architecture for database systems was developed and published in 1971 by the Database Task Group appointed by the Conference on Data Systems and Languages, or **CODASYL DBTG.** A similar vocabulary and architecture was developed and published in 1975 by The Standards Planning and Requirements Committee of the American National Standards Institute Committee on Computers and Information Processing, or **ANSI/X3/SPARC.** As a result of these and later reports, databases can be viewed at three levels of abstraction. The levels form a layered **three-level architecture** and are described by three **schemas,** which are written descriptions of their structures. The purpose of the three-level architecture is to separate the user's model from the physical structure of the database. There are several reasons why this separation is desirable:

- Different users need different views of the same data.

- The way a particular user needs to see the data may change over time.

- Users should not have to deal with the complexities of the database storage structures.

- The DBA should be able to make changes to the conceptual model of the database without affecting all users.

- The DBA should be able to change the logical model, and to data structures and file structures, without affecting the conceptual model or users' views.

- Database structure should be unaffected by changes to the physical aspects of storage, such as changes to storage devices.

Figure 2.4 shows the three-level architecture of database systems. The way users think about data is called the **external level.** The **internal level** is the way the data is actually stored using standard data structures and file organizations (see Appendix A). However, there are many different users' views and many physical structures, so there must be some method of mapping the external views to the physical structures. A direct mapping is undesirable, since changes made to physical structures or storage devices would require a corresponding change in the external to physical mapping. Therefore there is a middle level that provides both the mapping and the desired independence between the external and physical levels. This is the **logical** level.

2.6.1 External Views

The **external level** consists of many different **external views** or **external models** of the database. Each user has a model of the real world represented in a form that is suitable for that user. Figure 2.5 presents a more

FIGURE 2.4

Simplified Three-Level Architecture for Database Systems

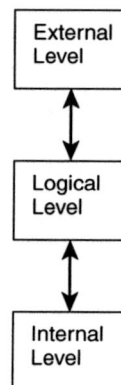

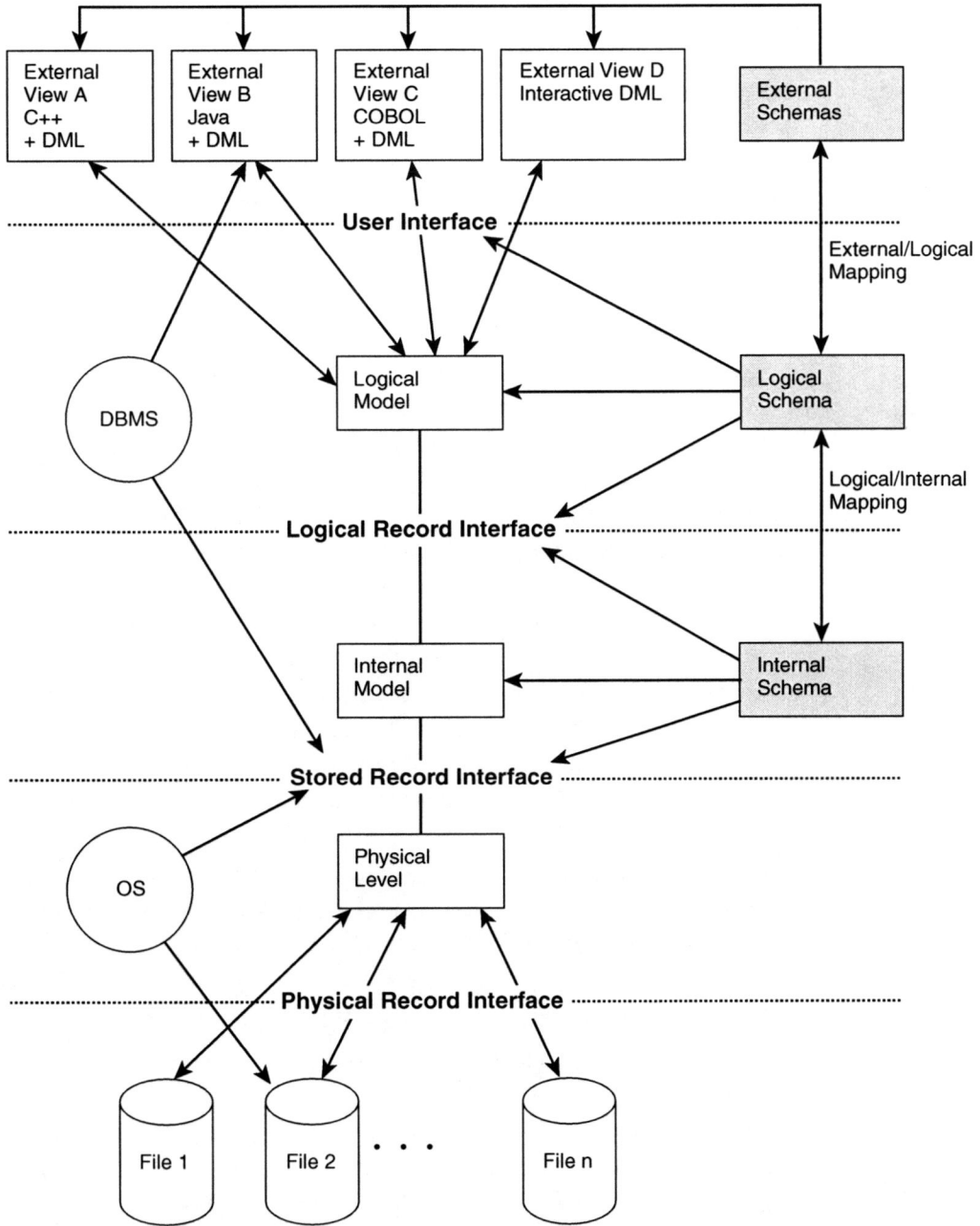

FIGURE 2.5

Three-Level Database Architecture

detailed picture of the three-level database architecture. The top level of Figure 2.5 shows several external views. A particular user interacts with only certain aspects of the miniworld, and is interested in only some entities, and only some of their attributes and relationships. Therefore, that user's view will contain only information about those aspects. Other entities or other attributes or relationships may actually be represented in the database, but the user will be unaware of them. Besides including different entities, attributes, and relationships, different views may have different representations of the same data. For example, one user may believe dates are stored in the form month, day, year, while another may believe they are represented as year, month, day. Some views might include **virtual** or calculated data, which is data not actually stored as such, but created when needed. For example, age may not be actually stored, but dateOfBirth may be, and age may be calculated by the system when the user refers to it. Views may even include data combined or calculated from several records. An **external record** is a record as seen by a particular user, a part of his or her external view. An external view is actually a collection of external records. The external views are described in **external schemas** (also called **subschemas**) that are written in the data definition language (DDL). Each user's schema gives a complete description of each type of external record that appears in that user's view. The schemas are compiled by the DBMS and stored in object form for use by the system data dictionary/directory in retrieving records. They should also be kept in source form as documentation. The DBMS uses the external schema to create a **user interface,** which is both a facility and a barrier. An individual user sees the database through this interface. It defines and creates the working environment for that user, accepting and displaying information in the format the user expects. It also acts as a boundary below which the user is not permitted to see. It hides the logical, internal, and physical details from the user.

To develop a user's view, the DBA first interviews the user and examines reports and transactions he or she creates or receives. After the entire design of the database is planned, the DBA determines what data will be available to that user and what representation the user will see, and writes an external schema for that user. Whenever possible, this external schema includes all the information the user has requested. Over time, the user's needs might change and modifications can be made to the view. Often, the new data required is already present in the database, and the user's external schema is re-written to allow access to it.

2.6.2   Logical and Conceptual Models

The middle level in the three-level architecture is the **logical level,** as shown in Figure 2.5. This model includes the entire information structure of the database, as seen by the DBA. It is the "community view" of data, and includes a description of all of the data that is available to be shared. It is a comprehensive model or view of the workings of the organization in the miniworld. All the entities, with their attributes and relationships, are represented in the logical model using the data model that the DBMS supports. The model includes any constraints on the data and semantic information about the data meanings. The logical model supports the external views, in that any data available to any user must be present in or derivable from the logical model. The logical model is relatively constant. When the DBA originally designs it, he or she tries to determine present and future information needs and attempts to develop a lasting model of the organization. Therefore, as new data needs arise, the logical model might already contain the objects required. If that is not the case, the DBA expands the logical model to include the new objects. A good logical model will be able to accommodate this change and still support the old external views. Only users who need access to the new data should be affected by the change. The **logical schema** is a complete description of the information content of the database. It is written in DDL, compiled by the DBMS, and stored in object form in the data dictionary/directory and in source form as documentation. The DBMS uses the logical schema to create the **logical record interface,** which is a boundary below which everything is invisible to the logical level and which defines and creates the working environment for the logical level. No internal or physical details such as how records are stored or sequenced cross this boundary. The logical model is actually a collection of logical records. The logical data model is the heart of the database. It supports all the external views and is, in turn, supported by the internal model. However, the internal model is merely the physical implementation of the logical model. The logical model is itself derived from the conceptual model. Developing the conceptual model is the most challenging, interesting, and rewarding part of database design. The database designer must be able to identify, classify, and structure objects in the design. The process of **abstraction,** which means identifying common properties of a set of objects rather than focusing on details, is used to categorize data. In computer science, abstraction is used to simplify concepts and hide complexity. For example, abstract data types are considered apart from their implementation; the behavior of queues and stacks can be described without considering how they are represented. The designer can look at different levels of abstraction, so that an abstract object on one level becomes a component of a higher level abstraction. During the conceptual design process, there might be many errors and several false starts. Like many other problem-solving processes, conceptual database design is an art, guided by knowledge. There may be many possible solutions, but some are better than others. The process itself is a learning situation. The designer gradually comes to understand the workings of the organization and the meanings of its data, and expresses that understanding in the chosen model. If the designer produces a good conceptual model, it is a relatively easy task to convert it to a logical model and complete the internal and physical design. If the conceptual model is a good one, the external views are easy to define as well. If any data that a user might be interested in is included in the conceptual model, it is an easy task to put it into the user's external view. On the other hand, a poor conceptual model can be hard to implement, particularly if data and relationships are not well defined. It will also be inadequate to provide all the needed external models. It will continue to cause problems during the lifetime of the database, because it will have to be "patched up" whenever different information needs arise. The ability to adjust to change is one of the hallmarks of good conceptual design. Therefore, it is worthwhile to spend all the time and energy necessary to produce the best possible conceptual design. The payoff will be felt not only at the logical and internal design stages but in the future.

2.6.3   Internal Model

The **internal level** covers the physical implementation of the database. It includes the data structures and file organizations used to store data on physical storage devices. The DBMS chosen determines, to a large extent, what structures are available. It works with the operating system access methods to lay out the data on the storage devices, build the indexes, and/or set the pointers that will be used for data retrieval. Therefore, there is actually a physical level below the one the DBMS is responsible for— one that is managed by the operating system under the direction of the DBMS. The line between the DBMS responsibilities and the operating system responsibilities are not clear cut and actually vary from system to system. Some DBMSs take advantage of many of the operating system access method facilities, while others ignore all but the most basic I/O managers and create their own alternative file organizations. The DBA must be aware of the possibilities for mapping the logical model to the internal model, and choose a mapping that supports the logical view and provides suitable performance. The **internal schema,** written in DDL, is a complete description of the internal model. It includes such items as how data is represented, how records are sequenced, what indexes exist, what pointers exist, and what hashing scheme, if any, is used. An **internal record** is a single stored record. It is the unit that is passed up to the internal level. The **stored record interface** is the boundary between the physical level, for which the operating system may be responsible, and the internal level, for which the DBMS is responsible. This interface is provided to the DBMS by the operating system. In some cases where the DBMS performs some operating system functions, the DBMS itself may create this interface. The physical level below this interface consists of items only the operating system knows, such as exactly how the sequencing is implemented and whether the fields of internal records are actually stored as contiguous bytes on the disk. The operating system creates the **physical record interface,** which is a lower boundary where storage details, such as exactly what portion of what track contains what data, are hidden.

The data dictionary/directory not only stores the complete external, logical, and internal schemas, but it also stores the mappings between them. The **external/logical mapping** tells the DBMS which objects on the logical level correspond to which objects in a particular user's external view. There may be differences in record names, data item names, data item order, data types, and so forth. If changes are made to either an external view or the logical model, the mappings must be changed. Similarly, the **logical/internal mapping** gives the correspondence between logical objects and internal ones, in that it tells how the logical objects are physically represented. If the stored structure is changed, the mapping must be changed accordingly.

To understand the distinctions among the three levels, we will examine what each level receives and passes on when we request the record of a particular employee. Refer to Figure 2.6 along with Figure 2.7. When user A requests a record such as the (external) record of Employee 101, the DBMS intercepts the request. If the request is entered online or at a workstation using the interactive data manipulation language (DML), the DBMS receives the request from the data communications system. If the request is submitted as part of a program, the DBMS takes it out of the program and

FIGURE 2.6
Retrieving Record of E101 for User A

```
┌─────────────────────────────────────┐
│ User A requests record of employee   │
│ E101 through User Interface          │
└─────────────────────────────────────┘
                   │
                   ▼
┌─────────────────────────────────────┐
│ DBMS receives request                │
└─────────────────────────────────────┘
                   │
                   ▼
┌─────────────────────────────────────┐
│ DBMS checks user A's external        │
│ schema, external/logical mapping,    │
│ logical schema in DD                 │
└─────────────────────────────────────┘
                   │
                   ▼
┌─────────────────────────────────────┐
│ DBMS checks to see if user A is      │
│ authorized. If not, rejects request  │
└─────────────────────────────────────┘
                   │
                   ▼
┌─────────────────────────────────────┐
│ DBMS checks logical/internal         │
│ mapping, determines corresponding    │
│ internal structures                  │
└─────────────────────────────────────┘
                   │
                   ▼
┌─────────────────────────────────────┐
│ DBMS uses stored record interface to │
│ request stored record from OS        │
└─────────────────────────────────────┘
                   │
                   ▼
┌─────────────────────────────────────┐
│ OS identifies desired physical record│
│ and asks access method to retrieve it│
└─────────────────────────────────────┘
                   │
                   ▼
┌─────────────────────────────────────┐
│ Access method retrieves block of     │
│ records to buffer, passes address of │
│ stored record to DBMS                │
└─────────────────────────────────────┘
                   │
                   ▼
┌─────────────────────────────────────┐
│ DBMS checks logical/internal         │
│ mapping, edits stored record, passes │
│ logical record to logical level      │
└─────────────────────────────────────┘
                   │
                   ▼
┌─────────────────────────────────────┐
│ DBMS checks external/logical         │
│ mapping, edits logical record, passes│
│ external record to User A            │
└─────────────────────────────────────┘
```

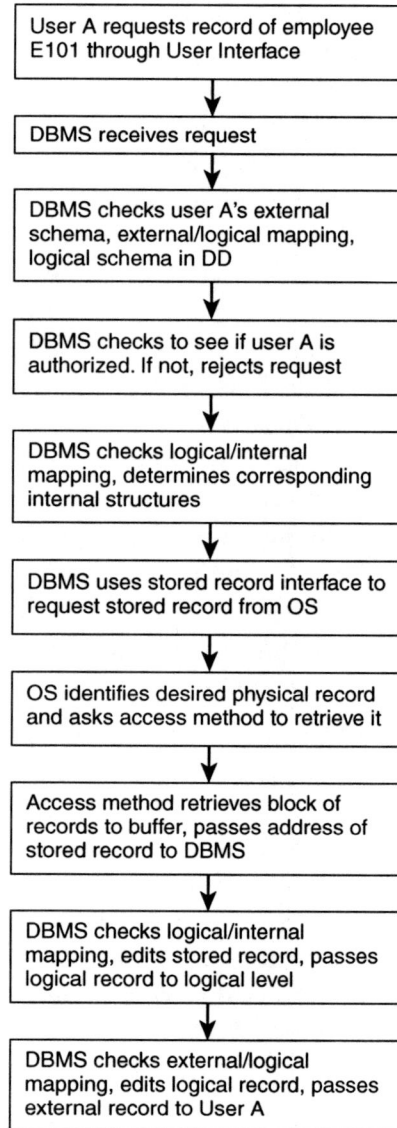

substitutes a subroutine call for it. In either case, once the DBMS receives the request, it checks the user's external view and the external/logical mapping. Both the views and the mapping are stored in object form in the data dictionary/directory, so the checking can be accomplished easily. The DBMS also checks the user's authorization to access the items and to perform the operations requested. If there is no such authorization, the request is denied. If the user is authorized, the DBMS notes what logical

External Employee Record:		
employeeName	empNumber	dept
JACK JONES	E101	Marketing

Logical Employee Record:				
empId	lastName	firstName	dept	salary
E101	Jones	Jack	12	55000

Stored Employee Record:						
empId	lastName	firstName	dept	salary	forward pointer	backward pointer

E101bbbbbb**Jones**bbbbbb**Jack**bbbbbbbbbb**12**bbbbbbbbb**55000**bbbb**10101**bbbbbb**10001**

Physical Record:				
Block header	rec of E90	rec of E95	**rec of E101**	rec of E125

FIGURE 2.7

Differences in External, Logical, Stored, and Physical Record

level objects are needed, and the request is passed down to the logical level. Next, the logical/internal mapping is checked to see what internal structures correspond to the logical items. Once again, the data dictionary/directory has stored both of the models and the mapping in object form. The DBMS identifies the internal objects that are required, and it passes the request to the operating system.

On the physical level, an employee record is contained in a physical record, a page or block that can hold several employee records. This is the unit that is brought to the buffer from the disk. The operating system is responsible for performing the basic job of locating the correct block for the requested record and managing its retrieval. When the retrieval is complete, the proper block is in the buffer, and the operating system passes to the DBMS the exact location within the buffer at which the stored record appears. The DBMS accesses only the requested employee record, not all the records in the block. However, it receives the complete stored record, exactly as it is coded or encrypted, together with any pointers that may appear in it, but without its header. This is a description of an internal record, which is the unit that passes up through the stored record interface. The DBMS uses the logical/internal mapping to decide what items to pass up through the logical record interface to the logical level.

At the logical level, the record appears as a logical record, with encryption and special coding removed. Pointers that are used for establishing relationships do not appear on the logical level, since that level is only concerned with the existence of relationships, not how they are implemented. Similarly, pointers used for sequencing are not of interest on the logical level, nor are indexes. The logical level record therefore contains only the information for that particular employee, but it contains all the fields stored for the employee, in the order in which they are stored. The DBMS checks the external/logical mapping to decide what the user's external record should look like.

When the record is passed up through the user interface to the external level, certain fields can be hidden, some can have their names changed, some can be rearranged, some can appear in a form different from their stored form, and some can be virtual, created from the stored record. Some external records might be combinations of stored records, or the result of operations such as calculations on stored records. The user then performs operations on the external record. That is, he or she can manipulate only those items that appear in the external record. These changes, if legal, are eventually made to the stored record. Figure 2.6 summarizes the steps in this process, and Figure 2.7 illustrates the differences in the appearance of the employee record as it is passed up to the external level.

2.6.4   Data Independence

A major reason for the three-level architecture is to provide **data independence,** which means that upper levels are unaffected by changes to lower levels. There are two kinds of data independence: **logical** and **physical.** Logical data independence refers to the immunity of external models to changes in the logical model. Logical model changes such as addition of new record types, new data items, and new relationships should be possible without affecting existing external views. Of course, the users for whom the changes are made need to be aware of them, but other users should not be. In particular, existing application programs should not have to be rewritten when logical level changes are made.

Physical data independence refers to the immunity of the logical model to changes in the internal model. Internal or physical changes such as a different physical sequencing of records, switching from one access method to another, changing the hashing algorithm, using different data

FIGURE 2.8
Logical and Physical Data
Independence

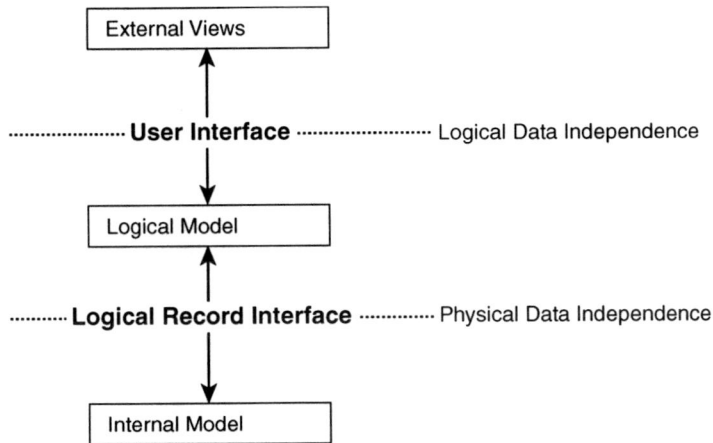

```
        ┌─────────────────┐
        │ External Views  │
        └─────────────────┘
                 ▲
                 │
 ············· User Interface ················· Logical Data Independence
                 │
                 ▼
        ┌─────────────────┐
        │  Logical Model  │
        └─────────────────┘
                 ▲
                 │
 ········· Logical Record Interface ············ Physical Data Independence
                 │
                 ▼
        ┌─────────────────┐
        │ Internal Model  │
        └─────────────────┘
```

structures, and using new storage devices should have no effect on the logical model. On the external level, the only effect that may be felt is a change in performance. In fact, a deterioration in performance is the most common reason for internal model changes. Figure 2.8 shows where each type of data independence occurs.

2.7   Overview of Data Models

A **data model** is a collection of tools usually including a type of diagram and specialized vocabulary for describing the structure of the database. A data model provides a description of the database structure including the data, the relationships within the data, constraints on the data, and sometimes data semantics or meanings. This structure is called the **intension** of the database, and it is relatively permanent. It is described in the database schema. The schema may change occasionally if new data needs arise, a process called **schema evolution.** The data stored in the database at a given moment is called an **extension** of the database, a **database instance,** or a **database state.** The extension changes whenever records are added, deleted, or updated. The extension should always be a **valid state,** which means it should satisfy all the constraints specified in the schema. The intension of the database is actually a complex abstract data structure that formally defines all possible extensions.

The data models in this section describe representation methods. There is much disagreement over what constitutes a data model, and that is reflected in the dozens of proposed models and methodologies found in the literature.

2.7.1   The Entity-Relationship Model

The Entity-Relationship model is an example of what is called a **semantic model.** Semantic models are used to describe the conceptual and external levels of data, and are independent of the internal and physical aspects. In addition to specifying what is to be represented in the database, they attempt to incorporate some meanings or semantic aspects of data such as explicit representation of objects, attributes, and relationships, categorization of objects, abstractions, and explicit data constraints. Some of the concepts of the E-R model were introduced in Section 2.2.2, when we described the four levels of abstraction in the discussion of data. The model was introduced by Chen in the mid 1970s and is widely used for conceptual design. It is based on identifying objects called entities that are representations of real objects in the miniworld. Entities are described by their attributes and are connected by relationships. We described entities as persons, places, events, objects, or concepts about which we collect data. A more proper description is that an entity is any object that exists and is distinguishable from other objects. The attributes describe the entities and distinguish them from one another. We defined an entity set as a collection of entities of the same type. Now we also define a relationship set as a set of relationships of the same type, and we add the fact that relationships themselves might have descriptive attributes. The E-R model also allows us to express constraints, or restrictions, on the entities or relationships. Chapter 3 contains a more complete description of the E-R model, including details about constraints.

One of the most useful and attractive features of the E-R model is that it provides a graphical method for depicting the conceptual structure of the database. E-R diagrams contain symbols for entities, attributes, and relationships. Figure 2.9 shows some of the symbols, along with their names, meanings, and usages. Figure 2.10 illustrates a simple E-R diagram for a students and classes database similar to the one we discussed in Section 1.2. It shows an entity set called Student, with the attributes stuId, lastName, firstName, major, and credits. Class information, to be kept for each class offered during the current term, includes the classNumber, the schedule, and the room. The Student and Class entity sets are connected by a relationship set, Enroll, which tells us which students are enrolled in which classes. It has its own descriptive attribute, grade. Note that grade is not an attribute of Student, since knowing the grade for a student is meaningless unless we know the course as well. Similarly, grade is not an

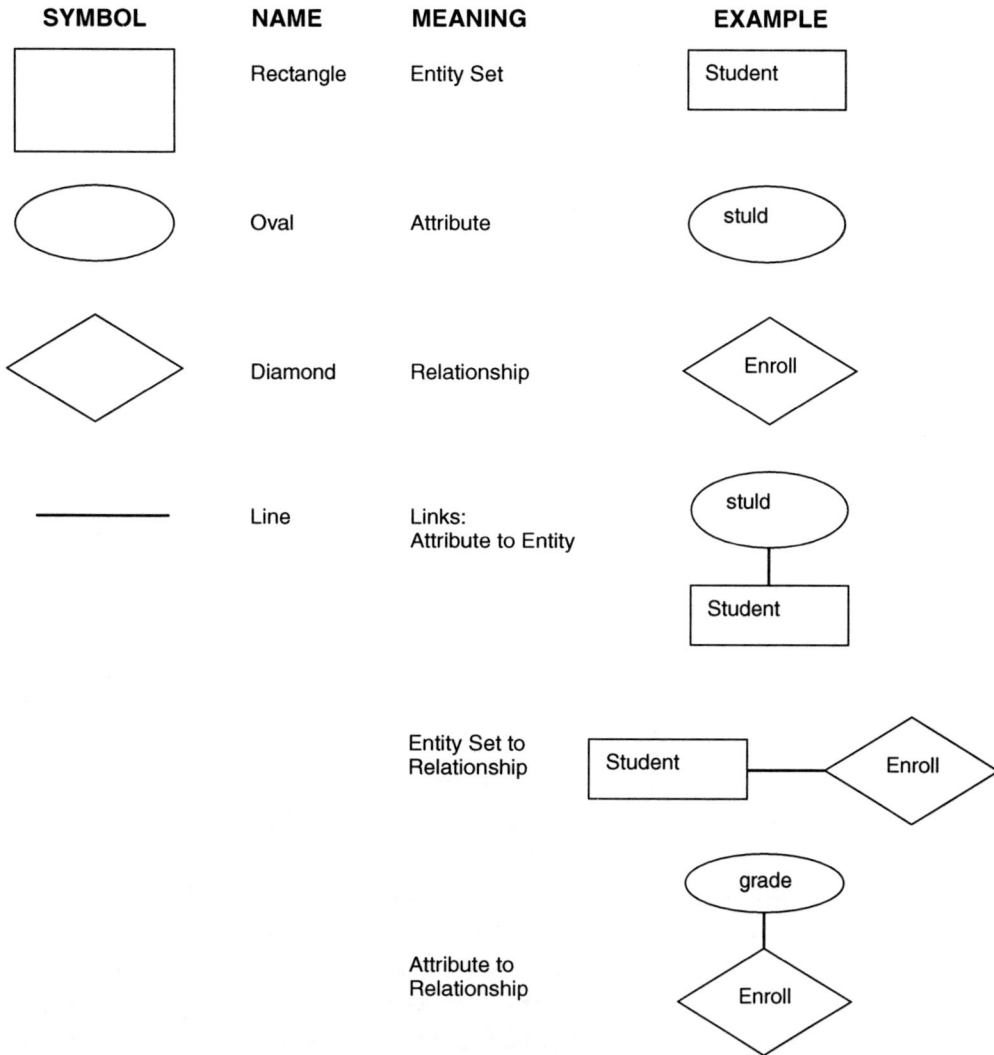

SYMBOL	NAME	MEANING	EXAMPLE
▭	Rectangle	Entity Set	Student
⬭	Oval	Attribute	stuId
◇	Diamond	Relationship	Enroll
──	Line	Links: Attribute to Entity	stuId ── Student
		Entity Set to Relationship	Student ── Enroll
		Attribute to Relationship	grade ── Enroll

FIGURE 2.9

Basic Symbols for E-R Diagrams

attribute of Class, since knowing that a particular grade was given for a class is meaningless unless we know to which student the grade was given. Therefore, since grade has meaning only for a particular combination of student and class, it belongs to the relationship set. Since the E-R model describes only a conceptual structure for the database, we do not attempt to describe how the model could or should be represented internally.

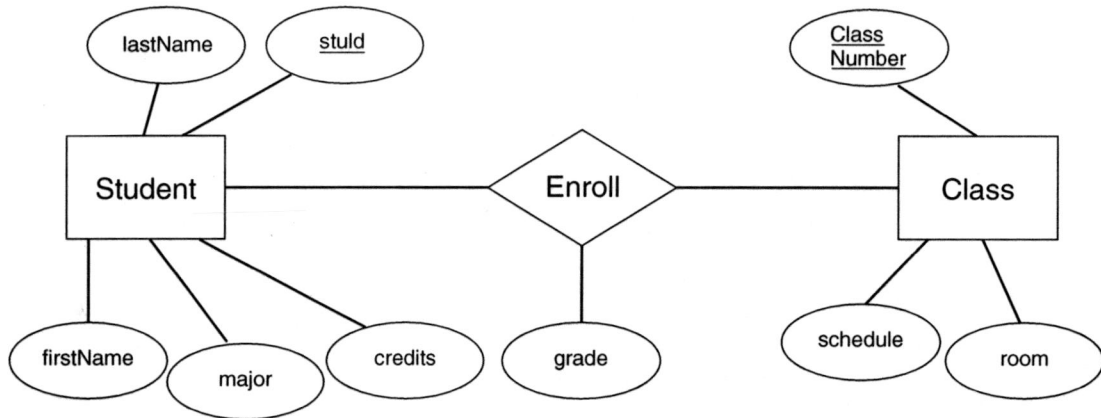

FIGURE 2.10
Simplified E-R Diagram

Therefore, the material in Section 2.2.2 in which we described data items, records, and files is not part of the E-R model itself.

2.7.2   Relational Model

The relational model is an example of a **record-based model.** Record-based models are used to describe the external, logical, and to some extent the internal levels of the database. They allow the designer to develop and specify the logical structure and provide some options for implementation of the design. They are implemented using a variety of database systems. However, they do not provide much semantic information such as categorization of objects, relationships, abstraction, or data constraints. The relational model was proposed by Codd in 1970 and continues to be the widely used, because of its simplicity from the user's point of view and its power. The relational model began by using the theory of relations in mathematics and adapting it for use in database theory. The same type of theoretical development of the subject, complete with formal notation, definitions, theorems, and proofs that we usually find in mathematics can be applied to databases using this model. The results of this theoretical development are then applied to practical considerations of implementation. In the relational model, entities are represented as relations, which are physically represented as tables or two-dimensional arrays, and attributes as columns of those tables. Relationships may also be represented as relations or tables, since this model regards a relationship as a special type of entity. Figure 1.1 (a)–(d) showed a sample relational database for data about students and their classes. We have a table for the student entity set, one for the class entity set, one for the faculty entity set, and one for the relationship between the student and the class. A student is related to a class by being enrolled in that class. The columns of the Student table have headings for the Student attributes: stuId, lastName, firstName, major, and credits. The Class table has a column for each of its attributes, classNumber, facId, schedule, and room. The Faculty table has columns for facId, name, department, and rank. The Enroll table is used to show the relationship between the Student and Class tables by including the columns stuId and classNumber, the primary keys of those two tables. It also has the attribute grade, which belongs to the relationship. Note that the records in the Enroll table show what students are enrolled in what classes. We will study the relational model, including a standard language for the model called SQL, in later chapters. Two older record-based models are the **network** and the **hierarchical** models mentioned in Section 1.7. They are primarily of historic interest, since they are no longer widely used for developing new databases. However, many legacy databases based on these models still exist, with code that is still being used and that must be maintained. Appendix B discusses the network model and Appendix C covers the hierarchical model.

2.7.3   Object-Oriented Model

The object-oriented model is a semantic model similar to the E-R. It extends the E-R concepts by adding **encapsulation,** a means of incorporating both data and functions in a unit where they are protected from modification from outside. As opposed to entities having attributes as in E-R, this model uses **objects** that have both a **state** and a **behavior.** The state of an object is determined by the values of its attributes (instance variables). The behavior is the set of methods (functions) defined for the object. In creating an object-oriented database, the designer begins by defining **classes,** which specify the attributes and methods for a set of objects. Each object is then created by instantiating (creating an instance of) the class, using one of the class's own methods called a **constructor.** The structure of objects can be quite complex. Every object in a database must have a unique **object identifier** that functions as a permanent primary key, but that does not take its value from any of the object's attributes. Classes that are related to one another are grouped to form **class hierarchies.** Readers who are familiar with object-oriented programming will recognize these concepts. An important difference between program objects and database objects is **persistence.** Unlike a program object that exists only while the program is executing, a database object remains in existence after execution of an application program completes.

2.7.4   Object-Relational Model

The object-relational model extends the relational model by adding some complex data types and methods to it. Instead of atomic, single-valued attributes as required in the relational model, this model allows attributes to be structured and have sets or arrays of values. It also permits methods and type inheritance. The SQL language was extended in 1999 to create and manipulate the more complex data types that this model supports. Therefore the language used to manage an object-relational database is closer to the type of language used for relational databases than that used for strictly object-oriented databases.

2.7.5   Semistructured Data Model

Most data models require that entity types (or objects or records, depending on the model) have the same structure. The structure is defined in the schema, and remains unchanged unless the DBA changes the schema. By contrast, the semi-structured model allows a collection of nodes, each containing data, possibly with different schemas. The node itself contains information about the structure of its contents. Semi-structured databases are especially useful when existing databases having different schemas must be integrated. The individual databases can be viewed as documents, and XML (Extensible Markup Language) tags can be attached to each document to describe its contents. XML is a language similar to HTML (Hypertext Markup Language), but is used as a standard for data exchange rather than data presentation. XML tags are used to identify elements, sub-elements, and attributes that store data. The schema can be specified using a Document Type Definition (DTD) or by an XML schema that identifies the elements, their attributes, and their relationships to one another.

2.8   Chapter Summary

A corporation's operational data is a corporate resource, an asset that is of value to the organization and incurs cost. A database, which is shared by many users, protects operational data by providing data security, integrity constraints, reliability controls, and professional management by a DBA.

Data means facts, while information is processed data in a form useful for making decisions. There are four levels of discussion about data: **reality** (the real world) containing the **miniworld** (Universe of Discourse) that we are modeling, the **conceptual model** of the miniworld, **metadata** (data about data), and **database data** (data instances). From objects in the miniworld we identify **entities, entity sets, attributes,** and **relationships.** The structure of the database is called the **logical model of the database.** The database **schema,** a description of the structure, is recorded in the data dictionary. The data dictionary contains **metadata,** or data about data, and it tells us what **record types, data item types,** and **data aggregates** exist in the database. The database itself contains **data instances** or occurrences. There is a record in the database for each entity in the real world. A **file** is a named collection of record occurrences. A **database** is a collection of files.

A staged approach to database design is a top-down approach that allows the designer to develop a conceptual model that mirrors the operations of the organization, allows changes, supports many user views, is independent of physical implementation, and does not depend on the model of a particular DBMS. This approach allows the database to evolve as needs change. In staged database design the designer must analyze the user environment, develop a conceptual data model, choose the DBMS, create the logical model by mapping the conceptual model to the data model of the DBMS, develop the internal and physical models, evaluate the physical model, perform tuning if needed, and implement the physical model. Steps may be repeated until the design is satisfactory.

Design methodologies can be general techniques described in the literature or commercial products such as **CASE** packages. A **data dictionary** can be **integrated** (part of the DBMS) or **freestanding** (independent of a DBMS). An integrated data dictionary can be used by the DBMS whenever the database is accessed and automatically updated by the DBMS. A freestanding dictionary is useful early in the design process before a DBMS is chosen. A data dictionary is a valuable tool for collecting and organizing information about data. It is useful for collecting information about data in a central location, securing agreement about data item meanings, communicating with users, identifying redundancy and inconsistency (including **synonyms** and **homonyms**), recording changes to database structure, determining the impact of such changes, identifying sources of and responsibility for the correctness of items, recording external, logical, and physical models and their mappings, recording access control information, and providing audit information.

The **database administrator** must be technically competent, a good manager, and have excellent interpersonal and communication skills. He or she has primary responsibility for planning, designing, developing, and managing the operating database. In the planning and designing stage, responsibilities include preliminary planning, identifying user requirements, developing and maintaining the data dictionary, designing the conceptual model, choosing a DBMS, developing the logical model, and developing the internal and physical models. In the development phase, responsibilities are creating and loading the database, developing user views, writing and maintaining documentation, developing and enforcing data standards, developing and enforcing application program standards, developing operating procedures, and training users. Responsibilities for managing the database include monitoring performance, tuning and reorganizing, and keeping current on database improvements.

Standard database architecture uses three levels of abstraction: **external, logical,** and **internal.** An **external view** is the model seen by a particular user and consists of **external records,** which may be subsets or combinations or actual records. An **external schema** is an external model description written in the **data definition language,** which is part of the **data sublanguage** for the particular DBMS being used. The **user interface** creates the user's working environment and hides lower levels from the user. The **logical schema** is a complete DDL description of the logical model. It specifies the information content of the database, including all record types and fields, but does not contain details of storage or physical representation. The logical model is the heart of the database. Conceptual design is a challenging and rewarding task. A good conceptual design is easy to implement and supports the desired external views. The **logical record interface** is a boundary below which the logical level cannot see. The **internal schema** is a DDL description of the internal model. It specifies how data is represented, how records are sequenced, what indexes and pointers exist, and what hashing scheme is used. The **stored record interface** is the boundary below which the DBMS does not see. The operating system should be responsible for all physical details below this interface, including creating a **physical record interface** for itself to handle low-level physical details such as track placement. The **external/logical mapping** tells how the external views correspond to the logical items. The **logical/internal** mapping tells how logical items correspond to internal ones. **Data independence** makes each level immune to changes on lower levels. **Logical data independence** means that the logical level can be changed without changing external views. **Physical data independence** means internal and physical changes will not affect the logical model.

Some data models are the **entity-relationship, object-oriented, object-relational,** and **semistructured** models. There are also **record-based** models, including the **relational** as well as the older **network** and **hierarchical** models. The entity-relationship model uses **E-R diagrams** to show entity sets, attributes of entities, relationship sets, and descriptive attributes of relationships. The relational model uses **tables** to represent data and relationships. The object-oriented model uses the concept of a **class,** having attributes and methods. An **object** is created as an instance of a class. Object-oriented databases contain **persistent** objects. Object-relational databases are extensions of relational model databases to allow complex objects and methods. Semistructured databases consist of nodes that are self-describing using XML.

Exercises

2.1   Name four resources of a typical business organization.

2.2   Distinguish between data and information.

2.3   Identify the four levels of abstraction in discussing data. For each, give an example of an item that appears on that level.

2.4   Distinguish between an entity set and an entity instance, giving an example of each.

2.5   Distinguish between a record type and a record occurrence, giving an example of each.

2.6   What level of data abstraction is represented in the data dictionary? Give examples of the types of entries that would be stored there.

2.7   Explain why a staged design approach is more appropriate for database design than the traditional systems analysis approach.

2.8   Name five desirable characteristics of a conceptual model of an enterprise.

2.9   Name the eight major design stages in staged database design, along with the activities and possible outcomes of each.

2.10   Explain what is meant by saying staged database design is a "top-down" method.

2.11   Explain how a CASE package can be used in database design.

2.12   Name two advantages and two disadvantages of the following:

a. integrated data dictionaries

b. freestanding data dictionaries

2.13   Explain why users should not have access to the data dictionary.

2.14   Name eight uses for a data dictionary.

2.15   What types of skills must a database administrator possess? For what tasks are they needed?

2.16   List the major functions of the DBA.

2.17   Define each of the following terms:

a. operational data

b. corporate resource

c. metadata

d. entity

e. attribute

f. data item

g. data aggregate

h. data record

i. data file

j. system lifecycle

k. prototype

l. system tuning

      m. CASE

      n. integrated data dictionary

      o. data dictionary synonym

      p. data dictionary homonym

      q. data standards

      r. DBA

2.18   Describe the three-level architecture for databases.

2.19   Describe the two parts of data sublanguages.

2.20   Give five reasons why it is desirable to separate the physical representation from the conceptual structure of a database.

2.21   Distinguish between the following: user interface, logical record interface, stored record interface, physical record interface.

2.22   Describe each of the following: external schema, logical schema, internal schema.

2.23   Explain the purpose of the external/logical mapping and of the logical/internal mapping.

2.24   Distinguish between logical and physical data independence, and give examples of possible changes they allow.

2.25   Explain why the logical model is called the heart of the database.

2.26   Describe abstraction and explain how it is used in database design.

2.27   Distinguish between the intension and extension of a database.

2.28   Explain how record-based data models differ from semantic models.

Lab Exercises

Lab Exercise 2.1: Exploring a Diagramming Tool

Drawing tool software such as SmartDraw, Microsoft Visio, or similar products should be used for this laboratory exercise. If these are not available, the drawing tool in Microsoft Word can be used. Since each tool has slightly different requirements and conventions, explore the menus to find the right symbols to use.

Using a drawing tool, draw an E-R diagram for the University example similar to the one shown in Figure 2.10. If not all elements are available in the tool, write in any missing elements by hand.

Lab Exercise 2.2: Exploring a Project Management Tool

Using a project management tool such as Microsoft Project, explore the options of the tool, examining the various types of diagrams and charts available. Construct a diagram that illustrates the phases of a programming project, with a set of resources (programmers) for each task, and a timeline for completion of each phase. If you have Microsoft Project or Visio, choose a Gantt or PERT chart for this exercise. If neither of these is available, use a spreadsheet program such as Microsoft Excel. Use Figure 2.12 as a guide.

Lab Exercise 2.3: Constructing a Simple Data Dictionary

Using a word processor, make a list of the data items in the University example, providing a definition of each data item. Indicate grouped items by giving the name of the group and a list of the individual items in the group.

SAMPLE PROJECT: APPLYING PLANNING TECHNIQUES TO THE ART GALLERY PROJECT

- Step 2.1. Designing the Data Dictionary for The Art Gallery

Write out a user-oriented data dictionary, consisting of an alphabetical list of every data item referenced in any report or routine transaction, and an informal definition for each term.

The user-oriented data dictionary for The Art Gallery is as follows:

amountRemittedtoOwner   The dollar amount of money sent to an owner for the sale of an artwork.

artistAddress   The mailing address of an artist.

artistAreaCode   The telephone area code of an artist.

artistCity   The city of the mailing address of an artist.

artistFirstName   The given first name that an artist uses.

artistInterviewDate   The date an artist was interviewed by a representative of the gallery.

artistInterviewerName   The first and last name of the gallery representative who interviewed an artist.

artistLastName   The last name (surname) of an artist.

artistPhone   The complete telephone number of the artist.

artistSalesLastYear   The total dollar amount of sales of an artist's works during the entire previous year.

artistSalesYearToDate   The total dollar amount of sales of an artist's works from the first day of the current year to the date of the report or transaction on which it appears.

artistSocialSecurityNumber   The social security number of an artist.

artistState   The state of the mailing address of an artist.

artistStreet   The house number and street of the mailing address of an artist.

artistTelephoneNumber   The telephone number of an artist, not including area code.

artistTotalSalesforPeriod   The total dollar amount of sales of an artist's works for the period covered in a report or transaction.

artistTotalAskingPriceforPeriod   The total dollar value of an artist's unsold works for sale in the gallery for the period covered in a report or transaction, computed as the sum of their asking prices.

artistZip   The postal ZIP code of the mailing address of an artist.

askingPrice   The asking price of a work of art.

buyerAddress   The mailing address of a buyer of an artwork of the gallery.

buyerAreaCode   The telephone area code of a buyer of an artwork of the gallery.

buyerCity   The city of the mailing address of a buyer of an artwork of the gallery.

buyerFirstName   The first name of a buyer of an artwork of the gallery.

buyerLastName   The last name (surname) of a buyer of an artwork of the gallery.

buyerPhone   The complete telephone number of a buyer of an artwork of the gallery.

buyerState   The state of the mailing address of a buyer of an artwork of the gallery.

buyerStreet   The house number and street of the mailing address of a buyer of an artwork of the gallery.

buyerTelephoneNumber   The telephone number of a buyer of an artwork of the gallery, not including area code.

buyerZip   The postal ZIP code of the buyer of a work of art.

collectionArtistFirstName   The first name of the artist featured in a group of artworks owned by a collector.

collectionArtistLastName   The last name of the artist featured in a group of artworks owned by a collector.

collectionMedium   The medium used for a group of artworks owned by a collector.

collectionStyle   The style of a group of artworks owned by a collector.

collectionType   The type of a group of artworks owned by a collector.

collectorAddress   The mailing address of a collector of works of art.

collectorAreaCode   The telephone area code of a collector of works of art.

collectorCity   The city of the mailing address of a collector of works of art.

collectorFirstName   The given first name of a collector of works of art.

collectorInterviewDate   The date a collector of works of art was interviewed by a representative of the gallery.

collectorInterviewerName   The first and last name (surname) of the representative of the gallery who interviewed a collector of works of art.

collectorLastName   The last name (surname) of a collector of works of art.

collectorPhone   The complete telephone number of a collector of works of art.

collectorSalesLastYear   The total dollar amount of sales of the collectors' artworks during the entire previous year.

collectorSalesYeartoDate   The total dollar amount of sales of the collecor's artworks from the first day of the current year to the date of the report or transaction on which it appears.

collectorSocialSecurityNumber   The social security number of a collector of works of art.

collectorState   The state of the mailing address of a collector of works of art.

collectorStreet   The house number and street of the mailing address of a collector of works of art.

collectorTelephoneNumber   The telephone number of a collector of works of art, not including area code.

collectorTotalSalesforPeriod   The total dollar amount of sales of the collector's works for the period covered in a report or transaction.

collectorTotalAskingPriceforPeriod   The total dollar value of the collector's unsold works for sale in the gallery for the period covered in a report or transaction, computed as the sum of their asking prices.

collectorZip   The postal ZIP code of the mailing address of a collector of works of art.

potentialCustomerAddress   The mailing address of a potential customer of the gallery.

potentialCustomerAreaCode   The telephone area code of a potential customer of the gallery.

potentialCustomerCity   The city of the mailing address of a potential customer of the gallery.

potentialCustomerDateFilledIn   The date a customer information form was filled in.

potentialCustomerFirstName   The first name of a potential customer of the gallery.

potentialCustomerLastName   The last name (surname) of a potential customer of the gallery.

potentialCustomerPhone   The complete telephone number of a potential customer of the gallery.

potentialCustomerState   The state of the mailing address of a potential customer of the gallery.

potentialCustomerStreet   The house number and street of the mailing address of a potential customer of the gallery.

potentialCustomerTelephoneNumber   The telephone number of a potential customer of the gallery, not including area code.

potentialCustomerZip   The postal ZIP code of the mailing address of a potential customer of the gallery.

dateListed   The date a work of art is first offered for sale in the gallery.

dateReturned   The date a work of art is returned to its owner.

dateShown   The date a work of art is featured in an art show by the gallery.

dateOfReport   The date that a report was generated.

medium   The medium of a work of art. Examples of valid values are oil, pastel, watercolor, watermedia, acrylic, marble, steel, copper, wood, fiber, other.

ownerAddress   The mailing address of the owner of a work of art.

ownerAreaCode   The telephone area code of the owner of a work of art.

ownerCity   The city of the mailing address of the owner of a work of art.

ownerFirstName   The given first name that the owner of a work of art uses.

ownerLastName   The last name (surname) of the owner of a work of art.

ownerPhone   The complete telephone number of the owner of a work of art.

ownerSocialSecurityNumber   The social security number of the owner of a work of art.

ownerState   The state of the mailing address of the owner of a work of art.

ownerStreet   The house number and street of the mailing address of the owner of a work of art.

ownerTelephoneNumber   The telephone number of the owner of a work of art, not including area code.

ownerZIP   The postal ZIP code of the mailing address of the owner of a work of art.

preferredArtist   The name of the artist chosen as a preference by a potential customer of the gallery.

preferredMedium   The medium chosen as a preference by a potential customer of the gallery.

preferredStyle   The style chosen as a preference by a potential customer of the gallery.

preferredType   The type chosen as a preference by a potential customer of the gallery.

purchasesLastYear   The total dollar amount of sales to a buyer during the entire previous year.

purchasesYearToDate　　The total dollar amount of sales to a buyer from the first day of the current year to the date of the report or transaction on which it appears.

reportStartingDate　　The date chosen as the earliest date for information to be used in a report.

reportEndingDate　　The date chosen as the latest date for information to be used in a report.

saleDate　　The date a work of art was sold by the gallery.

saleInvoiceNumber　　The number printed on the invoice for a sale of a work of art.

salePrice　　The price at which a work of art was sold by the gallery.

salesPersonAddress　　The full address of a sales associate who works in the gallery.

salesPersonFirstName　　The given first name of a sales associate who works in the gallery.

salesPersonLastName　　The last name (surname) of a sales associate who works in the gallery.

salesPersonSocialSecurityNumber　　The social security number of a sales associate who works in the gallery.

saleSalesPersonCommission　　The dollar amount of commission for a salesperson for the sale of a work of art.

saleSalesPersonName　　The first and last name of the salesperson who sold a work of art.

saleTax　　The dollar amount of sales tax for the sale of an artwork.

saleTotal　　The total dollar amount of a sale, including price and tax, for an artwork.

salespersonCommissionforPeriod　　The total dollar amount of commission earned by a salesperson for a specific period.

salespersonTotalSalesforPeriod　　The total dollar amount of sales, not including tax, made by a salesperson during a specific period.

showClosingDate　　The final date that an art show is open to the public.

showFeaturedArtist　　The name of an artist featured in an art show.

showTheme　　The theme of an art show.

showTitle   The title given to an art show.

showOpeningDate   The first date that an art show is open to the public.

size   The size of a work of art, expressed in inches. For two-dimensional works, given as length by width; for three-dimensional works, given as length by width by height.

status   The sales status of a work of art. Possible values are sold or unsold.

style   The artistic style of a work of art. Examples of valid values are contemporary, impressionist, folk, other.

title   The title of a work of art.

totalAllSalesforWeek   The total dollar amount of sales for the gallery for a specific week, not including tax.

totalAskingPriceForPeriod   The sum of asking prices for all works during the period chosen for a report.

type   The type of a work of art. Examples of valid values are painting, sculpture, collage, other.

usualMedium   The medium the artist usually uses. Examples of valid values are oil, pastel, watercolor, watermedia, acrylic, marble, steel, copper, wood, fiber, other.

usualStyle   The usual artistic style of the artist's works. Examples of valid values are contemporary, impressionist, folk, other.

usualType   The type of artwork the artist normally produces. Examples of valid values are painting, sculpture, collage, other.

yearCompleted   The year that a work of art was completed.

- Step 2.2. Modify the List of Assumptions (as needed)

  The list of assumptions has no changes at this point. It remains as shown in Step 1.4.

- Step 2.3. Write a Cross-Reference Table (showing what data items appear on what forms, reports, or transactions)

To construct the cross-reference table, write the names of all forms, reports, and transactions as column headings across the top of the table. Write the items from the data dictionary down the first column, making a form similar to a spreadsheet. If a data item on a given row appears on a particular form, report, or transaction, place a check mark in the cell for the corresponding column-row intersection. The cross-reference table for The Art Gallery appears in Figure 2.11.

- Step 2.4. Create a project management chart using either Gantt or PERT format

We can use a project management tool such as Microsoft Project to make a chart that lists the major steps of the project and assign a timeline for the completion of the entire project, whether done by an individual or by a group. Figure 2.12 shows a simplified diagram for completion of parts of the database project for The Art Gallery as a Gantt chart created using Microsoft Visio. We assume that there are three people (listed under Resources) working on the project.

STUDENT PROJECTS: APPLYING PLANNING TECHNIQUES TO STUDENT PROJECTS

- Step 2.1. Design the Data Dictionary for the Student Project

Write out a user-oriented data dictionary, consisting of an alphabetical list of every data item referenced in any report or routine transaction, and an informal definition for each term.

- Step 2.2. Modify the List of Assumptions

  Make any changes needed to the assumptions.

- Step 2.3. Write a Cross-Reference Table

To construct the cross-reference table, write the names of all forms, reports, and transactions as column headings across the top of the table. Write the items from the data dictionary down the first column, making a form similar to a spreadsheet. If a data item on a given row appears on a particular form, report, or transaction, place a check mark in the cell for the corresponding column-row intersection.

- Step 2.4. Project Management Planning for the Student Project

  Using a project management tool such as Microsoft Project or a spreadsheet, make a chart that lists the major tasks of the project and assign a timeline for the completion of the entire project. Divide the major tasks into subtasks. If the project is being done by a group, assign the subtasks to the group members. Indicate dependency of one task on another by drawing arrows. Establish deadlines as necessary to complete the project on time.

Document or Form on Which Item Appears

Item	ArtistInfo	CollInfo	ArtwrkInfo	SaleInv	MailList	ActvArtsts	IndArtstSa	CollSum	IndColSal	WksForSal	SalThisWk	BuyerSals	PrefCust	SalsPerfor	AgedArt	PaymtStub	ArtShow
amountRemittedtoOwner																X	
artistAddress	X					X	X										
artistAreaCode	X					X	X										
artistCity	X					X	X										
artistFirstName	X		X	X		X	X		X	X	X		X	X	X	X	X
artistInterviewDate	X																
artistInterviewerName	X																
artistLastName	X		X	X		X	X		X	X	X		X	X	X	X	X
artistPhone	X					X	X										
artistSalesLastYear						X											
artistSalesYearToDate						X											
artistSocialSecurityNumber	X																
artistState	X					X	X										
artistStreet	X					X	X										
artistTelephoneNumber	X					X	X										
artistTotalSalesforPeriod							X										
artistTotalAskingPriceforPeriod							X										
artistZip	X					X											
askingPrice			X				X		X	X					X		X
buyerAddress				X							X						
buyerAreaCode				X							X						
buyerCity				X							X						
buyerFirstName				X							X	X					
buyerLastName				X							X	X					
buyerphone				X							X						
buyerState				X							X						
buyerStreet				X							X						
buyerTelephoneNumber				X							X						
buyerZip				X							X						
collectionArtistFirstName		X															

FIGURE 2.11

Cross Reference Table

114

	ArtistInfo	CollInfo	ArtwrkInfo	SaleInv	MailList	ActvArtsts	IndArtstSa	CollSum	IndColSal	WksForSal	SalThisWk	BuyerSals	PrefCust	SalpPerfor	AgedArt	PaymtStub	ArtShow
collectionArtistLastName	X																
collectionMedium	X																
collectionStyle	X																
collectionType	X																
collectorAddress		X						X	X								
collectorAreaCode		X						X	X								
collectorCity		X						X	X								
collectorFirstName		X						X	X								
collectorInterviewDate		X															
collectorInterviewName		X															
collectorLastName		X						X	X								
collectorPhone		X						X	X								
collectorSalesLastYear								X									
collectorSalesYearToDate								X									
collectorSocialSecurityNumber		X															
collectorState		X						X	X								
collectorStreet		X						X	X								
collectorTelephoneNumber		X						X	X								
collectorTotalSalesforPeriod									X								
collectorTotalAskingPriceforPeriod									X								
collectorZip		X						X	X								
dateListed			X				X		X	X				X			
dateReturned			X				X		X								
dateShown										X							
dateOfReport						X	X			X		X			X		
medium			X				X			X			X			X	
ownerAddress			X													X	
ownerAreaCode			X														
ownercity			X													X	
ownerFirstName			X								X				X	X	
ownerLastName			X								X				X	X	
ownerhone			X												X		
ownerSocialSecurityNumber			X													X	
ownerState			X													X	

115

	ArtistInfo	CollInfo	ArtwrkInfo	SaleInv	MailList	ActvArtsts	IndArtstSa	CollSum	IndColSal	WkForSal	SalThisWk	BuyerSals	PrefCust	SalpPerfor	AgedArt	PaymtStub	ArtShow
ownerStret			X													X	
ownerTelephoneNumber			X												X		
ownerZip			X										X				
potentialCustomerAddress					X								X				
potentialCustomerAreaCode					X								X				
potentialCustomerCity					X								X				
potentialCustomerDateFilledIn					X												
potentialCustomerFirstName					X								X				
potentialCustomerLastName					X								X				
potentialCustomerPhone					X												
potentialCustomerState					X								X				
potentialCustomerStreet					X								X				
potentialCustomerTelephoneNumber					X												
potentialCusomerZip					X								X				
preferredArtist					X			X					X				
preferredMedium					X			X					X				
preferredStyle					X			X					X				
preferredType					X			X					X				
purchasedLastYear												X					
purchasesYearToDate												X					
reportStartingDate														X			
reportEndingDate														X			
saleDate				X			X		X		X			X			
saleInvoiceNumber				X													
salePrice				X			X		X		X			X	X		
salesPersonAddress														X			
salesPersonFirstName				X							X			X	X		
salesPersonLastName				X							X			X	X		
salesPersonSocialSecurityNumber														X			
saleSalesPersonCommission											X						
saleSalesPersonName				X							X				X		
saleTax				X											X		
saleTotal				X											X		
salespersonCommissionForPeriod														X			

	ArtistInfo	CollInfo	ArtwrkInfo	SaleInv	MailList	ActvArtsts	IndArtstSa	CollSum	IndColSal	WksForSal	SalThisWk	BuyerSals	PrefCust	SalpPerfor	AgedArt	PaymtStub	ArtShow
salespersonTotalSalesForPeriod											X			X			
showClosingDate																	X
showFeaturedArtist																	X
showTheme																	X
showTitle																	X
showOpeningDate																	X
size			X												X		
status															X		X
style			X						X	X			X		X		
title			X	X					X	X	X		X	X	X		
totalAllSalesForWeek											X						
totalAskingPriceForPeriod							X		X			X					
type			X				X		X	X			X	X			
usualMedium	X					X											
usualStyle	X					X											
usualType	X					X											
yearCompleted			X				X		X								

ID	Task Name	Resource Names	Start	Finish	Duration
1	Define specifications		1/5/2004	1/8/2004	4d
2	Interview users	Adam	1/5/2004	1/6/2004	2d
3	Identify transactions, reports needed	Adam, Beth	1/7/2004	1/7/2004	1d
4	Begin data dict, x-ref table	Beth,Colin	1/8/2004	1/8/2004	1d
5	Create E-R diagram		1/9/2004	1/13/2004	3d
6	Identify entities,attributes,relationships	Adam	1/9/2004	1/9/2004	4h
7	Identify cardinality,participation constraints	Adam, Beth	1/12/2004	1/12/2004	4h
8	Draw diagram	Adam, Colin	1/13/2004	1/13/2004	1d
9	Map E-R to relational model	Beth	1/14/2004	1/14/2004	1d
10	Normalize relational model	Adam	1/15/2004	1/15/2004	1d
11	Create relational database	Colin	1/16/2004	1/19/2004	2d
12	Create EER diagram	Adam, Beth, Colin	1/19/2004	1/20/2004	2d
13	Map EER model to object-relational model	Adam	1/21/2004	1/21/2004	1d
14	Create object-relational database	Beth	1/22/2004	1/23/2004	2d
15	Create UML diagram	Beth	1/23/2004	1/26/2004	2d
16	Map UML diagram to object-oriented model	Colin	1/27/2004	1/27/2004	1d
17	Create object-oriented database	Adam	1/28/2004	1/29/2004	2d

FIGURE 2.12

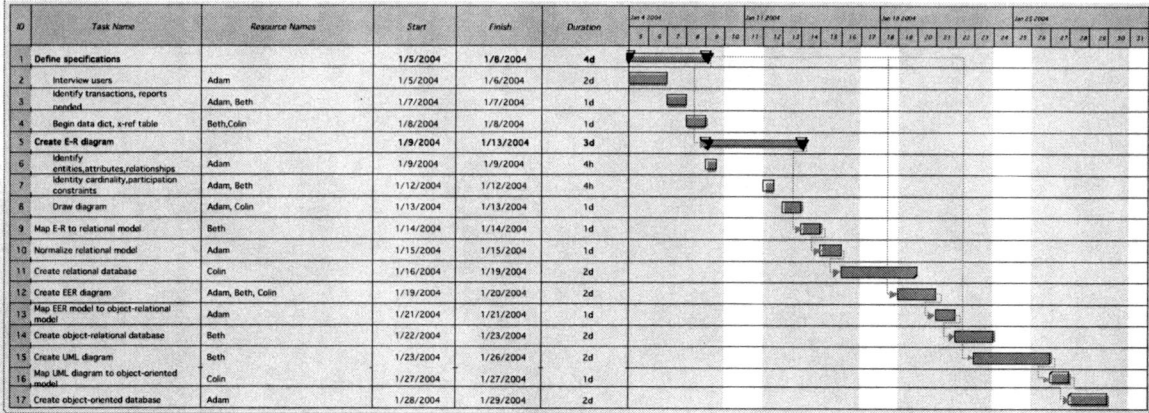

Gantt Chart for The Art Gallery Database Project

CHAPTER 3

The Entity-Relationship Model

Chapter Objectives

In this chapter you will learn the following:

- What an enterprise schema is

- The meaning of entity type, entity set, and entity instance

- How to represent entities on the entity-relationship (E-R) diagram

- The meaning of attribute

- How attributes are associated with entities

- The meaning of attribute domain

- What a null value is

- The meaning of multivalued, composite, and derived attributes

- The meaning of superkey, candidate key, primary key, alternate key, secondary key, and foreign key

- The meaning of relationship type, relationship set, and relationship instance

- How to represent relationship sets as ordered pairs, ordered triples, or ordered n-tuples

- How to represent relationship sets and their attributes on an E-R diagram

- The meaning and representation of the cardinality of a relationship

- The meaning and representation of participation constraints

- When and how to indicate roles on an E-R diagram

- The meaning of existence dependency and weak entity sets

Exercises

Lab Exercises: Drawing E-R Diagrams

SAMPLE PROJECT: Creating the E-R Diagram for The Art Gallery Project

STUDENT PROJECTS: Creating E-R Diagrams for the Student Projects

3.1   Purpose of the E-R Model

The entity-relationship model was developed by P. P. Chen in 1976 to facilitate database design by allowing the designer to express the conceptual properties of the database in an **enterprise schema.** The word enterprise is widely used in database discussions to mean the organization for which the database is kept. The enterprise could be a small business, a corporation, a university, a government agency, a hospital, or some other organization. The enterprise schema is a description that corresponds to the conceptual model. It is independent of any particular DBMS. Therefore, it is not limited to the data definition language of any particular DBMS. It uses its own E-R diagrams to express the structure of the model. Some of the diagram symbols and their uses were described in Figure 2.9 and Figure 2.10. Because of its independence from a DBMS, the enterprise schema will be valid regardless of the management system chosen, and it can remain correct even if the DBMS is changed. Unlike a schema written in a DDL, the E-R diagrams that we will use are not generally available to be used by the DBMS for creating the logical structure or doing external/logical or logical/internal relationships. We note that there are software tools that actually use E-R diagrams to create the database structures. However, we will view the diagrams as design tools and discuss how they could be useful in implementing a variety of systems. We also note that the discussion of the E-R model here differs slightly from that of Chen's. We have added concepts and used terminology that will be useful in later discussions.

The E-R model was classified in Section 2.7 as a semantic model, one that attempts to capture meaning as well as structure. There is a real effort to have the items in the model represent "things" in the miniworld, the part of the real world that the database is to model, and to express the relationships between real-world "things" by relationships in the model. The model describes the environment of the miniworld in terms of **entities, attributes,** and **relationships.** Figure 2.9 shows the basic symbols for E-R diagrams. A **rectangle** is used to represent an entity, an **oval** to represent an attribute, and a **diamond** to represent a relationship. These elements are connected by lines, as shown in Figure 2.9 and Figure 2.10. Figure 3.1 is an enhanced version of Figure 2.10, showing a simplified E-R diagram for a university database that represents information about students, faculty, and classes. The Student entity set,

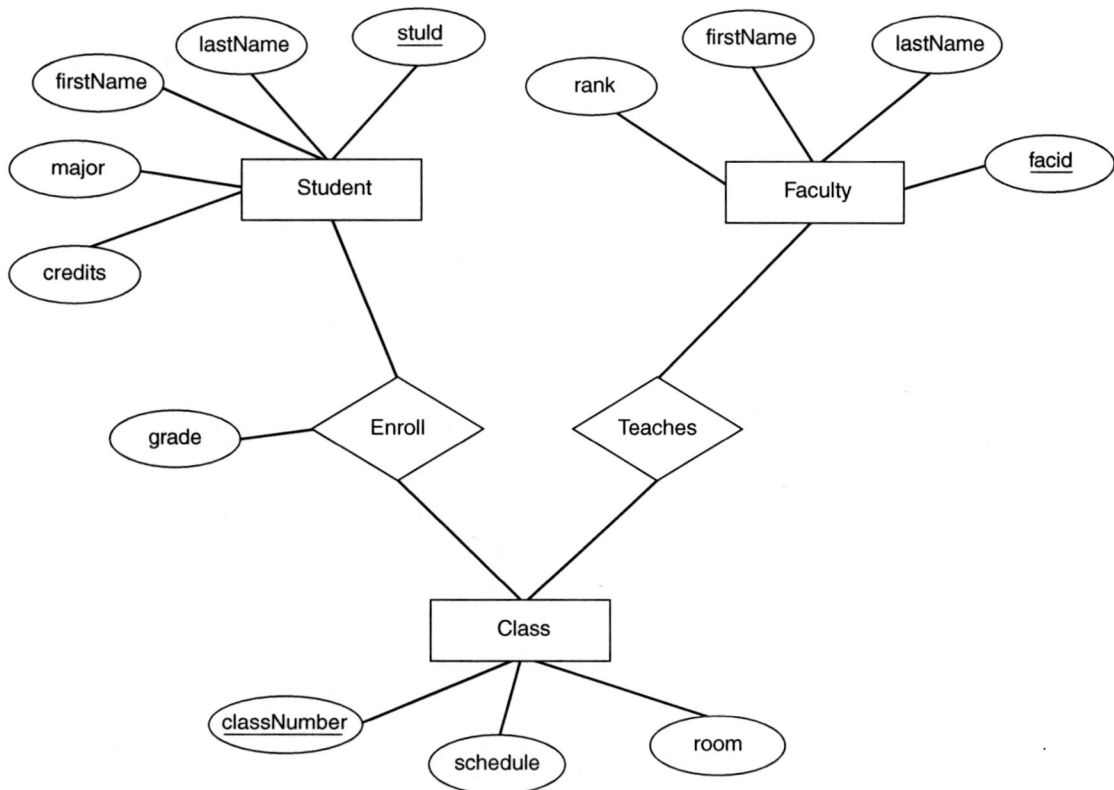

FIGURE 3.1

A Simplified E-R diagram for the University Database

shown as a rectangle, has attributes stuId, lastName, firstName, major, and credits, each shown as an oval connected to the rectangle for the Student entity. The Faculty entity set has attributes facid, lastName, first-Name, and rank. The class entity set has attributes classNumber, schedule, and room. The diamond marked Enroll shows there is a relationship between students and the classes they are taking. The Teaches relationship connects faculty to the classes they teach.

3.2   Entities

We will not give a formal definition of the term **entity** but, informally, we describe it as any object that exists and can be distinguished from other objects. It can represent a person, place, event, object, or concept in the real world that we plan to model in the database. It may be a physical object or an abstraction. Different designers may disagree about what entities exist in the miniworld. Entity **instances** represent a particular student, a specific class, an individual customer, a particular employee, an account, a patient, a conference, an invention, or a club, depending on what the enterprise is and what parts of it we wish to represent. Applying abstraction, we can identify the common properties of entity instances that are of interest in the database, and define an **entity type,** which is a representation in the data model of a category of entities. For example, if the enterprise is a university, we can consider all students in the university and identify the common properties of interest for the Student entity type. The entity type forms the **intension** of the entity, the permanent definition part. A collection of entities of the same type is called an **entity set.** The set must be **well-defined,** meaning that it must be possible to determine whether a particular entity instance belongs to it or not. All the entity instances that fulfill the definition at the moment form the **extension** of the entity. The members of the Student entity set change as students come and go, but the student entity type remains constant. Entity sets can intersect, that is, have common members. For example, in the model of the university we might have a faculty entity type and an administrator entity type. A particular person may satisfy the definition of both types, being simultaneously both a faculty member and an administrator in the university, and would therefore be an instance in both of these entity sets. As shown in Figure 3.1, an entity type is represented in E-R diagrams by a rectangle having the name of the entity inside.

3.3 Attributes

The **attributes** of an entity represent the defining properties or qualities of the entity type. For the student entity type, the defining properties might be the student's ID, name, major, and number of credits accumulated. The attributes are the representation in the model of those properties, namely stuId, stuLastName, stuFirstName, major, and credits. Normally, an entity will have a value for each of its attributes. An attribute is represented in an E-R diagram by an oval with the name of the attribute inside. A line connects the attribute oval to the rectangle for the entity set it describes. Figure 3.1 shows several examples of attributes connected to their entity types. Just as with entities, different designers may disagree about the attributes for an entity set. For example, another designer may choose to include stuAddress, stuPhone, and stuStatus, but not credits. In addition, what appears to be an attribute to one designer may be an entity to another. For example, major might be seen as an entity in a different design. In choosing whether an object should be an entity or an attribute, the designer should consider whether the object describes another object and whether it has values for its instances. In that case, it is best to represent the object as an attribute. If it is difficult to identify possible values, the object is more likely to be an entity.

3.3.1 Domains

The set of values permitted for each attribute is called the **domain** of that attribute. For the Student example, the domain of the credits attribute might be the set of integer values between 0 and 150 inclusive, depending on how the university computes credit hours. The domain of the stuLastName attribute is somewhat more difficult to define, since it consists of all legal last names of students. It is certainly a string, but it might consist not only of letters but also apostrophes, blanks, hyphens, or other special characters. Different attributes may have the same domains. For example, a subset of the set of positive integers is often used as a domain for attributes with quite different meanings, such as credits and age. An attribute actually maps an entity set to the domain of the attribute. For example, the attribute credits is a function that takes the set of students, and maps each student to a specific value in the domain $\{0, . . ., 150\}$. Figure 3.2 illustrates credits as a function majoring the Student entity set to the credits domain. (Note: This figure is not part of an E-R diagram, but a means

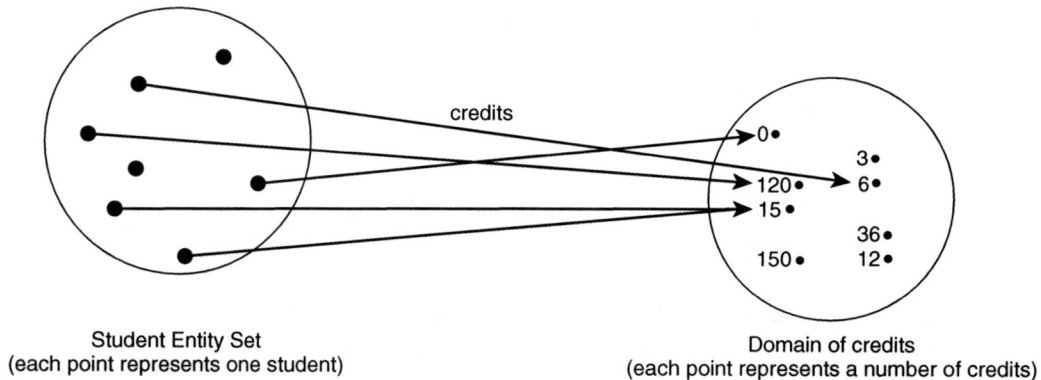

Student Entity Set
(each point represents one student)

Domain of credits
(each point represents a number of credits)

FIGURE 3.2

Credits as Mapping of Student Entity to Credits Domain

of illustrating this concept visually.) You may notice that the word domain as used here does not fit the mathematical notion of domain as the set on which a function is defined. In fact, the domain of the attribute is actually the range of a mathematical function. A particular entity instance could be described as a set of ordered pairs, with each pair being the name of an attribute and the value of the attribute. For a specific student, such a set might be {(stuId, S1001), (stuLastName, Smith), (stuFirstName, Jack), (major, History), (credits, 90)}. The named attribute itself and its domain are part of the intension of the model, while the attribute values are part of the extension. Note that some members of both sets are unmapped in Figure 3.2.

3.3.2   Null Values

Sometimes the value of that attribute is unknown at the present time or is undefined for a particular instance. In a database, some attributes may be permitted to have **null values** for some entity instances. In that case, the entity instance will not map to the domain of the attribute, although other instances of the same entity set will map to the attribute domain. In Figure 3.2 some members of the student entity set were not connected by arrows to the domain of credits. Note that values of zero or a blank string for a character-string field are considered to be non-null entries. Null means no value.

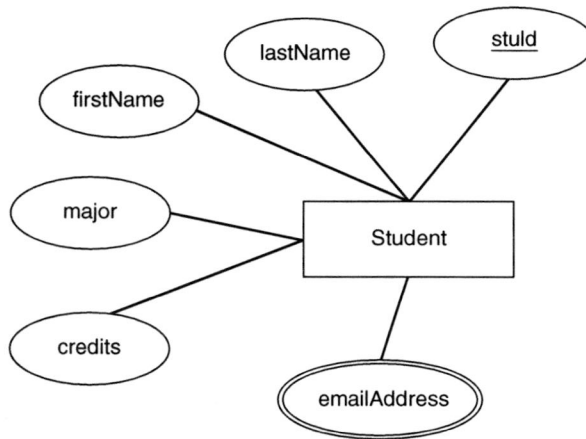

FIGURE 3.3
Student Entity Set with
Multivalued Attribute
emailAddress

3.3.3   Multivalued Attributes

Some attributes may have **multiple values** for an entity instance. For example, students may have more than one e-mail address. If it is possible for any entity instance to have multiple values for a particular attribute, we use a **double oval** around the attribute's name. The double oval should not be interpreted to mean that all instances must have multiple values, only that some instances may. Figure 3.3 illustrates how the multiple e-mail addresses for a student would appear on an E-R diagram.

3.3.4   Composite Attributes

Some attributes can be decomposed into smaller elements. For example address can be broken down into street, city, state, and zip. If we examine classNumber, we see that it consists of a department code, a course number within that department, and a letter for a section. If we used stuName as an attribute, we could decompose that into firstName and lastName. Similarly, telephoneNumber might be decomposed into areaCode, phoneNumber,or into countryCode, areaCode, exchange,and extension. An attribute is a **composite** attribute if it is possible to decompose it further. We indicate that an attribute is a composite by writing its name in an oval in the usual manner, and then drawing ovals for the individual components, which we connect by lines to the composite attribute's oval. Figure 3.4 illustrates address as a composite attribute.

FIGURE 3.4
Faculty Entity Set with Composite Attribute address and Derived Attribute age

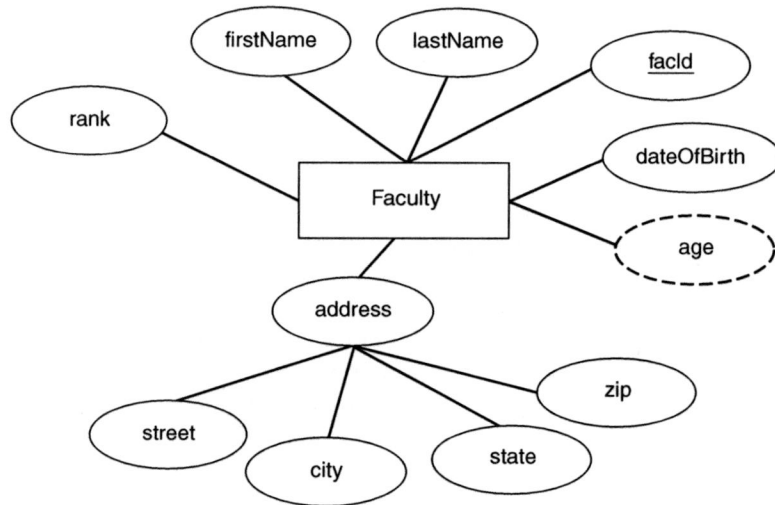

FIGURE 3.4
Faculty Entity Set with Composite Attribute address and Derived Attribute age

3.3.5   Derived Attributes

We might sometimes want to include in a design an attribute whose value can be calculated when needed. For example, we might want to treat age as if it were an attribute, but if we already stored dateOfBirth there is no need to store age as well, since it is easily calculated. Attributes that are not to be stored, but whose values are to be calculated or obtained from other sources, are called **derived.** These are indicted by a **dashed oval** on an E-R diagram. Figure 3.4 also shows age as a derived attribute. Attributes can also be derived from other entities or from relationships. For example, we could have an attribute currentEnrollment for Class, showing the number of students enrolled. The value could be derived from the number of enrollment relationships for the class entity. If we had stored Department as an entity, we could have a derived attribute, numberOfFaculty, which would hold a count of the faculty members for each department. This could be derived from the faculty entity.

3.4   Keys

Intuitively, we think of a **key** as a data item that allows us to tell records apart. We need a more exact definition of the concept of key. We begin with the notion of superkey.

3.4.1   Superkeys

A **superkey** is an attribute or a set of attributes that uniquely identifies an entity. This means it always allows us to tell one entity instance from another. For example, for the Student entity set, {stuId} is a superkey because it can be used to uniquely identify each student. If you have a list of all students—with their IDs, last names, first names, majors, and credits—and you are told the stuId value, there is only one student on the list with that value. If you are told the student's last name, you might not be sure which student to choose, since two or more students might have the same last name. Therefore {stuLastName} is not a superkey. If you have a superkey, then any set of attributes containing that superkey is also a superkey. Therefore, the combination of stuId and credits, written {stuId,credits}, is also a superkey. Note that a superkey provides unique identification for all extensions of the database, not just for one or two examples. We can use examples to help us fix our ideas about superkeys, but an example might be misleading. For instance, it might happen that at the moment no two students in the university have the same last name and we might incorrectly infer from the particular extension that {stuLast-Name} is a superkey. To identify a superkey requires that we consider the meaning of the attributes, a semantic notion, before deciding whether we have uniqueness over all extensions. Superkeys represent a constraint that prevents two entities from ever having the same value for those attributes. It represents an assumption we make about the miniworld we are using in the model.

3.4.2   Candidate Keys

Since a superkey such as {stuId,credits} might contain extra attributes that are not necessary for unique identification of entity instances, we are interested in finding superkeys that do not contain these extra attributes. In this example, the extra attribute is clearly credits. A **candidate key** is one that does not contain extra attributes. We define a candidate key as a superkey such that no proper subset of its attributes is itself a superkey. In our example, {stuId,credits} is not a candidate key because it contains a subset, {stuId}, that is a superkey. However, {stuId} by itself is a candidate key, since it has no proper subset that identifies entities. There may be several candidate keys for an entity set. If we stored social security numbers of students, then {socSecNo} would also be a candidate key, provided each student had a social security number. Note that a candidate key can consist of a single attribute, as {stuId} and {socSecNo} both do, or it can be a combination of attributes. For example, the combination {lastName,firstName,Address}, if it is always unique, can be a candidate key for some entity set. When a key consists of more than one attribute, we call it a **composite key.** For convenience, we will now drop the set braces in identifying keys, and simply list the attribute(s) in the key.

3.4.3   Primary Keys

An entity set might have several candidate keys. The database designer chooses among them and identifies one of them as the normal way of identifying entities and accessing records. This becomes the **primary key.** In other words, the primary key is the "successful" candidate key—the one actually chosen. The primary key may be a single attribute key or a composite key. Often, the other candidate keys become **alternate keys,** whose unique values provide another method of accessing records. The term **secondary key** usually means an attribute or set of attributes whose values, not necessarily unique, are used as a means of accessing records. In our example, stuId might be the primary key for the Student entity set. If socSecNo is also stored, it might be an alternate key. The attribute lastName can be used as a secondary key. While duplicate last names are allowed, we can use the last name to help us find a student record if we do not know the student ID or social security number. Usually an index is created on a secondary key field, permitting quick retrieval of records with a particular value of the indexed attribute. The records can then be examined individually to find the one desired. For the Class entity set, course# might be the primary key, and facId might be the primary key for the Faculty entity set. An important characteristic of a primary key is that none of its attributes have null values. If we permitted null values in keys, we would be unable to tell entities apart, since two entities with null values for the same key attribute might be indistinguishable. This follows from the definition of candidate key, which specified that no subset of a candidate key is itself a candidate key, so all attributes in a candidate key are necessary for unique identification of entity instances. To insure data correctness, we also have to insist that no attribute of a candidate key be permitted to have null values. In creating a database, typically we identify the primary key so that the system will enforce the no null and uniqueness properties, and we enforce the key status of candidate keys by specifying that they be unique. We underline the primary key of an entity in the E-R diagram, as shown in Figure 3.1.

For the sake of completeness, we note here that there is a concept called **foreign key.** However, it belongs to the relational model, and it is not part of the Entity-Relationship model. We will discuss it in Chapter 4.

3.5   Relationships

Entities are often linked by associations or **relationships,** which are connections or interactions among the entity instances. A student may be related to a class by being enrolled in that class. By abstraction, we can identify the common properties of certain relationships and define a **relationship type** and a corresponding well-defined **relationship set** as the collection of relationships of that type. The relationships that satisfy the requirements for membership in the relationship set at any moment are the **instances,** or members, of the relationship set. As with entities and attributes, the relationship type is part of the **intension** and the instances are part of the **extension** of the model. For example, we have a relationship type that links each student with each of the classes in which he or she is enrolled. We then have an Enroll relationship set, which contains all instances of the relationship. The name given to a relationship set is chosen by the designer. It is a good practice to choose a verb that captures the meaning of the relationship. If no name is given, we will refer to the relationship by using the names of the related entities, with a hyphen between them, e.g., Student-Class or Department-Faculty. Figure 3.1 shows two relationships, Enroll and Teaches, represented by diamonds on the E-R diagram.

3.5.1   Types of Relationships

Enroll is an example of a **binary** relationship set, one that links two entity sets. It is possible to describe this relationship set more formally as a set of ordered pairs, in which the first element represents a student and the second a class that the student is taking. At a given moment, the instances of this relationship set might be thought of as

```
Enroll = { (The student with Id S1001, The class with classNumber ART103A),
           (The student with Id S1020, The class with classNumber CS201A),
           (The student with Id S1002, The class with classNumber CS201A),
           (The student with Id S1010, The class with classNumber ART103A),
           (The student with Id S1002, The class with classNumber ART103A),
           (The student with Id S1020, The class with classNumber MTH101B),
           (The student with Id S1001, The class with classNumber HST205A),
           (The student with Id S1010, The class with classNumber MTH103C),
           (The student with Id S1002, The class with classNumber MTH103C) }
```

Each ordered pair shows that a particular student is enrolled in a particular class. For example, the first pair shows that the student whose ID is S1001 is enrolled in the class with class number ART103A. The set of the ordered pairs of the related entities is the relationship set, and each ordered pair is an instance of the relationship.

The entity sets involved in a relationship set need not be distinct. For example, we could define a roommate relationship within the Student entity set. Such a relationship is called **recursive.** Assuming only two students share a room, this would be a binary relationship called Roommate of the form

```
Roommate = {(Student1, Student2) | Student1 ∈ Student, Student2 ∈
Student, Student1 is the roommate of Student2}.
```

Instances of this relationship would be ordered pairs of students, as in

```
Roommate = { (The student with Id S1001, The student with Id S1020),
             (The student with Id S1020, The student with Id S1001),
             (The student with Id S1002, The student with Id S1005),
             . . . }
```

If we had an entity set of employees, we might have a recursive Manages relationship that links each employee to his or her manager, who is also an employee. That set would be defined as

```
Manages = {(Employee1, Employee2) | Employee1 ∈ Employee, Employee2 ∈
Employee, Employee1 is the manager of Employee2}.
```

Instances would be ordered pairs of employees, as in

```
Manages = { (The Employee with Id E101, The Employee with Id E301),
            (The Employee with Id E101, The Employee with Id E421),
            The Employee with Id E102, The Employee with Id E555),
            . . . }
```

A relationship might involve more than two entity sets. For example, we could have a ternary relationship, one involving three entity sets, linking classes, faculty, and textbooks used in the class. Then the relationship set could be defined as a set of ordered triples, in which the first element represents a class, the second a faculty member, and the third a textbook. Using course numbers to represent class entities, faculty IDs to represent faculty entities, and isbn numbers to represent textbooks, this relationship, which we call Class-Faculty-Text, might be thought of as

```
Class-Faculty-Text= { (Class ART103A, Faculty F101, Text '0-89134-573-6'),
                      (Class CSC201A, Faculty F105, Text '0-13-101634-1'),
                      (Class CSC203A, Faculty F105, Text '0-13-090955-5'),
```

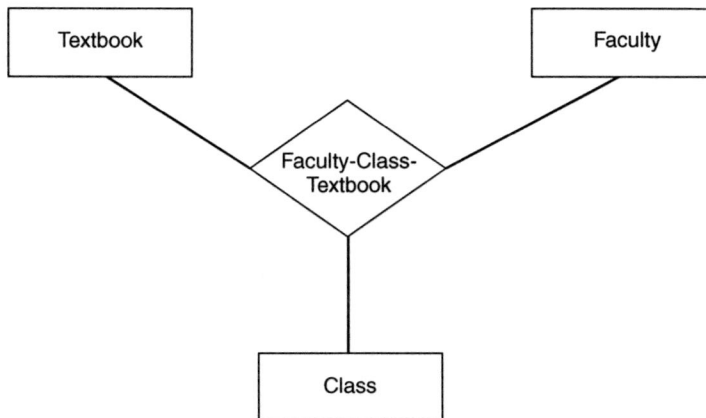

FIGURE 3.5
A Ternary Relationship

```
(Class HST205A, Faculty F115, Text '0-78-531220-4'),
(Class MTH101B, Faculty F110, Text '0-618-04239-3'),
(Class MTH103C, Faculty F110, Text '0-618-733214-6')}
```

Here, each ordered triple is an instance that shows that a particular text is used in a particular class which is taught by a particular professor. For example, the ordered triple (Class ART103A, Faculty F101, Text '0-89134-573-6'), means that the class ART103A, which is taught by the professor whose ID is F101, is using the text with isbn '0-89134-573-6' as the textbook. Figure 3.5 illustrates how a ternary relationship appears on an E-R diagram.

Although most relationships in a data model are binary or at most ternary, we could define a relationship set linking any number of entity sets. Therefore, the general relationship set can be thought of as a subset of an n-ary relation of the form

$$\{(e_1, e_2, \ldots .e_n) \mid e_1 \in E_1, e_2 \in E_2, \ldots, e_n \in E_n\}$$

where the E_i are entity sets, the e_i are entity instances, and each ordered n-tuple represents an instance of the relationship. You may recognize the notation used for the cross-product or Cartesian product of sets in mathematics. In fact, a relationship set is a subset of the Cartesian product of the entity sets involved; that is, if R is a relationship set and $E_1, E_2, \ldots, E_2$ are entity sets, then

$$R \subset E_1 \times E_2 \times \ldots \times E_n$$

3.5.2   Attributes of Relationship Sets

Sometimes a relationship set has **descriptive attributes** that belong to the relationship rather than to any of the entities involved. For example, in Figure 3.1, the attribute grade is a descriptive attribute for the Enroll relationship set. On an E-R diagram, we place a descriptive attribute of a relationship in an oval and connect it to the relationship diamond. Since students are still enrolled in the classes, we will assume this attribute represents the mid-term grade. The attribute grade does not describe the Student entity, since each student can have grades for several classes, nor does it describe the Class entity, since there are different grades given in a particular class for different students. For a grade to have meaning, it must be associated with a particular student for a particular class. Since grade is an attribute of Enroll, it can be described as a mapping of instances of Enroll to the domain of grade. Figure 3.6 shows grade as a function mapping the instance (Student S1001,Class Art103A) to the domain of grade. Note that the relationship Enroll is pictured as a set of ordered pairs. This diagram is not part of the E-R diagram, but is included only to illustrate this relationship concept.

3.5.3   Cardinality of a Relationship

It is important to identify restrictions or constraints on relationships so that the possible extensions of the relation correspond to real-world connections or associations. Two types of constraints on relationships are participation constraints and cardinality. The **cardinality** of a relationship is the number of entities to which another entity can map under that relationship. Let X and Y be entity sets and R a binary relationship from X to Y. If there were no cardinality constraints on R, then any number of entities in X could relate to any number of entities in Y. Usually, however,

FIGURE 3.6

Attribute of Relationship Set as a Function

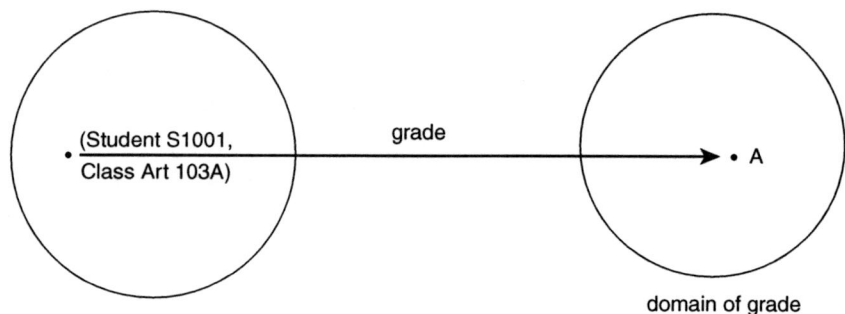

there are restrictions on the number of corresponding entities. We distinguish four types of binary relationships.

1. **one-to-one.** A relationship R from X to Y is **one-to-one** if each entity in X is associated with at most one entity in Y and, conversely, each entity in Y is associated with at most one entity in X. An example of a one-to-one relationship is the Chairperson to Department relationship. Each chairperson chairs at most one department, and each department has at most one chairperson. In family life, an example of a one-to-one relationship is the monogamous marriage relationship. At any given time, each husband is be married to only one wife, and each wife to one husband.

2. **one-to-many.** A relationship R from X to Y is **one-to-many** if each entity in X can be associated with many entities in Y but each entity in Y is associated with at most one entity in X. The word "many" applies to the possible number of entities another is associated with. For a given instance, there might be zero, one, two, or more associated entities, but if it is *ever* possible to have more than one, we use the word "many" to describe the association. The relationship between Faculty and Class is one-to-many, assuming there is no team teaching. Each faculty member can teach several classes, but each class is taught by only one faculty member. In a family, the traditional mother-to-child relationship is one-to-many. A mother can have many children, but each child has only one (birth) mother.

3. **many-to-one.** A relationship R from X to Y is **many-to-one** if each entity in X is associated with at most one entity in Y, but each entity in Y can be associated with many entities in X. The relationship between Student and his or her major Department is many-to-one, assuming there are no double or triple majors. Each student can have at most one major, but a department can have many student majors in it. In family life, the child-to-(birth) mother relationship is many-to-one. Each child has at most one birth mother, but each mother can have many children. A many-to-one relationship is actually the same as a one-to-many, but viewed from the opposite side.

4. **many-to-many.** A relationship R from X to Y is **many-to-many** if each entity in X can be associated with many entities in Y and

each entity in Y can be associated with many entities in X. The relationship between Student and Class is many-to-many. Each student can be enrolled in many classes (i.e., more than one), and each class can have many students enrolled in it. In a family, the grandparent-to-grandchild relationship illustrates a many-to-many relationship. A grandparent can have many grandchildren, and a grandchild can have many grandparents. The parent-to-child relationship is also many-to-many, since each child can have two parents, and each parent many children.

If entity sets A, B, and C are related in a ternary relationship, R, we can determine cardinality constraints for the participation of each entity set in the relationship. For each particular combination of B and C entities, if there is only one A value, then A participates as a "one." If there can be more than one A value for a particular B-C combination, then A participates as a "many." Similarly, B participates as a "one" or a "many" depending on how many B values can exist for each A-C combination, and C participates as a "one" or a "many" depending on the number of C values for each A-B combination. The notion can be extended to any degree relation.

3.5.4   Showing Cardinalities on an E-R Diagram

In an E-R diagram, lines connect the rectangles representing entity sets to the diamonds representing the relationship sets that show their association. There are several alternate methods of showing the cardinality of the relationship. The traditional one, shown as Method 1 at the top in Figure 3.7 is to put a "1" to show a "one" relationship cardinality and an "M" or "N" to show a "many" cardinality on the line connecting an entity to a relationship set. Thus if one faculty member is associated with each class, the line between the Faculty entity set rectangle and the Faculty-Class relationship set diamond has a "1" on it. Since many classes can be associated with the faculty member, the line between the Faculty-Class relationship set diamond and the Class rectangle has an "M" on it. If we choose to represent the one-to-one Chairperson-Department relationship, we would put a "1" on the line connecting the Chairperson rectangle to the Chairperson-Department relationship set diamond, and another "1" on the line connecting the relationship set diamond to the Department rectangle. For the Enroll relationship, we would have an "M" from the Student entity set rectangle to the Enroll diamond and an "N" from the Enroll diamond to the Class entity set rectangle.

FIGURE 3.7
Showing Cardinalities on E-R Diagram

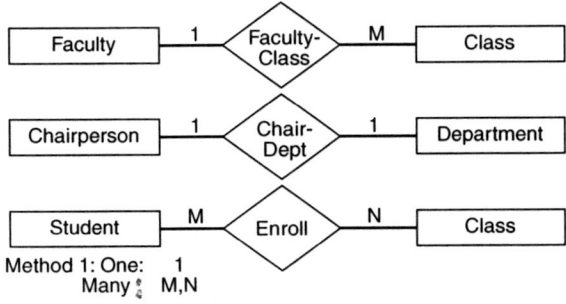

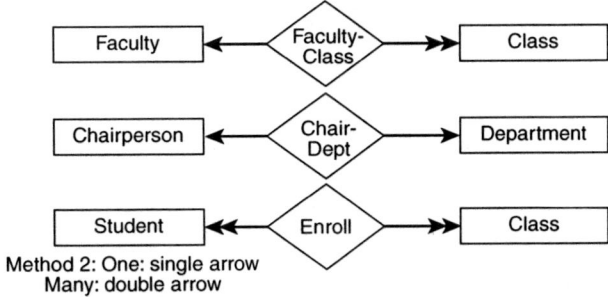

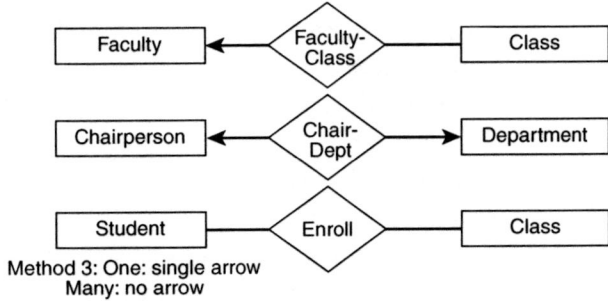

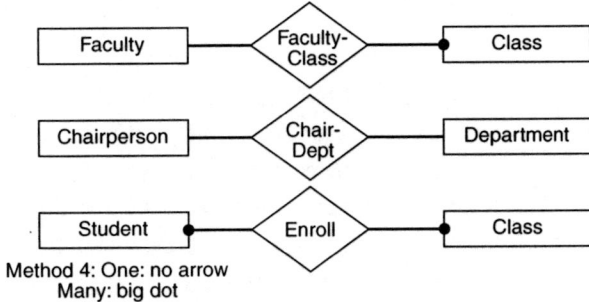

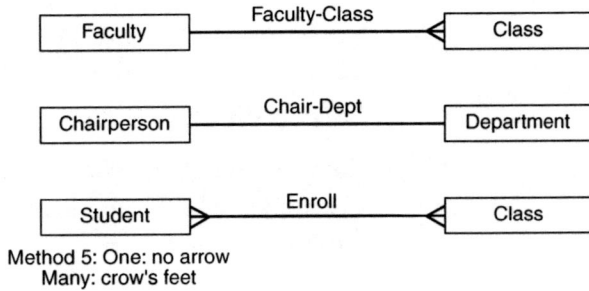

FIGURE 3.8
Cardinalities for Ternary Relationship

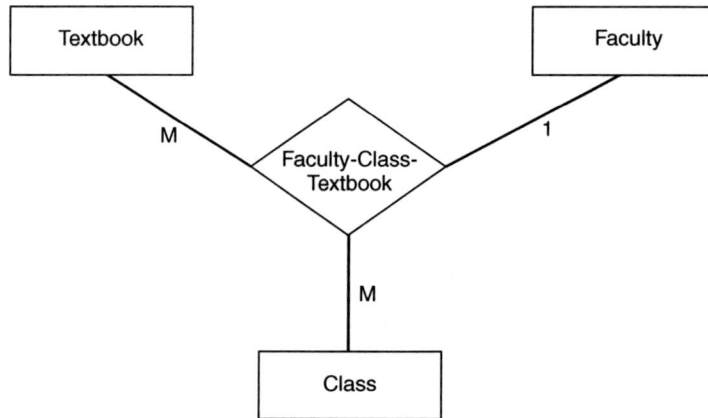

An alternate notation to the "1" is to put a single-headed arrow on the line from a relationship diamond pointing to an entity set rectangle that participates as a "one" and a double-headed arrow on the line pointing to an entity set that participates as a "many." Some authors or diagram-drawing software tools use a single arrow for a "one" and no arrowhead for a "many," while others use a "big dot" at the end of a "many" line and nothing at the end of a "one" line. Still another notation is to use lines to connect related entities, without a diamond, with a branched "crow's foot" at the end for a "many," and an unbranched end for a "one." Figure 3.7 summarizes these methods applied to these three examples.

For ternary relations, we place a "1" or an "M" or "N" on the arc from an entity to the relationship set, depending on whether the entity participates as a "one" or as a "many." We determine the participation by asking, "For each combination of the other two entities, how many of these participate?" Figure 3.8 shows the cardinalities for the Faculty-Class-Textbook ternary relationship. It indicates that for each Faculty-Class combination there may be many texts, for each combination of faculty and text there may be many classes, but for each combination of class and text there is only one faculty.

3.5.5 Participation Constraints

It is possible that not all members of an entity set participate in a relationship. For example, some faculty members may not be teaching this semester, or some students may not be enrolled in any class this semester,

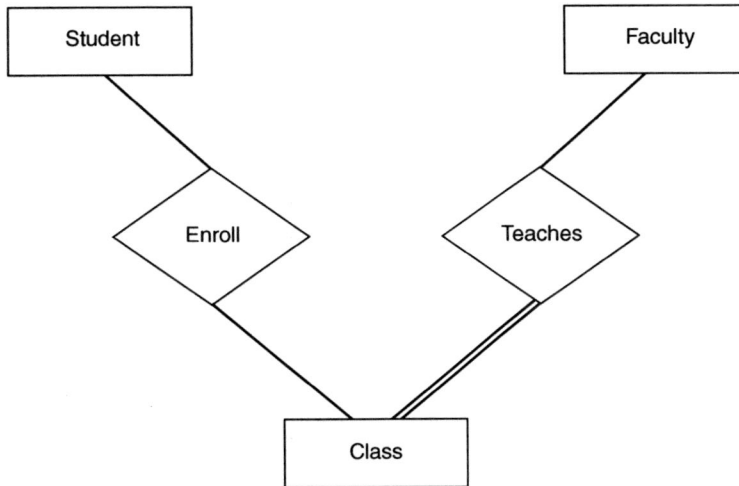

FIGURE 3.9

Total vs. Partial Participation in a Relationship

although they are maintaining their student status. If every member of an entity set must participate in a relationship, refer to this as **total participation** of the entity set in the relationship. We denote this by drawing a double line from the entity rectangle to the relationship diamond. A single line indicates that some members of the entity set may not participate in the relationship, a situation called **partial participation.** For example, if there are students who do not take classes, the participation of Student in the Enroll relationship is partial, and the line linking the Student entity set rectangle to the Enroll relationship diamond is a single line. A double line would imply that a person is not a student unless he or she is enrolled in some class. The single lines in Figure 3.9 shows that some students may not be enrolled in any class, some classes may have no students enrolled, and some faculty members may not be teaching any class. However, the double line shows that every class must have a faculty member teaching it. There are also alternate methods of representing participation constraints.

3.6   Roles

In a relationship, each entity has a function called its **role** in the relationship. Usually it is clear from the context what role an entity plays in a relationship. Thus in the relationship connecting Faculty and Class, it is understood that the Faculty entity plays the "is the teacher of" role in the relationship, while the Class entity plays the "is taught by" role. However,

FIGURE 3.10(a)

Recursive Relationship

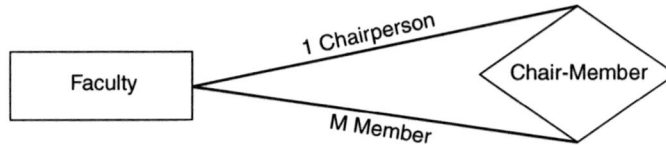

FIGURE 3.10(a) Recursive Relationship

FIGURE 3.10(b)

Entity Sets with Two Relationships

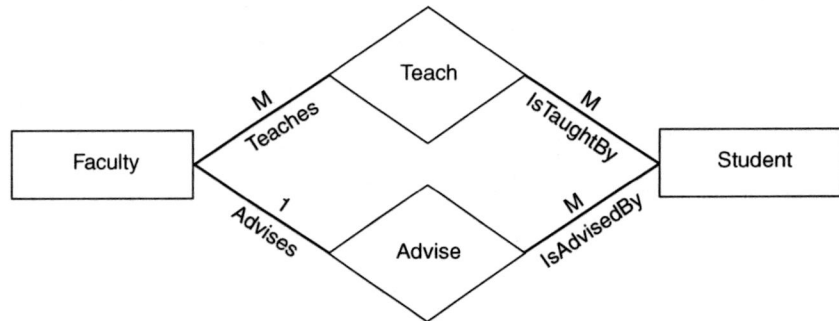

FIGURE 3.10(b) Entity Sets with Two Relationships

not all relationships involve distinct entity sets. When an entity set is related to itself, we have a **recursive** relationship, and it is necessary to indicate the roles that members play in the relationship. For example, one faculty member in each department is the chairperson. If we choose not to represent the chairperson as a separate entity, but to keep him or her in the Faculty entity set, then we might want to represent the Chair-Member relationship that links other department members to their chairperson. Figure 3.10(a) shows the Chair-Member relationship set defined on the Faculty entity set, with roles for the chairperson and the other members. The Roommate relationship on the Student entity set, which we described in Section 3.5.1, is a recursive one-to-one relationship, in which one student has the "has roommate" role and another has the "is roommate of" role. The Manages relationship between a manager-employee and the other employees he or she manages, shown in Section 3.5.1, is a recursive one-to-many relationship. The manager plays the "manages" role and the other employees play the "is managed by" role. Another instance where role names are helpful occurs when the same two entity sets are related in two different ways. For example, suppose we wanted to represent two different relationship types between faculty members and students. One type would be the usual Teacher-Student relationship, in which the Faculty entity has the "teaches" and the Student entity has the "is taught by" role. Another is the Advisor relationship, in which the Faculty entity has the "advises" role and the Student entity has the "is advised by" role. When entity sets are connected by multiple relationships, the roles can be written on the appropriate links. Figure 3.10(b) shows two entity sets, Faculty and Student, connected by two relationships, with roles appearing on the links. Although not necessary in all cases, we can use role names to help clarify any relationship, whether required or not.

3.7   Existence Dependency and Weak Entities

At times we need to store data about an entity that we would not be interested in unless we had a related entity already in the database. For example, we would not need to store data about sales orders unless we had customers. An existence constraint, or **existence dependency,** can occur between two entities. If X and Y are entities and each instance of Y must have a corresponding instance of X, then we say that Y is **existence dependent** on X. This means a Y entity cannot exist without some X entity. If Y is existence dependent on X, then Y must have **total participation** in its relationship set with X. A special type of existence dependency occurs when the dependent entity set does not have a candidate key, and its instances are indistinguishable without a relationship with another entity. For example, assume that teaching evaluations of faculty members are conducted by senior faculty or by the dean, and the ratings are stored in the database. For simplicity, we assume a single rating is given for each evaluation, so that an evaluation entity has attributes Date, RaterName, and Rating. Since there might be several instances with identical values for all three attributes, an Evaluation entity must be associated with the correct Faculty instance to have meaning. In this case, X (Faculty, in this example) is referred to as the **strong entity** (also called the parent, owner, or dominant entity) and Y (Rating, in this example) as the **weak entity** (also called the child, dependent, or subordinate entity). A weak entity is depicted in the E-R diagram by drawing a double rectangle around the entity, and making the relationship diamond a double diamond. Figure 3.11 shows the E-R diagram with the weak Evaluation entity and its identifying relationship. When an entity is weak, it has no primary key of its own, but is unique only in reference to its relationship to its owner. However, it often has a partial key, also called a discriminator, that allows us to uniquely identify the weak entities that belong to the same owner. The partial key may be a single attribute or a composite. For Evaluation, Date alone cannot be sufficient, if it is possible for a faculty member to be evaluated by two different people on the same date. Therefore, we will use the combination

FIGURE 3.11
Weak Entity Set

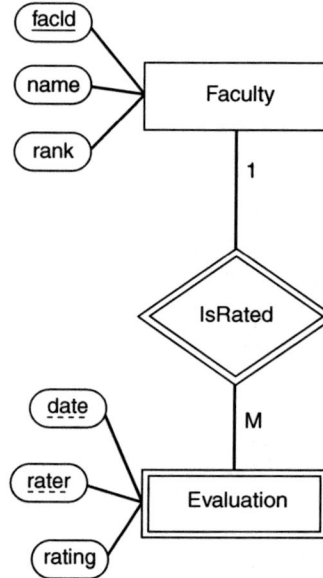

of Date and RaterName as the discriminator. The discriminator is indicated by a dashed underline on the E-R diagram.

3.8   A Sample E-R Diagram

Figure 3.12 shows an E-R diagram incorporating many of the entities and relationships discussed in this chapter. The entities and attributes are:

- Student: stuId, lastName, firstName, major, credits

We are assuming each student has a unique ID and has at most one major.

- Department: deptCode, deptName, office

We are assuming that each department has a unique code and a unique name, and that each department has one office designated as the departmental office.

- Faculty: facId, lastName, firstName, rank

We are assuming that FacId is unique and that every faculty member must belong to a department. One faculty member in each department is the chairperson.

- Class: classNumber, sched, room

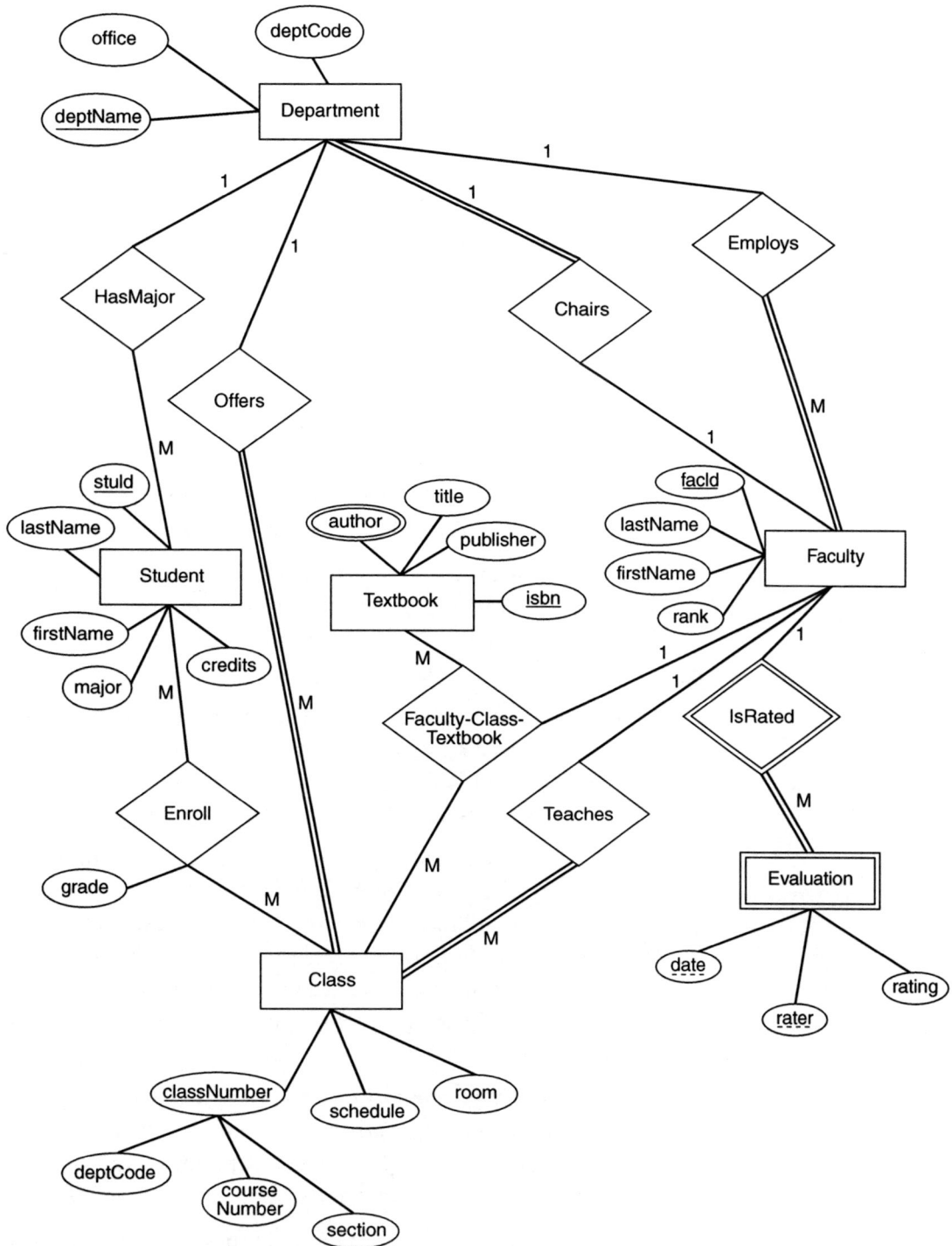

FIGURE 3.12
An E-R Diagram

We are assuming the classNumber consists of a department code, a number that identifies the course within the department, and a section code. We are keeping data for current classes only. If we want to store historical data about past class offerings or data about planned classes, we would need to add a date attribute.

- Textbook: <u>isbn,</u> author, title, publisher

We assume a book can have multiple authors.

- Evaluation: <u>date, rater,</u> rating

Evaluation is a weak entity, dependent on Faculty.

Note that we do not make the enterprise one of the entities. We have no entity set called university, since this is the entire enterprise. Everything in the diagram represents some facet of the university. The relationship sets are:

1. HasMajor, which is a one-to-many relationship that connects students to their major departments. We are assuming students have at most one major. Not every department has majors, and not every student has declared a major.

2. Offers, which is a one-to-many relationship that connects departments to the classes they offer. Only offerings for the current semester are kept in this database. A department may have no class offerings this semester, but every class has a department that offers it.

3. Enroll, which is a many-to-many relationship that connects students to the classes in which they are enrolled. We are assuming only current enrollments are kept. Grade is a descriptive attribute for this relationship set. Since the students are still enrolled in the classes, this attribute represents a mid-term grade. Some students are not enrolled in any class, and some class offerings may have no students enrolled.

4. Employs, which is a one-to-many relationship that connects departments to faculty members assigned to them. Faculty members must belong to exactly one department. A department might or might not have faculty assigned to it, but it can also have many faculty.

5. Chairs, which is a one-to-one relationship that connects departments to faculty. One faculty member in each department is the chairperson of the department. Every department must have a chairperson, but not every faculty member must be a chairperson.

We are assuming a chairperson is a regular faculty member who has the additional responsibility of chairing the department.

6. Teaches, which is a one-to-many relationship that connects faculty members to the classes they teach. We assume a faculty member may teach zero or many classes, and each class has exactly one faculty member assigned to it.

7. IsRated, a one-to-many relationship between Faculty and the weak entity, Evaluation. Not every faculty member has a rating, but every rating must belong to a faculty member.

8. Faculty-Class-Textbook, which is a ternary relationship among the three entities. We could have used two binary relationships, the Teaches one that already exists connecting Faculty and Class, and a new one UsesText, connecting Class and Textbook, as indicated in Figure 3.13. However, the meaning would be slightly different. The UsesText binary relationship would indicate that the class would use that text regardless who the instructor is, while the ternary relationship indicates that the text depends on the instructor. The cardinalities are more difficult to identify in a ternary relationship than in a binary one, but the ones pictured in Figure 3.12 preserve the meanings. To identify the cardinality for each entity, it is necessary to determine how many instances of that entity are related to each combination of instances of the other two entities.

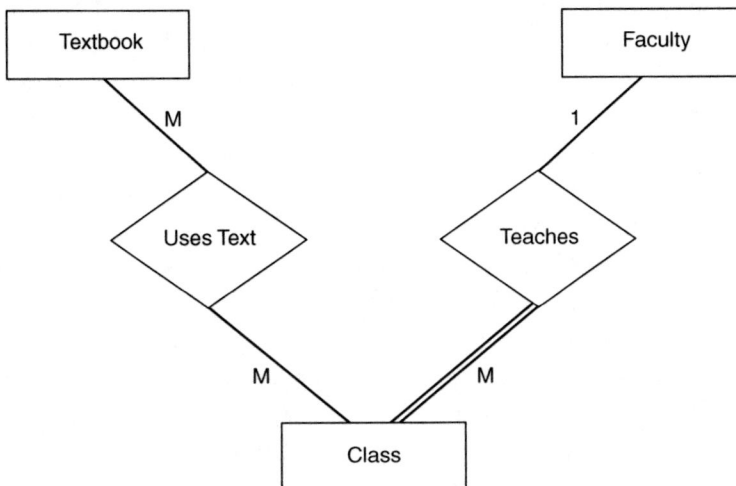

FIGURE 3.13

Example of Two Binary Relationships Replacing the Ternary Relationship

3.9   Chapter Summary

The **entity-relationship** model uses E-R **diagrams** to represent an enterprise schema, a conceptual level description that is independent of any DBMS. An **entity** is any distinguishable object in the miniworld that the database models. Entities are categorized into **entity types,** and a collection of entities of the same type forms an **entity set.** The individual entities that belong to the set at a given moment are **entity instances.** On an E-R diagram, a **rectangle** represents an entity type. **Attributes** are representations of properties of the real-world entities. They are represented as **ovals** on an E-R diagram. The set of values permitted for an attribute are its domain. The attribute is actually a mapping of the entity set into the domain of the attribute. **Null** values occur when an entity instance is missing a value for a particular attribute. Attributes can also be **multivalued, composite,** and/or **derived.**

A **superkey** is an attribute set that uniquely identifies entity instances. A minimal superkey, one with no proper subset that is also a superkey, is called a **candidate key.** The **primary key** of an entity is the candidate key that the designer chooses for unique identification. The other candidate keys can become **alternate keys.** A **secondary key,** which provides another way to access records, might or might not have unique values. A **composite key** is one that has more than one attribute. No attribute of a primary key can have null values.

A **relationship** is an association or interaction between entities. A **relationship set** consists of all relations of a given relationship type. Relationships may be **binary,** linking two entities, **ternary,** linking three entities, or **n-ary,** linking n entities. Binary relationship instances can be represented as ordered pairs, ternary instances as ordered triples, and n-ary instances as ordered n-tuples of entity instances. A relationship set is a subset of the Cartesian product of the related entity sets. A **diamond** is used to represent a relationship set on an E-R diagram. A relationship set may have descriptive attributes. On an E-R diagram, a descriptive attribute appears in an oval connected to the relationship diamond. Relationships have **cardinality constraints,** that specify how many entity instances may be related. For binary relationships, these may be one-to-one, one-to-many, many-to-one, or many-to-many. For ternary or higher-degree relationships, cardinality is determined for each entity by examining how many instances of that entity can occur for each combination of the other entities in the relationship. Cardinalities can be shown on E-R diagrams in several ways, the usual one being to write "1" or "M" on the arc from each entity set to the relationship diamond to indicate the cardinality of the participation of that entity set. Relationships also have participation constraints, which can be **total,** indicating that all members of the entity set must participate in the relationship, or **partial,** if not all members have to participate.

If a relationship is **recursive,** i.e., defined on a single entity set, or if two entity sets are related in more than one way, the **role** or function an entity plays in a relationship can be identified. This is done by placing the role name on the arc from the entity set to the relationship diamond on the E-R diagram.

An entity is **existence dependent** on another if it cannot exist in the database without a corresponding instance of the other entity. If such an entity has no key of its own, but must use the primary key attribute of the entity it depends on, it is called **weak.** The entity it depends on is called **strong.** A weak entity is shown on an E-R diagram within a double rectangle with its identifying relationship shown as a double diamond.

Exercises

3.1 **Define each of the following terms.**

   a. entity type

   b. entity set

   c. well-defined set

   d. intension of an entity

   e. extension of an entity

   f. attribute

   g. domain of an attribute

   h. null value

   i. superkey

   j. candidate key

   k. composite key

   l. primary key

m. alternate key

n. secondary key

o. relationship type

p. relationship set

q. binary relationship

r. ternary relationship

s. n-ary relationship

t. cardinality of a relationship

u. recursive relationship

v. existence dependency

w. weak entity

3.2   Consider the entity set Employee with attributes empId, socSec-No, empName, jobtitle, and salary

a. Show how the entity set and its attributes would be represented on an E-R diagram.

b. Describe the domain of the salary attribute, making assumptions as needed.

c. Identify a superkey for the Employee entity set.

d. Identify all candidate keys for the entity set.

e. Identify a primary key for the entity set and underline it on the E-R diagram.

3.3   a. Assume in the same enterprise as in Exercise 3.2, that there is an entity set called Project with attributes projName, startDate, end-Date, and budget. Show how this entity set and its relationship to Employee would be represented on the E-R diagram. Assume you want to represent the number of hours an employee is assigned to work on a project, and show that in the diagram.

b. Stating any necessary assumptions, make a decision about the cardinality and participation constraints of the relationship, and add appropriate symbols to the E-R diagram.

c. Assume there is another entity called Department to be added. Each employee works for only one department. Projects are not directly sponsored by a department. Making up attributes as needed, add this entity and appropriate relationship(s) to the diagram.

3.4 Design a database to keep data about college students, their academic advisors, the clubs they belong to, the moderators of the clubs, and the activities that the clubs sponsor. Assume each student is assigned to one academic advisor, but an advisor counsels many students. Advisors do not have to be faculty members. Each student can belong to any number of clubs, and the clubs can sponsor any number of activities. The club must have some student members in order to exist. Each activity is sponsored by exactly one club, but there might be several activities scheduled for one day. Each club has one moderator, who might or might not be a faculty member. Draw a complete E-R diagram for this example. Include all constraints.

3.5 A dentist's office needs to keep information about patients, the number of visits they make to the office, work that must be performed, procedures performed during visits, charges and payments for treatment, and laboratory supplies and services. Assume there is only one dentist, so there is no need to store information about the dentist in the database. There are several hundred patients. Patients make many visits, and the database should store information about the services performed during each visit, and the charges for each of the services. There is a standard list of charges, kept outside the database. The office uses three dental laboratories that provide supplies and services, such as fabricating dentures. Draw a complete E-R diagram for this example.

3.6 An interior design firm would like to have a database to represent its operations. A client (customer) requests that the firm perform a job such as decorating a new home, redecorating rooms, locating and purchasing furniture, and so forth. One of the firm's decorators is placed in charge of each job. For each job, the firm provides an estimate of the amount of time and money required for the entire job. Some of the work for a job, such as planning furniture placement, is done by the decorator in charge of the job. In addition, the firm might hire contractors to work on a daily or hourly basis on a particular job. A job might also include several activities, such as painting, installing floor covering, fabricating draperies, wallpapering, constructing, installing cabinets, and so on. These activities are done by contractors hired by the firm. The contractor provides an estimate for each activity. An activity or job might also require materials such as paint or lumber, and the firm has to keep track of the cost of materials for each activity or job, in order to bill the client. The database should store the estimated costs and actual costs of all activities and all jobs. Draw a complete E-R diagram for this example

3.7   An automobile body repair shop needs to keep information about its operations. Customers initially bring their cars to the shop for an estimate of repairs. A mechanic looks at the car and estimates the cost and time required for the entire job. If the customer accepts the estimate, a job number is assigned and the customer's name and contact information; the car's license plate number, make, model, and year; and a list of the repairs needed are recorded. The customer then makes an appointment to bring in the car on a specified date. When the car is brought in for repairs, the work begins. The shop keeps track of the charges for parts and labor as they accumulate. Only one mechanic works on the car for the entire job. A job might include several repairs (e.g., replacing the left fender, painting the passenger door.) The time actually spent for each repair is recorded and used to calculate the cost of labor, using a fixed hourly rate. Draw a complete E-R diagram for this example.

3.8   A database is needed to keep track of the operations of a physical therapy center. Every patient must be referred by a physician and have a prescription for physical therapy in order to receive treatments. A patient may have different physicians at different times. The database keeps all information about prescriptions and treatments, both past and current. When appointments are made, the information about scheduled date and time is recorded. No patient is ever scheduled for two visits on one day. The center has several physical therapists, and a patient may be treated by different physical therapists at different visits. When a patient makes a visit at an appointed time, the name of the therapist, the treatment, the date, time, and the equipment used are all recorded for that visit. Each of these has only one value for the visit. This information will be used later for insurance billing, which is not part of this database. Draw a complete E-R diagram for this example.

Lab Exercises: Drawing E-R Diagrams

Drawing tool software such as SmartDraw, Microsoft Visio, or similar products should be used for this laboratory exercise. If these are not available, the Paint program or the drawing tool in Microsoft Word can be used.

Using a drawing tool, draw an E-R diagram for the Employee-Project-Department example described in Exercises 3.2 and 3.3.

SAMPLE PROJECT: CREATING THE E-R DIAGRAM FOR THE ART GALLERY PROJECT

- Step 3.1. Make a list of all entities and their associated attributes.

This may take several attempts, and different designers will arrive at different solutions. In identifying entities, we examine the data dictionary and the cross-reference table that we developed in previous steps. Most of the data items there represent attributes rather than entities. We should avoid the temptation to make all reports or transactions entities. Our job is to try to use abstraction to group the attributes into entities for the mini-world we are modeling, which covers only a small part of the gallery's activities. Besides examining the documents we developed in Chapter 2, we need to think about the enterprise and ask ourselves what are the persons, places, events, objects, or concepts in the miniworld that we want to keep information about. The cross-reference table can help here. If several attributes tend to appear together on reports, they can be attributes of the same entity. The original data dictionary might have some items that we do not need to store in the database. They can be dropped from the list of attributes. By examining the data dictionary and asking ourselves what people are important in the Art Gallery, we can with certainty identify artists, collectors, and buyers as entities, and probably those potential customers who filled out the forms and whom we want to place on our mailing list, along with the buyers. Thinking about what events are important, the sale of an artwork is a central event, and an art show is an event of some importance. The salesperson who sells a work of art could also be an entity. The work of art is an object of great importance to the gallery, so it could be an entity. Note that we do not make the gallery itself an entity, since it is the enterprise.

The entities are:

```
Artist
Artwork
Buyer
Collector
Potential customer
Sale
Show
Salesperson
Owner
```

1. Artist

    In identifying the attributes for an entity, we try to find data items that tell a single fact about an entity instance. For the Artist entity, we look for attributes whose value would tell us one piece of information about a particular artist. Grouping the items from the data dictionary, the attributes that seem to describe the artist (as opposed to his or her artworks or the sale or show thereof), are:

    ```
    artistAddress, artistAreaCode, artistCity, artistFirstName,
    artistInterviewDate, artistInterviewerName, artistLastName, artistPhone,
    artistSalesLastYear, artistSalesYearToDate, artistSocialSecurityNumber,
    artistState, artistStreet, artistTelephoneNumber,
    artistTotalSalesforPeriod, artistTotalAskingPriceforPeriod,
    usualMedium, usualStyle, usualType.
    ```

    Examining these more closely, we see that some of them form composite attributes, including:

    `artistAddress`, consisting of `artistStreet, artistCity, artistState, artistZip`

    `artistName`, consisting of `artistFirstName, artistLastName`

    `artistPhone`, consisting of `artistAreaCode, artistTelephoneNumber`

    We notice that some of the items are produced for a single report and have no meaning if we don't know the parameters for the report, so they should be considered temporary (ephemeral) data that will not be stored. We include as ephemeral data artistTotal-SalesforPeriod and artistTotalAskingPriceForPeriod, since they are dependent on the start and end date the user chooses to run the report for, and have little meaning without the report. We might consider treating artistSalesLastYear and artistSalesYearToDate the same way. However, the value of artistSalesLastYear could be computed at the end of each year, as required for tax reporting purposes, and is a constant for the entire year that follows, so it is a value we could compute once and store. Similarly, the artistSalesYearToDate could be computed once each week or once each month and stored. These two items have meaning that is independent of the report that produces them provided, of course, that they are updated on a regular schedule. With these changes, the attribute list is shortened. Dropping the prefix artist that we listed in the data dictionary for some of the attributes, we now have:

`Artist` attributes are: `address(street, city, state, zip), interviewDate, interviewerName,` <u>`name`</u>`(first, last), phone(areaCode, number), salesLastYear, salesYearToDate, socialSecurityNumber, usualMedium, usualStyle, usualType`

We would normally choose socialSecurityNumber as the primary key, since it has unique values. If the gallery sells only works owned by the artists who create them, this could work well, since the social security number would have to be provided by the artist for tax reporting purposes, so it would always be available. However, we cannot be sure that we will have the social security numbers of artists whose works are owned by collectors. It is also possible that we will have works for foreign artists, who do not have a social security number. Therefore, we might have null values for this attribute, so we cannot use it as the primary key. Instead, we will choose the artist name, which we have assumed is unique, and which should always be available.

2. Artwork
   When we examine the data dictionary for items that describe the work of art, we find the candidates for attributes are:

   `askingPrice, dateListed, dateReturned, dateShown, status, medium, size, style, title, type, yearCompleted`

   We do not include on the list the attributes that describe the artist, which is a different entity. We also ignore the attributes that describe the owner of the work, since that person will be either the artist or a collector, which will be a separate entity. This leaves just a few attributes for the work.

   `Artwork` attributes are: `askingPrice, dateListed, dateReturned, dateShown, status, medium, size, style,` <u>`title`</u>`, type, yearCompleted`

We note that Artwork does not have a key. If we knew the artist of the work, then title would be the key. Since it requires the key of another entity to be used, Artwork is a weak entity, dependent on Artist. We use title as a partial key, a discriminator for this entity.

3. Buyer
   Potential attributes are:

   buyerAddress, buyerAreaCode, buyerCity, buyerFirstName,
   buyerLastName, buyerState, buyerStreet, buyerTelephoneNumber,
   buyerZip, purchasesLastYear, purchasesYearToDate

   Grouping the composites, as before, and dropping the buyer prefix, we get the following:

   Buyer with attributes: <u>name</u>(firstName, lastName), address(street, city,
   state, zip), <u>phone</u>(areaCode, telephoneNumber), purchasesLastYear,
   purchasesYearToDate

   We do not have social security number, which would provide unique values for a key, and we do not want to ask buyers to provide their social security numbers for privacy reasons. We assume names of buyers are not unique, so we cannot use name as a key. Phone appears to be a possibility for a key, but only if no two buyers have the same telephone number. To allow for the possibility that, for example, two members of the same household might both be buyers, we will add the name to the phone number and use the combination as the composite primary key.

4. Collector
   Looking through the data dictionary for attributes of Collector the candidates include:

   collectionArtistFirstName, collectionArtistLastName, collectionMedium,
   collectionStyle, collectionType, collectorAddress, collectorAreaCode,
   collectorCity, collectorFirstName, collectorInterviewDate,
   collectorInterviewerName, collectorLastName, collectorPhone,
   collectorSalesLastYear, collectorSalesYearToDate,
   collectorSocialSecurityNumber, collectorState, collectorStreet,
   collectorTelephoneNumber, collectorTotalSalesforPeriod,
   collectorTotalAskingPriceforPeriod

   Some of these form composite attributes, including:

   address, consisting of street, city, state, and zip
   name, consisting of firstName and lastName
   phone, consisting of areaCode and telephoneNumber

We drop ephemeral data, including `collectorTotalSalesforPeriod` and `collectorTotalAskingPriceforPeriod`, but we keep `collectorSalesLastYear` and `collectorSalesYearToDate`, which have meaning independent of the reports that generate them.

Again dropping the prefix, this leaves the following:

`Collector` with attributes: `name(firstName, lastName), address(street, city, state, zip), interviewDate, interviewerName, phone(areaCode, telephonenumber), salesLastYear, salesYearToDate, collectionArtistFirstName, collectionArtistLastName, collectionMedium, collectionStyle, collectionType, SalesLastYear, SalesYearToDate, `SocialSecurityNumber`

We note that, unlike buyers, collectors must provide their social security numbers, since the gallery is obliged to report to the government the social security number of the recipient and the amount for any payments for works sold. We will use the social security number as the primary key.

5. Potential customer

    Recall that a potential customer is a person who has filled out a form indicating an interest in the gallery's works, but who has yet not bought any artwork. Attributes to be considered are as follows:

    `potentialCustomerAddress, potentialCustomerAreaCode, potentialCustomerCity, potentialCustomerDateFilledIn, potentialCustomerFirstName, potentialCustomerLastName, potentialCustomerState, potentialCustomerStreet, potentialCustomerTelephoneNumber, potentialCustomerPreferredArtist, potentialCustomerPreferredMedium, potentialCustomerPreferredStyle, potentialCustomerPreferredType, potentialCustomerZip`

    Grouping the composite attributes and dropping the prefix, we have the following:

    `Potential customer` with attributes: `address(street, city, state, zip), `phone`(areaCode, telephoneNumber), `name`(firstName, lastName),dateFilledIn, preferredArtist, preferredMedium, preferredStyle, preferredType.`

    For the same reasons as we did with buyer, we will add the name to the phone number and use the combination as the composite primary key.

6. Show
Potential attributes are: `showFeaturedArtist,`
`showClosingDate, showTheme, showTitle,`
`showOpeningDate`

We note that a show always has a unique title, and it may have either a featured artist or a theme. None of the attributes are composites or ephemeral, so we keep all of them. Since the title is unique, we use that as the key. We have: `Show` with attributes `FeaturedArtist,` `ClosingDate,` `Theme,` `Title,` `OpeningDate`

7. Sale
Potential attributes are: `amountRemittedtoOwner saleDate,`
`saleInvoiceNumber, salePrice, saleSalesPerson-`
`Commission saleTax, SaleTotal`

We could have considered the title of the artwork, the buyer's name, the artist's name, the name of the collector (if any), and the salesperson's name, but we note that there are separate entities for artwork, buyer, artist, collector, and salesperson, so we do not include these attributes here. We will keep the salesperson commission, since that attribute describes a single sale, and will have different amounts for different sales by the same salesperson.

Since none of the listed attributes are composite or ephemeral data, we leave all of them, so we have: `Sale` with attributes `amountRemittedToOwner,` `saleDate,` `InvoiceNumber,` `salePrice,` `saleSalesPersonCommission,` `saleTax,` `SaleTotal`. We will use the invoice number as the primary key.

8. Salesperson
In choosing attributes for Salesperson we will not include information about the individual sales that a salesperson has made, since the sale data is already listed for that entity. Salesperson then has potential attributes such as:

`salesPersonAddress, salesPersonFirstName, salesPersonLastName,`
`salesPersonName, salespersonSocialSecurityNumber,`
`salespersonCommissionForPeriod, salespersonTotalSalesForPeriod`

We can specify the individual components of the address and telephone number, and make a composite attribute for the name. We drop the sales and commission total for a period, because this is ephemeral data. This leaves the entity as: `Salesperson` with attributes `name(firstName, lastName),` `socialSecurityNumber`, `address(street, city, state, zip).`

We will use socialSecurityNumber as the primary key, since we will always have that value for any employee of the gallery.

9. Owner
    Potential attributes are: `ownerAddress, ownerAreaCode,
    ownercity, ownerFirstName, ownerLastName,
    ownerPhone, ownerSocialSecurityNumber,
    ownerState, ownerStreet, ownerTelephone
    Number,ownerZip`
    However, since an owner is either the artist of the work or a collector, and we have data items that correspond to these for both of those entities, we already have the values of all the owner data items, so we drop the Owner entity.

Examining the data dictionary to see if there are any attributes unaccounted for, we see `dateOfReport, reportEndingDate, reportStartingDate, totalAskingPriceforPeriod, total-AllSalesforWeek,` all of which appear on reports. We note that all of these are either calculated or ephemeral data that does not have to be stored. We also see several attributes for the owner of an artwork, but we note that since an owner is either an artist or a collector, we already have the values of those attributes stored for those entities.

- Step 3.2. Make a list of relationships to be represented, and any descriptive attributes for them.

  Our entities are Artist, Collector, Buyer, PotentialCustomer, Artwork, Show, Sale, and Salesperson. Looking for relationships among them, we find the following.

1. Creates: Artist is related to Artwork. Every artwork in the gallery has an artist who created it. In fact, Artwork does not have a key without Artist, since title is not unique. Therefore, we will make Artwork a weak entity, dependent on Artist through the Creates relationship.

2. Owns: In some instances the artwork is not owned by the artist who created it. For those entity instances, Artwork is also related to Collector, through the Owns relationship.

3. SoldIn: Artwork is related to Sale.

4. SoldBy: Sale is related to Salesperson.

5. SoldTo: Sale is related to Buyer.

6.   ShownIn: Artwork is related to Show

7.   PreferredBy: PotentialCustomer does not appear to be strongly related to any other entity. However, a potential customer can identify an artist as a preference, so we could relate PotentialCustomer to Artist.

8.   CollectedBy: Since a collector might collect works predominantly by one artist, we can add a relationship between Artist and Collector.

9.   FeaturedIn: We add this relationship to connect an artist to the "one-person" shows where that person's work is featured.

Since there were no remaining attributes on the data dictionary, there are no attributes that depend on relationships in this example.

- Step 3.3. Draw an E-R diagram to represent the enterprise. Be sure to identify relationship participation and cardinality constraints, any weak entity sets, and role names, if needed.

An E-R diagram is shown in Figure 3.14. To construct it, we use the following steps. We start the diagram with the Artist entity. We concluded previously that Artwork is a weak entity with reference to Artist, so we draw a double rectangle for Artwork, and a double diamond for the Creates relationship. Each artist may have zero or many artworks in the gallery. We use a single line to allow for the possibility that an artist has been interviewed but none of his or her artworks have been selected yet. Each artwork must have exactly one artist, so Artwork has total participation in the relationship. An artist can create many works of art, but an artwork has only one artist. This is a 1:M relationship.

Next we add the Collector entity. The Owns relationship between Collector and Artwork is also 1:M. A collector might not yet have a work of art in the gallery (partial participation), but an artwork must have an owner. However, the owner may be the artist rather than a collector, so we choose partial participation for Artwork as well.

The CollectedBy relationship connects an artist to the collector(s), if any, who collect his or her works. Each artist may have many collectors, but a collector can optionally name one artist on the form, making this a 1:M relationship with partial participation on both sides.

Now we add the Sale entity. IsSold, the Artwork to Sale relationship is 1:1. In our list of assumptions, we said that each artwork is sold once, at most,

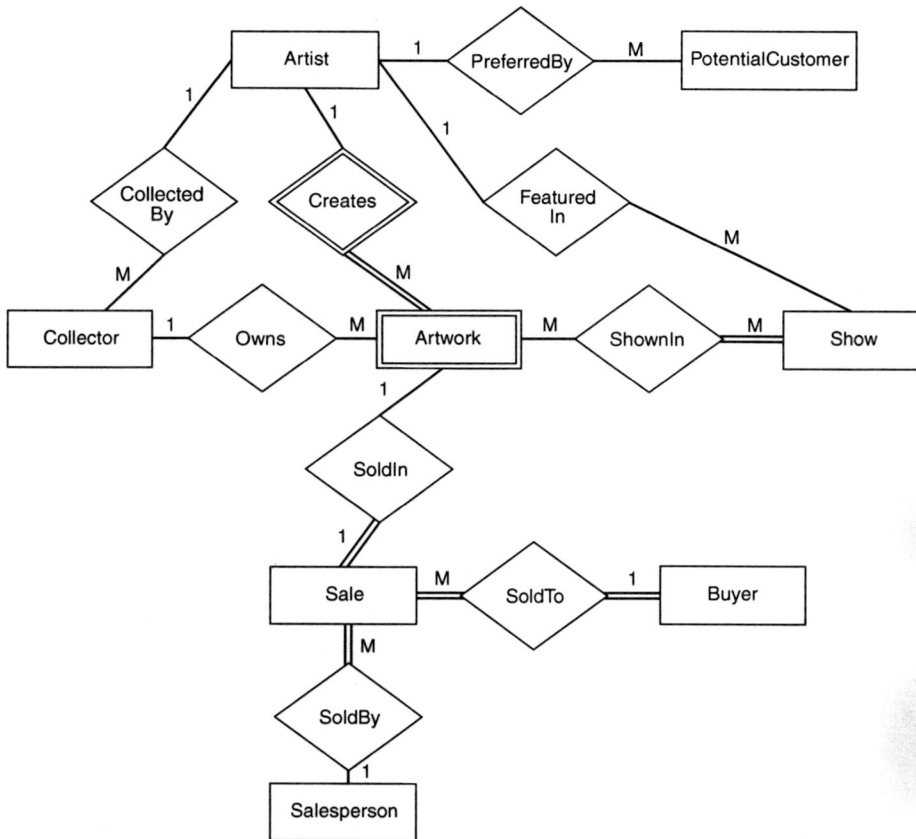

Artist: address (street, city, state, zip), interviewDate, interviewerName,
name(firest, last), phone(areaCode, telephoneNumber), salesLastYear, salesYearToDate,
socialSecurityNumber, usualMedium, usualStyle, usualType

Artwork: askingPrice, dateListed, dateReturned, dateShown, status,workMedium, workSize,
workStyle, workTitle, workType, workYearCompleted

Buyer: name(firstName, lastName), address(street, city, state, zip), phone(areaCode,
telephoneNumber), purchasesLastYear, purchasesYearToDate

Collector: name(firstName, lastName), address(street, city, state, zip), interviewDate,
interviewerName, phone(areaCode, telephonenumber), salesLastYear, salesYearToDate,
collectionArtistFirstName, collectionArtistLastName, collectionMedium, collectionStyle,
collectionType, SalesLastYear, SalesYearToDate, SocialSecurityNumber

PotentialCustomer: address(street, city, state, zip), phone(areaCode, telephoneNumber),
name(firstName, lastName), dateFilledIn, preferredArtist, preferredMedium, preferredStyle,
preferredType.

Show: showFeatureArtist, showClosingDate, showTheme, showTitle, showOpeningDate

Sale: amoutRemittedToOwner, saleDate, InvoiceNumber, salePrice,
sale SalesPersonCommission, saleTax, SaleTotal (calculated field)

Salesperson: name(firstName, lastName), socialSecurityNumber, address(street, city,
state, zip)

FIGURE 3.14

E-R Diagram for the Art Gallery

and each sale is for one artwork. An artwork may or may not be sold (partial participation), but a sale must have an artwork (total participation).

Next we add the Show entity. The Artwork to Show relationship, ShownIn, is M:N, since an artwork can appear in more than one show, and each show can show many works of art. It is partial participation for the Artwork, since not all artworks appear in shows, and total for Show, since a show must include at least one work of art.

The Artist to Show relationship, FeaturedIn, is 1:M, since a show has, at most, one featured artist, but an artist could be featured in more than one show. The participation is partial on both sides, since an artist does not have to be featured in any show, and a show does not have to feature an artist.

We can add the Salesperson entity. Sale to Salesperson, SoldBy, is M:1. Each sale is made by just one salesperson, but a salesperson can make many sales. A sale requires a salesperson (total participation) but a new salesperson cannot have made any sales yet (partial participation). We can also add the Buyer entity. SoldTo, the Sale to Buyer relationship is M:1. A sale is to one buyer, but the same buyer can be involved in many sales. A sale must have a buyer (total participation) and a buyer, by definition, must be someone who has bought an artwork (total participation).

Lastly we add the PotentialCustomer entity. PreferredBy, the Artist to PotentialCustomer relationship, is 1:M, since a potential customer can identify one artist, but an artist might have many potential customers who prefer him or her. This is a partial relationship on both sides, since a potential customer does not have to state a preference for any artist, and an artist may have no potential customers who have chosen him or her as preferred.

- Step 3.4. Update the data dictionary and list of assumptions as needed.

Revised Data Dictionary. Changes are in *italics*.

amountRemittedtoOwner   The dollar amount of money sent to an owner for the sale of an artwork.

artistAddress   The mailing address of an artist; *composite consisting of artistStreet, artistCity, artistState, artistZip.*

artistAreaCode   The telephone area code of an artist; *part of the composite artistPhone.*

artistCity   The city of the mailing address of an artist; *part of the composite artistAddress.*

artistFirstName The given first name that an artist uses; *part of the composite artistName.*

artistInterviewDate The date an artist was interviewed by a representative of the gallery.

artistInterviewerName The first and last name of the gallery representative who interviewed an artist.

artistLastName The last name (surname) of an artist; *part of the composite artistName.*

artistName The first and last name of an artist; *composite consisting of artistFirstName, artistLastName.*

artistPhone The complete telephone number of the artist; *composite consisting of artistAreaCode and artistTelephoneNumber.*

artistSalesLastYear The total dollar amount of sales of an artist's works during the entire previous year.

artistSalesYearToDate The total dollar amount of sales of an artist's works from the first day of the current year to the present.

artistSocialSecurityNumber The social security number of an artist.

artistState The state of the mailing address of an artist; *part of the composite artistAddress.*

artistStreet The house number and street of the mailing address of an artist; *part of the composite artistAddress.*

artistTelephoneNumber The telephone number of an artist, not including area code; *part of the composite artistPhone.*

artistTotalSalesforPeriod *The total dollar amount of sales of an artist's works for the period covered in a report or transaction. (Item deleted.)*

artistTotalAskingPriceforPeriod *The total dollar value of an artist's unsold works for sale in the gallery for the period covered in a report or transaction, computed as the sum of their asking prices. (Item deleted.)*

artistZip The postal zip code of the mailing address of an artist; *part of the composite artistAddress.*

askingPrice The asking price of a work of art.

buyerAddress The mailing address of a buyer of an artwork of the gallery; *composite consisting of buyerStreet, buyerCity, buyerState, buyerZip.*

buyerAreaCode   The telephone area code of a buyer of an artwork of the gallery; *part of the composite buyerPhone.*

buyerCity   The city of the mailing address of a buyer of an artwork of the gallery; *part of the composite buyerAddress.*

buyerFirstName   The first name of a buyer of an artwork of the gallery; *part of the composite buyerName.*

buyerLastName   The last name of a buyer of an artwork of the gallery; *part of the composite buyerName.*

buyerName   The first and last name of a buyer of an artwork of the gallery; *composite consisting of buyerFirstName, buyerLastName.*

buyerPhone   The complete telephone number of a buyer of an artwork of the gallery; *composite consisting of buyerAreaCode and buyerTelephoneNumber.*

buyerState   The state of the mailing address of a buyer of an artwork of the gallery; *part of the composite buyerAddress.*

buyerStreet   The house number and street of the mailing address of a buyer of an artwork of the gallery; *part of the composite buyerAddress.*

buyerTelephoneNumber   The telephone number of a buyer of an artwork of the gallery, not including area code; *part of the composite buyerPhone.*

buyerZip   The postal zip code of the buyer of a work of art; *part of the composite buyerAddress.*

collectionArtistFirstName   The first name of the artist featured in a group of artworks owned by a collector; *part of composite collectionArtistName.*

collectionArtistLastName   The last name of the artist featured in a group of artworks owned by a collector; *part of composite collectionArtistName.*

collectionArtistName   The first and last name of the artist featured in a group of artworks owned by a collector; *composite consisting of collectionArtistFirstName, collectionArtistLastName.*

collectionMedium   The medium used for a group of artworks owned by a collector.

collectionStyle   The style of a group of artworks owned by a collector.

collectionType   The type of a group of artworks owned by a collector.

collectorAddress   The mailing address of a collector of works of art; *composite consisting of collectorStreet, collectorCity, collectorState, collectorZip.*

collectorAreaCode   The telephone area code of a collector of works of art; *part of composite collectorPhone.*

collectorCity   The city of the mailing address of a collector of works of art; *part of composite collectorAddress.*

collectorFirstName   The given first name of a collector of works of art; *part of composite collectorName.*

collectorInterviewDate   The date a collector of works of art was interviewed by a representative of the gallery.

collectorInterviewerName   The first and last name of the representative of the gallery who interviewed a collector of works of art.

collectorLastName   The last name (surname) of a collector of works of art; *part of composite collectorName.*

collectorName   The first and last name of a collector of works of art; *composite consisting of collectorFirstName, collectorLastName.*

collectorPhone   The complete telephone number of a collector of works of art; *composite consisting of collectorAreaCode, collectorTelephoneNumber.*

collectorSalesLastYear   The total dollar amount of sales of the collector's artworks during the entire previous year.

collectorSalesYearToDate   The total dollar amount of sales of the collector's artworks from the first day of the current year to the present.

collectorSocialSecurityNumber   The social security number of a collector of works of art.

collectorState   The state of the mailing address of a collector of works of art; *part of composite collectorAddress.*

collectorStreet   The house number and street of the mailing address of a collector of works of art; *part of composite collectorAddress.*

collectorTelephoneNumber   The telephone number of a collector of works of art, not including area code; *part of composite collectorPhone.*

collectorTotalSalesforPeriod   The total dollar amount of sales of the collector's works for the period covered in a report or transaction. (Item deleted.)

collectorTotalAskingPriceforPeriod   The total dollar value of the collector's unsold works for sale in the gallery for the period covered in a report or transaction, computed as the sum of their asking prices. (Item deleted.)

collectorZip   The postal zip code of the mailing address of a collector of works of art; *part of composite collectorAddress.*

dateListed   The date a work of art is first offered for sale in the gallery.

dateReturned   The date a work of art is returned to its owner.

dateShown   The date a work of art is featured in an art show by the gallery.

dateOfReport   The date that a report was generated. (Item not stored.)

medium   The medium of a work of art. Examples of valid values are oil, pastel, watercolor, watermedia, acrylic, marble, steel, copper, wood, fiber, other.

ownerAddress   The mailing address of the owner of a work of art. (Item deleted; owner replaced by either Artist or Collector.)

ownerAreaCode   The telephone area code of the owner of a work of art. (Item deleted; owner replaced by either Artist or Collector.)

ownerCity   The city of the mailing address of the owner of a work of art. (Item deleted; owner replaced by either Artist or Collector.)

ownerFirstName   The given first name that the owner of a work of art uses. (Item deleted; owner replaced by either Artist or Collector.)

ownerLastName   The last name (surname) of the owner of a work of art. (Item deleted; owner replaced by either Artist or Collector.)

ownerPhone   The complete telephone number of the owner of a work of art. (Item deleted; owner replaced by either Artist or Collector.)

ownerSocialSecurityNumber   The social security number of the owner of a work of art. (Item deleted; owner replaced by either Artist or Collector.)

ownerState   The state of the mailing address of the owner of a work of art. (Item deleted; owner replaced by either Artist or Collector.)

ownerStreet   *The house number and street of the mailing address of the owner of a work of art. (Item deleted; owner replaced by either Artist or Collector.)*

ownerTelephoneNumber   *The telephone number of the owner of a work of art, not including area code. (Item deleted; owner replaced by either Artist or Collector.)*

ownerZip   *The postal zip code of the mailing address of the owner of a work of art. (Item deleted; owner replaced by either Artist or Collector.)*

potentialCustomerAddress   The mailing address of a potential customer of the gallery; *composite consisting of potentialCustomerStreet, potentialCustomerCity, potentialCustomerState, potentialCustomerZip.*

potentialCustomerAreaCode   The telephone area code of a potential customer of the gallery; *part of the composite potentialCustomerPhone.*

potentialCustomerCity   The city of the mailing address of a potential customer of the gallery; *part of the composite potentialCustomerAddress.*

potentialCustomerDateFilledIn   The date a customer information form was filled in.

potentialCustomerFirstName   The first name of a potential customer of the gallery; *part of the composite potentialCustomerName.*

potentialCustomerLastName   The last name of a potential customer of the gallery; *part of the composite potentialCustomerName.*

potentialCustomerName.   The first and last name of a potential customer of the gallery; *composite consisting of potentialCustomerFirstName, potentialCustomerLastName.*

potentialCustomerPhone   The complete telephone number of a potential customer of the gallery; *composite consisting of potentialCustomerAreaCode, potentialCustomerTelephoneNumber.*

potentialCustomerState   The state of the mailing address of a potential customer of the gallery; *part of the composite potentialCustomerAddress.*

potentialCustomerStreet   The house number and street of the mailing address of a potential customer of the gallery; *part of the composite potentialCustomerAddress.*

potentialCustomerTelephoneNumber   The telephone number of a potential customer of the gallery, not including area code; *part of the composite potentialCustomerPhone.*

potentialCustomerZip   The postal zip code of the mailing address of a potential customer of the gallery; *part of the composite potentialCustomerAddress.*

preferredArtist   The name of the artist chosen as a preference by a potential customer of the gallery.

preferredMedium   The medium chosen as a preference by a potential customer of the gallery.

preferredStyle   The style chosen as a preference by a potential customer of the gallery.

preferredType   The type chosen as a preference by a potential customer of the gallery.

purchasesLastYear   The total dollar amount of sales to a buyer during the entire previous year.

purchasesYearToDate   The total dollar amount of sales to a buyer from the first day of the current year to the present.

reportStartingDate   The date chosen as the earliest date for information to be used in a report. Item deleted.

reportEndingDate   The date chosen as the latest date for information to be used in a report. (Item deleted.)

saleDate   The date a work of art was sold by the gallery.

saleInvoiceNumber   The number printed on the invoice for a sale of a work of art.

salePrice   The price at which a work of art was sold by the gallery.

salesPersonAddress   The full address of a sales associate who works in the gallery; *composite consisting of salesPersonStreet, salesPersonCity, salesPersonState, salesPersonZip.*

salesPersonFirstName   The given first name of a sales associate who works in the gallery; *part of composite salesPersonName.*

salesPersonLastName   The last name (surname) of a sales associate who works in the gallery; *part of composite salesPersonName.*

salesPersonName   The first and last name of a sales associate who works in the gallery; composite consisting of salesPersonFirstName, salesPersonLastName.

salesPersonSocialSecurityNumber   The social security number of a sales associate who works in the gallery.

salesPersonCommissionForPeriod   The total dollar amount of commission earned by a salesperson for a specific period. (Item deleted.)

salesPersonTotalSalesForPeriod   The total dollar amount of sales, not including tax, made by a salesperson during a specific period. (Item deleted.)

saleSalesPersonCommission   The dollar amount of commission for a salesperson for the sale of a work of art.

saleTax   The dollar amount of sales tax for the sale of an artwork.

saleTotal   The total dollar amount of a sale, including price and tax, for an artwork; *(Item deleted; calculated from salePrice and saleTax.)*

showClosingDate   The final date that an artshow is open to the public.

showFeaturedArtist   The first and last name of an artist featured in an artshow.

showTheme   The theme of an artshow.

showTitle   The title given to an artshow.

showOpeningDate   The first date that an artshow is open to the public.

size   The size of a work of art, expressed in inches. For two-dimensional works, given as length by width; for three-dimensional works, given as length by width by height.

status   The sales status of a work of art. Possible values are sold or unsold.

style   The artistic style of a work of art. Examples of valid values are contemporary, impressionist, folk, other.

title   The title of a work of art.

totalAllSalesForWeek   The total dollar amount of sales for the gallery for a specific week, not including tax. (Item deleted.)

totalAskingPriceForPeriod   The sum of asking prices for all works during the period chosen for a report. (Item deleted.)

type   The type of a work of art. Examples of valid values are painting, sculpture, collage, other.

usualMedium   The medium the artist usually works in. Examples of valid values are oil, pastel, watercolor, watermedia, acrylic, marble, steel, copper, wood, fiber, other.

usualStyle.   The usual artistic style of the artist's works. Examples of valid values are contemporary, impressionist, folk, other.

usualType   The type of artwork the artist normally produces. Examples of valid values are painting, sculpture, collage, other.

yearCompleted   The year that a work of art was completed.

The list of assumptions has some minor changes, indicated in italics as follows:

1. Artist names are unique, but customer names and collector names are not.

2. For privacy reasons, only people who receive payments from the gallery are asked to provide their social security numbers, because these payments have to be reported for income tax purposes. Therefore, the gallery keeps social security numbers for salespersons, collectors, and artists, but not for buyers or potential customers.

3. An artist might have many works for sale in the gallery.

4. Each work is an original, one-of-a-kind piece. No prints or reproductions are sold.

5. Two works of art can have the same title, but the combination of title and artist name is unique.

6. A work of art can be owned either by the artist who created it or by another person, referred to here as a collector.

7. Even if the work of art is owned by a collector, it is important to keep information about the artist who created it, since that is a factor in determining its value.

8. A work of art is sold by the gallery only once. The gallery does not re-sell its own works.

9. A work of art might appear in more than one show. Some works do not appear in any show.

10. Payment for all sales is made immediately and in full at the time of purchase. Payment may be by credit, cash, or check. The owner is paid the balance and the salesperson is paid the commission at the end of the week.

11. The database does not include payroll information, except for the commission to be paid to salespeople for sales of artwork.

12. There are lists of valid values for type, style, and medium of artworks. Each has a value "other" for works that do not fit existing values.

13. Information about works not selected to be listed by the gallery is discarded.

14. Lists of artists, collectors, buyers, and potential customers are evaluated periodically to determine whether they should be dropped.

15. *Titles of art shows are unique. Each art show also has either a single featured artist or a theme.*

16. *An art show normally features many works of art, but it is possible that a single important piece of art is shown.*

STUDENT PROJECTS: CREATING E-R DIAGRAMS FOR STUDENT PROJECTS

For the project you have chosen, do the following:

- Step 3.1. Make a list of all entities and their associated attributes.

- Step 3.2. Make a list of relationships to be represented, and any descriptive attributes for them.

- Step 3.3. Draw an E-R diagram to represent the enterprise. Be sure to identify relationship participation and cardinality constraints, weak entity sets, and role names if needed.

- Step 3.4. Update the data dictionary and list of assumptions as needed.

4 CHAPTER

The Relational Model

Chapter Objectives

In this chapter you will learn the following:

- The origins of the relational model

- Some advantages of the relational model

- How tables are used to represent data

- The connection between mathematical relations and relational-model relations

- Characteristics of database relations

- How to identify relation keys

- The meaning of entity integrity and referential integrity

- How to write out a relational schema

Exercises

SAMPLE PROJECT: Initial Mapping of the E-R Model to Tables for
  The Art Gallery

STUDENT PROJECTS: Initial Mapping to Tables for the Student Projects

- The categories of relational languages
- How to write queries in relational algebra
- How relational calculus queries are expressed
- How views are defined in the relational model
- How to transform an E-R diagram into a relational model for a database

4.1   Brief History of the Relational Model

The relational model was first proposed by Codd in 1970, in a paper called "A Relational Model of Data for Large Shared Data Banks." Much of the early research on the model was done by Codd and his associates at the IBM Research Laboratory, formerly in San Jose, California. At that time, the market was dominated by hierarchical and network model database management systems, which used complex data and storage structures and were difficult for users to understand. A prototype relational database management system, called **System R,** was developed by IBM researchers during the late 1970s. This project was designed to demonstrate the practicality of the relational model by providing an implementation of its data structures and operations. It also proved to be an excellent source of information about related implementation techniques such as concurrency control, query optimization, transaction management, data security and integrity, recovery, human factors, and user interfaces, and led to many research papers and other prototypes. System R is the basis for DB2, IBM's relational database management system. The **Peterlee Relational Test Vehicle** was a more theoretical early project developed at the IBM UK Scientific Laboratory.

INGRES was another early relational model research project, developed at the University of California at Berkeley at about the same time as the System R project. The research led to a "university" version of INGRES, as well as a commercial product. **ORACLE** was developed and marketed using many of the System R results. Among early microcomputer-based relational database management systems were **dBase, R:base,** and **Paradox.** Microsoft's **Access,** which uses the relational model, is now the most widely used microcomputer-based database management system. **Oracle,**

DB2, Informix, Sybase, and Microsoft's **SQL Server**—all of which use the relational model—are currently the most popular enterprise database management systems.

4.2   Advantages of the Relational Model

The relational model is based on the mathematical notion of a **relation.** Codd and others extended the notion to apply to database design. Thus they were able to take advantage of the power of mathematical abstraction and of the expressiveness of mathematical notation to develop a simple but powerful structure for databases. The relational model is the subject of a large body of research literature.

Much of the literature treats the model theoretically, developing aspects of the model by using the mathematical approach of theorem and proof. This abstract approach has the advantage that the results are general, meaning they do not depend on a particular example, and can be applied to many different applications. Fortunately, we can use the results of the theory to design relational models without necessarily following the intricate process of theorem proving. The theory assists in database design by identifying potential flaws in proposed designs, and providing tools to allow us to correct those flaws. Chapter 6 contains a detailed discussion of some of these techniques.

The basic structure of the relational model is simple, making it easy to understand on an intuitive level. It allows separation of the conceptual and physical levels, so that conceptual design can be performed without considering storage structures. Users and designers find that the model allows them to express conceptual data notions in a manner that is easily understood. Data operations are also easy to express, and do not require users to be familiar with the storage structures used. The model uses a few very powerful commands to accomplish data manipulations that range from the simple to the complex. For these reasons, the relational model has become the most popular model for databases.

4.3   Relational Data Structures

The data structures used in the relational model are tables with relationships among them (Figure 4.1).

4.3.1 Tables

The relational model is based on the concept of a **relation,** which is physically represented as a **table** or two-dimensional array. In this model, tables are used to hold information about the objects to be represented in the database. Using the terms of the Entity Relationship model, both entity sets and relationship sets are shown using tables. A relation is represented as a two-dimensional table in which the rows of the table correspond to individual records and the columns correspond to attributes. For example, the Student relation is represented by the `Student` table, having columns for attributes `stuId`, `lastName`, `firstName`, `major`, and `credits`. Figure 4.1(a), which is a copy of Figure 1.1(a), shows an instance of the `Student` table. Note that the column names, `stuId`, `lastName`, `firstName`, `major`, and `credits`, are the same as the attribute names. As you can see from

Student

stuId	lastName	firstName	major	credits
S1001	Smith	Tom	History	90
S1002	Chin	Ann	Math	36
S1005	Lee	Perry	History	3
S1010	Burns	Edward	Art	63
S1013	McCarthy	Owen	Math	0
S1015	Jones	Mary	Math	42
S1020	Rivera	Jane	CSC	15

FIGURE 4.1
The University Tables

FIGURE 4.1(a)
The Student Table

Faculty

facId	name	department	rank
F101	Adams	Art	Professor
F105	Tanaka	CSC	Instructor
F110	Byrne	Math	Assistant
F115	Smith	History	Associate
F221	Smith	CSC	Professor

FIGURE 4.1(b)
The Faculty Table

FIGURE 4.1(c)

The Class Table

Class			
classNo	facId	schedule	room
ART103A	F101	MWF9	H221
CSC201A	F105	TuThF10	M110
CSC203A	F105	MThF12	M110
HST205A	F115	MWF11	H221
MTH101B	F110	MTuTh9	H225
MTH103C	F110	MWF11	H225

FIGURE 4.1(d)

The Enroll Table

Enroll		
stuId	classNo	grade
S1001	ART103A	A
S1001	HST205A	C
S1002	ART103A	D
S1002	CSC201A	F
S1002	MTH103C	B
S1010	ART103A	
S1010	MTH103C	
S1020	CSC201A	B
S1020	MTH101B	A

this example, a column contains values of a single attribute; for example, the stuId column contains only IDs of students. The **domain** of an attribute is the set of allowable values for that attribute. Domains may be distinct, or two or more attributes may have the same domain. Each row of the table corresponds to an individual record or entity instance. In the relational model, each row is called a **tuple**.

A table that represents a relation has the following characteristics:

- Each cell of the table contains only one value.

- Each column has a distinct name, which is the name of the attribute it represents.

- The values in a column all come from the same domain, since they are all values of the corresponding attribute.

- Each tuple or row is distinct; there are no duplicate tuples.

- The order of tuples or rows is immaterial.

To show what these restrictions mean, we use the `Student` table as an example. Since each cell should contain only one value, it is illegal to store multiple values for an attribute of a single entity. For example, we cannot store two majors for a student in a single cell. The column names written at the tops of the columns correspond to the attributes of the relation. The values in the `stuId` column are all from the domain of `stuId`; we would not allow a student's name to appear in this column. There can be no duplicate rows, because each individual student is represented just once. For example, the row containing (S1001, Smith, Tom, History, 90) appears only once. The rows can be interchanged at will, so the records of S1001 and S1002 can be switched, with no change in the relation.

4.3.2 Mathematical Relations

To understand the strict meaning of the term relation, we need to review some notions from mathematics. Suppose we have two sets, D_1 and D_2, with $D_1 = \{1,3\}$ and $D_2 = \{a,b,c\}$. We could form the Cartesian product of these two sets, written $D_1 \times D_2$, which is the set of all ordered pairs such that the first element is a member of D_1 and the second element is a member of D_2. Another way of thinking of this is to find all combinations of elements with the first from D_1 and the second from D_2. Thus we find the following:

$D_1 \times D_2 = \{(1,a), (1,b), (1,c), (3,a), (3,b), (3,c)\}$

A relation is simply some subset of this Cartesian product. For example,

$R = \{(1,a), (3,a)\}$

is a relation. Often, we specify which ordered pairs will be in the relation by giving some rule for their selection. For example, R includes all those ordered pairs in which the second element is a, so we could write R as,

$R = \{(x,y) \mid x \in D_1, y \in D_2, \text{ and } y = a\}$

Using these same sets, we could form another relation, S, in which the first element is always 3. Thus,

$S = \{(x,y) \mid x \in D_1, y \in D_2, \text{ and } x = 3\}$

Alternatively, **S** = {(3, a), (3, $\overset{b}{6}$), (3, c)}, since there are only three ordered pairs in the Cartesian product that satisfy the condition.

We could extend the notion of a relation to three sets in a natural way. Let **D₁**, **D₂**, and **D₃** be three sets. Then the Cartesian product **D₁ × D₂ × D₃** of these three sets is the set of all ordered triples such that the first element is from **D₁**, the second element is from **D₂**, and the third element is from **D₃**. A relation is then any subset of this Cartesian product. For example, suppose we define the sets as,

$D_1 = \{1,3\}$ $D_2 = \{2,4,6\}$ $D_3 = \{3,6,9\}$
Then $D_1 \times D_2 \times D_3 = \{(1,2,3), (1,2,6), (1,2,9), (1,4,3), (1,4,6), (1,4,9),$
$(1,6,3), (1,6,6), (1,6,9), (3,2,3), (3,2,6), (3,2,9), (3,4,3), (3,4,6),$
$(3,4,9), (3,6,3), (3,6,6), (3,6,9)\}$

A relation is any subset of these ordered triples. For example, we could define a relation **T** as those ordered triples in which the third element is the sum of the first two. Then we have,

$T = \{(x,y,z) \mid x \in D_1, y \in D_2, z \in D_3 \text{ and } z = x + y\}$
or $T = \{(1,2,3), (3,6,9)\}.$

We can go beyond three sets and define a general relation on n domains. Let **D₁, D₂, . . ., Dₙ** be n sets. Their Cartesian product is defined as,

$D_1 \times D_2 \times \ldots \times D_n = \{(d_1, d_2, \ldots, d_n) \mid d_1 \in D_1, d_2 \in D_2, \ldots, d_n \in D_n\}$

The Cartesian product is usually written,

$\Pi_{i=1}^{n} D_i$

A relation on the n sets is any set of n-tuples chosen from this Cartesian product. Notice that in defining relations we had to specify the domains, or the sets from which we chose values.

4.3.3   Database Relations and Tables

Applying these concepts to databases, let **A₁, A₂, . . ., Aₙ** be attributes with domains **D₁, D₂, . . ., Dₙ**. A relation schema **R** is such a set of attributes with their corresponding domains. Thus the set {**A₁, A₂, . . ., Aₙ**} with corresponding domains {**D₁, D₂, . . ., Dₙ**} is a relation schema. A **relation r** on a relation schema **R** is a set of mappings from the attribute names to their corresponding domains. Thus relation **r** is a set of n-tuples $(A_1{:}d_1, A_2{:}d_2, \ldots, A_n{:}d_n)$ such that $d_1 \in D_1, d_2 \in D_2, \ldots, d_n \in D_n$. Each element in one of these n-tuples consists of an attribute and a value of that attribute. Normally, when we write out a relation as a table, we list the attribute names as column headings and simply write out the tuples using values chosen from the appropriate domains, so we think of the n-tuples as having the form $(d_1, d_2, . . ., d_n)$. In this way we can think of a relation in the relational model as any subset of the Cartesian product of the domains of the attributes. A table is simply a representation of such a relation.

For our university example, the relation `Student` would have attributes `stuId`, `lastName`, `firstName`, `major`, and `credits`, each with their corresponding domains. The `Student` relation is any subset of the Cartesian product of the domains, or any set of 5-tuples in which the first element is a student ID, the second is a student's last name, the third is student's first name, the fourth is a major, and the fifth is a number of credits. Some of the 5-tuples are:

```
{
(S1001, Smith, Tom, History, 90),
(S1002, Chin,  Ann, Math,    36)
. . .}
```

More properly, these 5-tuples are:

```
{
(stuId:S1001, lastName:Smith, firstName:Tom, major:History, credits:90),
(stuId:S1002, lastName:Chin, firstName:Ann, major:Math, credits:36)
. . .}
```

The `Student` table, shown in Figure 4.1(a) is a convenient way of writing out all the 5–tuples that satisfy the relation at the moment. The 5-tuples are, of course, the rows of the table, which explains why table rows in the relational model are called **tuples.** The table, with all its rows written out, is an instance or **extension** of the relation. The structure of the table, together with a specification of the domains and any other restrictions on possible values, shows the **intension** of the relation, also called the **database schema.** Strictly speaking, the schema also includes domains, views, character sets, constraints, stored procedures, authorizations, and other related information. We can represent relation schemas by giving the name of each relation, followed by the attribute names in parentheses, as in,

```
Student (stuId, lastName, firstName, major, credits)
```

The attribute `stuId` is underlined because it is customary to underline the primary key in the relation schema.

4.3.4   Properties of Relations

Most of the characteristics specified for tables result from the properties of relations. Since a relation is a set, the order of elements does not count. Therefore, in a table, the order of rows is immaterial. In a set, no elements are repeated. Similarly, in a table, there are no duplicate rows. When we found the Cartesian products of sets with simple, single-valued elements such as integers, each element in each tuple was single valued. Similarly, each cell of a table contains only one value. In a relation, the possible values for a given position are determined by the set or domain on which the position is defined. In a table, the values in each column must come from the same attribute domain. In a mathematical relation, the order of elements in a tuple is important. For example, the ordered pair (1,2) is quite different from the ordered pair (2,1), as you realize when you locate the two points in a plane using Cartesian coordinates. However, in tables, the order of columns is immaterial. We consider the Student table to be the same even if we put the columns in different order, as long as we use the same data. The reason is that the column headings tell us which attribute the value belongs to. However, once the structure of the table is chosen, the order of elements within the rows of the extension must match the order of column names.

4.3.5   Degree and Cardinality

The number of columns in a table is called the **degree** of the relation. The degree of the Student relation is five, since the Student table has five columns. This means each row of the table is a 5–tuple, containing 5 values. A relation with only one column would have degree one and be called a **unary** relation. A relation with two columns is called **binary,** one with three columns is called **ternary** and, after that, the term **n-ary** is usually used. The degree of a relation is part of the intension of the relation and never changes.

By contrast, the number of rows in a table, called the **cardinality** of the relation, changes as new tuples are added or old ones are deleted. The cardinality is a property of the extension of the relation, the particular instance of the relation at any given moment.

4.3.6   Relation Keys

Since a relation is a set and a set has no duplicate elements, it is always possible to tell elements of a set apart. In a database relation, the tuples are the set elements, so it must always be possible to tell tuples apart. This means that there must always be some attribute, or some combination of attributes, that makes the tuples distinct. Therefore there will always be a superkey for every relation, and this implies that there will always be a minimal superkey, which means there is always a candidate key. Therefore we can always find a primary key for every relation. In the worst case, the entire set of attributes would need to be examined to tell tuples apart. Usually, however, some smaller set of attributes is sufficient to distinguish among tuples. Applying our definitions from Chapter 3, a **superkey** for a relation is a set of attributes that uniquely identifes a tuple, a **candidate key** is a superkey such that no proper subset is a superkey, and a **primary key** is the candidate key that is actually chosen to uniquely identify tuples. Note that an instance of the table cannot be used to prove that an attribute or combination of attributes is a candidate key. The fact that there are no duplicates for the values that appear at a particular moment does not guarantee that duplicates are not possible. However, the presence of duplicates in an instance can be used to show that some attribute combination is not a candidate key. Identifying a candidate key requires that we consider the meaning of the attribute(s) involved so that we can make a decision about whether duplicates are possible in the miniworld. Only by using this semantic information and identifying the assumptions for the model can we be sure that an attribute combination is a candidate key.

A **foreign key** is an attribute or attribute combination of a relation that is not the primary key of that relation but that is the primary key of some relation, usually a different one. Foreign keys are very important in the relational model, because they are used to represent logical connections between relations. Consider an employee relation with schema,

```
Employee(empId, lastName, firstName, departmentName)
```

and also a Department relation with schema,

```
Department(departmentName, office)
```

The attribute departmentName, which is a primary key in the Department relation, is a foreign key in Employee. Notice that although it has unique values in the Department table, it is not unique in the Employee table, since several employees may belong to the same department. Having that attribute in the Employee table allows us to tell what department an employee belongs to. When we have a foreign key, we call the relation in which the attribute or combination is the primary key its **home relation.** Department is the home relation for departmentName.

In the tables shown in Figure 4.1(a)–(d), `facId` is a foreign key in `Class`. It is not the primary key of that table, but it is the primary key of a different table, `Faculty`. Having that attribute in the `Class` table allows us to connect a class with the faculty member who teaches it, showing the relationship between these tables. In the `Enroll` table, `stuId` is a foreign key. It is not, by itself, the primary key of `Enroll`, but it is the primary key of `Student`. Similarly, `classNo` is a foreign key in `Enroll`, but it is the primary key of `Class`. These two attributes in `Enroll` allow us to tell what classes a student is enrolled in, and what students are enrolled in each class.

The home relation does not have to be a separate table. For example, suppose an employee schema appears as,

```
Employee(empId, firstName, lastName, managerEmpId)
```

Although `empId` is the primary key of this table, `managerEmpId` is a foreign key that actually refers to the `empId` of another tuple in the same table. Each employee's record contains the `empId` of that person's manager, which of course occurs in the manager's employee record as his or her `empId`.

4.4   Integrity Constraints: domain, key, foreign key, general constraints

It is important to preserve the **integrity,** which means the correctness and internal consistency, of the data in the database by not allowing users to enter data that would make the database incorrect. The relational model allows us to define **integrity constraints (ICs)**, which are rules or restrictions that apply to all instances of the database. A **legal state** of the database is one that obeys all the integrity constraints. Part of the job of a database management system is to enforce the integrity constraints—to ensure that any data entered creates a legal instance of the database.

Since every attribute has an associated domain, there are restrictions on the set of values allowed for attributes of relations. These are called **domain constraints,** and they can be enforced in SQL by defining the domain for an attribute when we create a table. An alternative is to use one of the built-in data types, and to add a constraint called the CHECK option, which allows us to specify that the value of an attribute must be within a specified set of values, or that it must obey a condition that we specify using logical predicates.

A primary key constraint, called **entity integrity,** states that in a relation **no attribute of a primary key can have a null value.** By definition, a primary key is a minimal identifier that is used to uniquely identify tuples. This means that no subset of the primary key is sufficient to provide unique identification of tuples. If we were to allow a null value for any part of the primary key, we would be demonstrating that not all of the attributes are needed to distinguish between tuples, which would contradict the definition. All relation keys, both primary and candidate, must have unique values. In SQL, we can identify the primary key using a primary key constraint when we create the table. The system will then enforce both the non-null and uniqueness constraints automatically. For candidate keys, most systems allow us to specify both a uniqueness constraint and a not null constraint.

An integrity rule called **referential integrity** applies to foreign keys. Referential integrity states that, if a foreign key exists in a relation, then either the foreign key value must match the primary key value of some tuple in its home relation, or the foreign key value must be completely null. SQL allows us to specify foreign key constraints when we create a table.

There are several other types of constraints, referred to as **general constraints,** which we will discuss in later chapters. Many such constraints can be expressed in SQL as **table constraints,** which are rules governing values permitted within a table, or as **SQL assertions,** which are statements specifying that a given logical predicate must be true for all states of the database. General constraints are enforced by the database management system whenever changes are made to the data. The system verifies that the changes do not violate the constraints before permitting them to be made permanent.

4.5   Representing Relational Database Schemas

A relational database schema can have any number of relations. We can represent relation schemas by giving the name of each relation, followed by the attribute names in parentheses, with the primary key underlined. There is no simple standard way of indicating foreign keys unambiguously, but we will use italics to indicate that an attribute is a foreign key, or part of a foreign key. Unfortunately, this method will not always tell us clearly what the home relation is. Also, if we have composite foreign keys, and the attributes overlap, we would have difficulty identifying exactly what the foreign key is. The clearest way of showing foreign keys is by drawing arrows from the foreign keys to the primary keys they refer to. Recall that the schema actually also includes domains, views, character sets, constraints, stored procedures, authorizations and other related information, so our representation is actually only a part of the schema. For the university example, a simple database might contain relations for `Student`, `Class`, `Faculty`, and `Enroll`. The relation schemas would be written as:

```
Student (stuId, lastName, firstName, major, credits)
Class (classNo, facId, schedule, room)
Faculty (facId, name, department, rank)
Enroll(stuId,classNo, grade)
```

The relation schema gives us the table name for each relation and column headings for each of its attributes. The logical model schema is the set of all these schemas for the database. Figure 4.1 shows an instance of this database.

Notice that some attributes, such as foreign keys, appear in more than one relation. For example, `stuId` appears in both `Student` and `Enroll`. When we want to distinguish between the two appearances of `stuId`, we use the relation name, followed by a period, followed by the attribute name. The two qualified names for `stuId` are `Student.stuId` and `Enroll.stuId`. An even more explicit name would start with the database name, then the table name, then the attribute name, as in `University.Student.stuId`. When an attribute appears in more than one relation, its appearance usually represents a relationship or interaction between tuples of the two relations. These common attributes play an important role in performing data manipulation, as we shall see in later sections.

4.6   Relational Data Manipulation Languages

There are a variety of languages used by relational database management systems.

4.6.1   Categories of DMLs

Some of the languages are **procedural** or proscriptive, meaning the user tells the system exactly how to manipulate the data. **Relational algebra** is an example of a procedural language that we will discuss.

Others are **nonprocedural** or declarative, which means the user states what data is needed but not exactly how it is to be located. **Relational calculus** and **SQL** are nonprocedural languages. Some languages are **graphical,** allowing the user to give an example or illustration of what data should be found. **QBE** (QueryByExample) is a graphical language that allows users to provide examples of data they would like retrieved. Another category is **fourth-generation language** (4GL), which allows a complete customized application to be created using a few commands in a user-friendly, often menu-driven, environment. Some systems accept a variety of **natural language,** sometimes called a **fifth-generation language,** a restricted version of natural English.

Both relational algebra and relational calculus are formal, non-user-friendly languages. They are not implemented in their native form in database management systems, but both have been used as the basis for other, higher level data manipulation languages for relational databases. They are of interest because they illustrate the basic operations required of any data manipulation language, and because they serve as the standard of comparison for other relational languages.

4.6.2   Relational Algebra

Relational algebra is a theoretical language with operators that are applied on one or two relations to produce another relation. Thus, both the operands and the result are tables. Date originally proposed eight operations, but several others have been developed. Three very basic operations, SELECT, PROJECT, and JOIN, allow us to perform most of the data retrieval operations that interest us. We will use the university database example from Figure 4.1 to illustrate these operations. There are several variations of syntax of relational algebra commands, and we will use a fairly simple English-like one here and present it informally. We also include the more formal symbolic notation for the commands. There are many variations of the operations that are included in relational algebra. We assume we have the option of assigning the results to a table that we name in the command. (Note: In a more formal discussion, we would use a special "rename" operation to do this.)

The SELECT Operator, σ

The SELECT command is applied to a single table and takes rows that meet a specified condition, copying them into a new table. Informally, the general form is:

SELECT *tableName* WHERE *condition* [GIVING *newTableName*]

Symbolically, the form is:

[*newTableName* =] σ $_{predicate}$ (*table-name*)

or simply

σ$_θ$(*table-name*)

For example, if we wanted to find all information in the Student table about student S1013, we would write informally,

SELECT Student WHERE stuId = 'S1013' GIVING Result

or symbolically,

Result = σ $_{STUID='S1013'}$ (Student)

The command produces a new table that we call Result, which looks like this:

Result:

stuId	lastName	firstName	major	credits
S1013	McCarthy	Owen	Math	0

The SELECT operation can be used to find more than one row. For example, to find all classes that meet in room H225, we would write,

SELECT Class WHERE room = 'H225' GIVING Answer

or symbolically,

Answer = σ $_{room='H225'}$ (Class)

This command produces the following table:

Answer:

classNo	facId	schedule	room
MTH101B	F110	MTuTh9	H225
MTH103C	F110	MWF11	H225

Note that the operation is performed on an existing table, *tableName*, and produces a new table that is a horizontal subset of the old one and which we can name and indicate by *newTableName*. The square brackets indicate that the part of the statement enclosed in them is optional. The old table still continues to exist under its old name and both it and the new table are available for additional operations. If we simply wish to find and display the rows that satisfy the condition, but do not plan further operations on the new table, we omit its name. The selection predicate is referred to as the **theta-condition.** The Greek letter theta, written θ, is often used in mathematics to represent any kind of operator. It was used by the developers of relational theory to represent predicates involving any of the comparison operators, namely,

<, <=, >, >=, =, ≠, ∧ (AND), ∨ (OR), ¬ (NOT)

We can form complex selection predicates by using more than one comparison operator in the θ-condition. For example, to find all math majors who have more than 30 credits, we write:

SELECT Student WHERE major = 'Math' AND credits> 30

or symbolically,

$\sigma_{major='Math' \land credits > 30}(Student)$

This command produces the following unnamed table:

stuId	lastName	firstName	major	credits
S1002	Chin	Ann	Math	36
S1015	Jones	Mary	Math	42

The PROJECT Operator, Π

The PROJECT command also operates on a single table, but it produces a vertical subset of the table, extracting the values of specified columns, eliminating duplicates, and placing the values in a new table. Informally, its form is,

PROJECT tableName OVER (colName, . . ., colName) [GIVING newTableName]

or, symbolically,

[newTableName =] Π colName, . . ., colName (tableName)

To illustrate projection over a single column, we find all the different majors that students have by the command,

PROJECT Student OVER major GIVING Temp

or Temp = $\Pi_{major}(Student)$

The resulting table, Temp, looks like this:

Temp <u>major</u>
    History
    Math
    Art
    CSC

Notice that we get all the values that appear in the `major` column of the `Student` table, but duplicates have been eliminated.

When we project over two or more columns, duplicates of combinations of values are eliminated. For example, suppose we want to find the room where each faculty member teaches. We could do so by using the command,

```
PROJECT Class OVER (facId,room)
```

or,

$\Pi_{\text{facId,room}}$ (Class)

This gives the result in an unnamed table,

facId	room
F101	H221
F105	M110
F115	H221
F110	H225

While we have repetition in the room values, with H221 appearing twice, we notice that the repeated room values appear with different `facId` values. As long as the combination has not appeared before, it is added to the projection. Notice that the third and the last rows of `Class` did not contribute to the projection result, since their combination of values for `facId` and `room` appeared previously.

We can combine the SELECT and PROJECT operations to give us only specific columns of certain rows, but doing so requires two steps. For example, suppose we want to see the names and IDs of all history majors. Since we want only history majors, we need a SELECT, but since we want only certain columns of those records, we need a PROJECT. We can express the query as,

```
SELECT Student WHERE major = 'History' GIVING Temp
PROJECT Temp OVER (lastName, firstName, stuId) GIVING Result
```

After the first command is executed, we have the table,

Temp:

stuId	lastName	firstName	major	credits
S1001	Smith	Tom	History	90
S1005	Lee	Perry	History	3

The second command is performed on this temporary table, and the result is,

Result:

lastname	firstname	stuid
Smith	Tom	S1001
Lee	Perry	S1005

Notice that the PROJECT operation allowed us to reverse the order of the two columns in the final result. We could have written the commands symbolically as,

$$\Pi_{\text{lastName,firstName,stuId}}(\sigma_{\text{major='History'}}(\text{Student}))$$

Note that we can compose the operations using the result of the first as the argument for the second. The intermediate table resulting from the selection operation, which we called `Temp` when we used the English-like syntax, does not need a name when we use symbolic notation, since we use the expression as an operand. Observe that we could not reverse the order of the SELECT and PROJECT. If we had done the PROJECT first, we would have an intermediate table with only `lastName`, `firstName`, and `stuId` columns, so we could not then try to do a SELECT on `major` on the intermediate table, since it does not contain that attribute.

The Product and Joins—Theta Join, Equijoin, Natural Join, Semijoin, and Outerjoin Given two tables, A and B, we can form their product, written A TIMES B or A × B, in much the same way as we formed the Cartesian product of sets in Section 4.3.2. A × B is a table formed by concatenating all rows of A with all rows of B. Its columns are the columns of A followed by the columns of B, and its width is the width of A plus the width of B. It can be produced in several ways. One method is to use a "nested loop" algorithm. We start with the first row of A, combine it with the first row of B, then with the second row of B, and so forth until all combinations of the first row of A with all rows of B have been formed. Then the procedure is repeated for the second row of A, then the third row, and so forth. If A has x rows and B has y rows, then A TIMES B, written A × B, has x*y rows.

Suppose we form the product of Student and Enroll, written Student × Enroll. This table will have seven columns, but two of them will be called `stuId`. To distinguish these two, we use the qualified names from the original tables, `Student.stuId` and `Enroll.stuId`. The product, which has 63 rows, is shown in Figure 4.2.

We can define several operations based on the product of tables. The most general one is called the **THETA JOIN**. The theta join is defined as the result of performing a SELECT operation on the product. For example, we might want only those tuples of the product where the `credits` value is greater than 50. Here, theta is >, and we could write the query as,

```
Student TIMES Enroll WHERE credits > 50
```

FIGURE 4.2

Student X Enroll

Student.stuId	lastname	firstName	major	Enroll.stuId	classNo	grade
S1001	Smith	Tom	History	S1002	ART103A	D
S1001	Smith	Tom	History	S1002	MTH103C	B
S1001	Smith	Tom	History	S1010	ART103A	
S1001	Smith	Tom	History	S1020	MTH101B	A
S1001	Smith	Tom	History	S1001	HST205A	C
S1001	Smith	Tom	History	S1002	CSC201A	F
S1001	Smith	Tom	History	S1010	MTH103C	
S1001	Smith	Tom	History	S1001	ART103A	A
S1001	Smith	Tom	History	S1020	CSC201A	B
S1002	Chin	Ann	Math	S1002	MTH103C	B
S1002	Chin	Ann	Math	S1010	ART103A	
S1002	Chin	Ann	Math	S1002	CSC201A	F
S1002	Chin	Ann	Math	S1010	MTH103C	
S1002	Chin	Ann	Math	S1002	ART103A	D
S1002	Chin	Ann	Math	S1001	HST205A	C
S1002	Chin	Ann	Math	S1001	ART103A	A
S1002	Chin	Ann	Math	S1020	MTH101B	A
S1002	Chin	Ann	Math	S1020	CSC201A	B
S1005	Lee	Perry	History	S1010	MTH103C	
S1005	Lee	Perry	History	S1001	HST205A	C
S1005	Lee	Perry	History	S1002	MTH103C	B
S1005	Lee	Perry	History	S1020	CSC201A	B
S1005	Lee	Perry	History	S1002	ART103A	D
S1005	Lee	Perry	History	S1010	ART103A	
S1005	Lee	Perry	History	S1020	MTH101B	A
S1005	Lee	Perry	History	S1001	ART103A	A
S1005	Lee	Perry	History	S1002	CSC201A	F

Student X Enroll						
Student.stuId	lastname	firstName	major	Enroll.stuId	classNo	grade
S1010	Burns	Edward	Art	S1002	ART103A	D
S1010	Burns	Edward	Art	S1001	HST205A	C
S1010	Burns	Edward	Art	S1002	CSC201A	F
S1010	Burns	Edward	Art	S1001	ART103A	A
S1010	Burns	Edward	Art	S1002	MTH103C	B
S1010	Burns	Edward	Art	S1010	MTH103C	
S1010	Burns	Edward	Art	S1020	MTH101B	A
S1010	Burns	Edward	Art	S1020	CSC201A	B
S1010	Burns	Edward	Art	S1010	ART103A	
S1013	McCarthy	Owen	Math	S1010	ART103A	
S1013	McCarthy	Owen	Math	S1002	ART103A	D
S1013	McCarthy	Owen	Math	S1001	HST205A	C
S1013	McCarthy	Owen	Math	S1002	MTH103C	B
S1013	McCarthy	Owen	Math	S1020	CSC201A	B
S1013	McCarthy	Owen	Math	S1010	MTH103C	
S1013	McCarthy	Owen	Math	S1002	CSC201A	F
S1013	McCarthy	Owen	Math	S1001	ART103A	A
S1013	McCarthy	Owen	Math	S1020	MTH101B	A
S1015	Jones	Mary	Math	S1001	ART103A	A
S1015	Jones	Mary	Math	S1020	MTH101B	A
S1015	Jones	Mary	Math	S1001	HST205A	C
S1015	Jones	Mary	Math	S1020	CSC201A	B
S1015	Jones	Mary	Math	S1010	MTH103C	
S1015	Jones	Mary	Math	S1002	ART103A	D
S1015	Jones	Mary	Math	S1010	ART103A	
S1015	Jones	Mary	Math	S1002	CSC201A	F
S1015	Jones	Mary	Math	S1002	MTH103C	B

(Continued)

FIGURE 4.2
(Continued)

Student.stuId	lastname	firstName	major	Enroll.stuId	classNo	grade
				Student X Enroll		
S1020	Rivera	Jane	CSC	S1001	HST205A	C
S1020	Rivera	Jane	CSC	S1002	ART103A	D
S1020	Rivera	Jane	CSC	S1010	ART103A	
S1020	Rivera	Jane	CSC	S1020	CSC201A	B
S1020	Rivera	Jane	CSC	S1001	ART103A	A
S1020	Rivera	Jane	CSC	S1002	CSC201A	F
S1020	Rivera	Jane	CSC	S1002	MTH103C	B
S1020	Rivera	Jane	CSC	S1020	MTH101B	A
S1020	Rivera	Jane	CSC	S1010	MTH103C	

This is equivalent to,

```
Student TIMES Enroll GIVING Temp
SELECT Temp WHERE credits > 50
```

or symbolically,

$$\sigma_{credits>50} \ (\text{Student} \times \text{Enroll})$$

The symbol X_θ is sometimes used to stand for the theta join. We note that for any two relations, X and Y, the theta join is defined symbolically as,

```
A Xθ B = σθ (A × B)
```

Since the product is a slow operation requiring, in the example above, 63 concatenations, it would be more efficient to perform the selection first and then do the product, provided that sequence of operations gives the same result. A more efficient form, requiring only 18 concatenations, is:

```
SELECT Student WHERE credits > 50 GIVING Temp2
Temp2 TIMES Enroll
```

or,

$$(\sigma_{credits>50} \ (\text{Student})) \times \text{Enroll}$$

Although the product is a valid operation, we would rarely be interested in forming concatenations of rows of Student with rows of Enroll having a different stuId. A more common operation involving the product of tables is the one in which we ask for only those rows of the product in

					Student Equijoin Enroll		
Student.stuId	lastName	firstName	major	credits	Enroll.stuId	classNo	grade
S1001	Smith	Tom	History	90	S1001	HST205A	C
S1001	Smith	Tom	History	90	S1001	ART103A	A
S1002	Chin	Ann	Math	36	S1002	MTH103C	B
S1002	Chin	Ann	Math	36	S1002	CSC201A	F
S1002	Chin	Ann	Math	36	S1002	ART103A	D
S1010	Burns	Edward	Art	63	S1010	MTH103C	
S1010	Burns	Edward	Art	63	S1010	ART103A	
S1020	Rivera	Jane	CSC	15	S1020	MTH101B	A
S1020	Rivera	Jane	CSC	15	S1020	CSC201A	B

FIGURE 4.3

Student EQUIJOIN Enroll

which the values of the common columns are equal. When the theta is equality on the common columns, we have the **EQUIJOIN** of tables. To form the equijoin, then, we start with two tables having a common column or columns. We compare each tuple of the first with each tuple of the second and choose only those concatenations in which the values in the common columns are equal. We would form the equijoin of `Student` and `Enroll` by choosing those tuples of the product with matching `stuId` values. Figure 4.3 shows:

```
Student EQUIJOIN Enroll
```

written symbolically as,

Student $\times_{\text{Student.stuId=Enroll.stuId}}$ Enroll

Note that this is equivalent to,

```
Student TIMES Enroll GIVING Temp3
SELECT Temp3 WHERE Student.stuId = Enroll.stuId
```

or,

σ Student.stuId=Enroll.stuId (Student $\times$ Enroll)

If we had more than one common column, both sets of values would have to match.

You may notice that, by definition, we always have at least two identical columns in an equijoin. Since it seems unnecessary to include the repeated column, we can drop it and we define a **NATURAL JOIN** as an equijoin in which the repeated column is eliminated. This is the most common form of the JOIN operation—so common, in fact, that this is what is usually meant by JOIN. When we mean the natural join we simply write:

```
tableName1 JOIN tableName2 [GIVING newTableName]
```

We can use the symbol $|x|$ for the natural join, as in,

```
tableName1 |x| tableName2
```

The natural join of `Student` and `Enroll` would produce a table identical to the one in Figure 4.3, except the second `stuId` column would be dropped. Since `Faculty` and `Class` have a common column, `facId`, we will find their natural join. The result of the command,

```
Faculty JOIN Class
```

or,

```
Faculty |x|Class
```

is shown in Figure 4.4. The resulting table gives us all the details about faculty members and the classes they teach. The join allows us to recombine pieces of information about an entity, even though they appear on different tables. We do not keep the data about faculty and classes in a single table, because we would have a lot of repetition in the table. Notice that data about Tanaka and Byrne is repeated, because they each teach two classes.

FIGURE 4.4
Faculty |x| Class

Faculty Natural Join Class

facId	name	department	rank	classNo	schedule	room
F101	Adams	Art	Professor	ART103A	MWF9	H221
F105	Tanaka	CSC	Instructor	CSC203A	MThf12	M110
F105	Tanaka	CSC	Instructor	CSC201A	TuTHF10	M110
F110	Byrne	Math	Assistant	MTH103C	MWF11	H225
F110	Byrne	Math	Assistant	MTH101B	MTuTh9	H225
F115	Smith	History	Associate	HST205A	MWF11	H221

More complicated queries can require use of the SELECT, PROJECT, and JOIN commands. For example, suppose we want to find the classes and grades of student Ann Chin. We notice that the `Student` table contains the student's name, but not classes or grades, while the `Enroll` table contains the classes and grades, but not the name. Whenever we need to use more than one table to answer a query, we must use a join or product. If the result needs to contain only some, but not all, columns of the original tables, we also need a PROJECT. If not all rows will be used, we need a SELECT as well. To decide what operations to do and in what order, examine the tables to see how you would answer the question "by hand" and then try to formulate the operations required in terms of relational algebra commands. Here, we would start with the `Student` table, and locate the record for Ann Chin (a SELECT operation). We would then consult the `Enroll` table, look for records with stuId that matches Ann Chin's stuId (a JOIN operation), and read off only the classNo and grade values (a PROJECT operation). One way to find the data required is the following, expressed using our English-like language:

```
SELECT Student WHERE lastName='Chin' AND firstName ='Ann' GIVING Temp1
Temp1 JOIN Enroll GIVING Temp2
PROJECT Temp2 OVER (classNo, grade) GIVING Answer
```

or symbolically as,

$$\Pi_{classNo,grade}\big((\sigma_{lastName='Chin' \wedge firstName='Ann'}(Student)) |x| Enroll\big)$$

After the SELECT in the first line we have this result:

Temp1:

stuid	lastname	firstname	major	credits
S1002	Chin	Ann	Math	36

After the JOIN in the second line we have this result:

Temp2:

stuId	lastName	firstName	major	credits	classNo	grade
S1002	Chin	Ann	Math	36	ART103A	D
S1002	Chin	Ann	Math	36	CSC201A	F
S1002	Chin	Ann	Math	36	MTH103C	B

After the PROJECT in the third line, we have this result:

Answer:

classNo	grade
CSC201A	F
ART103A	D
MTH103C	B

You may have observed that all we really needed from `Temp1` was the `stuId` column, since this was used for the comparison for the join, and none of the other columns was used later. Therefore, if we preferred, we could have used a PROJECT on `Temp1` to give us only the `stuId` column before doing the JOIN, as in,

$$\Pi_{classNo,grade}(\Pi_{stuId}\ (\sigma_{lastName='Chin'\wedge firstName='Ann'}(Student))\ |x|\ Enroll)$$

A third way to do the query is,

```
JOIN Student, Enroll GIVING Tempa
SELECT Tempa WHERE lastName='Chin' AND firstName = 'Ann' GIVING Tempb
PROJECT Tempb OVER (classNo, grade)
```

or,

$$\Pi_{classNo,grade}(\sigma_{lastName='Chin'\wedge firstName='Ann'}(Student\ |x|\ Enroll))$$

As you may have observed, this method is less efficient, since the first line requires 54 comparisons to form a joined table, a relatively slow operation. Doing the selection first reduces the number of comparisons to nine, thus optimizing the query.

We can do joins of joined tables. Suppose we wanted to find the IDs of all students in Professor Adams's classes. We would need data from the `Faculty`, `Class`, and `Enroll` tables to answer this query. One method is,

```
SELECT Faculty WHERE name = 'Adams' GIVING Temp1
Temp1 JOIN Class GIVING Temp2
Temp2 JOIN Enroll GIVING Temp3
PROJECT Temp3 OVER stuId GIVING Result
```

or symbolically,

$$\Pi_{stuId}(((\sigma_{name='Adams'}(Faculty))\ |x|\ Class)\ |x|\ Enroll)$$

In this example, `Temp2` has seven columns and `Temp3` has nine columns. Since only one of the `Faculty` columns, `facId`, is used for the join and none of its other columns is needed later, we could do a PROJECT before the first join. Alternatively, since only one of `Temp2`'s columns, `classNo`, is needed for the join and none of its other columns is used again, we could do a PROJECT between the two joins.

Several other types of join operators can be defined. One variation is the **SEMIJOIN** of two tables. If A and B are tables, then the left-semijoin A |x B, is found by taking the natural join of A and B and then projecting the result onto the attributes of A. The result will be just those tuples of A that participate in the join. For the `Student` and `Enroll` tables shown in Figure 4.1, the left-semijoin of `Student` by `Enroll`, written as:

```
Student LEFT-SEMIJOIN Enroll
```

Student LEFT-SEMIJOIN Enroll			
stuId	**lastName**	**firstName**	**major**
S1001	Smith	Tom	History
S1002	Chin	Ann	Math
S1010	Burns	Edward	Art
S1020	Rivera	Jane	CSC

FIGURE 4.5
Student LEFT-SEMIJOIN Enroll

or symbolically,

    Student |x Enroll

is shown in Figure 4.5. Note that semijoin is not commutative. For example, Student LEFT SEMIJOIN Enroll is different from Enroll LEFT SEMIJOIN Student. In addition to the left-semijoin, we can define the right-semijoin of A and B, written A x| B, which is found by taking the natural join of A and B and then projecting the result onto the attributes of B. For Student x| Enroll, this is the projection onto the Enroll table of the natural join, that is, those tuples of Enroll that participate in the join (namely, all of them). Its columns are stuId, classNo, and grade, and it has the same tuples as the Enroll table.

Another type of join operation is the OUTERJOIN. This operation is an extension of a THETA JOIN, an EQUIJOIN, or a NATURAL JOIN operation. When forming any of these joins, any tuple from one of the original tables for which there is no match in the second table does not enter the result. For example, in an equijoin for tables with a common column, a row in the first table does not participate in the result unless there is a row in the second table with the same value for the common column. We saw, for example, that the row "S1015 Jones Mary Math 42" from the Student table was not represented in the Student EQUIJOIN Enroll table, shown in Figure 4.3, because there was no row of Enroll having S1015 as the stuId value. Neither were there rows for S1005 nor S1013. In an outerjoin, such unmatched rows appear, with null values for the attributes that the other table contributes to the result. For example, let us form the outer-equijoin of Student and Faculty where we compare Student.lastName with Faculty.name. As shown in Figure 4.6(a), we include all the rows in Student EQUIJOIN Faculty (i.e., all the student tuples with the faculty tuples having the same last name), and add in the rows from Student

FIGURE 4.6

Outerjoins

FIGURE 4.6(a)

Student OUTERJOIN Faculty

Student OUTER-EQUIJOIN Faculty

stuId	lastName	firstName	major	facId	name	department	rank
S1001	Smith	Tom	History	F221	Smith	CSC	Professor
S1001	Smith	Tom	History	F115	Smith	History	Associate
S1002	Chin	Ann	Math				
S1005	Lee	Perry	History				
S1010	Burns	Edward	Art				
S1013	McCarthy	Owen	Math				
S1015	Jones	Mary	Math				
S1020	Rivera	Jane	CSC				
				F101	Adams	Art	Professor
				F105	Tanaka	CSC	Instructor
				F110	Byrne	Math	Assistant

FIGURE 4.6(b)

Student LEFT-OUTER-EQUIJOIN Faculty

Student LEFT-OUTER-EQUIJOIN Faculty

stuId	lastName	firstName	major	facId	name	department	rank
S1001	Smith	Tom	History	F221	Smith	CSC	Professor
S1001	Smith	Tom	History	F115	Smith	History	Associate
S1002	Chin	Ann	Math				
S1005	Lee	Perry	History				
S1010	Burns	Edward	Art				
S1013	McCarthy	Owen	Math				
S1015	Jones	Mary	Math				
S1020	Rivera	Jane	CSC				

that have no matching `Faculty` rows, placing null values in the `facId`, name, `department`, and rank columns. We also include any rows of `Faculty` for which the name value does not have a match in the `Student` table.

A variation of the outer equijoin shown is a LEFT OUTER EQUIJOIN, which means only unmatched rows from the first (left) table appear in

Student RIGHT-OUTER-EQUIJOIN Faculty

stuId	lastName	firstName	major	facId	name	department	rank
S1001	Smith	Tom	History	F221	Smith	CSC	Professor
S1001	Smith	Tom	History	F115	Smith	History	Associate
				F101	Adams	Art	Professor
				F105	Tanaka	CSC	Instructor
				F110	Byrne	Math	Assistant

FIGURE 4.6(c)
Student RIGHT-OUTER-EQUIJOIN Faculty

the result. The left outer equijoin of Student and Faculty is shown in Figure 4.6(b). In a RIGHT OUTER EQUIJOIN we include unmatched rows from the second (right) table, as shown for Student and Faculty in Figure 4.6(c). We can also define the general outer theta join, the left outer theta join, and the right outer theta join in a similar manner.

The outer natural join is similar to the outer equijoin, except that we drop the repeated column(s) as usual for a natural join. If the joined rows have an equal non-null value for a repeated column, we use that value in the common column. If both have null values, we use a null, and if one has a null value and the other not, we use the non-null value in the result.

Division

Division is a binary operation that can be defined on two relations where the entire structure of one (the divisor) is a portion of the structure of the other (the dividend). It tells us which values in the attributes that appear only in the dividend appear with all the rows of the divisor. An example is shown in Figure 4.7. Here, the structure of the Stu table shown in Figure 4.7(b) is contained within the structure of the Club table shown in Figure 4.7(a), so we can divide Club by Stu. The results, shown in Figure 4.7 (c) will be those values of ClubName appear with every value of StuNumber and StuLastName, that is, the names of the clubs that all of the students belong.

Notice that this division is equivalent to the following operations:

```
PROJECT Club OVER (ClubName) GIVING Temp1
Temp1 TIMES Stu GIVING Temp2
Temp2 MINUS Club GIVING Temp3
PROJECT Temp3 OVER ClubName GIVING Temp4
Temp1 MINUS Temp4 GIVING Quotient
```

FIGURE 4.7
Division Tables

FIGURE 4.7
Division Tables

FIGURE 4.7(a)
The Club Table

Club		
ClubName	**StuNumber**	**StuLastName**
Computing	S1001	Smith
Computing	S1002	Chin
Drama	S1001	Smith
Drama	S1002	Chin
Drama	S1005	Lee
Karate	S1001	Smith
Karate	S1002	Chin
Karate	S1005	Lee

FIGURE 4.7(b)
The Stu Table

Stu	
StuNumber	**StuLastName**
S1001	Smith
S1002	Chin
S1005	Lee

FIGURE 4.7(c)
Club ÷ Stu

Club DividedBy Stu
ClubName
Drama
Karate

Set Operations: Union, Difference, Intersection

Since relations are basically sets of n-tuples, relational algebra includes a version of the basic set operations of union, intersection, and set difference. For these binary operations to be possible, the two relations on which they are performed must be **union compatible.** This means that it is possible to do a union operation since they have the same basic structure. In particular, they must have the same degree and attributes in the corresponding position in both relations must have the same domains. For example, the third column in the first table must have the same domain as the third column in the second table, although the column names could be different. The result of each of the set operations is a new table with the same structure as the two original tables. The four tables we have been working with all have different structures, so no pair of them is union-compatible. Therefore we will use the two tables in Figure 4.8(a) for set operations. We assume that the `MainFac` table contains records of faculty members teaching at the main campus, while the `BranchFac` table contains records of those teaching at the branch campus of the university. Some faculty members teach at both locations.

The union of two relations is the set of tuples in either or both of the relations. For example, we can find the union of `MainFac` and `BranchFac` as follows:

```
MainFac UNION BranchFac
```

or symbolically,

```
MainFac ∪ BranchFac
```

The result is shown in Figure 4.8 (b).

The intersection of two relations is the set of tuples in both of the relations simultaneously. The intersection of `MainFac` and `BranchFac`,

```
MainFac INTERSECTION BranchFac
```

or symbolically,

```
MainFac ∩ BranchFac
```

is shown in Figure 4.8(c).

The difference between two relations is the set of tuples that belong to the first relation but not to the second. Therefore,

```
MainFac MINUS BranchFac
```

or symbolically,

```
MainFac − BranchFac
```

is the table shown in Figure 4.8(d).

Many extensions of relational algebra exist. Methods of treating null values in a systematic fashion have been added to the standard operators, and aggregate functions such as SUM, AVG, MAX, MIN, and COUNT have been defined by various researchers.

FIGURE 4.8
The Set Operations

FIGURE 4.8(a)
Union-Compatible Relations MainFac and BranchFac

MainFac

FacID	name	department	rank
F101	Adams	Art	Professor
F105	Tanaka	CSC	Instructor
F221	Smith	CSC	Professor

BranchFac

FacId	name	department	rank
F101	Adams	Art	Professor
F110	Byre	Math	Assistant
F115	Smith	History	Associate
F221	Smith	CSC	Professor

FIGURE 4.8(b)
MainFac UNION BranchFac

MainFac UNION BranchFac

FacId	name	department	rank
F101	Adams	Art	Professor
F105	Tanaka	CSC	Instructor
F110	Byrne	Math	Assistant
F115	Smith	History	Associate
F221	Smith	CSC	Professor

FIGURE 4.8(c)
MainFac INTERSECTION BanchFac

MainFac INTERSECTION BranchFac

FacId	name	department	rank
F101	Adams	Art	Professor
F221	Smith	CSC	Professor

FIGURE 4.8(d)
MainFac MINUS BanchFac

MainFac MINUS BranchFac

FacId	name	department	rank
F105	Tanaka	CSC	Instructor

4.6.3   Relational Calculus

Relational calculus is a non-procedural formal relational data manipulation language in which the user simply specifies what data should be
retrieved, but not how to retrieve it. It is an alternate standard for relational
data manipulation languages. This section presents only a brief discussion
for comparison purposes, and is not intended as a complete treatment of
the language. The relational calculus is not related to the familiar differen-
tial and integral calculus in mathematics, but it uses a branch of symbolic
logic called the **predicate calculus.** When applied to databases, it comes in
two forms: **tuple-oriented** relational calculus and **domain-oriented** relational calculus. Both use concepts from symbolic logic.

In logic, a **predicate** is a declarative sentence that can be either true or
false. For example, the sentences "Mary Jones is a student" and "Mary
Jones has 500 credits" are both predicates, since we can decide whether
they are true or false. On the other hand, "What a day!" is not a predicate.
If a predicate contains a variable, as in "x is a student," there must be an
associated replacement set or **range** for x. When some values of the range
are substituted for x, the predicate may be true; for other values, it may be
false. For example, if the range is the set of all people, and we replace x by
Mary Jones, the resulting predicate, "Mary Jones is a student" is true. If we
replace x by Professor Adams, the predicate is probably false.

If we use P to stand for a predicate, then $\{x \mid P(x)\}$ means the set of all
values x such that P is true. We could have used Q,R, or any other letter for
the predicate. Similarly, we could have used y, z, w, or any other letter to
stand for the variable, so,

   $\{t \mid P(t)\}$, $\{s \mid Q(s)\}$, $\{x \mid R(x)\}$

all mean the set of values in the replacement set for which the corresponding predicate is true.

We may connect predicates by the logical connectives AND ($\wedge$), OR ($\vee$) and
NOT ($\neg$) to form **compound predicates** such as:

   P(x)AND Q(x)   P(x) OR Q(x)   NOT(P(x)) OR Q(x)

which can be written as,

   $P(x) \wedge Q(x)$ $P(x) \vee Q(x)$ $\neg P(x) \vee Q(x)$

A **conjunction** consists of predicates connected by AND, a **disjunction** consists of predicated connected by OR, and a negation is a predicate preceded

by a NOT. In logic there are two **quantifiers** used with predicates to tell how many instances the predicate applies to. The **existential** quantifier, **EXISTS,** means "There exists." It is used in **assertions,** or statements that must be true for at least one instance, such as:

    EXISTS x (P(x)}

"There exists at least one value variable x such that P(x) is true." The symbol $\exists$ is sometimes used for "There exists," so we could write the assertion as,

    ∃ x (P(x))

The **universal** quantifier, **FORALL,** means "For all." It is sometimes written $\forall$. It is used in assertions about every instance, such as:

    FORALL s(P(s)) or ∀ s(P(s))

which means P(S) is true for all values, s, in the range. A variable without a quantifier ($\exists$ or $\forall$) is called a **free variable,** and one with a quantifier is called a **bound variable.**

Tuple-oriented Relational Calculus In tuple-oriented relational calculus we use **tuple variables,** which are variables that take on the tuples of some relation or relations as values. Intuitively, we express a **query** in a form such as:

    {S | P(S)}

which means "Find the set of all tuples, say s, such that P(S) is true when S=s." Here, S is the tuple variable and P(S) is a **formula** that describes S. Since S stands for a tuple of a relation, we can refer to an attribute of the tuple using dot notation. For example:

    {S | S ∈ Student ∧ S.credits > 50}

means "Find all students having more than 50 credits." Similarly,

    {S.stuId | S ∈ Student ∧ S.major='History' ∧ S.credits < 30}

means "Find the stuId of all students who are history majors with fewer than 30 credits." These queries are evaluated by instantiating the tuple variable, S, with each tuple, s, of its range, Student, in turn, and testing the predicate for that tuple. The tuples for which the predicate is true form the result of the query.

Now we will define the concept of formula more formally. We begin with the definition of an **atomic formula** or **atom.** Let S,T represent tuple variables having attributes a and b respectively; let θ represent one of the comparison operators ($<$, $<=$, $>$, $>=$, $=$, $\neq$); and let r represent a relation. An atomic formula is one that has one of the following forms:

- $S \in r$

- $S.a \; \theta \; R.b$

- $S.a \; \theta \; constant$

Formulas are constructed recursively from atomic formulas using these rules:

- An atomic formula is a formula

- If F_1 and F_2 are formulas, then so are $F_1 \wedge F_2$, $F_1 \vee F_2$, and $\neg F_1$

If S is a tuple variable that appears as a free variable in a formula F, then

- $\exists S \, (F(S))$ is a formula and

- $\forall \; S(F(S))$ is a formula

A tuple relational calculus expression, such as the queries shown earlier, has the form,

$\{S_1.a_1, S_2.a_2, \ldots, S_n.a_n \mid F(S_1, S_2, \ldots, S_n)\}$

where the S_1 are tuples variables having ranges which are the relations S_1, $S_2, \ldots, S_n$ and the a_1 are attributes of those relations. F is a formula, as previously defined.

Examples of Tuple-oriented Relational Calculus

- Example 1. Find the names of all faculty members who are Professors in the CSC Department.

   ```
   {F.name | F ∈ Faculty ∧ F.department = 'CSC' ∧ F.rank ='Professor'}
   ```

- Example 2. Find the last names of all students enrolled in CSC201A.

   ```
   {S.lastName | S ∈ Student ∧ EXISTS E (E ∈ Enroll ∧ E.stuId =
   S.stuId ∧ E.classNo = 'CSC201A')}
   ```

- Example 3. Find the first and last names of all students who are enrolled in at least one class that meets in room H221.

   ```
   {S.firstName, S.lastName | S ∈ Student ∧ EXISTS E (E ∈ Enroll
   ∧ E.stuId = S.stuId ∧ EXISTS C (C ∈ Class ∧C.classNo = E.classNo
   ∧ C.room = 'H221'))}
   ```

- Example 4. Find the names of faculty members who are in the CSC department but do not teach CSC201A.

  {F.name | F ∈ Faculty ∧ F.department= 'CSC' ∧ ¬ EXISTS C (C ∈ Class
  ∧ C.facId = F.facId ∧ C.classNo = 'CSC201A')}

- Example 5. Find the last names of students enrolled in every class offered.

  {S.lastName | S ∈ Student ∧ C ∈ Class ∧ FORALL C (EXISTS E (E ∈ Enroll
  ∧ E.stuId = S.stuId ∧ E.classNo = C.classNo))}

In creating an expression in tuple relational calculus, it is important that it be **safe**, that is, the conditions to be tested be restricted to a finite set of possibilities, so that we do not spend time trying to test a predicate that cannot be tested in a finite amount of time. For example, the expression,

{S | ¬ (S ∈ Student)}

is unsafe, since there are infinite number of possible tuples that are not in Student. To avoid such queries, we define the **domain** of an expression to be the set of all values that either appear explicitly in the expression (e.g., constants such as 'H221') or that appear in one or more of the relations that show up in the expression. An expression is safe if all the values in its result are in its domain. We limit queries to safe expressions.

It can be demonstrated that the relational algebra is logically equivalent to the safe relational calculus, so that any expression in one can be translated into an equivalent expression in the other.

Domain-oriented Relational Calculus

In domain-oriented relational calculus, we use variables that take their values from domains instead of tuples of relations. If $P(x_1, x_2, \ldots, x_m)$ stands for a predicate with variables $x_1, x_2, \ldots, x_n$, where $n <= m$, then,

{< $x_1, x_2, \ldots, x_n$ > | $P(x_1, x_2, \ldots, x_m)$}

will mean the set of all domain variables $x_1, x_2, \ldots, x_n$ for which the predicate $P(x_1, x_2, \ldots, x_m)$ is true. The predicate must be a formula composed of atoms. In domain relational calculus, an **atom** must have one of the following forms:

- <$x_1, x_2, \ldots, x_n$> ∈ R, where R is a relation having n attributes and each x_i is a domain variable or a constant.

- $x_i \ \theta \ x_j$ where x_i and x_j are domain variables and θ is one of the comparison operators ($<, <=, >, >=, =, \neq$), provided x_i and x_j have domains that can be compared using θ.

- $x_i \ \theta \ c$, where c is a constant in the domain of x_i and θ is a comparison operator as before.

A formula is constructed from atoms using rules, as follow:

- An atom is a formula.

- If F_1 and F_2 are formulas, then so are $F_1 \wedge F_2$, $F_1 \vee F_2$, and $\neg \ F_1$.

- If $F(x)$ is a formula having domain variable x, then $\exists \ x \ (F(x))$ is a formula and $\forall \ x \ (F(x))$ are both formulas.

Examples

In the domain-oriented relational calculus, we often want to test for a **membership condition,** to determine whether values belong to a relation. The expression `<x, y, z>` $\in$ `X` evaluates to true if, and only if, there is a tuple in relation `X` with values x, y, z for its three attributes.

In Examples 6–10, we will use the domain variables `SI` for `stuId`, `LN` for `lastName`, `FN` for `firstName`, `MJ` for `major`, `CR` for `credits`, `CN` for `classNo`, `FI` for `facId`, `SH` for `schedule`, `RM` for `room`, `DP` for `department`, `RK` for `rank`, and `GR` for `grade`. Notice that when an attribute such as `LN` appears in more than one relation we need only one domain variable for both of its appearances, since the same domain is used. We will assume we can use `LN` for faculty names as well as student last names. We will use the notation $\exists$ x,y,z $(F(x,y,x))$ as a shorthand for $\exists$ x($\exists$ y($\exists$ z(F(x,y,z)))).

- Example 1. Find the names of all faculty members who are professors in the CSC Department.

  ```
  {LN | ∃ FI,DP,RK(<FI,LN,DP,RK> ∈ Faculty ∧ RK = 'Professor' ∧
  DP = 'CSC')}
  ```

- Example 2. Find the last names of all students enrolled in CSC201A.

  ```
  {LN | ∃ SI,FN,MJ,CR(<SI,LN,FN,MJ,CR> ∈ Student ∧ ∃ CN,GR(<SI,CN,GR>
  ∈ Enroll ∧ CN = 'CSC201A'))}
  ```

Example 3. Find the first and last names of all students who are enrolled in at least one class that meets in room H221.

```
{FN,LN | ∃ SI,MJ,CR(<SI,LN,FN,MJ,CR> ∈ Student ∧ ∃ CN,GR(<SI,CN,GR ∈ Enroll
  ∧ ∃ FI,SH,RM(<CN,FI,SH,RM> ∈ Class ∧ RM = 'H221')))}
```

Example 4. Find the names of faculty members who are in the CSC Department but do not teach CSC201A. (Note: For this example, let FI′ also represent FacId.)

```
{LN | ∃ FI,DP,RK(<FI,LN,DP,RK> ∈ Faculty ∧ DP = 'CSC' ∧ ¬ ∃
CN,FI′,SH,RM(<CN,FI′,SH,RM> ∈ CLASS ∧ CN = 'CSC201A' ∧ FI′ = FI))}
```

Example 5. Find the last names of students enrolled in every class offered. (Note: For this example, let SI′ also represent StudId).

```
{LN | ∃ SI,FN,MJ,CR(<SI,LN,FN,MJ,CR> ∈ Student ∧ ∀ CN ∃
SI′,GR(<SI′,CN,GR> ∈ Enroll ∧ SI′= SI))}
```

All of the domain relational calculus queries shown here are safe. We can ensure safety of domain relational calculus, as we did for tuple relational calculus, by restricting values in tuples of the expression to those in the domain of the formula.

4.7   Views

In the standard three-level architecture, the top level consists of external views. An external view is the structure of the database as it appears to a particular user. In the relational model, the word "view" has a slightly different meaning. Rather than being the entire external model of a user, a view is a virtual table—a table that does not actually exist but can be constructed by performing operations such as relational algebra selection, projection, or join or other calculations on the values of existing tables. Thus, an external model can consist of both actual conceptual-level tables and views derived from tables.

The view mechanism is desirable because it allows us to hide portions of the database from certain users. The user is not aware of the existence of any attributes that are missing from his or her view. It also permits users to access data in a "customized" manner. The view should be designed to create an external model that the user finds familiar and comfortable. For example, a user might need `Enroll` records that contain student names as well as the three attributes already in `Enroll`. This view would be created by joining the Enroll and Student tables, and then projecting on the four attributes of interest. Another user might need to see Student records without the credits attribute. For this user, a projection is done so that his or her view does not have the credits column. Attributes may be renamed, so that the user accustomed to calling the ID of students by the name stuNumber can see that column heading, and the order of columns can be changed, so that lastName, firstName can appear as the first and second columns in a view. Selection operations can also be used to create a view. For example, a department chairperson can see faculty records for only that department. Here, a select operation is performed so that only a horizontal subset of the Faculty table is seen. View tables are not permanently stored as such. Instead, their definitions are stored in the data dictionary and the system creates the view dynamically as the user requests it. When the user finishes with a view, the view table is erased, but the underlying tables from which it was created remain.

Although all of the previous examples demonstrate that a view provides logical independence, views allow more significant logical independence when the logical level is reorganized. If a new column is added to a table, existing users can be unaware of its existence if their views are defined to exclude it. When new tables are added, of course there is no change to the external models of existing users. However, if an existing table is rearranged or split up, a view can be defined so that users can continue to see their old models. In the case of splitting up a table, the old table can be recreated by defining a view from the join of the new tables, provided the split is done in such a way that the original can be reconstructed. We can ensure that this is possible by placing the primary key in both of the new tables. Thus, if we originally had a Student table of the form,

    Student(stuId, lastName, firstName, ssn, major, credits)

we could reorganize this into two new tables,

    PersonalStu(stuId, lastName, firstName, ssn)
    AcademicStu(stuId, major, credits)

Users and applications could still access the data using the old table structure, which would be recreated by defining a view called Student as the natural join of personalStu and academicStu, with stuId as the common column.

Many views act as "windows" into tables, allowing the user to see portions of actual tables. Others that contain joined, calculated, or summary information from actual tables are not windows, but more like "snap-shots," pictures of the data as it existed when the view was invoked during the session. In the "window" case, the view is dynamic, meaning changes made to the actual table that affect view attributes are immediately reflected in the view. When users make permitted changes to the "window" view, those changes are made to the underlying tables. There are restrictions on the types of modifications that can be made through views. For example, a view that does not contain the primary key should not be update-able at all. Also, views constructed from summary information are not update-able. When a view user writes a DML command, he or she uses the view name, and the system automatically converts the command into an equivalent one on the underlying tables. The necessary external/logical mapping information is stored in the data dictionary. The (permitted) operations are performed on the actual tables, and the system returns results in the form that a user expects, based on the view used.

4.8   Mapping an E-R Model to a Relational Model

An E-R diagram can be converted to a relational model fairly easily. To convert our University E-R diagram to a relational model, refer to Figure 3.12.

- The **strong entity sets** represented by rectangles become relations represented by tables. The table name is the same as the entity name, which is the name written inside the rectangle. For strong entity sets, **non-composite, single-valued attributes,** represented by simple ovals, become attributes of the relation, or column headings of the table. The strong entity sets, `Department`, `Student`, and `Faculty` can be represented immediately by the following tables:

```
Department (deptName, deptCode, office)
Student (stuId, lastName, firstName, major, credits)
Faculty (facId, lastName, firstName, rank)
```

- For E-R attributes that are **composites,** the pure relational model does not directly allow us to represent the fact that the attribute is a composite. Instead, we can simply make a column for each of the simple attributes that form the composite, or we can choose to leave the composite as a single attribute. For example, if we had a composite, `address`, we would not have a column with that name, but instead have individual columns for its components: `street`, `city`, `state`, and `zip`. For example, if we included an address in the `Student` table, we could use the schema,

```
Student1 (stuId, lastName, firstName, street, city, state, zip, major,
credits)
```

or, keeping address as a single attribute,

```
Student2 (stuId, lastName, firstName, address, major, credits)
```

The second choice would make it more difficult to select records on the basis of the value of parts of the address, such as zip code or state. In Figure 3.12, we saw that `classNo` is actually a composite consisting of `deptCode`, `courseNumber`, and `section`. Here, we are choosing to leave that composite as a single attribute. Therefore for the present we form the `Class` table as,

```
Class (classNo, schedule, room)
```

- **Multivalued** attributes pose a special problem when converting to a pure relational model, which does not allow multiple values in a cell. The usual solution is to remove them from the table and to create a separate relation in which we put the primary key of the entity, along with the multivalued attribute. The key of this new table is the combination of the key of the original table and the multivalued attribute. If there are multiple multivalued attributes in the original table, we have to create a new table for each one. These new tables are treated as if they are weak entities, with the original table (without the multivalued attributes) acting as the owner entity. It is convenient to name the new tables using the plural form of the multivalued attribute name. As an illustration of how to handle multivalued attributes, let us consider what we would do if students could have more than one major. To represent this, we would change the `Student` table by removing `major` from it, and create instead two tables,

```
Student3(stuId, lastName, firstName, credits)
StuMajors(stuId, major)
```

However, we are assuming that students have at most one major, so we will retain the original `Student` table instead. Another solution is to put in additional columns for the multiple values in the original table. Using this solution, if students could have at most two majors, the `Student` table would become,

```
Student4(stuId, lastName, firstName, major1, major2, credits)
```

If telephone numbers were included for faculty, and faculty members could have more than one telephone number stored in the database, the multiple column solution would produce the schema,

```
Faculty (facId, lastName, firstName, rank, phone, alternatePhone)
```

In Figure 3.12, we saw that the attribute `author` for `Textbook` can have multiple values. We will choose the first method, representing the authors in a separate table, giving us,

```
Textbook(isbn, title, publisher)
TextAuthors(isbn, author)
```

- **Weak entity sets** are also represented by tables, but they require additional attributes. Recall that a weak entity is dependent on another (owner) entity and has no candidate key consisting of just its own attributes. Therefore, the primary key of the corresponding owner entity is used to show which instance of the owner entity a weak entity instance depends on. To represent the weak entity, we use a table whose attributes include all the attributes of the weak entity, plus the primary key of the owner entity. The weak entity itself should have a discriminant—some attribute or attribute set that, when coupled with the owner's primary key, enables us to tell instances apart. We use the combination of the owner's primary key and the discriminant as the key. In Figure 3.12, the weak entity set, `Evaluation`, was given the primary key of its owner entity set, `Faculty`, resulting in the table,

```
Evaluation(facId, date, rater, rating)
```

- **Relationship sets** can be translated directly into tables as well. A relationship set can be represented by a table having the primary keys of the associated entities as attributes. If the relationship set has no descriptive (non-key) attributes, we can construct the corresponding relationship table simply be creating column headings consisting of the primary keys of the associated entities. If the relationship set has descriptive attributes, these also become attributes of the relation, so we have columns for them as well as for the primary keys of the related entities.

  - For **1-1 or 1-M binary relationships,** we can choose not to represent relationship sets by a separate relationship table. Whenever the relationship is one-to-one or one-to-many, it is possible to use foreign keys to show the relationship.

- If A:B is **one-to-many,** we can place the key of A (the one side) in the table for B, the many side, where it becomes a foreign key. Teaches is a one-to-many relationship set connecting the strong entity sets, Class and Faculty. This relationship could be represented by the table,

Teaches(<u>classNo</u>, facId)

We would choose classNo as the key of Teaches, since facId does not give unique values for this combination of attributes. Instead, we will use a foreign key to represent this relationship, by placing facId, the key of the "one" side, Faculty, in the table for the "many" side, Class. We therefore change the Class table to,

Class (<u>classNo</u>, *facId*, schedule, room)

and we do not store the Teaches table.

- For a **weak entity,** the relationship with the owner is already represented, because the primary key of the owner entity is already in the table for the weak entity, so it is not necessary to use another table to represent their connection.

- All entity sets that have a **one-to-one** relationship should be examined carefully to determine whether they are actually the same entity. If they are, they should be combined into a single entity. If A and B are truly separate entities having a one-to-one relationship, then we can put the key of either relation in the other table to show the connection (i.e., either put the key of A in the B table, or vice-versa, but not both). For example, if students can get a parking permit to park one car on campus, we might add a Car entity, which would have a one-to-one relationship with Student. Each car belongs to exactly one student and each student can have at most one car. The initial schema for Car might be,

Car(<u>licNo</u>, make, model, year, color)

We assume licNo includes the state where the car is licensed. To store the one-to-one relationship with Student, we could put stuId in the Car table, getting,

Car(<u>licNo</u>, make, model, year, color, *stuId*).

Alternatively, we could add `licNo` to the `Student` table.

- For a binary relationship, the only case where it is impossible to drop the relationship set is the **many-to-many** case. Here, the only way the connection can be shown is by a table. The `Enroll` relationship represents a many-to-many relationship. The table that represents it must contain the primary keys of the associated `Student` and `Class` entities, `stuId` and `classNo` respectively. Since the relationship also has a descriptive attribute, `grade`, we include that as well. Note that we would need a relationship table even if there were no such descriptive attribute for the M:M relationship. The relationship table is,

Enroll (<u>stuId, classNo</u>, grade)

- When we have a **ternary,** or **n-ary relationship** involving three or more entity sets, we must construct a table for the relationship, in which we place the primary keys of the related entities. If the ternary or n-ary relationship has a descriptive attribute, it goes in the relationship table. Figure 3.12 showed a ternary relationship, `Faculty-Class-Textbook`. We represented it by the table,

Faculty-Class-Textbook(facId, <u>classNo, isbn</u>)

We chose the combination of `classNo` and `isbn` as the key because, as the diagram shows, for each combination of `classNo` and `isbn` values, there is only one `facId`.

- When we have a **recursive** relationship, its representation depends on the cardinality. We can always represent such a relationship by a separate table, regardless of its cardinality. If the cardinality is many-to-many, we must create a corresponding relationship table. If it is one-to-one or one-to-many, the foreign key mechanism can be used. For example, `Chair-Member` could have been included as a one-to-many recursive relationship on `Faculty`. It could be represented by a table that shows pairs of `facId` values, in which the first `facId` represents a faculty member and the second represents the chairperson for that faculty member. The relationship table therefore would have the form,

Chair-Member (<u>memberFacId</u>, chairFacId)

The two attributes have the same domain, the set of `facId` values, but we have renamed them to distinguish between members and chairpersons. The key is `memberFacId`, since each faculty member has only one chairperson, but a chairperson may be associated with several department members. The alternative would be to place the `chairFacId` as a foreign key in the `Faculty` table. The `Faculty` table would then have the structure,

`Faculty (`facID`, lastName, firstName, department, rank, `chairFacId`).`

If we assume each student can have exactly one roommate, we could represent the one-to-one recursive roommate relationship either as a separate table,

`Roommate(`stuId`, roommateStuId)`

or by adding an attribute to the Student table, as in

`Student(`stuId`, lastName, firstName, major, credits, `roommateStuId`)`

Whenever we have a choice of how to represent relationships, as in the one-to-one or one-to-many cases for binary relationships, how do we know whether or not to use a separate table? The answer can depend on the applications for which we are designing a particular database. Having a separate relationship table gives maximum flexibility, allowing us to change the associations easily. However, it requires doing joins whenever the relationship is used, which can produce poor performance if many applications require the joins. The designer must choose between flexibility and efficiency, depending on the criteria for the applications.

There are eight relationship sets represented in Figure 3.12 by diamonds. The 1:M `HasMajor` relationship set connecting `Department` to `Student` has attributes `deptname` and `stuId`, the primary keys of the associated entity sets. Therefore, if we chose to represent the relationship as a table, we would use,

`HasMajor(deptName, `stuId`)`

We would underline `stuId` as the primary key, since this attribute gives unique values for each tuple, even without deptname. We could choose not to create this relationship table at all, since it is a one-to-many relationship, and in doing so we will represent the relationship by a foreign key. To do so, we place the primary key of the "one" side, `Department`, in the table for the "many" side, `Student`. We note that `Student` already contains `major`, an attribute which is actually a foreign key. (We are assuming here that the names of all major programs are actually just the department names. If that is not the case, i.e., program majors can differ from department names, then we would need to add the department name as a foreign key in Student.) If we decide to create the relationship table, we could drop the major attribute from the Student table. Then we would need to do a join whenever we needed to find a student's major. Our choice will be to keep major in Student and not use a separate table for this relationship.

The Enroll relationship represents a many-to-many relationship, which always requires a separate table. In addition, it has a descriptive attribute, the presence of which indicates that a separate table is desirable. This table must contain the primary keys of the associated Student and Class entities, stuId and classNo respectively. The relationship table is:

```
Enroll (stuId, classNo, grade)
```

Note that in a many-to-many relationship, we need the primary keys for both of the related entities as the primary key of the relationship. Recall that the grade here means the mid-term grade, since these records are for the current semester.

Offers is a one-to-many relationship that connects Department to Class. We can represent this relationship by the table,

```
Offers(deptname, classNo)
```

An alternative is to put the key of Department, deptName, in the Class table. We will choose to use the relationship table here. Teaches is a one-to-many relationship set connecting the strong entity sets, Class and Faculty. This relationship could be represented by the table,

```
Teaches (classNo, facId)
```

We would choose classNo as the key, since facId does not give unique values for this combination of attributes. Instead, we will use a foreign key to represent this relationship, by placing facId, the key of the "one" side, Faculty, in the table for the "many" side, Class. We therefore change the Class table to:

```
Class (classNo, facId, schedule, room)
```

Employs is a one-to-many relationship that represents the association between Department and Faculty. We have the option to represent the relationship explicitly by the table,

```
Employs (deptName, facId)
```

Again, we choose not to create this table, and use the foreign key mechanism, adding `deptName` as an attribute in the `Faculty` table, making that table,

    Faculty (facId, lastName, firstName, deptName, rank)

`Chairs` is a one-to-one relationship that connects `Department` to `Faculty`. We will push the primary key of `Faculty` into `Department` as a foreign key, making the `Department` schema,

    Department (deptName, deptCode, office, chairFacId)

As indicated previously, the ternary relationship connecting `Textbook`, `Faculty`, and `Class` should be represented by a table. The `isRated` relationship connecting the weak entity `Evaluation` to its owner, `Faculty`. It will be represented by having the primary key of the owner entity in the weak entity's table as part of its primary key.

Our entire schema, then, is:

    Department (deptName, deptCode, office, chairFacId)
    Student (stuId, lastName, firstName, major, credits)
    Class (classNo, facId, sched, room)
    Textbook (isbn, title, publisher)
    TextbookAuthors (isbn, author)
    Faculty (facId, lastName, firstName, deptName, chairFacId, rank)
    Evaluation (facId, date, rater, rating)
    Enroll (stuId, classNo, grade)
    Offers (deptName, classNo)
    Textbook-Class-Faculty (isbn, classNo, facId)

4.9 Codd's Rules for a Relational Database Management System

In two 1985 articles, Codd published rules or principles that a database management system must use to be considered "fully relational." (Codd, E. F., "Is Your DBMS Really Relational?", *Computerworld*, Oct. 14, 1985; "Does Your DBMS Run by the Rules?", *Computerworld*, Oct. 21, 1985). Codd wanted to maintain the integrity of the relational model and to make it clear that placing a relational user interface on top of a system that used some other model as its basic data model was not enough to make a DBMS truly relational. He identified 12 rules, along with a fundamental overarching rule that he called Rule Zero. The rules provided a set of standards for judging whether a DBMS is fully relational. The rules, which were the subject of much debate, are summarized as follows:

- **Rule Zero.** A relational database management system must manage its stored data using only its relational capabilities. This is the fundamental principle upon which the remaining 12 rules are based.

- **Rule 1–Information Representation.** All information must be represented, at the logical level, only as values in tables.

- **Rule 2–Guaranteed Access.** It must be possible to access any data item in the database by giving its table name, column name, and primary key value.

- **Rule 3–Representation of Null Values.** The system must be able to represent null values in a systematic way, regardless of the data type of the item. Null values must be distinct from zero or any other number, and from empty strings.

- **Rule 4–Relational Catalog.** The system catalog, which contains the logical description of the database, must be represented the same way as ordinary data.

- **Rule 5–Comprehensive Data Sublanguage.** Regardless of the number of other languages it supports, the database must include one language that allows statements expressed as character strings to support data definition, definition of views, data manipulation, integrity rules, user authorization, and a method of identifying units for recovery.

- **Rule 6–Updating Views.** Any view that is theoretically updateable can actually be updated by the system.

- **Rule 7–Insert, Delete, and Update Operations.** Any relation that can be handled as a single operand for retrieval can also be handled that way for insertion, deletion, and update operations.

- **Rule 8–Physical Data Independence.** The application programs are immune to changes made to storage representations or access methods.

- **Rule 9–Logical Data Independence.** Changes made to the logical level, such as splitting tables or combining tables, which do not affect the information content at the logical level, do not require modification of applications.

- **Rule 10–Integrity Rules.** Integrity constraints such as entity integrity and referential integrity must be specifiable in the data sublanguage and stored in the catalog. Application program statements should not be used to express these constraints.

- **Rule 11–Distribution Independence.** The data sublanguage should be such that if the database is distributed, the applications programs and users' commands need not be changed.

- **Rule 12–Nonsubversion.** If the system allows a language that supports record-at-a-time access, any program using this type of access cannot bypass the integrity constraints expressed in the higher-level language.

4.10 Chapter Summary

A mathematical **relation** is defined as a subset of the Cartesian product of sets. In database terms, a relation is any subset of the Cartesian product of the domains of the attributes. A relation is normally written as a set of **n-tuples,** in which each element is chosen from the appropriate domain. Relations are physically represented as **tables,** with the rows corresponding to individual records and the columns to the attributes of the relation. The structure of the table, with domain specifications and other constraints is the **intension** of the database, while the table with all its rows written out is an instance or **extension** of the database. Properties of database relations are: Each cell is single-valued, column names are distinct, a column's values all come from the same domain, row order is immaterial, and there are no duplicate rows.

The **degree** of a relation is the number of attributes or columns. A **unary** relation has one column, a **binary** relation has two, a **ternary** relation has three and an **n-ary** relation has n columns. The **cardinality** of a relation is the number of rows or tuples. Degree is a property of the intension, while cardinality is a property of the extension of a relation. A **superkey** is a set of attributes that uniquely identifies tuples of the relation, while a **candidate key** is a minimal superkey. A **primary key** is the candidate key chosen for use in identification of tuples. A relation must always have a primary key. A **foreign key** is an attribute of a relation that is not the primary key of that relation, but that is the primary key of some (usually other) relation, called its **home relation. Entity integrity** is a constraint that states that no attribute of a primary key may be null. **Referential integrity** states that foreign key values must match the primary key values of some tuple in the home relation or be completely null. Other integrity rules include **domain constraints, table constraints,** and **general constraints.**

Relational data manipulation languages may be **procedural** or **nonprocedural, graphical, fourth-generation,** or **fifth-generation. Relational algebra** is a formal procedural language. Its operators include select, project, product, union, intersection, difference, division, and several type of joins, semijoins, and outerjoins. **Relational calculus** is a formal nonprocedural language that uses predicates. The most common type of query in tuple-oriented relational calculus has the form $\{x \mid P(x)\}$, which means "Find the set of all tuple variables x such that predicate $P(x)$ is true." A typical query in domain-oriented relational calculus has the form $\{<x_1, x_2, \ldots, x_n> \mid P(x_1, x_2, \ldots, x_n)\}$, which means "Find the set of all domain variables for which the predicate is true." Relational algebra is logically equivalent to a safe subset of relational calculus.

A **view** in the relational model is not a complete external model, but a **virtual table.** The view protects security and allows the designer to customize a user's model. Views are created dynamically when the user makes a data request.

In converting an E-R to a relational model, strong entities become tables having a column for each of the entity's simple, single-valued attributes. Composite attributes can either be stored as a single attribute, or the simple attributes that comprise the composite are each represented by a column, with no representation of the composite. Each multivalued attribute is removed and placed in a separate table, along with the primary key of the original table. Tables for weak entities have columns for the key attributes of the associated owner entity as well as for the attributes of the weak entity. Relationship tables have columns for the primary key attributes of the related entities, plus a column for each descriptive attribute of the relation. Many-to-many relations require a separate relationship table, but one-to-one and one-to-many relationships can be represented by foreign keys instead of by tables. The designer can choose whichever method fits the application best, trading off flexibility for efficiency. Ternary and n-ary relationships are best represented as separate tables. Recursive relationships can be represented by foreign keys, provided they are one-to-one or one-to-many, or by a separate relationship table, which is required if they are many-to-many relationships.

Exercises

4.1 Let S = {red, yellow, green} and T = {plaid, stripe, dot}. Find the Cartesian product of S and T.

4.2 Let Q = {Tom, Mary, Jim} and R = {walking, running}. Create a relation with Q and R as domains.

4.3 Consider the relation schema containing book data for a bookstore: Book (title, author, isbn, publisher, pubDate, city, qtyOnHand)

a. Write out the table for an instance of this relation.

b. Identify a superkey, a candidate key, and the primary key, writing out any assumptions you need to make to justify your choice.

4.4 Consider the following database instance that contains information about employees and the projects to which they are assigned:

Emp

empId	lastName
E101	Smith
E105	Jones
E110	Adams
E115	Smith

Assign

empId	projNo	hours
E101	P10	200
E101	P15	300
E105	P10	400
E110	P15	700
E110	P20	350
E115	P10	300
E115	P20	400

Proj

projNo	projName	budget
P10	Hudson	500000
P15	Columbia	350000
P20	Wabash	350000
P23	Arkansas	600000

Show ALL the tables (including the intermediate ones) that would be produced by each of the following relational algebra commands:

a. SELECT Emp WHERE lastName = 'Adams' GIVING T1

   JOIN T1, Assign GIVING T2

   Symbolically this is,

   $(\sigma_{lastName='Adams'}(Emp)) \, |X| \, Assign$

b. SELECT Proj WHERE budget > 400000 GIVING T1

   JOIN T1, Assign GIVING T2

   PROJECT T2 OVER empId GIVING T3

   Symbolically this is,

   $\Pi_{empId}((\sigma_{budget>400000}(Proj)) \, |X| \, Assign)$

c. PROJECT Assign OVER projNo GIVING T1

   JOIN T1, Proj GIVING T2

   PROJECT T2 OVER budget GIVING T3

   Symbolically this is,

   $\Pi_{budget}(\Pi_{projNo}(Assign) \, |X| \, Proj)$

4.5   Using the Emp, Proj, and Assign tables shown in Exercise 4.4, show what results would be produced by each of the following tuple relational calculus commands.

a. {E.empId | E ∈ Emp ∧ E.lastName = 'Smith'}

b. {P | P ∈ Proj ∧ P.budget < 500000}

c. {E.lastName | E ∈ Emp ∧ ∃ A(A ∈ Assign ∧ (A.empId = E.empId) ∧ (A.projNo ='P10'))}

d. {E | E ∈ Emp ∧ ∃ A(A ∈ Assign ∧ (E.empId = A.empId) ∧ ∃ P(P ∈ Proj ∧ (A.projNo = P.projNo) ∧ (P.projName = 'Columbia')))}

4.6   Using the Emp, Proj, and Assign tables of Exercise 4.4, show what results would be produced by each of the following domain relational algebra commands. Assume variable EI and EI′ stand for empId, LN for lastName, PN for projNo, PM for projName, BG for budget, and HR for hours

a. {EI | ∃ LN(<EI,LN> ∈ Emp ∧ LN = 'Smith'}

b. {LN | ∃ EI(<EI,LN> ∈ Emp ∧ ∃ PN,HR(<EI,PN,HR> ∈ Assign ∧ PN = 'P15'))}

c. {EI| ∃ LN(<EI,LN> ∈ Emp ∧ ∃ PN,HR(<EI,PN,HR ∈ Assign
   ∧ ∃ PM,BG(<PN,PM,BG> ∈ Proj ∧ BG>= 500000)))}

d. {LN | ∃ EI(<EI,LN> ∈ Emp ∧ ¬∃ EI',PN,HR(<EI',PN,HR> ∈ Assign
   ∧ PN = 'P20' ∧ EI' = EI))}

4.7 Consider the following schema for a database that keeps information about business trips and their associated expenses by employees:

EMPLOYEE (SSN, Name, DeptNo, JobTitle, Salary)

TRIP(TripId, DepartureCity, DestinationCity, DepartureDate, ReturnDate, SSN)

EXPENSE(TripID, Item, Date, Amount)

Write relational algebra queries for each of the following:

a. Get a list of all the different destination cities where the employees have taken trips.

b. Find all the employee information for employees who work in Department 10.

c. Get complete trip records (but not their associated expenses) for all trips with departure dates after January 1 of the current year.

d. Find the names of all employees who have departed on trips from London.

e. Find the SSN of all employees who have any single expense item of more than $1000 for any trip.

f. Find the names of all employees who have any expense item with value "Entertainment."

g. Find the destination cities of all trips taken by employees who have the job title of "Consultant."

h. Find the names and departments of all employees who have a single expense item of over $1000 since January 1 of this year.

i. Find the items and amounts of all expenses for a trip to Cairo beginning on January 3 of this year taken by employee Jones.

j. Find the names, departments, and job titles of all employees who have any expense item with value "Service Charge" for trips taken to Melbourne last year, along with the date and amount of the expense.

4.8   Using the `Employee, Trip, Expense` schema from Exercise 4.7, write tuple relational calculus commands for each of the following queries.

a. Find the names of all employees who work in Department 10.

b. Find the social security numbers and names of all employees who have taken a business trip to Hong Kong.

c. Find the social security numbers and names of all employees who have any expense for an item called "Miscellaneous."

d. Find all the expense items and amounts for any business expense incurred by employee Smith.

4.9   Using the `Employee, Trip, Expense` schema from Exercise 4.7, write domain relational calculus commands for each of the following queries.

a. Find the social security numbers of all employees who have the job title Programmer.

b. Find the names of all employees who have taken a business trip departing from San Francisco.

c. Find the names of employees who have not taken any business trips.

d. Find all the expense items for a business trip taken by employee Jones with departure date of January 10 of this year.

4.10   Design a relational database schema corresponding to the diagram shown in Figure 4.9.

4.11   Design a relational database schema for the data described in Exercises 3.2 and 3.3.

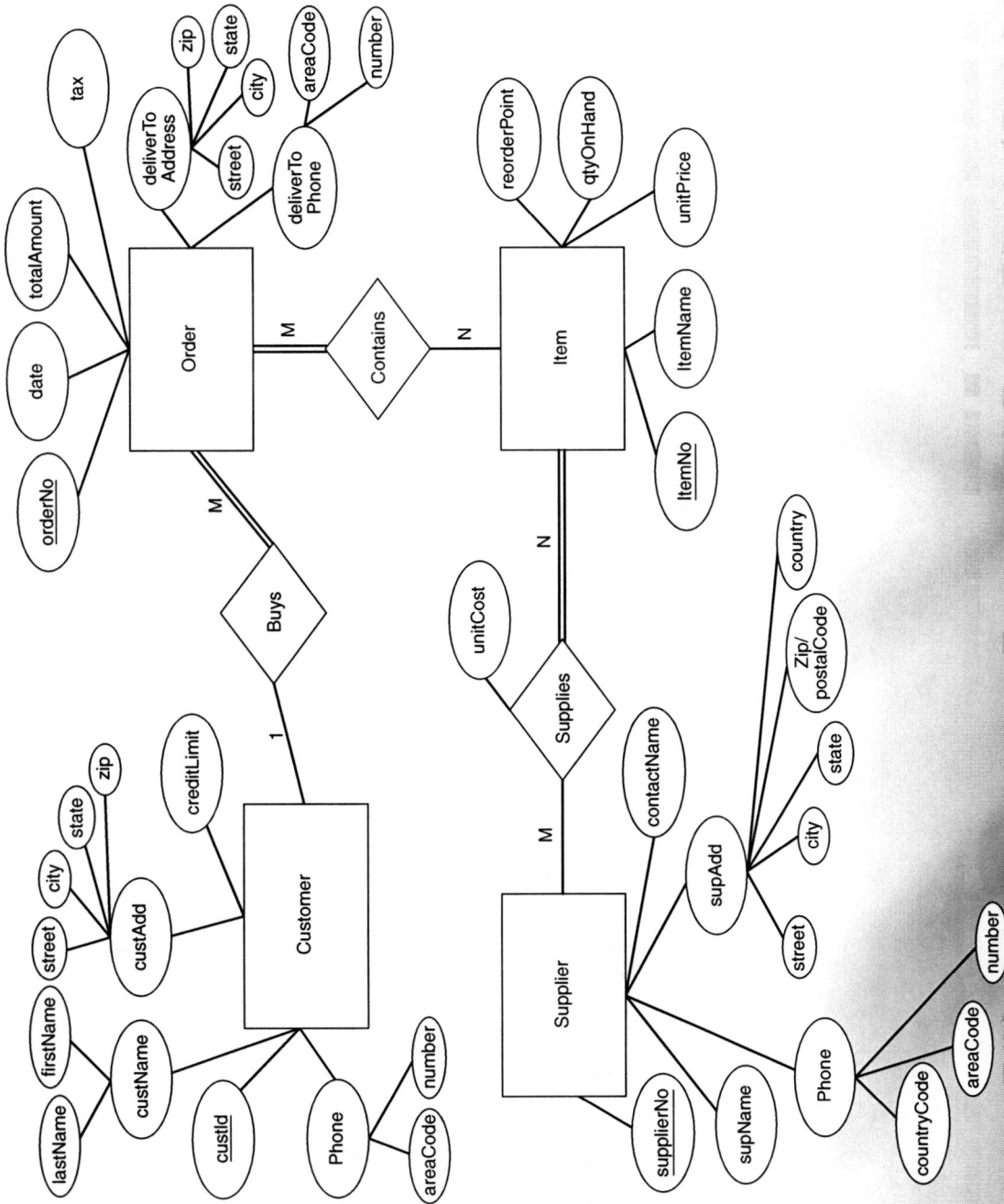

FIGURE 4.9
E-R Diagram for CustomerOrder Example

4.12   Design a relational database schema for the data described in Exercise 3.4.

4.13   Design a relational database schema for the data described in Exercise 3.5.

4.14   Design a relational database schema for the data described in Exercise 3.6.

4.15   Design a relational database schema for the data described in Exercise 3.7.

4.16   Design a relational database schema for the data described in Exercise 3.8.

SAMPLE PROJECT: INITIAL MAPPING OF THE E-R MODEL TO TABLES FOR THE ART GALLERY

- Step 4.1. Map the E-R model developed at the end of Chapter 3 to relational model, using the guidelines presented in Section 4.9.

The E-R diagram developed at the end of Chapter 3 showed the strong entities `Artist`, `PotentialCustomer`, `Collector`, `Show`, `Sale`, `Buyer`, and `Salesperson`, and a weak entity, `Artwork`.

The strong entities map to the following tables. Note that we replaced composite attributes by their simple components, and we underlined primary keys. Although it is not necessary, it is customary to list the primary keys as the first columns in the tables.

```
Artist(firstName, lastName, street, city, state, zip, interviewDate, interviewerName,
areaCode, telephoneNumber, salesLastYear, salesYearToDate, socialSecurityNumber,
usualMedium, usualStyle, usualType)

PotentialCustomer(firstName, lastName, street, city, state, zip, areaCode,
telephoneNumber, dateFilledIn, preferredArtist, preferredMedium,
preferredStyle, preferredType)

Collector(SocialSecurityNumber, firstName, lastName, street, city, state, zip,
interviewDate, interviewerName, areaCode, telephonenumber, salesLastYear,
salesYearToDate, collectionArtistFirstName, collectionArtistLastName,
collectionMedium, collectionStyle, collectionType, SalesLastYear, SalesYearToDate)

Show(showTitle, showFeaturedArtist, showClosingDate, showTheme,
showOpeningDate)
```

```
Sale(invoiceNumber, amountRemittedToOwner, saleDate, salePrice,
saleSalesPersonCommission, saleTax, SaleTotal)

Buyer(firstName, lastName, street, city, state, zip, areaCode,
telephoneNumber, purchasesLastYear, purchasesYearToDate)

Salesperson(socialSecurityNumber, firstName, lastName, street, city,
state, zip)
```

Since the weak entity `Artwork` depends on `Artist`, we add the key of `Artist` to the `Artwork` table and combined it with the weak entity's partial key to form a primary key, as follows:

```
Artwork(artistLastName, artistFirstName, workTitle, askingPrice, dateListed,
dateReturned, dateShown, status, workMedium, workSize, workStyle, workType,
workYearCompleted)
```

The relationship sets are: `PreferredBy`, `CollectedBy`, `Creates`, `FeaturedIn`, `Owns`, `ShownIn`, `SoldIn`, `SoldTo`, and `SoldBy`.

The one-to-many `PreferredBy` relationship could be a separate table having the primary keys of `Artist` and `PotentialCustomer` as columns, but instead we choose to represent it by a foreign key. Therefore we need to put `artistLastName` and `artistFirstName` in the `PotentialCustomer` table. We note that `preferredArtist` is already in that table. We replace it by the two attributes, which we call `preferredArtistLastName` and `preferredArtistFirstName`, which together will form a foreign key, indicated by italics in the schema shown below in boldface.

The `CollectedBy` relationship is also one-to-many, and can be represented by placing the key of `Artist` in `Collector`. We notice that `Collector` already has `collectionArtistLastName`, `collectionArtistFirstName`, so the relationship is already represented.

The `Creates` relationship has already been represented by placing the primary key of `Artist` in `Artwork`. We show by using italics that these attributes, although part of the primary key, also form a foreign key in `Artwork`.

`FeaturedIn` is a one-to-many relationship that can be represented using a foreign key. We note that `Show` already has an attribute called `showFeaturedArtist`. We change that to `showFeaturedArtistLastName, showFeaturedArtistFirstName`.

The one-to-many `Owns` relationship can be represented by placing the primary key of `Collector` in the `Artwork` table, so we add `collectorSocialSecurityNumber` to that table, using italics to show that it is a foreign key.

The `ShownIn` relationship is many-to-many, so we must construct a table with the primary keys of `Artwork` and `Show` to represent it. Since there are no descriptive attributes on the E-R diagram, this is an "all key" table, with no non-key attributes. We also note that its attributes are foreign keys, referring to the tables where they are primary keys.

The `SoldIn` relationship is one-to-one. If we do not wish to construct a new table, we have the options of placing the key of `Artwork` in `Sale`, or of `Sale` in `Artwork`. Note that we do not need to do both. We will choose the first alternative.

The `SoldTo` relationship is many-to-one. We choose to represent it by placing the key of the "one" side, `Buyer`, in the table for the "many" side, `Sale`, where it is the foreign key `buyerLastName, buyerFirstName, areaCode, telephoneNumber`.

Similarly, to represent the one-to-many `SoldBy` relationship, we place the primary key of `Salesperson` in the `Sale` table, where it becomes the foreign key `salespersonSocialSecurityNumber`.

The resulting tables in the conceptual level relational schema are the following.

Artist (<u>firstName, lastName</u>, street, city, state, zip, interviewDate, interviewerName, areaCode, telephoneNumber, salesLastYear, salesYearToDate, socialSecurityNumber, usualMedium, usualStyle, usualType)

PotentialCustomer(<u>firstName, lastName</u>, street, city, state, zip, <u>areaCode, telephoneNumber</u>, dateFilledIn, *preferredArtistLastName, preferredArtistFirstName*, preferredMedium, preferredStyle, preferredType)

Artwork(<u>*artistLastName, artistFirstName, workTitle*</u>, askingPrice, dateListed, dateReturned, dateShown, status, workMedium, workSize, workStyle, workType, workYearCompleted, *collectorSocialSecurityNumber*)

ShownIn (<u>*artistLastName, artistFirstName, workTitle, showTitle*</u>)

Collector (<u>SocialSecurityNumber</u>, firstName, lastName, street, city, state, zip, interviewDate, interviewerName, areaCode, telephonenumber, salesLastYear, salesYearToDate, *collectionArtistFirstName, collectionArtistLastName*, collectionMedium, collectionStyle, collectionType, SalesLastYear, SalesYearToDate)

Show (<u>showTitle</u>, *showFeaturedArtistLastName, showFeaturedArtistFirstName*, showClosingDate, showTheme, showOpeningDate)

Sale (<u>InvoiceNumber</u>, *artistLastName, artistFirstName, workTitle*, amountRemittedToOwner, saleDate, salePrice, saleSalesPersonCommission, saleTax, SaleTotal, *buyerLastName, buyerFirstName, buyerAreaCode, buyerTelephoneNumber, salespersonSocialSecurityNumber*)

```
Buyer(firstName, lastName, areaCode, telephoneNumber, street, city, state,
zip, purchasesLastYear, purchasesYearToDate)
```

```
Salesperson (socialSecurityNumber, firstName, lastName, street, city, state,
zip)
```

We note that the primary keys of `Artist`, `Buyer`, and `PotentialCustomer` consist of two or more character string attributes. We observe that it becomes burdensome to include these multiple attributes when we use them as foreign keys. We will address this issue in a later chapter.

STUDENT PROJECTS: INITIAL MAPPING TO TABLES FOR STUDENT PROJECTS

- Step 4.1. Map the E-R model developed at the end of Chapter 3 to a relational model, using the guidelines presented in Section 4.8 and illustrated in the Sample Project..

5 CHAPTER

Normalization

Chapter Objectives

In this chapter you will learn the following:

- Why relations should be normalized

- The meaning of functional dependency and its relationship to keys

- How inference rules for functional dependencies can be used

- The definition of first normal form and how to achieve it

- The meaning of full functional dependency

- The definition of second normal form and how to achieve it

- The meaning of transitive dependency
- The definition of third normal form and how to achieve it
- The definition of Boyce-Codd Normal Form and how to achieve it
- The meaning of multivalued dependencies
- The definition of fourth normal form and how to achieve it
- The meaning of join dependency
- The definition of fifth normal form (Projection-Join Normal Form)
- The definition of domain-key normal form
- When to stop the normalization process

5.1   Objectives of Normalization

The basic objective of logical modeling is to develop a "good" description of the data, its relationships, and its constraints. For the relational model, this means we must identify a suitable set of relations. However, the task of choosing the relations is a difficult one, because there are many options for the designer to consider. This chapter explains some methods of improving logical design. The techniques presented here are based on a large body of research into the logical design process generally called normalization.

The purpose of normalization is to produce a stable set of relations that is a faithful model of the operations of the enterprise. By following the principles of normalization, we achieve a design that is highly flexible, allowing the model to be extended when needed to account for new attributes, entity sets, and relationships. We design the database in such a way that we can enforce certain types of integrity constraints easily. We can also reduce redundancy in the database, both to save space and to avoid inconsistencies in data. We also ensure that the design is free of certain update, insertion, and deletion anomalies. An anomaly is an inconsistent, incomplete, or contradictory state of the database. If these anomalies were present, we would be unable to represent some information, we might lose information when certain updates were performed, and we would run the risk of having data become inconsistent over time.

5.2   Insertion, Update, and Deletion Anomalies

Consider the following relation.

```
NewClass(classNo, stuId, stuLastName, facId, schedule, room, grade)
```

An instance of this relation appears in Figure 5.1. In this example, we will assume that there is only one faculty member for each class (i.e., no team teaching). We also assume each class is always scheduled for the same room. This relation exhibits update, insertion, and deletion anomalies.

- **Update anomaly.** Suppose we wished to change the schedule of ART103A to MWF12. It is possible we might update the first two records of the NewClass table but not the third, resulting in an inconsistent state in the database. It would then be impossible to tell the true schedule for that class. This is an update anomaly.

- **Insertion anomaly.** An insertion anomaly occurs when we try to add information about a course for which no student has yet registered. For example, suppose we create a new class, with values MTH110A, F110, MTuTh10, H225 for classNumber, facId, schedule, and room. We are unable to record the course information, even though we have the values for these attributes. Since the key is {courseNo,stuId}, we are not permitted to insert a record with a null value for stuId. Because we are not able to represent this class information, we have an insertion anomaly. The same problem would occur if we tried to insert information about a student who had not yet registered for any course.

- **Deletion anomaly.** When we delete the record of the only student taking a particular course, a deletion anomaly occurs. For exam-

courseNo	stuId	stuLastName	facId	schedule	room	grade
ART103A	S1001	Smith	F101	MWF9	H221	A
ART103A	S1010	Burns	F101	MWF9	H221	
ART103A	S1006	Lee	F101	MWF9	H221	B
CSC201A	S1003	Jones	F105	TUTHF10	M110	A
CSC201A	S1006	Lee	F105	TUTHF10	M110	G
HST205A	S1001	Smith	F202	MWF11	H221	

FIGURE 5.1

The NewClass Table

ple, if student S1001 dropped out of HST205A, we would lose all information about that course. It would be desirable to keep the course information, but we cannot do so without a corresponding `stuId`. Similarly, if a student drops the only course he or she is taking, we lose all information about that student.

Research into these anomalies was first done by Codd, who identified the causes and defined the first three "normal forms." A relation is in a specific normal form if it satisfies the set of requirements or constraints for that form. Note that the constraints we discuss are schema constraints, permanent properties of the relation, not merely of some instance of the relation. They are properties of the intension, not just of a particular extension. Later research by Boyce and Codd led to a refinement of the third of these forms. Additional research by Fagin, Zaniolo, and Delobel (each independently) resulted in the definition of three new normal forms. All of the normal forms are nested, in that each satisfies the constraints of the previous one, but is a "better" form because each eliminates flaws found in the previous form. Figure 5.2 shows how the seven normal forms are related. The largest circle represents all relations. Among the set of all relations those that satisfy certain conditions are in first normal form, and they are represented by the second largest circle. Of those in first normal form, there are some that have additional conditions and that are second normal form as well; these fall into the next circle, and so forth. Our design objective should be to put the schema in the highest normal form that is practical and appropriate for the data in the database. Normalization means putting a relation into a higher normal form. Normalization requires that we have a clear grasp of the semantics of the model. Merely examining an instance or extension is not sufficient, because an

FIGURE 5.2
Relationships of Normal Forms

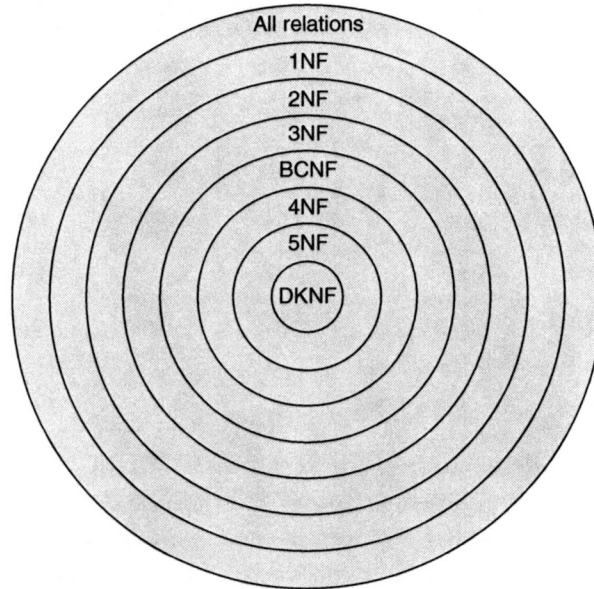

instance does not provide enough information about all the possible values or combinations of values for relation attributes.

In attempting to pinpoint the causes of update, insertion, and deletion anomalies, researchers have identified three kinds of dependencies: **functional dependencies, multivalued dependencies,** and **join dependencies.** Additional dependencies appear in the research literature.

5.3 Functional Dependency

A **functional dependency (FD)** is a type of relationship between attributes, as described in the following definition:

> **Definition:** If R is a relation schema and A and B are non-empty sets of attributes in R, we say that B is **functionally dependent** on A if, and only if, each value of A in R has associated with it exactly one value of B in R.

We write this as,

$$A \rightarrow B$$

which we read as "A functionally determines B." The definition says that if two tuples in an extension of R have the same value for A, they must also

			NewStudent		
stuId	**LastName**	**major**	**credits**	**status**	**socSecNo**
S1001	Smith	History	90	Senior	100429500
S1003	Jones	Math	95	Senior	010124567
S1006	Lee	CSC	15	Freshman	088520876
S1010	Burns	Art	63	Junior	099320985
S1060	Jones	CSC	25	Freshman	064624738

FIGURE 5.3

Instance of NewStudent Table (assume each student has only one major)

have the same values for B. More formally, for every pair of tuples, t_1 and t_2, in every instance of R, we have the following rule:

If $t_1.A = t_2.A$ then $t_1.B = t_2.B$

Here, the notation $t_1.A$ means the projection of tuple t_1 onto the attributes of set A. This rule does not mean that A **causes** B or that the value of B can be calculated from the value of A by a formula, although sometimes that is the case. It simply means that if we know the value of A and we examine the table of relation R, we will find only one value of B in all the rows that have the given value of A at any one time. Thus, when two rows have the same A value, they must also have the same B value. However, for a given B value, there may be several different A values. A functional dependency is actually a **many-to-one relationship** from attribute set A to attribute set B. It is an **integrity constraint** that every instance of the database must obey. Note that A or B can be sets that consist of a single attribute. When a functional dependency exists, the set of attributes on the left side of the arrow (A in this example) is called a **determinant** and the set of attributes on the right side of the arrow is called the **dependent.**

To illustrate functional dependency, consider the following relation:

```
NewStudent(stuId, lastName, major, credits, status, socSecNo)
```

Figure 5.3 shows an instance of the relation. This relation stores information about students in a college. Here, we will assume that every student has a unique ID and social security number and that each student has at most one major. We will assume that last names are not unique, that two different students may have the same last name. The attribute `credits` means the number of credits completed, and `status` refers to the year the student is in—freshman, sophomore, junior, or senior. Although we will use this instance to help us detect functional dependencies, we are trying to determine permanent characteristics of the relation, not simply of the instance. Examining the table, we see that if we are given a specific value of stuId, there is only one value of lastName associated with that particular stuId. For example, for stuId S1006, the associated lastName is Lee. Because we understand that each student is given a unique ID, we know that this is a characteristic of the relation, not just of this instance, so {lastName} is functionally dependent on {stuId}, and we can write,

> {stuId} → {lastName}

However, for a given value of lastName there may be more than one stuId. We note that for the lastName Jones there are two stuId values, S1003 and S1060. Therefore we cannot turn the functional dependency around and write {lastName} → {stuId}. For each of the other attributes, there is only one value associated with a particular value of stuId, so all the attributes are functionally dependent on stuId. We have,

> {stuId} → {stuId}
> {stuId} → {lastName}
> {stuId} → { major}
> {stuId} → {credits}
> {stuId} → {status}
> {stuId} → {socSecNo}

which we will write in abbreviated form as,

> {stuId } → {stuId, lastName, major, credits, status, socSecNo}

to indicate that each of the attributes on the right is functionally dependent on stuId. Similarly we have,

> {socSecNo} → {socSecNo, stuId, lastName, major, credits, status}

Also note that status is functionally dependent on credits. For example, if the value of credits is known to be 15, the status is automatically freshman. We write,

> {credits} → {status}

For sets consisting of a single attribute like these, we will write just the attribute name, and drop the set braces. For this case of functional dependency, the determinant, credits, does **not** functionally determine all the other attributes of the relation. Note also that the value of credits is not necessarily unique. Several students could have the same number of credits, so uniqueness is not a necessary characteristic of determinants. The instance in Figure 5.3 did not really demonstrate the lack of uniqueness of credits, which shows that we must be careful in making judgments from instances only. We need to concentrate on the meanings of the attributes and their constraints in identifying functional dependencies. Note that we do not have the FD `status → credits`, since, for example, two freshmen may have a different number of credits, as we see in the records of S1006 and S1060.

Certain functional dependencies are called **trivial** because they are always satisfied in every relation. In trivial functional dependencies, the dependent is a subset of the determinant. If all the attributes in the set on the right-hand side are included in the set on the left-hand side of the dependency, or if the two sides are the same, the FD is trivial. For example, the following FDs are trivial:

```
{A,B}→ A
{A,B}→ B
{A,B}→ {A,B}
```

5.4   Superkeys, Candidate Keys, and Primary Keys

Recall from Chapter 3 that a **superkey** is an attribute or a set of attributes that uniquely identifies an entity. In a table, a superkey is any column or set of columns whose values can be used to distinguish one row from another. Therefore, a superkey is any unique identifier. Since a superkey uniquely identifies each entity, it functionally determines all the attributes of a relation. For the `Student` table in Figure 5.3, `{stuId}` is a superkey. So is the combination of `{stuId, lastName}`. In fact, `{stuId, any other attribute}` is a superkey for this relation. The same is true for `{socSecNo, any other attribute}`. In fact, any set of attributes containing a superkey is also a superkey. However, a superkey may contain additional attributes that are not needed for uniqueness, and we are interested in finding superkeys that do not contain such extra attributes.

A **candidate key** is a superkey such that no proper subset of its attributes is itself a superkey. Therefore, a candidate key must be a **minimal** identifier. In our example, the superkey `{stuId, lastName}` is not a candidate key because it contains a proper subset, `{stuId}`, that is a superkey. However, `stuId` by itself is a candidate key. Similarly, `socSecNo` is a candidate key. If no two students are permitted to have the same combination of name and major values, the combination `{lastName, major}` would also be a candidate key. Therefore, we see that a relation may have several candidate keys. We will use the term composite key to refer to a key that consists of more than one attribute.

A **primary key** is a candidate key that is actually used to identify tuples in a relation. In our example, stuId might be the primary key and socSecNo an alternate key. These two attributes functionally determine each other, and all of the attributes are functionally dependent on each of them. When making a decision about which candidate key to use as the primary key, it is important to consider which choice is a better representation of the real world in which the enterprise functions. We choose stuId rather than socSecNo because, since the university assigns stuId values, we can always be sure of having that value for each student. It is possible we might not have the social security number of every student. For example, international students may not have social security numbers. There are also privacy rules that limit the use of social security numbers as identifiers, so it is better to avoid using them for the university database. Although not explicitly stated in the definition, an important characteristic of a primary key is that none of its attributes may have null values. If we permitted null values in keys, we would be unable to tell records apart, since two records with null values in the same key field might be indistinguishable. For candidate keys, we should specify that their values are also unique in the database. This helps to ensure the quality of data, since we know that duplicate values would be incorrect for these items. It is also desirable to enforce the "no nulls" rule for candidate keys, provided we can be sure the value of the candidate key will be available.

5.5   The Normalization Process Using Primary Keys

In practice, database designers usually develop an initial logical model for a relational database by mapping an E-R diagram or other conceptual model to a set of relations. They identify the primary key and possibly functional dependencies during the conceptual design process. By mapping the E-R diagram to a relational model using the method described in Section 4.8, the designer creates a relational model that is already fairly well normalized. To complete the relational design process, the designer checks each relation, identifies a set of functional dependencies for it if any exist other than the ones involving the primary key, and normalizes it further if necessary. A well-developed set of rules of thumb, or heuristics, is used to guide the normalization process based on primary keys. In the next section we describe this process, using informal definitions of the normal forms. In later sections we will formalize these notions.

5.5.1 First Normal Form

We will use a counterexample to describe first normal form. If we assume that a student is permitted to have more than one major, and we try to store multiple majors in the same field of the student record, our NewStu table might appear as in Figure 5.4(a). This example violates the definition of first normal form, which follows.

> **Definition:** A relation is in **first normal form** (1NF) if, and only if, every attribute is single-valued for each tuple.

This means that each attribute in each row, or each "cell" of the table, contains only one value. An alternate way of describing first normal form is to say that the domains of the attributes of the relation are **atomic.** This means that no sets, lists, repeating fields, or groups are allowed in the domain. The values in the domain must be single values that cannot be broken down further. In the table in Figure 5.4(a), we see this rule violated in the records of students S1006 and S1010, who now have two values listed for major. This is the first such example we have seen, because all the relations we considered until now were in first normal form. In fact, most of relational theory is based on relations in at least first normal form, although non-first normal form relations appear in the literature. It is important to have first normal form so that the relational operators, as we have defined them, will work correctly. For example, if we perform the relational algebra operation SELECT NewStu WHERE major = 'Math' on the table in Figure 5.4(a), should the record of student S1006 be included? If we were to do a natural join with some other table using major as the joining column, would this record be paired with only those having both CSC and Math as major, or with those having either CSC or Math? What would happen on the join if another record had a double major listed as Math CSC? To avoid these ambiguities, we will insist that every relation be written in first normal form. If a relation is not already in 1NF, we can rewrite it, creating a new relation consisting of the key of the original relation, plus the multivalued attribute. Therefore, we would rewrite the NewStu table as in Figure 5.4(b) and create a new Majors table. We also note that the key of the new table is not stuId, since any student with more than one major appears at least twice. We need {stuId, major} to uniquely identify a record in that table.

Another method of normalizing to first normal form in the case where we know the maximum number of repeats an attribute can have is to add

FIGURE 5.4

First Normal Form Examples

FIGURE 5.4(a)

NewStu Table (assume students can have double majors)

StuId	lastName	major	credits	status	socSecNo
S1001	Smith	History	90	Senior	100429500
S1003	Jones	Math	95	Senior	010124567
S1006	Lee	CSC Math	15	Freshman	088520876
S1010	Burns	Art English	63	Junior	099320985
S1060	Jones	CSC	25	Freshman	064624738

FIGURE 5.4(b)

NewStu2 Table and Majors Table

NewStu2				
stuId	lastName	credits	status	socSecNo
S1001	Smith	90	Senior	100429500
S1003	Jones	95	Senior	010124567
S1006	Lee	15	Freshman	088520876
S1010	Burns	63	Junior	099320985
S1060	Jones	25	Freshman	064624738

Majors	
stuId	major
S1001	History
S1003	Math
S1006	CSC
S1006	Math
S1010	Art
S1010	English
S1060	CSC

stuId	lastName	major1	major2	credits	status	socSecNo
S1001	Smith	History		90	Senior	100429500
S1003	Jones	Math		95	Senior	010124567
S1006	Lee	CSC	Math	15	Freshman	088520876
S1010	Burns	Art	English	63	Junior	099320985
S1060	Jones	CSC		25	Freshman	064624738

FIGURE 5.4(c)

NewStu3 Table with Two Attributes for Major

stuId	lastName	major	credits	status	socSecNo
S1001	Smith	History	90	Senior	100429500
S1003	Jones	Math	95	Senior	010124567
S1006	Lee	CSC	15	Freshman	088520876
S1006	Lee	Math	15	Freshman	088520876
S1010	Burns	Art	63	Junior	099320985
S1010	Burns	English	63	Junior	099320985
S1060	Jones	CSC	25	Freshman	064624738

FIGURE 5.4(d)

NewStu Table Rewritten in 1NF, with {Stuld, major} as Primary Key

new columns for the attribute. For example, if we know students can have at most two majors, we could rewrite NewStu with two columns for major, major1 and major2, as shown in Figure 5.4(c). The disadvantage of this approach is that you must know the maximum number of repeats, and that queries become more complex. To form a relational algebra selection on the major, you would need to test both major1 and major2 columns.

An alternate method of making the original table 1NF is to make the multivalued attribute part of the key. Using this method, the new table would contain multiple rows for students with multiple majors, as shown in Figure 5.4(d). This solution can cause difficulties to arise when the designer attempts to put the relation into higher normal forms.

5.5.2   Full Functional Dependency and Second Normal Form

For the relation shown in both Figure 5.1 and Figure 5.5(a), we have the following functional dependencies in addition to the trivial ones:

```
{courseNo,stuId} → {lastName}
{courseNo,stuId} → {facId}
{courseNo,stuId} → {schedule}
{courseNo,stuId} → {room}
{courseNo,stuId} → {grade}
```

Since there is no other candidate key, we chose `{courseNo,stuId}` for the primary key. Again, ignoring trivial functional dependencies, we also have the functional dependencies,

```
courseNo → facId
courseNo → schedule
courseNo → room
stuId → lastName
```

So we find attributes that are functionally dependent on the combination `{courseNo,stuId}`, but also functionally dependent on a subset of that combination. We say that such attributes are not **fully** functionally dependent on the combination.

> **Definition:** In a relation R, attribute A of R is **fully functionally dependent** on an attribute or set of attributes X of R if A is functionally dependent on X but not functionally dependent on any proper subset of X.

In our example, although `lastName` is functionally dependent on `{courseNo,stuId}`, it is also functionally dependent on a proper subset of that combination, namely `stuId`. Similarly, `facId`, `schedule`, and `room` are functionally dependent on the proper subset `courseNo`. We note that `grade` is fully functionally dependent on the combination `{courseNo,stuId}`.

> **Definition:** A relation is in **second normal form** (2NF) if, and only if, it is in first normal form and all the non-key attributes are fully functionally dependent on the key.

Clearly, if a relation is 1NF and the key consists of a single attribute, the relation is automatically 2NF. We have to be concerned about 2NF only when the key is composite. From the definition, we see that the `Class` relation is not in second normal form since, for example, `lastName` is not fully functionally dependent on the key `{courseNo,stuId}`. Although

classNo	stuId	stuLastName	facId	schedule	room	grade
ART103A	S1001	Smith	F101	MWF9	H221	A
ART103A	S1010	Burns	F101	MWF9	H221	
ART103A	S1006	Lee	F101	MWF9	H221	B
CSC201A	S1003	Jones	F105	TUTHF10	M110	A
CSC201A	S1006	Lee	F105	TUTHF10	M110	C
HST205A	S1001	Smith	F202	MWF11	H221	

FIGURE 5.5

Second Normal Form Example

FIGURE 5.5(a)

The NewClass Table, Not in 2NF

Register

classNo	stuId	grade
ART103A	S1001	A
ART103A	S1010	
ART103A	S1006	B
CSC201A	S1003	A
CSC201A	S1006	C

Stu

stuId	stuLastName
S1001	Smith
S1010	Burns
S1006	Lee
S1003	Jones

Class2

classNo	facId	schedule	room
ART103A	F101	MWF9	H221
CSC201A	F105	TUTHF10	M110
HST205A	F202	MWF11	H221

FIGURE 5.5(b)

The Register, Stu, and Class2 Tables in 2NF

there are other non-full functional dependencies here, one is sufficient to show that the relation is not 2NF.

A 1NF relation that is not 2NF can be transformed into an equivalent set of 2NF relations. The transformation is done by performing **projections** on the original relation in such a way that it is possible to get back the original by taking the join of the projections. Projections of this type are called **lossless projections,** and will be discussed in more detail in Section 5.6.3. Essentially, to make a relation 2NF, you identify each of the non-full functional dependencies and form projections by removing the attributes that depend on each of the determinants identified as such. These determinants are placed in separate relations along with their dependent attributes. The original relation will still contain the composite key and any attributes that are fully functionally dependent on it. Even if there are no attributes fully functionally dependent on the key of the original relation, it is important to keep the relation (even with only the key attributes) in order to be able to reconstruct the original relation by a join. This "connecting relation" shows how the projections are related.

Applying this method to our example we first identify all the functional dependencies that concern us. For brevity, we will combine attributes that appear as dependents having the same determinant and we drop the set braces on both sides. It is important to note that when we use this less formal notation, attributes on the right-hand side of the arrow can be "broken up" and listed as separate FDs but attributes on the left-hand side must remain together, since it is the combination of them that is a determinant. The functional dependencies are,

```
courseNo → facId, schedule, room
stuId → lastName
courseNo,stuId → grade (and, of course, facId,schedule,room,lastName)
```

Using projection, we break up the NewClass relation into the following set of relations:

```
Register (courseNo, stuId, grade)
Class2 (courseNo, facId, schedule, room)
Stu (stuId, stuLastName)
```

The resulting relations are shown in Figure 5.5(b). Note that we could reconstruct the original relation by taking the natural join of these three relations. Even if there were no grade attribute, we would need the relation Register(courseNo,stuId) in order to show which students are enrolled in which courses. Without it, we could not join Class2 and Stu, which have no common attributes. Using these new relations, we have eliminated the update, insertion, and deletion anomalies discussed earlier. We can change the course schedule for ART103A by updating the schedule column in a single record in Class2. We can add new course information to Class2 without having any student registered in the course, and we can insert new student information by adding a record to Stu, without having to insert course information for that student. Similarly, we can drop a registration record from Register and still retain the information about the course in Class2 and about the student in Stu.

5.5.3   Transitive Dependency and Third Normal Form

Although second normal form relations are better than those in first normal form, they may still have update, insertion, and deletion anomalies. Consider the following relation:

```
NewStudent (stuId, lastName, major, credits, status)
```

Figure 5.6(a) shows an instance of this relation. Here, the only candidate key is `stuId`, and we will use that as the primary key. Every other attribute of the relation is functionally dependent on the key, so we have the following functional dependency, among others,

```
stuId → credits
```

However, since the number of credits determines `status`, as discussed in Section 5.3, we also have,

```
credits → status
```

Thus, `stuId` functionally determines `status` in two ways, directly and transitively, through the non-key attribute `status`. Using transitivity we have,

```
(stuId → credits) ∧ (credits → status) ⇒ (stuId → status)
```

> **Definition:** If A, B, and C are attributes of relation R, such that A → B, and B → C, then C is **transitively dependent** on A.

For third normal form, we want to eliminate certain transitive dependencies. Transitive dependencies cause insertion, deletion, and update anomalies. For example, in the `NewStudent` table in Figure 5.6(a), we cannot insert the information that any student with 30 credits has Soph status until we have such a student, because that would require inserting a record without a `stuId`, which is not permitted. If we delete the record of the only student with a certain number of credits, we lose the information about the status associated with those credits. If we have several records with the same `credits` value and we change the status associated with that value (for example, making 24 credits now have the status of Soph), we might accidentally fail to update all of the records, leaving the database in an inconsistent state. Because of these problems, it is desirable to remove transitive dependencies and create a set of relations that satisfy the following definition.

> **Definition:** A relation is in **third normal form** (3NF) if, whenever a non-trivial functional dependency X → A exists, then either X is a superkey or A is a member of some candidate key.

FIGURE 5.6

Third Normal Form Example

FIGURE 5.6(a)

NewStudent Table Not in 3NF

NewStudent

stuId	lastName	major	credits	status
S1001	Smith	History	90	Senior
S1003	Jones	Math	95	Senior
S1006	Lee	CSC	15	Freshman
S1010	Burns	Art	63	Junior
S1060	Jones	CSC	25	Freshman

FIGURE 5.6(b)

NewStu2 and Stats Tables in 3NF

NewStu2

stuId	lastName	major	credits
S1001	Smith	History	90
S1003	Jones	Math	95
S1006	Lee	CSC	15
S1010	Burns	Art	63
S1060	Jones	CSC	25

Stats

credits	status
15	Freshman
25	Freshman
63	Junior
90	Senior
95	Senior

Paraphrasing Kent (see references), you can remember the characteristics of third normal form by saying that each non-key attribute must depend on the key, the whole key, and nothing but the key.

In checking for third normal form, we look to see if any non-candidate key attribute (or group of attributes) is functionally dependent on another non-key attribute (or group). If such a functional dependency exists, we remove the functionally dependent attribute from the relation, placing it in a new relation with its determinant. The determinant can remain in the original relation. For our NewStudent example, since the undesirable dependency is credits → status, and status is not part of any candidate key, we form the set of relations:

```
NewStu2 (stuId, lastName, major, credits)
Stats (credits, status)
```

This decompostion is shown in Figure 5.6(b). In fact, we may decide not to store status in the database at all, and calculate the status for those views that need it. In that case, we simply drop the `Stats` relation. This example did not involve multiple candidate keys. If we had a second candidate key, `socialSecurityNumber`, in the original relation, we would have,

```
socialSecurityNumber → status
```

but this is permissible since `socialSecurityNumber` is a superkey for the relation, so we would have left the social security number in the `NewStu2` relation, along with the `stuId` and the other attributes there.

The definition of third normal form is the original one developed by Codd. It is sufficient for relations that have a single candidate key, but was found to be deficient when there are multiple candidate keys that are composite and overlapping. Therefore, an improved definition of third normal form, named for its developers, Boyce and Codd, was formulated to take care of all cases.

5.5.4 Boyce-Codd Normal Form

Boyce-Codd Normal Form is slightly stricter than 3NF.

> **Definition:** A relation is in Boyce/Codd Normal Form (BCNF) if, whenever a non-trivial functional dependency X → A exists, then X is a superkey.

Therefore, to check for BCNF, we simply identify all the determinants and verify that they are superkeys.

Returning to our earlier examples to check directly for BCNF, we see that for our `NewStudent` relation shown in Figure 5.6(a), the determinants are `stuId` and `credits`. Since `credits` is not a superkey, this relation is not BCNF. Performing the projections as we did in the previous section, the resulting relations are BCNF. For the relation `NewClass` shown in Figure 5.5(a), we found the determinants `courseNo`, which is not (by itself) a superkey, and `stuId`, also not a superkey. Therefore the `Class` relation is not BCNF. However, the relations resulting from the projections are BCNF. Consider an example in which we have 3NF but not BCNF.

```
NewFac (facName, dept, office, rank, dateHired)
```

For this example, shown in Figure 5.7(a) we will assume that, although faculty names are not unique, no two faculty members within a single department have the same name. We also assume each faculty member has only one office, identified in office. A department may have several faculty offices, and faculty members from the same department may share offices.

FIGURE 5.7

Boyce-Codd Normal Form Example

FIGURE 5.7(a)

NewFac Table in 3NF, but Not BCNF

Faculty

facName	dept	office	rank	dateHired
Adams	Art	A101	Professor	1975
Byrne	Math	M201	Assistant	2000
Davis	Art	A101	Associate	1992
Gordon	Math	M201	Professor	1982
Hughes	Math	M203	Associate	1990
Smith	CSC	C101	Professor	1980
Smith	History	H102	Associate	1990
Tanaka	CSC	C101	Instructor	2001
Vaughn	CSC	C105	Associate	1995

FIGURE 5.7(b)

Fac1 and Fac2 in BCNF

Fac1

office	dept
A101	Art
C101	CSC
C105	CSC
H102	History
M201	Math
M203	Math

Fac2

facName	office	rank	dateHired
Adams	A101	Professor	1975
Byrne	M201	Assistant	2000
Davis	A101	Associate	1992
Gordon	M201	Professor	1982
Hughes	M203	Associate	1990
Smith	C101	Professor	1980
Smith	H102	Associate	1990
Tanaka	C101	Instructor	2001
Vaughn	C105	Associate	1995

From these assumptions, we have the following FDs. Again, we are dropping set braces and combining dependents with the same determinant.

```
office → dept
facName,dept → office, rank, dateHired
facName,office → dept, rank, dateHired
```

We have overlapping candidate keys of {facName,dept} and {facName,office}. If we choose {facName,dept} as our primary key, we are left with a determinant, office, that is not a superkey. This violates BCNF. Note that the relation is 3NF since office is part of a candidate key. To reach BCNF, we can decompose the Faculty relation by projection into,

```
Fac1 (dept, office)
Fac2 (facName, office, rank, dateHired)
```

The key of the first relation is office, since a department may have several offices, but each office belongs to only one department. It is clearly BCNF, since the only determinant is the key. The key of the second is {facName,office}. It is also BCNF, since its only determinant is the key. Note, however, that our final scheme does not preserve the functional dependency facName,dept → office, rank, dateHired, since these attributes do not remain in the same relation.

(Note: If we had chosen facName,office as the primary key of the original NewFac relation, we would have office → dept. Since office is not a superkey, the relation would not be BCNF. In fact, it would not be 2NF, since dept would not be fully functionally dependent on the key, facName,office.)

Any relation that is not BCNF can be decomposed into BCNF relations by the method just illustrated. However, it might not always be desirable to transform the relation into BCNF. In particular, if there is functional dependency that is not preserved when we perform the decomposition, then it becomes difficult to enforce the functional dependency in the database since two or more tables would have to be joined to verify that it is enforced, and an important constraint is lost. In that case, it is preferable to settle for 3NF, which always allows us to preserve dependencies. Our NewFac relation provided an example in which we lost a functional dependency by normalizing to BCNF. In the resulting relations, the attributes facName and dept appeared in different relations, and we had no way to express the fact that they determined all other attributes.

5.5.5   Comprehensive Example of Functional Dependencies

To summarize the various normal forms defined by functional dependencies, consider the following relation that stores information about projects in a large business:

```
Work (projName, projMgr, empId, hours, empName, budget, startDate, salary,
empMgr, empDept, rating)
```

Figure 5.8(a) shows an instance of this relation.

We make the following assumptions:

1. Each project has a unique name.

2. Although project names are unique, names of employees and managers are not.

3. Each project has one manager, whose name is stored in `projMgr`.

4. Many employees can be assigned to work on each project, and an employee can be assigned to more than one project. The attribute `hours` tells the number of hours per week a particular employee is assigned to work on a particular project.

5. `budget` stores the amount budgeted for a project, and `startDate` gives the starting date for a project.

6. `salary` gives the annual salary of an employee.

7. `empMgr` gives the name of the employee's manager, who might not be the same as the project manager.

8. `empDept` gives the employee's department. Department names are unique. The employee's manager is the manager of the employee's department.

9. `rating` gives the employee's rating for a particular project. The project manager assigns the rating at the end of the employee's work on that project.

Using these assumptions, we find the following functional dependencies to begin with,

```
projName → projMgr, budget, startDate
empId → empName, salary, empMgr, empDept
projName, empId → hours, rating
```

Since we assumed people's names were not unique, `empMgr` does not functionally determine `empDept`. (Two different managers may have the same

FIGURE 5.8
Normalization Example

projName	projMgr	empId	hours	empName	budget	startDate	salary	empMgr	empDept	rating
Jupiter	Smith	E101	25	Jones	100000	01/15/04	60000	Levine	10	9
Jupiter	Smith	E105	40	Adams	100000	01/15/04	55000	Jones	12	
Jupiter	Smith	E110	10	Rivera	100000	01/15/04	43000	Levine	10	8
Maxima	Lee	E101	15	Jones	200000	03/01/04	60000	Levine	10	
Maxima	Lee	E110	30	Rivera	200000	03/01/04	43000	Levine	10	
Maxima	Lee	E120	15	Tanaka	200000	03/01/04	45000	Jones	15	

FIGURE 5.8(a)
The Work Table

Proj

projName	projMgr	budget	startDate
Jupiter	Smith	100000	01/15/04
Maxima	Lee	200000	03/01/04

Dept

empDept	empMgr
10	Levine
12	Jones
15	Jones

Emp1

EmpId	empName	salary	empDept
E101	Jones	60000	10
E105	Adams	55000	12
E110	Rivera	43000	10
E120	Tanaka	45000	15

Work1

projName	empId	hours	rating
Jupiter	Jones	25	9
Jupiter	Adams	40	
Jupiter	Rivera	10	8
Maxima	Jones	15	
Maxima	Rivera	30	
Maxima	Tanaka	15	

FIGURE 5.8(b)
The Normalized Tables Replacing Work

name and manage different departments, or possibly a manager may manage several departments—see Jones in Figure 5.8(a).) Similarly, `projMgr` does not determine `projName`. However, since department names are unique and each department has only one manager, we need to add,

```
empDept → empMgr
```

You may ask whether `projMgr` → `budget`. Although it may be the case that the manager determines the budget in the English sense of the word, meaning that the manager comes up with the figures for the budget, you should recall that functional dependency does not mean to cause or to figure out. Similarly, although the project manager assigns a rating to the employee, there is no functional dependency between `projmgr` and `rating`. (If there were, it would mean that each manager always gives the same ratings to those he or she evaluates. For example, it would mean that if the manager's name is Levine the employee always gets a rating of 9.)

Since we see that every attribute is functionally dependent on the combination `projName, empId`, we will choose that combination as our primary key, and see what normal form we have. We begin by checking to see whether it is already in BCNF.

BCNF: We look to see if there is a determinant that is not a superkey. Any one of `empId`, `empDept`, or `projName` is sufficient to show that the `Work` relation is not BCNF. Since we know it is not BCNF, let us begin the normalization process by checking the lower normal forms, normalizing the relation(s) as we go along.

First Normal Form: With our composite key, each cell would be single valued, so `Work` is in 1NF.

Second Normal Form: We found partial (non-full) dependencies.

```
projName → projMgr, budget, startDate
empId → empName, salary, empMgr, empDept
```

We can take care of these, transforming the relation into an equivalent set of 2NF relations by projection, resulting in,

```
Proj (projName, projMgr, budget, startDate)
Emp (empId, empName, salary, empMgr, empDept)
Work1 (projName, empId, hours, rating)
```

Third Normal Form: Using the set of projections, {`Proj`, `Emp`, `Work1`}, we test each relation to see if we have 3NF. Examining `Proj`, we see that no non-key attribute functionally determines another non-key attribute, so `Proj` is 3NF. In `Emp`, we have a transitive dependency, since `empdept` → `empmgr`, as previously explained. Since `empdept` is not a superkey, nor is `empmgr` part of a candidate key, this violates 3NF. Therefore we need to rewrite `Emp` as,

```
Emp1 (empId, empName, salary, empDept)
Dept (empDept, empMgr)
```

`Work1` has no transitive dependency involving hours or rating, so that relation is already 3NF. Our new set of 3NF relations is therefore,

```
Proj (projName, projMgr, budget, startDate)
Emp1 (empId, empName, salary, empDept)
Dept (empDept, empMgr)
Work1 (projName, empId, hours, rating)
```

BoyceCodd Normal Form revisited: Our new 3NF set of relations is also BCNF, since, in each relation, the only determinant is the primary key.

Figure 5.8(b) shows the new tables that replace the original `Work` table. Note that they can be joined to produce the original table exactly.

5.6   Properties of Relational Decompositions

Although normalization can be carried out using the heuristic approach based on primary keys and demonstrated in the previous sections, a more formal approach to relational database design is based strictly on functional dependencies and other types of constraints. This approach uses formal normalization algorithms to create relation schemas. To begin, all the attributes in the database are placed in a single large relation called the **universal relation.** Using functional dependencies and other constraints, the universal relation is decomposed into smaller relational schemas until the process reaches a point where no further decomposition is preferred. We would like the results of the decomposition process to have some important qualities, if possible. It is desirable to have each relation schema be in BCNF or at least 3NF. Other important properties include attribute preservation, dependency preservation, and lossless joins.

5.6.1   Attribute Preservation

When the universal relation is constructed it contains, by definition, every attribute in the database. In the process of decomposing the universal relation into smaller relations and moving attributes into them, we want to ensure that every attribute appears in at least one of the relations, so no data item is lost. As we saw in our examples, the database schema usually contains some repetition of attributes in order to represent relationships among the tables. However, the attributes have to placed in relations in a manner that preserves all of the information, not just all of the attributes.

5.6.2   Dependency Preservation

A functional dependency represents a constraint that should be enforced in the database. Whenever an update is performed, the DBMS should check that the constraint is not violated. It is much easier to check constraints within one table than to check one involving multiple tables, which would require doing a join first. To avoid having to do such joins, we would like to be sure that in a decomposition the functional dependencies involve attributes that are all in the same table, if possible. Given a decomposition of a relation R, with a set of functional dependencies on it, into a set of individual relations $\{R_1, R_2, \ldots, R_n\}$, for each functional dependency $X \rightarrow Y$ it is desirable for all the attributes in $X \cup Y$ to appear in the same relation, R_i. This property is called **dependency preservation.** It is always possible to find a dependency preserving decomposition that is 3NF, but it is not always possible to find one that is BCNF, as illustrated by the example shown in Figure 5.7 and discussed in Section 5.5.4.

5.6.3   Lossless Decomposition

In splitting relations by means of projection in our earlier examples, we were very explicit about the method of decomposition to use. In particular, we were careful to use projections that could be undone by joining the resulting tables, so that the original table would result. By the term original table we do not mean merely the structure of the table, that is, the column names, but the actual tuples as well. Such a decomposition is called a nonloss or **lossless decomposition,** because it preserves all the information in the original relation. Although we have used the word decomposition, we have not written a formal definition, and we do so now.

> **Definition:** A **decomposition** of a relation R is a set of relations $\{R_1, R_2, \ldots, R_n\}$ such that each R_i is a subset of R and the union of all of the R_i is R.

Now we are ready for the definition of lossless decomposition.

> **Definition:** A decomposition $\{R_1, R_2, \ldots, R_n\}$ of a relation R is called a **lossless decomposition** for R if the natural join of $R_1, R_2, \ldots, R_n$ produces exactly the relation R.

Not all decompositions are lossless, because there are projections whose join does not give us back the original relation. As an example of a lossy projection, consider the relation `EmpRoleProj(`_`empName, role,`_ _`projName`_`)` shown in Figure 5.9(a). The table shows which employees play which roles for which projects. We can decompose the table by projection into the two tables, `Table 1` and `Table 2` shown in Figure 5.9(b). However, when we join those two tables, in Figure 5.9(c), we get an extra tuple that did not appear in the original table. This is a **spurious** (false) tuple, one created by the projection and join processes. Since, without the original table, we would have no way of identifying which tuples were genuine and which were spurious, we would actually lose information (even though we have more tuples) if we substituted the projections for the original relation.

We can guarantee lossless decomposition by making sure that, for each pair of relations that will be joined, the set of common attributes is a superkey of one of the relations. We can do this by placing functionally dependent attributes in a relation with their determinants and keeping the determinants themselves in the original relation.

More formally, for binary decompositions, if R is decomposed into two relations {R1,R2} then the join is lossless if, and only if, either of the following holds in the set of FDs for R, or is implied by the FDs in R:

    R1 ∩ R2 → R1 − R2

or,

    R1 ∩ R2 → R2 − R1

In the example shown in Figure 5.9, `role` was not a determinant for either `projName` or `empName`, so the intersection of the two projections, `role`, did not functionally determine either projection. We saw many examples of lossless projection when we normalized relations.

For a decomposition involving more than two relations, the previous test cannot be used, so we present an algorithm for testing the general case.

FIGURE 5.9
Example of Lossy Projection

FIGURE 5.9(a)
Original Table EmpRoleProj

EmpRoleProj

empName	role	projName
Smith	designer	Nile
Smith	programmer	Amazon
Smith	designer	Amazon
Jones	designer	Amazon

FIGURE 5.9(b)
Projections of EmpRoleProj

Table 1

empName	role
Smith	designer
Smith	programmer
Jones	designer

Table 2

role	projName
designer	Nile
programmer	Amazon
designer	Amazon

FIGURE 5.9(c)
Join of Table 1 and Table 2

empName	role	projName	
Smith	designer	Nile	
Smith	designer	Amazon	
Smith	programmer	Amazon	
Jones	designer	Nile	←spurious tuple
Jones	designer	Amazon	

Algorithm to Test for Lossless Join

Given a relation R(A1,A2, . . . An), a set of functional dependencies, F, and a decomposition of R into relations R1,R2, . . . Rm, to determine whether the decomposition has a lossless join

1. Construct an *m* by *n* table, *S*, with a column for each of the *n* attributes in *R* and a row for each of the *m* relations in the decomposition.

2. For each cell *S(i,j)* of *S*,
     if the attribute for the column, *Aj*, is in the relation for the row, *Ri*,
       then place the symbol *a(j)* in the cell
       else place the symbol *b(i,j)* there

3. Repeat the following process until no more changes can be made to S:

   for each FD $X \rightarrow Y$ in F

       for all rows in S that have the same symbols in the columns corresponding to the attributes of X, make the symbols for the columns that represent attributes of Y equal by the following rule:

           if any row has an a value, $a(j)$, then set the value of that column in all the other rows equal to $a(j)$

           if no row has an a value, then pick any one of the b values, say $b(i,j)$, and set all the other rows equal to $b(i,j)$

4. if, after all possible changes have been made to S, a row is made up entirely of a symbols, $a(1), a(2), \ldots, a(n)$, then the join is lossless. If there is no such row, the join is lossy.

Example:

Consider the relation $R(A,B,C,D,E)$ having decomposition consisting of $R1(A,C)$, $R2(A,B,D)$, and $R3(D,E)$ with FDs $A \rightarrow C$, $AB \rightarrow D$, and $D \rightarrow E$. Figure 5.10 illustrates the algorithm. Referring to Figure 5.10(a), we construct one row for each relation in the decomposition and one column for each of the five attributes of R. For each row, we place the value a with the column subscript in any column whose heading represents an attribute in that relation, and the value b with the usual row and column subscript in the column for any attribute not in that relation. For example, in the first row, for relation $R1(A,C)$, we place $a(1)$ in the first column, for A, and $a(3)$ in the third column, for C. Since B does not appear in $R1$, we place $b(1,2)$ in its column. Similarly, we place $b(1,4)$ in the D column and $b(1,5)$ in the E column, since these attributes do not appear in $R1$. Now we consider the FD $A \rightarrow C$, and look for rows that agree on the value of the left-hand side, A. We find that rows 1 and 2 agree on the value $a(1)$. Therefore, we can set the C values equal. We find that row 1 has an a value, $a(3)$, in the C column, so we set the C column value of row 2 equal to $a(3)$ in Figure 5.10(b). Considering the second FD, $AB \rightarrow D$, we cannot find any two rows that agree on both their A and B values, so we are unable to make any changes. Now considering the FD $D \rightarrow E$, we find that row 2 and row 3 agree on their D values, $a(4)$, so we can set their E values equal. Since row 3 has an E value of $a(5)$, we change the E value of row 2 to $a(5)$ as well in Figure 5.10(b). Now we find that the second row of Figure 5.10(b) has all a values, and we conclude that the projection has the lossless join property.

FIGURE 5.10

Testing for Lossless Join

R(A,B,C,D,E)
Decomposition: R1(A, C), R2(A, B, D), R3(D, E)
FDs: $A \rightarrow C$, $AB \rightarrow D$, $D \rightarrow E$

FIGURE 5.10(a)

Initial Placement of Values

	A	B	C	D	E
R1(A, C)	a(1)	b(1,2)	a(3)	b(1,4)	b(1,5)
R2(A, B, D)	a(1)	a(2)	b(2,3)	a(4)	b(2,5)
R3(D, E)	b(3,1)	b(3,2)	b(3,3)	a(4)	a(5)

FIGURE 5.10(b)

Table after Considering All FDs

	A	B	C	D	E
R1(A, C)	a(1)	b(1,2)	a(3)	b(1,4)	b(1,5)
R2(A, B, D)	a(1)	a(2)	a(3)	a(4)	a(5)
R3(D, E)	b(3,1)	b(3,2)	b(3,3)	a(4)	a(5)

The test for the lossless join property for the general case is much more complex than that for the binary decomposition case. However, if we limit our projections to successive binary projections, each of which is lossless, the final result will also be lossless. If we have a decomposition D consisting of the set $\{R_1, R_2\}$ which has the lossless join property (easily confirmed by the test for the binary case), and R_2 in turn has a lossless projection $\{T_1, T_2\}$ (also easily tested since it is binary), then the decomposition D_2 consisting of $\{R_1, T_1, T_2\}$ is lossless.

It is always possible to find a BCNF decomposition that is lossless. We will present such an algorithm is Section 5.7.8.

5.7   Formal Relational Design

5.7.1   Inference Rules: Armstrong's Axioms

To begin the more formal approach to normalization, we need a set of axioms that provide rules for working with functional dependencies. Rules of inference for functional dependencies, called **inference axioms** or **Armstrong's Axioms,** after their developer, can be used to find all the FDs logically implied by a set of FDs. These rules are **sound,** meaning they are an immediate consequence of the definition of functional dependency and that any functional dependency that can be derived from a given set of FDs using them is true. They are also **complete,** meaning they can be used to derive every valid inference about dependencies, so that if a particular FD cannot be derived from a given set of FDs using these rules, then the given set of FDs does not imply that particular FD.

Let A, B, C, and D be subsets of attributes of a relation R. The following axioms hold (note that AC means the union of set A and set C here):

- **Reflexivity.** If B is a subset of A, then $A \to B$. This also implies that $A \to A$ always holds. Functional dependencies of this type are called **trivial functional dependencies.**

- **Augmentation.** If $A \to B$, then $AC \to BC$.

- **Transitivity.** If $A \to B$ and $B \to C$, then $A \to C$.

The following rules can be derived from the previous three:

- **Additivity** or Union. If $A \to B$ and $A \to C$, then $A \to BC$

- **Projectivity** or Decomposition. If $A \to BC$, then $A \to B$ and $A \to C$

- **Pseudotransitivity.** If $A \to B$ and $CB \to D$, then $AC \to D$.

These rules can be used to develop a formal theory of functional dependencies, but we will concentrate instead on their practical applications.

5.7.2 Closure of a Set of Functional Dependencies

For normalization, it is necessary to identify superkeys, candidate keys, and other determinants, which we can do if we have identified all the functional dependencies in a relation. We also need to be able to reason about all the functional dependencies implied by a given set of functional dependencies. Doing so requires the notion of the closure of a set of FDs. If F is a set of functional dependencies for a relation R, then the set of all functional dependencies that can be derived from F, F^+, is called the **closure of F.** Armstrong's axioms are sufficient to compute all of F^+; that is, if we were to apply these rules repeatedly, we would find all the functional dependencies in F^+. However, the task would obviously be very complex and take a lot of time. It would simplify matters if we could find a smaller set of FDs that we could use instead of all of F^+.

5.7.3   Closure of an Attribute

Given a set of functional dependencies F of a relation R, we are often interested in finding all the attributes in R that are functionally dependent on a certain attribute or set of attributes, A, in R. We call this set of attributes the **closure of A** or A^+. Clearly, if A^+ is all of R, then A is a superkey for R. We could find A^+ by computing all of F^+ and then choosing only those functional dependencies where A is the determinant, but there is a shortcut. The following algorithm can be used to find A^+, given a set F of functional dependencies:

Closure Algorithm for Attribute Set A

```
result ← A;
while (result changes) do
    for each functional dependency B → C in F
        if B is contained in result then result ← result ∪ C;
end;
A+ ← result;
```

For example, let R be a relation with attributes W,X,Y,Z and functional dependencies,

$W \to Z$
$\{Y,Z\} \to X$
$\{W,Z\} \to Y$

Let us compute $\{W \cup Z\}^+$. We assign $\{W \cup Z\}$ to `result` and enter the while for the first time. We look for an FD whose determinant is contained in `result`, which has only $W \cup Z$ at the moment. The FD $\{W,Z\} \to Y$, satisfies this requirement, so we assign $\{W \cup Z\} \cup Y$ to `result`. Since we had a change in `result`, we enter the while again. Now we look for an FD where W, Z, Y or any combination of these three is a determinant. We can use $\{Y,Z\} \to X$, and now we assign $\{\{W \cup Z\} \cup Y)\} \cup X$ to `result`. Since we have found that every attribute of R is in $\{W \cup Z\}+$, $W \cup Z$ is a superkey.

To find W^+ we assign W to `result` and enter the while for the first time. The FD $W \to Z$ has W as a determinant, so we assign $W \cup Z$ to `result`. Since we had a change to `result`, we enter the while again. This time we use $\{W,Z\} \to Y$, so we assign $\{W \cup Z\} \cup Y$ to `result`. Now we look for an FD where any combination of attributes W,Z,Y appears as the determinant. This time we can use $\{Y,Z\} \to X$, and now we assign $\{\{W \cup Z\} \cup Y\} \cup X$ to `result`. Since we have found that every attribute of R is in W^+, W is a superkey for this relation. Because it has no proper subset which is also a superkey, W is a candidate key as well. Note that we now know that $W \cup Z$ is not a candidate key.

It is easy to verify that {Y∪Z} is not a superkey. We start with `result` ← {Y∪Z}. Using {Y,Z} → X, `result` becomes {Y∪Z] ∪X. Now we look for an FD where some combination of Y,Z,X is the determinant. Since there is none, we cannot add any new attributes to `result`. This means that {Y∪Z}+ is only {{Y∪Z}∪X}, so W is not functionally dependent on {Y∪Z}, which means {Y∪Z} is not a superkey.

The closure algorithm also allows us to determine whether a particular functional dependency exists in R. For attribute sets A and B, if we wish to determine whether A → B, we can calculate A+, and see if it includes B.

5.7.4 Identifying Redundant Functional Dependencies

Given a set of functional dependencies, we would like to be able to replace them by a smaller but equivalent set of FDs. One way to do so is to determine whether any of them is **redundant,** meaning that it can be derived from the others. To do so, we can use the following algorithm:

Algorithm for Determining Redundancy in a Set of of FDs

    1.   Choose a candidate FD, say X → Y, and remove it from the set of FDs.

    2.   result ← X;
            while (result changes and Y is not contained in result) do
                for each FD, A → B, remaining in the reduced set of FDs
                    if A is a subset of result, then result ← result ∪ B
            end

    3.   if Y is a subset of result, then the FD X → Y is redundant.

We could then remove the FD X → Y from the set, since it can be derived from the other FDs. By testing every FD in the set in turn and removing any that can be derived from the others, then repeating this process with the remaining FDs we can find a nonredundant set of FDs equivalent to the original set.

For example, suppose we have the following set of FDs:

    (1) W → Z
    (2) W → Y
    (3) {Y,Z} → X
    (4) {W,Z} → Y

We begin by testing (1), W → Z. We assign W to `result`. Now we search for an FD (other than (1)) in which W is the determinant. We find one in (2), W → Y. Now we assign W ∪ Y to `result`. Searching for an FD having a determinant which is contained in W ∪ Y, we find none. Therefore we are unable to show that Z is contained in `result`, and we conclude that (1) is not redundant.

Next we test (2), W → Y. We assign W to `result`. Searching for an FD other than (2) whose determinant is W, we find one in (1), so we can assign W∪Z to `result`. Now we seek an FD whose determinant is contained in W∪Z. We find (4), {W,Z} → Y, and now we can assign {W∪Z}∪Y to `result`. Since Y is now contained in `result`, we can exit the while and conclude that (2) is redundant. We now eliminate (2) from the set of FDs.

Testing (3), we assign Y∪Z to `result`. We look for an FD other than (3) or (2) (which we eliminated in the previous step) whose determinant is contained in Y∪Z. Finding none, we conclude that (3) is not redundant.

Testing (4), we assign W∪Z to `result`. In (1), we see that the determinant, W, is contained in `result`, so we could add the right side of (1), Z, to `result`, but it is already there. There is no other FD whose determinant is contained in W∪Z, except for (2), which we have eliminated. Therefore we conclude that (4) is not redundant in the reduced set of FDs since we are unable to get Y in `result`. Our final set of FDs is,

(1) W → Z
(3) {Y,Z} → X
(4) {W,Z} → Y

5.7.5   Covers and Equivalent Sets of FDs

If F and G are two sets of FDs for some relation R, then F is a **cover** for G if every FD in G is also in F$^+$. This means that every FD in G can be derived from the FDs in F, or that G$^+$ is a subset of F$^+$. To prove that F is a cover for G, we examine each FD X → Y in G. We then calculate X$^+$ in F and demonstrate that X$^+$ contains the attributes of Y. If this holds true for all the FDs in G, then F is a cover for G. For a relation R, two sets of FDs, F and G, are said to be **equivalent** if and only if F is a cover for G and G is also a cover for F, (i.e., F$^+$ = G$^+$). To prove equivalence, we prove F and G are covers for each other.

If G is a set of FDs in R, and G is large, we would like to be able to find a smaller set of FDs such that all the FDs in G are also implied by that smaller set, that is, the smaller set is a cover for G.

5.7.6   Minimal Set of Functional Dependencies

A set of FDs, F, is said to be **minimal** if it satisfies these conditions

- The right side of every FD in F has a single attribute. This form is called standard or **canonical** form for FDs.

- No attribute on the left side of any FD in F is **extraneous.** This means that if $X \rightarrow Y$ is an FD in F then there is no proper subset S of X such that $S \rightarrow Y$ can be used in place of $X \rightarrow Y$ and the resulting set is equivalent to F.

- F has no redundant FDs.

5.7.7   Finding a Minimal Cover for a Set of FDs

A cover, F, for G, is said to be a **minimal cover** (also called a **nonredundant** cover) if F is a cover for G but no proper subset of F is a cover for G. A set of FDs may have several minimal covers, but we can always find one of them. To do so, we begin with the set of FDs, G. We express each FD in G in canonical form, that is, with one attribute on the right side. Then we examine the left side of each FD, checking each attribute, A, on the left side to see if deleting it does not effect G^+. If the deletion of A has no effect, we delete it from the left side. This eliminates extraneous attributes from all the FDs. Next we examine each remaining FD and check to see if it is redundant, that is, if deleting it has no effect on G^+. If it is redundant, we eliminate it. The final set of FDs, which we will call F, is irreducible and equivalent to the original set. The algorithm follows.

Algorithm for Finding a Minimal Cover, F, for a Given Set of FDs, G

1. Set $F \leftarrow G$;
2. For each FD in F that is not in canonical form, i.e. of the form $X \rightarrow \{Y1, Y2, . . . Yn\}$, replace it by the n FDs $X \rightarrow Y1$, $X \rightarrow Y2$, . . ., $X \rightarrow Yn$;
3. Eliminate extraneous attributes:
   For each FD $X \rightarrow Y$ in F
   for each attribute A that is an element of X
   if $((F-\{X \rightarrow Y\}) \cup \{(X - \{A\}) \rightarrow Y\}$ is equivalent to F
   then replace $X \rightarrow Y$ with $\{X - \{A\}\} \rightarrow Y$ in F;
4. Eliminate redundant FDs:
   For each remaining FD $X \rightarrow Y$ in F
   If $(F-\{X \rightarrow Y\})$ is equivalent to F
   Then remove $X \rightarrow Y$ from F

5.7.8 Decomposition Algorithm for Boyce-Codd Normal Form with Lossless Join

It is always possible to find a decomposition, D, that is Boyce-Codd Normal Form and that has the lossless join property. The process involves finding each violation of BCNF and removing it by decomposing the relation containing it into two relations. The process is repeated until all such violations are removed. The algorithm is,

Given a Universal Relation R and a Set of Functional Dependencies on the Attributes of R:

1. $D \leftarrow R$;

2. while there is some relation schema S in D that is not already BCNF
   {
       a. Find a functional dependency $X \rightarrow Y$ in S that violates BCNF
       b. Replace S by two relation schemas (S-Y) and (X,Y)
   }

5.7.9 Synthesis Algorithm for Third Normal Form Decomposition

We can always find a third normal form decomposition that is lossless and that preserves dependencies. The algorithm for the third normal form decomposition is,

Given a Universal Relation R and a Set of Functional Dependencies, G, on R,

1. Find a minimal cover F for G, using the algorithm given in Section 5.7.7.
2. Examine the left-hand sides of all the functional dependencies. If there is more than one functional dependency in F with the same left-hand side; for example, there is some attribute or set of attributes X, and one or more attributes Ai such that

   $X \rightarrow A1, X \rightarrow A2, . . ., X \rightarrow An$;

   then combine X with the attributes on the right-hand side to form a relation having the schema R1($\underline{X}$, A1, A2, . . . An) in which X is the key
   Repeat this for all such determinants in F.
3. if none of the resulting relation schemas contains a key for the universal relation, R, then create a new relation containing attributes that form a key for R.

5.8   Multivalued Dependencies and Fourth Normal Form

Although Boyce-Codd Normal Form is sufficient to remove any anomalies due to functional dependencies, further research by Fagin led to the identification of another type of dependency that can cause similar design problems. These are multivalued dependencies. To illustrate the concept of multivalued dependencies, consider the following relation:

```
JointAppoint(facId, dept, committee)
```

Here we will assume that a faculty member can belong to more than one department. For example, a professor can be hired jointly by the CSC and Math departments. A faculty member can belong to several college-wide committees, each identified by the committee name. There is no relationship between department and committee. Figure 5.11(a) shows an unnormalized version of this relation. In order to make the relation 1NF, we must rewrite it so that each cell has only one value. Although the preferred method is to create a separate relation for each multivalued attribute, another method of creating 1NF is by "flattening" the table as shown in Figure 5.11(b). Notice that we are forced to write all the combinations of `dept` values with `committee` values for each faculty member, or else it would appear that there is some relationship between `dept` and `committee`. For example, without the second row, it would appear that F101 is on the Budget committee only as a member of the CSC department, but not as a member of the Math department. Also note that the key of the relation is now {`facId, dept, committee`}. The resulting relation is BCNF, since the only determinant is the key. Although we have taken care of all functional dependencies, there are still update, insertion, and deletion anomalies. If we want to update a committee that F101 belongs to from Budget to Advancement, we need to make two changes. If we want to insert the record of a faculty member who is not on any committee we are unable to do so, since `committee` is part of the key, so null values are not permitted in that column. This is an insertion anomaly. Similarly, if F221 drops membership on the Library committee, we lose all the rest of the information stored for him or her, since we are not permitted to have a null value for an attribute of the key. Earlier, we found similar problems were caused by functional dependencies, but there are none in this

FIGURE 5.11

Fourth Normal Form Example

FIGURE 5.11(a)

JointAppoint Table Not in 1NF

JointAppoint

facId	dept	committee
F101	CSC Math	Budget Curriculum
F221	Biology	Library
F330	English	Budget Admissions

FIGURE 5.11(b)

JointAppoint1 Table in 1NF Showing Multivalued Dependencies

JointAppoint1

facId	dept	committee
F101	CSC	Budget
F101	Math	Budget
F101	CSC	Curriculum
F101	Math	Curriculum
F221	Biology	Library
F330	English	Budget
F330	English	Admissions

FIGURE 5.11(c)

Appoint1 and Appoint2 Tables in 4NF

Appoint1

facId	dept
F101	CSC
F101	Math
F221	Biology
F330	English

Appoint2

facId	Committee
F101	Budget
F101	Curriculum
F221	Library
F330	Admissions
F330	Budget

example, so we need to identify a new cause. Although a faculty member is not associated with only one department, he or she is certainly associated with a particular set of departments. Similarly, a faculty member is associated with a specific set of committees at any given time. The set of departments for a particular `facId` is independent of the set of committees for that faculty member. This independence is the cause of the problems. To see how we can correct them, we need another definition.

> **Definition:** Let R be a relation having attributes or sets of attributes A, B, and C. There is a **multivalued dependency** of attribute B on attribute A if and only if the set of B values associated with a given A value is independent of the C values.

We write this as A —>> B and read it as A multi-determines B. If R has at least three attributes, A, B, and C, then in R(A,B,C), if A —>> B, then A—>> C as well.

Unlike rules for functional dependencies, which made certain tuples illegal in relations, multivalued dependencies make certain tuples essential in a relation. In the normalized `JointAppoint1` table shown in Figure 5.11(b), we were forced to write certain tuples because we had included others. For example, when we wrote the combination of F101 with both the CSC and Math department values, we had to write two tuples for each of the committee values, Budget and Curriculum, and place each department value in a tuple with each committee value. An exact definition of multivalued dependency describes the tuples that must appear.

Alternate Definition of Multivalued Dependency

More generally, if R is a relation with multivalued dependency,

   A —>> B

then in any table for R, if two tuples, t1 and t2, have the same A value, then there must exist two other tuples t3 and t4 obeying the following rules:

1. t3 and t4 have the same A value as t1 and t2
2. t3 has the same B value as t1
3. t4 has the same B value as t2
4. if R - B represents the attributes of R that are not in B, then the t2 and t3 have the same values for R - B and
5. t1 and t4 have the same values for R - B

The dependency A —>> B is called a **trivial multivalued dependency** if B is a subset of A or A ∪ B is all of R. Now we are ready to consider fourth normal form.

> **Definition:** A relation is in **fourth normal form** (4NF) if, and only if, it is in BoyceCodd normal form and there are no nontrivial multivalued dependencies.

Our `JointAppoint1` relation shown in Figure 5.11(b) is not in fourth normal form because of the two nontrivial multivalued dependencies,

```
facId —>> dept
facId —>> committee
```

When a relation is BCNF but not 4NF, we can transform it into an equivalent set of 4NF relations by projection. We form two separate relations, placing in each the attribute that multi-determines the others, along with one of the multidetermined attributes.

For our `JointAppoint1` relation, we form the two projections,

```
Appoint1 (facId, dept)
Appoint2 (facId, committee)
```

Both of these relations are in 4NF. They are shown in Figure 5.11(c).

5.9   Lossless Decomposition and Fifth Normal Form

As discussed in Section 5.6.3, not all decompositions are lossless, because there are projections whose join does not give us back the original relation. We used as an example of a lossy projection the relation `EmpRoleProj(empName, role, projName)` shown again in Figure 5.12(a). The table shows which employees play which roles for which projects. We can decompose the table by projection into the two tables, `Table 1` and `Table 2`, shown in Figure 5.12(b). (For the moment, we ignore `Table 3`.) However, when we join those two tables, in Figure 5.12(c), we get an extra spurious tuple that did not appear in the original table, thereby losing information. The original table can be recreated only by joining the result with `Table 3`, as shown in Figure 5.12(d). The recreation depends on this join—that is, the final join is needed to get back the table. A **join dependency** exists when for a relation R with subsets of its attributes A, B, . . ., Z, R is equal to the join of its projections on A, B, . . ., Z.

> **Definition:** A relation is in **fifth normal form** if every join dependency is implied by the candidate keys.

FIGURE 5.12

Example of Join Dependency

EmpRoleProj		
empName	role	projName
Smith	designer	Nile
Smith	programmer	Amazon
Smith	designer	Amazon
Jones	designer	Amazon

FIGURE 5.12(a)

Original Table EmpRoleProj

Table 1	
empName	role
Smith	designer
Smith	programmer
Jones	designer

Table 2	
role	proName
designer	Nile
programmer	Amazon
designer	Amazon

Table 3	
empName	projName
Smith	Nile
Smith	Amazon
Jones	Amazon

FIGURE 5.12(b)

Projections of EmpRoleProj

empName	role	projName	
Smith	designer	Nile	
Smith	designer	Amazon	
Smith	programmer	Amazon	
Jones	designer	Nile	←spurious tuple
Jones	designer	Amazon	

FIGURE 5.12(c)

First Join Using Table 1 and Table 2

empName	role	projName
Smith	designer	Nile
Smith	designer	Amazon
Smith	programmer	Amazon
Jones	designer	Amazon

FIGURE 5.12(d)

Join of First Join with Table 3 over EmpName, projName

Essentially, this means that the only valid decompositions are those involving candidate keys. Join dependencies are related to multivalued dependencies, but they can be very difficult to identify because they are subtle. If a design consists of relations that are all 5NF, they are in their simplest useful form so there is nothing to be gained by decomposing them further, since that would result in a loss of information. Unfortunately, there is no simple test for 5NF. Join dependencies are believed to be relatively rare, so designers often stop the normalization process at 4NF, BCNF, or 3NF (to preserve functional dependencies).

5.10   Domain-Key Normal Form

The final normal form to be defined by Fagin involves the concepts of domain, key, and constraint. Fagin demonstrated that a relation in this form cannot have update, insertion, or deletion anomalies. Therefore, this form represents the ultimate normal form with respect to these defects.

> **Definition:** A relation is in **Domain-Key Normal Form** (DKNF) is every constraint is a logical consequence of domain constraints or key constraints.

The definition uses the terms domain, key, and constraint. As usual, the domain of an attribute is the set of allowable values for that attribute. Fagin uses the word key to mean what we have described as a superkey, a unique identifer for each entity. Constraint is a general term meaning a rule or restriction that can be verified by examining static states of the database. For a constraint to exist, then, we must be able to state it as a logical predicate and we must be able to determine whether that predicate is true or false by examining instances of the relation. Although functional dependencies, multivalued dependencies, and join dependencies are constraints, there are other types, called general constraints, as well. We may have rules about relationships between attributes of a relation (intrarelation constraints) that are not expressed as dependencies, or there may be rules about relationships between relations (interrelation constraints). For example, consider the relation Student (`stuId`, . . ., `credits`). Suppose we have a rule that the `stuId` has a prefix that changes as the student progresses; for example, all freshman have a 1, all sophomores a 2, etc. at the beginning of their IDs. This could be expressed as the general constraint,

- If the first digit of `stuId` is 1, then `credits` must be between 0 and 30.

- If the first digit of `stuId` is 2, . . .

- . . .

A familiar example of an interrelation constraint is a referential integrity constraint. Consider `Student(stuId, lastName,. . .)` and `Enroll(stuId,courseNo, grade)`. An interrelation constraint here is,

- For each tuple in Enroll there must be a tuple in `Student` with the same `stuId`.

For a relation to be DKNF, intra-relation constraints must be expressible as domain constraints or key constraints. We could express our constraint on `Student` by splitting `Student` into four different relations. For example, for freshman, we might have,

`Stu1(stuId, . . ., credits)` with the domain constraints
- `stuId` must begin with a 1
- `credits` must be between 0 and 30.

We would then have `STU2` with similar domain constraints for sophomores, `STU3` for juniors, and `STU4` for seniors. For our inter-relation constraint, we would have to restrict the domain of `stuId` in `Student` to the values actually represented in `Enroll`. However, Fagin's definition does not extend to inter-relation constraints, since his objective was to define a form that would allow general constraints to be checked within a relation by checking only that relation's domain and key constraints. Since an inter-relation constraint such as a referential integrity constraint involves two relations, it is not considered in DKNF.

Unfortunately, although the concept of Domain-Key Normal Form is simple, there is no proven method of converting a design to this form.

5.11 The Normalization Process

As we stated at the beginning of this chapter, the objective of normalization is to find a stable set of relations that are a faithful model of the enterprise. We found that normalization eliminated some problems of data representation and resulted in a good schema for the database. There are two different processes that could be used to develop the set of normalized relations, called analysis and synthesis. Most designers choose instead to start with an Entity-Relationship diagram and work from there.

5.11.1 Analysis

The analysis or decomposition approach begins with a list of all the attributes to be represented in the database and assumes that all of them are in a single relation called the universal relation for the database. The designer then identifies functional dependencies among the attributes and uses the techniques of decomposition explained in this chapter to split the universal relation into a set of normalized relations. Our normalization examples in Section 5.5 were all decomposition examples. In particular, in Section 5.5.5 we considered an example in which we had a single relation called `Work`. `Work` was actually a universal relation, since all the attributes to be stored in the database were in it. We then wrote out our assumptions and identified four functional dependencies. The functional dependencies enabled us to perform lossless projections, so that we developed a set of relations in BCNF that preserved all functional dependencies. Since there were no multivalued dependencies they are also in 4NF, and since there were no remaining non-trivial lossless projections, they are in 5NF. All the constraints expressed in our list of assumptions and all the dependencies we identified in our discussion were considered in developing the final set of relations. The constraints are represented as key constraints in the resulting relations, so we actually have a set of DKNF relations. This example illustrates the process of analysis from a universal relation. The algorithm given in Section 5.7.8 for finding a BCNF decomposition is an analysis algorithm.

5.11.2 Synthesis

Synthesis is, in a sense, the opposite of analysis. In analysis we begin with a single big relation and break it up until we reach a set of smaller normalized relations. In synthesis we begin with attributes and combine them into related groups, using functional dependencies to develop a set of normalized relations. If analysis is a top-down process, then synthesis is bottom-up. The algorithm we presented in Section 5.7.9 for creating a set of 3NF relations is a synthesis algorithm.

5.11.3 Normalization from an Entity-Relationship Diagram

In practice, when a complete E-R diagram exists, the process of normalization is significantly more efficient than either pure analysis or pure synthesis. Using the mapping techniques discussed in Section 4.8, the resulting set of tables is usually fairly well normalized. The designer can begin by checking each relation to see if it is BCNF. If not, the determinants that cause the problems can be examined and the relation normalized. This process is illustrated in the Sample Project for The Art Gallery at the end of this chapter.

5.12 When to Stop Normalizing

Regardless of the process used, the end result should be a set of normalized relations that preserve dependencies and form lossless joins over common attributes. An important question is how far to go in the normalization process. Ideally, we try to reach DKNF. However, if that results in a decomposition that does not preserve dependencies, then we settle for less. Similarly, if we try for 5NF, 4NF or BCNF, we may not be able to get a decomposition that preserves dependencies, so we would settle for 3NF in that case. It is always possible to find a dependency preserving decomposition for 3NF. Even so, there may be valid reasons for choosing not to implement 3NF as well. For example, if we have attributes that are almost always used together in applications and they end up in different relations, then we will always have to do a join operation when we retrieve them. A familiar example of this occurs in storing addresses. Assume we are storing an employee's name and address, in the relation,

```
Emp (empId, lastName, firstName, street, city, state, zip)
```

As usual we are assuming names are not unique. We have the functional dependency,

```
zip → city, state
```

which means that the relation is not 3NF. We could normalize it by decomposition into,

```
Emp1 (empid, name, street, zip)
Codes (zip, city, state)
```

However, this would mean that we would have to do a join whenever we wanted a complete address for a person. In this case, we might settle for 2NF and implement the original EMP relation. In general, performance requirements should be taken into account in deciding what the final form will be. The Art Gallery sample project illustrates tradeoffs in normalization.

5.13 Chapter Summary

This chapter dealt with a method for developing a suitable set of relations for the logical model of a relational database. Three types of dependencies, **functional dependencies, multivalued dependencies,** and **join dependencies** were found to produce problems in representing information in the database. Many problems involved **update, insertion,** and **deletion anomalies.** A set of attributes B is said to be **functionally dependent** on a set of attributes A in a relation R if each A value has exactly one B value associated with it.

Normalization is often done by starting with a set of relations designed from the mapping of an E-R diagram and using heuristic methods to create an equivalent set of relations in a higher normal form. **First normal form** means that a relation has no multiple-valued attributes. We can normalize a relation that is not already in 1NF by creating a new table consisting of the key and the multivalued attribute, by adding additional columns for the expected number of repeats, or by "flattening," making the multivalued attribute part of the key. Relations in 1NF can have update, insertion, and deletion anomalies, due to **partial dependencies** on the key. If a non-key attribute is not **fully functionally dependent** on the entire key, the relation is not in **second normal form.** In that case, we normalize it by projection, placing each determinant that is a proper subset of the key in a new relation with its dependent attributes. The original composite key must also be kept in another relation. Relations in 2NF can still have update, insertion, and deletion anomalies. **Transitive dependencies,** in which one or more non-key attribute functionally determines another non-key attribute, cause such anomalies. **Third normal form** is achieved by eliminating transitive dependencies using projection. The determinant causing the transitive dependency is placed in a separate relation with the attributes it determines. It is also kept in the original relation. In third normal form, each non-key attribute is functionally dependent on the key, the whole key, and nothing but the key. **Boyce-Codd Normal Form** requires that every determinant be a superkey. This form is also achieved by projection, but in some cases the projection will separate determinants from their functionally dependent attributes, resulting in the loss of an important constraint. If this happens, 3NF is preferable.

Three desirable properties for relational decompositions are **attribute preservation, dependency preservation,** and **lossless decomposition.** Lossy projections can lose information because when they are undone by a join, spurious tuples can result. For binary projections, we can be sure a decomposition is lossless if the intersection of the two projections is a determinant for one of them. For binary decompositions, there is a simple test for lossless decomposition. There is also an algorithm to test for lossless decomposition in the general case. However, if decomposition is done by repeated binary decomposition, the simpler test can be applied to each successive decomposition. Functional dependencies can be manipulated formally by using **Armstrong's axioms** or rules of inference. The set, F+, of all functional dependencies logically implied by a given set, F, of functional dependencies is called its **closure**. The closure can be constructed by repeated application of Armstrong's axioms, but it is a long procedure. Similarly, the closure, A+, of an attribute A in a set of functional dependencies is the set of all attributes that A functionally determines. We can compute A+ by a simple algorithm. The algorithm for attribute closure can be used to answer some very important questions, such as whether A is a superkey, whether A is a candidate key, and whether a particular functional dependency appears in F+. For a set of FDs, F there is a simple algorithm to determine whether a particular FD is **redundant** in the set, which means it can be derived from the other FDs in F. If F and G are two sets of FDs for some relation R, then F is a **cover** for G if every FD in G is also in F+. If F is a cover for G and G is also a cover for F, then F and G are said to be **equivalent**, and F+ = G+. A set of functional dependencies is **minimal** if it is written in canonical form (i.e., every FD has only one attribute on the right-hand side), no attribute of a determinant is extraneous, and there are no redundant FDs. A cover, F, for G, is said to be a **minimal cover** (**nonredundant** cover) if F is a cover for G but no proper subset of F is a cover for G. A set of FDs may have several minimal covers, but we can always find one of them by a simple algorithm. If a relation is not already BCNF, we can use a decomposition algorithm to find an equivalent set of BCNF relations that forms a lossless projection. It is not always possible to find a BCNF decomposition that also preserves dependencies. However, it is always possible to find a 3NF decomposition that is both lossless and dependency-preserving. A synthesis algorithm that starts with a minimal cover for the set of FDs exists to do so.

Multivalued dependencies can occur when there are three attributes in a relation key, and two of them have independent multiple values for each distinct value of the third. Fourth normal form requires that a relation be BCNF and have no multivalued dependencies. We can achieve 4NF by projection, but usually we do so only if the resulting projections preserve functional dependencies. A relation is in fifth normal form if there are no remaining nontrivial nonloss projections. Alternatively, a relation is in fifth normal form if every join dependency is implied by the candidate keys. There is no proven method for achieving fifth normal form. **Domain key normal form** requires that every constraint be a consequence of domain constraints or key constraints. No proven method exists for producing domain key normal form.

In analysis we began with a relation, identify dependencies, and use projection to achieve a higher normal form. The opposite approach, called synthesis, begins with attributes, finds functional dependencies, and groups together functional dependencies with the same determinant, forming relations.

In deciding what normal form to choose for implementation, we consider attribute preservation, lossless projection, and dependency preservation. We generally choose the highest normal form that allows for all of these. We must also balance performance against normalization in implementation, so we sometimes accept a design that is in a lower normal form for performance reasons.

Exercises

5.1   Consider the following universal relation that holds information about books in a bookstore:

```
Books (title, isbn, author, publisherName, publisherAdd,
totalCopiesOrdered, copiesInStock, publicationDate, category,
sellingPrice, cost)
```

Assume:

- The isbn uniquely identifies a book. (It does not identify each copy of the book, however.)

- A book may have more than one author.

- An author may have more than one book.

- Each publisher name is unique. Each publisher has one unique address—the address of the firm's headquarters.

- Titles are not unique.

- totalCopiesOrdered is the number of copies of a particular book that the bookstore has ever ordered, while copiesInStock is the number still unsold in the bookstore.

- Each book has only one publication date. A revision of a book is given a new ISBN.

- The category may be biography, science fiction, poetry, etc. The title alone is not sufficient to determine the category. The sellingPrice, which is the amount the bookstore charges for a book, is always 20 percent above the cost, which is the amount the bookstore pays the publisher or distributor for the book.

a. Using these assumptions and stating any others you need to make, list all the non-trivial functional dependencies for this relation.

b. What are the candidate keys for this relation? Identify the primary key.

c. Is the relation in third normal form? If not, find a 3NF lossless join decomposition of Books that preserves dependencies.

d. Is the relation or resulting set of relations in Boyce-Codd Normal Form? If not, find a lossless join decomposition that is in BCNF. Identify any functional dependencies that are not preserved.

5.2   Consider the following relation that stores information about students living in dormitories at a college:

```
College (lastName, stuId, homeAdd, homePhone, dormRoom, roommateName,
dormAdd, status, mealPlan, roomCharge, mealPlanCharge)
```

Assume:

- Each student is assigned to one dormitory room and may have several roommates.

- Names of students are not unique.

- The college has several dorms. dormroom contains a code for the dorm and the number of the particular room assigned to the student. For example, A221 means Adams Hall, room 221. Dorm names are unique.

- The dormAdd is the address of the dorm building. Each building has its own unique address. For example, Adams Hall may be 123 Main Street, Anytown, NY 10001.

- status tells the student's status: Freshman, Sophomore, Junior, Senior, or Graduate Student.

- mealPlan tells how many meals per week the student has chosen as part of his or her meal plan. Each meal plan has a single mealPlanCharge associated with it.

- The roomCharge is different for different dorms, but all students in the same dorm pay the same amount.

Answer questions (a)–(d) as in Exercise 5.1 for this example.

5.3   Consider the following attributes for tables in a relational model designed to keep track of information for a moving company that moves residential customers, usually from one home or apartment to another:

customerID, customerName, customerCurrentAddress, customerCurrentPhone,
customerNewAddress, customerNewPhone, pickupLocation, dropOffLocation,
dateOfMove, startingTime, estimatedWeight, estimatedCost,
truck#Assigned, driverName, driverLicNo, actualCost, amountOfDamages,
truckCapacity, costOfTolls, tax, finalAmount, invoiceNumber, amountPaid,
datePaid, checkNumber, amountDue

Assume:

- Although in most cases the `pickupLocation` is the customer's old address and the `dropOffLocation` is the new address, there are exceptions, such as when furniture is moved to or from storage.

- An estimate is provided before the move using a pre-printed invoice containing a unique invoice number. The actual cost is recorded on the same form once the move is complete. The actual cost may differ from the estimated cost. The final amount includes the actual cost of the move, plus tax and tolls.

- In most cases, the customer pays the final amount immediately, but sometimes he or she pays only part of the bill, especially if the amount of damages is high. In those cases, there is an amount due, which is the difference between the final amount and amount paid.

(a)–(d) Answer questions (a)–(d) as in Exercise 5.1 for this example.

(e) What tables would you actually implement? Explain any denormalization, omissions or additions of attributes.

5.4   The owner of catering company wants a database to keep track of various aspects of the business. Clients may be individuals or businesses who make arrangements for events such as weddings, dances, corporate dinners, fundraisers, etc. The company owns a catering hall in which only one event can take place at a time. In addition, clients can use the services of the company to cater events at their homes, places of business, or places that the client rents, such as historic mansions. Several of these off-site events can take place at the same time. Clients who rent the catering hall must guarantee a minimum of 150 guests, but the hall can accommodate up to 200. Reservations for the hall are accepted up to two years in advance. Clients who provide their own space can have any number of guests. Reservations for off-site events are usually made several months in advance. The firm provides the food, table settings (dishes, silverware, and glassware), linens, waiters, and bartenders for the event, regardless of whether it is in the catering hall or elsewhere. Customers can choose the color of the linen. The firm has set menus that are identified by number. For a given menu number, there is one appetizer, one salad, one main course, and one dessert. (For example, menu number 10 may include shrimp cocktail, Caesar salad, prime rib, and chocolate mousse.) The firm quotes a total price for its services, based on the number of guests, the menu, the location, and intangible factors such as how busy they are on that date. The firm can also contract for floral arrangements, musicians, entertainers, and photographers, if the client requests. The client pays the catering company, which then pays the contractor. The price charged the customer for each of these is always 10% above the cost to the catering company. Assume names are unique. Also assume musicians and entertainers provide only one type of music or entertainment.

Assume the following attributes have been identified:

```
clientLName, cFName, cPhone, cStreet, cCity, cState, cZip, eventDate,
eventStartTime, eventDuration, eventType, numberGuests, locationName,
locationStreet, locationCity, locationState, locationZip,
linenColorRequested, numberWaiters, numberBartenders, totalPrice,
floristName, floristPhone, floristCost, floristPrice, musicContact,
musicContactPhone, musicType, musicCost, musicPrice, entertainerName,
entertainerPhone, entertainerType, entertainerCost, entertainerPrice,
photographerName, photographerPhone, photographerCost,
photographerPrice, menuNumberChosen, menuAppetizer, menuSalad,
menuMain, menuDessert.
```

(a)–(d) Answer questions (a)–(d) as in Exercise 5.1 for this example.

(e) What tables would you actually implement? Explain any denormalization, omissions or additions of attributes.

5.5 Consider the following relations, and identify the highest normal form for each, as given, stating any assumptions you need to make.

a. Work1 (empId, empName, dateHired, jobTitle, jobLevel)

b. Work2 (empId, empName, jobTitle, ratingDate, raterName, rating)

c. Work3 (empId, empName, projectNo, projectName, projBudget, empManager, hoursAssigned)

d. Work4 (empId, empName, schoolAttended, degreeAwarded, graduationDate)

e. Work5 (empId, empName, socialSecurityNumber, dependentName, dependentAddress, relationToEmp)

5.6 For each of the relations in Exercise 5.5, identify a primary key and,

a. if the relation is not in third normal form, find a 3NF lossless join decomposition that preserves dependencies.

b. if the relation or resulting set of relations is not in Boyce-Codd Normal Form, find a lossless join decomposition that is in BCNF. Identify any functional dependencies that are not preserved.

5.7 Consider instances of relation R(A,B,C,D) shown in Figure 5.13. For each of the following sets of FDs, determine whether each of the instances is consistent with the FDs given:

a. A → B,C
   B → D

b. AB → C
   B → D

c. AB → CD
   AC → B

5.8 Given the following set, S, of FDs:

S = {A→ B, B → C, AC → D}

a. Find the closure of A, A⁺.

b. Is A a superkey? Explain.

Instance 1			
A	**B**	**C**	**D**
a1	b1	c1	d1
a2	b2	c1	d2
a3	b1	c2	d3
a4	b3	c2	d3

Instance 2			
A	**B**	**C**	**D**
a1	b1	c1	d1
a2	b1	c2	d1
a3	b2	c1	d2
a4	b2	c2	d2

Instance 3			
A	**B**	**C**	**D**
a1	b1	c1	d1
a2	b1	c2	d1
a1	b2	c3	d2
a2	b2	c4	d2

FIGURE 5.13

Instances of R(A,B,C,D)

    c. Is B a superkey? How do you know?

    d. Is the FD B → D in S⁺? How do you know?

    e. Find the closure of the set of FDs, S+.

5.9   Examine each of the following sets of FDs and find any redundant FDs in each. Give a minimal cover for each.

    a. B → D
       E → C
      AC → D
      CD → A
      BE → A

    b. A → CDE
       B → CE
      AD → E
      CD → F
      BD → A
     CED → ABD

    c. D → C
      AB → C
      AD → B
      BD → A
      AC → B

5.10   Consider the relation:

R (A,B,C,D,E)

with FDs

A → B
BC → D
D → BC
C → A

a. Identify the candidate keys of this relation.

b. Suppose the relation is decomposed into,

R1 (A, B)
R2 (B, C, D)

Does this decompostion have a lossless join?

SAMPLE PROJECT: NORMALIZING THE RELATIONAL MODEL FOR THE ART GALLERY

In the sample project section at the end of Chapter 3, we created an E-R diagram for The Art Gallery. At the end of Chapter 4, we saw how to map that diagram to tables. In the present section, we want to normalize the relations. Although we could begin the normalization process by making a single universal relation that lists all attributes and then trying to isolate functional dependencies among the attributes, we can make our job easier by using the entities and relationships we identified in Chapter 3 and the tables to which they mapped at the end of Chapter 4. In practice, tables that result from such mappings are usually almost normalized already. Therefore, we use our mapped tables as a starting point.

- Step 5.1. Begin with the list of the tables that the entities and relationships from the E-R diagram mapped to naturally, from the sample project section at the end of Chapter 4. For each table on the list, identify functional dependencies and normalize the relation to BCNF. Then decide whether the resulting tables should be implemented in that form. If not, explain why.

The following tables resulted from the mapping:

Artist(<u>firstName, lastName</u>, street, city, state, zip, interviewDate,
interviewerName, areaCode, telephoneNumber, salesLastYear, salesYearToDate,
socialSecurityNumber, usualMedium, usualStyle, usualType)

PotentialCustomer(<u>firstName, lastName, areaCode, telephoneNumber</u>, street, city, state, zip, dateFilledIn, *preferredArtistLastName, preferredArtistFirstName,* preferredMedium, preferredStyle, preferredType)

Artwork(<u>*artistLastName, artistFirstName,* workTitle</u>, askingPrice, dateListed, dateReturned, dateShown, status, workMedium, workSize, workStyle, workType, workYearCompleted, *collectorSocialSecurityNumber*)

ShownIn(<u>*artistLastName, artistFirstName, workTitle, showTitle*</u>)

Collector(<u>socialSecurityNumber</u>, firstName, lastName, street, city, state, zip, interviewDate, interviewerName, areaCode, telephoneNumber, salesLastYear, salesYearToDate, *collectionArtistFirstName, collectionArtistLastName,* collectionMedium, collectionStyle, collectionType, salesLastYear, salesYearToDate)

Show(<u>showTitle</u>, *showFeaturedArtistLastName, showFeaturedArtistFirstName,* showClosingDate, showTheme, showOpeningDate)

Sale(<u>invoiceNumber,</u> *artistLastName, artistFirstName, workTitle,* amountRemittedToOwner, saleDate, salePrice, saleSalesPersonCommission, saleTax, saleTotal, *buyerLastName, buyerFirstName, salespersonSocialSecurityNumber*)

Buyer(<u>firstName, lastName</u>, street, city, state, zip, <u>areaCode, telephoneNumber</u>, purchasesLastYear, purchasesYearToDate)

Salesperson(<u>socialSecurityNumber</u>, firstName, lastName, street, city, state, zip)

For the Artist table, let us identify FDs.

firstName + lastName → all attributes

It would appear that

socialSecurityNumber → all attributes

Recall that BCNF permits determinants that are candidate keys to remain in the table, so we do not have a problem with leaving socialSecurityNumber in the table. However, we recall that we assumed that we would not always have the social security number of artists whose works were owned by collectors, so the value of this attribute may be null for some artists. However, when it appears, it is unique in the table.

zip → city, state

We might want to consider,

areaCode → ? city, state

We conclude that with mobile telephones (cell phones), the area code is not necessarily associated with the city and state of the artist's residence or studio, so we do not have this as a functional dependency. We also consider whether the complete telephone number determines the address.

```
areaCode + telephoneNumber → ? street, city, state, zip
```

Is it possible for two artist records with the same telephone number to have two different addresses? If the telephone is a home or studio telephone, the addresses should be the same (the address of the location of the telephone). If it is a mobile telephone, the two artists would have to be sharing it for the same number to appear in two different records, so it is likely that they share the same address in that case also. We will keep this as a functional dependency. We might then want to ask,

```
areaCode + telephoneNumber → ? all attributes
```

We decide this is not the case, since we consider the possibility that two artists may share the same home or studio and the same telephone number there, but still have different names, styles, and so on. The table is in 1NF and 2NF, but not 3NF or BCNF because of the dependencies we have listed. We therefore decompose the Artist table as follows:

```
Artist1(firstName, lastName, interviewDate, interviewerName, areaCode,
telephoneNumber, salesLastYear, salesYearToDate, socialSecurityNumber,
usualMedium, usualStyle, usualType)
Phones(areaCode, telephoneNumber, street, zip)
Zips(zip, city, state)
```

However, this design would require that we use the telephone number in order to get the street and ZIP code of an artist, and that we do two joins whenever we want to get an artist's complete address. For the sake of efficiency, we will compromise and put the street and ZIP back in the Artist1 table. We choose to leave the Zips table as it is, noting that complete ZIP code tables are available for purchase in electronic form. Now our form for the Artist tables is,

```
Artist2 (firstName, lastName, interviewDate, interviewerName, areaCode,
telephoneNumber, street, zip, salesLastYear, salesYearToDate,
socialSecurityNumber, usualMedium, usualStyle, usualType)
Zips(zip, city, state)
```

We note that the primary key of Artist2 is a composite, and that it will become a composite foreign key in other tables. Composite foreign keys require checking multiple fields in joins. In practice, it is better to use a numeric field for a key value than a character string, which is subject to differences in spelling, capitalization, and punctuation in entering data. Data entry errors or variations in entering string data can cause errors when we try to compare values; in particular, when the fields are used as foreign keys. Therefore, we will create a unique numeric identifier for each artist, which we will call `artistId`, and make that the primary key of the first table. All the attributes of the first table will be functionally dependent on it. This type of key is called a **surrogate key,** and most database management systems have a mechanism to generate values and to keep track of values for surrogate keys. Oracle uses a concept called a **sequence** for this purpose. Microsoft Access uses an **autonumber** data type for the same purpose. In fact Access prompts the user to allow it to generate a key field of this type if the user neglects to specify one. We therefore have as our final artist tables,

(1) `Artist3(`<u>`artistId`</u>`, firstName, lastName, interviewDate, interviewerName, areaCode, telephoneNumber, street, `*`zip`*`, salesLastYear, salesYearToDate, socialSecurityNumber, usualMedium, usualStyle, usualType)`

(2) `Zips(`<u>`zip`</u>`, city, state)`

For `PotentialCustomer` we have many of the same FDs that we saw for Artist.

    `firstName + lastName + areaCode + telephoneNumber → all attributes`

    `areaCode + telephoneNumber → street, city, state, zip`

    `zip → city, state`

Using the same reasoning as we did for `Artist`, we will add a unique identifier, `potentialCustomerId`, to use as the primary key. We might question whether there is a functional dependency between the preferred artist and other preferences. Although there may be some connection, it is not a true functional dependency, since, for example, two people who admire the same artist might prefer works that are in different mediums or styles, perhaps even produced by the same artist.

For strict BCNF we would break up `PotentialCustomer` as follows:

```
Customer1(potentialCustomerId, firstName, lastName, areaCode,
telephoneNumber, dateFilledIn, preferredArtistLastName,
preferredArtistFirstName, preferredMedium, preferredStyle, preferredType)

Phones(areaCode, telephoneNumber, street, zip)

Zips(zip, city, state)
```

Using the same logic that we used for artist information, we choose instead to create a table that keeps the street and ZIP code with the other customer data, and to use the `Zips` table that already exists to determine city and state. We also want to use the `preferredArtistId` instead of first and last name. Therefore, we add to the design the table,

(3) `PotentialCustomer2` (*potentialCustomerId*, firstName, lastName, areaCode, telephoneNumber, street, *zip*, dateFilledIn, *preferredArtistId*, preferredMedium, preferredStyle, preferredType)

For `Artwork`, we have the following FDs:

```
artistLastName + artistFirstName + workTitle → all attributes
```

We were using the artist name as a foreign key here. Since we changed the primary key of `Artist` to `artistId`, we will change the foreign key as well, replacing the name by the Id in the `Artwork` table. Although there is some logical connection between the dates, there is no functional dependency between them. We will also create a unique identifier for each work, `artworkId`,

(4) `Artwork` (*artworkId*, *artistId*, workTitle, askingPrice, dateListed, dateReturned, dateShown, status, workMedium, workSize, workStyle, workType, workYearCompleted, *collectorSocialSecurityNumber*)

For the `ShownIn` table there are no non-trivial functional dependencies, so we could keep the table in its current form. However, we wish to use artworkId to identify the artwork.

(5) `ShownIn` (*artworkId*, *showTitle*)

In the `Collector` table, we have the FDs,

```
socialSecurityNumber → all attributes
```

as well as the FDs we saw previously involving telephone numbers and ZIP codes. We also want to use `artistId` in place of the artist's first and last name. We therefore chose to create the table shown below, and to make use of the existing `Zips` table.

(6) Collector1 (<u>socialSecurityNumber</u>, firstName, lastName, street, *zip*,
interviewDate, interviewerName, areaCode, telephoneNumber, salesLastYear,
salesYearToDate, *collectionArtistId,* collectionMedium, collectionStyle,
collectionType, salesLastYear, salesYearToDate)

For the `Show` table, we have the FD,

showTitle → all attributes

However, we wish to substitute the `artistId` for the name, as we did for earlier tables. There may be some connection between the featured artist and the show title, but they are not necessarily functionally dependent. For example, two different shows may both feature the same artist, but their titles will be different. The same is true of the theme and the title. There is also some connection between the opening date and closing date of the show. If we assumed that only one show can open on a given date, then there would be only one closing date associated with that opening date, and we would have a transitive dependency that we would need to remove. Let us add to the assumptions that more than one show can open at the same time. This is a reasonable assumption if the gallery is large enough. In that case, there may be shows that have the same opening date but different closing dates. Given these assumptions, the `Show` table is already normalized.

(7) Show (<u>showTitle</u>, *showFeaturedArtistId,* showClosingDate, showTheme,
showOpeningDate)

For `Buyer`, we have the FD,

firstName + lastName + areaCode + telephoneNumber → all attributes

as well as the FDs involving telephone numbers and ZIP codes, as we saw earlier for `Artist` and for `Collector`. As we did for `Artist`, we will create a numeric primary key, `buyerId`. Using the same pattern as for those tables, we design a new `Buyer` table and make use of the `Zips` table designed previously.

(8) Buyer (<u>buyerId</u>, firstName, lastName, street, *zip*, areaCode,
telephoneNumber, purchasesLastYear, purchasesYearToDate)

For the `Sale` table, we have the FD,

invoiceNumber → all attributes

Since each artwork is sold at most once, we also have,

```
artworkId → all attributes
```

Since it is permissible to keep a candidate key in the relation, this does not present a problem. Again, we will substitute the `artworkId` for the artist name and title, and the `buyerId` for the buyer name as foreign keys. If the commission is a constant percentage of the sale price, then we have,

```
salePrice → saleSalesPersonCommission
```

We do not assume that sale price determines tax, since some buyers, such as nonprofit organizations, may be tax-exempt. However, the sale total is just the sum of sale price and tax, so we have,

```
salePrice + tax → saleTotal
```

Actually, any two of these determine the other. We might think we have the FD between the `salePrice` and the `amountRemittedToOwner`. However, it is possible that there may be a delay between the time a work is sold and the time an owner is paid, so we could have two sales with the same sale price and different amounts remitted to the owner, because one has not yet been paid. Removing the FDs identified here, we form the new table,

(9) Sale1 (<u>InvoiceNumber</u>, *artworkId,* amountRemittedToOwner, saleDate, salePrice, saleTax, buyerId, *salesPersonSocialSecurityNumber*)

We could also have the table,

```
Commissions(salePrice, saleSalesPersonCommission)
```

but we do would not need to store this, since the commission is easily calculated. Similarly, because of the arithmetic relationship among the attributes, we do not need to store the table,

```
Totals(salePrice, saleTax, saleTotal)
```

For `Salesperson` we have,

```
socialSecurityNumber → all attributes
zip → city, state
```

Removing the transitive dependency and making use of the existing `Zips` table, we have,

(10) Salesperson (<u>socialSecurityNumber</u>, firstName, lastName, street, *zip*)

The tables numbered 1–10 will be used as the final set of tables for the relational design for this database.

- Step 5.2. Update the data dictionary and list of assumptions as needed.

We need to add to the data dictionary the new identifiers we created, as follows:

artistId   A unique numeric identifier created for each artist.

artworkId   A unique numeric identifier created for each work of art.

buyerId   A unique numeric identifier created for each buyer.

potentialCustomerId   A unique numeric identifier created for each potential customer.

We make a note of the calculated items that are not to be stored.

saleTotal   The total dollar amount of a sale, including price and tax, for an artwork; *calculated from salePrice and saleTax. Calculated item.*

saleSalesPersonCommission   The dollar amount of commission for a salesperson for the sale of a work of art. *Calculated item.*

We see that Artist, Buyer, Collector, PotentialCustomer, and Salesperson share attributes that have the same meanings, so we drop distinctions based on sources for the following attributes: name, firstName, lastName, address, street, city, state, zip, phone, areaCode, telephoneNumber, and socialSecurityNumber.

There are no changes to the list of assumptions.

STUDENT PROJECTS: NORMALIZING THE RELATIONAL MODEL FOR THE STUDENT PROJECTS

- Step 5.1. Begin with the list of the tables that the entities and relationships from the E-R diagram mapped to naturally, from the student project section at the end of Chapter 4. For each table on the list, identify functional dependencies and normalize the relation to BCNF. Then decide whether the resulting tables should be implemented in that form. If not, explain why. Give the final schema for the relational model.

- Step 5.2. Update the data dictionary and the list of assumptions as needed.

6 CHAPTER

Relational Database Management Systems and SQL

Chapter Objectives

In this chapter you will learn the following:

- The history of relational database systems and SQL

- How the three-level architecture is implemented in relational database management systems

- How to create and modify a logical-level database structure using SQL DDL

- How to retrieve and update data in a relational database using SQL DML

- How to enforce constraints in relational databases

- How to terminate relational transactions

- How SQL is used in a programming environment

- How to create relational views

- When and how to perform operations on relational views

- The structure and functions of a relational database system catalog

- The functions of the various components of a relational database management system

6.1   Brief History of SQL in Relational Database Systems

As described in Chapter 4, the relational model was first proposed by E. F. Codd in 1970. D. D. Chamberlin and others at the IBM San Jose Research Laboratory developed a language now called SQL, or Structured Query Language, as a data sublanguage for the relational model. Originally spelled SEQUEL, the language was presented in a series of papers starting in 1974, and it was used in a prototype relational system called System R, which was developed by IBM in the late 1970s. Other early prototype relational database management systems included INGRES, which was developed at the University of California at Berkeley, and the Peterlee Relational Test Vehicle, developed at the IBM UK Scientific Laboratory. System R was evaluated and refined over a period of several years, and it became the basis for IBM's first commercially available relational database management system, SQL/DS, which was announced in 1981. Another early commercial database management system, Oracle, was developed in the late 1970s using SQL as its language. IBM's DB2, also using SQL as its language, was released in 1983. Microsoft SQL Server, MySQL, Informix, Sybase, dBase, Paradox, r: Base, FoxPro, and many other relational database management systems have incorporated SQL.

Both the American National Standards Institute (ANSI) and the International Standards Organization (ISO) adopted SQL as a standard language for relational databases and published specifications for the SQL language in 1986. This standard is usually called SQL1. A minor revision, called SQL-89, was published three years later. A major revision, SQL2, was adopted by both ANSI and ISO in 1992. The first parts of the SQL3 standard, referred to as SQL:1999, were published in 1999. Major new features included object-oriented data management capabilities and user-defined data types. Most vendors of relational database management systems use their own extensions of the language, creating a variety of dialects around the standard.

SQL has a complete data definition language (DDL) and data manipulation language (DML) described in this chapter, and an authorization language, described in Chapter 9. Readers should note that different implementations of SQL vary slightly from the standard syntax presented here, but the basic notions are the same.

6.2   Architecture of a Relational Database Management System

Relational database management systems support the standard three-level architecture for databases described in Section 2.6. As shown in Figure 6.1, relational databases provide both logical and physical data independence because they separate the external, logical, and internal levels. The logical level for relational databases consists of base tables that are physically stored. These tables are created by the database administrator using a CREATE TABLE command, as described in Section 6.3. A base table can have any number of indexes, created by the DBA using the CREATE INDEX command. An index is used to speed up retrieval of records based on the value in one or more columns. An index lists the values that exist for the indexed column(s), and the location of the records that have those values. Most relational database management systems use B trees or B+ trees for indexes. (See Appendix A.) On the physical level, the base tables are represented, along with their indexes, in files. The physical representation of the tables may not correspond exactly to our notion of a base table as a two-dimensional object consisting of rows and columns. However, the rows of the table do correspond to physically stored records, although their order and other details of storage may be different from our concept

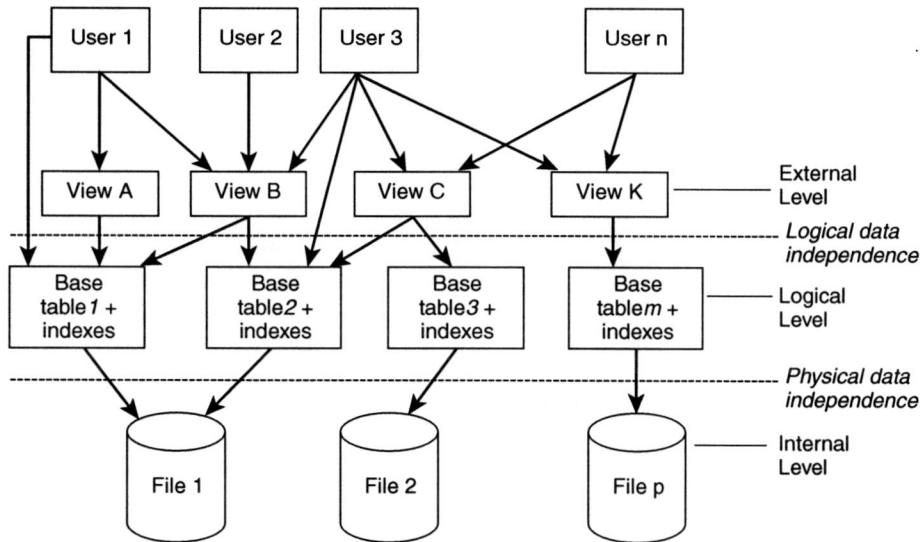

FIGURE 6.1

Three Level Architecture for Relational Databases

of them. The database management system, not the operating system, controls the internal structure of both the data files and the indexes. The user is generally unaware of what indexes exist, and has no control over which index will be used in locating a record. Once the base tables have been created, the DBA can create "views" for users, using the CREATE VIEW command, described in Section 6.8. A view may be a subset of a single base table, or it may be created by combining base tables. Views are "virtual tables," not permanently stored, but created when the user needs to access them. Users are unaware of the fact that their views are not physically stored in table form. In a relational system, the word "view" means a single virtual table. This is not exactly the same as our term "external view," which means the database as it appears to a particular user. In our terminology, an external view may consist of several base tables and/or views.

One of the most useful features of a relational database is that it permits dynamic database definition. The DBA, and users he or she authorizes to do so, can create new tables, add columns to old ones, create new indexes, define views, and drop any of these objects at any time. By contrast, many other systems require that the entire database structure be defined at creation time, and that the entire system be halted and reloaded when any structural changes are made. The flexibility of relational databases encourages users to experiment with various structures and allows the system to be modified to meet their changing needs. This enables the DBA to ensure that the database is a useful model of the enterprise throughout its life cycle.

6.3   Defining the Database: SQL DDL

The most important SQL Data Definition Language (DDL) commands are the following:

> CREATE TABLE
> CREATE INDEX
> ALTER TABLE
> RENAME TABLE
> DROP TABLE
> DROP INDEX

These statements are used to create, change, and destroy the logical structures that make up the logical model. These commands can be used at any time to make changes to the database structure. Additional commands are available to specify physical details of storage, but we will not discuss them here, since they are specific to the system.

We will apply these commands to the following example, which we have used in previous chapters:

```
Student (stuId, lastName, firstName, major, credits)
Faculty (facId, name, department, rank)
Class (classNumber, facId, schedule, room)
Enroll (classNumber, stuId, grade)
```

6.3.1   Create Table

This command is used to create the base tables that form the heart of a relational database. Since it can be used at any time during the lifecycle of the system, the database developer can start with a small number of tables and add to them as additional applications are planned and developed. A base table is fairly close to the abstract notion of a relational table. It consists of one or more **column headings,** which give the **column name** and **data type,** and zero or more **data rows,** which contain one data value of the specified data type for each of the columns. As in the abstract rela-

tional model, the rows are considered unordered. However, the columns
are ordered left-to-right, to match the order of column definitions in the
CREATE TABLE command. The form of the command is:

```
CREATE TABLE base-table-name (colname datatype [column constraints -
NULL/NOT NULL, DEFAULT . . . , UNIQUE, CHECK . . . , PRIMARY KEY . . .]]
[,colname datetype [column constraints]
. . .
[table constraints - PRIMARY KEY . . . , FOREIGN KEY . . . , UNIQUE
. . . , CHECK . . .]
[storage specifications]);
```

Here, base-table-name is a user-supplied name for the table. No SQL keywords may be used, and the table name must be unique within the database. For each column, the user must specify a name that is unique within
the table, and a data type. The optional storage specifications section of
the CREATE TABLE command allows the DBA to name the tablespace
where the table will be stored. If the tablespace is not specified, the database management system will create a default space for the table. Those
who wish to can ignore system details and those who desire more control
can be very specific about storage areas.

Figure 6.2 shows the commands to create the base tables for a database for
the University example.

6.3.1.1 Data Types

Built-in data types include various numeric types, fixed-length and
varying-length character strings, bit strings, and user-defined types. The
available data types vary from DBMS to DBMS. For example, the most
common types in Oracle are CHAR(N), VARCHAR2(N),
NUMBER(N,D), DATE, and BLOB (binary large object). In DB2, types
include SMALLINT, INTEGER, BIGINT, DECIMAL/NUMERIC, REAL,
DOUBLE, CHAR(N), VARCHAR(N), LONG VARCHAR, CLOB,
GRAPHIC, DBCLOB, BLOB, DATE, TIME, and TIMESTAMP. Microsoft
SQL Server types include NUMERIC, BINARY, CHAR, VARCHAR DATE-
TIME, MONEY, IMAGE, and others. Microsoft Access supports several
types of NUMBER, as well as TEXT, MEMO, DATE/TIME, CURRENCY,
YES/NO, and others. In addition, some systems, such as Oracle, allow
users to create new domains, built on existing data types. Rather than
using one of the built-in data types, users can specify domains in advance,
and they can include a check condition for the domain. SQL:1999 allows

```
CREATE TABLE Student          (
stuId                         CHAR(6),
lastName                      CHAR(20) NOT NULL,
firstName                     CHAR(20) NOT NULL,
major                         CHAR(10),
credits                       SMALLINT DEFAULT 0,
CONSTRAINT Student_stuId_pk PRIMARY KEY (stuId),
CONSTRAINT Student_credits_cc CHECK (CREDITS>=0 AND credits < 150);
```

```
CREATE TABLE Faculty          (
facId                         CHAR(6),
name                          CHAR(20) NOT NULL,
department                    CHAR(20) NOT NULL,
rank                          CHAR(10),
CONSTRAINT Faculty_facId_pk PRIMARY KEY (facId));
```

```
CREATE TABLE Class            (
classNumber                   CHAR(8),
facId                         CHAR(6) NOT NULL,
schedule                      CHAR(8),
room                          CHAR(6),
CONSTRAINT Class_classNumber_pk PRIMARY KEY (classNumber),
CONSTRAINT Class_facId_fk FOREIGN KEY (facId) REFERENCES Faculty (facId));
```

```
CREATE TABLE Enroll           (
stuId                         CHAR(6),
classNumber                   CHAR(8),
grade                         CHAR(2),
CONSTRAINT Enroll_classNumber_stuId_pk PRIMARY KEY (classNumber, stuId),
CONSTRAINT Enroll_classNumber_fk FOREIGN KEY (classNumber) REFERENCES Class
    (classNumber),
CONSTRAINT Enroll_stuId_fk FOREIGN KEY (stuId) REFERENCES Student (stuId) ON DELETE CASCADE);
```

the creation of new **distinct** data types using one of the previously defined types as the source type. For example, we could write:

```
CREATE DOMAIN creditValues INTEGER
    DEFAULT 0
    CHECK (VALUE >=0 AND VALUE <150);
```

Once a domain has been created, we can use it as a data type for attributes. For example, when we create the Student table, for the specification of `credits` we could then write:

```
credits creditValues, . . .
```

in place of,

```
credits SMALLINT DEFAULT 0,
. . .
CONSTRAINT Student_credits_cc CHECK (credits>=0 AND credits < 150)
```

However, when we create distinct types, SQL:1999 does not allow us to compare their values with values of other attributes having the same underlying source type. For example, if we use the `creditValues` domain for `credits`, we cannot compare `credits` with another attribute whose type is also SMALLINT—for example, with `age`, if we had stored that attribute. We cannot use the built-in SQL functions such as COUNT, AVERAGE, SUM, MAX, or MIN on distinct types, although we can write our own definitions of functions for the new types.

6.3.1.2 Column and Table Constraints

The database management system has facilities to enforce data correctness, which the DBA should make use of when creating tables. Recall from Section 4.4 that the relational model uses integrity constraints to protect the correctness of the database, allowing only legal instances to be created. These constraints protect the system from data entry errors that would create inconsistent data. Although the table name, column names, and data types are the only parts required in a CREATE TABLE command, optional constraints can and should be added, both at the column level and at the table level.

The column constraints include options to specify NULL/NOT NULL, UNIQUE, PRIMARY KEY, CHECK and DEFAULT for any column, immediately after the specification of the column name and data type. If we do not specify NOT NULL, the system will allow the column to have null values, meaning the user can insert records that have no values for those fields. When a null value appears in a field of a record, the system is able to distinguish it from a blank string or zero value, and treats it differently in computations and logical comparisons. It is desirable to be able to insert null values in certain situations; for example, when a college student has not yet declared a major we might want to set the `major` field to null. However, the use of null values can create complications, especially in operations such as joins, so we should use NOT NULL when it is appropriate. We can also specify a default value for a column, if we wish to do so. Every record that is inserted without a value for that field will then be given the default value automatically. We can optionally specify that a given field is to have unique values by writing the UNIQUE constraint. In that case, the system will reject the insertion of a new record that has the same value in that field as a record that is already in the database. If the primary key is not composite, it is also possible to specify PRIMARY KEY as a column constraint, simply by adding the words PRIMARY KEY after the data type for the column. Clearly we cannot allow duplicate values for the primary key. We also disallow null values, since we could not distinguish between two different records if they both had null key values, so the specification of PRIMARY KEY in SQL carries an implicit NOT NULL constraint as well as a UNIQUE constraint. However, we may wish to ensure uniqueness for candidate keys as well, and we should specify UNIQUE for them when we create the table. The system automatically checks each record we try to insert to ensure that data items for columns that have been described as unique do not have values that duplicate any other data items in the database for those columns. If a duplication might occur, it will reject the insertion. It is also desirable to specify a NOT NULL constraint for candidate keys, when it is possible to ensure that values for these columns will always be available. The CHECK constraint can be used to verify that values provided for attributes are appropriate. For example, we could write:

```
credits SMALLINT DEFAULT 0 CHECK ((credits>=0) AND (credits < 150)),
```

Table constraints, which appear after all the columns have been declared, can include the specification of a primary key, foreign keys, uniqueness, checks, and general constraints that can be expressed as conditions to be checked. If the primary key is a composite, it must be identified using a table constraint rather than a column constraint, although even a primary key consisting of a single column can be identified as a table constraint. The PRIMARY KEY constraint enforces the uniqueness and not null constraints for the column(s) identified as the primary key. The FOREIGN

KEY constraint requires that we identity the referenced table where the column or column combination is a primary key. The SQL standard allows us to specify what is to be done with records containing the foreign key values when the records they relate to are updated or deleted in their home table. For the University example, what should happen to a `Class` record when the record of faculty member assigned to teach the class is deleted or the `facId` of the `Faculty` record is updated? For the deletion case, the DBMS could automatically:

- Delete all `Class` records for that faculty member, an action performed when we specify ON DELETE CASCADE in the foreign key specification in SQL.

- Set the `facId` in the `Class` record to a null value, an action performed when we write ON DELETE SET NULL in SQL.

- Set the `facId` to some default value such as F999 in the `Class` table, an action performed when we write ON DELETE SET DEFAULT in SQL. (This choice requires that we use the DEFAULT column constraint for this column prior to the foreign key specification.)

- Not allow the deletion of a `Faculty` record if there is a `Class` record that refers to it, an action performed when we specify ON DELETE NO ACTION in SQL.

The same actions, with similar meanings, can be specified in an ON UPDATE clause; that is,

```
ON UPDATE CASCADE/SET NULL/SET DEFAULT/NO ACTION
```

For both deletion and update, the default is NO ACTION, essentially disallowing changes to a record in a home relation that would cause inconsistency with records that refer to it. As shown in Figure 6.2, for the `Class` table we have chosen the default. Also note the choices we made for the `Enroll` table, for changes made to both `classNumber` and `stuId`.

The table uniqueness constraint mechanism can be used to specify that the values in a combination of columns must be unique. For example, to ensure that no two classes have exactly the same schedule and room, we would write:

```
CONSTRAINT Class_schedule_room_uk UNIQUE (schedule, room)
```

Recall from Section 4.4 that the uniqueness constraint allows us to specify candidate keys. The above constraint says that {`schedule`, `room`} is a candidate key for Class. We could also specify that {facId, schedule} is a candidate key by,

```
CONSTRAINT Class_facId_schedule_uk UNIQUE (facId, schedule)
```

since a faculty member cannot teach two classes with exactly the same schedule.

Constraints, whether column or table level, can optionally be given a name, as illustrated in the examples. If we do not name them, the system will generate a unique constraint name for each constraint. The advantage of naming constraints is that we can then refer to them easily. There are SQL commands to allow us to disable, enable, alter, or drop constraints at will, provided we know their names. It is good practice to use a consistent pattern in naming constraints. The pattern illustrated here is the table-name, column name(s) and an abbreviation for the constraint type (pk, fk, nn, uk, cc), separated by underscores.

6.3.2   Create Index

We can optionally create indexes for tables to facilitate fast retrieval of records with specific values in a column. An index keeps track of what values exist for the indexed column, and which records have those values. For example, if we have an index on the lastName column of the Student table, and we write a query asking for all students with last name of Smith, the system will not have to scan all Student records to pick out the desired ones. Instead, it will read the index, which will point it to the records with the desired name. A table can have any number of indexes, which are stored as B-trees or B+ trees in separate index files, usually close to the tables they index. (See Appendix A for a description of tree indexes.) Indexes can be created on single fields or combinations of fields. However, since indexes must be updated by the system every time the underlying tables are updated, additional overhead is required. Aside from choosing which indexes will exist, users have no control over the use or maintenance of indexes. The system chooses which, if any, index to use in searching for records. Indexes are not part of the SQL standard, but most DBMSs support their creation. The command for creating an index is:

```
CREATE [UNIQUE] INDEX indexname ON basetablename (colname [order]
[,colname [order]] . . .) [CLUSTER] ;
```

If the UNIQUE specification is used, uniqueness of the indexed field or combination of fields will be enforced by the system. Although indexes can be created at any time, we may have a problem if we try to create a unique index after the table has records stored in it, because the values stored for the indexed field or fields may already contain duplicates. In this case, the system will not allow the unique index to be created. To create the index on `lastName` for the `Student` table we would write:

```
CREATE INDEX Student_lastName ON STUDENT (lastName);
```

The name of the index should be chosen to indicate the table and the field or fields used in the index. Any number of columns, regardless of where they appear on the table, may be used in an index. The first column named determines major order, the second gives minor order, and so on. For each column, we may specify that the order is ascending, ASC, or descending, DESC. If we choose not to specify order, ASC is the default. If we write,

```
CREATE INDEX Faculty_department_name ON Faculty (department ASC, name ASC);
```

then an index file called `Faculty_Department_Name` will be created for the `Faculty` table. Entries will be in alphabetical order by department. Within each department, entries will be in alphabetical order by faculty name.

Some DBMSs allow an optional CLUSTER specification for only one index for each table. If we use this option, the system will store records with the same values for the indexed field(s) close together physically, on the same page or adjacent pages if possible. If we create a clustered index for the field(s) used most often for retrieval, we can substantially improve performance for those applications needing that particular order of retrieval, since we will be minimizing seek time and read time. However, it is the system, not the user, that chooses to use a particular index, even a clustered one, for data retrieval.

Oracle automatically creates an index on the primary key of each table that is created. The user should create additional indexes on any field(s) that are often used in queries, to speed up execution of those queries. Foreign key fields, which are often used in joins, are good candidates for indexing.

6.3.3   ALTER TABLE, RENAME TABLE

Once a table has been created, users might find it more useful if it contained an additional data item, did not have a particular column, or had different constraints. Here, the dynamic nature of a relational database structure makes it possible to change existing base tables. For example, to add a new column on the right of the table, we use a command of the form:

```
ALTER TABLE basetablename ADD columnname datatype;
```

Notice we cannot use the NULL specification for the column. An ALTER TABLE ..ADD command causes the new field to be added to all records already stored in the table, and null values to be assigned to that field in all existing records. Newly inserted records, of course, will have the additional field, but we are not permitted to specify no nulls even for them.

Suppose we want to add a new column, cTitle, to our Class table. We can do so by writing

```
ALTER TABLE Class ADD cTitle CHAR(30);
```

The schema of the Class table would then be:

```
Class(classNumber,facId,schedule,room,cTitle)
```

All old Class records would now have null values for cTitle, but we could provide a title for any new Class records we insert, and update old Class records by adding titles to them. We can also drop columns from existing tables by the command:

```
ALTER TABLE basetablename DROP COLUMN columnname;
```

To drop the cTitle column and return to our original structure for the Class table, we would write:

```
ALTER TABLE Class DROP COLUMN cTitle;
```

If we want to add, drop, or change a constraint, we can use the same ALTER TABLE command. For example, if we created the Class table and neglected to make facId a foreign key in Class, we could add the constraint at any time by writing:

```
ALTER TABLE Class ADD CONSTRAINT Class_facId_fk FOREIGN KEY (facId) REFERENCES
Faculty (facId));
```

We could drop an existing named constraint using the ALTER TABLE command. For example, to drop the check condition on the credits attribute of Student that we created earlier, we could write:

```
ALTER TABLE Student DROP CONSTRAINT Student_credits_cc;
```

We can change the name of an existing table easily by the command:

```
RENAME TABLE old-table-name TO new-table-name;
```

6.3.4 DROP Statements

Tables can be dropped at any time by the SQL command:

```
DROP TABLE basetablename;
```

When this statement is executed, the table itself and all records contained in it are removed. In addition, all indexes and, as we will see later, all views that depend on it are dropped. Naturally, the DBA confers with potential users of the table before taking such a drastic step. Any existing index can be destroyed by the command:

```
DROP INDEX indexname;
```

The effect of this change may or may not be seen in performance. Recall that users cannot specify when the system is to use an index for data retrieval. Therefore, it is possible that an index exists that is never actually used, and its destruction would have no affect on performance. However, the loss of an efficient index that is used by the system for many retrievals would certainly affect performance. When an index is dropped, any access plans for applications that depend on it are marked as invalid. When an application calls them, a new access plan is devised to replace the old one.

6.4 Manipulating the Database: SQL DML

SQL's query language is **declarative,** also called **non-procedural,** which means that it allows us to specify what data is to be retrieved without giving the procedures for retrieving it. It can be used as an interactive language for queries, embedded in a host programming language, or as a complete language in itself for computations using SQL/PSM (Persistent Stored Modules).

The SQL DML statements are:

> SELECT
> UPDATE
> INSERT
> DELETE

6.4.1 Introduction to the SELECT Statement

The SELECT statement is used for retrieval of data. It is a powerful command, performing the equivalent of relational algebra's SELECT,

PROJECT, and JOIN, as well as other functions, in a single, simple statement. The general form of SELECT is,

```
SELECT    [DISTINCT] col-name [AS newname], [,col-name..] . . .
FROM      table-name [alias] [,table-name] . . .
[WHERE    predicate]
[GROUP BY col-name [,col-name] . . . [HAVING predicate]
```

or,

```
[ORDER BY col-name [,col-name] . . .];
```

The result is a table that may have duplicate rows. Since duplicates are allowed in such a table, it is not a relation in the strict sense, but is referred to as a **multi-set** or a **bag.** As indicated by the absence of square brackets, the SELECT and the FROM clauses are required, but not the WHERE or the other clauses. The many variations of this statement will be illustrated by the examples that follow, using the `Student`, `Faculty`, `Class`, and/or `Enroll` tables as they appear in Figure 6.3

- Example 1. Simple Retrieval with Condition

    Question: Get names, IDs and number of credits of all Math majors.

    Solution: The information requested appears on the `Student` table. From that table we select only the rows that have a value of 'Math' for `major`. For those rows, we display only the `lastName`, `firstName`, `stuId`, and `credits` columns. Notice we are doing the equivalent of relational algebra's SELECT (in finding the rows) and PROJECT (in displaying only certain columns). We are also rearranging the columns.

    SQL Query:

    ```
    SELECT    lastName, firstName, stuId, credits
    FROM      Student
    WHERE     major = 'Math';
    ```

    Result:

lastName	firstName	stuId	credits
Chin	Ann	S1002	36
McCarthy	Owen	S1013	0
Jones	Mary	S1015	42

Notice that the result of the query is a table or a multi-set.

Student

stuId	lastName	firstName	major	credits
S1001	Smith	Tom	History	90
S1002	Chin	Ann	Math	36
S1005	Lee	Perry	History	3
S1010	Burns	Edward	Art	63
S1013	McCarthy	Owen	Math	0
S1015	Jones	Mary	Math	42
S1020	Rivera	Jane	CSC	15

Faculty

facId	name	department	rank
F101	Adams	Art	Professor
F105	Tanaka	CSC	Instructor
F110	Byrne	Math	Assistant
F115	Smith	History	Associate
F221	Smith	CSC	Professor

Class

classNumber	facId	schedule	room
ART103A	F101	MWF9	H221
CSC201A	F105	TuThF10	M110
CSC203A	F105	MThF12	M110
HST205A	F115	MWF11	H221
MTH101B	F110	MTuTh9	H225
MTH103C	F110	MWF11	H225

Enroll

stuId	classNumber	grade
S1001	ART103A	A
S1001	HST205A	C
S1002	ART103A	D
S1002	CSC201A	F
S1002	MTH103C	B
S1010	ART103A	
S1010	MTH103C	
S1020	CSC201A	B
S1020	MTH101B	A

FIGURE 6.3

The University Database (Same as Figure 1.1)

- Example 2. Use of Asterisk Notation for "all columns"

  Question: Get all information about CSC Faculty.

  Solution: We want the entire `Faculty` record of any faculty member whose department is 'CSC'. Since many SQL retrievals require all columns of a single table, there is a short way of expressing "all columns," namely by using an asterisk in place of the column names in the SELECT line.

SQL Query:

```
SELECT      *
FROM        Faculty
WHERE       department = 'CSC';
```

Result:

facId	name	department	rank
F105	Tanaka	CSC	Instructor
F221	Smith	CSC	Professor

Users who access a relational database through a host language are usually advised to avoid using the asterisk notation. The danger is that an additional column might be added to a table after a program was written. The program will then retrieve the value of that new column with each record and will not have a matching program variable for the value, causing a loss of correspondence between database variables and program variables. It is safer to write the query as:

```
SELECT      facId, name, department, rank
FROM        Faculty
WHERE       department = 'CSC';
```

- Example 3. Retrieval without Condition, Use of "Distinct," Use of Qualified Names

Question: Get the course number of all courses in which students are enrolled.

Solution: We go to the `Enroll` table rather than the `Class` table, because it is possible there is a `Class` record for a planned class in which no one is enrolled. From the `Enroll` table, we could ask for a list of all the `classNumber` values, as follows.

SQL Query:

```
SELECT      classNumber
FROM        Enroll;
```

Result:

<u>classNumber</u>
ART103A
CSC201A
CSC201A
ART103A
ART103A
MTH101B
HST205A
MTH103C
MTH103C

Since we did not need a predicate, we did not use the WHERE line. Notice that there are several duplicates in our result; it is a multi-set, not a true relation. Unlike the relational algebra PROJECT, the SQL SELECT does not eliminate duplicates when it "projects" over columns. To eliminate the duplicates, we need to use the DISTINCT option in the SELECT line. If we write,

```
SELECT DISTINCT classNumber
FROM Enroll;
```

The result would be:

<u>classNumber</u>
ART103A
CSC201A
HST205A
MTH101B
MTH103C

In any retrieval, especially if there is a possibility of confusion because the same column name appears on two different tables, we specify *tablename.colname.* In this example, we could have written:

```
SELECT    DISTINCT Enroll.classNumber
FROM      Enroll;
```

Here, it is not necessary to use the qualified name, since the FROM line tells the system to use the `Enroll` table, and column names are always unique within a table. However, it is never wrong to use a qualified name, and it is sometimes necessary to do so when two or more tables appear in the FROM line.

- Example 4: Retrieving an Entire Table

  Question: Get all information about all students.

  Solution: Because we want all columns of the Student table, we use the asterisk notation. Because we want all the records in the table, we omit the WHERE line.

  SQL Query:

  ```
  SELECT    *
  FROM      Student;
  ```

  Result: The result is the entire Student table.

- Example 5. Use of "ORDER BY" and AS

  Question: Get names and IDs of all Faculty members, arranged in alphabetical order by name. Call the resulting columns Faculty-Name and FacultyNumber.

  Solution: The ORDER BY option in the SQL SELECT allows us to order the retrieved records in ascending (ASC—the default) or descending (DESC) order on any field or combination of fields, regardless of whether that field appears in the results. If we order by more than one field, the one named first determines major order, the next minor order, and so on.

  SQL Query:

  ```
  SELECT    name AS FacultyName, facId AS
            FacultyNumber
  FROM      Faculty
  ORDER BY  name;
  ```

  Result:

FacultyName	FacultyNumber
Adams	F101
Byrne	F110
Smith	F202
Smith	F221
Tanaka	F105

The column headings are changed to the ones specified in the AS clause. We can rename any column or columns for display in this way. Note the duplicate name of 'Smith'. Since we did not specify minor order, the system will arrange these two rows in any order it chooses. We could break the "tie" by giving a minor order, as follows:

```
SELECT    name AS FacultyName, facId AS
          FacultyNumber
FROM      Faculty
ORDER BY  name, department;
```

Now the Smith records will be reversed, since F221 is assigned to CSC, which is alphabetically before History. Note also that the field that determines ordering need not be one of the ones displayed.

- Example 6. Use of Multiple Conditions

  Question: Get names of all math majors who have more than 30 credits.

  Solution: From the Student table, we choose those rows where the major is 'Math' and the number of credits is greater than 30. We express these two conditions by connecting them with 'AND.' We display only the lastName and firstName.

  SQL Query:

```
SELECT    lastName, firstName
FROM      Student
WHERE     major = 'Math'
          AND credits > 30;
```

  Result:

lastName	firstName
Jones	Mary
Chin	Ann

The predicate can be as complex as necessary by using the standard comparison operators =, <>, <, <=, >, >= and the standard logical operators AND, OR and NOT, with parentheses, if needed or desired, to show order of evaluation.

6.4.2   SELECT Using Multiple Tables

- Example 7. Natural Join

Question: Find IDs and names of all students taking ART103A.

Solution: This question requires the use of two tables. We first look in the `Enroll` table for records where the `classNumber` is 'ART103A.' We then look up the `Student` table for records with matching `stuId` values, and join those records into a new table. From this table, we find the `lastName` and `firstName`. This is similar to the JOIN operation in relational algebra. SQL allows us to do a natural join, as described in Section 4.6.2, by naming the tables involved and expressing in the predicate the condition that the records should match on the common field.

SQL Query:

```
SELECT     Enroll.stuId, lastName, firstName
FROM       Student, Enroll
WHERE      classNumber = 'ART103A'
           AND Enroll.stuId = Student.stuId;
```

Result:

stuId	lastName	firstName
S1001	Smith	Tom
S1010	Burns	Edward
S1002	Chin	Ann

Notice that we used the qualified name for `stuId` in the SELECT line. We could have written `Student.stuId` instead of `Enroll.stuId`, but we needed to use one of the table names, because `stuId` appears on both of the tables in the FROM line. We did not need to use the qualified name for `classNumber` because it does not appear on the `Student` table. The fact that it appears on the `Class` table is irrelevant, as that table is not mentioned in the FROM line. Of course, we had to write both qualified names for `stuId` in the WHERE line.

Why is the condition "`Enroll.stuId=Student.stuId`" necessary? The answer is that it is essential. When a relational database system performs a join, it acts as if it first forms a Cartesian product, as described in Section 4.6.2, so an intermediate table containing the combinations of all records from the `Student` table with the records of the `Enroll` table is (theoretically) formed. Even if the system restricts itself to records in `Enroll` that satisfy the condition "`classNumber='ART103A'` ", the intermediate table numbers 6*3 or18 records. For example, one of those intermediate records is:

S1015   Jones   Mary   Math   42   ART103A   S1001   A

We are not interested in this record, since this student is not one of the people in the ART103A class. Therefore, we add the condition that the `stuId` values must be equal. This reduces the intermediate table to three records.

- Example 8. Natural Join with Ordering

  Question: Find `stuId` and `grade` of all students taking any course taught by the `Faculty` member whose `facId` is F110. Arrange in order by `stuId`.

  Solution: We need to look at the `Class` table to find the `classNumber` of all courses taught by F110. We then look at the `Enroll` table for records with matching `classNumber` values, and get the join of the tables. From this we find the corresponding `stuId` and `grade`. Because we are using two tables, we will write this as a join.

  SQL Query:

```
SELECT     stuId,grade
FROM       Class,Enroll
WHERE      facId = 'F110' AND Class.classNumber
           = Enroll.classNumber
ORDER BY   stuId ASC;
```

  Result:

stuId	grade
S1002	B
S1010	
S1020	A

- Example 9. Natural Join of Three Tables

  Question: Find course numbers and the names and majors of all students enrolled in the courses taught by `Faculty` member F110.

  Solution: As in the previous example, we need to start at the `Class` table to find the `classNumber` of all courses taught by F110. We then compare these with `classNumber` values in the `Enroll` table to find the `stuId` values of all students in those courses. Then we look at the `Student` table to find the names and majors of all the students enrolled in them.

SQL Query:

```
SELECT    Enroll.classNumber, lastName,
          firstName, major
FROM      Class, Enroll, Student
WHERE     facId = 'F110'
          AND Class.classNumber =
          Enroll.classNumber
          AND Enroll.stuId = Student.stuId;
```

Result:

classNumber	lastName	firstName	major
MTH101B	Rivera	Jane	CSC
MTH103C	Burns	Edward	Art
MTH103C	Chin	Ann	Math

This was a natural join of three tables, and it required two sets of common columns. We used the condition of equality for both of the sets in the WHERE line. You may have noticed that the order of the table names in the FROM line corresponded to the order in which they appeared in our plan of solution, but that is not necessary. SQL ignores the order in which the tables are named in the FROM line. The same is true of the order in which we write the various conditions that make up the predicate in the WHERE line. Most sophisticated relational database management systems choose which table to use first and which condition to check first, using an optimizer to identify the most efficient method of accomplishing any retrieval before choosing a plan.

- Example 10. Use of Aliases

  Question: Get a list of all courses that meet in the same room, with their schedules and room numbers.

  Solution: This requires comparing the `Class` table with itself, and it would be useful if there were two copies of the table so we could do a natural join. We can pretend that there are two copies of a table by giving it two "aliases," for example, COPY and COPY2, and then treating these names as if they were the names of two distinct tables. We introduce the "aliases" in the FROM line by writing them immediately after the real table names. Then we have the aliases available for use in the other lines of the query.

SQL Query:

```
SELECT  COPY1.classNumber, COPY1.schedule, COPY1.room,
        COPY2.classNumber, COPY2.schedule
FROM    Class COPY1, Class COPY2
WHERE   COPY1.room = COPY2.room
        AND COPY1.classNumber < COPY2.classNumber ;
```

Result:

COPY1.classNumber	COPY1.schedule	COPY1.room	COPY2.classNumber	COPY2.schedule
ART103A	MWF9	H221	HST205A	MWF11
CSC201A	TUTHF10	M110	CSC203A	MTHF12
MTH101B	MTUTH9	H225	MTH103C	MWF11

Notice we had to use the qualified names in the SELECT line even before we introduced the "aliases." This is necessary because every column in the `Class` table now appears twice, once in each copy. We added the second condition "COPY1.`classNumber` < COPY2.C0URSE#" to keep every course from being included, since every course obviously satisfies the requirement that it meets in the same room as itself. It also keeps records with the two courses reversed from appearing. For example, because we have,

ART103A   MWF9   H221   HST205A   MWF11

we do not need the record

HST205A   MWF11   H221   ART103A   MWF9

Incidentally, we can introduce aliases in any SELECT, even when they are not required.

- Example 11. Join without Equality Condition

    Question: Find all combinations of students and `Faculty` where the student's major is different from the `Faculty` member's department.

    Solution: This unusual request is to illustrate a join in which the condition is not an equality on a common field. In this case, the fields we are examining, `major` and `department`, do not even have the same name. However, we can compare them since they have the same domain. Since we are not told which columns to show in the result, we use our judgment.

SQL Query:

```
SELECT   stuId, lastName, firstName, major, facId, name, department
FROM     Student, Faculty
WHERE    Student.major <> Faculty.department;
```

Result:

stuId	lastName	firstName	major	facId	name	department
S1001	Smith	Tom	History	F101	Adams	Art
S1001	Smith	Tom	History	F105	Tanaka	CS
S1001	Smith	Tom	History	F110	Byrne	Math
S1001	Smith	Tom	History	F221	Smith	CS
S1010	Burns	Edward	Art	F202	Smith	History
....						
....						
....						
S1013	McCarthy	Owen	Math	F221	Smith	CS

As in relational algebra, a join can be done on any two tables by simply forming the Cartesian product. Although we usually want the natural join as in our previous examples, we might use any type of predicate as the condition for the join. If we want to compare two columns, however, they must have the same domains. Notice that we used qualified names in the WHERE line. This was not really necessary, because each column name was unique, but we did so to make the condition easier to follow.

- Example 12. Using a Subquery with Equality

Question: Find the numbers of all the courses taught by Byrne of the math department.

Solution: We already know how to do this by using a natural join, but there is another way of finding the solution. Instead of imagining a join from which we choose records with the same facId, we could visualize this as two separate queries. For the first one, we would go to the Faculty table and find the record with name of Byrne and department of Math. We could make a note of the corresponding facId. Then we could take the result of that query, namely F110, and search the Class table for records with that value in facId. Once we found them, we would display the classNumber. SQL allows us to sequence these queries so that the result of the first can be used in the second, shown as follows:

SQL Query:

```
SELECT    classNumber
FROM      Class
WHERE     facId =
          (SELECT   facId
          FROM      Faculty
          WHERE     name = 'Byrne'
                    AND department = 'Math');
```

Result:

```
classNumber
MTH101B
MTH103C
```

Note that this result could have been produced by the following SQL
query, using a join:

```
SELECT    classNumber
FROM      Class, Faculty
WHERE     name = 'Byrne' AND department = 'Math' AND Class.facId
          = Faculty.facId;
```

A subquery can be used in place of a join, provided the result to be displayed
is contained in a single table and the data retrieved from the subquery consists of only one column. When you write a subquery involving two tables,
you name only one table in each SELECT. The query to be done first, the
subquery, is the one in parentheses, following the first WHERE line. The
main query is performed using the result of the subquery. Normally you
want the value of some field in the table mentioned in the main query to
match the value of some field from the table in the subquery. In this example, we knew we would get only one value from the subquery, since `facId` is
the key of `Faculty`, so a unique value would be produced. Therefore, we
were able to use equality as the operator. However, conditions other than
equality can be used. Any single comparison operator can be used in a subquery from which you know a single value will be produced. Since the subquery is performed first, the SELECT . . . FROM . . . WHERE of the
subquery is actually replaced by the value retrieved, so the main query is
changed to the following:

```
SELECT    classNumber
FROM      Class
WHERE     facId = ('F110');
```

- Example 13. Subquery Using 'IN'

  Question: Find the names and IDs of all `Faculty` members who teach a class in Room H221.

  Solution: We need two tables, `Class` and `Faculty`, to answer this question. We also see that the names and IDs both appear on the `Faculty` table, so we have a choice of a join or a subquery. If we use a subquery, we begin with the `Class` table to find `facId` values for any courses that meet in Room H221. We find two such entries, so we make a note of those values. Then we go to the `Faculty` table and compare the `facId` value of each record on that table with the two ID values from `Class`, and display the corresponding `facId` and name.

  SQL Query:

```
SELECT    name, facId
FROM      Faculty
WHERE     facId IN
          (SELECT    facId
          FROM      Class
          WHERE     room = 'H221');
```

  Result:

name	facId
Adams	F101
Smith	F202

In the WHERE line of the main query we used IN, rather than =, because the result of the subquery is a set of values rather than a single value. We are saying we want the `facId` in `Faculty` to match any member of the set of values we obtain from the subquery. When the subquery is replaced by the values retrieved, the main query becomes:

```
SELECT    name, facId
FROM      Faculty
WHERE     FACID IN ('F101','F202');
```

The IN is a more general form of subquery than the comparison operator, which is restricted to the case where a single value is produced. We can also use the negative form 'NOT IN', which will evaluate to true if the record has a field value which is not in the set of values retrieved by the subquery.

- Example 14. Nested Subqueries

Question: Get an alphabetical list of names and IDs of all students in any class taught by F110.

Solution: We need three tables, Student, Enroll, and Class, to answer this question. However, the values to be displayed appear on one table, Student, so we can use a subquery. First we check the Class table to find the classNumber of all courses taught by F110. We find two values, MTH101B and MTH103C. Next we go to the Enroll table to find the stuId of all students in either of these courses. We find three values, S1020, S1010, and S1002. We now look at the Student table to find the records with matching stuId values, and display the stuId, lastName, and firstName, in alphabetical order by name.

SQL Query:

```
SELECT    lastName, firstName, stuId
FROM      Student
WHERE     stuId IN
          (SELECT   stuId
           FROM     Enroll
           WHERE    classNumber IN
                    (SELECT classNumber
                     FROM    Class
                     WHERE   facId = 'F110'))
ORDER BY lastName, firstName ASC;
```

Result:

lastName	firstName	stuId
Burns	Edward	S1010
Chin	Ann	S1002
Rivera	Jane	S1020

In execution, the most deeply nested SELECT is done first, and it is replaced by the values retrieved, so we have:

```
SELECT    lastName, firstName, stuId
FROM      Student
WHERE     stuId IN
          (SELECT   stuId
           FROM     Enroll
```

```
          WHERE     classNumber IN
                       ('MTH101B', 'MTH103C'))
          ORDER BY  lastName, firstName ASC;
```

Next the subquery on `Enroll` is done, and we get:

```
SELECT    lastName, firstName, stuId
FROM      Student
WHERE     stuId IN
             ('S1020', 'S1010', 'S1002')
ORDER BY  lastName, firstName ASC;
```

Finally, the main query is done, and we get the result shown earlier. Note that the ordering refers to the final result, not to any intermediate steps. Also note that we could have performed either part of the operation as a natural join and the other part as a subquery, mixing both methods.

- Example 15. Query Using EXISTS

    Question: Find the names of all students enrolled in CSC201A.

    Solution: We already know how to write this using a join or a subquery with IN. However, another way of expressing this query is to use the existential quantifier, EXISTS, with a subquery.

    SQL Query:

    ```
    SELECT    lastName, firstName
    FROM      Student
    WHERE     EXISTS
              (SELECT  *
               FROM    Enroll
               WHERE   Enroll.stuId = Student.stuId
               AND     classNumber = 'CSC201A');
    ```

    Result:

lastName	firstName
Rivera	Jane
Chin	Ann

This query could be phrased as "Find the `lastName` and `firstName` of all students such that there exists an `Enroll` record containing their `stuId` with a `classNumber` of CSC201A". The test for inclusion is the existence of such a record. If it exists, the "EXISTS (SELECT FROM . . .;" evaluates to true.

Notice we needed to use the name of the main query table (`Student`) in the subquery to express the condition `Student.stuId = Enroll.stuId`. In general, we avoid mentioning a table not listed in the FROM for that particular query, but it is necessary and permissible to do so in this case. This form is called a **correlated** subquery, since the table in the subquery is being compared to the table in the main query.

- Example 16. Query Using NOT EXISTS

Question: Find the names of all students who are not enrolled in CSC201A.

Solution: Unlike the previous example, we cannot readily express this using a join or an IN subquery. Instead, we will use NOT EXISTS.

SQL Query:

```
SELECT    lastName, firstName
FROM      Student
WHERE     NOT EXISTS
          (SELECT    *
          FROM      Enroll
          WHERE     Student.stuId = Enroll.stuId
          AND       classNumber = 'CSC201A');
```

Result:

lastName	firstName
Smith	Tom
Burns	Edward
Jones	Mary
McCarthy	Owen
Lee	Perry

We could phrase this query as "Select student names from the `Student` table such that there is no `Enroll` record containing their STUID values with `classNumber` of CSC201A."

6.4.3 SELECT with Other Operators

- Example 17. Query Using UNION

Question: Get IDs of all `Faculty` who are assigned to the history department or who teach in Room H221.

Solution: It is easy to write a query for either of the conditions, and we can combine the results from the two queries by using a UNION operator. The UNION in SQL is the standard relational algebra operator for set union, and works in the expected way, eliminating duplicates.

SQL Query:

```
SELECT    facId
FROM      Faculty
WHERE     department = 'History'
UNION
SELECT    facId
FROM      Class
WHERE     room ='H221';
```

Result:

```
facId
F115
F101
```

- Example 18. Using Functions

Question: Find the total number of students enrolled in ART103A.

Solution: Although this is a simple question, we are unable to express it as an SQL query at the moment, because we have not yet seen any way to operate on collections of rows or columns. We need some functions to do so. SQL has five built-in functions: COUNT, SUM, AVG, MAX, and MIN. We will use COUNT, which returns the number of values in a column.

SQL Query:

```
SELECT    COUNT (DISTINCT stuId)
FROM      Enroll
WHERE     classNumber = 'ART103A';
```

Result:

```
3
```

The built-in functions operate on a single column of a table. Each of them eliminates null values first, and operates only on the remaining non-null values. The functions return a single value, defined as follows:

COUNT	returns the number of values in the column
SUM	returns the sum of the values in the column

AVG	returns the mean of the values in the column
MAX	returns the largest value in the column
MIN	returns the smallest value in the column.

COUNT, MAX, and MIN apply to both numeric and nonnumeric fields, but SUM and AVG can be used on numeric fields only. The collating sequence is used to determine order of nonnumeric data. If we want to eliminate duplicate values before starting, we use the word DISTINCT before the column name in the SELECT line. COUNT(*) is a special use of the COUNT. Its purpose is to count all the rows of a table, regardless of whether null values or duplicate values occur. Except for COUNT(*). we must always use DISTINCT with the COUNT function, as we did in the above example. If we use DISTINCT with MAX or MIN it will have no effect, because the largest or smallest value remains the same even if two tuples share it. However, DISTINCT usually has an effect on the result of SUM or AVG, so the user should understand whether or not duplicates should be included in computing these. Function references appear in the SELECT line of a query or a subquery.

Additional Function Examples:

Example (a) Find the number of departments that have `Faculty` in them. Because we do not wish to count a department more than once, we use DISTINCT here.

```
SELECT   COUNT(DISTINCT department)
FROM     Faculty;
```

Example (b) Find the average number of credits students have. We do not want to use DISTINCT here, because if two students have the same number of credits, both should be counted in the average.

```
SELECT   AVG(credits)
FROM     Student;
```

Example (c) Find the student with the largest number of credits. Because we want the student's credits to equal the maximum, we need to find that maximum first, so we use a subquery to find it.

```
SELECT   stuId, lastName, firstName
FROM     Student
WHERE    credits =
         (SELECT   MAX(credits)
          FROM     Student);
```

Example (d) Find the ID of the student(s) with the highest grade in any course. Because we want the highest grade, it might appear that we should use the MAX function here. A closer look at the table reveals that the grades are letters A, B, C, etc. For this scale, the best grade is the one that is earliest in the alphabet, so we actually want MIN. If the grades were numeric, we would have wanted MAX.

```
SELECT      stuId
FROM        Enroll
WHERE       grade =
            (SELECT   MIN(grade)
             FROM     Enroll);
```

Example (e) Find names and IDs of students who have less than the average number of credits.

```
SELECT      lastName, firstName, stuId
FROM        Student
WHERE       credits <
            (SELECT   AVG(credits)
             FROM     Student);
```

- Example 19. Using an Expression and a String Constant

    Question: Assuming each course is three credits list, for each student, the number of courses he or she has completed.

    Solution: We can calculate the number of courses by dividing the number of credits by three. We can use the expression `credits/3` in the SELECT to display the number of courses. Since we have no such column name, we will use a string constant as a label. String constants that appear in the SELECT line are simply printed in the result.

    SQL Query:

```
SELECT      stuId, 'Number of courses =', credits/3
FROM        Student;
```

    Result:

```
stuId
S1001 Number of courses =   30
S1010 Number of courses =   21
S1015 Number of courses =   14
S1005 Number of courses =    1
```

```
S1002 Number of courses =  12
S1020 Number of courses =   5
S1013 Number of courses =   0
```

By combining constants, column names, arithmetic operators, built-in functions, and parentheses, the user can customize retrievals.

- Example 20. Use of GROUP BY

  Question: For each course, show the number of students enrolled.

  Solution: We want to use the COUNT function, but need to apply it to each course individually. The GROUP BY allows us to put together all the records with a single value in the specified field. Then we can apply any function to any field in each group, provided the result is a single value for the group.

  SQL Query:

  ```
  SELECT      classNumber, COUNT(*)
  FROM        Enroll
  GROUP BY    classNumber;
  ```

  Result:

className	
ART103A	3
CSC201A	2
MTH101B	1
HST205A	1
MTH103C	2

Note that we could have used COUNT(DISTINCT stuId) in place of COUNT(*) in this query.

- Example 21. Use of HAVING

  Problem: Find all courses in which fewer than three students are enrolled.

  Solution: This is a question about a characteristic of the groups formed in the previous example. HAVING is used to determine which groups have some quality, just as WHERE is used with tuples to determine which records have some quality. You are not permitted to use HAVING without a GROUP BY, and the predicate in the HAVING line must have a single value for each group.

SQL Query:

```
SELECT     classNumber
FROM       Enroll
GROUP BY   classNumber
HAVING     COUNT(*) < 3 ;
```

Result:

classNumber
CSC201A
MTH101B
HST205A
MTH103C

- Example 22. Use of LIKE

  Problem: Get details of all MTH courses.

  Solution: We do not wish to specify the exact course numbers, but we want the first three letters of `classNumber` to be MTH. SQL allows us to use LIKE in the predicate to show a pattern string for character fields. Records whose specified columns match the pattern will be retrieved.

  SQL Query:

  ```
  SELECT     *
  FROM       Class
  WHERE      classNumber LIKE 'MTH%';
  ```

  Result:

classNumber	facId	schedule	room
MTH101B	F110	MTUTH9	H225
MTH103C	F110	MWF11	H225

In the pattern string, we can use the following symbols:

  % The percent character stands for any sequence of characters of any length >= 0.
  _ The underscore character stands for any single character.

All other characters in the pattern stand for themselves.

Examples:

- **classNumber** LIKE 'MTH%' means the first three letters must be MTH, but the rest of the string can be any characters.

- **stuId** LIKE 'S_ _ _ _' means there must be five characters, the first of which must be an S

- **schedule** LIKE '%9' means any sequence of characters, of length at least one, with the last character a nine.

- **classNumber** LIKE '%101%' means a sequence of characters of any length containing 101. Note the 101 could be the first, last, or only characters, as well as being somewhere in the middle of the string.

- **name** NOT LIKE 'A%' means the name cannot begin with an A.

- Example 23. Use of NULL

Question: Find the stuId and classNumber of all students whose grades in that course are missing.

Solution: We can see from the Enroll table that there are two such records. You might think they could be accessed by specifying that the grades are not A, B, C, D, or F, but that is not the case. A null grade is considered to have "unknown" as a value, so it is impossible to judge whether it is equal to or not equal to another grade. If we put the condition "WHERE grade <>'A' AND grade <>'B' AND grade <>'C' AND grade <>'D' AND grade <>'F'" we would get an empty table back, instead of the two records we want. SQL uses the logical expression,

columnname IS [NOT] NULL

to test for null values in a column.

SQL Query:

```
SELECT      classNumber,stuId
FROM        Enroll
WHERE       grade IS NULL;
```

Result:

classNumber	stuId
ART103A	S1010
MTH103C	S1010

Notice that it is illegal to write "WHERE `grade` = NULL," because a predicate involving comparison operators with NULL will evaluate to "unknown" rather than "true" or "false." Also, the WHERE line is the only one on which NULL can appear in a SELECT statement.

- Example 24. Recursive Queries

    SQL:1999 allows recursive queries, which are queries that execute repeatedly until no new results are found. For example, consider a CSCCOURSE table, as shown in Figure 6.4(a). Its structure is:

    CSCCourse(*courseNumber*, courseTitle, credits,
    prerequisiteCourseNumber)

    For simplicity, we assume a course can have at most one immediate prerequisite course. The prerequisite course number functions as a foreign key for the CSCCourse table, referring to the primary key (course number) of a different course.

    Problem: Find all of a course's prerequisites, including prerequisites of prerequisites for that course.

    SQL Query:

```
WITH RECURSIVE
Prereqs (courseNumber, prerequisiteCourseNumber) AS
    ( SELECT courseNumber, prerequisiteCourseNumber
      FROM CSCCourse
      UNION
      SELECT (COPY1.courseNumber, COPY2.prerequisiteCourseNumber
      FROM Prereqs COPY1, CSCCourse COPY2
      WHERE COPY1.prerequisiteCourseNumber = COPY2.courseNumber);

SELECT *
FROM Prereqs
ORDER BY courseNumber, prerequisiteCourseNumber;
```

This query will display each course number, along with all of that course's prerequisites, including the prerequisite's prerequisite, and so on, all the way back to the initial course in the sequence of its prerequisites. The result is shown in Figure 6.4(b).

6.4.4   Operators for Updating: UPDATE, INSERT, DELETE

The UPDATE operator is used to change values in records already stored in a table. It is used on one table at a time, and can change zero, one, or many records, depending on the predicate. Its form is:

```
UPDATE    tablename
SET       columnname = expression
          [columnname = expression] . . .
[WHERE    predicate];
```

Note that it is not necessary to specify the current value of the field, although the present value may be used in the expression to determine the new value. The SET statement is actually an assignment statement, and works in the usual way.

- Example 1. Updating a Single Field of One Record

  Operation: Change the major of S1020 to Music.

  SQL Command:

  ```
  UPDATE    Student
  SET       major = 'Music'
  WHERE     stuId = 'S1020';
  ```

- Example 2. Updating Several Fields of One Record

  Operation: Change Tanaka's department to MIS and rank to Assistant.

  SQL Command:

  ```
  UPDATE    Faculty
  SET       department = 'MIS'
            rank = 'Assistant'
  WHERE     name = 'Tanaka';
  ```

CSCCourse			
courseNumber	courseTitle	credits	prerequisiteCourseNumber
101	Intro to Computing	3	
102	Computer Applications	3	101
201	Programming 1	4	101
202	Programming 2	4	201
301	Data Structures & Algorithms	3	202
310	Operating Systems	3	202
320	Database Systems	3	301
410	Advanced Operating Systems	3	310
420	Advanced Database Systems	3	320

FIGURE 6.4(a)

CSCCourse table to demonstrate recursive queries

FIGURE 6.4(b)

Result of recursive query

Prereqs

courseNumber	prerequisiteCourseNumber
101	
102	
102	101
201	
201	101
202	
202	101
202	201
301	
301	101
301	201
301	202
310	
310	101
310	201
310	202
320	
320	101
320	201
320	202
320	301
410	
410	101
410	201
410	202
410	310
420	
420	101
420	201
420	202
420	301
420	320

- Example 3. Updating Using NULL

Operation: Change the major of S1013 from Math to NULL.
To insert a null value into a field that already has an actual value, we must use the form:

SET *columnname* = NULL

SQL Command:

```
UPDATE    Student
SET       major = NULL
WHERE     stuId = 'S1013';
```

- Example 4. Updating Several Records

Operation: Change grades of all students in CSC201A to A.

SQL Command:

```
UPDATE    Enroll
SET       grade = 'A'
WHERE     classNumber = 'CSC201A';
```

- Example 5. Updating All Records.

Operation: Give all students three extra credits.

SQL Command:

```
UPDATE    Student
SET       credits = credits + 3;
```

Notice we did not need the WHERE line, because all records were to be updated.

- Example 6. Updating with a Subquery

Operation: Change the room to B220 for all courses taught by Tanaka.

SQL Command:

```
UPDATE    Class
SET       room = 'B220'
WHERE     facId =
          (SELECT  facId
           FROM    Faculty
           WHERE   name = 'Tanaka');
```

The INSERT operator is used to put new records into a table. Normally, it is not used to load an entire table, because the database management system usually has a load utility to handle that task. However, the INSERT is useful for adding one or a few records to a table. Its form is:

```
INSERT
INTO      tablename [(colname [,colname]. . .)]
VALUES    (constant [,constant] . . .);
```

- Example 1. Inserting a Single Record, with All Fields Specified

Operation: Insert a new `Faculty` record with ID of F330, name of Jones, department of CSC and rank of Instructor.

SQL Command:

```
INSERT
INTO    Faculty (facId, name, department, rank)
VALUES  ('F330', 'Jones', 'CSC', 'Instructor');
```

- Example 2. Inserting a Single Record, without Specifying Fields

Operation: Insert a new student record with ID of S1030, name of Alice Hunt, major of art, and 12 credits.

SQL Query:

```
INSERT
INTO    Student
VALUES  ('S1030', 'Hunt', 'Alice', 'Art', 12);
```

Notice it was not necessary to specify field names, because the system assumes we mean all the fields in the table. We could have done the same for the previous example.

- Example 3. Inserting a Record with Null Value in a Field

Operation: Insert a new student record with ID of S1031, name of Maria Bono, zero credits, and no major.

SQL Command:

```
INSERT
INTO    Student (lastName, firstName, stuId, credits)
VALUES  ('Bono', 'Maria', 'S1031', 0);
```

Notice we rearranged the field names, but there is no confusion because it is understood that the order of values matches the order of fields named in the INTO, regardless of their order in the table. Also notice the zero is an actual value for `credits`, not a null value. `major` will be set to null, since we excluded it from the field list in the INTO line.

- Example 4. Inserting Multiple Records

  Operation: Create and fill a new table that shows each course and the number of students enrolled in it.

  SQL Command:

```
CREATE TABLE Enrollment
    (classNumber CHAR(7) NOT NULL,
    Students SMALLINT);
INSERT
INTO Enrollment      (classNumber, Students)
    SELECT           classNumber, COUNT(*)
    FROM             Enroll
    GROUP BY         classNumber;
```

Here, we created a new table, `Enrollment`, and filled it by taking data from an existing table, `Enroll`. If `Enroll` is as it appears in Figure 6.3, `Enrollment` now looks like this:

Enrollment	classNumber	Students
	ART103A	3
	CSC201A	2
	MTH101B	1
	HST205A	1
	MTH103C	2

The `Enrollment` table is now available for the user to manipulate, just as any other table would be. It can be updated as needed, but it will not be updated automatically when the `Enroll` table is updated.

The DELETE is used to erase records. The number of records deleted may be zero, one, or many, depending on how many satisfy the predicate. The form of this command is:

```
DELETE
FROM      tablename
WHERE     predicate;
```

- Example 1. Deleting a Single Record

Operation: Erase the record of student S1020.

SQL Command:

```
DELETE
FROM      Student
WHERE     stuId = 'S1020';
```

- Example 2. Deleting Several Records

Operation: Erase all enrollment records for student S1020.

SQL Command:

```
DELETE
FROM      Enroll
WHERE     stuId = 'S1020';
```

- Example 3. Deleting All Records from a Table

Operation: Erase all the class records.

If we delete `Class` records and allow their corresponding `Enroll` records to remain, we would lose referential integrity, because the `Enroll` records would then refer to classes that no longer exist. However, if we have created the tables using Oracle and the commands shown in Figure 6.2, the delete command will not work on the `Class` table unless we first delete the `Enroll` records for any students registered in the class, because we wrote,

```
CONSTRAINT Enroll_classNumber_fk FOREIGN KEY (classNumber) REFERENCES Class
(classNumber)
```

for the Enroll table. However, assuming that we have deleted the `Enroll` records, then we can delete `Class` records.

SQL Command:

```
DELETE
FROM      Class;
```

This would remove all records from the `Class` table, but its structure would remain, so we could add new records to it at any time.

- Example 4. DELETE with a Subquery

Operation: Erase all enrollment records for Owen McCarthy.

SQL Command:

```
DELETE
FROM      Enroll
WHERE     stuId =
          (SELECT    stuId
           FROM      Student
           WHERE     lastName = 'Mc Carthy'
           AND firstName = 'Owen');
```

Because there were no such records, this statement will have no effect on
`Enroll`.

6.5   Active Databases

The DBMS has more powerful means of insuring integrity in a database
than the column and table constraints discussed in Section 6.3. An **active
database** is one in which the DBMS monitors the contents in order to prevent illegal states from occurring, using constraints and triggers.

6.5.1   Enabling and Disabling Constraints

The column and table constraints described in Section 6.3 are identified
when the table is created, and are checked whenever a change is made to
the database, to ensure that the new state is a valid one. Changes that could
result in invalid states include insertion, deletion, and updating of records.
Therefore, the constraints are checked by the DBMS whenever one of these
operations is performed, usually after each SQL INSERT, DELETE, or
UPDATE statement. This is called the IMMEDIATE mode of constraint
checking, and it is the default mode. However, there are times when a
transaction or application involves several changes and the database will be
temporarily invalid while the changes are in progress—while some but not
all of the changes already have been made. For example, assume we have a
Department table in our University example with a `chairPerson` column
in which we listed the `facId` of the chairperson, and we use a NOT NULL
specification for that field, and make it a foreign key, by writing:

```
CREATE TABLE Department (
    deptName        CHAR(20),
    chairPerson     CHAR(20) NOT NULL,
    CONSTRAINT Department_deptName_pk PRIMARY KEY(deptName),
    CONSTRAINT Department_facId_fk FOREIGN KEY REFERENCES Faculty (facId));
```

For the Faculty table definition in Figure 6.2, we already have a NOT NULL for the department, but now we could make `department` a foreign key with the new `Department` table as the home table, by writing:

```
ALTER TABLE Faculty ADD CONSTRAINT Faculty_department_fk FOREIGN KEY
department REFERENCES Department(deptName);
```

What will happen when we try to create a new department and add the faculty for that department to the `Faculty` table? We cannot insert the department record unless we already have the chairperson's record in the `Faculty` table, but we cannot insert that record unless the department record is already there, so each SQL INSERT statement would fail. For such situations, SQL allows us to defer the checking until the end of the entire transaction, using statements such as,

```
SET CONSTRAINT Department_facId_fk DEFERRED;
```

or,

```
SET CONSTRAINT Faculty_department_fk DEFERRED;
```

We can enable or disable constraints to allow such transactions to succeed, using the statement such as:

```
DISABLE CONSTRAINT Department_facId_fk;
```

At the end of the transaction, we should write,

```
ENABLE CONSTRAINT Department_facId_fk;
```

to allow enforcement again. Although not recommended, SLQ allows us to write,

```
DISABLE ALL CONSTRAINTS;
```

which suspends all integrity checking until a corresponding,

```
ENABLE ALL CONSTRAINTS;
```

command is encountered. These statements can be used both interactively and within applications.

6.5.2   SQL Triggers

Like constraints, **triggers** allow the DBMS to monitor the database. However, they are more flexible than constraints, apply to a broader range of situations, and allow a greater variety of actions. A trigger consists of three parts:

- An **event,** which is normally some change made to the database

- A **condition,** which is a logical predicate that evaluates to true or false

- An **action,** which is some procedure that is done when the event occurs and the condition evaluates to true, also called firing the trigger

A trigger has access to the inserted, deleted, or updated data that caused it to fire (i.e., to be activated or raised), and the data values can be used in the code both for the condition and for the action. The prefix :OLD is used to refer to the values in a tuple just deleted or to the values replaced in an update. The prefix :NEW is used to refer to the values in a tuple just inserted or to the new values in an update. Triggers can be fired either before or after the execution of the insert, delete or update operation. We can also specify whether the trigger is fired just once for each triggering statement, or for each row that is changed by the statement. (Recall that, for example, an update statement may change many rows.) In Oracle, you specify the SQL command (INSERT, DELETE, or UPDATE) that is the event; the table involved; the trigger level (ROW or STATEMENT); the timing (BEFORE or AFTER); and the action to be performed, which can be written as one or more SQL commands in PL/SQL. Section 6.7 discusses PL/SQL in more detail. The Oracle trigger syntax has the form:

```
CREATE OR REPLACE TRIGGER trigger_name
    [BEFORE/AFTER] [INSERT/UPDATE/DELETE] ON table_name
    [FOR EACH ROW] [WHEN condition]
    BEGIN
        trigger body
    END;
```

For example, let us add to the Class table two additional attributes, currentEnroll, which shows the number of students actually enrolled in each class, and maxEnroll, which is the maximum number of students allowed to enroll. The new table, RevClass, is shown in Figure 6.5, along with a new version of the Enroll table, RevEnroll. Since currentEnroll is a derived attribute, dependent on the RevEnroll table, its value should be updated when there are relevant changes made to RevEnroll. Changes that affect currentEnroll are:

1. A student enrolls in a class

2. A student drops a class

3. A student switches from one class to another

In an active database, there should be triggers for each of these changes. For change (1), we should increment the value of `currentEnroll` by one. We can refer to the `classNumber` of the new `RevEnroll` record by using the prefix :NEW. The corresponding trigger is shown in Figure 6.5(b) Note that we did not use the WHEN because we always want to make this change after a new enrollment record is inserted, so no condition was needed. For change (2), we need to decrement the value of `currentEnroll` by one, and we use the prefix :OLD to refer to the `revEnroll` record being deleted. The trigger is shown in Figure 6.5(c). Change (3) could be treated as a drop followed by an enrollment, but instead we will write a trigger for an update to demonstrate an action with two parts, as shown in Figure 6.5(d).

While these triggers are sufficient if there is room in a class, we also need to consider what should happen if the class is already fully enrolled. The value of `maxEnroll` should have been examined before we allowed a student to enroll in the class, so we need to check that value before we do change (1) or change (3). Assume that if a change would cause a class to be overenrolled, we call a procedure called RequestClosedCoursePermission that takes as parameters the student's ID, the class number, the current enrollment, and maximum enrollment. The action should be taken before we make the change. The trigger is shown in Figure 6.5(e).

Triggers are automatically enabled when they are created. They can be disabled by the statement:

> ALTER TRIGGER *trigger_name* DISABLE;

After disabling, they can enabled again by the statement:

> ALTER TRIGGER *trigger_name* ENABLE;

They can be dropped by the statement:

> DROP TRIGGER *trigger_name*;

Oracle provides an INSTEAD OF form that is especially useful when a user tries to update the database through a view. This form specifies an action to be performed instead of the insert, delete, or update that the user requested. It will be discussed in Section 6.8. Triggers can also be used to provide an audit trail for a table, recording all changes, the time they were made, and the identity of the user who made them, an application that will be discussed in Section 9.6.

RevClass					
classNumber	facId	schedule	room	currentEnroll	maxEnroll
ART103A	F101	MWF9	H221	3	25
CSC201A	F105	TuThF10	M110	2	20
CSC203A	F105	MThF12	M110	0	20
HST205A	F115	MWF11	H221	1	35
MTH101B	F110	MTuTh9	H225	1	25
MTH103C	F110	MWF11	H225	2	25

RevEnroll		
stuId	classNumber	grade
S1001	ART103A	A
S1001	HST205A	C
S1002	ART103A	D
S1002	CSC201A	F
S1002	MTH103C	B
S1010	ART103A	
S1010	MTH103C	
S1020	CSC201A	B
S1020	MTH101B	A

FIGURE 6.5(a)

Tables for Triggers

```
CREATE TRIGGER ADDENROLL
AFTER INSERT ON RevEnroll
FOR EACH ROW
BEGIN
   UPDATE RevClass
   SET currentEnroll = currentEnroll +1
   WHERE RevClass.classNumber = :NEW.classNumber;
END;
```

Figure 6.5(b)

Trigger for Student Enrolling in a Class

Figure 6.5(c)

Trigger for Student Dropping a Class

```
CREATE TRIGGER DROPENROLL
AFTER DELETE ON RevEnroll
FOR EACH ROW
BEGIN
    UPDATE RevClass
    SET currentEnroll = currentEnroll −1
    WHERE RevClass.classNumber = OLD.classNumber;
END;
```

Figure 6.5(d)

Trigger for Student Changing Classes

```
CREATE TRIGGER SWITCHENROLL
AFTER UPDATE OF classNumnber ON RevEnroll
FOR EACH ROW
    BEGIN
        UPDATE RevClass
        SET currentEnroll = currentEnroll + 1
        WHERE RevClass.classNumber = :NEW.classNumber;
        UPDATE RevClass
        SET currentEnroll = currentEnroll −1
        WHERE RevClass.classNumber = :OLD.classNumber;
    END;
```

Figure 6.5(e)

Trigger for Checking for Over-enrollment Before Enrolling Student

```
CREATE TRIGGER ENROLL_REQUEST
BEFORE INSERT OR UPDATE OF classNumber ON REVenroll
FOR EACH ROW
DECLARE
    numStu number;
    maxStu number;
BEGIN
    select   maxEnroll into maxStu
    from     RevClass
    where  RevClass.classNumber = :NEW.classNumber;

    select   currentEnroll +1 into numStu
    from     RevClass
    where  RevClass.classNumber = :NEW.classNumber;

    if numStu > maxStu
    RequestClosedCoursePermission(:NEW.stuId, :NEW.classNumber, RevClass.currentEnroll,
    RevClass.maxEnroll);
    end if;
END;
```

6.6   Using COMMIT and ROLLBACK Statements

Any changes made to a database using SQL commands are not permanent until the user writes a COMMIT statement. As discussed in Chapter 10, an SQL transaction ends when either a COMMIT statement or a ROLLBACK statement is encountered. The COMMIT makes permanent the changes made since the beginning of the current transaction, which is either the beginning of the session or the time since the last COMMIT or ROLLBACK. The ROLLBACK undoes changes made by the current transaction. It is wise to write COMMIT often to save changes as you work.

6.7   SQL Programming

For the interactive SQL statements shown so far, we assumed that there was a user interface that provided an environment to accept, interpret, and execute the SQL commands directly. An example is Oracle's SQLPlus facility. Though some users can interact with the database this way, most database access is through programs.

6.7.1   Embedded SQL

One way that SQL can be used is to embed it in programs written in a general-purpose programming language such as C, C++, Java, COBOL, Ada, Fortran, Pascal, PL/1, or M, referred to as the **host language.** Any interactive SQL command, such as the ones we have discussed, can be used in an application program, with minor modifications. The programmer writes the source code using both host language statements, which provide the control structures, and SQL statements, which manage the database access. Executable SQL statements are preceded by a prefix such as the keyword EXEC SQL, and end with a terminator such as a semicolon. An executable SQL statement can appear wherever an executable host language statement can appear. The DBMS provides a precompiler, which scans the entire program and strips out the SQL statements, identified by the prefix. The SQL is compiled separately into some type of access module, and the SQL statements are replaced, usually by simple function calls in the host language. The resulting host language program can then be compiled as usual. Figure 6.6 illustrates this process.

The data exchange between the application program and the database is accomplished through the host-language program variables, for which

FIGURE 6.6
Processing Embedded SQL Programs

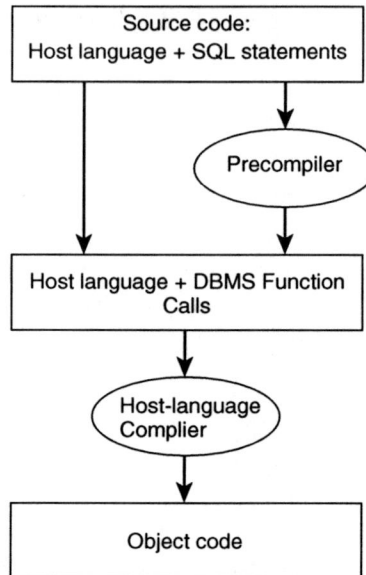

attributes of database records provide values or from which they receive their values. These **shared variables** are declared within the program in an SQL declaration section such as the following:

```
EXEC SQL BEGIN DECLARE SECTION;
char stuNumber[5];
char stuLastName[15];
char stuFirstName[12];
char stuMajor[10];
int stuCredits;
char SQLSTATE[6];
EXEC SQL END DECLARE SECTION;
```

The first five program variables declared here are designed to match the attributes of the Student table. They can be used to receive values from Student tuples, or to supply values to tuples. Because the data types of the host language might not match those of the database attributes exactly, a type cast operation can be used to pass appropriate values between program variables and database attributes. SQL:1999 provides language bindings that specify the correspondence between SQL data types and the data types of each host language.

The last variable declared, SQLSTATE, is a character array that is used for communicating error conditions to the program. When an SQL library function is called, a value is placed in SQLSTATE indicating which error condition may have occurred when the database was accessed. A value of '00000' indicates no error, while a value '02000' indicates that the SQL statement executed correctly but no tuple was found for a query. The value of SQLSTATE can be tested in host language control statements. For example, some processing may be performed if the value is '00000', or a loop may be written to read a record until the value of '02000' is returned.

Embedded SQL SELECT statements that operate on a single row of a table are very similar to the interactive statements we saw earlier. For example, a SELECT statement that retrieves a single tuple is modified for the embedded case by identifying the shared variables in an INTO line. Note that when shared variables are referred to within an SQL statement, they are preceded by colons to distinguish them from attributes, which might or might not have the same names. The following example begins with a host-language statement assigning a value to the host variable stuNumber. It then uses an SQL SELECT statement to retrieve a tuple from the Student table whose stuId matches the shared variable stuNumber (referred to as :stuNumber in the SQL statement). It puts the tuple's attribute values into four shared variables that were declared previously:

```
stuNumber = 'S1001';
EXEC SQL  SELECT  Student.lastName, Student.firstName, Student.major,
Student.credits
    INTO :stuLastName, :stuFirstName, :stuMajor, :stuCredits
    FROM Student
    WHERE Student.stuId = :stuNumber;
```

This segment should be followed by a host-language check of the value of SQLSTATE.

To insert a database tuple, we can assign values to shared variables in the host language and then use an SQL INSERT statement. The attribute values are taken from the host variables. For example, we could write:

```
stuNumber = 'S1050';
stuLastName = 'Lee';
stuFirstName = 'Daphne';
stuMajor = 'English';
stuCredits = 0;
EXEC SQL    INSERT
           INTO Student (stuId, lastName, firstName, major, credits)
           VALUES(:stuNumber,:stuLastName, :stuFirstName,:stuMajor,
:stuCredits);
```

We can delete any number of tuples that we can identify using the value of a host variable:

```
stuNumber = 'S1015';
EXEC SQL    DELETE
        FROM Student
        WHERE stuId = :stuNumber;
```

We can also update any number of tuples in a similar manner:

```
stuMajor = 'History';
EXEC SQL UPDATE Student
        SET CREDITS = CREDITS + 3
        WHERE major = :stuMajor;
```

Instead of checking the value of SQLSTATE after each SQL statement, we can use the error-handling WHENEVER statement which has the form:

```
EXEC SQL WHENEVER [SQLERROR/NOT FOUND] [CONTINUE/GO TO statement];
```

As mentioned earlier, a NOT FOUND condition means that the value of SQLSTATE is 02000, while SQLERROR condition is any exception. A WHENEVER remains in effect for the entire program for the condition specified, unless a new WHENEVER for the same condition appears, overriding the first.

A special problem called an **impedance mismatch** occurs when a SELECT statement returns more than one tuple (a multi-set). Although the relational model uses sets, a host language is generally capable of handling only one record at a time rather than an entire set of records. We need a device called a **cursor,** a symbolic pointer that points to one row of a table or multi-set at a time, provides access to that row to the application, then moves on to the next row. For an SQL query that returns a multi-set, the cursor can be used to step through the results of the query, allowing values to be provided to the host language tuple-by-tuple. A cursor is created and positioned so that it can point to one row in the table or in the multi-set at a time. The form for declaring a cursor is:

```
EXEC SQL DECLARE cursorname [INSENSITIVE] [SCROLL] CURSOR FOR query
    [FOR {READ ONLY | UPDATE OF attributeNames}];
```

For example, to create a cursor that will later be used to go through CSC student records that we plan to retrieve only, we would write:

```
EXEC SQL DECLARE CSCstuCursor CURSOR FOR
    SELECT stuId, lastName, firstName, major, credits
    FROM student
    WHERE major='CSC';
```

Note that this is a declaration, not an executable statement. The SQL query is not executed yet. After declaring the cursor, we write a statement to open it. This executes the query so that the results multi-set is created. Opening the cursor also positions it just before the first tuple of the results set. For this example, we write:

```
EXEC SQL OPEN CSCstuCursor;
```

To retrieve the first row of the results, we then use the FETCH command which has the form,

```
EXEC SQL FETCH cursorname INTO hostvariables;
```

as in,

```
EXEC SQL FETCH CSCstuCursor INTO :stuNumber,:stuLastName,
:stuFirstName,:stuMajor,:stuCredits
```

The FETCH statement advances the cursor and assigns the values of the attributes named in the SELECT statement to the corresponding shared variables named in the INTO line. A loop controlled by the value of SQL-STATE (e.g., WHILE (SQLSTATE = 00000)) should be created in the host language so that additional rows are accessed. The loop also contains host language statements to do whatever processing is needed. After all data has been retrieved, we exit the loop, and close the cursor in a statement such as:

```
EXEC SQL CLOSE CSCstuCursor;
```

If we plan to update multiple rows using the cursor, we must initially declare it to be updatable, by using a more complete declaration such as:

```
EXEC  SQL DECLARE stuCreditsCursor CURSOR FOR
      SELECT stuId, credits
      FROM Student
FOR UPDATE OF credits;
```

We must name in both the SELECT statement and the update attribute list any attribute that we plan to update using the cursor. Once the cursor is open and active, we can update the tuple at which the cursor is positioned, called the **current** of the cursor, by writing a command such as:

```
EXEC SQL UPDATE Student
SET credits = credits +3
WHERE CURRENT OF stuCreditsCursor;
```

Similarly, the current tuple can be deleted by a statement such as:

```
EXEC SQL DELETE FROM Student
WHERE CURRENT OF stuCreditCursor;
```

Users may wish to be able to specify the type of access they need at run time rather than in a static fashion using compiled code of the type just described. For example, we might want a graphical front end where the user could enter a query that can be used to generate SQL statements that are executed dynamically, like the interactive SQL described earlier. Besides the version of SQL just discussed, which is classified as static, there is a **dynamic SQL,** which allows the type of database access to be specified at run time rather than at compile time. For example, the user may be prompted to enter an SQL command that is then stored as a host-language string. The SQL PREPARE command tells the database management system to parse and compile the string as an SQL command, and to assign the resulting executable code to a named SQL variable. An EXECUTE command is then used to run the code. For example, in the following segment the host-language variable userString is assigned an SQL update command, the corresponding code is prepared and bound to the SQL identifier userCommand, and then the code is executed.

```
char userString[]='UPDATE Student SET credits = 36 WHERE stuId= S1050';
EXEC SQL PREPARE userCommand FROM :userString;
EXEC SQL EXECUTE userCommand;
```

6.7.2 API, ODBC, and JDBC

For embedded SQL, a precompiler supplied by the DBMS compiles the SQL code, replacing it with function calls in the host language. A more flexible approach is for the DBMS to provide an **Application Programming Interface,** API, that includes a set of standard library functions for database processing. The library functions can then be called by the application, which is written in a general purpose language. Programmers use these library functions in essentially the same way they use the library of the language itself. The functions allow the application to perform standard operations such as connecting to the database, executing SQL commands, presenting tuples one at a time, and so on. However, the application would still have to use the precompiler for a particular DBMS and be linked to the API library for that DBMS, so the same program could not be used with another DBMS.

Open Database Connectivity (ODBC) and **Java Database Connectivity (JDBC)** provide standard ways of integrating SQL code and general purpose languages by providing a common interface. This standardization allows applications to access multiple databases using different DBMSs.

```
+-----------------------------------+
| Application                       |
+-----------------------------------+
| Driver Manager                    |
+---------+---------+---------------+
| Driver  | Driver  | Driver        |
+---------+---------+---------------+
    |         |         |
  (Database)(Database)(Other
                        Data
                        Source)
```

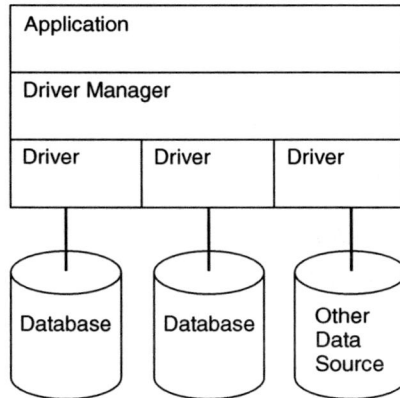

FIGURE 6.7
ODBC/JDBC Architecture

The standard provides a high degree of flexibility, allowing development of client-server applications that work with a variety of DBMSs, instead of being limited to a particular vendor API. Most vendors provide ODBC or JDBC drivers that conform to the standard. An application using one of these standard interfaces can use the same code to access different databases without recompilation. ODBC/JDBC architecture requires four components— the application, driver manager, driver, and data source (normally a database), as illustrated in Figure 6.7. The application initiates the connection with the database, submits data requests as SQL statements to the DBMS, retrieves the results, performs processing, and terminates the connection, all using the standard API. A driver manager loads and unloads drivers at the application's request, and passes the ODBC or JDBC calls to the selected driver. The database driver links the application to the data source, translates the ODBC or JDBC calls to DBMS-specific calls, and handles data translation needed because of any differences between the DBMS's data language and the ODBC/JDBC standard, and error-handling differences that arise between the data source and the standard. The data source is the database (or other source, such as a spreadsheet) being accessed, along with its environment, consisting of its DBMS and platform. There are different levels of conformance defined for ODBC and JDBC drivers, depending on the type of relationship between the application and the database.

6.7.3 SQL PSM

Most database management systems include an extension of SQL itself, called **Persistent Stored Modules** (PSM), to allow users to write stored procedures, called **internal routines,** within the database process space, rather than externally. These facilities are used to write SQL routines that can be saved with the database schema and invoked when needed. (In contrast, programs written in a host language are referred to as external routines.) Oracle's PL/SQL, which can be accessed from within the SQLPlus environment, is this type of facility. The SQL/PSM standard is designed to provide complete programming language facilities, including declarations, control structures, and assignment statements.

SQL/PSM modules include functions, procedures, and temporary relations. To declare a procedure, we write:

```
CREATE PROCEDURE procedure_name  (parameter_list)
    declarations of local variables
    procedure code
```

Each parameter in the parameter list has three items—mode, name, and datatype. The mode can be IN, OUT, or INOUT, depending on whether it is an input parameter, an output parameter, or both. The name and data type of the parameter must also be given. Next we have declarations of local variables, if any, and the code for the procedure, which may contain SQL statements of the type we have seen previously for embedded SQL, plus assignment statements, control statements, and error handling.

A function has a similar declaration, as follows:

```
CREATE FUNCTION function_name (parameter list)
    RETURNS SQLdatatype
declarations of local variables
function code (must include a RETURN statement)
```

Functions accept only parameters with mode IN, to prevent side effects. The only value returned should be the one specified in the RETURN statement.

Declarations have this form,

```
DECLARE identifier datatype;
```

as in,

```
DECLARE     status              VARCHAR2;
DECLARE     number_of_courses   NUMBER;
```

The SQL assignment statement, SET, permits the value of a constant or an expression to be assigned to a variable. For example, we could write:

```
SET status = 'Freshman'; //However, Oracle uses := for assignment
SET number_of_courses = credits/3;
```

Branches have the form:

```
IF (condition) THEN statements;
   ELSEIF (condition) statements;
   . . .
   ELSEIF (condition) statements;
   ELSE statements;
END IF;
```

for example,

```
IF (Student.credits <30) THEN
   SET status = 'Freshman';
   ELSEIF (Student.credits <60) THEN
      SET status = 'Sophomore';
   ELSEIF (Student.credits <90) THEN
      SET status = 'Junior';
   ELSE SET status = 'Senior';
END IF;
```

The CASE statement can be used for selection based on the value of a variable or expression.

```
CASE selector
    WHEN value1          THEN statements;
    WHEN value2          THEN statements;
    . . .
    END CASE;
```

Repetition is controlled by LOOP ... ENDLOOP, WHILE ... DO ... END WHILE REPEAT, ... UNTIL ... END REPEAT, and FOR ... DO ... END FOR structures. We can use cursors as we did for embedded SQL. For example, we could write:

```
...
DECLARE CSCstuCursor CURSOR FOR
   SELECT stuId, lastName, firstName, major, credits
   FROM student
   WHERE major= 'CSC';
OPEN CSCstuCursor;
WHILE (SQLCODE = '00000') DO
   FETCH CSCstuCursor INTO stuNumber,stuLastName,stuFirstName,
   stuMajor,stuCredits;
      //statements to process these values
END WHILE;
CLOSE CSCstuCursor;
```

The language also provides predefined exception handlers, and allows the user to create user-defined exceptions as well.

Once a procedure has been created, it can be executed by this command:

```
EXECUTE procedure_name(actual_ parameter_ list);
```

As with most languages, the actual parameter list consists of the values or variables being passed to the procedure, as opposed to the formal parameter list that appears in the declaration of the procedure.

A function is invoked by using its name, typically in an assignment statement. For example:

```
SET newVal = MyFunction (val1, val2);
```

6.8   Creating and Using Views

Views are an important tool for providing users with a simple, customized environment and for hiding data. As explained in Section 6.2, a relational view does not correspond exactly to the general external view, but is a virtual table derived from one or more underlying base tables. It does not exist in storage in the sense that the base tables do, but is created by selecting specified rows and columns from the base tables, and possibly performing operations on them. The view is dynamically produced as the user works with it. To make up a view, the DBA decides which attributes the user needs to access, determines what base tables contain them, and constructs one or more views to display in table form the values the user should see. Views allow a dynamic external model to be created for the user easily. The reasons for providing views rather than allowing all users to work with base tables are as follows:

- Views allow different users to see the data in different forms, permitting an external model that differs from the logical model.

- The view mechanism provides a simple authorization control device, easily created and automatically enforced by the system. View users are unaware of, and cannot access, certain data items.

- Views can free users from complicated DML operations, especially in the case where the views involve joins. The user writes a simple SELECT statement using the view as the named table, and the system takes care of the details of the corresponding more complicated operations on the base tables to support the view.

- If the database is restructured on the logical level, the view can be used to keep the user's model constant. For example, if the table is split by projection and the primary key appears in each resulting new table, the original table can always be reconstructed when needed by defining a view that is the join of the new tables.

The following is the most common form of the command used to create a view:

```
CREATE VIEW viewname
   [(viewcolname [,viewcolname] . . .)]
   AS  SELECT    colname [,colname] . . .
       FROM      basetablename [,basetablename] . . .
       WHERE     condition;
```

The view name is chosen using the same rules as the table name, and should be unique within the database. Column names in the view can be different from the corresponding column names in the base tables, but they must obey the same rules of construction. If we choose to make them the same, we need not specify them twice, so we leave out the *viewcolname* line. In the AS SELECT line, we list the names of the columns from the underlying base tables that we wish to include in the view. The order of these names should correspond exactly to the *viewcolnames,* if those are specified. However, columns chosen from the base tables may be rearranged in any desired manner in the view. As in the usual SELECT . . . FROM . . . WHERE, the condition is a logical predicate that expresses some restriction on the records to be included. A more general form of the CREATE VIEW uses any valid subquery in place of the SELECT we have described.

- Example 1. Choosing a Vertical and Horizontal Subset of a Table

  Assume a user needs to see IDs and names of all history majors. We can create a view for this user as follows:

```
CREATE VIEW HISTMAJ (last, first, StudentId)
   AS SELECT  lastName, firstName,stuId
      FROM    Student
      WHERE   major = 'History';
```

Here we renamed the columns from our base table. The user of this view need not know the actual column names.

- Example 2. Choosing a Vertical Subset of a Table

If we would like a table of all courses with their schedules and room, we could create this as follows:

```
CREATE VIEW    ClassLoc
AS SELECT      classNumber, schedule, room
FROM           Class;
```

Notice we did not need a condition here, since we wanted these parts of all `Class` records. This time we kept the names of the columns as they appear in the base table.

- Example 3. A View Using Two Tables

Assume a user needs a table containing the IDs and names of all students in course CSC101. The virtual table can be created by choosing records in `Enroll` that have `classNumber` of CSC101, matching the `stuId` of those records with the `stuId` of the `Student` records, and taking the corresponding `lastName`, and `firstName` from `Student`. We could express this as a join or a subquery.

```
CREATE VIEW ClassList
   AS  SELECT   Student.stuId,lastName,
                firstName
       FROM     Enroll,Student
       WHERE    classNumber = 'CSC101'
                AND Enroll.stuId =
                Student.stuId;
```

- Example 4. A View of a View

We can define a view derived from a view. For example, we can ask for a subset of the ClassLoc (virtual) table by writing:

```
CREATE VIEW ClassLoc2
   AS  SELECT   classNumber, room
       FROM     ClassLoc;
```

- Example 5. A View Using a Function

In the SELECT statement in the AS line we can include built-in functions and GROUP BY options. For example, if we want a view of `Enroll` that gives `classNumber` and the number of students enrolled in each class, we write:

```
CREATE VIEW ClassCount (classNumber, TotCount)
   AS  SELECT   classNumber, COUNT(*)
       FROM     Enroll
                GROUP BY classNumber;
```

Notice we had to supply a name for the second column of the view, since there was none available from the base table.

- Example 6. Operations on Views

Once a view is created, the user can write SELECT statements to retrieve data through the view. The system takes care of mapping the user names to the underlying base table names and column names, and performing whatever functions are required to produce the result in the form the user expects. Users can write SQL queries that refer to joins, ordering, grouping, built-in functions, and so on, of views just as if they were operating on base tables. Since the SELECT operation does not change the underlying base tables, there is no restriction on using it with views. The following is an example of a SELECT operation on the ClassLoc view:

```
SELECT   *
FROM     ClassLoc
WHERE    room LIKE 'H%';
```

INSERT, DELETE, and UPDATE present certain problems with views. For example, suppose we had a view of student records such as:

```
StudentVw1(lastName, firstName, major, credits)
```

If we were permitted to insert records, any records created through this view would actually be Student records, but would not contain stuId, which is the key of the Student table. Since stuId would have the NOT NULL constraint, we would have to reject any records without this field. However, if we had the following view,

```
StudentVw2(stuId,lastName, firstName,credits)
```

we should have no problem inserting records, since we would be inserting Student records with a null major field, which is allowable. We could accomplish this by writing:

```
INSERT
INTO    StudentVw2
VALUES  ('S1040' 'Levine', 'Adam', 30);
```

However, the system should actually insert the record into the Student table. We can use an INSTEAD OF trigger to make sure this happens.

```
CREATE TRIGGER InsertStuVw2
  INSTEAD OF INSERT ON StudentVw2
  FOR EACH ROW
```

```
BEGIN
    INSERT
    INTO Student
    VALUES (:NEW.stuId, :NEW.lastName,
    :NEW.firstName, NEW. Credits);
END;
```

Now let us consider inserting records into the view `ClassCount`, as described earlier in Example 5. This view used the COUNT function on groups of records in the `Enroll` table. Obviously, this table was meant to be a dynamic summary of the `Enroll` table, rather than being a row and column subset of that table. It would not make sense for us to permit new `ClassCount` records to be inserted, since these do not correspond to individual rows or columns of a base table.

The problems we have identified for INSERT apply with minor changes to UPDATE and DELETE as well. As a general rule, these three operations can be performed on views that consist of actual rows and columns of underlying base tables, provided the primary key is included in the view, and no other constraints are violated. INSTEAD OF triggers can be used to ensure that the database updates the underlying tables.

6.9   The System Catalog

The **system catalog** or **system data dictionary** can be thought of as a database of information about databases. It contains, in table form, a summary of the structure of each database as it appears at a given time. Whenever a base table, view, index, constraint, stored module, or other item of a database schema is created, altered, or dropped, the DBMS automatically updates its entries in the catalog. The system also uses the catalog to check authorizations and to store information for access plans for applications. Users can query the data dictionary using ordinary SQL SELECT commands. However, since the data dictionary is maintained by the DBMS itself, the SQL UPDATE, INSERT, and DELETE commands cannot be used on it.

The **Oracle data dictionary** contains information about all schema objects, but access to it is provided through three different views, called USER, ALL, and DBA. In Oracle, each user is automatically given access to all the objects he or she creates. The **USER view** provides a user with information about all the objects created by that user. Users can be given access to objects that are created by others. The **ALL view** provides information about those objects in addition to the one the user has created.

The **DBA view,** which provides information about all database objects, is available to the database administrator. Each of the views is invoked by using the appropriate term as a prefix for the object(s) named in the FROM clause in a query. For example, if a user wants a list of the names of all the tables he or she has created, the query is:

```
SELECT TABLE_NAME
FROM USER_TABLES;
```

Queries can be written by using the appropriate prefix (USER_, ALL_, DBA_) in the FROM clause, followed by one of the categories CATALOG, CONSTRAINTS, CONS_COLUMNS (columns that have constraints), DICTIONARY, IND_COLUMNS (columns that have indexes), INDEXES, OBJECTS, TAB_COLUMNS (table columns), TRIGGERS, ROLES, PROFILES, SEQUENCES, SOURCE (source code for a module), SYS_PRIVS, USERS, TABLES, TABLESPACES, VIEWS, and other objects in the schema. For each of these categories, each of the three views (USER, ALL, DBA) has several columns. Generally, you can assume that each category has a column for the name of the object, which you can use to write a query such as:

```
SELECT VIEW_NAME
FROM USER_VIEWS;
```

To determine what all the available columns are, you can use the wild card (*) in the SELECT clause. For example,

```
SELECT*
FROM USER_TAB_COLUMNS;
```

will display all the recorded information about the columns in the tables you have created. Then you can use the view's column names (e.g., COLUMN_NAME, DATA_TYPE) in a more targeted query, such as:

```
SELECT COLUMN_NAME, DATA_TYPE
FROM USER_TAB_COLUMNS
WHERE TABLE_NAME = 'STUDENT';
```

Another way to learn about the objects is to use the DESCRIBE command. Once you know the name of an object (e.g., a table, constraint, column), which you can obtain by one of the methods just illustrated, you can ask for a description of it. For example, you can write,

```
DESCRIBE STUDENT;
```

to see what is known about the Student table, or,

```
DESCRIBE HISTMAJ;
```

to see what is known about the HISTMAJ view that we created in Section 6.8. If we want to learn what information is available about constraints in the USER view, we would write:

```
DESCRIBE USER_CONSTRAINTS;
```

We can then write a query using the names of the columns that are displayed, such as:

```
SELECT CONSTRAINT_NAME, CONSTRAINT_TYPE, TABLE_NAME
FROM USER_CONSTRAINTS;
```

For information about triggers, the command,

```
SELECT TRIGGER_NAME, TRIGGERING_EVENT, TRIGGER_TYPE
FROM USER_TRIGGERS;
```

provides useful information about them.

IBM's **DB2 Universal Database** has a system catalog that is also kept in the form of tables in a schema called SYSIBM, usually with restricted access. Two views of the tables, SYSCAT and SYSSTAT, are available for users. The **SYSCAT schema** has many tables, all of which are read-only. Some of the most important ones are the following:

```
TABLES (TABSCHEMA, TABNAME, DEFINER, TYPE, STATUS, COLCOUNT,
KEYCOLUMNS, CHECKCOUNT, ...)
COLUMNS (TABSCHEMA, TABNAME, COLNAME, COLNO, TYPENAME, LENGTH,
DEFAULT, NULLS, ...)
INDEXES (INDSCHEMA, INDNAME, DEFINER, TABSCHEMA, TABNAME, COLNAMES,
UNIQUERULE, COLCOUNT, ...)
TRIGGERS (TRIGSCHEMA, TRIGNAME, DEFINER, TABSCHEMA, TABNAME,
TRIGTIME, TRIGEVENT, ...)
VIEWS (VIEWSCHEMA, VIEWNAME, DEFINER, TEXT ...)
```

You can write queries for these tables using SQL, as in,

```
SELECT TABSCHEMA, TABNAME
FROM TABLES
WHERE DEFINER = 'JONES';
```

which gives the names of all the tables created by Jones.

The query,

```
SELECT *
FROM COLUMNS
WHERE TABNAME = 'STUDENT'
GROUP BY COLNAME;
```

gives all the available information about the columns of the Student table.

6.10   Chapter Summary

Oracle, IBM's DB2, MySQL, SQL Server and other relational database management systems use **SQL,** a standard relational DDL and DML. On the logical level, each relation is represented by a **base table.** The external level consists of **views,** which are created from subsets, combinations, or other operations on the base tables. A base table can have **indexes,** one of which can be a clustered index, defined on it. Dynamic database definition allows the structure to be changed at any time.

SQL DDL commands **CREATE TABLE** and **CREATE INDEX** are used to create the base tables and their indexes. Several built-in **data types** are available, and users can also define new types. **Constraints** can be specified on the column or table level. The **ALTER TABLE** command allows changes to existing tables, such as adding a new column, dropping a column, changing data types, or changing constraints. The **RENAME TABLE** command allows the user to change a table's name. **DROP TABLE** and **DROP INDEX** remove tables and indexes, along with all the data in them, from the database.

The **DML** commands are **SELECT, UPDATE, INSERT,** and **DELETE.** The SELECT command has several forms, and it performs the equivalent of the relational algebra SELECT, PROJECT, and JOIN operations. Options include **GROUP BY, ORDER BY, GROUP BY ... HAVING, LIKE,** and built-in functions **COUNT, SUM, AVG, MAX,** and **MIN.** The SELECT statement can operate on joins of tables, and can handle **subqueries,** including correlated subqueries. Expressions and set operations are also possible. The UPDATE command may be used to update one or more fields in one or more records. The INSERT command can insert one or more records, possibly with null values for some fields. The DELETE operator erases records, while leaving the table structure intact.

An active database is one where the DBMS actively monitors changes to ensure that only legal instances of the database are created. A combination of constraints and **triggers** may be used to create an active database.

The **COMMIT** statement makes permanent all changes that have been made by the current transaction. The **ROLLBACK** statement undoes all changes that were made by the current transaction. The current transaction begins immediately after the last COMMIT or ROLLBACK, or if neither of these occurred, then at the beginning of the current user session.

SQL is often used in a programming environment rather than interactively. It can be **embedded** in a host programming language and separately compiled by a **precompiler.** It can be used with a standard API through **ODBC** or **JDBC.** It can also be used as a complete language using its own **SQL PSMs.** Oracle's PL/SQL is an example of a complete programming environment for creating SQL PSMs.

The **CREATE VIEW** command is used to define a virtual table, by selecting fields from existing base tables or previously defined views. The SELECT operation can be used on views, but other DML commands are restricted to certain types of views. An **INSTEAD OF trigger** is useful for replacing user's DML commands written on a view with corresponding commands on the base table(s) used for the view. A view definition can be destroyed by a DROP VIEW command.

The **system catalog** or **system data dictionary** is a database containing information about the user's database. It keeps track of the tables, columns, indexes, and views that exist, as well as authorization information and other data. The system automatically updates the catalog when structural changes and other modifications are made.

Exercises

6.1   Write the commands needed to create indexes for the `Student`, `Faculty`, `Class`, and `Enroll` tables in this chapter.

6.2   For each of the join examples (Examples 7–11) in Section 6.4.2, replace the join by a subquery, if possible. If not possible, explain why not.

Directions for exercises 6.3–6.25: For the schema that follows, write the indicated commands in SQL. Figure 6.8 shows the DDL for creating these tables. It shows that `departmentName` is a foreign key in the `Worker` table, that `mgrId` is a foreign key in the `Dept` table, that `projMgrId` is a foreign key in the `Project` table, and that `projNo` and `empId` are foreign keys in the `Assign` table. We assume each department has a manager, and each project has a manager, but these are not necessarily related. (Note: It is recommended that you do Lab Exercise 1 in conjunction with these exercises. If Oracle is not available, you can use another relational DBMS, including the freeware MySQL, which you can download. Depending on

```
CREATE TABLE Dept (
departmentName VARCHAR2 (15),
mgrld Number(6),
CONSTRAINT Dept_departmentName_pk PRIMARY KEY (departmentName));
CREATE TABLE Worker (
empld NUMBER (6),
lastName VARCHAR2 (20) NOT NULL,
firstName VARCHAR2 (15) NOT NULL,
departmentName   VARCHAR2 (15),
birthDate DATE,
hireDate DATE,
salary NUMBER (8, 2),
CONSTRAINT Worker_empid_pk PRIMARY KEY (empid),
CONSTRAINT Worker_departmentNumber_fk FOREIGN KEY (departmentNumber) REFERENCES
Dept (departmentName));

ALTER TABLE Dept Add CONSTRAINT Dept_mgrld_fk FOREIGN KEY (mgrld) REFERENCES
Worker (empld)) ON UPDATE

CREATE TABLE Project (
projNo NUMBER (6),
projName VARCHAR2 (20),
projMgrld VARCHAR2 (20),
budget NUMBER (8, 2),
startDate DATE,
expectedDurationWeeks NUMBER (4),
CONSTRAINT Project_projNo_pk PRIMARY KEY (projNo),
CONSTRAINT Project_projMgrld_fk FOREIGN KEY (projMgrid) REFERENCES WORKER
(empld));
```

(continued)

FIGURE 6.8

DDL and Insert Statements for Worker-Project-Assign Example

```
CREATE TABLE Assign (
projNo NUMBER (6),
empId NUMBER (6),
hoursAssigned NUMBER (3),
rating NUMBER (1),
CONSTRAINT Assign_projNo_empId_pk PRIMARY KEY (projNo, empId),
CONSTRAINT Assign_projNo_fk FOREIGN KEY (projNo) REFERENCES Project (projNo) ON UPDATE
CONSTRAINT Assign_empId_fk FOREIGN KEY (empId) REFERENCES Worker (empId) ON
ON DELETE CASCADE);

INSERT INTO Dept VALUES ('Accounting',);
INSERT INTO Dept VALUES ('Research',);

INSERT INTO Worker VALUES(101,'Smith', 'Tom','Accounting', '01-Feb-1960', '06-Jun-1983', 50000);
INSERT INTO Worker VALUES(103,'Jones','Mary' ,'Accounting', '15-Jun-1965', '20-Sep-1985', 48000);
INSERT INTO Worker VALUES(105,'Burns','Jane', 'Accounting', '21-Sep-1970' ,'12-Jun-1990', 39000);
INSERT INTO Worker VALUES(110,'Burns','Michael', 'Research', '05-Apr-1967', '10-Sep-1990', 70000);
INSERT INTO Worker VALUES(115,'Chin','Amanda', 'Research', '22-Sep-1965', '19-Jun-1985', 60000);

UPDATE Dept SET mgrId = 101 WHERE departmentName = 'Accounting';
UPDATE Dept SET mgrId = 101 WHERE departmentName = 'Research';

INSERT INTO Project VALUES (1001,'Jupiter', 101, 300000,'01-Feb-2004', 50);
INSERT INTO Project VALUES (1005,'Saturn', 101, 400000,'01-Jun-2004', 35);
INSERT INTO Project VALUES (1019,'Mercury', 110, 350000,'15-Feb-2004', 40);
INSERT INTO Project VALUES (1025,'Neptune', 110, 600000,'01-Feb-2005', 45);
INSERT INTO Project VALUES (1030,'Pluto', 110, 380000,'15-Sept-2004', 50);

INSERT INTO Assign(projNo, empId, hoursAssigned) VALUES (1001, 101, 30);
INSERT INTO Assign VALUES (1001, 103, 20, 5);
INSERT INTO Assign(projNo, empId, hoursAssigned)VALUES (1005, 103, 20);
INSERT INTO Assign(projNo, empId, hoursAssigned)VALUES (1001, 105, 30);
INSERT INTO Assign VALUES (1001, 115, 20, 4);
INSERT INTO Assign VALUES (1019, 110, 20, 5);
INSERT INTO Assign VALUES (1019, 115, 10, 4);
INSERT INTO Assign(projNo, empId, hoursAssigned)VALUES (1025, 110, 10);
INSERT INTO Assign(projNo, empId, hoursAssigned)VALUES (1030, 110, 10);
```

FIGURE 6.8—Continued

the product, you may need to make some changes to the DDL. If you do not plan to do Lab Exercise 1, you can simply write out the commands.)

```
Worker (empId, lastName, firstName, departmentName, birthDate, hireDate,
salary)
Dept (departmentName, mgrId)
Project (projNo, projName, projMgrId, budget, startDate,
expectedDurationWeeks)
Assign (projNo, empId, hoursAssigned, rating)
```

6.3   Get the names of all workers in the accounting department.

6.4   Get an alphabetical list of names of all workers assigned to project 1001.

6.5   Get the name of the employee in the research department who has the lowest salary.

6.6   Get details of the project with the highest budget.

6.7   Get the names and departments of all workers on project 1019.

6.8   Get an alphabetical list of names and corresponding ratings of all workers on any project that is managed by Michael Burns.

6.9   Create a view that has project number and name of each project, along with the IDs and names of all workers assigned to it.

6.10   Using the view created in Exercise 6.9, find the project number and project name of all projects to which employee 110 is assigned.

6.11   Add a new worker named Jack Smith with ID of 1999 to the research department.

6.12   Change the hours, which employee 110 is assigned to project 1019, from 20 to 10.

6.13   For all projects starting after May 1, 2004, find the project number and the IDs and names of all workers assigned to them.

6.14   For each project, list the project number and how many workers are assigned to it.

6.15   Find the employee names and department manager names of all workers who are not assigned to any project.

6.16   Find the details of any project with the word "urn" anywhere in its name.

6.17   Get a list of project numbers and names and starting dates of all projects that have the same starting date.

6.18   Add a field called `status` to the `Project` table. Sample values for this field are `active`, `completed`, `planned`, `cancelled`. Then write the command to undo this change.

6.19   Get the employee ID and project number of all employees who have no ratings on that project.

6.20   Assuming that `salary` now contains annual salary, find each worker's ID, name, and monthly salary.

6.21   Add a field called `numEmployeesAssigned` to the `Project` table. Use the UPDATE command to insert values into the field to correspond to the current information in the `Assign` table. Then write a trigger that will update the field correctly whenever an assignment is made, dropped, or updated. Write the command to make these changes permanent.

6.22 a)   Write an Oracle data dictionary query to show the names of all the columns in a table called `Customers`.

   b)   Write a corresponding query for the DB2 UDB SYSCAT tables for this example.

6.23 a)   Write an Oracle data dictionary query to find all information about all columns named PROJNO.

   b)   Write a corresponding query for the DB2 UDB SYSCAT tables for this example.

6.24 a)   Write an Oracle data dictionary query to get a list of names of people who have created tables, along with the number of tables each has created. Assume you have DBA privileges.

   b)   Write a corresponding query for the DB2 UDB SYSCAT tables for this example.

6.25 a)   Write an Oracle data dictionary query to find the names of tables that have more than two indexes.

   b)   Write a corresponding query for the DB2 UDB SYSCAT tables for this example.

Lab Exercises

Lab Exercise 6.1. Exploring the Oracle Database for Worker-Dept-Project-Assign Example

A script to create an Oracle database for the example used in exercises 6.3–6.25 appears in Figure 6.8 and on the website that accompanies this book. The script was written using Notepad. Find the script on the website, copy it into your own directory, and open it with Notepad. Open Oracle's SQLPlus facility. You will switch back and forth between Notepad and SQLPlus, because the editor in SQLPlus is hard to use.

a. In Notepad, highlight and copy the command to create the first table, then switch to SQLPlus and paste that command in the SQLPlus window and execute the command. You should see the message "Table created." If you get an error message instead, go back to the Notepad file and correct the error.

b. Continue to create the remaining tables one at a time in the same manner.

c. Run the INSERT commands to populate the tables. Explain why the two UPDATE statements were used.

d. Using that implementation, execute the Oracle SQL statements for Exercises 6.3–6.25.

Lab Exercise 6.2. Creating and Using a Simple Database in Oracle

a. Write the DDL commands to create the Student, Faculty, Class, and Enroll tables for the University database shown in Figure 6.2.

b. Using the INSERT command, add the records as they appear in Figure 6.3 to your new Oracle database.

c. Write SQL queries for the following questions, and execute them.

   i. Find the names of all history majors.

   ii. Find the class number, schedule, and room for all classes that Smith of the history department teaches.

   iii. Find the names of all students who have fewer than average number of credits.

iv. Find the names of all the teachers that Ann Chin has, along with all her classes and midterm grades from each.

v. For each student, find the number of classes he or she is enrolled in.

SAMPLE PROJECT: CREATING AND MANIPULATING A RELATIONAL DATABASE FOR THE ART GALLERY

In the sample project section at the end of Chapter 5, we created a normalized relational model for The Art Gallery database. Renaming the tables slightly, we concluded that the following model should be implemented:

(1) Artist (<u>artistId</u>, firstName, lastName, interviewDate, interviewerName, areaCode, telephoneNumber, street, *zip*, salesLastYear, salesYearToDate, socialSecurityNumber, usualMedium, usualStyle, usualType)

(2) Zips (<u>zip</u>, city, state)

(3) PotentialCustomer (<u>potentialCustomerId</u>, firstname, lastName, areaCode, telephoneNumber, street, *zip*, dateFilledIn, *preferredArtistId*, preferredMedium, preferredStyle, preferredType)

(4) Artwork (artworkId, *artistId*, workTitle, askingPrice, dateListed, dateReturned, dateShown, status, workMedium, workSize, workStyle, workType, workYearCompleted, *collectorSocialSecurityNumber*)

(5) ShownIn (<u>*artworkId,showTitle*</u>)

(6) Collector (<u>socialSecurityNumber,</u> firstName, lastName, street, *zip*, interviewDate, interviewerName, areaCode, telephonenumber, salesLastYear, salesYearToDate, *collectionArtistId*, collectionMedium, collectionStyle, collectionType, SalesLastYear, SalesYearToDate)

(7) Show (<u>showTitle</u>, *showFeaturedArtistId*, showClosingDate, showTheme, showOpeningDate)

(8) Buyer (<u>buyerId,</u> firstName, lastName, street, *zip*, areaCode, telephoneNumber, purchasesLastYear, purchasesYearToDate)

(9) Sale (<u>InvoiceNumber,</u> *artworkId*, amountRemittedToOwner, saleDate, salePrice, saleTax, *buyerId*, *salespersonSocialSecurityNumber*)

(10) Salesperson (<u>socialSecurityNumber,</u> firstName, lastName, street, *zip*)

- Step 6.1. Update the data dictionary and list of assumptions if needed. For each table, write the table name and write out the names, data types, and sizes of all the data items, identify any constraints, using the conventions of the DBMS you will use for implementation.

No changes were made to the list of assumptions. No further changes to the data dictionary are needed. For an Oracle database, the tables will have the structures as follows:

TABLE Zips

Item	Datatype	Size	Constraints	Comments
Zip	CHAR	5	PRIMARY KEY	
city	VARCHAR2	15	NOT NULL	
state	CHAR	2	NOT NULL	

TABLE Artist

Item	Datatype	Size	Constraints	Comments
artistId	NUMBER	6	PRIMARY KEY	
firstName	VARCHAR2	15	NOT NULL; (firstName, lastName) UNIQUE	
lastName	VARCHAR2	20	NOT NULL; (firstName, lastName) UNIQUE	
interviewDate	DATE			
interviewerName	VARCHAR2	35		
areaCode	CHAR	3		
telephoneNumber	CHAR	7		
street	VARCHAR2	50		
zip	CHAR	5	FOREIGN KEY REF Zips	
salesLastYear	NUMBER	8,2		
salesYearToDate	NUMBER	8,2		
socialSecurityNumber	CHAR	9	UNIQUE	
usualMedium	VARCHAR	15		
usualStyle	VARCHAR	15		
usualType	VARCHAR	20		

TABLE Collector

Item	Datatype	Size	Constraints	Comments
socialSecurityNumber	CHAR	9	PRIMARY KEY	
firstName	VARCHAR2	15	NOT NULL	
lastName	VARCHAR2	20	NOT NULL	
interviewDate	DATE			
interviewerName	VARCHAR2	35		
areaCode	CHAR	3		
telephoneNumber	CHAR	7		
street	VARCHAR2	50		
zip	CHAR	5	FOREIGN KEY Ref Zips	
salesLastYear	NUMBER	8,2		
salesYearToDate	NUMBER	8,2		
collectionArtistId	NUMBER	6	FOREIGN KEY REF Artist	
collectionMedium	VARCHAR	15		
collectionStyle	VARCHAR	15		
collectionType	VARCHAR	20		

TABLE PotentialCustomer

Item	Datatype	Size	Constraints	Comments
potentialCustomerId	NUMBER	6	PRIMARY KEY	
firstname	VARCHAR2	15	NOT NULL	
lastName	VARCHAR2	20	NOT NULL	
areaCode	CHAR	3		
telephoneNumber	CHAR	7		
street	VARCHAR2	50		
zip	CHAR	5	FOREIGN KEY REF Zips	
dateFilledIn	DATE			
preferredArtistId	NUMBER	6	FOREIGN KEY REF Artist	
preferredMedium	VARCHAR2	15		
preferredStyle	VARCHAR2	15		
preferredType	VARCHAR2	20		

TABLE Artwork

Item	Datatype	Size	Constraints	Comments
artworkId	NUMBER	6	PRIMARY KEY	
artistId	NUMBER	6	FOREIGN KEY REF Artist; NOT NULL; (artistId, workTitle) UNIQUE	
workTitle	VARCHAR2	50	NOT NULL; (artistId, workTitle) UNIQUE	
askingPrice	NUMBER	8,2		
dateListed	DATE			
dateReturned	DATE			
dateShown	DATE			
status	VARCHAR2	15		
workMedium	VARCHAR2	15		
workSize	VARCHAR2	15		
workStyle	VARCHAR2	15		
workType	VARCHAR2	20		
workYearCompleted	CHAR	4		
collectorSocialSecurityNumber	CHAR	9	FOREIGN KEY REF Collector	

TABLE Show

Item	Datatype	Size	Constraints	Comments
showTitle	VARCHAR2	50	PRIMARY KEY	
showFeaturedArtistId	NUMBER	6	FOREIGN KEY REF Arist	
showClosingDate	DATE			
showTheme	VARCHAR2	50		
showOpeningDate	DATE			

TABLE ShownIn

Item	Datatype	Size	Constraints	Comments
artworkId	NUMBER	6	PRIMARY KEY(artworkId, showTitle); FOREIGN KEY REF Artwork	
showTitle	VARCHAR2	50	PRIMARY KEY(artworkId, showTitle); FOREIGN KEY REF Show	

TABLE Buyer

Item	Datatype	Size	Constraints	Comments
buyerId	NUMBER	6	PRIMARY KEY	
firstName	VARCHAR2	15	NOT NULL	
lastName	VARCHAR2	20	NOT NULL	
street	VARCHAR2	50		
zip	CHAR	5	FOREIGN KEY REF Zips	
areaCode	CHAR	3		
telephoneNumber	CHAR	7		
purchasesLastYear	NUMBER	8,2		
purchasesYearToDate	NUMBER	8,2		

TABLE Salesperson

Item	Datatype	Size	Constraints	Comments
socialSecurityNumber	CHAR	9	PRIMARY KEY	
firstName	VARCHAR2	15	NOT NULL; (firstName,lastName) UNIQUE	
lastName	VARCHAR2	20	NOT NULL; (firstName,lastName) UNIQUE	
street	VARCHAR2	50		
zip	CHAR	5	FOREIGN KEY REF Zips	

TABLE Sale

Item	Datatype	Size	Constraints	Comments
invoiceNumber	NUMBER	6	PRIMARY KEY	
artworkId	NUMBER	6	NOT NULL; UNIQUE; FOREIGN KEY REF Artwork	
amountRemittedToOwner	NUMBER	8,2	DEFAULT 0.00	
saleDate	DATE			
salePrice	NUMBER	8,2		
saleTax	NUMBER	6,2		
buyerId	NUMBER	6	NOT NULL; FOREIGN KEY REF Buyer	
salespersonSocialSecurityNumber	CHAR	9		

- Step 6.2. Write and execute SQL statements to create all the tables needed to implement the design.

Because we wish to specify foreign keys as we create the tables, we must be careful of the order in which we create, because the "home table" has to exist before the table containing the foreign key is created. Therefore, we will use the following order: Zips, Artist, Collector, Potential Customer, Artwork, Show, ShownIn, Buyer, Salesperson, Sale. The DDL statements to create the tables are shown in Figure 6.9. We are using Oracle syntax, but the DDL statements should work, with minor modifications, for any relational DBMS.

- Step 6.3. Create indexes for foreign keys and any other columns that will be used most often for queries.

The DDL statements to create the indexes are shown in Figure 6.10.

- Step 6.4. Insert about five records in each table, preserving all constraints. Put in enough data to demonstrate how the database will function.

Figure 6.11 shows the INSERT statements. Because we wish to make use of Oracle's system-generated values for surrogate keys, we created sequences for each of `artistId`, `potentialCustomerId`, `artworkId`, and `buyerId`, using this command:

```
CREATE SEQUENCE sequence-name
[START WITH starting-value]
[INCREMENT BY step] . . .;
```

We chose to start with one and increment by one, the defaults. To generate each new value, we use the command *<sequence_name>*.NEXTVAL, as shown in the INSERT commands. We assume `invoiceNumber` is a number preprinted on the invoice form, not system-generated, so we do not need a sequence for that number.

- Step 6.5. Write SQL statements that will process five non-routine requests for information from the database just created. For each, write the request in English, followed by the corresponding SQL command.

1. Find the names of all artists who were interviewed after January 1, 2004, but who have no works of art listed.

```
SELECT firstName, lastName
FROM Artist
WHERE interviewDate > '01-Jan-2004' AND NOT EXISTS
    (SELECT *
    FROM Artwork
    WHERE artistId =Artist.artistId);
```

```
CREATE TABLE Zips (
      zip CHAR (5),
      city VARCHAR2 (15) NOT NULL,
      state CHAR (2) NOT NULL,
      CONSTRAINT Zips_zip__pk PRIMARY KEY (zip));

CREATE TABLE Artist (
      ArtistId NUMBER (6),
      firstName VARCHAR2 (15) NOT NULL,
      lastName VARCHAR2 (20) NOT NULL,
      interviewDate DATE,
      interviewerName VARCHAR2 (35),
      areaCode   CHAR (3),
      telephoneNumber   CHAR (7),
      street VARCHAR2 (50),
      zip   CHAR (5),
      salesLastYear NUMBER (8, 2),
      salesYearToDate   NUMBER (8, 2),
      socialSecurityNumber CHAR (9),
      usualMedium VARCHAR (15),
      usualStyle VARCHAR (15),
      usualType VARCHAR (20),
      CONSTRAINT Artist_ArtistId_pk PRIMARY KEY (ArtistId),
      CONSTRAINT Artist_SSN_uk UNIQUE (socialSecurityNumber),
      CONSTRAINT Artist_fName_lName_uk UNIQUE (firstName,   lastName),
      CONSTRAINT Artist_zip_fk FOREIGN KEY (zip) REFERENCES Zips (zip));

CREATE TABLE Collector (
      socialSecurityNumber CHAR (9),
      firstName VARCHAR2 (15) NOT NULL,
      lastName VARCHAR2 (20) NOT NULL,
      interviewDate DATE,
      interviewerName VARCHAR2 (35),
      areaCode CHAR (3),
      telephoneNumber    CHAR (7),
```

FIGURE 6.9

Oracle DDL Statements for The Art Gallery Tables

```
          street VARCHAR2 (50),
          zip CHAR (5),
          salesLastYear NUMBER (8, 2),
          salesYearToDate    NUMBER (8, 2),
          collectionArtistId NUMBER (6),
          collectionMedium VARCHAR (15),
          collectionStyle VARCHAR (15),
          collectionType VARCHAR (20),
          CONSTRAINT Collector_SSN_pk PRIMARY KEY
          (socialSecurityNumber).
          CONSTRAINT Collector_collArtistid_fk FOREIGN KEY (collectionArtistId)
REFERENCES Artist (artistId)
          CONSTRAINT Collector_zip_fk FOREIGN KEY (zip) REFERENCES Zips (zip));

CREATE TABLE PotentialCustomer (
          potentialCustomerId NUMBER (6),
          firstname VARCHAR2 (15) NOT NULL,
          lastName VARCHAR2 (20) NOT NULL,
          areaCode CHAR (3),
          telephoneNumber CHAR (7),
          street VARCHAR2 (50),
          zip CHAR (5),
          dateFilledIn DATE,
          preferredArtistId NUMBER (6),
          preferredMedium VARCHAR2 (15),
          preferredStyle VARCHAR2 (15),
          preferredType VARCHAR2 (20),
          CONSTRAINT PotentialCustomer_potCusId_pk PRIMARY KEY
          (potentialCustomerId),
          CONSTRAINT PotentialCustomer_zip_fk FOREIGN KEY (zip)
          REFERENCES Zips (zip)
          CONSTRAINT Potential Customer_prefAId_fk FOREIGN KEY
          (preferredArtistId) REFERENCES Artist (artist_Id)) ;

CREATE TABLE Artwork (
          artworkId NUMBER (6),
          artistId NUMBER (6) NOT NULL,
```

(continued)

FIGURE 6.9—Continued

```
        workTitle VARCHAR2 (50) NOT NULL,
        askingPrice NUMBER (8, 2),
        dateListed DATE,
        dateReturned DATE,
        dateShown DATE,
        status VARCHAR2 (15),
        workMedium VARCHAR2 (15),
        workSize VARCHAR2 (15),
        workStyle VARCHAR2 (15),
        workType VARCHAR2 (20),
        workYearCompeted CHAR (4),
        collectorSocialSecurityNumber CHAR (9),
        CONSTRAINT Artwork_artworkId_pk PRIMARY KEY (artworkId).
        CONSTRAINT Artwork_artId_wTitle_uk UNIQUE (artistId, workTitle),
        CONSTRAINT Artwork_artId_fk FOREIGN KEY (artistId) REFERENCES Artist (artistId)
        CONSTRAINT Artwork_collSSN_fk FOREIGN KEY
(collectorSocialSecurityNumber)   REFERENCES Collector (socialSecurityNumber);

CREATE TABLE Show (
        showTitle VARCHAR2 (50),
        showFeaturedArtistId NUMBER (6),
        showClosingDate DATE,
        showTheme VARCHAR2 (50),
        showOpeningDate DATE,
        CONSTRAINT Show_showTitle_pk PRIMARY KEY (showTitle),
        CONSTRAINT Show_showFeaturedArtId_fk FOREIGN KEY (showFeaturedArtistId)
REFERENCES Artist (artistId);

CREATE TABLE ShownIn (
        artworkId NUMBER (6),
        showTitle VARCHAR2 (50),
        CONSTRAINT ShownIn_artId_showTitle_pk PRIMARY KEY (artworkId, showTitle),
        CONSTRAINT ShownIn_artId_fk FOREIGN KEY (artworkId) REFERENCES Artwork
        (artworkId)
```

FIGURE 6.9—Continued

```
        CONSTRAINT ShownIn_showTitle_fk FOREIGN KEY (showTitle) REFERENCES Show
        (showTitle));

CREATE TABLE Buyer (
        buyerId NUMBER (6),
        firstName VARCHAR2 (15) NOT NULL,
        lastName VARCHAR2 (20) NOT NULL,
        street VARCHAR2 (50),
        zip CHAR (5),
        areaCode CHAR (3),
        telephoneNumber CHAR (7),
        purchasesLastYear NUMBER (8, 2),
        purchasesYearToDate NUMBER (8, 2),
        CONSTRAINT Buyer_buyerId_pk PRIMARY KEY (buyerId),
        CONSTRAINT Buyer_zip_fk FOREIGN KEY (zip) REFERENCES Zips (zip));

CREATE TABLE Salesperson (
        socialSecurityNumber CHAR (9),
        firstName VARCHAR2 (15) NOT NULL,
        lastName VARCHAR2 (20) NOT NULL,
        street VARCHAR2 (50),
        zip CHAR (5),
        CONSTRAINT Salesperson_SSN_pk PRIMARY KEY
        socialSecurityNumber),
        CONSTRAINT Salesperson_fName_lName_uk UNIQUE (firstName, lastName),
        CONSTRAINT Salesperson_zip_fk FOREIGN KEY (zip) REFERENCES Zips (zip));

CREATE TABLE Sale (
        invoiceNumber NUMBER (6),
        artworkId NUMBER (6) NOT NULL,
        amountRemittedToOwner NUMBER (8, 2) DEFAULT 0.00,
        saleDate DATE,
        salePrice NUMBER (8, 2),
        saleTax NUMBER (6, 2),
        buyerId NUMBER (6) NOT NULL,
```

(continued)

FIGURE 6.9—Continued

```
salespersonSocialSecurityNumber CHAR (9),
CONSTRAINT Sale_invoiceNumber_pk PRIMARY KEY (invoiceNumber),
CONSTRAINT Sale_artworkId_uk UNIQUE (artworkId),
CONSTRAINT Sale_artworkId_fk FOREIGN KEY (artworkId) REFERENCES Artwork (artworkId),
CONSTRAINT Sale_buyerId_fk FOREIGN KEY (buyerId) REFERENCES Buyer (buyerId));
```

```
CREATE UNIQUE INDEX Artist_lastName_firstName ON Artist(lastName, firstName);
CREATE INDEX Artist_zip ON Artist(zip);

CREATE INDEX Collector_collectionArtistId On Collector(collectionArtistId);
CREATE INDEX Collector_zip ON Collector(zip);
CREATE INDEX Collector_lastName_firstName ON Collector(lastName, firstName);

CREATE INDEX PotentialCustomer_zip ON PotentialCustomer(zip);
CREATE INDEX PotentialCustomer_lastName_firstName ON PotentialCustomer(lastName,
firstName);

CREATE UNIQUE INDEX Artwork_artistId_workTitle ON Artwork (artistId, workTitle);
CREATE INDEX Artwork_artistId ON Artwork(artistId);
CREATE INDEX Artwork_collectorSocialSecurityNumber ON Artwork
(collectorSocialSecurityNumber);

CREATE INDEX Show_showFeaturedArtistId On Show (showFeaturedArtistId);

CREATE INDEX Shownin_artworkId ON Shownin (artworkId);
CREATE INDEX Shownin_show Title ON ShownIn (showTitle);

CREATE INDEX Buyer_zip ON Buyer(zip);
CREATE INDEX Buyer_lastName_firstName ON Buyer (lastName, firstName);

CREATE UNIQUE INDEX Salesperson_lastName_firstName ON Salesperson (lastName, firstName);
CREATE INDEX Salesperson_zip ON Salespeson (zip);

CREATE INDEX Sale_buyerId ON Sale (buyerId);
```

FIGURE 6.10

Oracle DDL Statements for The Art Gallery Indexes

```
INSERT INTO Zips VALUES ('10101','New York','NY');
INSERT INTO Zips VALUES ('10801','New Rochelle','NY');
INSERT INTO Zips VALUES ('92101','San Diego','CA');
INSERT INTO Zips VALUES ('33010','Miami','FL');
INSERT INTO Zips VALUES ('60601','Chicago','IL');

CREATE SEQUENCE artistId_sequence;
INSERT INTO Artist VALUES(artistId_sequence.NEXTVAL,'Leonardo','Vincenti','10-Oct-1999',
'Hughes','212','5559999','10 Main Street','10101',9000,4500,'099999876','oil','realism','painting');
INSERT INTO Artist VALUES(artistId_sequence.NEXTVAL,'Vincent','Gogh','15-Jun-2004',
'Hughes','914','5551234','55 West 18 Street','10801',9500,5500,'099999877','oil',
'impressionism','painting');
INSERT INTO Artist VALUES(artistId_sequence.NEXTVAL,'Winslow','Homes','05-Jan-2004',
'Hughes','619','1234567','100 Water Street','92101',14000,4000,'083999876','watercolor',
'realism','painting');
INSERT INTO Artist VALUES(artistId_sequence.NEXTVAL,'Alexander','Calderone','10-Feb-
1999','Hughes','212','5559999','10 Main Street','10101',20000,20000,'123999876','steel',
'cubism','sculpture');
INSERT INTO Artist VALUES(artistId_sequence.NEXTVAL,'Georgia','Keefe','05-Oct-2004',
'Hughes','305','1239999','5 Chestnut Street','33010',19000,14500,'987999876','oil','realism',
'painting');

INSERT INTO Collector VALUES('102345678','John','Jackson','01-Feb-2004','Hughes','917',
'7771234','24 Pine Avenue','10101',4000,3000,1,'oil','realism','collage');
INSERT INTO Collector VALUES ('987654321','Mary','Lee','01-Mar-2003','Jones','305',
'5551234','10 Ash Street',33010,'2000',3000,2,'watercolor','realism','painting');
INSERT INTO Collector VALUES('034345678','Ramon','Perez','15-Apr-2003','Hughes','619',
'8881234','15 Poplar Avenue','92101',4500,3500,3,'oil','realism','painting');
INSERT INTO Collector VALUES('888881234','Rick','Lee','20-Jun-2004','Hughes','212',
'9991234','24 Pine Avenue','10101',4000,3000,3,'oil','realism','sculpture');
INSERT INTO Collector VALUES('777345678','Samantha','Torno','05-May-2004','Jones','305',
'5551234','10 Ash Street','33010',40000,30000,1,'acrylic','realism','painting');

CREATE SEQUENCE potentialCustomerId-sequence;
INSERT INTO PotentialCustomer VALUES(potentialCustomerId_sequence.NEXTVAL,'Adam',
'Burns','917','3456789','1 Spruce Street','10101','12-Dec-2003',1,'watercolor','impressionism',
'painting');
INSERT INTO PotentialCustomer VALUES(potentialCustomerId sequence.NEXTVAL,'Carole','Burns',
'917','3456789','1 Spruce Street','10101','12-Dec-2003',2,'watercolor','realism',sculpture');
INSERT INTO PotentialCustomer VALUES(potentialCustomerId_sequence.NEXTVAL,'David',
'Engel','914','7777777','715 North Avenue','10801','08-Aug-2003',3,'watercolor','realism',
'painting');
```

FIGURE 6.11

INSERT statements to populate The Art Gallery Tables

```
INSERT INTO PotentialCustomer VALUES(potentialCustomerId_sequence.NEXTVAL,'Frances',
'Hughes','619','3216789','10 Pacific Avenue','92101','05-Jan-2004',2,'oil','impressionism',
'painting');
INSERT INTO PotentialCustomer VALUES(potentialCustomerId_sequence.NEXTVAL,'Irene',
'Jacobs','312','1239876','1 Windswept Place','60601','21-Sep-2003',5,'watercolor','abstract
expressionism','painting');

CREATE SEQUENCE artworkId_sequence;
INSERT INTO Artwork VALUES(artworkid_sequence.NEXTVAL, 1,'Flight', 15000.00,'08-Sep-
2003',NULL ,NULL,'for sale','oil','36 in X 48 in','realism','painting','2001',NULL );
INSERT INTO Artwork VALUES(artworkid_sequence.NEXTVAL, 3,'Bermuda Sunset', 8000.00,
'15-Mar-2004',NULL ,'01-Apr-2004' ,'sold','watercolor','22 in X 28 in','realism','painting',
2003',NULL );
INSERT INTO Artwork VALUES(artworkid_sequence.NEXTVAL, 3,'Mediterranean Coast',
4000.00,'18-Oct-2003',NULL ,'01-Apr-2004','for sale','watercolor','22 in X 28 in','realism',
'painting','2000','102345678');
INSERT INTO Artwork VALUES(artworkid_sequence.NEXTVAL, 5,'Ghost orchid', 18000.00',
05-Jun-2003',NULL ,NULL ,'sold','oil','36 in X 48 in','realism','painting','2001','034345678' );
INSERT INTO Artwork VALUES(artworkid_sequence.NEXTVAL, 4,'Five Planes', 15000.00,
'10-Jan-2004',NULL ,'10-Mar-2004' ,'for sale','steel','36inX30inX60in','cubism''sculpture'
'2003','034345678' );

INSERT INTO Show VALUES('The Sea in Watercolor',3,'30-Apr-2004','seascapes','01-Apr-2004');
INSERT INTO Show VALUES('Calderone:Mastery of Space',4,'20-Mar-2004','mobiles','10-Mar-2004');

INSERT INTO ShownIn VALUES(2,'The Sea in Watercolor');
INSERT INTO ShownIn VALUES(3,'The Sea in Watercolor');
INSERT INTO ShownIn VALUES(5,'Calderone:Mastery of Space');

CREATE SEQUENCE buyerId_sequence;
INSERT INTO Buyer VALUES (BuyerId_sequence.NEXTVAL,'Valerie','Smiley','15 Hudson
Street','10101','718','5551234',5000,7500);
INSERT INTO Buyer VALUES (BuyerId_sequence.NEXTVAL,'Winston','Lee','20 Liffey Avenue',
'60601','312','7654321',3000,0);
INSERT INTO Buyer VALUES (BuyerId_sequence.NEXTVAL,'Samantha','Babson','25 Thames
Lane','92101','619','4329876',15000,0);
INSERT INTO Buyer VALUES (BuyerId_sequence.NEXTVAL,'John','Flagg','22 Amazon Street',
'10101','212','7659876',3000,0);
INSERT INTO Buyer VALUES (BuyerId_sequence.NEXTVAL,'Terrence','Smallshaw','5 Nile
Street','33010','305','2323456',15000,17000);

INSERT INTO Salesperson VALUES('102445566','John','Smith','10 Sapphire Row','10801');
INSERT INTO Salesperson VALUES('121344321','Alan','Hughes','10 Diamond Street','10101');
INSERT INTO Salesperson VALUES('101889988','Mary','Brady','10 Pearl Avenue','10801');
INSERT INTO Salesperson VALUES('111223344','Jill','Fleming','10 Ruby Row','10101');
INSERT INTO Salesperson VALUES('123123123','Terrence','DeSimone','10 Emerald Lane','10101');

INSERT INTO Sale VALUES(1234, 2,NULL ,'05-Apr-2004',7500,600, 1,'102445566');
INSERT INTO Sale VALUES(1235, 6,NULL ,'06-Apr-2004',17000,1360, 5,'121344321');
```

2. Find the total commission for salesperson John Smith earned between the dates April 1, 2004, and April 15, 2004. Recall that the gallery charges 10% commission, and the salesperson receives one-half of that, which is 5% of the selling price.

```
SELECT .05 * SUM(salePrice)
FROM Sale
WHERE saleDate > = '01-Apr-2004' AND
    saleDate < = '15-Apr-2004' AND
    salespersonSocialSecurityNumber = (SELECT socialSecurityNumber
                                       FROM Salesperson
                                       WHERE firstName= 'John' AND lastName
                                       ='Smith');
```

3. Find the collector names, artist names, and titles of all artworks that are owned by collectors, not by the artists themselves, in order by the collector's last name.

```
SELECT Collector.firstName, Collector.lastName, Artist.firstName,
Artist.lastName, workTitle
FROM Artist, Artwork, Collector
WHERE   Artist.artistId = Artwork.artistId AND
        Artwork.collectorSocialSecurityNumber =
        Collector.socialSecurityNumber AND
        collectorSocialSecurityNumber IS NOT NULL
ORDER BY Collector.lastName, Collector.firstName;
```

4. For each potential buyer, find information about shows that feature his or her preferred artist.

```
SELECT firstName, lastName, showTitle, showOpeningDate, showClosingDate,
potentialCustomerId
FROM Show, PotentialCustomer
WHERE showFeaturedArtistId = PotentialCustomer.preferredArtistId
ORDER BY potentialCustomerId;
```

5. Find the average sale price of works of artist Georgia Keefe.

```
SELECT AVG(salePrice)
FROM Sale
WHERE artworkId IN (SELECT artworkId
    FROM Artwork
    WHERE artistId = (SELECT ArtistId
                      FROM Artist
                      WHERE lastName = 'Keefe' AND firstName ='Georgia'));
```

- Step 6.6. Create at least one trigger and write the code for it. This trigger will update the amount of the buyer's purchases year-to-date whenever a sale is completed.

```
CREATE TRIGGER UPDATEBUYERYTD
AFTER INSERT ON Sale
FOR EACH ROW
BEGIN
    UPDATE Buyer
    SET purchasesYearToDate = purchasesYearToDate + :NEW.salePrice
    WHERE Buyer.buyerId = :NEW.buyerId;
END;
```

STUDENT PROJECTS: CREATING AND USING A RELATIONAL DATABASE FOR THE STUDENT PROJECTS

For the normalized tables you developed at the end of Chapter 5 for the project you have chosen, carry out the following steps to implement the design using a relational database management system such as Oracle, SQLServer, or MySQL.

- Step 6.1. Update the data dictionary and list of assumptions as needed. For each table, write the table name and write out the names, data types, and sizes of all the data items, and identify any constraints, using the conventions of the DBMS you will use for implementation.

- Step 6.2. Write and execute SQL statements to create all tables needed to implement the design. The website for this book has directions for using SQL to create an Access database.

- Step 6.3. Create indexes for foreign keys and for any other columns as needed.

- Step 6.4. Insert at least five records in each table, preserving all constraints. Put in enough data to demonstrate how the database will function.

- Step 6.5. Write SQL statements that will process five non-routine requests for information from the database just created. For each, write the request in English, followed by the corresponding SQL command.

- Step 6.6. Create at least one trigger and write the code for it.

CHAPTER 7

The Enhanced Entity-Relationship Model and the Object-Relational Model

Chapter Objectives

In this chapter you will learn the following:

- Why the E-R model has been extended to the EE-R model

- The meaning of generalization and specialization

- How to represent a generalization hierarchy on an EE-R diagram

- How to represent generalization constraints

- The meaning of union

- How to use (*min..max*) notation for relationship constraints

- How to map an EE-R model to a strictly relational model

- How to use the object-oriented extensions to the relational model with SQL

- How to map an EE-R model to an object-relational model

- How Oracle implements the object-relational model

7.1 Rationale for Extending the E-R Model

Although the E-R model is sufficient to represent data needs for traditional applications in business, it is not semantically rich enough to model the more complex environments used for more advanced applications. The databases used for geographic information systems, search engines, data mining, multimedia, computer-aided design and computer-aided manufacturing (CAD/CAM), software development, engineering design, and many other sophisticated applications must be capable of representing more semantic information than the standard E-R model can express. The **Extended Entity-Relationship (EE-R)** model extends the E-R model to allow various types of abstraction to be included, and to express constraints more clearly. Addition symbols have been added to standard E-R diagrams to create EE-R diagrams that express these concepts.

7.2 Generalization and Specialization

The process of generalization and its inverse, specialization, are two abstractions that are used to incorporate more meaning in EE-R diagrams.

7.2.1 Specialization

Often an entity set contains one or more subsets that have special attributes or that participate in relationships that other members of the same entity set do not have. For instance, in the University example whose E-R diagram is shown in Figure 3.12, the `Faculty` entity set can be broken up into subsets, `AdjunctFac` and `FullTimeFac`. Adjunct faculty members teach part-time and are usually appointed on a temporary basis, while full-time faculty are regular employees who work on a continuing basis. Adjunct faculty members are paid per course, while full-time faculty are paid an annual salary. All faculty have attributes `facId`, `lastName`, `firstName`, and `rank`, but `AdjunctFac` members have a local attribute called `coursePayRate` whereas `FullTimeFac` have a local attribute called `annualSalary`.

The method of identifying subsets of existing entity sets, called **specialization,** corresponds to the notion of subclass and class inheritance in object-oriented design, where it is represented by class hierarchies, as discussed in Chapter 8. Figure 7.1(a) shows how this superclass-subclass relationship is represented in EE-R diagrams. In this diagram, the superclass, `Faculty`, has been specialized into two subclasses, `AdjunctFac` and `FullTimeFac`. The circle below `Faculty` is called the **specialization circle,** and it is connected by a line to the superclass. Each subclass is connected to the circle by a line having an **inheritance symbol,** a subset symbol or cup, with the open side facing the superclass. The subclasses inherit the attributes of the superclass, and may optionally have distinct local attributes, such as `coursePayRate` for `AdjunctFac` and `annualSalary` for `FullTimeFac`. Since each member of a subclass **is a** member of the superclass, the specialization circle is sometimes referred to as an *isa* **relationship.**

Sometimes an entity has just one subset with special properties or relationships that we want to keep information about. It contains only one subclass for a specialization. In that case, on the EE-R diagram we omit the circle and simply show the subclass connected by a subset line to the superclass. For example, if some university `Class` entity instances have a lab component for which we want to keep information about the lab used and lab schedule, we could design a subclass just of those entities, as shown in Figure 7.1(b). Note that `LabClass` inherits all the attributes of `Class`, (i.e., `LabClass` *isa* `Class`) in addition to having its local attributes of `labNumber` and `labSched`.

Subclasses may also participate in local relationships that do not apply to the superclass or to other subclasses in the same hierarchy. For example, only regular faculty members can subscribe to a pension plan. We assume each full-time faculty member can choose one of several companies, and has a unique contract number for his or her pension plan with that company. Each company has several contact persons, of whom one is assigned to correspond with the faculty member. Figure 7.1(c) illustrates this possibility.

7.2.2 Generalization

By the process of specialization, we developed the Faculty class hierarchy by breaking up an existing class into subclasses. Class hierarchies can also be created by recognizing that two or more classes have common properties and identifying a common superclass for them, a process called **generalization**. These two processes are inverses of each other, but they both result in the same type of hierarchy diagram. For example, since students and faculty both have IDs and names as attributes, we could generalize these two entity sets into a new superclass, `Person`, having the common attributes. The subclasses `Student` and `Faculty` would each retain their special attributes, as shown in Figure 7.1(d). Using generalization, we developed this diagram from the bottom up. Note that we would have the same diagram if we had started with `Person` and specialized it into `Student` and `Faculty`, but we would have been working from the top down.

FIGURE 7.1 (a)

Specialization with Two Subclasses

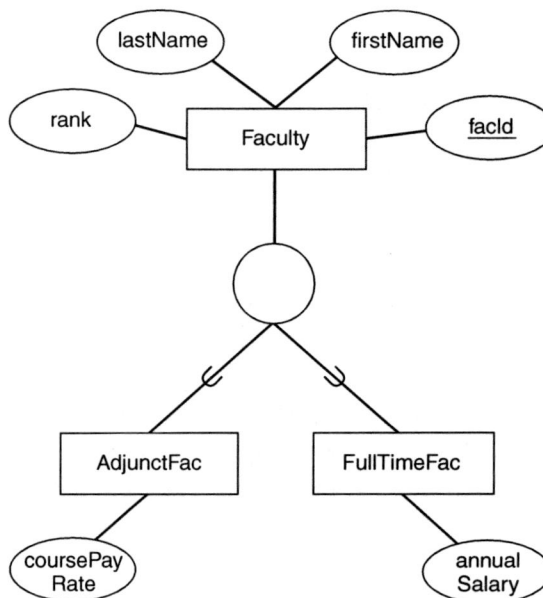

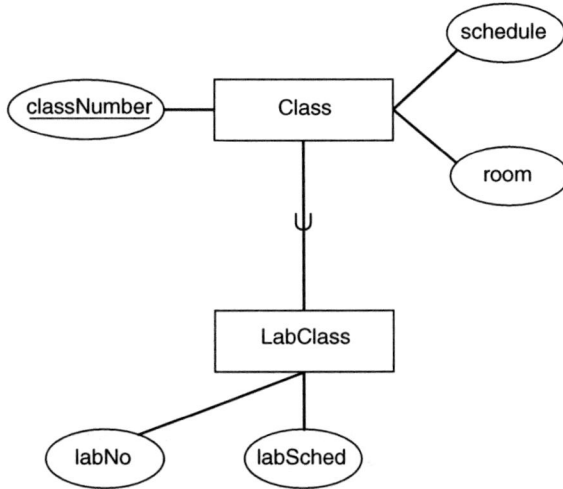

FIGURE 7.1 (b)
Specialization with One Subclass

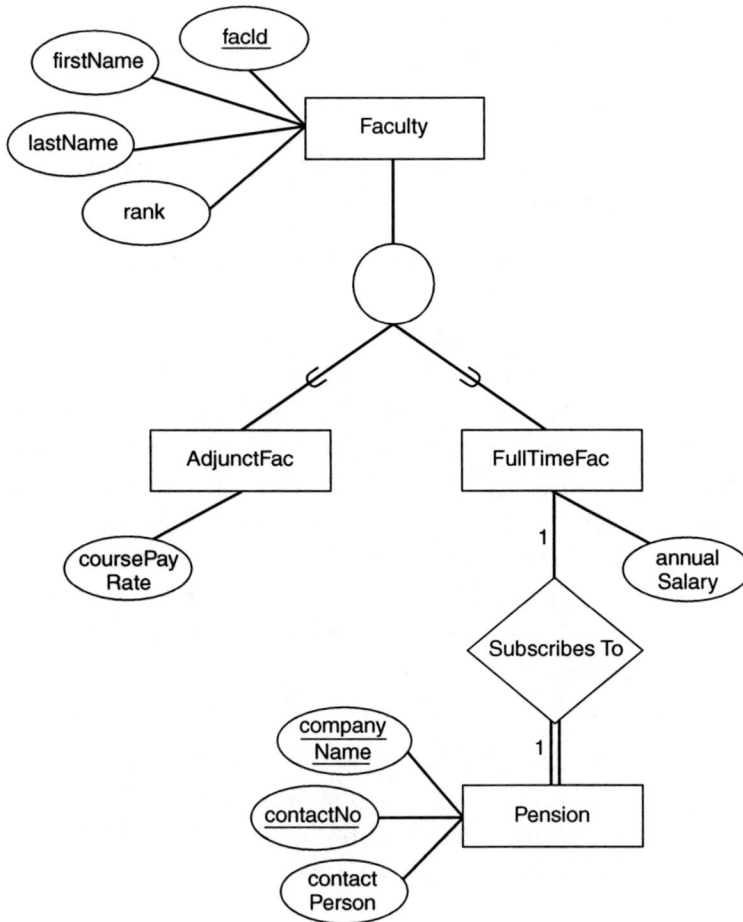

FIGURE 7.1 (c)
Subclass with Relationship

FIGURE 7.1 (d)

Generalization with Person Superclass

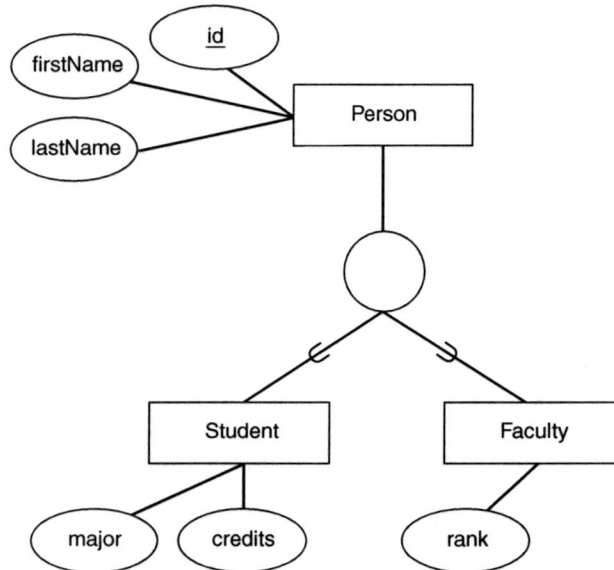

7.2.3 Generalization Constraints—Disjointness, Completeness, Definition Method

Subclasses can be **overlapping,** which means the same entity instance can belong to more than one of the subclasses, or **disjoint,** which means they have no common members. This is referred to as the **disjointness** constraint, and it is expressed by placing an appropriate letter, d or o, in the specialization circle. A d indicates disjoint subclasses, and an o indicates overlapping subclasses. For example, since a faculty member cannot be both adjunct and full-time, we place a d in the circle for that specialization, as shown on the bottom left in Figure 7.2(a). We have placed an o in the specialization circle of Person into Faculty and Student to indicate that a person can be both a faculty member and a student. We are assuming, just for this diagram, that a faculty member might be able to take graduate courses, for example, and therefore he or she could be a member of the Student entity set as well as of the Faculty set.

Students are also specialized disjointly in this diagram into undergraduate and graduate. Both types of students have attributes id, lastName, and firstName inherited from Person, both have the attribute credits, but undergraduates have major as an attribute, while graduate students have `program`. Undergraduates are further disjointly specialized into class years, as shown by the d in the circle for that specialization. Although we have not listed them, we will assume that each class year has some distinguishing attribute. For example, freshmen could have a peer mentor, seniors could have a thesis supervisor, and so on.

A specialization also has a **completeness** constraint, which shows whether every member of the entity set must participate in it. If every member of the superclass must belong to some subclass, we have a **total** specialization. If some superclass members can be permitted not to belong to any

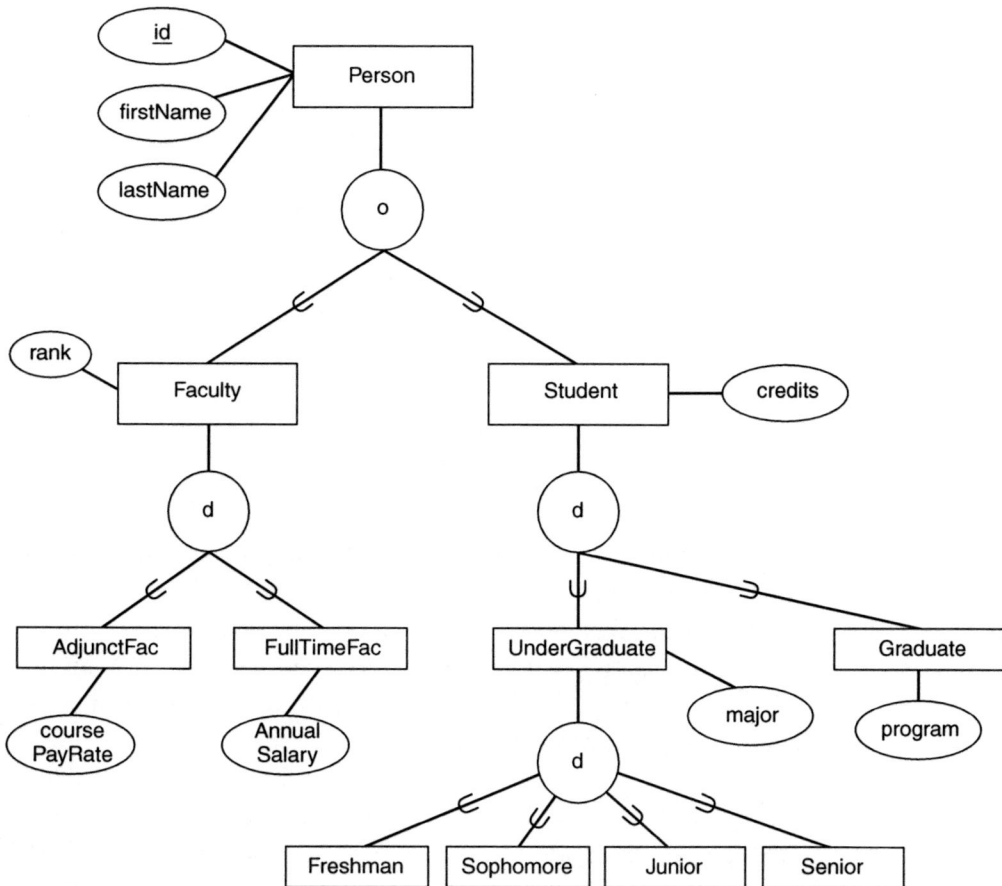

FIGURE 7.2 (a)
Disjoint vs Overlapping Subclasses

FIGURE 7.2 (b)

**Total and Partial Partici-
pation in Specialization**

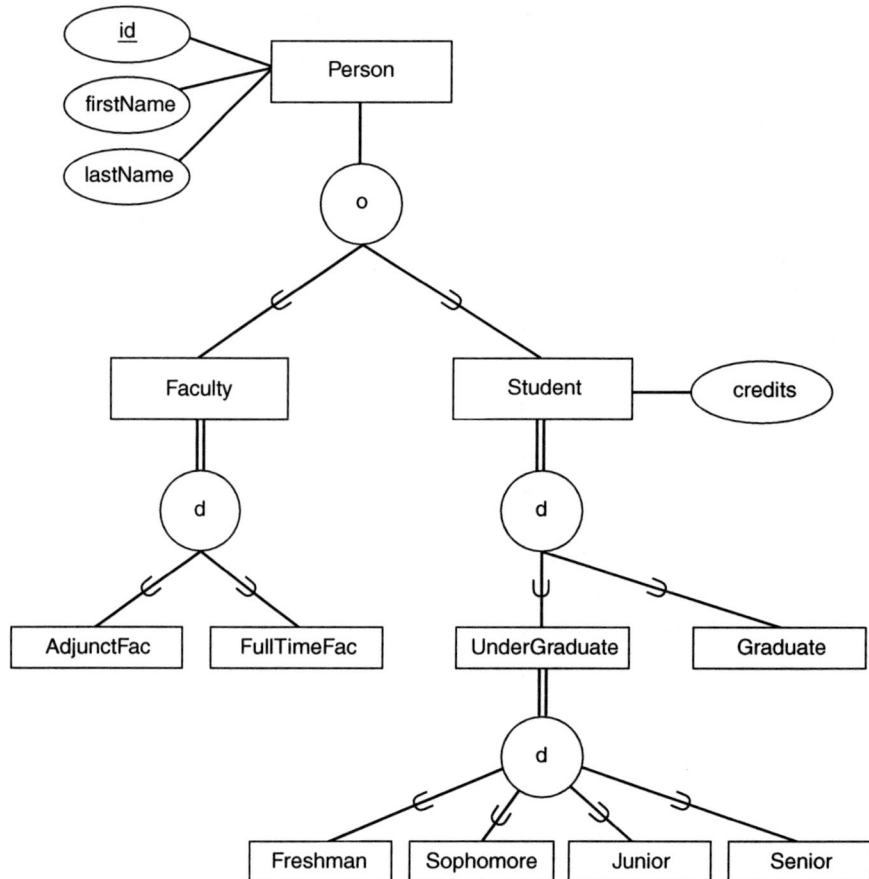

subclass, the specialization is **partial.** For example, since every faculty member must be either AdjunctFac or FullTimeFac, we have total specialization. In Figure 7.2(b), this is indicated by the double line connecting the superclass, Faculty, to the specialization circle on the bottom left of the diagram. The single line connecting Person to its specialization circle indicates that the specialization into Faculty and Student is partial. There may be some Person entities who are neither faculty nor students. The double line below Student indicates a total specialization into graduate or undergraduate. The double line below undergraduates shows a total specialization into class years, implying that every undergraduate student must belong to one of the class years.

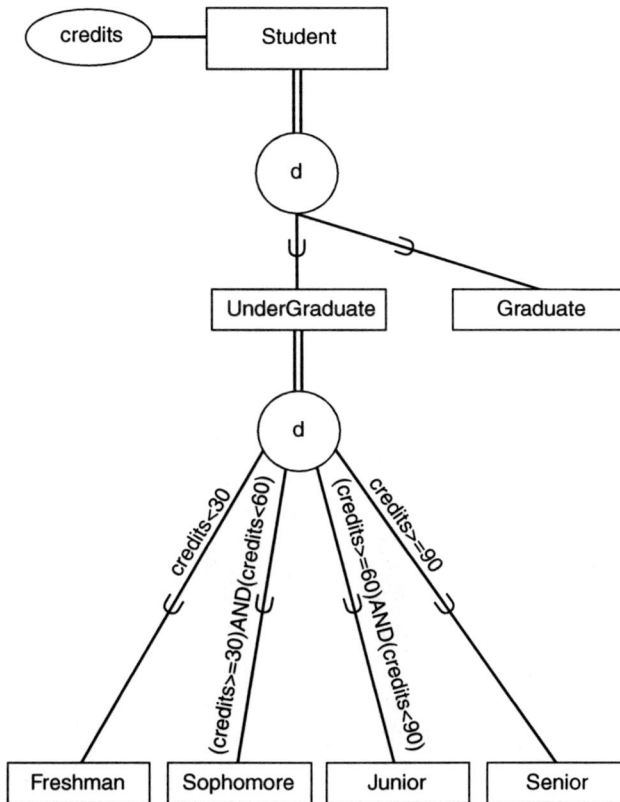

FIGURE 7.2 (c)
**Predicate-Defined
Specialization**

In some specialization hierarchies, it is possible to identify the subclass that an entity belongs to by examining a specific condition or predicate for each subclass. In the specialization of UnderGraduates, if the predicate "credits <30" is true, the student belongs to the freshman subclass, while if the predicate "credits > = 30 AND credits <60" is true, the student is a sophomore, and so on for the other two subclasses. This is an example of a **predicate-defined** specialization, since subclass membership is determined by a predicate. On an EE-R diagram, we can write the defining predicate on the line from the specialization circle to the subclass as shown in Figure 7.2(c).

Some predicate-defined specializations, including this one, use the value of the same attribute in the defining predicate for all the subclasses. These are called **attribute-defined** specializations. We indicate the defining

FIGURE 7.2 (d)

Attribute-Defined Specialization

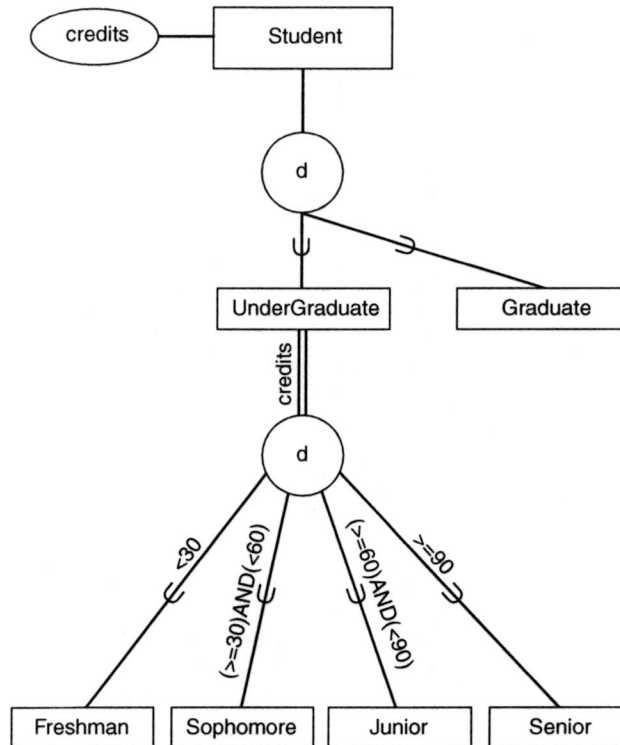

attribute on the line from the circle to the superclass, and the distinguishing value for each subclass on the line from the subclass to the circle, as shown for the class year specialization in Figure 7.2(d). Specializations that are not predicate-defined are said to be **user-defined,** since the user is responsible for placing the entity instance in the correct subclass. In our example, the specialization of Person into Faculty and Student; of Faculty into Adjunct and FullTime; and Student into Undergraduate and Graduate are all user-defined.

7.2.4 Multiple Hierarchies and Inheritance

In addition to specializing undergraduate students according to the class year, a database designer could decide that is important to specialize them by their residence status. Figure 7.3(a) shows this further specialization of UnderGraduate by residence according to whether a student lives in an on-campus dormitory, an off-campus university property, or at home. The class year specialization and the residence specialization are independent of each other, and both can appear on the same diagram. In this way, the EE-R model allows us to give the same superclass more than one specialization.

Sometimes the same entity set can be a subclass of two or more superclasses. Such a class is called a **shared subclass,** and it has **multiple inheritance** from its superclasses. For example, adding to our University example, as shown in Figure 7.3(b), some graduate students might be Teaching Assistants. Teaching Assistants receive funding for their tuition from a `fundingSource`, and they assist in some introductory classes at the university, for which they receive a salary. Members of the `TeachingAssistant` subclass inherit all the attributes of `Faculty` and of `Graduate`, and of the superclasses of those classes, `Student` and `Person`, in addition to having their own distinguishing attribute of `fundingSource`. As with all subclasses, shared subclasses can participate in relationships, as we see `TeachingAssistant` participating in the `Assist` relationship with the `Class` entity set.

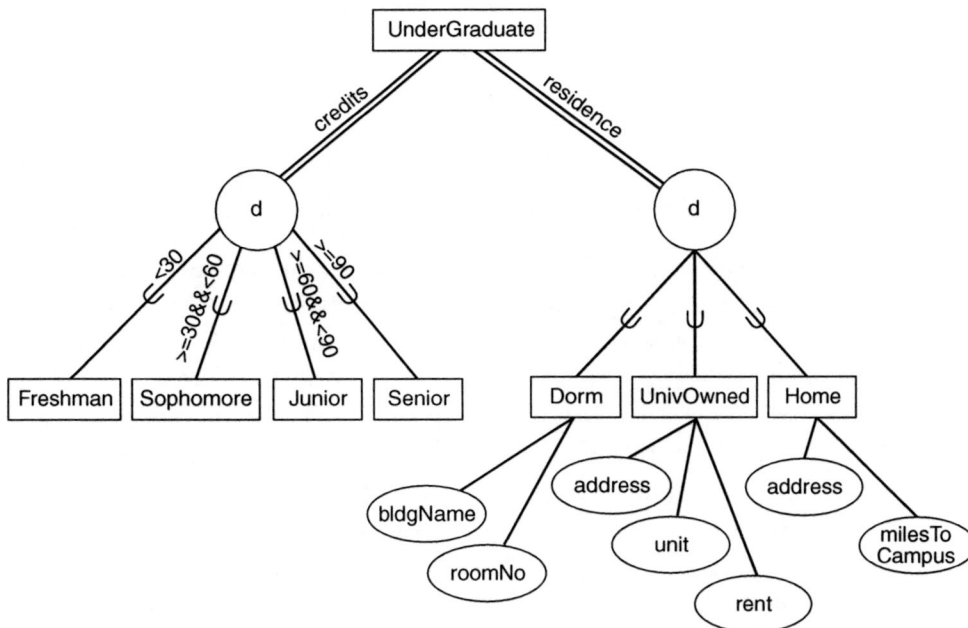

FIGURE 7.3 (a)

Multiple Specializations—by Class Year and by Residence

FIGURE 7.3 (b)

Multiple Inheritance

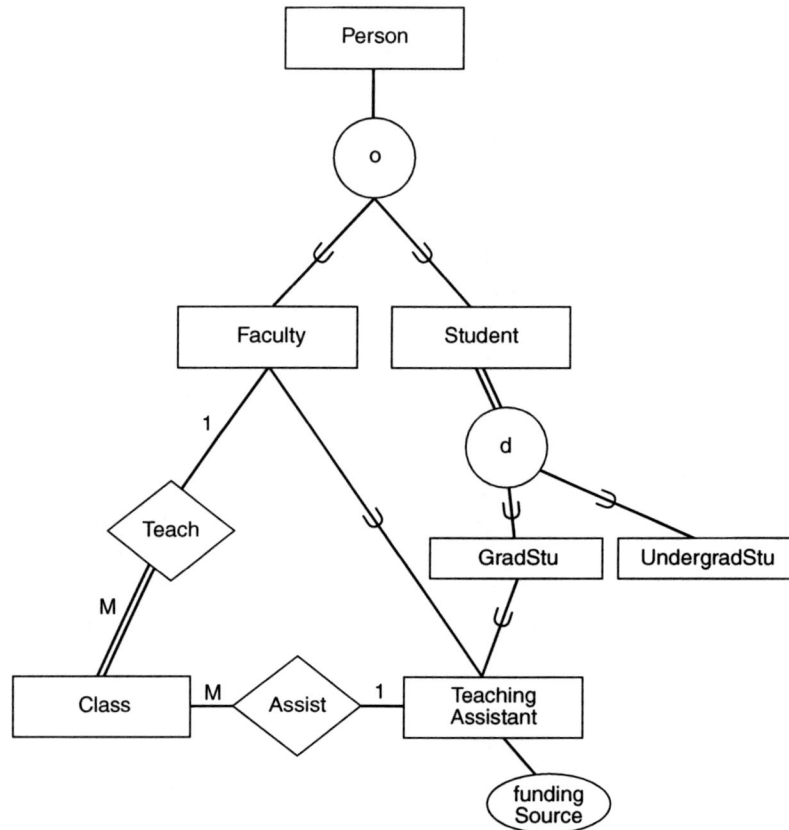

7.3   Union

Whereas a shared subclass, as described in the previous section, is a member of all its superclasses and inherits attributes from all of them, a subclass can be related to one of a collection, called a **union** or **category,** of superclasses, rather than belonging to all of them. In that case, an instance of the subclass inherits the attributes of only one of the superclasses, depending on which member of the union that it belongs to. Expanding on our University example, suppose we want to represent sponsors of campus-wide events, which can be sponsored by teams, departments, or clubs. We assume here that a campus-wide event must have exactly one sponsor, but it can be a team, a department, or a club. We could form a union of Team, Department, and Club, which is then the set of all of these entities. Sponsor is a subclass of the union. The attributes of a particular sponsor will depend on which type it is. Figure 7.4(a) illustrates a union of Club,

`Team,` and `Dept,` represented by the union circle below them. The union has subclass `Sponsor,` which is related to `CampusWideEvent.` The three classes are connected to the circle with a set union symbol in it. The circle is connected to the subclass, `Sponsor,` by a line with the subset symbol (cup) on it, facing the circle.

Categories can be partial or total, depending on whether every member of the sets that make up the union must participate in it. The line connecting `Sponsor` to its union circle in Figure 7.4(a) is single, indicating a **partial category.** This indicates that not every `Club,` `Team,` or `Dept` has to be a `Sponsor.` Elaborating on this example in Figure 7.4(b) we show that `CampusWideEvent` is a union of `Concert` or `Fair.` This indicates that every campus-wide event is either a concert or a fair, and a particular campus-wide event will have the attributes of one of these superclasses.

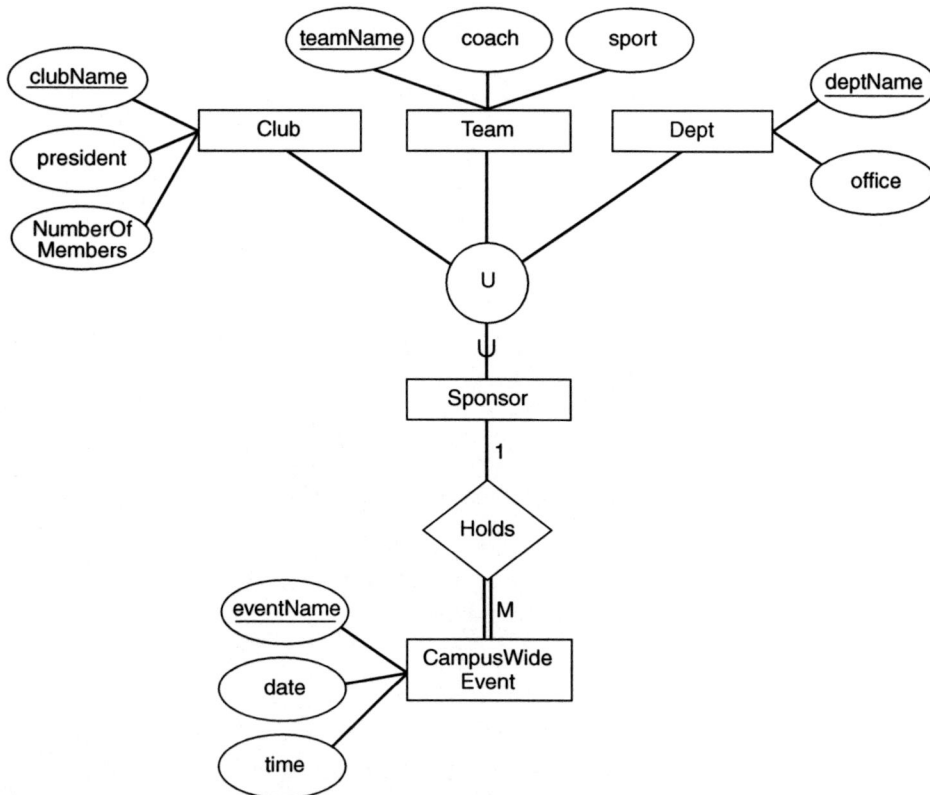

FIGURE 7.4 (a)

Example of Union

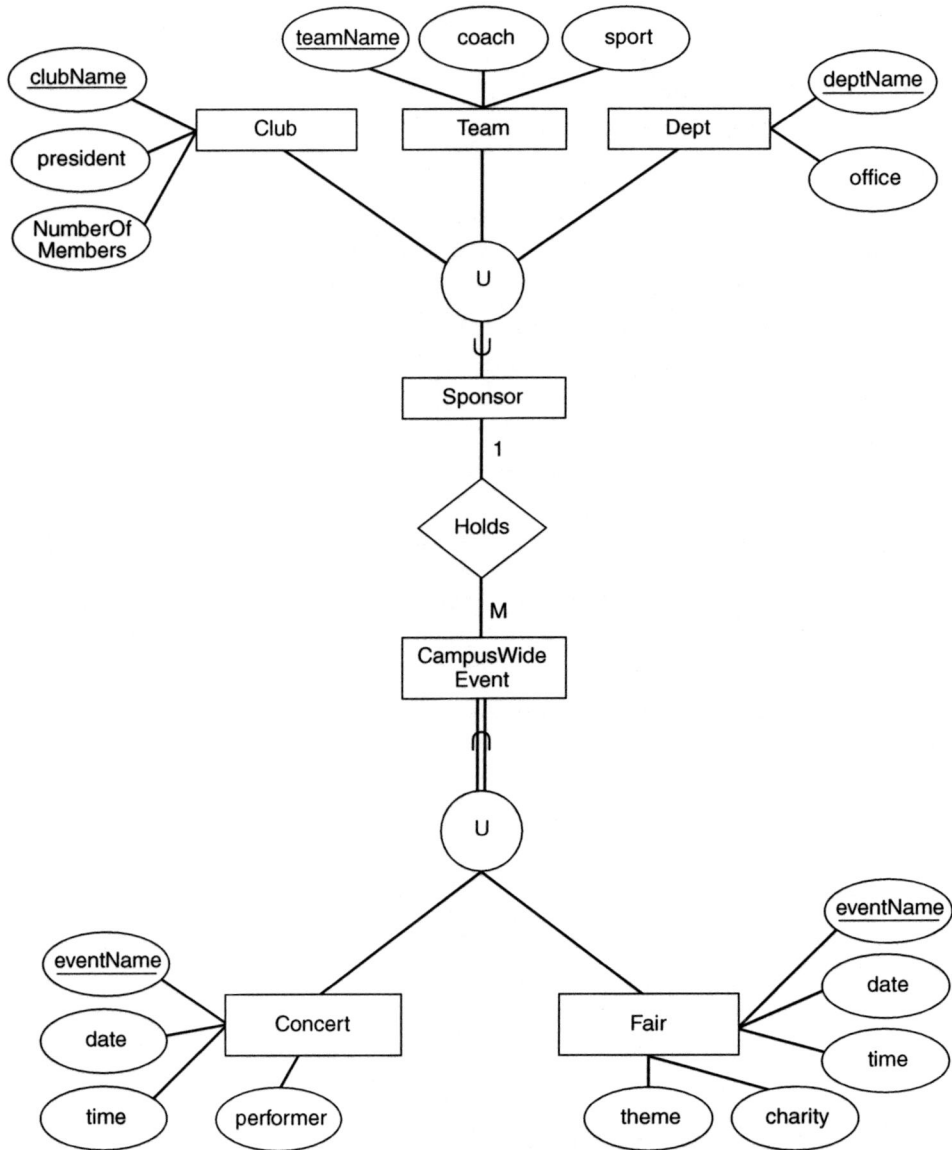

FIGURE 7.4 (b)
Partial vs Total Union

The line connecting CampusWideEvent to the union circle is double, indicating a **total category,** which means every Concert and Fair must be a member of CampusWideEvent.

Different designers can make different choices about when to use a union or a specialization abstraction. If a union is total, and the superclasses share

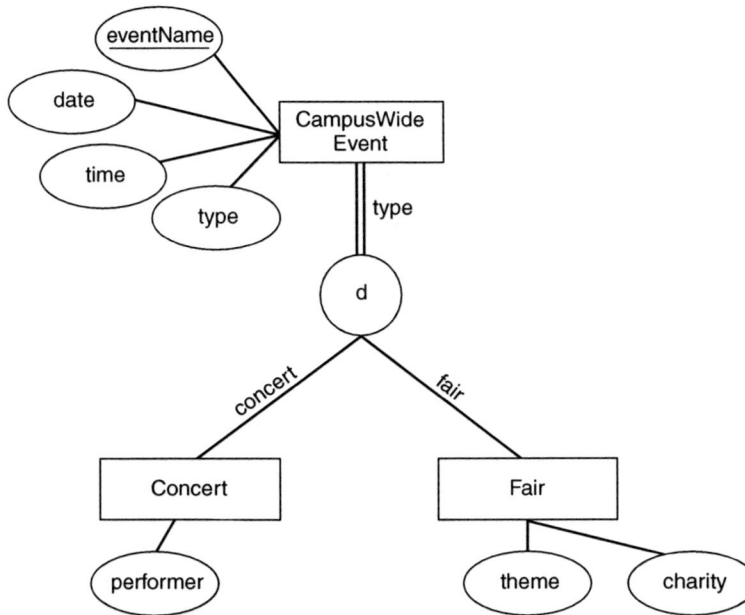

FIGURE 7.5
Total Union replaced by Specialization/ Generalization

many attributes, it might be preferable to use specialization. Figure 7.5 shows a specialization of campus-wide events into two subclasses, instead of using the union of concerts and fairs into campus-wide events as we did in Figure 7.4(b). Here we show an attribute-defined specialization, with type as the defining attribute. Notice that as a specialization/generalization, it is clear that every concert or fair is a campus event because, in specialization/generalization, every member of a subclass is automatically a member of the superclass. It is a total specialization, as shown by the double line connecting CampusWideEvent to the specialization circle, indicating that all campus-wide events are either fairs or concerts.

7.4 Using (*min..max*) Notation for Cardinality and Participation

In the E-R and EE-R diagrams thus far, we have used single lines or double lines to show participation constraints for relationships. We have shown relationship cardinality by using "1" for "one" and "M" (or "N") for "many" on the appropriate lines. An alternative representation that shows both participation and cardinality constraints is the (*min, max*) notation illustrated in the E-R diagram in Figure 7.6 for part of the University example. It can be used with either E-R or EE-R diagrams. Each line

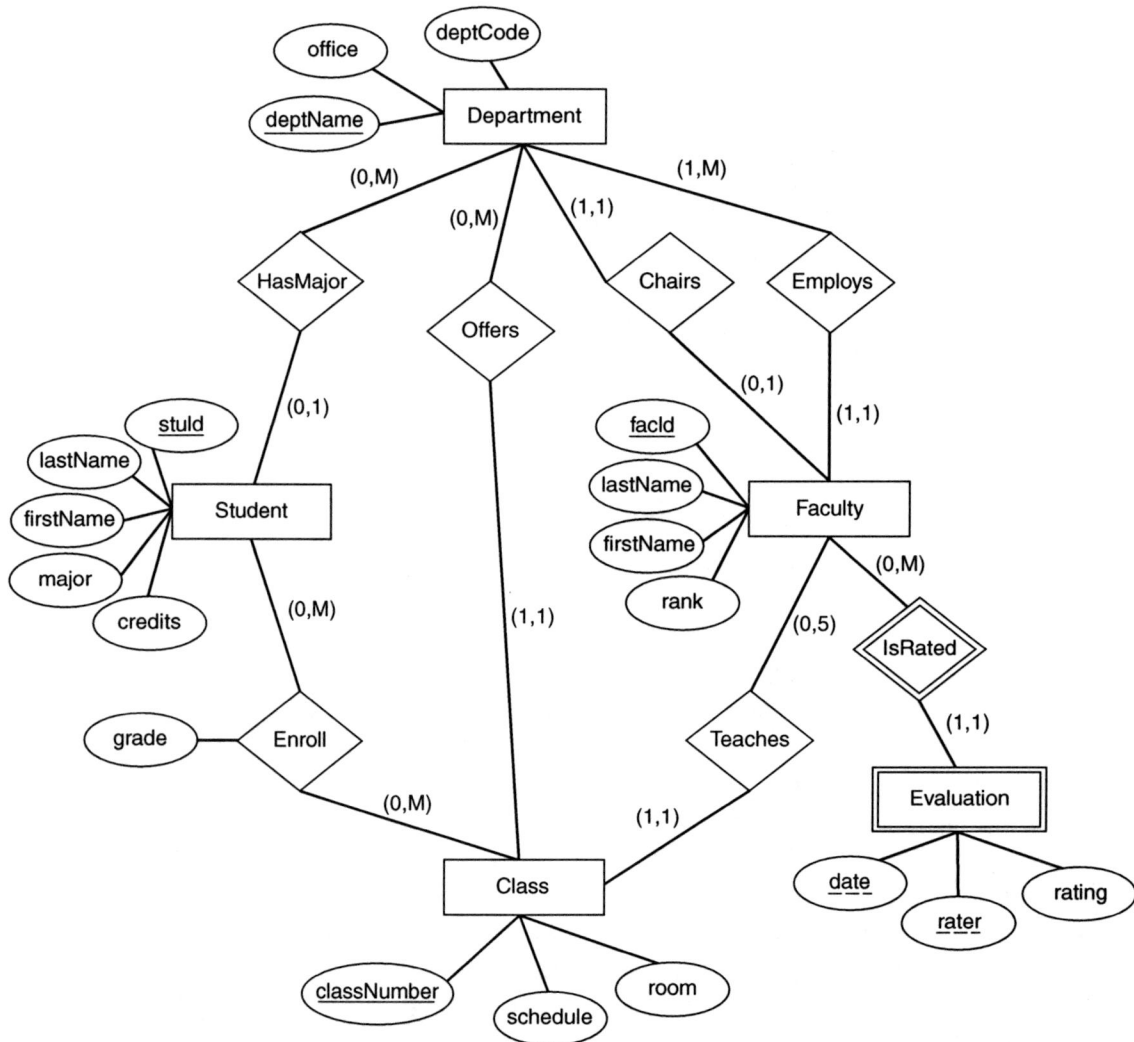

FIGURE 7.6

Part of University ER Diagram with (*min, max*) notation.

connecting an entity rectangle to a relationship diamond has a pair of integers, (*min, max*), written in parenthesis above it. The first integer of the pair, *min*, specifies the least number of relationship instances an entity instance must participate in. If *min* is 0, it means that there might be entity instances that do not participate in instances of the relationship, so the participation is partial. If *min* is 1 or more, the participation is total. The value of *max* is the greatest number of relationship instances the entity can participate in. This value could be 1, N (to represent *many*), or some constant integer, such as 10. Some notations use * in place of N to represent *many*. In Figure 7.6, the line connecting `Department` to the `HasMajor` relationship diamond has a min of 0, indicating that a department does not need to have a student majoring in it, and a max of M, indicating that a department can have many student majors. The line from `Student` to the `HasMajor` relationship diamond has (0,1), which means a student does not have to have any major, and has at most one major. The (1,M) on the line connecting `Department` to the `Employs` relationship has a min of 1, meaning a department must have at least one faculty member, and a max of M, since a department can have many faculty. The line from `Faculty` to the relationship has (1,1), indicating that a faculty member belongs to exactly one department. Other participation and cardinality constraints are indicated on the diagram. We note that all of these constraints reflect assumptions about this particular university and that the constraints might be different in another institution.

7.5   A Sample EE-R Diagram

We now modify our University E-R diagram to show some of the generalizations discussed in previous sections. Figure 7.7 shows an EE-R diagram for the University example, modified to illustrate the use of generalization/specialization, union, and (*min..max*), notation.

7.6   Mapping an EE-R Model to a Relational Model

The techniques discussed in Section 4.8 for mapping an E-R model to a relational model must be extended to take into account the additional features of the EE-R model, namely specialization/generalization, and union.

7.6.1   Summary of E-R to Relational Mapping Concepts

For entity sets and relationships that are not part of generalizations or unions, the mapping proceeds as for the E-R model.

- We map strong entity sets to tables having a column for each single-valued, non-composite attribute.
  - For composite attributes, we create a column for each component and do not represent the composite. Alternatively, we can create a single column for the composite and ignore the components.

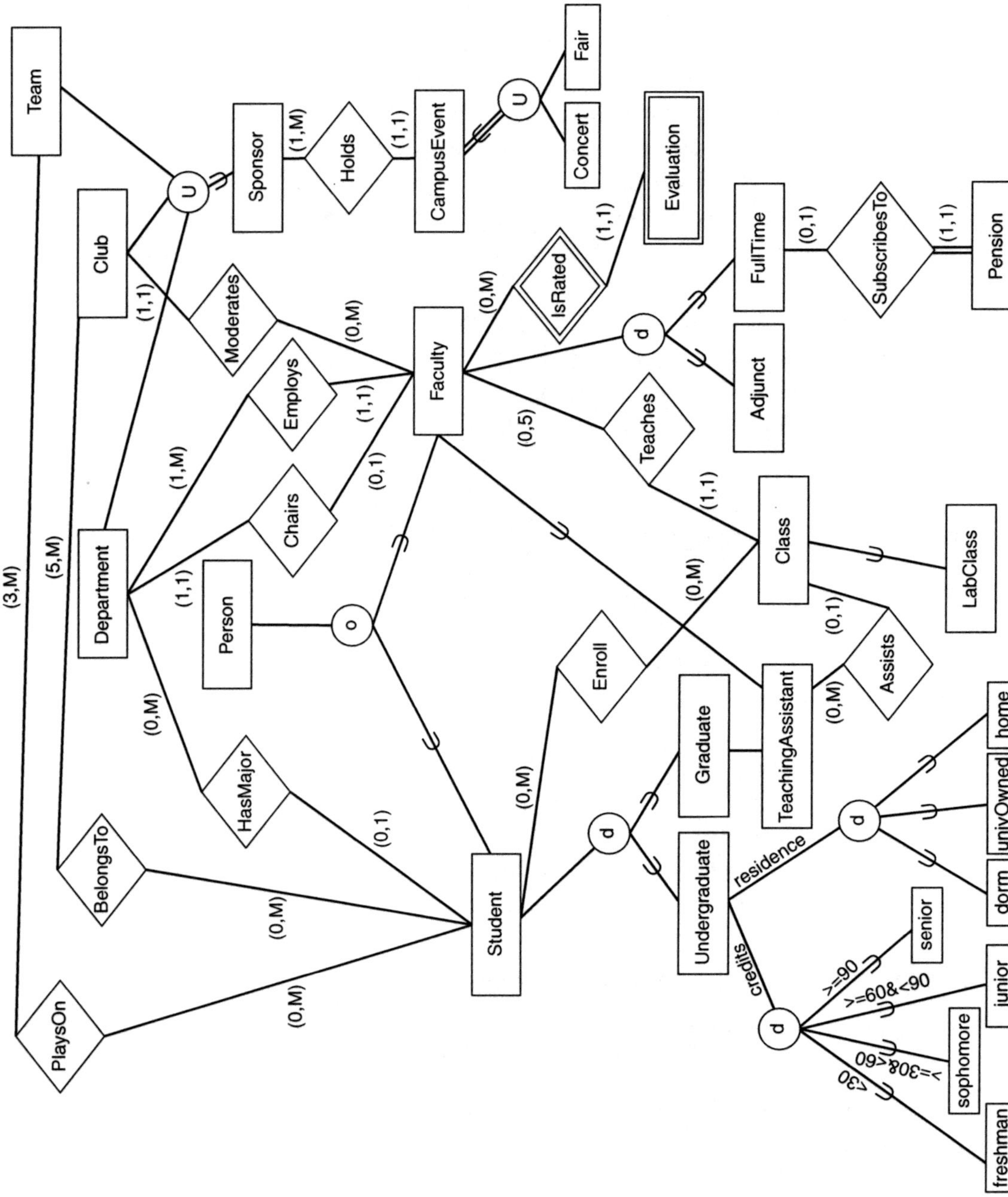

FIGURE 7.7

An EE-R Diagram for the University Example

- For each multi-valued attribute, we create a separate table having the primary key of the entity, along with a column for the multi-valued attribute. Alternatively, if we know the maximum number of values for the attribute, we can create multiple columns for these values. Another method is to use the multi-valued attribute of the primary key, thus "flattening" the table.

- For weak entity sets, we create tables that include the primary key of the owner entity along with the attributes of the weak entity set.

- For one-to-many binary relationships we place the primary key of the one side in the table of the many side, creating a foreign key.

- For one-to-one binary relationships, we place either one of the primary keys in the table for the other entity.

- For many-to-many binary relationships, and for all higher-level relationships, we create a relationship table that consists of the primary keys of the related entities, along with any descriptive attributes of the relationship.

7.6.2　Mapping EE-R Class Hierarchies to Relational Tables

To illustrate the representation of subclasses, we will use Figure 7.1(a), which shows `Faculty` with subclasses `AdjunctFac` and `FullTimeFac`. We can choose one of the following methods.

- **Method 1.** Create a table for the superclass and one for each of the subclasses, placing the primary key of the superclass in each subclass table. For Figure 7.1(a), we create three tables, `Faculty`, `AdjunctFac`, and `FullTimeFac`. Faculty has the attributes shown on the diagram, including a primary key, `facId`. Both `AdjunctFac` and `FullTimeFac` tables have columns for their own attributes, plus columns for the primary key of the superclass, `facId`, which functions both as the primary key and a foreign key in those tables. The tables are:

  ```
  Faculty(facId, lastName, firstName, rank)
  AdjunctFac(facId, coursePayRate)
  FullTimeFac(facId, annualSalary)
  ```

- **Method 2.** Create tables for each of the subclasses, and no table for the superclass. Place all of the attributes of the superclass in each of the subclass tables. For this example, we would have tables for `AdjunctFac` and `FullTimeFac`, and none for `Faculty`. The tables are:

```
AdjunctFac(facId, lastName, firstName, rank, coursePayRate)
FullTimeFac(facId, lastName, firstName, rank, annualSalary)
```

- **Method 3.** Create a single table that contains all the attributes of the superclass, along with all the attributes of all subclasses. For our example, we could create the table:

```
AllFac(facId, lastName, firstName, rank, annualSalary,
coursePayRate)
```

A variation of Method 3 is to add a "type field" to the record, indicating which subclass the entity belongs to. For attribute-defined disjoint specializations, this is simply the defining attribute. For overlapping specializations, we could add a membership field for each specialization, indicating whether or not the entity belongs to each of the subclasses.

There are tradeoffs to be considered for each of these methods. The first works for all types of subclasses, regardless of whether the specialization is disjoint or overlapping; partial or total; and attribute-defined or user-defined. For our example, queries about faculty that involve only the common attributes are easily answered using the superclass table. However, queries about members of a subclass will, in general, require a join with the superclass table. The second method handles queries about the subclasses well, since one table has all the information about each subclass. However, it should not be used if the subclasses are overlapping, because data about the instances that belong to more than one subclass will be duplicated. It cannot be used if the specialization is partial, because the entity instances that do not belong to any subclass cannot be represented at all using this method. The third method allows us to answer queries about all the subclasses and the superclass without doing joins, but it will result in storing many null values in the database.

7.6.3 Mapping Unions

To represent unions (categories), we create a table for the union itself, and individual tables for each of the superclasses, using foreign keys to connect them. A problem that often arises with mapping unions is that the superclasses can have different primary keys. Figure 7.4(a) shows `Sponsor` as the union of `Club`, `Team`, and `Department`, which have primary keys `clubName`, `teamName`, and `deptName` respectively.

Although these are all names, they might not be comparable because of differences in length. Other unions might involve grouping together entity sets with radically different keys. The solution is to create a surrogate key that will be the primary key of the union. It will be a foreign key in the tables for each of the superclasses. For the `Sponsor` example, we create a surrogate key for sponsor, which we call `sponsorId`, and we insert that attribute as a foreign key in the tables for `Club`, `Team`, and `Department`. We also add `SponsorType` to indicate whether the sponsor is a club, team, or department. The schema will be:

```
Sponsor(sponsorId, sponsorType)
Club(clubName, president, numberOfMembers, sponsorId)
Team(teamName, coach, sport, sponsorId)
Department(deptName, office, sponsorId)
```

If the primary keys of the superclasses are the same, it is not necessary to create a surrogate key. The table for the union will consist of the common primary key field and a type field. The common primary key field will also function as a foreign key for the superclass tables. For the `CampusWideEvent` example shown in Figure 7.4(b), the schema will be:

```
CampusWideEvent(eventName, eventType)
Concert(eventName, date, time, performer)
Fair(eventName, date, time, theme, charity)
```

7.7 Extending the Relational Model

The relational model was designed to represent data that consists of single-valued attributes of a small collection of data types, related in relatively simple ways, typically used in traditional data processing. As discussed in Section 7.1, the model lacks some features needed to represent the more complex types and relationships necessary for advanced applications. The industry responded to this challenge initially by proposing an entirely new data model, the object data model, which is discussed in Chapter 8. Vendors of relational database management systems, including Oracle, IBM, Sybase, Informix, and Microsoft have met this competition by capturing some of the features of the object data model, and extended their relational products to incorporate them. The SQL:1999 standard also extended the SQL language to use these new features. The object-relational model can be viewed as a compromise between the strictly relational model and the object-oriented model.

Some of the additional features needed are:

- Richer fundamental data types, including types for multimedia—text, images, video, audio, and so on
- Collection types that can hold multiple attributes
- User-defined data types, including user-written operations to manipulate them
- Representation of class hierarchies, with inheritance of both data structures and methods
- Reference or pointer types for objects, to enable us to refer to large objects such as multimedia files that are stored elsewhere.

7.7.1 New Fundamental Data Types

To address the first requirement, SQL:1999 added two new fundamental data types, LARGE OBJECT (LOB) and BOOLEAN, as well as two type constructors, ARRAY and ROW, to the SQL standard.

The **LOB** type can be used to store text, audio, video, and other multimedia objects. Besides images and audio or video clips, an attribute such as a student's signature might be stored in LOB format. The LOB type has variants **BLOB** (BINARY LARGE OBJECT), and **CLOB** (CHARACTER LARGE OBJECT). LOB types have very restricted functions, such as substring operations. They allow comparisons only for equality or inequality, and they cannot be used for ordering or in GROUP BY or ORDER BY clauses. Since they are large files, LOBs are normally stored and rarely retrieved again. They can be manipulated by using a **LOB locator,** a system-generated binary surrogate for the actual value. If we wish to add a student's signature to the Student record, we would add the signature attribute in the CREATE TABLE command for the Student table, using the attribute declaration:

```
signature CLOB REF IS sigid SYSTEM GENERATED,
```

The sigid is a pointer to the file containing an image of the signature. We will discuss its use in Section 7.7.5.

The SQL:1999 **BOOLEAN** data type can be used for attributes with possible values of true, false, or unknown. In the table for students, we could add a Boolean attribute, matriculated, to indicate whether the student is matriculated or not, using a declaration such as the following within the CREATE TABLE command:

```
matriculated BOOLEAN DEFAULT false,
```

7.7.2   Collection Types

SQL:1999 includes two structured collection types, **array** and **row.** The current version does not support any unstructured collection types, although it is expected that future versions will include them. Both sets (unordered collections of distinct elements) and multisets (unordered collections that allow repetition of elements), were considered for the standard, but inclusion of them was postponed.

ARRAY[n] is a structured type that allows an ordered collection of values of the same base data type to be stored as a single attribute. We must specify the base type for the n values to be stored in the array, using the form:

attribute-name basetype ARRAY [*n*]

For example, if we wish to allow students to have double majors, we could declare the `majors` attribute in the CREATE TABLE command as VAR-CHAR (10) ARRAY[2]. with the rest of the command appearing as it did in Figure 6.2.

```
CREATE TABLE Stu (
    stuId         CHAR(6),
    lastName      CHAR(20) NOT NULL,
    firstName     CHAR(20) NOT NULL,
    matriculated  BOOLEAN DEFAULT false;
    majors        VARCHAR(10) ARRAY[2],
    credits       SMALLINT DEFAULT 0,
CONSTRAINT Student_stuId_pk PRIMARY KEY (stuId),
CONSTRAINT Student_credits_cc CHECK ((credits>=0) AND (credits < 150)));
```

The standard square bracket notation is used in SQL:1999 to refer to individual elements of an array. For example, if we assume the indexing starts at 1, we can access the first major listed for a student by:

```
SELECT Stu.majors[1]
FROM Stu
WHERE stuId = 'S999';
```

To insert a record into a table with an array type, we use the array constructor (ARRAY), listing the values to be inserted into the array, as in:

```
INSERT INTO Stu VALUES ('S555', 'Quirk','Sean', true,
ARRAY ['French','Psychology'], 30);
```

Multidimensional arrays and arrays of arrays are not supported in SQL:1999.

The declaration of the components of **ROW type** consists of a sequence of pairs of field names and data types, like the list of attributes and their data types in a traditional table definition. In fact, we can use the ROW type declaration to create a data type and then use the type to create a table, as illustrated by the following:

```
CREATE ROW TYPE team_row_type(
    teamName    CHAR(20),
    coach       CHAR(30),
    sport       CHAR(15));

CREATE TABLE Team OF TYPE team_row_type;
```

All of the types that are defined using SQL's type constructors have built-in methods that are available for users, as we saw illustrated for arrays. For the ROW type, we can refer to an individual field using the dot notation. For example, for the Team table, we can refer to the coach for a particular record by using the notation: Team.coach, as in

```
SELECT Team.coach
FROM Team
WHERE Team.sport= 'soccer';
```

An attribute of a table can itself have a row-type, allowing nested tables. For example, we can have an attribute of a NewStu table to represent one team the student belongs to, as follows:

```
CREATE TABLE NewStu (
    stuId     CHAR(6),
    . . .
    team      team_row_type,
    . . .);
```

The ROW constructor can use any data type for its fields, including ROW and ARRAY. For example, we could have put several teams in the student's record by creating the table with an array of the team row type, which we call teams, as follows:

```
CREATE TABLE NewStu2 (
    stuId         CHAR(6),
    lastName      CHAR(20) NOT NULL,
    firstName     CHAR(20) NOT NULL,
    matriculated  BOOLEAN DEFAULT false;
    teams         team_row_type ARRAY[3],
    majors        CHAR(10) ARRAY[2],
    credits       SMALLINT DEFAULT 0,
CONSTRAINT Student_stuId_pk PRIMARY KEY (stuId),
CONSTRAINT Student_credits_cc CHECK ((credits>=0) AND (credits < 150)));
```

Now each row of the NewStu2 table contains a table of up to three teams (with their names, coaches, and sports) that the student belongs to, so we have nested tables. Since rows of a table can now be defined as a data type, we can pass rows as parameters to modules (procedures or functions), or return rows from functions.

If we have a row nested in a table, as in the `NewStu2` table described above, we can refer to the individual attributes using nested dot notation, as in:

```
SELECT NewStu2.teams.coach
FROM NewStu2
WHERE stuId = "S999";
```

If the student belongs to several teams, this will give us several coaches. If we wanted only the coach of the first team, we would have used `NewStu2.teams[1].coach` in the SELECT line. We can use the same notation to perform the other DML operations on row attributes. To insert a `NewStu2` record, we use constructors, as shown in this example:

```
INSERT INTO NewStu2 VALUES('S999', 'Smith', 'Michael', true, ARRAY[ROW('Angels',
'Jones', 'soccer'), ROW('Devils', 'Chin', 'swimming'), ROW('Tigers', 'Walters',
'basketball')], ARRAY['Math', 'Biology'], 60);
```

7.7.3　User-defined Data Types (UDT)

SQL:1999 also allows a user-defined data type, **DISTINCT,** to be constructed from a base type. For example, if we write,

```
CREATE DISTINCT TYPE studentAgeType AS INTEGER;
```

and also,

```
CREATE DISTINCT TYPE numberOfCreditsType AS INTEGER;
```

then, even though both are integers, we cannot compare a studentAgeType attribute with a numberofCreditsType attribute.

SQL:1999 also allows users to create **structured data types,** which can have several attributes. The attributes can be any SQL type, including the traditional built-in types, the LOB types, ARRAY or ROW types, or other structured types, allowing nesting of structured types. Thus, a structured UDT can be either the type used for an attribute, or the type used for a table. Attributes can be stored items or they can be **virtual,** which means they are derived using a function defined for the type. Users can choose to make the new type **instantiable,** which allows instances of the type to be created. If the type is instantiable, SQL provides a default **constructor function** to allow new instances of the type to be created. This constructor always has the same name and data type as the user-defined data type, so we can invoke it by using the name of the type. The default constructor takes no parameters, and simply assigns default values to the instance attributes. Users can also create their own constructors when they define the new type. User-defined types can also be **non-instantiable,** which means no instances of that type can be created.

We saw in Chapter 6 how useful the SQL built-in functions such as SUM and COUNT are for a variety of queries. These functions can be used with many different data types. However, when users define their own data types, the built-in functions are not defined for these types, nor are any but a few very basic operations. Therefore, users must also define operations on the new types they create, building on the basic operations defined for the source types. The definition of a new type includes a list of its **attributes** and its **methods,** which are routines that are defined for the type. Methods are defined only for a single user-defined type, and do not apply to other types the user creates. Structured types can be manipulated using operations defined by the user as methods, functions, and procedures. To provide comparison of objects of the same user-defined type, the user can define equality and ordering relationships for the type. SQL:1999 provides some automatic functions for user-defined types. Besides the default constructor described earlier, there are automatic **observer** (sometimes called GET) methods that return the values of attributes, and **mutator** (sometimes called SET) methods that allow values to be assigned to attributes. Although the user can override these observer and mutator methods by redefining them, they cannot be overloaded, unlike the corresponding methods in some object-oriented languages.

As an example of a structured type definition we will define a new StudentType as follows:

```
CREATE TYPE StudentType AS (
stuId          VARCHAR(6),
lastName       VARCHAR(15),
firstName      VARCHAR(12),
advisorId      VARCHAR2(6),
credits        SMALLINT,
dateOfBirth    DATE)
METHOD         addCredits(smallint);
```

We can optionally add,

```
INSTANTIABLE
NOT FINAL
```

As this example illustrates, a type definition contains the name of the type (here, our new StudentType), a list of attributes with their data types within parentheses, and a list of methods (if any) for the type. Note that we do not indicate a primary key for the type, because we are defining a type, not a table. The attributes can themselves be previously defined UDTs. We indicate the argument types and return type (if any) for each method. When invoked, a method takes an instance of the type as an implicit parameter. Methods are invoked using dot notation because, like attributes, they are members of the type. For example, if `firstStudent` is an instance of the StudentType, we can write:

```
firstStudent.addCredits(3);
```

The code for the method `addCredits( )` is written separately. Within the method, the implicit parameter (firstStudent, in our example) is referred to as *self*. The code for the `addCredits` method might be:

```
CREATE METHOD addCredits (numberOfCredits smallint) FOR StudentType
    BEGIN
        SET self.credits = self.credits + numberOfCredits;
    END;
```

Using this new StudentType, we can create a new version of the `Student` table, which differs slightly from the version used in previous chapters, for purposes of illustration.

```
CREATE TABLE Student of StudentType
(CONSTRAINT Student_stuId_pk PRIMARY KEY(stuId),
CONSTRAINT Student_advisorId_fk FOREIGN KEY (advisorId) REFERENCES
Faculty (facId));
```

Any other constraints, including foreign keys, are specified for the table, since they apply to the table, not to the type. We can create as many tables as we wish using the same UDT. Although we can insert values in the usual way, it is preferable to use the StudentType type constructor, as in:

```
INSERT INTO Student
VALUES(StudentType('S999', 'Fernandes', 'Luis', 'F101', 0,
'25-Jan-1985'));
```

Besides the constructor `StudentType`, used in the INSERT here, the new type has the `addCredits( )` method that we wrote, as well as the built-in observer and mutator methods for each of its attributes. For example `firstName( )` is a method that returns the value of the `firstName` attribute of a tuple, and `credits (30)`, assigns a value of

30 to the `credits` attribute. These are invoked for an instance of the type, using dot notation, as in,

```
firstStudent.firstName( );
```

or

```
secondStudent.credits(30);
```

7.7.4   Type Hierarchies

Structured types can participate in type hierarchies, in which subtypes inherit all attributes and operations of their supertypes, but they may have additional attributes and operations of their own. Figure 7.7 shows a class hierarchy under `Student`. When defining a new type, the user can declare it as FINAL, which means that no subtypes can be defined for it, or NOT FINAL, which allows subtypes to be created. As discussed in Section 7.7.3, if a class is defined as NOT INSTANTIABLE, we cannot create instances of that type, but if it has subtypes, instances of the subtypes can be created, provided the subtypes themselves are made instantiable. Using our previously defined type, `StudentType`, which was NOT FINAL, we can define a subtype, `UndergraduateType`, by writing:

```
CREATE TYPE UndergraduateType UNDER StudentType AS (
    major varchar(10) ARRAY[2])
INSTANTIABLE,
NOT FINAL;
```

We can define a new function, `hasDoubleMajor`, for the subtype,

```
CREATE FUNCTION hasDoubleMajor (u UndergraduateType) RETURNS BOOLEAN
    BEGIN
      IF (u.major[2] IS NOT NULL)
        THEN
            RETURN TRUE;
        ELSE
            RETURN FALSE;
      END IF;
    END;
```

To create a table for the subtype, we create a subtable under the `Student` table that was previously created for the `StudentType`.

```
CREATE TABLE Undergraduate OF UndergraduateType UNDER Student;
```

Undergraduate tuples inherit all the attributes of `Student` tuples and have an additional attribute, which is an array of majors. They also inherit any functions, procedures, or methods defined for StudentType; their own constructor, observer, and mutator methods for majors; and their own user-defined function, hasDoubleMajor( ). Note that hasDoubleMajor( ) could have been defined as a method rather than a function, but we chose a function for purposes of illustration. To invoke the function we cannot use the *self*ish form, IF (thirdStudent.hasDoubleMajor( )) THEN . . . , that applies to methods. The *self*ish form provides an instance (*self*-thirdStudent, in this example) on which the method is performed. Instead, for a function, we must provide an actual parameter of UndergraduateType, as in:

```
IF (hasDoubleMajor(thirdStudent)) THEN . . .
```

In addition to methods and functions, user-defined types can have **procedures,** which are similar to functions, but have no return type. They can have input parameters, identified by the keyword **IN**; output parameters, identified by **OUT**; and two-way parameters, identified by **IN/OUT,** before the name of the formal parameter in the procedure heading. For example, we could have created a procedure to count the number of majors an undergraduate has. We chose a procedure rather than a method or function here only for purposes of illustration.

```
CREATE PROCEDURE countMajors(IN u UndergraduteStudent, OUT
numberOfMajors SMALLINT)
BEGIN
    numberOfMajors =0;
    IF (u.majors[1] is NOT NULL) THEN numberOfMajors =
    numberOfMajors +1;
    IF (u.majors[2] IS NOT NULL) THEN numberOfMajors =
    numberOfMajors +1;
END;
```

The procedure would be invoked and the output parameter used in statements such as

```
countMajors(fourthStudent, count);
IF (count = 2) THEN . . .
```

We could continue in this fashion, creating a type called FreshmanType under UndergraduateType. For freshmen, we would add an attribute for peerMentor, and any additional methods, functions, or procedures that apply to freshmen only. Since we have no subtypes for FreshmanType shown in Figure 7.7, we would make that type INSTANTIABLE FINAL.

```
CREATE TYPE FreshmanType UNDER UndergraduateType AS (
    peerMentor varchar(25))
INSTANTIABLE,
FINAL;
```

We could then create a `Freshman` subtable using SQL:1999 syntax:

```
CREATE TABLE Freshmen OF FreshmanType UNDER Undergraduate;
```

For graduate students, we would write a definition for GraduateStudentType under StudentType, similar to the one for UndergraduateType, this time specifying the graduate program that the student is enrolled in as an attribute. We could also create a subtype, TeachingAssistantType, under GraduateStudent-Type. Referring to Figure 7.7, we see that TeachingAssistant also appears as a subtype of Faculty. However, multiple inheritance is not allowed in the SQL:1999 standard. If we chose to make it a subtype of GraduateStudentType, we would not be able to make it a subtype of FacultyType as well.

7.7.5   Reference Types

In strictly relational databases, we saw that foreign keys are used to establish relationships between tables. For related entities, the value of an attribute of a tuple in a table is the primary key value of another tuple, usually from a different table. Object-relational systems use a similar mechanism, allowing attributes of a type that are actually **references** or pointers to another type. When reference types are used, the user must explicitly find and set the reference value when a tuple is inserted. For example, in the relational model, if we assume each student has an adviser who is a faculty member, the corresponding `facId` is identified as a foreign key when we create the `Student` table. In the object-relational model, we represent the connection by using a reference type instead. We will assume we have previously defined FacultyType and used that type to create the `Faculty` table. Now we will create a new Student-Type with a reference, `aId`, to FacultyType. We use the "CREATE OR REPLACE" form to handle the possibility that the type already exists.

```
CREATE OR REPLACE TYPE StudentType AS (
(stuId       VARCHAR(6),
lastName     VARCHAR(15),
firstName    VARCHAR(12),
aId          REF(FacultyType) SCOPE Faculty,
credits      SMALLINT,
dateOfBirth  DATE)
METHOD       addCredits(smallint));
```

Then we can create a new Student table:

```
CREATE TABLE Student OF StudentType;
```

The reference attribute, `aId`, which is a reference to a FacultyType, refers to tuples in an existing table, `Faculty`, as indicated by the scope specification for it. Note that the reference specifies the type of object referred to, while the scope specifies the table containing tuples of that type. We will use queries to set the reference values. SQL:1999 requires that a table that will have a reference to it contain an attribute for the identifier of each tuple, similar to a surrogate key. Therefore, when we create the `Faculty` table, we must add the reference attribute, whose value can be generated by the system,

```
CREATE TABLE Faculty of FacultyType
REF IS aid SYSTEM GENERATED;
```

The system generates a value for `aid` when we insert a `Faculty` tuple, and it can retrieve that value when needed, in response to a query. Note that the value is an internal one that would not appear as part of the tuple it refers to. Using SQL:1999 syntax, when we wish to insert a `Student` tuple, we must get the value of the `aid` of the adviser, using a query. We first insert a `Student` tuple with a null reference for the `aid`.

```
INSERT INTO Student VALUES('S555', 'Hughes','John', null, 0, '04-Jan-1988');
```

Then we set the reference by means of an update of that tuple, using a subquery on the `Faculty` table to find the correct `aid` value.

```
UPDATE Student
SET aid = (SELECT f.aid
   FROM Faculty AS f
   WHERE facId = 'F101')
WHERE f.stuId ='S555';
```

To find the referenced tuple in a query, we have to dereference `aid`. The form `DEREF(aid)` can be used to find the entire tuple referenced. An example is:

```
SELECT s.lastName, s.firstName, DEREF(s.aid), s.dateOfBirth
FROM Student s
WHERE s.lastName ='Smith';
```

This query returns the last name and first name of each student named Smith, along with the `facId`, `name`, `department`, and `rank` of the student's adviser (assuming those are the attributes of FacultyType), and the student's date of birth. In place of the DEREF operator, we can use the –> operator to retrieve the value of an attribute of the tuple referenced. For example,

```
aid -> lastName
```

retrieves the value of the `lastName` attribute of the `Faculty` tuple referenced.

Although the `aid` value functions like a foreign key, there are some important differences. References do not support the same strict constraints that foreign keys do. A major problem can occur if the referenced object is deleted, because we might be left with **dangling pointers** (pointers whose referenced objects no longer exist) in the database. Some systems allow us to specify **REFERENCES ARE CHECKED** and to add ON DELETE clauses for references. In addition to system-generated references, the standard allows for user-generated references (for which the user must provide and keep track of the unique identifiers), and derived references (for which the user must specify the attribute from which the reference attribute derives its value).

In Section 7.7.1, we saw that LOB types have a **LOB locator,** which is also a reference. Student signatures were declared using a reference type.

```
signature CLOB REF IS sigid SYSTEM GENERATED;
```

Here, the `sigid` is a reference to the file containing an image of the student's signature. The database stores the reference in the `Student` record. We can use a SELECT statement to find the value of this reference, as in:

```
SELECT s.sigid
FROM Student AS s
WHERE s.stuId ='S999';
```

This provides the value of the reference itself. To actually retrieve a signature, in the rare case where it is needed, we would have to dereference that pointer within a SELECT command. An application program or user-written methods, functions, or procedures would then manipulate the data as needed. For the signature, we might have a method to display it on a screen. If the LOB object were an audio file instead of a signature, a method might be defined to play a portion of the file, with starting and stopping points identified by parameters for the method. Similarly, if the LOB object were a video clip, we might locate the clip by dereferencing a LOB locator, and manipulate a portion of the video using methods.

7.8 Converting an EE-R Diagram to an Object-Relational Database Model

The object-relational model provides much more flexibility in mapping an EE-R diagram than does the strictly relational model. As illustrated in our examples, we can make use of new data types, collection types, user-defined structured types, inheritance, and reference types in creating our tables. We modify the mapping algorithm presented in Section 7.6.2 to incorporate the extensions.

For entity sets and relationships that are not part of generalizations or unions, the mapping can proceed in a manner similar to the relational model. Entity sets can be mapped to tables, either using the SQL2 syntax or creating a type and then using that type for the table creation. For composite attributes, we can define a structured type for the composite, with the components as attributes of the type. Multivalued attributes can be expressed as collection types, such as ARRAY. In representing relationships, reference types can be used in place of the foreign key mechanism. For specialization hierarchies, types and subtypes can be defined as needed. Then tables and subtables to correspond to the types can be created. However, since no subtypes can have multiple inheritance, the designer must choose among potential supertypes for a shared subtype. The subtype's relationship to the other supertype(s) should be expressed using references or foreign keys. There is no direct representation of unions (categories) in the object-relational model, but we can use the same method as we did for the relational model. We create a table for the union itself, and individual tables for each of the superclasses, using foreign keys or references to connect them.

7.9   Representing Objects in Oracle

Oracle's implementation of object-relational features differs from the SQL:1999 standard. Oracle provides both BLOB and CLOB data types that can hold up to four gigabytes of data, but it does not support Boolean as a built-in datatype. It provides **array types** and **user-defined object types.** Array types are declared using this form:

```
CREATE OR REPLACE TYPE arraytypename AS VARRAY (size) OF basetype;
```

The basetype of an array can be any valid datatype except LOBs, including user-defined ones, provided none of their attributes are LOBs. Oracle permits arrays of arrays. Note the use of parentheses in place of square brackets for the size. An example of an array type is:

```
CREATE OR REPLACE TYPE MajorsType AS VARRAY(2) OF VARCHAR2(10);
```

The array type can then be used as an attribute type for a table, as a component of a user-defined data type, or as a type for a parameter or variable in PL/SQL. Oracle supports structured UDTs in the form of **object types.** An Oracle object type is a structured type with attributes, which may be any valid type, including arrays or other objects, and methods, as we saw in the SQL:1999 standard. The object definition has this form:

```
CREATE OR REPLACE TYPE objecttypename AS OBJECT(
attribute definitions
method definitions);
```

For example:

```
CREATE OR REPLACE TYPE StudentType AS OBJECT (
stuId      VARCHAR2(5),
lastName   VARCHAR2(15),
firstName  VARCHAR2(12),
majors     MajorsType;
credits    NUMBER (3),
dateOfBirth DATE,
MEMBER FUNCTION findAge RETURN INTEGER)
INSTANTIABLE
NOT FINAL;
```

Types that have been created as NOT INSTANTIABLE can be changed later by this statement:

```
ALTER TYPE typename INSTANTIABLE;
```

However, altering a type from INSTANTIABLE to NOT INSTANTIABLE is possible only if the type has not been used to create columns, tables, or any other items that reference it.

The object type can be used as an attribute of another structured type (as MajorsType was used for StudentType), as the base type of an array, or as the only type in a table. Such tables are referred to as **object tables.** An example of an object table is the Student table we now create from the StudentType just defined:

```
CREATE TABLE Student of StudentType (
CONSTRAINT Student_stuId_pk PRIMARY KEY(stuId),
CONSTRAINT Student_credits_cc CHECK ((credits>=0) AND
(credits < 150)));
```

The rows of an object table are described as **row objects.**

Methods for a type can be classified as **member methods** or **static methods.** Member methods have the implicit parameter, *self,* as described in

Section 7.7.3. They can be implemented using PL/SQL, Java, or C. For example, the `findAge` member function can be coded as follows:

```
CREATE OR REPLACE TYPE BODY StudentType AS
MEMBER FUNCTION findAge RETURN INTEGER IS
BEGIN
   RETURN TRUNC((SYSDATE - dateOfBirth)/12);
END;
```

Member methods have the implicit *self parameter* and can be either **functions,** which have a single return type, or **procedures,** which have no return but may have input and/or output parameters. We can also create non-member or **static methods,** which are defined for the type, and which do not have an implicit *self* parameter. The system provides a default constructor for the type, but we could write our own constructors or additional functions or procedures using static methods. They are invoked using the name of the type, followed by a dot, then the name of the static method. As in the SQL standard, Oracle's automatic constructor for each type is invoked by writing the name of the type. Its parameters have the names and types of the attributes. For example, to insert a new **Student** record, we invoke the constructor for StudentType and MajorsType, by writing:

```
INSERT INTO Student VALUES StudentType ('S999', 'Smith', 'John',
MajorsType ('Math','Accounting'), 0,'05-Jan-1980');
```

User-defined types do not have any automatic ordering of their elements, but users can impose an order by identifying either a **map method** or an **order method** for the type. A **map method** directs Oracle to apply the comparison method it normally uses for one of its built-in types (normally, one of the attributes) as the comparison method for the entire type. For example, if we had defined a member function this way,

```
MAP MEMBER FUNCTION getstuId( ) RETURN VARCHAR2
```

and then coded this function to return the value of `stuId`, as follows,

```
CREATE OR REPLACE TYPE BODY StudentType AS
MEMBER FUNCTION getstuId( ) RETURN VARCHAR2 IS
BEGIN
   RETURN stuId;
END;
```

then Oracle would use its built-in method of comparing VARCHAR2 values applied to the `stuId` values whenever we compared StudentType objects, since we listed this method as MAP. Users can instead write their own comparison method, called an **order method,** to tell Oracle how to compare two objects of a user-defined type. If we chose to write a `compareAge( )` function and make it order method by declaring,

```
ORDER MEMBER FUNCTION compareAge(s StudentType) RETURN INTEGER
```

we could write code for the function as follows:

```
CREATE OR REPLACE TYPE BODY StudentType AS
MEMBER FUNCTION compareAge(s StudentType) RETURN INTEGER IS
BEGIN
    IF (self.dateOfBirth < s.dateOfBirth) THEN RETURN 1
    ELSE IF(self.dateOfBirth > s.dateOfBirth)THEN RETURN -1
    ELSE RETURN 0;
END;
```

Then Oracle would always compare two StudentType objects on the basis of age, not `stuId`. A UDT can have at most one map method or order method for the entire type. A subtype can create its own map method if its root supertype has one, but not its own order method.

When tables are created with only one object type, they are called object tables, and their rows are called row objects, as described previously. Each row object in an Oracle object table is given a unique identifier, called a logical object identifier (**OID**). The identifier can either be system generated (the default) or the user can specify that the primary key is to be used as the OID. A system generated OID is a 16-byte key to which the user has no access, although it can be used for finding and fetching objects. Oracle creates an index on the OID column of object tables. In a non-distributed, non-replicated environment, the user can choose the primary key as the OID. The selection is specified in the CREATE TABLE command, as in:

```
CREATE TABLE Student of StudentType (
CONSTRAINT Student_stuId_pk PRIMARY KEY(stuId),
CONSTRAINT Student_credits_cc CHECK ((credits>=0) AND (credits < 150))
OBJECT IDENTIFIER PRIMARY KEY);
```

The last line could have been replaced by OBJECT IDENTIFIER SYSTEM GENERATED.

Oracle also uses OIDs to help construct a **reference type** to refer to row objects. We can define a REF attribute, with an optional SCOPE clause that constrains the column to the table specified as the scope, as we saw for SQL:1999. The scope clause is required if the object identifier of the referenced object is the primary key. If we do not specify a scope, the reference can be to any row object of the specified type, regardless of where it appears. Since dangling pointers can result from deletion or update of row objects, Oracle provides a referential constraint mechanism, RESTRICT REFERENCES, for reference objects. There is also a test method, IS DANGLING, to determine whether the pointer is dangling, and a DEREF dereferencing operator for references.

Oracle also permits **nested tables.** A nested table is created from a single built-in type or object type, and then placed in another table. For example, we could create a nested contact list to hold names and telephone numbers of a student's parents, spouse, guardian, or other contacts, as:

```
CREATE OR REPLACE TYPE ContactType AS OBJECT(
    lastName       VARCHAR2(15),
    firstName      VARCHAR2(12),
    relationship   VARCHAR2(15),
    phoneNumber    VARCHAR2(10));
CREATE OR REPLACE TYPE ContactListType AS TABLE OF ContactType;
```

Then when we define StudentType we add as an attribute,

```
contactList contactListType;
```

immediately after the `dateOfBirth` attribute, and when we create the `Student` table, we specify:

```
CREATE TABLE Student OF StudentType(
CONSTRAINT Student_stuId_pk PRIMARY KEY stuId)
OBJECT IDENTIFIER PRIMARY KEY
NESTED TABLE contactList STORE AS contactListStorageTable(
    (PRIMARY KEY (NESTED_TABLE_ID, lastName, relationship, phoneNumber))
ORGANIZATION INDEX COMPRESS);
```

Note that we must identify a name for a storage table for the nested table, which we called `contactListStorageTable` here. This is a separate table from `Student`. We specify the primary key of the nested table to include `NESTED_TABLE_ID`, which is a hidden column created by Oracle that associates the rows of this contact table with the corresponding `Student` row. All the rows for contacts of a particular student have the same `NESTED_TABLE_ID`, so we added `lastName, relationship,` and `phoneNumber` to the primary key to guarantee uniqueness. The compressed indexed organization is specified so that rows belonging to the same student will be clustered together.

To insert data in the subtable, we first create a row for the owner table, `Student`, including a parameter-less call to the constructor for the subtable, as follows:

```
INSERT INTO Student VALUES StudentType ('S999', 'Smith', 'John', MajorsType('Math',
'Accounting'), 0, '05-Jan-1980', ContactListType( ));
```

The constructor creates an empty instance in the subtable, into which we can now insert data using an INSERT INTO TABLE statement as follows:

```
INSERT INTO TABLE(SELECT s.contactList
    FROM Student s
    WHERE s.stuId = 'S999')
VALUES('Smith', 'Marjorie', 'mother', '2017771234');
```

Note that here we created an alias in the FROM line, and then used it to refer to a column, which is the recommended Oracle practice for all UPDATE, DELETE, and SELECT statements and subqueries. We can continue to insert as many contacts as we wish for this student, or go on to create other Student tuples and their contact lists.

Nested tables can be unnested using the **TABLE** keyword to flatten the table as in:

```
SELECT s.lastName, s.firstName, c.*
FROM Student s, TABLE(s.contactList) c
WHERE s.credits <= 60
ORDER BY VALUE(s);
```

The result will be a multiset with a flattened list where student names will be repeated for each of their contacts (one contact per line). The order will be whatever order was specified when we created a map method or an order method for StudentType.

Oracle supports representation of object hierarchies. Subtypes can be created from user-defined types using almost the same syntax as SQL:1999. For example, assume we have created our StudentType as:

```
CREATE OR REPLACE TYPE StudentType AS OBJECT (
stuId       VARCHAR2(5),
lastName    VARCHAR2(15),
firstName   VARCHAR2(12),
credits     NUMBER(3),
dateOfBirth DATE,
MEMBER FUNCTION findAge RETURN INTEGER)
INSTANTIABLE
NOT FINAL;
```

To create UndergraduateType as a StudentType subtype, we write

```
CREATE OR REPLACE TYPE UndergraduateType UNDER StudentType (
majors VARCHAR2(10) VARRAY[2])
INSTANTIABLE,
NOT FINAL;
```

We can go on and create FreshmanType as a subtype of Undergraduate-Type by writing

```
CREATE OR REPLACE TYPE FreshmanType UNDER StudentType (
    peerMentor VARCHAR2(25) )
INSTANTIABLE,
FINAL;
```

The subtype inherits all the attributes and methods of its supertype, and can add its own attributes and methods, even overloading or overriding some methods from the supertype. In Oracle, subtypes can be substituted for supertypes as object columns or rows, in object tables or views. We can therefore insert Undergraduate records and Freshman records in the Student table. If we create the Student table,

```
CREATE TABLE Student OF StudentType;
```

then we can insert Student, Undergraduate, or Freshman records in the Student table by using the appropriate constructor, as follows:

```
INSERT INTO Student VALUES
(StudentType('S444', 'Klein', 'Susan', 36, '14-Mar-1976'));

INSERT INTO Student VALUES
(UndergraduateType('S555', 'Logan', 'Randolph', 12, '23-May-1982',
VARRAY('Spanish', 'French'));

INSERT INTO Student VALUES
(FreshmanType('S777', 'Miller', 'Terrence', 30, '30-Jun-1985',
VARRAY('Math',NULL), 'Tom Smith')
```

Every tuple in the table is, of course, a Student tuple, but some belong to other subtypes as well. Every tuple in a hierarchy has a **most specific type,** which is the "closest" subtype it belongs to, the subtype used when it is created.

To retrieve data from a hierarchical table, we can use the **VALUE** function, which ordinarily returns the attribute values of one or more tuples, including all subtypes in the result. For example, we can apply a VALUE query to all students, including subtypes, while searching for students whose last name is Smith by writing:

```
SELECT VALUE(s)
FROM Student s
WHERE s.lastName = 'Smith';
```

We can limit the query to the supertype and exclude the subtypes by writing the keyword **ONLY,** as in:

```
SELECT VALUE(s)
FROM ONLY(Student s)
WHERE s.lastName = 'Smith';
```

This query will find only those students who are not undergraduate or freshmen subtypes, or any other subtype of Student, if we had created others. It selects only those whose most specific subtype is StudentType. To limit the query to undergraduate students, we can specify that the tuple instances must be of type UndergraduateType, using **IS OF (*type*)** as follows:

```
SELECT VALUE(s)
FROM Student s
WHERE s.lastName = 'Smith' AND VALUE(s) IS OF
(UndergraduateType);
```

The results include all UndergraduateType tuples that satisfy the condition, including FreshmanType tuples. To eliminate the Freshman tuples, we could write:

```
SELECT VALUE(s)
FROM Student s
WHERE s.lastName = 'Smith' AND VALUE(s) IS OF (ONLY
UndergraduateType);
```

The ONLY clause limits the return to tuples whose most specific type is UndergraduateType.

If we wish to retrieve specific columns we can list them in the SELECT line, as usual. However, for columns that appear only in a subtype, we cannot simply list the column names in the SELECT line, since the column does not appear in the declaration of the type of the table listed in the FROM line. For example, peerMentor does not appear as a column in the Student table. There is a **TREAT( )** function that allows us to treat each Student tuple as if it were a Freshman tuple in order to examine the peerMentor attribute.

```
SELECT lastName, firstName, TREAT(VALUE(s) AS
FreshmanType).peerMentor
FROM Student s
WHERE VALUE(s) IS OF (FreshmanType);
```

If an Oracle type or subtype has a REF attribute, the DEREF operator can be used as in standard SQL. If a type or subtype has a nested table, the TABLE keyword can also be used, as we saw earlier, to unnest the table. ORDER BY and GROUP BY clauses can be used for queries on subtypes just as they were for other types.

Oracle supports other object-relational features besides the basic ones described here. It even allows users of strictly relational Oracle databases to view them as object-relational ones using a mechanism called an **object view**. An object view is constructed by defining an object type in which each attribute corresponds to a column of an existing relational table. The object view is created using a SELECT statement, in the same manner that we would create a relational view, except that we must specify an object identifier, saying which attribute(s) will be used to identify each row of the view. This identifier, which is usually the primary key, can be used to create reference attributes, if desired. To guarantee safety of updates in the object view, users can write INSTEAD OF triggers. The object view can then be treated as if it were an object table. If we had a purely relational `Faculty` table, defined as,

```
CREATE TABLE Faculty(
facId        NUMBER(4) PRIMARY KEY,
lastName     VARCHAR2(15),
firstName    VARCHAR2(10),
dept         VARCHAR2(10),
rank         VARCHAR2(10),
salary       NUMBER(8,2));
```

We could define a type, FacultyType, by writing:

```
CREATE OR REPLACE TYPE FacultyType (
facId        NUMBER(4),
lName        VARCHAR2(15),
fName        VARCHAR2(10),
department   VARCHAR2(10),
rank         VARCHAR2(10));
```

We could create an object view, `FacultyView`, by writing:

```
CREATE VIEW FacultyView OF FacultyType WITH OBJECT
IDENTIFIER (facId) AS SELECT f.facId, f.lastName,
f.firstName, f.dept, f.rank
FROM Faculty f;
```

Users can then refer to the attributes of the object using dot notation, write methods for the type, and use other object-relational features as if it were a user-defined structured type.

7.10 Chapter Summary

The E-R model is not semantically rich enough to represent the complex data and relationships needed for advanced applications. The EE-R model is an **enhanced E-R** model in which **specialization, generalization, union,** additional constraints, and other abstractions can be represented. **Specialization** means breaking up an entity set, or class, into the various types of subsets it contains. Its inverse process, **generalization,** means considering objects of different types that have some common features as subclasses of a higher-level class, called the superclass. On an EE-R diagram, generalization/specialization, also called an *isa* relationship, is represented by a line with a **specialization circle** connecting the higher-level class to its subclasses. An **inheritance symbol** (subset symbol) appears on the line(s) from the subclass(es) to the circle. If there is only one subclass, no circle is used, but the subset symbol appears on the line connecting the subclass to the superclass. Subclasses inherit the attributes and relationships of their superclasses, but they can have additional attributes or participate in additional relationships. Subclasses may be **disjoint** or **overlapping,** indicated by placing d or o in the specialization circle. The specialization can be **predicate-defined** (even **attribute-defined**) or **user-defined.** It may be **partial,** indicated by a single line, or **total,** indicated by a double line from the superclass to the specialization circle. A subclass can be **shared,** appearing as a subclass of more than one superclass, and having **multiple inheritance** from them.

A subclass may belong to one of a **category** or **union** of superclasses. A union is shown by a circle with the set union symbol, to which the superclasses are connected by lines. The subclass is connected by a line to the union circle. These subclasses inherit the attributes and relationships of only one of the superclasses. A category can be **partial** or **total,** indicated by a single or double line respectively from the subclass to the union circle. A total category may sometimes be replaced by a specialization. For both E-R and EE-R diagrams, an alternate notation for both relationship participation and cardinality is the (*min..max*) notation, indicating both the minimum and maximum number of relationship instances in which an entity instance participates.

An EE-R diagram can be converted to a relational model in much the same way as an E-R diagram, except for a generalization hierarchy. A hierarchy can be converted to tables in three different ways. In the first, there is a table for the superclass that contains the common attributes, and individual tables for the subclasses, each containing a column or columns for the key of the superclass and columns for their own attributes. In the second method, there is no table for the superclass, but each subclass table contains columns for all the attributes of the superclass in addition to columns for their own attributes. In the third, a single large table contains all the attributes of the superclass and all its subclasses. There can be a **type field** to indicate which subclass an entity belongs to, or a **membership field** for each specialization, especially in the case of overlapping subclasses. Categories are represented by creating a table for the subclass of the union, and individual tables for each of the superclasses, using their common primary key as a foreign key in the subclass table. However, if the superclasses have different primary keys, it might be necessary to create a surrogate key as the primary key of the union subclass table, and make it a foreign key for each of the superclasses.

The extended relational model has additional fundamental data types, collection types, user-defined data types (**UDTs**), class hierarchies, and reference types. **SQL:1999** added **LOB** and **Boolean** fundamental types. Collections include **array** and **row** types. Tables can be nested. **Distinct** types and **structured data types** can be defined by users. UDTs definitions include specification of attributes and methods. They can be **final** or not, **instantiable** or not. Built-in methods include **constructors, observers,** and **mutators.** Additional **member methods,** which can be functions or procedures, can be defined using the implicit *self* parameter. **Functions** return only one type, while **procedures** can have IN, OUT, and IN/OUT parameters, allowing several values to be passed back. **Static** methods, which do not have the *self* parameter, can be defined for the class. Tables can be created that use the type as the only column, or the type can appear as one of several columns. If the type is not final, subtypes that inherit all attributes and methods can be created, and we can add additional attributes and methods for the subtype. The hierarchy can be extended by creating subtypes of subtypes. However, multiple inheritance is not permitted. Subtables consisting of the subtype can be created under tables that consist of the supertype.

Reference types are pointers to another type. They can be used as attributes to represent relationships, similar to foreign keys. A **scope** can be specified that identifies the referenced table. References can be **system-generated, user-generated,** or **derived.** A **DEREF** operator retrieves the tuple referred to, or the –> operator can be used to retrieve the value of an attribute in the tuple referred to by a reference. **Dangling pointers** can result when referenced objects are deleted, but a **REFERENCES ARE CHECKED** clause provides some integrity protection. A **LOB locater** is a reference to a LOB object.

To convert an EE-R diagram to an object-relational model, we can modify the standard relational conversion mechanism, making use of new data types and collection types, which are useful for multivalued and composite attributes. Relationships can be represented by reference types instead of by foreign keys, if desired. Hierarchies can be represented using supertypes and subtypes.

Oracle syntax differs slightly from the SQL:1999 standard. UDTs can have a single method—either a **map method** or an **order method**—that defines the order of members. **Object tables,** which consist of only one UDT, are given unique **OIDs** for their **rows.** The OID can be system-generated or it can be the primary key, if globally unique. OIDs are used to create references to row objects. Nested tables and object hierarchies can be created. A single table can be created to hold all the objects in a hierarchy, and constructors can be used to insert instances of all the different classes in the hierarchy. Each tuple has **a most specific type** identified by the constructor used when it is inserted. The **VALUE** function is useful for retrieving data from a hierarchical table. The **ONLY** keyword and the **IS OF** *type* clause can be used to restrict the type of the result, and the **TREAT** keyword provides flexibility in retrieving subtypes.

An **object view** is a mechanism for treating a strictly relational database as if it were an object-relational one. It provides an object-relational view for users.

Exercises

7.1   Define the following terms:

a. specialization

b. generalization

c. union

d. superclass

e. subclass

f. local attribute

g. *isa* relationship

h. local relationship

i. disjointness constraint

j. completeness constraint

k. attribute-defined specialization

l. multiple inheritance

m. total category

n. LOB, BLOB

o. collection type

p. UDT

q. method

r. reference type

7.2   a. Assume the entity set Employees is specialized into Clerical, Sales, and Management. Show how the specialization is represented on an E-R diagram, making up attributes as needed, and stating any assumptions you need to make.

      b. For the specialization in part (a) add relationships that show:

        (i) All employees can have a pension plan

        (ii) Sales employees have clients

        (iii) Management employees have projects

      c. using (min,max) notation, add constraints for the relationships, stating any additional assumptions you need to make.

7.3   a. Convert the EE-R diagram you developed for Exercise 7.2 into a strictly relational model, writing out the schema.

      b. Convert the EE-R diagram you developed for Exercise 7.2 into an object-relational model, explaining what changes you would make to the relational schema from part (a).

7.4   Develop an EE-R diagram for the following application, which is an enhanced version of Exercise 3.5.

A dental group needs to keep information about patients, visits they make to the office, work that must be performed, procedures performed during visits, charges and payments for treatment, and laboratory supplies and services. Assume there are several dentists in the group. Patients make many visits, and can have several services or procedures performed during each visit. Although patients usually make appointments to see the same dentist, they can see another dentist in case of emergency or for other reasons. The database should store information about the services and procedures—including a code, description, and charges for each. Some services can span several visits. The office uses three dental laboratories, one for regular supplies, one for fabricating dentures, and one for other supplies and services.

7.5   a. Map the EE-R diagram you developed for Exercise 7.4 to a strictly relational model.

b. Convert the EE-R diagram you developed for Exercise 7.4 into an object-relational model, explaining what changes you would make to the relational schema from part (a).

7.6   Develop an EE-R diagram for the following application, which is an enhanced version of Exercise 3.6.

An interior design firm wants to have a database to represent its operations. A client requests that the firm perform services such as decorating a new house, redecorating rooms, locating and purchasing furniture, and so forth. Clients can be either private individuals or corporations. The client is matched with one of the firm's decorators, who works with the client until the job is completed. Clients can request a particular decorator, and they can change decorators for future jobs. For each job, the firm provides an estimate of the amount of time and money required to complete the job. A job can include several activities, such as painting, installing floor covering, fabricating and installing draperies, wallpapering, constructing and installing cabinets, and so on. These activities are done by contractors hired by the firm to work on a daily or hourly basis at a rate negotiated by both parties. The contractor provides an estimate of the time required for each activity. Some activities are done by the firm's decorator. Each activity requires materials such as paint or lumber, and the firm must keep track of the cost of materials as well as labor for each activity, for billing the client.

7.7   a. Map the EE-R diagram you developed for Exercise 7.6 to a strictly relational model.

        b. Convert the EE-R diagram you developed for Exercise 7.6 into an object-relational model, explaining what changes you would make to the relational schema from part (a).

Lab Exercise: Drawing an EE-R Diagram

Using drawing tool software such as Visio, SmartDraw, or the drawing tool in Word, draw an EE-R diagram for the example described in Exercise 7.2.

SAMPLE PROJECT: DRAWING AN EE-R DIAGRAM AND CREATING AN OBJECT-RELATIONAL DATABASE FOR THE ART GALLERY

- Step 7.1. Modify the E-R diagram and draw an EE-R diagram to represent the enterprise. Be sure to identify relationship participation and cardinality constraints using (min,max) notation. Identify any weak entity sets. Use generalization and union, as necessary, to express class relationships, adding appropriate constraint notation.

An E-R diagram is shown in Figure 7.8. Note that the initial diagram is missing some important features and has some confusing entities and relationships. For example, is a `Buyer` also a `PotentialCustomer`? Is an `Artist` a `Collector` of his or her own work? Also note that many attributes of `Customer`, `Buyer`, `Artist` and `Collector` are essentially the same. A more careful analysis is in order. The results are shown in the EE-R diagram in Figure 7.9, which you should compare with the E-R diagram in Figure 7.8.

In the E-R diagram, note that `Buyer` and `PotentialCustomer` have common attributes, with the only difference being that preferences are kept for customers but not for buyers. It makes good business sense to add

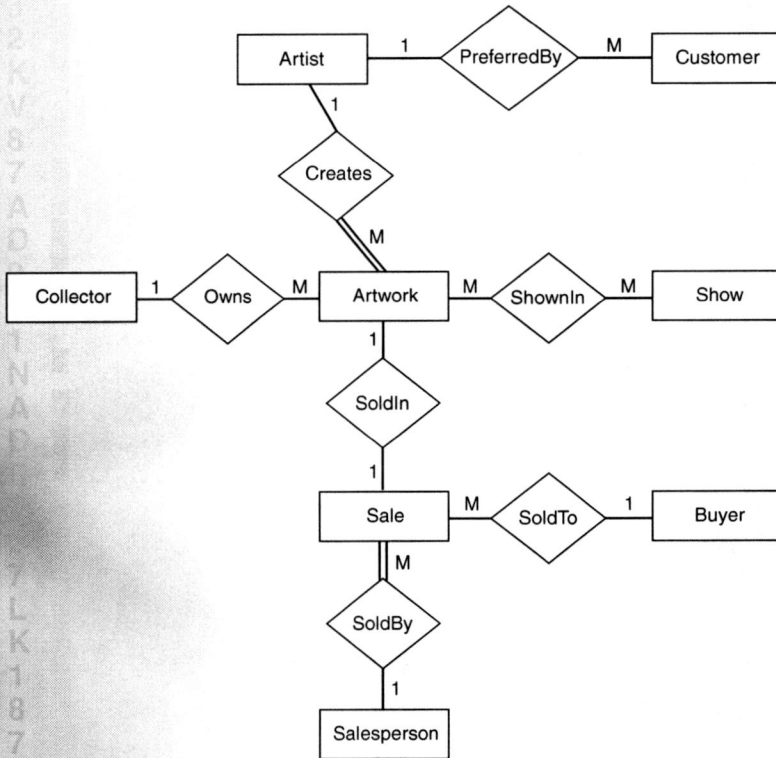

Artist Attributes: <u>artistId</u>, name(firstName, lastName), interviewDate, interviewerName, phone(areaCode, telephoneNumber), address(street, city, state, zip), salesLastYear, salesYearToDate, socialSecurityNumber, usualMedium, usualStyle, usualType

PotentialCustomer Attributes: <u>potentialCustomerId</u>, name(firstName, lastName), phone(areaCode, telephoneNumber), address(street, city, state, zip), dateFilledIn, preferredArtistId, preferredMedium, preferredStyle, preferredType

Artwork Attributes: <u>artworkId</u>, workTitle, askingPrice, dateListed, dateReturned, dateShown, status, workMedium, workSize, workStyle, workType, workyearCompleted

Collector Attributes: <u>socialSecurityNumber</u>, name(firstName, lastName), address(street, city, state, zip), interviewDate, interviewerName, phone(areaCode, telephonenumber), salesLastYear, salesYearToDate, collectionArtistId, collectionMedium, collectionStyle, collectionType, salesLastYear, salesYearToDate

Show Attributes: <u>showTitle</u>, showFeatureArtistId, showClosingDate, showTheme, showOpeningDate

Buyer Attributes: <u>buyerId</u>, name(firstName), address(street, city, state, zip), phone(areaCode, telephoneNumber), purchasesLastYear, purchasesYearToDate

Sale Attributes: <u>InvoiceNumber</u>, amountRemittedToOwner, saleDate, salePrice, saleTax

Salesperson Attributes: <u>socialSecurityNumber</u>, name(firstName, lastName), address(street, city, state, zip)

FIGURE 7.8
E-R Diagram for The Art Gallery

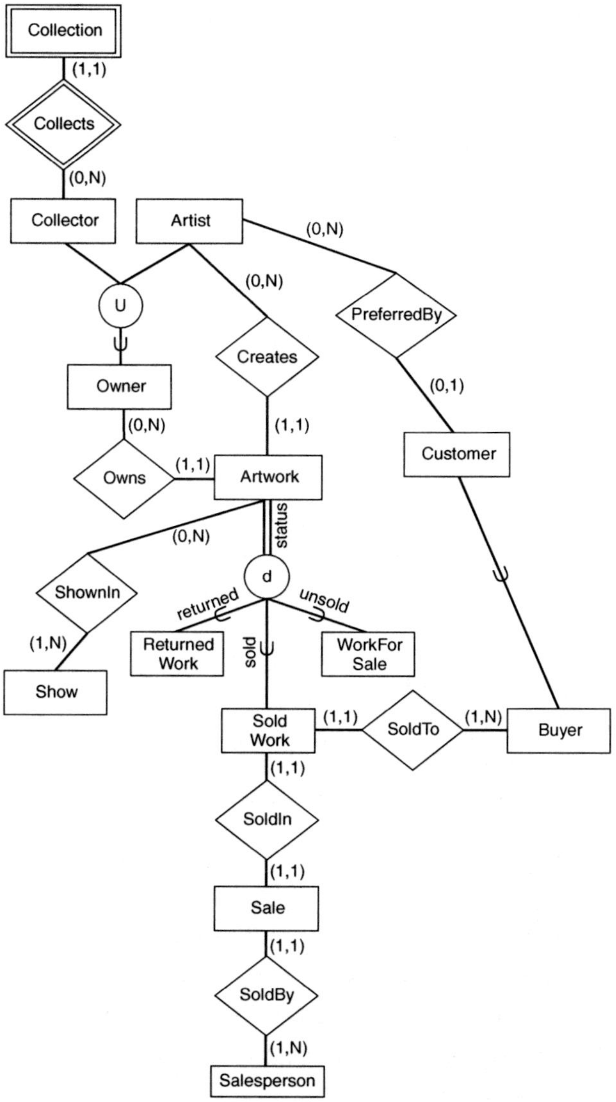

Artist Attributes: artistId, name(firstName, lastName), interviewerName, InterviewDate,
phone(areaCode,telephoneNumber), address(street,city,state,zip),salesLastYear,
salesYearToDate, socialSecurityNumber, usualMedium, usualStyle, usualType
Collector Attributes:socialSecurityNumber,name(firstName,lastName),address(street,city,state,zip),
interviewDate, interviewerName, phone(areaCode, telephoneNumber), salesLastYear,salesYearToDate)
Collection Attributes:collectorSocialSecurityNumber,collectionArtistId,collectionMedium,
collectionStyle,collectionType
Owner: union of Artist and Collector
Artwork Attributes: artworkId, workTitle, askingPrice, dateListed, dateShown, status, workMedium,
workSize, workStyle, workType, workYearCompleted
SoldWork subtype of Artwork. Additional attribute: dateSold
ReturnedWork subtype of Artwork. Additional attribute: dateReturned
WorkForSale subtype of Artwork: Additional attribute: location
Customer Attributes: CustomerId, name(firstName, lastName), phone(areaCode, telephoneNumber),
address(street, city, state, zip), dateFilledIn, preferredArtistId, preferredMedium,
preferredStyle, preferredType
Buyer Subtype of Customer. Additional Attributes: purchasesLastYear, purchasesYearToDate
Show Attributes: showTitle, showFeaturedArtistId, showClosingDate, showTheme, showOpeningDate
Sale Attributes: invoiceNumber, amountRemittedToOwner, saleDate, salePrice, saleTax
Salesperson Attributes: socialSecurityNumber, name(firstName, lastName),
address(street, city, state, zip)

FIGURE 7.9

EE-R Diagram for The Art Gallery

the preference information for Buyer. Because this makes their attributes identical, we will call both Customer. Now we can ask whether Buyer and Customer are the same. We conclude that a buyer is a customer who has actually made a purchase, i.e., a Buyer is someone who has a relationship with a Sale entity. Therefore, we can create a specialization within Customer, with Buyer as a subset having the relationship with Sale.

The Artwork entity is pictured as having a relationship to Sale but in fact only those works that have been sold have this relationship. The status attribute determines which artwork entities participate in the relationship. If we create an attribute-defined specialization on status, we can identify three disjoint subclasses of Artwork, namely, SoldWork, WorkForSale, and ReturnedWork, as shown in Figure 7.9. Of these, only SoldWork relates to Sale. We add an attribute, location, for WorkForSale. It will give the current location of the artwork.

The Artist and Collector attributes are very similar, and each entity relates to Artwork. Examining these entities more closely, we see that an artwork is sometimes owned by the artist and sometimes by a collector. Since the owner of a particular work is just one of these, not both, we use a union, with Owner as a subclass of the union of Artist and Collector. Owner participates in the Owns relationship with Artwork, as before. However, Artist always participates in the Creates relationship with Artwork, whether the artist is the owner or not. The Salesperson entity and SoldBy relationship remain as before, as do the Show and ShownIn relationship. We might consider creating a Person entity with subclasses Customer, Salesperson, Owner, since these are all people, but we choose not to do so, and to stop the abstraction process.

We still need to add constraint information. We would prefer to use the (*min..max*) notation for relationship participation and cardinality constraints, since it is more expressive than our earlier notation. In the Creates relationship, we decided earlier that Artist has partial participation, since we can keep data on interviewed artists who do not yet have artworks accepted by the gallery, so the min is 0. The max is n, because an artist can have created many accepted artworks, so we use (0..n) for Artist to Creates. The Artwork always participates in the Creates relationship with exactly one artist, so we use (1..1) for Artwork to Creates.

For `SoldWork` to `SoldIn` (because each sold work of art is sold exactly once) we use (1..1) for `SoldWork` to `SoldIn`. For `Sale` to `SoldIn`, both min and max are also 1, so we write (1..1) on this line.

For `Sale` to `SoldTo`, each sale has exactly one buyer, so we write (1..1). For `Buyer` to `SoldTo`, because a `Buyer` is by definition someone who has been involved in a `Sale`, the min is 1. A buyer can buy many artworks, therefore the max is n, so we use (1..n).

For `Sale` to `SoldBy`, each sale is made by exactly one salesperson, so we use (1..1). For `Salesperson` to `SoldBy`, because a salesperson might not have made any sales yet, the min is 0. A salesperson can make many sales, so the max is n, giving us (0..n).

For `Owner` to `Owns`, we agreed that we might store `Collector` or `Artist` information on people who have not yet had an artwork accepted, so we will assume we can store `Owner` information without an artwork, making the min 0. An `Owner` can have many works of art, so the max is n, giving us (0..n). For `Artwork` to `Owns`, each work of art has exactly one owner, making it (1..1).

For `Artwork` to `ShownIn`, the min is 0, because not all works are shown. The max is n, because an artwork can appear in many shows. For `Show` to `ShownIn`, we will make the min 1, assuming we could have a showing of a single, important piece of art. The max will be n, because a show would normally have many works of art.

Now we must decide whether the `Owner` union is partial or total. To be total, it would mean that every `Collector` and every `Artist` must be an `Owner`. Since we may have information about artists whose works are owned by collectors, this union is partial. An enhancement to the diagram that arises naturally, now that `Collector` is clearer, is that we might want to keep the `Collection` information separate from the `Collector`. This would also allow us to store data about multiple collections belonging to the same collector. Therefore, we add a `Collection` entity, with attributes `collectionArtist`, `collectionStyle`, `collectionMedium`, `collectionType`. This is a weak entity, depending on `Collector` for its primary key, with `Collects` as the relationship. We will use `collectionArtist` as the partial key. The `Collector` to `Collects` has min of 0, because a collector might not have any distinguished collections, but merely individual pieces. The max is n, as we now assume a collector might have several different collections, by various artists, so we use (0..n) for this line. For `Collects` to `Collector`, each `Collection` belongs to exactly one `Collector`, so we use (1..1).

We might consider treating `Customer` in a similar fashion, asking customers to name several preferred artists, styles, etc., but that would make the sign-up form tedious, and the resulting information might not be useful, so we choose to leave the EE-R diagram as it exists in Figure 7.9.

- Step 7.2. Map the EE-R diagram to an object-relational model. We will define structured types for addresses, names, and telephone numbers. We will use UDTs as often as possible: defining types and then creating tables of those types. To help distinguish between the type and the table, we will use the plural form for the name of the table. We will use REF types instead of foreign keys to represent relationships, when possible.

To translate the union, we will create a table for **Owners** having OwnerID and OwnerType as attributes. Then we will create tables for **Artists** and **Collectors,** each containing references to Owners. We will create a table for **Customers,** having a reference to the preferred artist. **Buyers** will be a subtable of Customers. For **Artworks,** we will replace the foreign key for Artist that we had in the strictly relational model by a reference to Artists, and add an Owners reference in place of the foreign key for Collector. We will create subtables for **ReturnedWorks, WorksForSale,** and **SoldWorks,** which will have a reference to Buyers. The **Shows** table will have a reference to Artists, to represent the featured artist. **ShownIn** is still needed for the many-to-many relationship, but both foreign keys will be replaced by references. We need a table for **Salespeople.** Then we will create the **Sales** table with references to SoldWorks and Salespeople. Finally, we will add a new table for **Collections,** with references to both Collectors and Artists.

- Step 7.3. Write the DDL to create the object-relational database, using Oracle 9i syntax, and execute the commands.

```
CREATE OR REPLACE TYPE AddressType AS OBJECT(
street      VARCHAR2(50),
city        VARCHAR2(15),
state       CHAR(2),
zip         CHAR(10));

CREATE OR REPLACE PhoneType AS OBJECT(
areaCode          CHAR(3),
telephoneNumber   CHAR(7));

CREATE OR REPLACE NameType AS OBJECT(
firstName   VARCHAR2(15),
lastName    VARCHAR2(20));

CREATE OR REPLACE OwnerType AS OBJECT (
ownerId     NUMBER(6),
ownerType   VARCHAR2(9));

CREATE TABLE Owners OF OwnerType(
CONSTRAINT Owners_ownerId_pk PRIMARY KEY (ownerId))
OBJECT IDENTIFIER PRIMARY KEY;

CREATE OR REPLACE TYPE ArtistType AS OBJECT (
artistId             NUMBER(6),
name                 NameType,
interviewDate        DATE,
interviewerName      NameType,
phone                PhoneType,
address              AddressType,
salesLastYear        NUMBER(8,2),
salesYearToDate      NUMBER(8,2),
socialSecurityNumber CHAR(9),
usualMedium          VARCHAR2(15),
usualStyle           VARCHAR2(15),
usualType            VARCHAR2(20);

CREATE TABLE Artists OF ArtistType(
CONSTRAINT Artists_artistId_pk PRIMARY KEY ArtistId,
CONSTRAINT Artists_SSN_uk UNIQUE socialSecurityNumber))
OBJECT IDENTIFIER PRIMARY KEY;
```

```
CREATE OR REPLACE CollectorType AS OBJECT (
socialSecurityNumber CHAR(9),
name                 NameType,
interviewDate        DATE,
interviewerName      NameType,
phone                Phonetype,
address              Addresstype,
salesLastYear        NUMBER (8,2),
salesYearToDate      NUMBER(8,2));

CREATE TABLE Collectors OF CollectorType(
CONSTRAINT Collectors_SSN_pk PRIMARY KEY (socialSecurityNumber));
OBJECT IDENTIFIER PRIMARY KEY;

CREATE OR REPLACE TYPE CustomerType AS OBJECT (
customerId           NUMBER(6),
Name                 NameType,
Phone                phoneType,
Address              ddressType,
dateFilledIn         DATE,
aid                  REFArtistType,
preferredMedium      VARCHAR2(15),
preferredStyle       VARCHAR2(15),
preferredType        VARCHAR2(20))
NOT FINAL

CREATE TABLE Customers OF CustomerType(
CONSTRAINT Customers_customerId_pk PRIMARY KEY (customerId))
OBJECT IDENTIFIER PRIMARY KEY;

CREATE OR REPLACE TYPE BuyerType UNDER CustomerType(
purchasesLastYear    NUMBER (8,2),
purchasesYearToDate NUMBER(8,2));

CREATE TABLE Buyers OF BuyerType;

CREATE OR REPLACE TYPE ArtworkType AS OBJECT (
artworkId    NUMBER(6),
aId          REF(ArtistType),
workTitle    VARCHAR2(50),
askingPrice NUMBER(8,2),
dateListed   DATE,
dateShown    DATE,
status       VARCHAR2(15),
workMedium   VARCHAR2(15),
workSize     VARCHAR2(15),
```

```
workStyle        VARCHAR2(15),
workType         VARCHAR2(20),
workYearCompleted CHAR(4),
ownId            REF OwnerType
NOT FINAL

CREATE OR REPLACE TABLE Artworks OF ArtworkType(
CONSTRAINT Artwork_artworkId_pk PRIMARY KEY (artworkId))
OBJECT IDENTIFIER PRIMARY KEY;

CREATE OR REPLACE TYPE ReturnedWorkType UNDER ArtworkType (
dateReturned DATE);

CREATE TABLE ReturnedWorks OF ReturnedWorkType (

CREATE OR REPLACE TYPE WorkForSaleType UNDER ArtworkType;
location         VARCHAR2(50));

CREATE OR REPLACE TABLE WorksForSale OF WorkForSaleType;

CREATE OR REPLACE TYPE SoldWorkType UNDER ArtworkType (
dateSold     DATE,
cid          REFCustomerType;

CREATE TABLE SoldWorks OF SoldWorkType;

CREATE OR REPLACE TYPE ShowType AS OBJECT (
ShowTitle        VARCHAR2(50),
aid              REFartistType,
showClosingDate DATE,
showTheme        VARCHAR2(50),
showOpeningDate DATE);

CREATE TABLE Shows of ShowType (
CONSTRAINT Shows_ShowTitle_pk PRIMARY KEY (ShowTitle))
OBJECT IDENTIFIER PRIMARY KEY;

CREATE TABLE ShownIn
(workId REFArtworkType,
showId   REF ShowType;

CREATE OR REPLACE TYPE SalespersonType AS OBJECT (
socialSecurityNumber CHAR(9),
name                 NameType,
address              AddressType);
```

```
CREATE TABLE Salespeople OF SalespersonType (
CONSTRAINT Salespeople_SSN_pk PRIMARY KEY (socialSecurityNumber))
OBJECT IDENTIFIER PRIMARY KEY;

CREATE OR REPLACE TYPE SaleType AS OBJECT (
invoiceNumber          NUMBER(6),
workId                 REFArtworkType,
amountRemittedToOwner  NUMBER(8,2),
saleDate               DATE,
salePrice              NUMBER(8,2),
saleTax                NUMBER(6,2),
sid                    REFSalespersonType;

CREATE TABLE Sales OF SaleType
CONSTRAINT Sales_invoiceNumber_pk PRIMARY KEY (invoiceNumber));

CREATE OR REPLACE TYPE CollectionType AS OBJECT (
cid                 REFCollectorType,
aid                 REFArtistType,
collectionMedium    VARCHAR2(15),
collectionStyle     VARCHAR2(15),
collectionType      VARCHAR2(20));

CREATE TABLE Collections OF CollectionType;
```

- Step 7.4. Write five DML commands for the new database, illustrating differences from the strictly relational DML.

  Note: When a table alias is used, Oracle allows dereferencing using the dot notation, which we will use in the queries.

1. Find the names of all artists who were interviewed after January 1, 2004, but who have no works of art listed.

```
SELECT a.name.firstName, a.name.lastName
FROM Artists a
WHERE a.interviewDate > '01-Jan-2004' AND NOT EXISTS
   (SELECT *
   FROM Artworks w
   WHERE w.aId.artistId=a.artistId);
```

2. Find the total commission for salesperson John Smith earned between the dates April 1, 2004, and April 15, 2004. Recall that the gallery charges 10% commission, and the salesperson receives one-half of that, which is 5% of the selling price.

```
SELECT .05 * SUM(s.salePrice)
FROM Sales s
WHERE s.saleDate >='01-Apr-2004' AND s.saleDate <='15-Apr-2004' AND
    s.sid.socialSecurityNumber = (SELECT p.socialSecurityNumber
            FROM Salesperson p
            WHERE p.name.firstName= 'John' AND p.name.lastName
            ='Smith');
```

3. Find the collector names, artist names and titles of all artworks that are owned by collectors, not by the artists themselves, in order by the collector's last name.

```
SELECT c.name, a,name, w.workTitle
FROM Collectors c, Artists a, Artworks w
WHERE a.artistId = w.aid.artistId AND w.ownid.ownerType = 'collector')
ORDER BY c.name.lastName;
```

4. For each potential buyer, find information about shows that feature his or her preferred artist. List in order of customer Id.

```
SELECT c.name, s.showTitle, s.showOpeningDate, s.showClosingDate
FROM Shows s , Customers c
WHERE s.aid.ArtistId = c.aid.artistId
ORDER BY c.customerId;
```

5. Find the average sale price of works of artist Georgia Keefe.

```
SELECT AVG(s.salePrice)
FROM Sales s
WHERE s.workId.artworkId IN (SELECT w.artworkid
    FROM Artworks w
    WHERE w.aid.artistId = (SELECT a.artistId
        FROM Artists a
        WHERE a.name.lastName = 'Keefe' AND a.name.firstName =
        'Georgia'));
```

STUDENT PROJECTS: DRAWING AN EE-R DIAGRAM AND CREATING AN OBJECT-RELATIONAL DATABASE FOR THE STUDENT PROJECT

- Step 7.1. Modify the E-R diagram and draw an EE-R diagram to represent the enterprise. Be sure to identify relationship participation and cardinality constraints using (min,max) notation. Identify any weak entity sets. Use generalization and union, as necessary, to express class relationships, adding appropriate constraint notation.

- Step 7.2. Map the EE-R diagram to an object-relational model.

- Step 7.3. Write the DDL to create the object-relational database, using Oracle 9i syntax or the syntax of the object-relational database management system you are using, and execute the commands.

- Step 7.4. Write five DML commands for the new database, illustrating differences from the strictly relational DML.

CHAPTER 8

The Object-Oriented Model

Chapter Objectives

In this chapter you will learn the following:

- The origins of the object-oriented data model

- Fundamental concepts of the object-oriented data model: object, class, inheritance, object identity

- How to construct a UML class diagram

- The basic concepts of the ODMG model

- How to write ODL for an object-oriented schema using a UML class diagram

- How to write simple queries using OQL

- How an object-oriented database is developed and used

SAMPLE PROJECT: Creating a UML Diagram for The Art Gallery and Converting the Diagram to an Object-Oriented Database Schema

STUDENT PROJECTS: Drawing a UML Diagram and Designing an Object-Oriented Database Model

8.1   Rationale for the Object-Oriented Data Model

The traditional relational model, in which data is represented as tables having rows of single-valued attributes, is limited in its ability to represent the complex data and relationships needed for advanced applications. Just as the E-R model was found to be lacking in its ability to represent a conceptual model for such applications as software development, computer-aided design, geographical information systems, engineering design, and many other advanced applications, the traditional relational model lacks the data structures to support the information requirements for these applications. **Object-oriented programming languages,** beginning with Simula and Smalltalk, presented an alternate way of designing programs, in which data structures and their operations had primary importance. Object-oriented programming is widely recognized as a method for producing highly reliable, reusable code. The promise of the early object-oriented languages, and the popularity of the object-oriented languages C++ and Java, have influenced database modeling as well. The challenge of extending these languages to databases is to move from the temporary objects created and manipulated by programs to **persistent objects** that can be stored in a database. Object-oriented database management systems allow the database designer to create highly complex, interrelated objects and to give them persistence. As discussed in Chapter 7, vendors of relational model database systems have responded to the challenges of object-oriented systems by extending the relational model to incorporate some object-oriented concepts. Because vendors have addressed some of the limitations of relational databases, and because users who have a heavy investment in relational systems are disinclined to migrate to an entirely new paradigm, the popularity of object-oriented databases has been limited. However, some strictly object-oriented database management systems (**OODBMS**), such as Objectivity, GemStone, ObjectStore, Ontos, and Versant, are in use.

8.2 Object-Oriented Data Concepts

8.2.1 Objects and Literals

The concept of an **object** is fundamental in the object-oriented model. An object has a state (value) and a unique identifier. An object is similar to an entity in our previous terminology, except that an object has not only **data elements** but also a set of **methods** (functions or procedures) that can be performed on it. Many examples of objects were presented in Chapter 7, in our discussion of how the relational model has been extended to include objects. In addition to the fundamental data types and user-defined structured types that correspond to records, object-oriented systems support collections types such as arrays, sets and others, and reference types, which are similar to pointers in programming. New types can be created incorporating previously defined types. Objects are **encapsulated,** which means that their data and methods form a unit, and that access to the data is restricted. Only the object's own methods, created and programmed by the designer of the object, are permitted to access the data, protecting it from changes by outside code. The external appearance of an object, visible to the outside world, is called its **interface.** The outside world interacts with the object through its interface, calling the object's own methods to perform any operations on its data elements. Figure 8.1 pictures two objects of a class called `Person`. Each `Person` object instance has its own identifier (`firstPerson` and `secondPerson`, in this example) and attributes `name`, `address`, and `telephone`, with its own values for those attributes. Each object is encapsulated, and the values of its attributes are accessible to the outside world only through its methods, `getName( )` and `setName( )`. From the names of these methods, we can assume that the programmer who designed these objects has written code for a function that returns the value of the `name` attribute (`getName( )`) and one that allows the user to provide a new value for the `name` attribute (`setName( )`). To make the other two attributes accessible as well, the programmer who designed these objects needs to add `get` and `set` methods for them as well.

A **literal** differs from an object in that it has a state (value) but no object identifier. Atomic literals are the values of the basic built-in types, but we can also have structured literals.

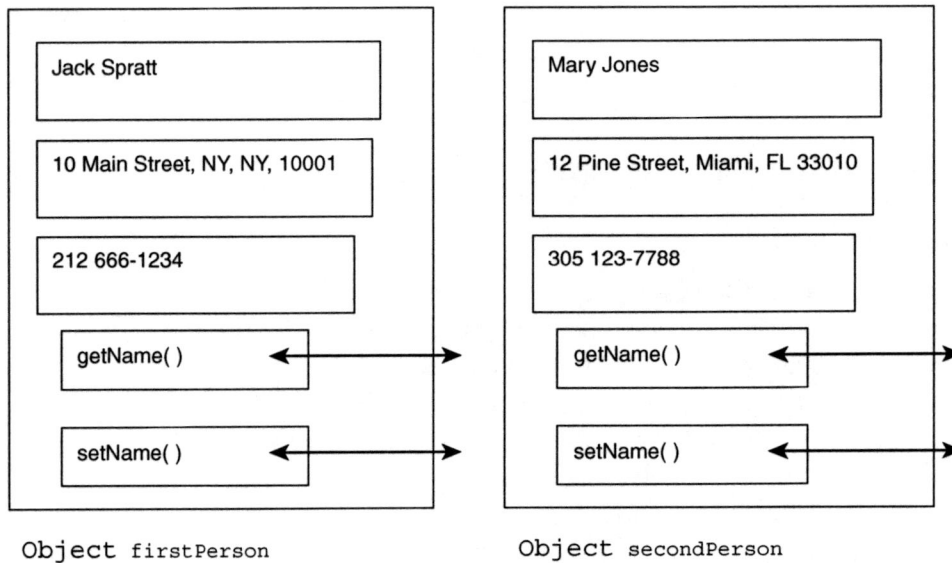

FIGURE 8.1
Two Person Objects

8.2.2   Classes

A **class** is a set of objects having the same structure, including the same variables with the same data types, and the same methods and relationships. A class is roughly equivalent to an entity type, except that it includes operations and relationships, not just data elements. Classes are defined by listing their components, which consist of **data members** (attributes, instance variables), member **methods** (functions or procedures that belong to the class), and the **relationships** that the class participates in. The general form we will use for a class definition is:

```
class classname {
    list of attributes, methods, relationships
}
```

For example, we can define a Person class as:

```
class Person {
   attribute string name;
   attribute string address;
   attribute string phone;
   void setName(string newName); // method
   string getName( ); //method
}
```

In this class definition, the three attributes are identified by their data types and names, and two methods are listed. The first, setName( ), has a single string parameter, but it has no return value, as indicated by void. As the name implies, it is intended to set the value of an object's name attribute. The code for this method is written by the designer of the class. It might be defined as follows:

```
void setName(string newName)
{
    self.name = newName;
}
```

The method is called from a user program to set the name of a Person object. For example, if firstPerson is created as a Person object within the user program, using a declaration such as,

```
Person          firstPerson;
```

or,

```
Person firstPerson = new Person();
```

the user is not able to set the person's name by referring directly to the name attribute of firstPerson, because of encapsulation of objects. Instead the user program should contain a command such as:

```
firstPerson.setName('Jack Spratt');
```

Here, firstPerson is the "calling object," the object used to call the method, and it becomes the implicit parameter for the method. Within the method, it is referred to as the *self* parameter. We referred to it by name in the assignment line of the method,

```
self.name = newName;
```

but we did not need to, and could have written just,

```
name = newName;
```

since it is understood that the unqualified attributes referred to within the method are those of the calling object, *self.*

For the getName( ) method, the code written by the designer of the class might be:

```
string getName( )
{
return name;
}
```

Within the user program we would call this method using an object as the implicit parameter. Continuing with our example, if we write as part the user program,

```
string employeeName = firstPerson.getName( );
```

the `firstPerson` object is the implicit parameter for the method, and the name of that object is returned, resulting in the value 'Jack Spratt' being assigned to the program variable `employeeName`.

The set of objects belonging to a class is called the **extent** of the class. An entity set is roughly equivalent to a class extent. The data types in a class can be predefined atomic types including integer, real, character, and Boolean, and more complex types as well as user-defined types. The individual objects in the class are called **instances, object instances,** or simply **objects,** and they are similar to entity instances.

8.2.3   Class Hierarchies and Inheritance

Classes are organized into **class hierarchies,** consisting of **superclasses** and **subclasses,** in which each subclass has an *isa* relationship with its superclass. This is similar to the concept of specialization and generalization that we saw in the EE-R model. Subclasses inherit the data members and methods of their superclasses, and they may have additional data members and methods of their own. Figure 8.2 shows an example of a class hierarchy. Note that this is not an EE-R diagram, as seen by the presence of the *isa* triangle, as opposed to the specialization circle we saw in EE-R diagrams. Figure 8.3 shows a simplified set of class declarations to correspond to the class hierarchy in Figure 8.2. All objects in the superclass, `Person`, have data members `name`, `address`, and `phone` that are common to all people. Those in the `Student` subclass inherit `name`, `address`, and `phone` and add data members of their own, `stuId` and `credits`. The `Faculty` subclass also inherits the `Person` attributes, but has its own data members, `facId`, `dept`, and `rank`. In turn, `Undergraduate` and `Graduate` subclasses inherit the attributes of both `Person` and `Student`. We have indicated subclasses by using *isa* and we have included some methods for each class. Along with attributes, methods of each superclass are also automatically inherited by the subclass, so that, for example, `Student` and `Faculty` subclasses, as well as `Student`'s `Undergraduate` and `Graduate` subclasses, have the `getName()` and `setName()` methods from `Person`. The subclasses can also have additional methods, as we see for the subclass `Student`,

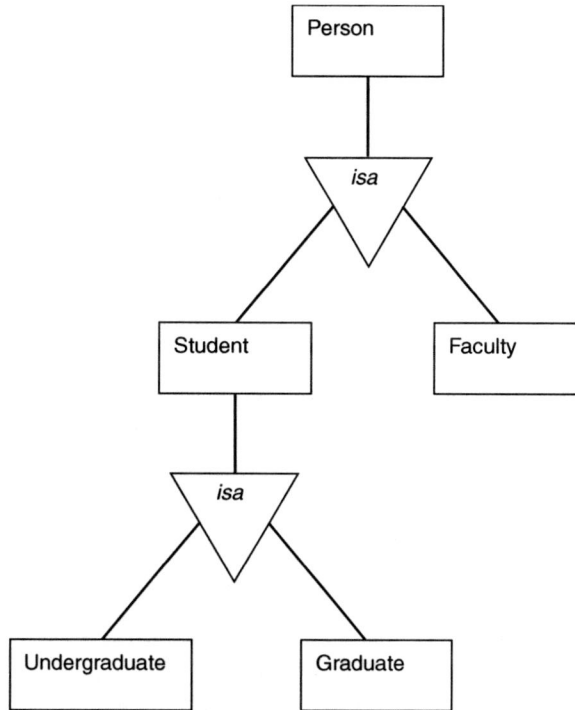

FIGURE 8.2
A Class Hierarchy

which has methods getCredits() and addCredits(). The Undergraduate and Graduate subclasses inherit these methods as well, and each has its own methods: setMajor() and getMajor() for Undergraduate, and getProgram() for Graduate. We could **override** a method by defining for the subclass a method that has the same **signature** as a method of the superclass, that is, the same name and the same number and types of parameters and return type. In that case the new method will be used on objects of the subclass.

Multiple inheritance means that a subclass belongs to more than one superclass, and that it inherits attributes and methods from the multiple superclasses. A simple example is shown in Figure 8.4, which shows a class for graduate teaching assistants as a subclass of both Student and Faculty. Each TeachingAssistant object has all the attributes and methods of Person, Faculty, Student, and Graduate, as well as any attributes and methods of its own. We could add its class definition shown in Figure 8.4 to the one in Figure 8.3. The class definition for TeachingAssistant includes a reference attribute assignedClassSection, which is a reference to another class, ClassSection, whose definition is not shown.

```
class Person {
    attribute name string;
    attribute Struct addr(string street, string city, string state,
        string zip) address;
    attribute phone string;
    string getName( );//method that returns a string
    void setName(string newName); // method with no return
};
class Student isa Person {
    attribute stuId string;
    attribute credits int;
    int getCredits( );
    void addCredits(int numCredits);
};
class Faculty isa Person {
    attribute facId string;
    attribute dept string;
    attribute enum FacultyRank{instructor, assistant, associate,
        professor} rank ;
    string getRank( );
};
class Undergraduate isa Student{
    attribute major string;
    string getMajor( );
    void setMajor(string newMajor);
};
class Graduate isa Student {
    attribute program string;
    string getProgram( );
};
```

8.2.4 Object Identity

Object identity is another fundamental concept for object-oriented models. Each object in the database is assigned its own unique object identifier, **OID,** which remains unchanged for the lifetime of the object. Unlike the relational model, where we must identify a primary key for each relation, the object-oriented model provides unique identifiers automatically. The

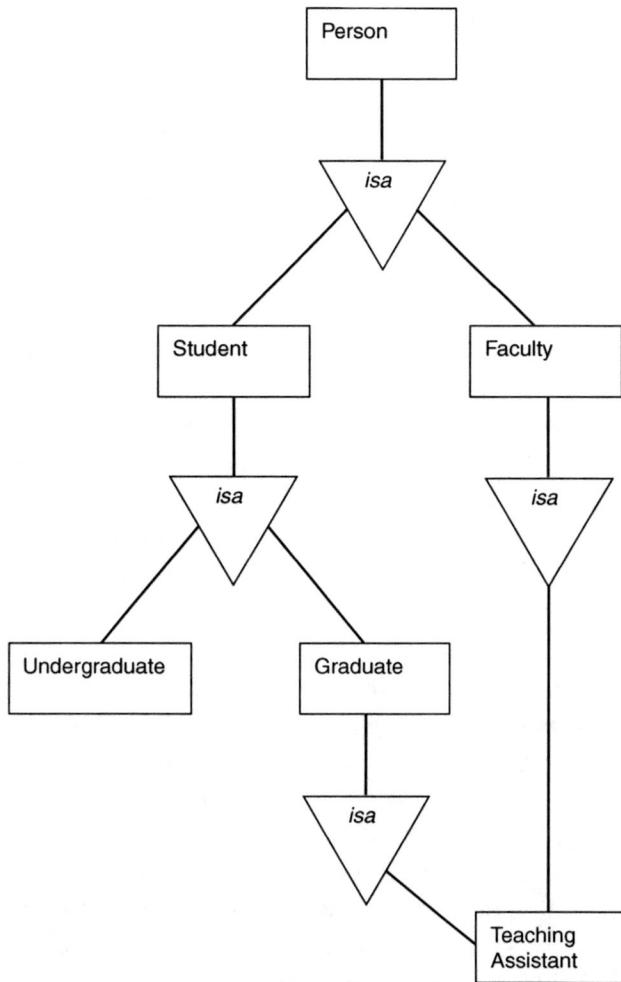

FIGURE 8.4
Multiple Inheritance

```
...
class TeachingAssistant isa Graduate isa Faculty{
      attribute fundingSource string;
      attribute annualStipend real(7,2);
      attribute assignedClassSection REF ClassSection;
};
```

value of the OID does not depend on the value of any attribute of the object. In the relational model, the primary key value could be updated. However, in the object-oriented model, the OID never changes. Since it is always possible to tell objects apart by their OIDs, it is also possible that two different objects have exactly the same values for all their data items, a situation forbidden in the relational model. References use the OIDs of the referenced objects.

8.3   Object-Oriented Data Modeling Using UML

E-R and EE-R diagrams are not well suited to representing objects, since they do not allow representation of methods. A widely used diagramming technique called **UML** (Unified Modeling Language) class diagrams allows us to express object-oriented concepts more naturally than either of the previous techniques. Figure 8.5 shows a UML class diagram for part of a University database, in which we show many of the features of such diagrams. The choices made in constructing this diagram are intended to demonstrate different features of the diagramming notation, and do not represent the only possible model for the example. In a UML diagram, **rectangles** represent classes. Class rectangles are subdivided into three sections, the top one for the class name, the middle for the attributes, and the bottom for the methods. In UML we distinguish between **associations,** which are either unidirectional or bidirectional relationships between classes, and **aggregation,** which is a type of relationship that connects a whole to its parts. **Associations,** or binary connections between classes, are represented by lines connecting the class rectangles. The name of the association may optionally appear on the line. Any descriptive attribute of the relationship is shown in a box connected to the association line by a dotted line, as shown in the `grade` attribute of the `Grading` relationship. **Role-names** can also appear on association lines, if they are needed for clarity, but their placement is opposite to that in an E-R diagram. For one of the associations between `Dept` and `Faculty` we have used rolenames `has chair` and `chairs` to show that it connects the chairperson with the department. **Aggregation** is a special type of relationship that connects a whole to its parts. If the phrase describing the relationship of a class to another is that it "is part of" the other, and the class is clearly subordinate to the other, then aggregation is the better representation of the relationship. We represented the relationship between `Course` and `ClassSection` as an aggregation. The aggregation is represented by a line with a diamond on the side of the class that is the aggregate. If the aggregation is not given a name, the aggregation line is interpreted to mean "has." Participation constraints and cardinality for both types of relationships are specified using a variation of the *(min, max)* notation discussed in Section 7.4. They are called **multiplicity indicators** in UML. They are written using the form *min . . max,* without parentheses, and are placed on the opposite side to their placement in an EE-R diagram. The * is used in place of M, and the abbreviation 1 means exactly one, that is, 1..1. Recursive relationships between members of the same class, called **reflexive associations** or **reflexive aggregations,**

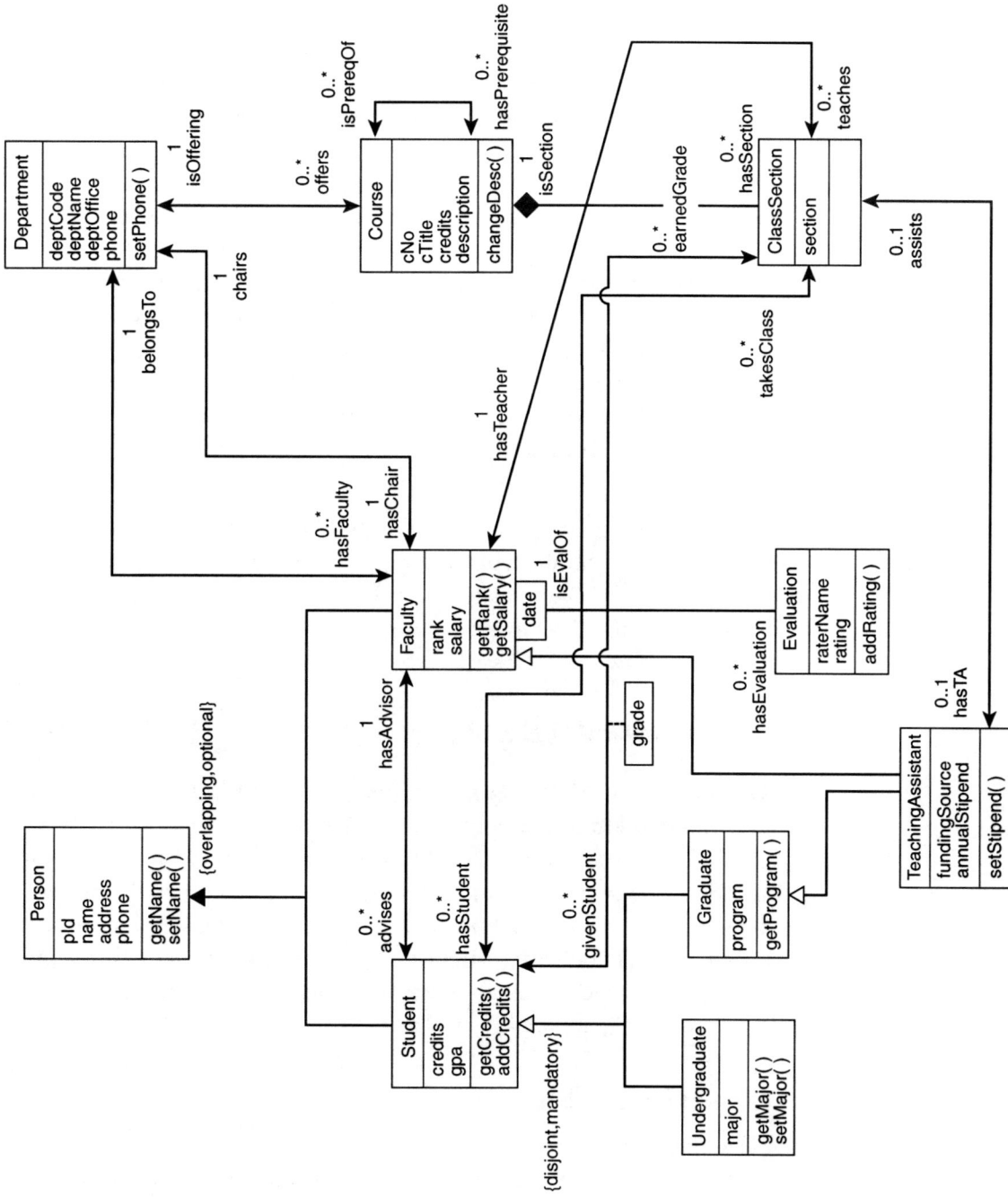

FIGURE 8.5

A UML Class Diagram

are shown by an association line or aggregation line going from a class back into itself. The relationship that connects courses and their prerequisites is a reflexive association. Rolenames appear on the line, with multiplicity indicators at each end. We show that a course may have zero to many prerequisites, and that a course may be a prerequisite for zero to many other courses. **Generalization hierarchies** are represented by lines connecting the subclasses to the superclass, with a triangle pointing toward the superclass. In Figure 8.5, `Person` is specialized into `Student` and `Faculty`, and `Student` is specialized into `Undergraduate` and `Graduate`. `Graduate` has a subclass, `Teaching Assistant`, which is also a subclass of `Faculty`, demonstrating multiple inheritance. A filled generalization triangle represents **overlapping** subclasses, while a blank (outline only) triangle represents **disjoint** ones. If each member of the superclass must belong to a subclass, we describe the specialization as **mandatory,** as opposed to **optional.** Specialization constraints can be written on the line near the triangle, enclosed in curly brackets. For example, we write {overlapping, optional} for the specialization of `Person` into `Student` and `Faculty`, and { disjoint, mandatory} for `Student` into `Undergraduate` and `Graduate`.

Weak entities can be represented by a box attached to the associated strong owner entity, with the **discriminator** (partial key) appearing in a box beneath the owner's class rectangle. We show Evaluation as a weak entity, dependent on Faculty. For this example, we assume the same faculty member is never evaluated twice on the same day, so we use date as the discriminator.

8.4   The ODMG Model and ODL

The **Object Database Management Group** (ODMG) is a group of vendors that has developed and published standards for object-oriented databases. The group has standards for the object model itself, **object definition language** (ODL), **object query language** (OQL), and language bindings for C++, Java, and Smalltalk. ODL is a standard language for describing schemas in object-oriented terms, serving the same function that DDL serves. Figure 8.6 shows the ODL definition for the university schema shown in Figure 8.5.

8.4.1   Class Declarations

Each class declaration begins with the keyword `class`, the name of the class, an optional extent and key declaration in parentheses, and a list of attributes, methods, and relationships enclosed in curly brackets.

```
class Person(
extent people
key pId)
{    attribute pId int;
     attribute name string;
     attribute Struct Addr(string street, string city, string state, string zip) address;
     attribute phone string;
     string getName( );
     void setName(string newName);
};

class Student extends Person
(extent students)
{    attribute credits int;
     attribute gpa real(3,2);
     int getCredits( );
     void addCredits(int numCredits);
     relationship Set<ClassSection> takesClass Inverse ClassSection::hasStudent;
     relationship Set<Grade> earnedGrade Inverse Grade::givenStudent
     relationship Faculty hasAdvisor Inverse Faculty::advises;
};

class Faculty extends Person
(extent facs)
{    attribute enum FacultyRank{instructor, assistant, associate, professor} rank;
     attribute salary real(8,2);
     string getRank( );
     real get salary( );
     relationship Department belongsTo Inverse Department::hasFaculty;
     relationship Set<ClassSection> teaches Inverse ClassSection::hasTeacher
     relationship Set<Student>advises Inverse Student::hasAdvisor;
     relationship Department chairs Inverse Department::hasChair;
};

class Undergraduate extends Student
(extent undergraduates)
{  attribute major string;
     string getMajor( );
     void setMajor(string newMajor);

};                                                              (Continued)
```

FIGURE 8.6
ODL Definition for University Schema

FIGURE 8.6—Continued

```
class Graduate extends Student
(extent graduates)
{   attribute program string;
    string getProgram( );
};
class TeachingAssistant extends Graduate
(extent teachingAssistants)
{    attribute fundingSource string;
    attribute annualStipend real(7,2);
    relationship ClassSection assists Inverse ClassSection::hasTA;
};
class Department
(extent departments
key deptCode, deptName)
{    attribute deptCode string;
    attribute deptName string;
    attribute deptOffice string;
    attribute phone string;
    relationship Set<Faculty> hasFaculty Inverse Faculty::belongsTo;
    relationship Faculty hasChair Inverse Faculty::chairs;
    relationship Set<Courses> offers Inverse Courses::isOffering
};
class Course
(extent courses
key cNo)
{    attribute cNo string;
    attribute cTitle string;
    attribute credits int;
    attribute description string;
    void change Desc(string newDesc);
    relationship Set<Course> hasPrerequisite Inverse isPrereqOf;
    relationship Set<Course> isPrereqOf Inverse hasPrerequisite;
    relationship Department isOffering Inverse Department::offers;
};
class ClassSection extends Course
(extent sections)
{    attribute section string
    relationship Set<Student> hasStudent Inverse Student::takesClass;
    relationship Faculty hasTeacher Inverse Faculty::Teaches
    relationship TeachingAssistant hasTA Inverse TeachingAssistant::assists;
    relationship Set<Grade>givenStudent Inverse Grade::earnedGrade
};
```

FIGURE 8.6—Continued

```
class Evaluation
(extent evaluations
key (date, isEvalOf)
{   attribute Struct DateType(int day, int month, int year) date;
    attribute string raterName;
    attribute int rating;
    relationship Faculty isEvalOf Inverse Faculty::hasEvaluation;
};
class Grade
(extent grades)
{   attribute string grade;
    relationship ClassSection section Inverse ClassSection::givenStudent;
    relationship Student givenStudent Inverse Student::earnedGrade;
};
```

8.4.2 Extent

The **extent** of a class can be thought of as the set of object instances for that class that are stored in the database at a given time. Using terms from Chapter 2, the class itself is part of the intension of the database, while the extent is part of the extension of the database. The class corresponds to a relation schema in relational systems, and the extent corresponds to the stored table that exists at a given moment, that is, the actual records. In E-R terms, the class is like the entity type, and the extent is the set of entity instances. The extent can be thought of as the name of the file where the objects in a class are stored. It is good practice to choose a name for the extent that is slightly different from the name of the class. For the `Person` class, we called the extent `people`. The parentheses can also contain the name of the key, which we discuss in a later section.

8.4.3 Attributes

The attributes for a class are listed, along with their datatypes, within curly brackets. A wide variety of types are permitted in ODL, including simple types and more complex types that can be built from them. **Atomic types** include integer, float, character, string, Boolean, and enumerated types. **Enumerated types** are identified by the keyword enum, the user-defined name of the type, a list of literals for the type within curly brackets, and the name of the attribute with that type. For example, we made attribute `rank` in `Faculty` have an enumerated type called `FacultyRank`. We can also have **structured types,** identified by the keyword `Struct`, the name of the type, and curly brackets containing each attribute with its data type. In the `Person` class definition, Addr is a structured type that we have used for the attribute `address`. Since we named the type, we can use it again for other classes, but we must identify the class it was defined in, using the form `Person::Addr`, called the **scoped name,** consisting of the class name, a double colon, and the structure name. This scoped form is used to refer to any property in a different class. Besides `Struct`, there are type constructors for five collection types, namely `Set`, `List`, `Array`, `Bag`, and `Dictionary`.

- A **set** consists of a finite number of values of one data type, which we specify in angled brackets, using notation Set<*typename*>. We can define an attribute as having a set of values, or we can use sets in relationships. For example, in the `Student` class we identify a relationship, `takesClass`, between each `student` instance and a set of `classSection` type instances, using Set<classSection>. This relationship connects each student to the classes he or she is taking.

- The **List** constructor is used to denote a finite list of elements of a single type, written List<*datatype*>. For example, since we have already defined the `Addr` structured type, we can use List<Person::Addr> to denote a list of address type values for some other class. Of course the type for a list could be an atomic type as well, as in List<integer>.

- An **array** consists of a set of elements all of the same type, with an index indicating position of each element. The array constructor requires that we specify the data type and the number of elements, as in Array<float, 5>.

- A **bag** or multiset is similar to a set, except that it permits duplicate values of a single data type. We denote it Bag<*datatype*>, as in Bag<string>.

- The **dictionary** type constructor has the form Dictionary <K,V> where K and V are some data types. It is used to construct pairs of values, <k,v> where k is a key type and v is some range type, and its purpose is to provide an efficient means of find the value of the range type for a given value of the key type.

8.4.4 Relationships

Relationships represent connections between object instances. For example, faculty members relate to class sections because they teach them, students relate to classes that they take, departments relate to faculty who are employed in them, and so on. The object-oriented model represents these connections using **references.** In ODL, the description of a relationship implies that the system stores and maintains such references. For example, there is a relationship called `takesClass` defined for the `Student` class in this line:

```
relationship Set<ClassSection> takesClass Inverse ClassSection::
hasStudent;
```

The first part of the declaration, `relationship Set<ClassSection> takesClass`, tells us that each `Student` instance can contain a set of references, called `takesClass`, to `ClassSection` instances. The keyword `Set` shows that this is a "many" relationship for each student; that is, a `Student` instance can be related to a set of `ClassSection` instances, not just one. The `takesClass` relationship can be seen as a way so that, given a `Student` instance, we can find out what classes the student is taking. We also expect that we would be able to turn the query around and, given a `ClassSection` instance, ask what students are in the class. We see that there is such an inverse relationship, `hasStudent`, defined for `ClassSection`. The phrase,

```
Inverse ClassSection::hasStudent;
```

means that each `ClassSection` object contains references to a set of the corresponding `Student` instances. We note that in addition to specifying in the `Student` class that the inverse exists, we also specify this relationship in the `ClassSection` class, in this line:

```
relationship Set<Student> hasStudent Inverse Student::takesClass;
```

The connection between `takesClass` and `hasStudent` is that if a class appears in the `takesClass` set of references for a student, that same student should appear in the `hasStudent` set of references for the class. These two relationships are therefore inverses of each other, as indicated. Note that when we identify the inverse relationship we normally use the scoped form for its name,

```
Inverse className::relationshipName,
```

since the inverse relationship is usually in another class definition. ODL allows relationships to have inverses or not. Those without inverses are described as **unidirectional,** while those with inverses are **bidirectional.** Relationships also have **cardinality,** which can be one-to-one, one-to-many, many-to-one, or many-to-many. The bidirectional Student—classSection relationship is many-to-many, and both relationship specifications included a **set** of references. If a relationship is one-to-many, like Department-Faculty, the relationship on the "one" side, Department, is a set. In this case we have Set<Faculty> since each Department instance has references to many Faculty instances as shown in the line.

```
relationship Set <Faculty>hasFaculty Inverse Faculty::belongsTo;
```

However, the relationship on the Faculty side,

```
relationship Department belongsTo Inverse Department::hasFaculty
```

specifies just Department (not Set<Department>), since a faculty record refers to only one department.

8.4.5 Methods

ODL class definitions can also contain declarations for methods for the class. Examples are the getName() and setName() methods listed for the Person class. A method is a function or procedure that can be performed on members of the class. Method declarations in ODL simply specify the **signature,** which is the name of the method, the return type, and the number and type of parameters, which may be identified as IN, OUT, or IN/OUT, as described previously. Class member methods are applied to an instance of the class, which is referred to as *self* in the code for the method. The actual code for the method is not part of the ODL, but is written in one of the host languages. Methods can be **overloaded,** which means the same method name can be used for different classes, and will have different code for them. Two methods for the same class can also have the same name, but if their signatures are different, they are considered different methods.

8.4.6 Classes and Inheritance

A subclass is identified by the keyword extends and the name of its superclass following the subclass name. The subclass inherits all the attributes, relationships, and methods of the superclass, and it can have some additional properties of its own that appear in the definition. For example, in Figure 8.6, Faculty extends Person, so it inherits,

```
name, address, phone, getName( ) and setName( )
```

from `Person`, but adds some additional properties. If the subclass has more than one superclass, we add a colon and the name of the second superclass immediately after the name of the first superclass. The second superclass must be an **interface,** a class definition without an associated extent.

8.4.7 N-ary Relationships and M:N Relationships with Attributes

Relationships in ODL are binary, but if we must model a ternary or higher-order relationship, we can do so by creating a class for the relationship itself. The class definition would include three or more relationships that connect the new class to the originally related classes. For example, in Section 3.5.1 we described a ternary relationship that connected a class, instructor, and text, shown in Figure 3.12 as `Faculty-Class-Textbook`. In the object-oriented model, we would define the class for the relationship, which we will call `BookOrder`, as shown in the following sketch:

```
Class BookOrder{
relationship Faculty teacher Inverse . . .
relationship Book bookFor Inverse . . .
relationship ClassSection uses Inverse . . .
}
```

If the relationship has any descriptive attributes, they would be listed as well. Note that this technique is similar to the way we treated higher order relationships in the relational model, where we created tables for such relationships.

Binary many-to-many relationships with descriptive attributes cannot be handled by the usual solution of making the relationship a set in both directions, since that leaves no place for descriptive attributes. Referring to the UML diagram in Figure 8.5, we see that `grade` is an example of a descriptive attribute. We use the same solution as for n-ary relationships, setting up a class for the relationship. We place the descriptive attributes as attributes of the new class, and we define two one-to-many relationships between the new class and the two original classes. We have done this in Figure 8.6 by defining the class `Grade`. Note that we also kept the many-to-many relationship between `Student` and `ClassSection` that represents enrollment in the section by defining set relationships in both.

8.4.8 Keys

Keys are optional in ODL, because the unique object identifier (OID) automatically given to each object instance allows the system to tell instances apart. However, the designer may choose to identify any candidate keys as well. This is done at the beginning of the class declaration within the same parentheses as the extent declaration. A key can be a single attribute or a composite, which is identified by placing parentheses around the names of component attributes. For example, we could have written:

```
class Faculty
(extent Fac
key facId, socSecNo, (name, department)
```

This means `facId` is a key, `socSecNo` is a key, and the combination of name and `department` is a key. Keys are not restricted to attributes. We can list a relationship or even a method as a key, provided it gives us unique values. Weak entity sets can often be represented as subclasses in which the relationship to the superclass is part of the key, with the discriminator as another part. For example, for the weak entity set `Evaluation`, we wrote:

```
class Evaluation
(extent Evaluations
key (date, IsEvalOf))
{. . .
relationship Faculty isEvalOf Inverse Faculty::hasEvaluation;
. . .
}
```

This means the composite key consists of the date of the evaluation and the related faculty member.

8.5   Object Query Language

Object Query Language (OQL) uses a syntax that is similar to SQL, but it operates on objects, not tables. The form for queries is:

```
SELECT expression list
FROM list of variables
WHERE condition;
```

Although the syntax is similar to SQL, there are some important differences. The expression list may contain the names of attributes of objects, identified by using the dot notation, as in:

```
SELECT s.stuId, s.credits
FROM students s;
```

The result will be the values of `stuId` and `credits` for each of the student instances in the students extent. In addition to attributes, we can use methods in the expression list. This retrieves the result of applying the method. We could write, for example,

```
SELECT p.getName( )
FROM people p;
```

which will return the value of the `name` attribute, provided the `getName( )` method has been written correctly to do that. We can also use a relationship in the expression list. This retrieves the object or set of objects related to the "calling" object through the relationship. For example,

```
SELECT s.stuId, s.takesClass
FROM students s
WHERE s.stuId = 'S999';
```

retrieves the set of classes that student S999 takes, as well as the `stuId`, S999.

The list of variables in the FROM line is similar to defining an alias in SQL. Usually we list the name of an extent, such as students or people, and an identifier for the name of the variable, such as s or p, as we saw above. The variable is actually an **iterator variable,** that ranges over the extent. There are alternate forms for declaring an iterator variable, such as:

```
FROM students s
FROM s in students
FROM students as s
```

In the WHERE clause, we are restricted to a Boolean expression having constants and variables defined in the FROM clause. We can use <, <=, >, >=, !=, AND, OR, and NOT in the expression. As in SQL, OQL does not eliminate duplicates, so the return is a bag (multiset) rather than a set. If we wish to eliminate duplicates, we can add the keyword DISTINCT as in SQL, producing a set. We can optionally add an ORDER BY clause, as in SQL.

- **Example 1.** Find the ID, name, and major of all undergraduates who have between 60 and 90 credits, in order by name.

OQL:
```
SELECT s.stuId, s.name, s.major
FROM students as s
WHERE s.credits >=60 AND s.credits<=90
ORDER BY s.name;
```

- **Example 2.** We can use a relationship to find records through references. For example, to find the names of all faculty in the biology department, we write the following query:

OQL:
```
SELECT f.name
FROM departments as d, d.hasFaculty as f
WHERE d.deptName = 'Biology';
```

The first part of the FROM clause says that d is an iterator variable that ranges over the objects in the `departments` extent, and the second part says that for each of the `department` objects, the set of faculty identified by the relationship `hasFaculty` for that department is to be identified with the iterator variable f. This is essentially setting up a nested loop that has d taking on each department in turn, and f taking on each faculty member in that department. The WHERE line restricts the results to the biology department, and the SELECT line displays just the faculty name.

- **Example 3.** We can also do subqueries in OQL. For example, the previous query can be broken up. We can first find the biology department object by writing:

```
OQL:
SELECT d
FROM d in departments
WHERE d.deptName = 'Biology';
```

We can use this as a subquery to provide the value for an iterator variable, b. Then we declare an iterator variable, f, for the relationship set `hasFaculty` for b. The entire query is expressed as follows.

```
OQL:
SELECT f.name
FROM (SELECT d
    FROM d in departments
    WHERE d.deptName = 'Biology') as b,
        b.hasFaculty as f;
```

- **Example 4.** It is possible to define structures for returned results right in a query. For example, we can find the name, rank, and salary of all faculty in the English department and put the results in a structure, in descending order by salary.

```
OQL:
SELECT struct(name: f.name, rank: f.rank, salary: f.salary)
FROM Faculty as f
WHERE f.belongsTo = 'English'
ORDER BY salary DESC;
```

- **Example 5.** Like SQL, OQL includes the operators COUNT, SUM, AVG, MAX, and MIN, but they are used differently. In OQL, the operator is applied to a collection rather than to a column. COUNT returns an integer, while the return from the other operators has the same type as the collection. The operators can be used on the results of a query. For example, to find the average salary of faculty members in the history department, we write the OQL query as follows:

```
OQL:
AVG(SELECT f.salary
    FROM fac as f
    WHERE f.belongsTo = 'History');
```

- **Example 6.** To find the number of undergraduates majoring in computer science, we can use the COUNT function.

```
OQL:
COUNT((SELECT u
    FROM students as u
    WHERE u.majorsIn = 'Computer Science');
```

To find all the class sections that have more than 30 students in them, we can put the COUNT in the WHERE line.

```
OQL:
SELECT   s
FROM     sections as s
WHERE COUNT(s.hasStudents >30);
```

- **Example 7.** Set operations of UNION, INTERSECTION, and EXCEPT (difference) are used as in SQL. For example, to find all students whose major or program is computer science, we write a union.

```
OQL:
(SELECT u
FROM undergraduates as u
WHERE u.major = 'Computer Science')
UNION
(SELECT g
FROM graduates as g
WHERE g.program = 'Computer Science');
```

We have chosen examples that are similar to SQL. OQL has many additional forms and capabilities that are not illustrated here.

8.6   Developing an OO Database

The process of creating an object-oriented database using an OODBMS such as Objectivity is meant to be a natural extension of application development in an object-oriented programming environment. As discussed previously, there are language bindings specified in the ODMG standard for C++, Java, and Smalltalk. The difference between using objects in programs written in these languages and database objects is the persistence of the database objects. Vendors who support the ODMG standard provide facilities to make program objects persist, and to provide access to database objects for manipulation within programs. A typical development process using, for example, C++ as the host language, is pictured in Figure 8.7. The database designer defines the schema using a data definition language such as ODL or C++ itself. The class definitions in the schema are essentially standard C++ ones that have been extended to provide persistence and to support relationships between objects, as well as inheritance. Persistence is provided by making all objects that are to be persistent inherit from a class provided by the OODBMS just for that purpose. For example, Objectivity provides the class ooOdb for C++. To make

FIGURE 8.7

Typical Object Oriented Database Development Process

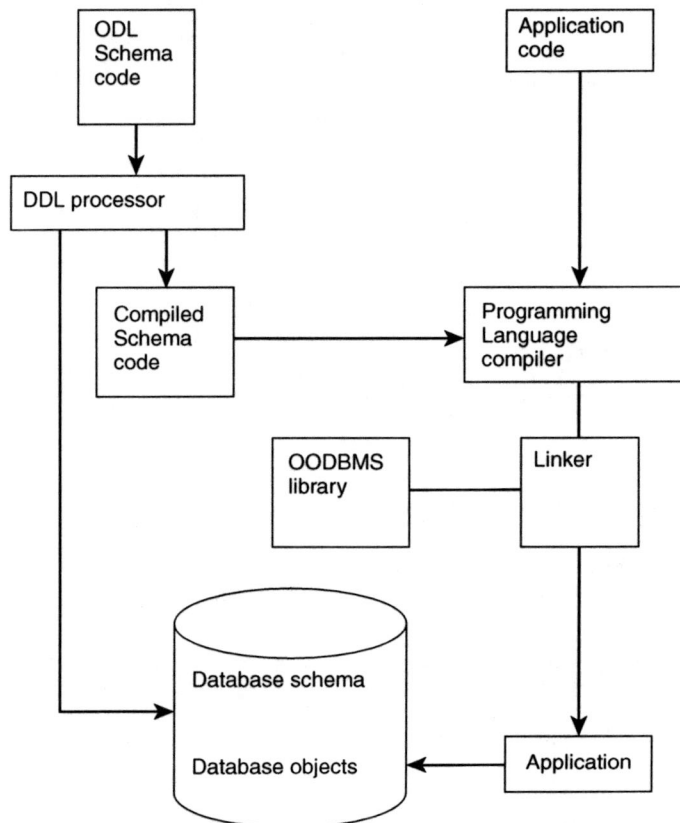

a class permanent, the programmer must specify that it extends ooOdb. For the `Person` class, we would write in C++,

```
class Person: public ooOjb
```

and then continue with the class definition. The persistence will be inherited by `Faculty`, `Student`, and their subclasses as well. If the schema is written in C++, any pointers used must be replaced by references, and the header file must be saved with the extension .ddl.

The DDL processor is then used to process the schema files. This creates the database schema on disk, and generates data model source files. Application code for populating objects in the database can be written in a separate C++ program. In C++, each class has at least one method, called a **constructor,** that generates new object instances. The objects to be stored in the database are created within the C++ application using constructors. Values of attributes of the object instances can be set either by the constructors using parameters or by methods such as `setName( )`. The program can also manipulate objects retrieved using OQL SELECT statements to update attributes or other properties. C++ classes can also have **destructors** whose function is to destroy objects that are no longer needed. These can be used to delete database objects. When the program is compiled, the C++ compiler uses the schema files created by the DDL processor. The result is then linked with the database run-time library to produce the executable code. The process is similar in Java and Smalltalk.

8.7   Chapter Summary

Object-oriented databases allow database designers and developers to express complex data structures, operations, and relationships more naturally than traditional relational databases. Object-oriented programming languages including C++, Java, and Smalltalk have been extended to allow **persistant** storage of the objects they create and manipulate. The fundamental concepts of the object-oriented paradigm involve an understanding of **objects, methods, encapsulation, classes,** and **inheritance.** In an object-oriented database, the class definitions correspond to class definitions for an object-oriented programming language. The set of object instances in a class is called the **extent** of the class. Each object instance is given a unique object identifier (**OID**) that is independent of any of the values of the object, and that is unchanging. OIDs are used to establish relationships between object instances. **Attributes** in a class can be **atomic**

types, enumerated types, **structured** types, or **collection** types, which include **set, bag, array, list,** and **dictionary** types.

UML diagrams are a useful method of representing classes and relationships, and fit well with the object-oriented data model. From a UML diagram, it is relatively easy to translate the design into class definitions that correspond directly to the items on the diagram, including the relationships between classes. A class is represented by a rectangle having three parts—the class name, the attributes, and the methods. Relationships are shown by lines, with multiplicity indicators of the form *min..max,* but placed on the opposite side to that used in EE-R diagrams. Relationships between classes, called **associations,** can be unidirectional or bidirectional, which is represented by defining an inverse for the relationship. They can specify a "one" relationship with a member of a class, or a "many," which is represented by specifying Set before the name of the related class. **Aggregation** is a special type of relationship that connects a whole to its parts. **Generalization** is indicated by lines connecting the subclasses to the superclass, with a triangle on the line into the superclass.

The Object Data Management Group (**ODMG**) has established standards for object-oriented databases, including standards for Object Definition Language (**ODL**) and Object Query Language (**OQL**). In ODL, we give class declarations, including the name of the class, any inheritance, extent, and keys, and descriptions of the attributes, relationships, and methods. OQL uses a syntax that is similar to SQL, but has greater flexibility for dealing with a variety of structures. Because of the ODMG standards for object-oriented language extensions, the process of developing a database using an OODBMS is closely linked to applications in those languages.

Exercises

8.1   Define the following terms:

   a. persistence

   b. encapsulation

   c. interface

   d. method

   e. extent

   f. class hierarchy

g. OID

h. association

i. aggregation

j. multiplicity indicator

k. reflexive association

l. mandatory specialization

m. inverse relationship

n. signature of a method

o. overloading

p. interface

q. constructor method

r. destructor method

s. iterator

8.2 Develop a UML class diagram for the dental group application described in Exercise 7.4.

8.3 Write an ODL schema that corresponds to the UML class diagram you developed in Exercise 8.2.

8.4 Develop a UML class diagram for the interior design firm application described in Exercise 7.6.

8.5 Write an ODL schema that corresponds to the UML class diagram you developed in Exercise 8.4.

8.6 a. Modify the UML diagram shown in Figure 8.5 by adding additional methods.

b. Modify the ODL schema shown in Figure 8.6 to include the new methods you added.

Lab Exercises

Creating UML Diagrams Using a Diagramming Tool If you have a diagramming tool such as Visio that supports UML diagrams, do exercises 8.2. and 8.4. using the diagramming tool.

SAMPLE PROJECT: CREATING A UML DIAGRAM FOR THE ART GALLERY AND CONVERTING THE DIAGRAM TO AN OBJECT-ORIENTED DATABASE SCHEMA

- Step 8.1. Create a UML diagram for The Art Gallery.

Figure 8.8 shows a sketch of a UML diagram for the sample project. To keep the diagram simple, class attributes and methods are not shown. We have created a `Person` class, with `Collector`, `Artist`, `Customer`, and `Salesperson` as subclasses. Because of the ease with which relationships can be defined, we have added relationships between `Artist` and `Collection`, and between `Artist` and `Show`, since either a collection or a show might feature a particular artist. We have chosen to make all relationships bidirectional, by providing inverses for each.

- Step 8.2. Convert the UML Diagram to an Object-Oriented Database Schema.

Figure 8.9 gives the ODL for a database that corresponds to the UML diagram. A few methods are included for the Person class. Methods should be

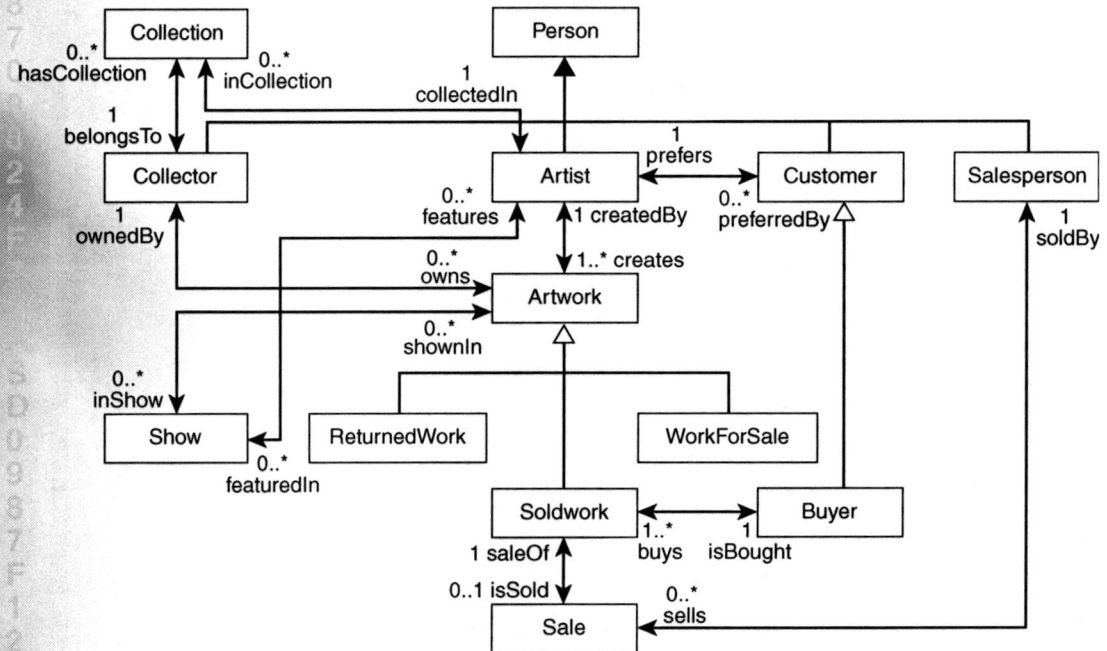

FIGURE 8.8
UML Diagram for The Art Gallery

added for the remaining classes. Note that we did not represent the union of `Collector` and `Artist` into `Owner`, since unions are difficult to represent. Instead, we added a method to the `Artwork` class, called `OwnerIsArtist`, that will return a Boolean value. It tests whether the reference to `Collector` is null and if so, returns true, indicating that the artist owns the work. However, if we wished to represent the union, we could have used the same solution as we used for the object-relational case.

STUDENT PROJECTS: DRAWING A UML DIAGRAM AND DESIGNING AN OBJECT-ORIENTED DATABASE MODEL

- **8.1.** Create a UML diagram for the Student Project
- **8.2.** Convert the UML diagram into an Object-Oriented database model and write the ODL for the schema.

```
class Person(
extent people
key pId)
{   attribute pId int;
    attribute Struct NameType(string first, string last) name;
    attribute Struct AddressType(string street, sting city, string state, string zip) address;
    attribute Struct PhoneType (string areaCode, string telephoneNumber) phone;
    int getPId( );
    void setPId(int newId);
    string getName( );
    void setName(string newName);
    string getAddress( );
    void setAddress(AddressType newAddress);
    string getPhone( );
    void setPhone(PhoneType newPhone);

};
                                                        (Continued)
```

FIGURE 8.9
ODL for The Art Gallery Schema

```
class Artist extends Person
{    attribute Struct DateType(int day, int month, int year) interviewDate;
     attribute NameType interviewerName;
     attribute real(10,2) salesLastYear;
     attribute real(10,2) salesYearToDate;
     attribute string socialSecurityNumber;
     attribute string usualMedium;
     attribute string usualStyle;
     attribute string usualType;
     DateType getinterviewDate();
     void setinterviewDate(DateType newartistinterviewDate);
     NameType getinterviewerName();
     void setinterviewerName(NameType newartistinterviewerName);
     real getsalesLastYear();
     void setsalesLastYear(real artistlastyearsalesAmount);
     real get salesYearToDate();
     void setsalesYearToDate(real artistsalesYTD);
     void updatesalesYearToDate(real artistNewSalesAmount);
     string getsocialSecurityNumber();
     void setsocialSecurityNumber(string artistnewSSN);
     string getusualMedium();
     void setusualMedium(string artistusualMedium);
     string getusualStyle();
     void setusualStyle(string artistusualStyle);
     string getusualType();
     void setusualType(string artistusualType);
     relationship Set<Artwork> creates Inverse Artwork::createdBy;
     relationship Set<Customer> preferredBy Inverse Customer::prefers;
     relationship Set<Show> featuredIn Inverse Show::features;
     relationship Set<Collection> inCollection Inverse Collection::collectedIn;
};

class Collector extends Person
{    attribute string socialSecurityNumber;
     attribute Artist::DateType interviewDate;
```

FIGURE 8.9—Continued

```
        attribute NameType interviewerName;
        attribute real(10,2) salesLastYear;
        attribute real(10,2) salesYearToDate;
        string getsocialSecurityNumber();
        void setsocialSecurityNumber(string collectornewSSN);
        Artist::DateType getinterviewDate();
        void setinterviewDate(Artist::DateType newcollectorinterviewDate);
        NameType getinterviewerName();
        void setinterviewerName(NameType newcollectorinterviewerName);
        real getsalesLastYear();
        void setsalesLastYear(real collectorsalesLastYearAmount);
        real getsalesYearToDate();
        void setsalesYearToDate(real collectorsalesYTDAmount);
        void updatesalesYearToDate(real collectornewSalesAmount);
        relationship Set<Collection> hasCollection Inverse Collection::belongsTo;
        relationship Set<Artwork> owns Inverse Artwork::ownedBy;
};

class Collection
{    attribute string collectionMedium;
     attribute string collectionStyle;
     attribute string collectionType;
     string getcollectionMedium();
     void setcollectionMedium(string medium);
     string getcollectionStyle();
     void setcollectionStyle(string style);
     string getcollectionType();
     void setcollectionType(string type);
     relationship Collector belongsTo Inverse Collector::hasCollection;
     relationship Artist collectedIn Inverse Artist::inCollection;
};

class Artwork
{    attribute string artworkId;
     attribute string workTitle;
     attribute real(6,2) askingPrice;
```

FIGURE 8.9—Continued

```
        attribute Artist::DateType dateListed;
        attribute Artist::DateType dateShown;
        attribute string status;
        attribute string workMedium;
        attribute string workSize;
        attribute string workStyle;
        attribute string workType;
        attribute int workYearCompleted;
        string getartworkId();
        void setartworkId(string newartworkId);
        string getartworkTitle();
        void setartworkTitle(string newartworkTitle);
        real getaskingPrice();
        void setaskingPrice(real newaskingPrice);
        Artist::DateType getdateListed();
        void setdateListed(Artist::DateType newdateListed);
        Artist::DateType getdateShown();
        void setdateShown(Artist::DateType newdateShown);
        string getstatus();
        void setstatus(string newstatus);
        string getworkMedium();
        void setstworkMedium(string newmedium);
        string getworkSize();
        void setstworkSize(string newsize);
        string getworkStyle();
        void setstworkStyle(string newStyle);
        string getworkType();
        void setstworkType(string newType);
        int getworkYearCompleted();
        void setworkYearCompleted(int newworkYearCompleted);
        boolean artistIsOwner( )//method to determine if the work is owned by the artist;
        relationship Artist createdBy Inverse Artist::creates;
        relationship Set<Show> inShow Inverse Show::shownIn;
        relationship Collector ownedBy Inverse Collector::owns;
};
```

FIGURE 8.9—Continued

```
class SoldWork extends Artwork
{    attribute Artist::DateType dateSold;
     Artist::DateType getdateSold();
     void setdateSold(DateType newdateSold);
     relationship Sale isSold Inverse Sale::saleOf;
     relationship Buyer isBought Inverse Buyer::buys;
};

class ReturnedWork extends Artwork
{    attribute Artist::DateType dateReturned;
     Artist::DateType getdateReturned();
     void setdateReturned(Artist::DateType newdateReturned);
};

class WorkForSale extends Artwork
{    attribute string location;
     string getlocation();
     void setlocation(string newlocation);
};

class Customer extends Person
{    attribute Artist::DateType dateFilledIn;
     attribute string preferredMedium;
     attribute string preferredStyle;
     attribute string preferredType;
     Artist::DateType getdateFilledIn();
     void setdateFilledIn(Artist::DateType newdateFilledIn);
     string getpreferredMedium();
     void setpreferredMedium(string newpreferredMedium);
     string getpreferredStyle();
     void setpreferredStyle(string newpreferredStyle);
     string getpreferredType();
     void setpreferredType(string newpreferredType);
     relationship Artist prefers Inverse Artist::preferredBy;
};
```

FIGURE 8.9—Continued

```
class Buyer extends Customer
{    attribute real(8,2) purchasesLastYear
     attribute real(8,2) purchasesYearToDate;
     real getpurchasesLastYear();
     void setpurchasesLastYear(real purchasesLastYearAmount);
     real getpurchasesYearToDate();
     void setpurchasesYearToDate(real purchasesYearToDateAmount);
     void updatepurchasesYearToDate(real amountNewPurchases);
     relationship SoldWork buys Inverse SoldWork::isBought;
};

class Show
{    attribute string showTitle;
     attribute string showClosingDate;
     attribute string showTheme;
     attribute string showOpeningDate;
     string getshowTitle();
     void setshowTitle(string newTitle);
     string getshowclosingDate();
     void setshowclosingDate(string newTitle);
     string getshowTheme();
     void setshowTheme(string newTitle);
     string getshowopeningDate();
     void setshowopeningDate(string newTitle);
     relationship Artist features Inverse Artist::featuredIn;
     relationship Set<Artwork> shownIn Inverse Artwork::inShow;
};

class Sale
{    attribute string invoiceNumber;
     attribute real(8,2) amountRemittedToOwner;
     attribute Artist::DateType saleDate;
     attribute real(8,2) salePrice;
     attribute real(6,2) saleTax;
     string getinvoiceNumber();
```

FIGURE 8.9—Continued

```
        void setinvoiceNumber(string newinvoiceNumber);
        real get amountremittedToOwner();
        void setamountremittedToOwner(real newamountRemitted);
        Artist::DateType getsaleDate();
        void setsaleDate(Artist::DateType newsaleDate);
        real getsalePrice();
        void setsalePrice(real newsalePrice);
        real getsaleTax();
        void setsaleTax(real newtaxAmount);
        relationship SoldWork saleOf Inverse SoldWork::isSold;
        relationship Salesperson soldBy Inverse Salesperson::sells;
};

class Salesperson extends Person
{   attribute string socialSecurityNumber;
    string getsocialSecurityNumber();
    void setsocialSecurityNumber(string newSSN);
    relationship Set<Sale> sells Inverse Sale::soldBy;
};
```

FIGURE 8.9—Continued

9 CHAPTER

Introduction to Database Security

Chapter Objectives

In this chapter you will learn the following:

- The meaning of database security

- The relationship between privacy and security

- Examples of accidental or deliberate threats to security

- Some physical security measures

- The meaning of user authentication

- The meaning of authorization

- How access control can be represented

- How the view functions as a security device

- The purpose of the security log and audit trail

- How and why data encryption is performed
- How security is enforced in some systems

9.1   Issues in Database Security

Database security means protecting the database from unauthorized access, modification, or destruction. Since the database represents an essential corporate resource, security is an important goal. In addition to the need to preserve and protect data for the smooth functioning of the organization, database designers have a responsibility to protect the privacy of individuals about whom data is kept. **Privacy** is the right of individuals to have some control over information about themselves. Many countries have laws designed to protect privacy, and every organization that collects and stores information about individuals is legally obliged to adopt policies that conform to local privacy legislation. The database design should reflect the organization's commitment to protection of individual privacy rights by including only those items that the organization has a right to know. In addition, privacy must be guarded by protecting stored information that is of a sensitive nature. Security threats can occur either **accidentally** or **deliberately.**

9.1.1   Accidental Security Threats

Some examples of accidental security violations are the following.

- The user may unintentionally request an object or an operation for which he should not be authorized, and the request could be granted because of an oversight in authorization procedures or because of an error in the database management system or operating system.

- A person may accidentally be sent a message that should be directed to another user, resulting in unauthorized disclosure of database contents.

- A communications system error might connect a user to a session that belongs to another user with different access privileges.

- The operating system might accidentally overwrite files and destroy part of the database, fetch the wrong files, and then inadvertently send them to the user, or might fail to erase files that should be destroyed.

9.1.2 Deliberate Security Threats

Deliberate security violations occur when a user intentionally gains unauthorized access and/or performs unauthorized operations on the database. A disgruntled employee who is familiar with the organization's computer system poses a tremendous threat to security. Industrial spies seeking information for competitors also threaten security. There are many ways deliberate security breaches can be accomplished, including:

- Wiretapping of communication lines to intercept messages to and from the database

- Electronic eavesdropping, to pick up signals from workstations, printers, or other devices within a building

- Reading display screens and reading or copying printouts carelessly left unsupervised by authorized users

- Impersonating an authorized user, or a user with greater access, by using his or her log-in and password

- Writing systems programs with illegal code to bypass the database management system and its authorization mechanism, and to access database data directly through the operating system

- Writing applications programs with code that performs unauthorized operations

- Deriving information about hidden data by clever querying of the database

- Removing physical storage devices from the computer facility

- Making physical copies of stored files without going through the database management system, thereby bypassing its security mechanisms

- Bribing, blackmailing, or otherwise influencing authorized users in order to use them as agents in obtaining information or damaging the database

9.2 Physical Security and User Authentication

Database security is best implemented as only one part of a broader security control plan. The plan should begin with physical security measures for the building itself, with special precautions for the computer facilities. Designing a physically secure building is clearly outside the domain of the database designer. However, the DBA or data administrator should be able to suggest measures that would control access to database facilities. Often these begin at the front door, where all employees must be identified visually by guards, or by using badges, handprints, sign-ins, or other mechanisms. Additional identification should be required to enter the computer facilities. Physical security measures should be extended to cover any location where offline data such as backups are stored as well.

Because physical security of individual workstations may be difficult to implement, security control of workstations requires **authentication** of users. Authentication means verifying the identify of the user—checking to ensure that the actual user is who he or she claims to be. It is usually implemented at the operating system level. When the user signs on, he or she enters a user ID, which is checked for validity. The system has a user profile for that ID, giving information about the user. The profile normally includes a password, which is supposed to be known only to the user. Passwords should be kept secret and changed frequently. A simple security precaution is for the system to require that passwords be changed monthly. The system should obviously never display passwords at log-in, and the stored profiles should be kept secure, possibly in encrypted form. Although passwords are the most widely used authentication method, they are not very secure, since users sometimes write them down, choose words that are easy to guess, or share them with others. In some organizations, users must insert badges or keys when they log on. In others, voice, fingerprints, retina scans, or other physical characteristics of the user are examined. Some use an authentication procedure rather than a single password. A procedure might consist of answering a series of questions and would take longer and be more difficult to reproduce than a password. Although authentication may be done only at the operating system level, it is possible to require it again at the database level. At the very least, the user should be required to produce an additional password to access the database.

9.3   Authorization

In addition to authentication, most database management systems designed for multiple users have their own security subsystems. These subsystems provide for **user authorization,** a method by which users are assigned rights to use database objects. Most multiple-user systems have an **authorization language** that is part of the data sublanguage. For example, SQL provides standard authorization commands to grant privileges to users, as discussed in Section 9.8. The DBA uses the authorization language to specify user's rights by means of **authorization rules,** statements that specify which users have access to what information, and what operations they are permitted to use on what data. The authorization mechanism is designed to protect the database by preventing individuals from unauthorized reading, updating, or destruction of database contents. These restrictions are added to the security mechanisms provided by the operating system. However, in a surprisingly large number of cases, database security subsystems are minimal or are not fully utilized. Recognizing that data is a valuable corporate resource, the designer should include available security mechanisms as an important factor in evaluating alternative database management systems, and should develop effective security policies utilizing whatever controls are available with the system chosen.

9.4   Access Control

Access control is the means by which authorizations are implemented. Access control means making sure that data or other resources are accessed only in authorized ways. In planning access, the DBA might use an **access control matrix** for the database, as shown in Figure 9.1. The column headings represent database objects, which may be the names of tables, views, data items, objects, modules, or other categories, depending on the database model and management system used. The row labels represent individuals, roles, groups of users, or applications. The cell entries

OBJECT

FIGURE 9.1

Access Control Matrix

SUBJECT	Student table	StuView1	WrapUp Procedure	Faculty table	Enroll table	. . .
User U101	read, update	read	execute	read		. . .
User U102		read				. . .
Role Advisor	read	read			read, insert, update, delete	. . .
. . .	. . .	. . .	. . .	. . .	. . .	. . .

specify the type of access permitted. Values of entries will also depend on the particular system used, but the choices usually include READ, INSERT, UPDATE, DELETE, and their combinations. Once the access control matrix is complete, the DBA must use the appropriate authorization language to implement it. The DBA, of course, is permitted to create and change the structure of the database, and to use the authorization language to grant data access to others or to revoke access. Some systems allow the DBA to delegate some of this authorization power as well. In that case, certain users might be permitted to modify existing database structures or to create new structures, and to update data occurrences. In a multiuser environment, such changes can have consequences for other users. Since the DBA is often the only one who has a comprehensive view of all user's data needs, it is often unwise to grant this authorization. The DBA can sometimes grant users the power to authorize other users to perform operations on the database. However, having many such "authorizers" can be extremely dangerous. Since authorizers can create other authorizers, the situation can get out of hand very quickly, making it difficult for the DBA to revoke authorizations.

9.5   Using Views for Access Control

The view is a widely used method for implementing access control. The view mechanism has a twofold purpose. It is a facility for the user, simplifying and customizing the external model through which the user deals with the database, freeing the user from the complexities of the underlying model. It is also a security device, hiding structures and data that the user

FIGURE 9.2(a)
Value-dependent View

```
CREATE VIEW CSCMAJ AS
    SELECT stuId, lastName, firstName, credits
    FROM Student
    WHERE major = 'CSC';
```

FIGURE 9.2(b)
Value-independent View

```
CREATE VIEW StuView1 AS
    SELECT stuId, lastName, firstName, major
    FROM Student;
```

should not see. In the relational model, a user's external model can consist entirely of views, or some combination of base tables and relational views. A relational view is derived from base tables by using a SELECT operation to pick out columns or rows, or by using other operations to obtain calculated or materialized data. By specifying restrictions in the WHERE line of the SELECT statement used to create views, the view can be made **value-dependent.** Figure 9.2 (a) gives an example of a view created from the `Student` table by including only data about students whose major is CSC. **Value-independent** views are created by specifying columns of base tables and omitting the WHERE line of the SELECT statement. Figure 9.2 (b) gives an example of a view of the `Student` table showing only columns `stuId`, `stuName`, and `major`.

9.6   Security Logs and Audit Trails

Another important security tool is the **security log,** which is a journal that keeps a record of all attempted security violations. The violation can be simply recorded in the log, or it can trigger an immediate message to the operator or to the DBA. Knowing about the existence of the log can be a deterrent in itself. If the DBA suspects that data is being compromised without triggering security log entries, it is possible to set up an **audit trail.** Such an auditing system records all access to the database, keeping information about the user who requested the access, the operation performed, the workstation used, the exact time of occurrence, the data item, its old value, and its new value, if any. The audit trail can therefore uncover the sources of suspicious operations on the database, even if they are performed by authorized users, such as disgruntled employees. **Trig-**

```
CREATE OR REPLACE TRIGGER EnrollAuditTrail
    BEFORE UPDATE OF grade ON Enroll
    FOR EACH ROW
    BEGIN
        INSERT INTO EnrollAudit
            VALUES(SYSDATE, USER, :OLD.stuld, :OLD.courseNo, :OLD.grade, :NEW.grade);
    END;
```

FIGURE 9.3
Audit Trail Using Trigger

gers can also be used to set up an audit trail for a table, recording all changes, the time they were made, and the identity of the user who made them. For example, in Oracle, if we wish to monitor changes to grades in the `Enroll` table, we would first set up a table to hold the audit records. The schema for that table might be:

EnrollAudit(<u>dateOfUpdate, userId</u>, oldStuid, oldCourseNo, oldGrade, newGrade)

The trigger should insert a record in the `EnrollAudit` table when a user tries to update a grade in the `Enroll` table. The code to do this is shown in Figure 9.3. It uses SYSDATE and USER, which are referred to as pseudocolumns in Oracle. Both act as functions that return appropriate values. SYSDATE returns the current date, while USER returns the ID of the current user.

9.7 Encryption

To counter the possibility of having files accessed directly through the operating system or having files stolen, data can be stored in the database in encrypted form. Only the database management system (DBMS) can unscramble the data, so that anyone who obtains data by any other means will receive jumbled data. When authorized users access the information properly, the DBMS retrieves the data and decodes it automatically. Encryption should also be used whenever data is communicated to other sites, so that wiretappers will also receive scrambled data. Encryption requires a **cipher system,** which consists of the following components:

- An **encrypting algorithm,** which takes the normal text (**plaintext**), as input, performs some operations on it, and produces the encrypted text (**ciphertext**), as output

- An **encryption key,** which is part of the input for the encrypting algorithm, and is chosen from a very large set of possible keys

- A **decrypting algorithm,** which operates on the ciphertext as input and produces the plaintext as output

- A **decryption key,** which is part of the input for the decrypting algorithm, and is chosen from a very large set of possible keys.

One widely used data encryption scheme is the **Data Encryption Standard** (DES) standard, devised by the National Bureau of Standards and adopted in 1977. In the DES scheme, the algorithm itself is public, while the key is private. It uses **symmetric** encryption, in which the decryption key is the same as the encryption key, and the decrypting algorithm is the inverse of the encrypting algorithm. Figure 9.4 gives an overview of the DES process. Because the algorithm is a standard, it is possible to put a hardware implementation of it on a single chip, so that encryption and decryption are very

FIGURE 9.4
Overview of DES Encryption

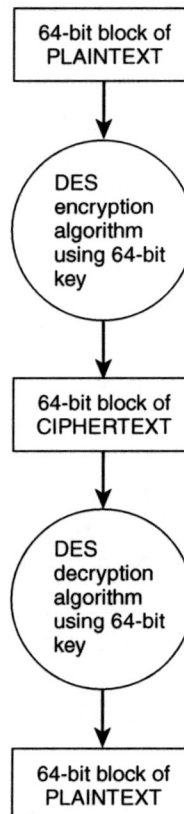

fast and cheap compared to a software implementation of the algorithm. The DES algorithm uses a 56-bit key on 64-bit blocks of plaintext, producing 64-bit blocks of ciphertext. When data is encoded, it is split up into 64-bit blocks. Within each block, characters are substituted and rearranged according to the value of the key. The decoding algorithm uses the same key to put back the original characters and to restore them to their original positions in each block. Two major challenges with the DES system involve key security and the ease of cracking the code. The key must be kept secure or the encryption is worthless, since anyone with the key has access to the data. Therefore, the security depends on the secrecy of the key, but all authorized users must be told the key. The more people who know the key, the more likely it is that the key will be disclosed to unauthorized users. Also, it is often necessary to distribute the key to receivers of encrypted messages. If telecommunications lines are used, transmitting the key in plaintext would allow wiretappers easy access to encrypted messages. Often, more secure lines are used for key distribution, or the key is distributed by mail or messenger. Although the DES standard is still widely used, it is not a very secure scheme, since it can be cracked in a reasonable amount of time. In 2000, an improved version called the **Advanced Encryption Standard** (AES) was developed and adopted as the new standard. It uses a symmetric scheme that is more sophisticated than the DES scheme, and it supports three possible key sizes of 128 bits, 192 bits, or 256 bits, depending on the level of security needed. Because of the larger key sizes, cracking the scheme is more challenging.

A second approach is **public-key encryption,** which uses pairs of prime numbers. Figure 9.5 provides an overview of public-key encryption. For each user, a pair of large prime numbers, (p, q) is chosen as the user's **private** key, and the product of the pair, p*q, becomes the **public** key of that user. Public keys are shared freely, so that anyone wishing to send a message to a user can find his or her public key easily. The public key is then used as input to an encryption algorithm, which produces the ciphertext for that user. When the user receives an encrypted message, he or she must produce the prime factors of the public key to decode it. Since there is no quick or easy method of finding the prime factors of a large number, it is extremely difficult for an intruder to find these factors. However, an intruder who is determined to break the key can do so, provided he or she is willing to commit substantial resources to the task. This method is only as secure as the private key, so users must be given their private keys in some secure fashion, and must protect the private keys against disclosure.

FIGURE 9.5
Overview of Public Key Encryption

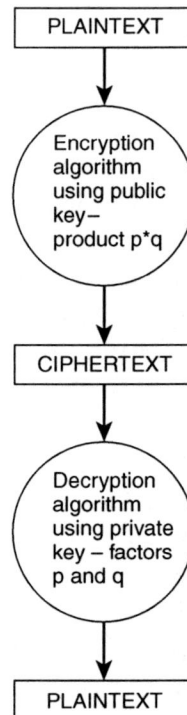

```
        ┌──────────────┐
        │  PLAINTEXT   │
        └──────────────┘
               │
               ▼
          ( Encryption
            algorithm
            using public
            key –
            product p*q )
               │
               ▼
        ┌──────────────┐
        │  CIPHERTEXT  │
        └──────────────┘
               │
               ▼
          ( Decryption
            algorithm
            using private
            key – factors
            p and q )
               │
               ▼
        ┌──────────────┐
        │  PLAINTEXT   │
        └──────────────┘
```

One well-known method of public key encryption is **RSA,** named for its developers Rivest, Shamir, and Adleman.

9.8   SQL Authorization Language

SQL has an authorization sublanguage that includes statements to grant privileges to, and to revoke privileges from users. A **privilege** is an action such as reading, updating, or deleting that a user is permitted to perform on database objects. In standard SQL, the creator of a schema is given all privileges on all the objects (tables, views, roles, modules) in it, and can pass those privileges on to others. Ordinarily, only the creator of the schema can modify the schema itself (adding tables, columns, and so on). The statement for granting privileges has the following form:

```
GRANT {ALL PRIVILEGES │ privilege-list}
ON {table-name│view-name}
TO {PUBLIC │ user-list│role-list} [WITH GRANT OPTION];
```

The possible privileges for base tables are SELECT, DELETE, INSERT, UPDATE, or REFERENCES*(col-name).* If a table is named in the ON clause, then ALL PRIVILEGES includes all of these operations. If a view is named in the ON clause, and the view was constructed in such a way that it is updatable, the SELECT, DELETE, INSERT and UPDATE privileges can be granted on that view. For views that are not updatable, only the SELECT can be granted. The UPDATE privilege can be made more restrictive by specifying a column list in parentheses after the word UPDATE, restricting the user to updating only certain columns, as in:

```
GRANT UPDATE ON Student(major) TO U101;
```

The REFERENCES privilege is applied to columns that may be used as foreign keys. This privilege allows the user to refer to those columns in creating foreign key integrity constraints. For example, to allow a user who can update the `Enroll` table to be able to reference `stuId` in the `Student` table in order to match its values for the `Enroll` table, we might write:

```
GRANT REFERENCES (stuId) ON Student TO U101;
```

The user list in the TO clause can include a single user or several users. SQL:1999 includes the capability to create user roles. A **role** can be thought of as a set of operations that should be performed by an individual or a group of individuals as part of a job. For example, in a university, advisors might need to be able to read student transcripts of selected students, so there may be an `Advisor` role to permit that. Depending on the policies of the university, the `Advisor` role might also include the privilege of inserting enrollment records for students at registration time. Students are permitted to perform SELECT but not UPDATE operations on their personal data, so there has to be a `Student` role that permits such access. Once the DBA has identified a role, a set of privileges is granted for the role, and then user accounts can be assigned the role. Some user accounts have several roles. If PUBLIC is specified in the TO clause, all users are given the privileges specified in the GRANT statement. The optional WITH GRANT OPTION clause gives the newly authorized user(s) permission to pass the same privileges to others. For example, we could write:

```
GRANT SELECT, INSERT, UPDATE ON Student TO U101, U102, U103 WITH GRANT OPTION;
```

Users U101, U102, and U103 would then be permitted to write SQL SELECT, INSERT and UPDATE statements for the `Student` table, and to pass that permission on to other users. Because of the ability of users with the grant option to authorize other users, the system must keep track of authorizations using a **grant diagram,** also called an **authorization graph.**

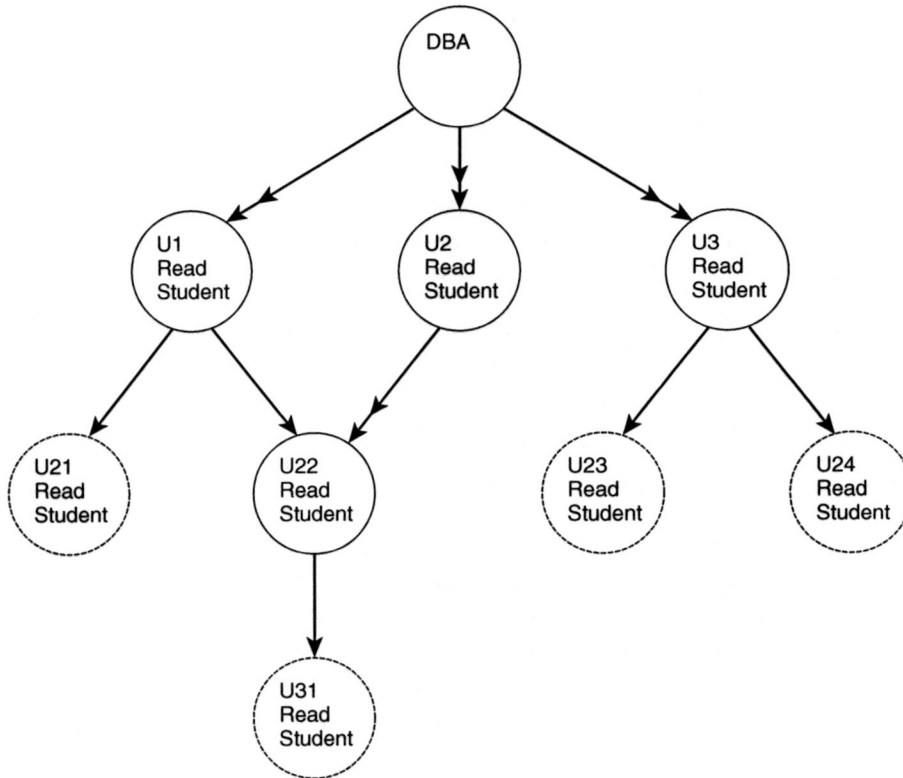

FIGURE 9.6
An Authorization Graph

Figure 9.6 shows an authorization graph. Here, the DBA, whom we assume is the creator of the schema, gave a specific privilege (for example, to read the `Student` table) WITH GRANT OPTION to users U1, U2, and U3. We will use a double arrowhead to mean granting with grant option, and a single arrowhead to mean without it. A solid outline for a node will mean that the node has received the grant option, and a dashed outline will mean it has not. U1 passed along the privilege to U21 and U22, both without the grant option. U2 also passed the privilege to U22, this time with the grant option, and U22 passed the privilege to U31, without the grant option. U3 authorized U23 and U24, both without the grant option. Note that if we give a different privilege to one of these users, we will need a new node to represent the new privilege. Each node on the graph represents a combination of a privilege and a user.

To create a role, we write a statement such as:

```
CREATE ROLE AdvisorRole;
CREATE ROLE FacultyRole;
```

We then grant privileges to the role just as we would to individuals, by writing statements such as:

```
GRANT SELECT ON Student TO AdvisorRole;
GRANT UPDATE ON Enroll TO AdvisorRole;
GRANT SELECT ON Enroll TO FacultyRole;
```

To assign a role to a user, we write a statement such as:

```
GRANT AdvisorRole TO U999;
```

We can even assign a role to another role by writing, for example:

```
GRANT FacultyRole TO AdvisorRole;
```

This provides a means of inheriting privileges through roles.

The SQL statement to remove privileges has this form:

```
REVOKE {ALL PRIVILEGES | privilege-list}
ON object-list
FROM {PUBLIC | user-list | role-list};
[CASCADE | RESTRICT];
```

For example, for U101 to whom we previously granted SELECT, INSERT, and UPDATE on Student with the grant option, we could remove some privileges by writing this:

```
REVOKE INSERT ON Student FROM U101;
```

This revokes U101's ability both to insert Student records and to authorize others to insert Student records. We can revoke just the grant option, without revoking the insert, by writing this:

```
REVOKE GRANT OPTION FOR INSERT ON Student FROM U101;
```

If an individual has the grant option for a certain privilege and the privilege or the grant option on it is later revoked, all users who have received the privilege from that individual have their privilege revoked as well. In this way, revocations **cascade,** or trigger other revocations. If a user obtained the same privilege from two authorizers, one of whom has authorization revoked, the user still retains the privilege from the other authorizer. Thus, if the DBA revoked the authorization of user U1 in

Figure 9.6, U21 would lose all privileges, but U22 would retain whatever privileges were received from U2. Since U22 has the grant option, user U21 could regain privileges from U22. In this way, unscrupulous users could conspire to retain privileges despite attempts by the DBA to revoke them. For this reason, the DBA should be very careful about passing the grant option to others. If the **RESTRICT** option is specified, the system checks to see if there are any cascading revocations, and returns an error if they exist, without executing the revoke statement. CASCADE is the default. When a privilege is revoked, the authorization graph is modified by removing the node(s) that lose their privileges.

9.9   Security in Oracle

Oracle provides robust security that goes far beyond the SQL authorization language commands. There are many different ways to set up and manage the security of an Oracle database besides the methods discussed here. The DBA normally handles the process of granting privileges to users. One way to do this is from SQL*Plus. The DBA writes a CREATE USER command which has this form:

CREATE USER *username* IDENTIFIED BY *password*;

For example:

```
CREATE USER U999 IDENTIFIED BY SESAME;
```

However, this command does not give any privileges to the user, so U999 will not be able to establish a session, unless the DBA also writes the following:

```
GRANT CREATE SESSION TO U999;
```

To test the account, the DBA can connect using the new name by writing, for example:

CONNECT U999/SESAME@*connectstring*;

The @*connectstring*, which is needed only if Oracle has been installed on a network, is known to the DBA. It is customary to require the user to change his or her password at the first actual log-in. This is done by the DBA using this command:

```
ALTER USER username
PASSWORD EXPIRE;
```

When the user tries to connect, he or she will be given a message saying the password has expired and prompting for a new one before being connected. Once connected, the user can also change his or her own password at any time by writing the following in SQL*Plus:

```
ALTER USER username
IDENTIFIED BY newpassword;
```

Although the user will be connected, he or she will not be able to access any data, since the only privilege given is the one to create a session. To actually use Oracle's facilities, the user needs to be given additional privileges, which can be either system privileges or object privileges.

9.9.1 Object Privileges

In Oracle an **object privilege** is the right to perform an action using DML commands on a table, view, procedure, function, sequence, or package. The creator of a schema automatically has all object privileges on all objects in the schema, and can grant the same object privileges to other users. For tables, the privileges include the SELECT, INSERT, UPDATE, DELETE, and REFERENCES as described in Section 9.8, but also ALTER (the right to use the ALTER TABLE command) and INDEX (the right to use the CREATE INDEX command). For updatable views, privileges are SELECT, INSERT, UPDATE, and DELETE. The syntax for these is the same as the standard SQL authorization language syntax shown in Section 9.8. For example, the DBA might give U999 wide privileges on the Student table by writing as follows:

```
GRANT ALL PRIVILEGES ON Student TO U999 WITH GRANT OPTION;
```

If there is a stored procedure called WrapUp, the DBA can give U999 permission to run the procedure by writing this command:

```
GRANT EXECUTE ON WrapUp TO U999;
```

9.9.2 System Privileges

In Oracle, **system privileges** include the right to perform actions using DDL commands on database data, schemas, tablespaces, or other Oracle resources, as well as the right to create user accounts. There are about 140 different system privileges possible. A list of them can be seen by writing the following SQL command:

```
SELECT name
FROM SYSTEM_PRIVILEGE_MAP;
```

System privileges can be given through SQL*Plus using a GRANT command of this form:

```
GRANT systemprivilege
TO username
[WITH ADMIN OPTION];
```

For example, we could allow U999 to create tables by writing:

```
GRANT CREATE TABLE TO U999 WITH ADMIN OPTION;
```

Additionally, privileges that are object privileges on single tables can be extended to become system privileges that extend to any table by using the keyword ANY, as in:

```
GRANT SELECT ANY TABLE TO U999;
```

The WITH ADMIN OPTION clause allows the user to pass the privilege on to others.

9.9.3   Roles

As in the SQL:1999 standard, Oracle allows privileges to be given to a role as well as to individuals or groups of users. A role consists of a group of privileges. Any number of roles can be granted to a user. Roles can also be granted to other roles, allowing inheritance of privileges. Roles can be created using the authorization language commands discussed in Section 9.8.

9.9.4   Using the Oracle Security Manager

The Oracle Enterprise Manager contains a module called the Security Manager, a facility that offers options for granting and revoking privileges. The DBA has to log in to access the Security Manager. From there, the DBA can choose *User* from the menu, then *Create* from the User submenu. The DBA fills in the new user name, chooses a profile, (which may be *default*), and chooses a method of authentication, which is usually *password*. He or she then enters a temporary password, and can choose to have the password expire immediately. This will cause the new user to be prompted for a new password the first time he or she uses the account. It is also possible to specify that authentication is to be done by the operating system instead of by password, by choosing *External* as the authentication mechanism. Having created one or more user accounts, the DBA is then able to use the Security Manager menus to grant both system and object privileges and to define roles.

9.9.5 Access Control for a Single Database

One way to obtain DBA privileges on a single database is to create a new Oracle 9i database. An easy way to do this is by using Oracle's Database Configuration Assistant, which is located in a directory created when Oracle is installed. This facility is a wizard that prompts users through the process of creating an empty database. The user is prompted to provide a name for the database and to choose other options. The system will then create a database with the name provided, set up SYS and SYSTEM accounts for the user, and ask the user for passwords for these accounts. The user then has all privileges on the new database, including the ability to create new users for it, and to grant authorizations as discussed earlier. To use the database through SQL*Plus, the user starts SQL*Plus and is immediately presented with a log-on window. The user can sign in using either SYS or SYSTEM, along with the appropriate password created earlier. The "host string," which is the name chosen for the database, must also be entered. Once in SQL*Plus, the user can then create the schema for the database using SQL DDL. The user who creates a database is automatically given a SYSTEM account, which is essentially a user account that has all privileges for that database. He or she can create accounts for other people too, by using either the SQL*Plus method discussed previously, or by using the Security Manager.

9.10 Statistical Database Security

Statistical databases are designed to provide data to support statistical analysis on populations. The data itself may contain facts about individuals, but the data is not meant to be retrieved on an individual basis. Users are granted permission to access statistical information such as totals, counts, or averages, but not information about individuals. For example, if a user is permitted statistical access to an employee database, he or she is able to write queries such as:

```
SELECT SUM(Salary)
FROM Employee
WHERE Dept = 10;
```

but not:

```
SELECT Salary
FROM Employee
WHERE empId = 'E101';
```

Special precautions must be taken when users are permitted access to statistical data, to ensure that they are not able to deduce data about individuals. For the preceding example, if there are no restrictions in place except that all queries must involve count, sum, or average, a user who wishes to find the employee of E101 can do so by adding conditions to the WHERE line to narrow the population down to that one individual, as in:

```
SELECT SUM (Salary)
FROM EMPLOYEE
WHERE Dept = 10 AND jobTitle = 'Programmer' AND dateHired > '01-Jan-2004';
```

The system can be modified to refuse to answer any query for which only one record satisfies the predicate. However, this restriction is easily overcome, since the user can ask for total salaries for the department and then ask for the total salary without that of E101. Neither of these queries is limited to one record, but the user can easily deduce the salary of employee E101 from them. To prevent users from deducing information about individuals, the system can restrict queries by requiring that the number of records satisfying the predicate must be above some threshold and that the number of records satisfying a pair of queries simultaneously cannot exceed some limit. It can also disallow sets of queries that repeatedly involve the same records.

9.11   Database Security and the Internet

Unless security software is used, all messages sent over the Internet are transmitted in plaintext, and can be detected by intruders using "packet sniffing" software. Obviously, customers who wish to purchase products need to have assurance that their credit card information is kept private when they send it over the Internet. Companies that allow Web connections to their internal networks for access to their database need to be able to protect it from attack. Both receivers and senders of messages need to have ways to be sure that the site they are communicating with is genuine and trustworthy. Several techniques are used to address these issues.

9.11.1 Firewalls

A **firewall** is a hardware and/or software barrier that is used to protect an organization's internal network (intranet) from unauthorized access. Various techniques are used to ensure that messages entering or leaving the intranet comply with the organization's standards. For example, a **proxy server,** a computer that intercepts all messages in both directions, can be used to hide the actual network address. Another technique is a **packet filter,** which examines each packet of information before it enters or leaves the intranet, making sure it complies with a set of rules. Various gateway techniques can apply security mechanisms to applications or connections.

9.11.2 Certification Authorities

Customers who wish to purchase goods from an e-commerce Web site need to feel confident that the site they are communicating with is genuine and that their ordering information is transmitted privately. A widely used method of verifying that a site is genuine is by means of **certification authorities** such as Verisign. The process uses public key encryption. The site begins the certification process by generating a public key and a private key, and sending a request to Verisign, along with the site's public key. Verisign issues an encrypted certificate to the site. When the customer wishes to place an order using a secure connection to the site, his or her browser asks the site for its Verisign certificate, which it receives in encrypted form. The browser decrypts the certificate using Verisign's public key, and verifies that this is indeed a Verisign certificate, and that the site's URL is the correct one. The certificate also contains the site's public key. The browser creates a session key, which it encrypts using the site's public key from the certificate, and sends the session key to the site. Since the session key is encrypted, only the actual site can decrypt it using its private key. Since both the browser and the site are the sole holders of the session key, they can now exchange messages encrypted with the session key, using a simpler protocol such as DES or AES. The process described here is the one used in the **Secure Sockets Layer** (SSL) protocol. A similar protocol, **Secure HTTP** (S-HTTP) guarantees security of individual messages rather than an entire session. An additional measure of security for transmission of credit card numbers is provided by the **Secure Electronic Transaction** (SET) protocol. When the customer is ready to transmit this information at the end of the order process, the browser sends the site most of the order information encoded with its public key, but the credit card information is encoded with the public key of the credit card company, so the site cannot decode it directly. Instead, the site has to send the credit card information directly to the card company site for approval and then for payment.

9.11.3 Digital Signatures

Digital signatures use a double form of public key encryption to create secure two-way communications that cannot be repudiated. They allow users to verify the authenticity of the person they are communicating with, and a means to prove that a message must have come from that person. Using a public key is not sufficient proof that the sender is authentic, since an impersonator can easily find another person's public key and use it to fabricate messages. One method of using digital signatures is for the sender to encode a message first with his or her own private key, and then with the public key of the receiver. The receiver decrypts the message first using his or her private key, and then using the sender's public key. The double encryption ensures that both parties are authentic, since neither one could have encoded or decoded the message without his or her private key. A variation of this technique involves using a Certification Authority, in a process similar to that used in SSL.

9.12   Chapter Summary

Database **security** means protecting the database from unauthorized access, modification, or destruction. **Privacy** is the right of individuals to have some control over information about themselves, and is protected by law in many countries. The privacy of individuals can be protected by database security. Security violations can be accidental or deliberate, and security breaches can be accomplished in a variety of ways. A security control plan should begin with physical security measures for the building and especially for the computer facilities. Security control of workstations involves user **authentication,** verifying the identity of users. The operating system normally has some means of establishing a user's identity, using user profiles, user IDs, passwords, authentication procedures, badges, keys, or physical characteristics of the user. Additional authentication can be required to access the database.

Most database management systems designed for multiple users have a security subsystem. These subsystems provide for **authorization,** by which users are assigned rights to use database objects. Most have an **authorization language** that allows the DBA to write **authorization rules** specifying which users have what type of access to database objects. **Access control** covers the mechanisms for implementing authorizations. An **access control matrix** can be used to identify what types of operations different users are permitted to perform on various database objects. The DBA can sometimes delegate authorization powers to others.

Views can be used as a simple method for implementing access control. A **security log** is a journal for storing records of attempted security violations. An **audit trail** records all access to the database, keeping information about the requester, the operation performed, the workstation used, the time, data items, and values involved. **Triggers** can be used to set up an audit trail. **Encryption** uses a **cipher system** that consists of an **encrypting algorithm** that converts **plaintext** into **ciphertext,** an **encryption key,** a **decrypting algorithm** that reproduces plaintext from ciphertext, and a **decryption key.** Widely used schemes for encryption are the **Data Encryption Standard (DES),** the **Advanced Encryption Standard (AES),** and **public key encryption.** DES/AES uses a standard algorithm, which is often hardware implemented. Public key encryption uses a product of primes as a public key, and the prime factors of the product as a private key.

SQL has an **authorization language** to provide security. The GRANT statement is used for authorization, and the REVOKE statement is used to retract authorization. Privileges can be given to individuals or to a role, and then the role is given to individuals. In Oracle, privileges include **object privileges** and **system privileges.** They can be granted using the authorization sublanguage or through the Oracle Security Manager.

When the database is accessible through the Internet, special security techniques are needed. These include firewalls, certifications authorities such as Verisign that issue digital certificates using SSL or S-HTTP, SET for financial information, and digital signatures.

Exercises

9.1   For each of the following, write SQL statements to create views where needed and to grant the indicated privileges for the University database with this schema:

```
Student(stuId, lastName, firstName, major, credits)
Faculty(facId, name, department, rank)
Class(classNumber, facId, schedule, room)
Enroll(stuId, classNumber, grade)
```

a. Give permission to read the tables Student and Class to user 201.

b. Create a view of Enroll that does not include the grade attribute, and give user 201 permission to read and update the view.

    c. Create a role that includes reading Student, Class, and the view created in (b). Give that role to all clerks in the dean's office, which includes users 202, 203, 204, and 205.

    d. Give permission to user 206, an assistant dean, to read and modify (insert, delete, update) the Faculty and Class tables. This user can authorize others to read and modify Class, but not Faculty.

    e. User 206 authorizes user 300 to read Class and Faculty. Write the command to do this.

    f. Create an authorization graph showing all the privileges given so far. You will need a separate node for each combination of privilege and user.

    g. Revoke the authorization privilege that the assistant dean was given in (d) but keep his or her own reading and modification privileges. How would you show this change on the authorization graph?

    h. Give permission to the Registrar, user 500, to read and modify Student, Class, and Enroll, and to grant those rights to others.

    i. For all academic advisors, give permission to read all Class records. For the advisor in the Math department, give permission to read the Student records of students majoring in Math, and to modify Enroll records for these students.

9.2   Assume you have a statistical database with the following schema. The only legal queries are those involving COUNT, SUM, and AVERAGE.

```
newFaculty(facId, lastName, firstName, department, salary, rank,
dateHired)
```

    a. Write a legal SQL query to find the salary of the only faculty member who is an Instructor in the Art Department.

    b. Assume the system will refuse to answer queries for which only one record satisfies the predicate as in (a). Write a legal set of queries that allows the user to deduce the salary of the art instructor.

    c. Assume that there are 10 faculty members in the Art Department. The system refuses to answer queries where the number of records satisfying the query is less than six. It will also refuse to answer pairs of queries where the number of records satisfying them simultaneously exceeds three. Would these restrictions make your query for (a) or (b) illegal? If so, is there another legal set of queries that will allow you to deduce the salary of the Art instructor?

9.3   a. Using the University schema shown in Exercise 9.1, write an SQL statement to create a value-dependent view of Student that includes only seniors.

       b. Write an SQL statement for a value-independent view of Faculty. Do not include the whole table.

       c. Write a statement to authorize user 125 to read both views.

9.4   Write a trigger to create an audit trail that will track all updates to the salary field of the newFaculty table shown in Exercise 9.2.

9.5   Log on to an e-commerce Web site, such as a large bookseller. Locate and read the information provided about security of online transactions. Determine whether SSL or some other secure protocol is used. If possible, display and print the information about the Verisign certificate for the site.

Lab Exercises: Exploring Oracle's Authorization System

If you have not already done so, create the Worker-Department-Project-Assign database, as directed in the lab exercise at the end of Chapter 6. As you do each of the following, keep an authorization graph, showing the privileges given.

       a. Create five users, U100, U101, U102, U103, and U104.

       b. Give user U100 all privileges on all tables, with grant option.

       c. Connect as U100 and pass the read privilege on all four tables to U101 and U102, with grant option.

       d. Still acting as U100, pass the read privilege on Worker to U103 and U104, without the grant option.

       e. Connect as U101 and pass the read privilege on Worker to U103 and U104, without the grant option.

       f. Connect as U100 and revoke all privileges you granted to U101.

g. From the graph, determine what privileges, if any, the remaining users should still have.

h. Test these privileges using appropriate SQL commands.

SAMPLE PROJECT: IMPLEMENTING SECURITY FEATURES FOR THE ART GALLERY DATABASE

We will work with the purely relational database created at the end of Chapter 6.

- Step 9.1. Create a value-independent view that hides some private information.

  The view will be of the `Artist` table, but without the social security number, sales, or interview information.

```
CREATE VIEW ArtistView1 AS
    SELECT artistId, firstName, lastName, areaCode, telephoneNumber,
    street, zip, usualMedium, usualStyle, usualType
    FROM Artist;
```

- Step 9.2. Create a user and authorize that person to read the view. Begin an authorization graph.

```
CREATE USER U1 IDENTIFIED BY SESAME;
GRANT SELECT ON VIEW ArtistView1 TO UI;
```

- Step 9.3. Authorize four other users to access and/or modify various parts of the database, and update the authorization graph.

```
GRANT SELECT ON Collector TO U2;
GRANT ALL PRIVILEGES ON Collector TO U3;
GRANT SELECT, INSERT ON Sale TO U4 WITH GRANT OPTION;
GRANT ALL PRIVILEGES ON Artwork TO U5;
```

The authorization graph is shown in Figure 9.7.

- Step 9.4. Write a trigger for an audit trail for updates to a sensitive item that users can update.

This trigger will monitor changes to the asking price of an artwork.

```
CREATE OR REPLACE TRIGGER ArtworkPriceAuditTrail
    BEFORE UPDATE OF askingPrice ON Artwork
    FOR EACH ROW
    BEGIN
        INSERT INTO ArtworkPriceAudit
            VALUES(SYSDATE, USER, :OLD.artworkId,:OLD.askingPrice,
                :NEW.askingPrice);
    END;
```

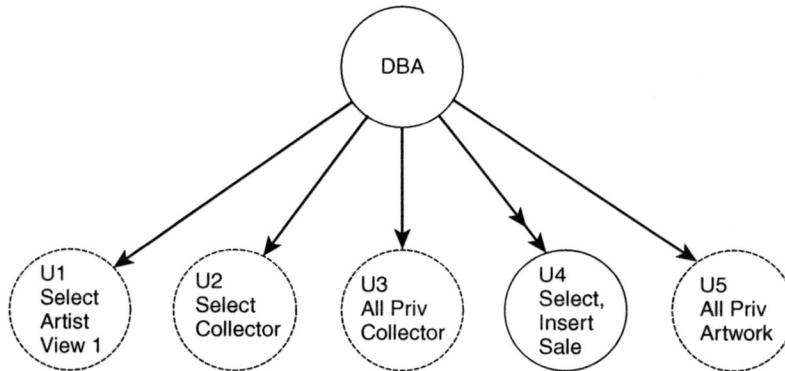

FIGURE 9.7
Authorization Graph for the Art Gallery

STUDENT PROJECTS: IMPLEMENTING SECURITY FEATURES FOR STUDENT PROJECTS

- Step 9.1. Create a value-independent view that hides some private information.

- Step 9.2. Create a user and authorize that person to read the view. Begin an authorization graph.

- Step 9.3. Authorize four other users to access and/or modify various parts of the database, and update the authorization graph.

- Step 9.4. Set up an audit trail for updates to a sensitive item that users can update and test it by updating the item.

10 CHAPTER

Transaction Management

Chapter Objectives

In this chapter you will learn the following:

- The characteristics of a transaction

- The meaning of concurrency control

- Why concurrency control is needed

- The meaning of serializability

- Why and how locking is done

- The meaning of deadlock

- How deadlock is detected

- How the two-phase locking protocol works

- What levels of locking may be used

- How timestamping is used for serializability

10.1 Properties of Transactions

Regardless of the care with which a database is designed and created, it can be easily damaged or destroyed unless proper concurrency controls and recovery techniques are in place. Database **recovery** means the process of restoring the database to a correct state in the event of a failure. **Concurrency control** is the ability to manage simultaneous processes involving the database without having them interfere with one another. Both are needed to protect the database from data contamination or data loss.

The notion of **transaction** is central to an understanding of both recovery and concurrency control. A transaction can be thought of as a logical unit of work on the database. It might be an entire program, a portion of a program, or a single command. It can involve any number of operations on the database. For the University database, we will use the following relational scheme:

```
Student (stuId, lastName, firstName, major, credits)
Faculty (facId, facname, department, rank)
Class (classNumber, facid, schedule, room)
Enroll (classNumber, stuId, grade)
```

A simple transaction against this database might be to update the number of credits in a `Student` record, given the `stuId`. This task involves locating the block containing the appropriate `Student` record on disk, bringing the block into the buffer, rewriting the value of the `credits` field in the record in the buffer, and finally writing the updated block out to disk. Figure 10.1 summarizes the steps in this transaction. A more complicated transaction would be to change the `stuId` assigned to a particular student. Obviously we need to locate the appropriate `Student` record, to bring its block into the buffer, to update the `stuId` in the buffer, and to write the update to disk as before, but we also need to find all the `Enroll` records having the old `stuId` and update them. If these updates are not made, we will have an inconsistent state of the database, a state in which the data is contradictory. A transaction should always bring the database from one consistent state to another. While the transaction is in progress, it is permissible to have a temporary inconsistent state. For example, during the `stuId` update, there will be some moment when one occurrence of the `stuId` contains the new value and another still contains the old one. However, at the end of the transaction, all occurrences will agree. A transaction is the entire series of steps necessary to accomplish a logical unit of work, in order to bring

- How optimistic concurrency control techniques operate
- The meaning of database recovery
- Some causes of database failure
- The nature and purpose of the database transaction log
- Why and how checkpoints are performed

FIGURE 10.1
**Steps in a Simple
Transaction**

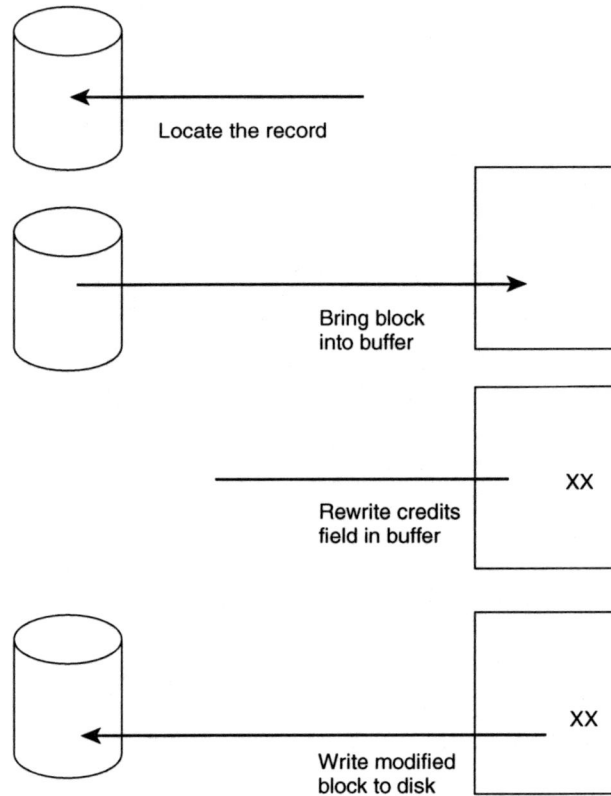

Locate the record

Bring block
into buffer

XX

Rewrite credits
field in buffer

XX

Write modified
block to disk

the database to a new consistent state. The transaction is an atomic process, a single "all or none" unit. We cannot allow only part of a transaction to execute—either the entire set of steps must be done or none can be done, because a partial transaction would leave the database in an inconsistent state.

There are two ways a transaction can end or terminate. If it executes to completion successfully, the transaction is said to be **committed,** and the database is brought to a new consistent state. The other possibility is that the transaction cannot execute successfully. In this case, the transaction is **aborted.** If a transaction is aborted, it is essential that the database be restored to the consistent state it was in before the transaction started. Such a transaction is undone or **rolled back.** A committed transaction cannot be aborted. If we decide that the committed transaction was a mistake, we must perform another **compensating transaction** to reverse its effects. However, an aborted transaction that has been rolled back can be

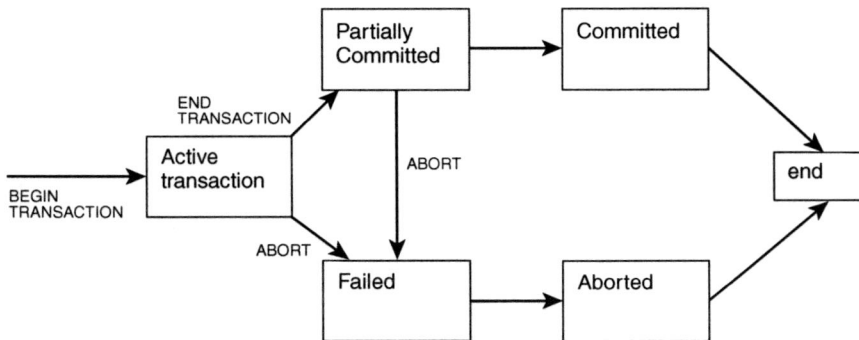

FIGURE 10.2
Transaction State Diagram

restarted at some future time and, depending on the cause of the failure, may successfully execute and commit at that time. Figure 10.2 shows the possible states of a transaction.

It is usually the responsibility of the programmer to identify the beginning and end of each transaction, since the database management system is unable to determine which updates form a single transaction. The words BEGIN TRANSACTION, END TRANSACTION, COMMIT, ABORT, and ROLLBACK are available in some DMLs to delimit transactions. If these delimiters are not used, the entire program is usually regarded as a single transaction, with the system automatically performing a COMMIT when the program terminates correctly and a ROLLBACK when it does not. The active state of the transaction starts with the BEGIN TRANSACTION statement and continues until the application program either aborts or terminates successfully. If the program terminates successfully, an END TRANSACTION is reached, and the DBMS prepares to check that it can commit. During this partially committed stage, the DBMS checks that the transaction will not violate the concurrency control protocols discussed beginning in Section 10.4, or any constraints, and that the system is able to make the required changes to the database itself. If no problems arise, the transaction is committed. On the other hand, if a fatal error arises while the transaction is active, it is marked as failed and aborted. If any updates were done to the database, they are rolled back. Even after the transaction has ended successfully, while in the partially committed state, if there is a problem with concurrency control, integrity, or a system failure, it can still be marked as failed and aborted.

All transactions should demonstrate four important properties, usually called the ACID properties, to ensure that the database maintains a correct state, despite transaction concurrency or system failure. **ACID** is an acronym for the properties, which are:

- **Atomicity.** The transaction is a single, "all or none" unit. Either the entire set of actions is carried out or none are. To ensure this property, the DBMS must be able to roll back transactions that will not be able to complete successfully, undoing their effects on the database. The DBMS' recovery subsystem maintains a **log** of all transaction writes to the database, which is used in the rollback process.

- **Consistency.** The user is responsible for ensuring that his or her transaction, if it were executed by itself, would leave the database in a consistent state. It is the job of the concurrency control subsystem of the DBMS to ensure consistency when multiple transactions execute at the same time.

- **Isolation.** Several transactions may execute at the same time, with interleaving of their operations. The isolation property requires that the final effect is as if the transactions were executed one after another rather than concurrently. Since each transaction leaves the database in a consistent state, the overall result would be a consistent state. The concurrency control system has to guarantee isolation.

- **Durability.** If a transaction has been committed, the DBMS must ensure that its effects are permanently recorded in the database, even if the system crashes before all its writes are made to the database. The recovery subsystem is responsible for guaranteeing durability. It uses the transaction log to ensure this property.

10.2   Need for Concurrency Control

One of the major objectives in developing a database is to create an information resource that can be shared by many users. If transactions execute one at a time, **serially,** with each transaction doing a commit before the next one begins, there is no problem of interference with one another's transactions. However, users often need to access data simultaneously. If all users are only reading data, there is no way they can interfere with one another and there is no need for concurrency control. If users are accessing different parts of the database, their transactions can run concurrently without a problem. However, when two users try to make updates simultaneously to the same data, or one updates while another reads the same data, there may be conflicts.

Multiprogramming means having two or more programs or transactions processing at the same time. For example, I/O control systems can handle I/O operations independently, while the main processor performs other operations. Such systems can allow two or more transactions to execute simultaneously. The system begins executing the first transaction until it reaches an input or output operation. While the I/O is being performed, the main processor, which would otherwise be idle during I/O, switches over to the second transaction and performs whatever operations it can on the second one. Control then returns to the first transaction and its operations are performed until it again reaches an I/O operation. In this way, operations of the two transactions are **interleaved,** with some operations from one transaction performed, then some from the other, and so forth, until all operations for both transactions are completed. Even though both transactions may be perfectly correct in themselves, the interleaving of operations may produce an incorrect outcome. Some examples of potential problems caused by concurrency are the **lost update problem,** the **uncommitted update problem,** the **problem of inconsistent analysis,** the **nonrepeatable read problem** and the **phantom data problem.** We illustrate the first three using schedules to show the chronological order in which operations are performed. A **schedule** is a list of the actions that a set of transactions performs, showing the order in which they are performed. In a schedule, we have a column for each transaction, showing the steps of that transaction. The order of operations in each transaction is preserved, but steps from another transaction can be performed during its execution, resulting in an interleaving of operations.

The Lost Update Problem

Suppose Jack and Jill have a joint savings account with a balance of $1000. Jill gets paid and decides to deposit $100 to the account, using a branch office near her job. Meanwhile, Jack finds that he needs some spending money and decides to withdraw $50 from the joint account, using a different branch office. If these transactions were executed serially, one after the other with no interleaving of operations, the final balance would be $1050 regardless of which was performed first. However, if they are performed concurrently, the final balance may be incorrect. Figure 10.3 shows a schedule for a concurrent execution that results in a final balance of $1100. The schedule shows sequential units of time as t1, t2, etc., to show the chronological order for operations. The only

FIGURE 10.3

The Lost Update Problem

TIME	Jack's Transaction	Jill's Transaction	BAL
t1	BEGIN TRANSACTION		
t2	read BAL*(reads 1000)*	BEGIN TRANSACTION	1000
t3	. . .	read BAL*(reads 1000)*	1000
t4	BAL = BAL − 50*(950)*	. . .	1000
t5	write BAL*(950)*	BAL = BAL + 100*(1100)*	950
t6	COMMIT	. . .	950
t7		write BAL *(1100)*	1100
t8		COMMMIT	1100

operations that involve the database are explicitly shown as *read <attribute>* or *write <attribute>*. As shown in Figure 10.1, these operations involve either bringing a value from the database into the buffer (read) or writing a new value to the database block in the buffer (write) and later copying the modified block out to the database. The transaction variables, which we assume for the sake of simplicity have the same name as the database attributes they correspond to, are separate from the database attributes. Updating a transaction variable has no effect on the database, until a *write <attribute>* command is encountered. The value that a transaction reads for a variable is the one it uses for calculations. Each transaction is unaware of any changes made to the database unless it makes them itself. As shown on the schedule, Jack's transaction reads a value of $1000 for BAL at time t2. Jill's transaction does the same slightly later at t3. Jack's transaction subtracts $50 from BAL, and then issues a write to the database at t5, as reflected in the BAL column. At time t5, Jill's transaction still uses the value it read for BAL, not the new value, which it has not read. Her transaction adds $100 and then writes a new value of $1100 to the database, overwriting Jack's update. According to the schedule, Jack's update is lost. If we had delayed Jill's reading until Jack's update had finished, we would have avoided this problem.

TIME	DEPOSIT Transaction	INTEREST Transaction	BAL
t1	BEGIN TRANSACTION		1000
t2	read BAL *(1000)*	. . .	1000
t3	BAL = BAL + 1000*(2000)*	. . .	1000
t4	write BAL *(2000)*	BEGIN TRANSACTION	2000
t5	. . .	read BAL *(2000)*	2000
t6	. . .	BAL = BAL * 1.05*(2100)*	2000
t7	ROLLBACK	. . .	1000
t8	. . .	write BAL *(2100)*	2100
t9		COMMIT	2100

FIGURE 10.4
The Uncommitted Update Problem

The Uncommitted Update Problem

The uncommitted update problem occurs with concurrent transactions when the first transaction is permitted to modify a value, which is then read by the second transaction, and the first transaction subsequently rolls back its update, invalidating the data that the second transaction is using. This is also called the **dirty read** problem, since it is caused by the reading of **dirty data,** intermediate results of an uncommitted transaction. Figure 10.4 shows a schedule containing an example of an uncommitted update that causes an error. Here, transaction INTEREST calculates the interest for a savings account, using a rate of 5%, while transaction DEPOSIT deposits $1000 in the account, but is rolled back. The starting balance in the account is $1000. If DEPOSIT actually updates the value of the balance to $2000 before INTEREST reads the balance, the amount that INTEREST will store is $2100. However, DEPOSIT is rolled back, which means the database state should show no effect due to DEPOSIT, so at time t6, the original value $1000 is restored as part of the rollback. Note that DEPOSIT is unaware that INTEREST has read its write, nor is INTEREST aware that DEPOSIT has rolled back. The reason for the rollback may be that the transaction itself was an error, or it may be the result of a system crash. At t8, the value calculated by INTEREST is written. Since the INTEREST was calculated on the incorrect balance, the final balance will be incorrect.

The Problem of Inconsistent Analysis

The problem of inconsistent analysis occurs when a transaction reads several values but a second transaction updates some of them during the execution of the first. Suppose we want to find the total balance of all savings accounts, but we allow deposits, withdrawals, and transfers to be performed during this transaction. Figure 10.5 contains a schedule that shows how an incorrect result could be produced. SUMBAL finds the sum of the balance on all accounts. We assume there are only three accounts to keep

Time	SUMBAL	TRANSFER	BAL_A	BAL_B	BAL_C	SUM
t1	BEGIN TRANSACTION		5000	5000	5000	–
t2	SUM = 0;	BEGIN TRANSACTION	5000	5000	5000	–
t3	read BAL_A (5000)	. . .	5000	5000	5000	–
t4	SUM = SUM + BAL_A (5000)	read BAL_A (5000)	5000	5000	5000	–
t5	read BAL_B (5000)	BAL_A = BAL_A −1000(4000)	5000	5000	5000	–
t6	SUM = SUM + BAL_B (10000)	write BAL_A (4000)	4000	5000	5000	–
t7	. . .	read BAL_C (5000)	4000	5000	5000	–
t8		BAL_C = BAL_C +1000 (6000)	4000	5000	5000	–
t9		write BAL_C (6000)	4000	5000	6000	–
t10	Read BAL_C (6000)	COMMIT	4000	5000	6000	–
t11	SUM = SUM + BAL_C (16000)		4000	5000	6000	–
t12	write SUM (16000)		4000	5000	6000	16000
t13	COMMIT		4000	5000	6000	16000

FIGURE 10.5
The Inconsistent Analysis Problem

the example small. Notice that this transaction does not update the accounts, but only reads them. Meanwhile transaction TRANSFER transfers $1000 from account A to account C. The TRANSFER transaction executes correctly and commits. However, it interferes with the SUMBAL transaction, which adds the same $1000 twice, once while it is in account A and again when it reaches account C.

There are two other famous problems that can arise from concurrency. They are the

a. **nonrepeatable read problem,** which occurs when a first transaction reads an item, another transaction then writes a new value for the item, and the first transaction then rereads the item and gets a different value.

b. **phantom data problem,** which occurs when a first transaction reads a set of rows (e.g., the tuples in the result of a query), another transaction inserts a row, and then the first transaction reads the rows again and sees the new row.

10.3 Serializability

Serial execution of transactions means that transactions are performed one after another, without any interleaving of operations. If A and B are two transactions, there are only two possible serial executions: all of transaction A is completed first and then all of transaction B is done, or all of B is completed and then all of A is done. In serial execution, there is no interference between transactions, since only one is executing at any given time. If the transactions shown in Figure 10.3 had been executed serially, regardless of whether the deposit or the withdrawal transaction were executed first, the results would have been correct. If the transactions in Figure 10.4 had been done serially, either the DEPOSIT transaction would have been rolled back before the INTEREST transaction started, or the INTEREST would have completed before the DEPOSIT started, so again they would not have interfered with each other. In Figure 10.5, if the TRANSFER transaction had been postponed until the SUMINT transaction completed, or if the TRANSFER had completed before the SUMINT started, the results would have been correct. The three problems that we described resulted from the concurrency and left the database in an inconsistent state. No serial execution would allow these problems to arise. However, there is no guarantee that the results of all serial executions of a given set of transactions will be identical. In banking, for example, it matters whether INTEREST is calculated for an account *before* a large deposit is made or *after*. In most cases, users do not care in what order their transactions are executed, as long as the results are correct and no user is made to wait too long. For n transactions, there are n! possible serial schedules. Regardless of which serial schedule is chosen, a serial execution will never leave the database in an inconsistent state, so every serial execution is considered to be correct, even though different results may be produced. Our goal is to find ways to allow transactions to execute concurrently while making sure they do not interfere with one another, and to produce a database state that could be produced by a truly serial execution.

If a set of transactions executes concurrently, we say the schedule is **serializable** if it produces the same results as some serial execution. It is essential to guarantee serializability of concurrent transactions in order to ensure database correctness. In serializability, the following factors are important:

- If two transactions are only reading data items, they do not conflict and order is not important

- If two transactions operate on (either reading or writing) completely separate data items, they do not conflict and order is not important

- If one transaction writes to a data item and another either reads or writes to the same data item, then the order of execution is important

Therefore, two operations **conflict** if all of the following is true:

- They belong to different transactions

- They access the same data item

- At least one of them writes the item

A serializable execution of transactions orders any conflicting operations in the same way as some serial execution, so that the results of the concurrent execution are the same as the results of at least one of the possible serial executions. This type of serializability is called **conflict serializability**. Figure 10.6 illustrates serial schedules and a serializable schedule for two transactions S and T. Figure 10.6(a) shows the serial schedule S,T while Figure 10.6(b) shows the serial schedule T,S. Figure 10.6(c) shows a serializable schedule that is conflict equivalent to the first serial schedule, S,T. The conflicting reads and writes of the data items are done in the

Time	S	T	S	T	S	T
t1	BEGIN TRANS			BEGIN TRANS	BEGIN TRANS	
t2	read x			read x	read x	BEGIN TRANS
t3	x = x*3			x=x+2	x=x*3	
t4	write x			write x	write x	
t5	read y			read y		read x
t6	y=y+2			y=y+5	read y	x=x+2
t7	write y			write y	y=y+2	write x
t8	COMMIT			COMMIT	write y	
t9		BEGIN TRANS	BEGIN TRANS		COMMIT	read y
t10		read x	read x			y=y+5
t11		x=x+2	x=x*3			write y
t12		write x	write x			COMMIT
t13		read y	read y			
t14		y=y+5	y=y+2			
t15		write y	write y			
t16		COMMIT	COMMIT			
	(a)Serial S,T		(b) Serial T,S		(c) serializable	

FIGURE 10.6

Two Serial schedules and a Serializable Schedule for Transactions S and T

same order in the serializable schedule as they are in the serial schedule S,T. Note that in (a) S reads and writes x before T reads and writes x, and S reads and writes y before T reads and writes y. The same order of reads and writes is preserved in the serializable schedule in (c). Also note that the two serial schedules here are not equivalent, but both are considered correct, and would leave the database in a consistent state. You can verify that the two serial schedules give different results by assigning initial values for x and y, and seeing what final values you get.

It is possible to determine whether a schedule is conflict serializable by examining the order of all its conflicting reads and writes, and comparing them with the order of the same reads and writes in the transactions' serial schedules, to determine if the order matches at least one of them. However, there is a graphical technique, called a **precedence graph,** that allows us to determine whether a schedule is conflict serializable. To construct

FIGURE 10.7
Precedence Graph for
Figure 10.5

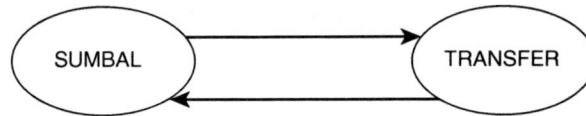

the graph, draw a node for each transaction, T1, T2, . . . Tn. Draw directed edges as follows:

- If Ti writes X, and then Tj reads X, draw edge from Ti to Tj
- If Ti reads X, and then Tj writes X, draw edge from Ti to Tj
- If Ti writes X, and then Tj writes X, draw edge from Ti to Tj

S is serializable if the precedence graph has **no cycles.** A cycle is a path that begins with a particular node and ends up back at the starting node. Figure 10.7 shows a precedence graph for the schedule in Figure 10.5. Since SUMBAL reads BAL_A and then TRANSFER writes BAL_A, we draw an edge from SUMBAL to TRANSFER. Since TRANSFER writes BAL_C and then SUMBAL reads it, we draw an edge from TRANSFER to SUMBAL, resulting in a cycle, and proving that the schedule is not serializable.

If a schedule is serializable, it is possible to use the precedence graph to find an equivalent serial schedule by examining the edges in the graph. Whenever an edge appears from Ti to Tj, put Ti before Tj in the serial schedule. If several nodes appear on the graph, you usually get a partial ordering of graph. There might be several possible serial schedules. If a cycle exists in the graph, no serial schedule is possible, since eventually you will need a node to precede itself.

Serializability can be achieved in several ways, but most systems use either locking or timestamping, the two techniques that will be described here. In general, the DBMS has a concurrency control subsystem that is "part of the package" and not directly controllable by either the users or the DBA. A facility called a **scheduler** is used to allow operations to be executed immediately, delayed, or rejected. If a transaction's operation is rejected, that transaction is aborted, but it may, of course, be restarted after the conflicting transaction completes.

10.4 Locking

Locking and timestamping are two techniques generally used to ensure serializability of concurrent transactions. Of these, locking is more com-

	Transaction 2 requests Shared lock	Transaction 2 requests Exclusive lock
Transactions 1 holds No lock	Yes	Yes
Transaction 1 holds Shared lock	Yes	No
Transaction 1 holds Exclusive lock	No	No

FIGURE 10.8
Lock Compatibility Matrix

monly used. A transaction "locks" a database object to prevent another transaction from modifying the object. Objects of various sizes, ranging from the entire database down to a single data item, may be locked. The size of the object determines the fineness, or **granularity,** of the lock. The actual lock might be implemented by inserting a flag in the data item, record, page, or file to indicate that portion of the database is locked, by keeping a list of locked parts of the database, or by other means. Often, there are two categories of locks: **shared** and **exclusive.** If a transaction has a shared lock on an item, it can read the item but not update it. Thus, many transactions can have shared locks on the same item at the same time. If a transaction has an exclusive lock on an item, it can both read and update the item. To prevent interference with other transactions, only one transaction can hold an exclusive lock on an item at any given time. Figure 10.8 illustrates a **lock compatibility matrix** that shows which type of lock requests can be granted simultaneously. If transaction 1 holds the type of lock indicated on the left, and transaction 2 requests the lock type indicated on the top of the column, the matrix shows whether the lock request can be granted. As shown, if the first transaction holds no lock, the second transaction can be granted either a shared or exclusive lock. If the first transaction holds a shared lock the second transaction can be granted only a shared, not an exclusive lock. All other lock requests will be denied.

If a system uses locks, any transaction that needs to access a data item must first lock the item, requesting a shared lock for read only access or an exclusive lock for write access. If the item is not already locked by another transaction, the lock will be granted. If the item is currently locked, the system determines whether the request is compatible with the existing lock. If a shared lock is requested on an item that has a shared lock on it, the request will be granted; otherwise, the transaction will have to wait until the existing lock is released. A transaction's locks are automatically released when the transaction terminates. In addition, a transaction can explicitly release locks that it holds prior to termination.

10.4.1 Deadlock

The set of items that a transaction reads is called its **read set,** and the items that a transaction writes is called its **write set.** In database processing, it is often difficult to identify the entire read set and write set of a transaction before executing the transaction. Often, records are accessed because of their relationship to other records. Usually it is impossible to tell in advance exactly which records will be related. For example, in the University database, if we ask for the name and department of all the teachers of a particular student, we are unable to predict exactly which Enroll records, Class records, and Faculty records will be needed.

Since we cannot always specify in advance which items need to be locked by a transaction, we make lock requests during the execution of the transaction. These requests can result in a situation called **deadlock,** which occurs when two transactions are each waiting for locks held by the other to be released. Figure 10.9 shows two transactions, S and T, which are deadlocked because each is waiting for the other to release a lock on an item it holds. At time t1, transaction S requests and obtains an exclusive lock (Xlock) on item a, and at time t2, transaction T obtains an exclusive lock on item b. Then at t3, S requests a lock on item b. Since T holds an exclusive lock on b, transaction S waits. Then at t4, T requests a shared

FIGURE 10.9

Deadlock with Two Transactions

Time	Transaction S	Transaction T
t1	Xlock a	. . .
t2	. . .	Xlock b
t3	request Xlock b	. . .
t4	wait	request Slock a
t5	wait	wait
t6	wait	wait
t7	wait	wait
. . .	. . .	. . .

lock (Slock) on item a, which is held with an exclusive lock by transaction S. Neither transaction can complete because each is waiting for a lock it cannot obtain until the other completes. Deadlocks involving several transactions can also occur. For example, Figure 10.10 shows four transactions, Q, R, S, and T that are deadlocked because Q is waiting for a data item locked by R, R is waiting for a data item locked by S, S is waiting for a data item locked by T, and T is waiting for a data item locked by Q. Once deadlock occurs, the applications involved cannot resolve the problem. Instead, the system has to recognize that deadlock exists and break the deadlock in some way.

There are two general techniques for handling deadlock: **deadlock prevention,** in which the system looks ahead to see if a transaction would cause a deadlock and never allows deadlock to occur, and **deadlock detection and recovery,** which allows deadlock to occur but, once it has, spots and breaks the deadlock. Since it is easier to test for deadlock and break it when it occurs than to prevent it, many systems use the detection and recovery method. Deadlock detection schemes use a **resource request graph** or **wait-for graph** to show which transactions are waiting for

Time	Trans Q	Trans R	Trans S	Trans T
t1	Xlock Q1	. . .	. . .	. . .
t2	. . .	Xlock R1	. . .	. . .
t3	. . .	. . .	Xlock S1	. . .
t4	. . .	. . .	. . .	Xlock T1
t5	request Slock R1	. . .	. . .	. . .
t6	wait	request Slock S1	. . .	. . .
t7	wait	wait	request Slock T1	. . .
t8	wait	wait	wait	request Slock Q1
t9	wait	wait	wait	wait
. . .	. . .	. . .	. . .	. . .

FIGURE 10.10
Deadlock with Four Transactions

FIGURE 10.11
Wait-for Graphs

FIGURE 10.11(a)
U Waits for V

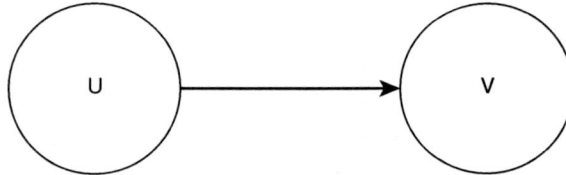

FIGURE 10.11(b)
S and T Deadlocked

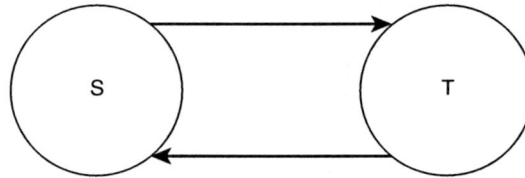

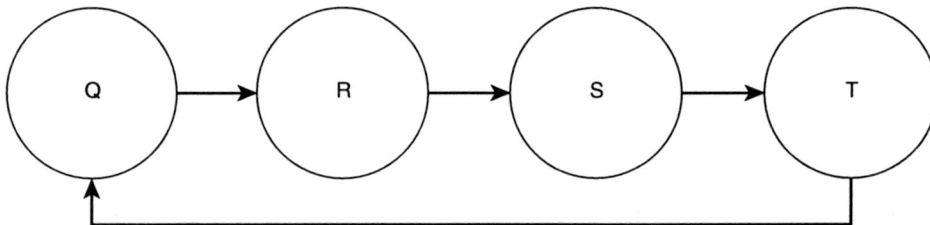

FIGURE 10.11(c)
Four Deadlocked Transactions

resources locked by other transactions. In such a graph, each node is a transaction. An edge indicates that one transaction is waiting for another to release a lock. For example, Figure 10.11 (a) shows two transactions, U and V, with the directed edge from U to V showing that U is waiting for a data item locked by V. The wait-for graph is maintained by the system. As new transactions start, new nodes are added to the graph. When a transaction makes a request for a locked resource, an edge is added to the graph. If the resource is unlocked and obtained by the transaction, the edge is erased. In deadlock, the graph will contain a **cycle.** Figure 10.11(b) shows a wait-for graph in which transactions S and T are deadlocked, because there is a cycle starting with S, going to T, and then going back to S. This cycle has length 2, because it contains 2 edges or directed paths, S to T, and T to S. (Of course, there is also a cycle starting at T.) Figure 10.11(c) shows a wait-for graph with a cycle of length 4. This pictures transactions Q, R, S, and T from Figure 10.10.

The system detects deadlock by periodically checking its wait-for graph for cycles. Note that it must check for cycles of any length, since a cycle might involve many transactions. Once a cycle is detected, the system must resolve the deadlock. It does so by choosing one of the transactions in the cycle as the **victim,** a transaction that will be made to fail and will be undone so that the other transactions can proceed. The victim may be the newest transaction, which has not done much work, or the transaction that has made the fewest updates, for example. Care must be taken to avoid always choosing the same transaction as the victim, a situation called **starvation,** because that transaction will never complete. If we chose transaction S shown in Figure 10.11(c) as the victim, then R would obtain its requested data items and could complete and release its locks, so that Q could also complete and, finally, T could obtain its data items. Then transaction S, the victim, could be restarted and could obtain its locks at a later time.

10.4.2 Two-Phase Locking

One locking scheme that ensures serializability is the **two-phase locking protocol.** According to the rules of this protocol, every transaction can go through two phases: first a **growing phase** in which it acquires all the locks needed for the transaction and then a **shrinking phase** in which it releases its locks. There is no requirement that all locks be obtained simultaneously. Normally the transaction acquires some locks, does some processing, and goes on to acquire additional locks as needed. However, it never releases any lock until it has reached a stage where no new locks will be needed. The rules are:

- A transaction must acquire a lock on an item before operating on the item. For read-only access, a shared lock is sufficient. For write access, an exclusive lock is required.

- Once the transaction releases a single lock, it can never acquire any new locks.

Figure 10.12 shows how the two-phase locking protocol could be applied to Figure 10.3. Note that both transactions needed an exclusive lock on BAL, since both were planning to update it. Jack's transaction requested and obtained the lock first, and held the lock until it finished the update on BAL. Then it released the lock and Jill's transaction, which had been suspended (put in a wait state) while it waited for the lock, could obtain it and complete.

FIGURE 10.12

Applying Two-Phase Locking Protocol to Figure 10.3

TIME	Jack's Transaction	Jill's Transaction	BAL
t1	BEGIN TRANSACTION		
t2	Xlock BAL		
t3	read BAL *(1000)*	BEGIN TRANSACTION	1000
t4	BAL = BAL − 50 *(950)*	request Xlock Bal	1000
t5	write BAL *(950)*	WAIT	950
t6	COMMIT/UNLOCK BAL	WAIT	950
t7		grant XlockBAL read BAL *(950)*	950
t8		BAL = BAL +100	950
t9		write BAL *(1050)*	1050
t10		COMMMIT/UNLOCK BAL	1050

In the **standard** two-phase locking protocol, described by the two rules given above, locks can be released before COMMIT, provided no new locks are requested after any are released. A problem that can arise is that an uncommitted transaction that has released its locks may be rolled back. If a second transaction has been permitted to read a value written by the rolled back transaction, it must also roll back, since it read dirty data. This problem is called a **cascading rollback.** Figure 10.13 shows a case of cascading rollbacks. Transaction R wrote a value of 4 for a, then released its lock, since it was no longer using a. Transaction S read the value of 4 that R had written, and wrote a new value, 8, for a. Transaction T read the value of 8 and calculated yet another value, 18. When R rolled back, the value of 4 that it wrote became invalid, which caused S to roll back as well. Then its write, 8, became invalid, so T had to roll back as well.

A variation called **strict** two phase locking requires that transactions hold their exclusive locks until COMMIT, preventing cascading rollbacks. An even stricter protocol is **rigorous** two-phase locking, which requires that transactions hold all locks, both shared and exclusive, until they commit.

The two-phase locking protocol can be refined slightly using **lock upgrading** to maximize concurrency. In this version of two-phase locking, a transaction may at first request shared locks that will allow other concurrent

Time	R	S	T	a
t1	BEGIN TRANS			1
t2	Xlock a	BEGIN TRANS		
t3	read a *(1)*	request Xlock a	BEGIN TRANS	
t4	a=a+3 *(4)*	wait	request Xlock a	
t5	write a *(4)*	wait	wait	4
t6	unlock a	wait	wait	
		grant Xlock a		
t7		read a*(4)*	wait	
t8		a = a*2 *(8)*	wait	
t9		write a*(8)*	wait	8
t10		unlock a	wait	
			grant Xlock a	
t11			read a *(8)*	
t12			a=a+10 *(18)*	
t13			write a *(18)*	18
t14	ROLLBACK			
t15		ROLLBACK		
t16			ROLLBACK	

FIGURE 10.13
Cascading Rollbacks

transactions read access to the items. Then when the transaction is ready to do an update, it requests that the shared lock be **upgraded,** or converted into an exclusive lock. Upgrading can take place only during the growing phase, and may require that the transaction wait until another transaction releases a shared lock on the item. Once an item has been updated, its lock can be downgraded—converted from an exclusive to a shared mode. Downgrading can take place only during the shrinking phase.

While all forms of the two-phase protocol guarantee serializability, they can cause deadlock, since transactions can wait for locks on data items. If two transactions each wait for locks on items held by the other, deadlock will occur, and the deadlock detection and recovery scheme described earlier will be needed.

10.4.3 Levels of Locking

Locks can be applied to a single data item, a single record, a file, a group of files, or the entire database. Few systems actually implement data item

FIGURE 10.14
Levels of Locking

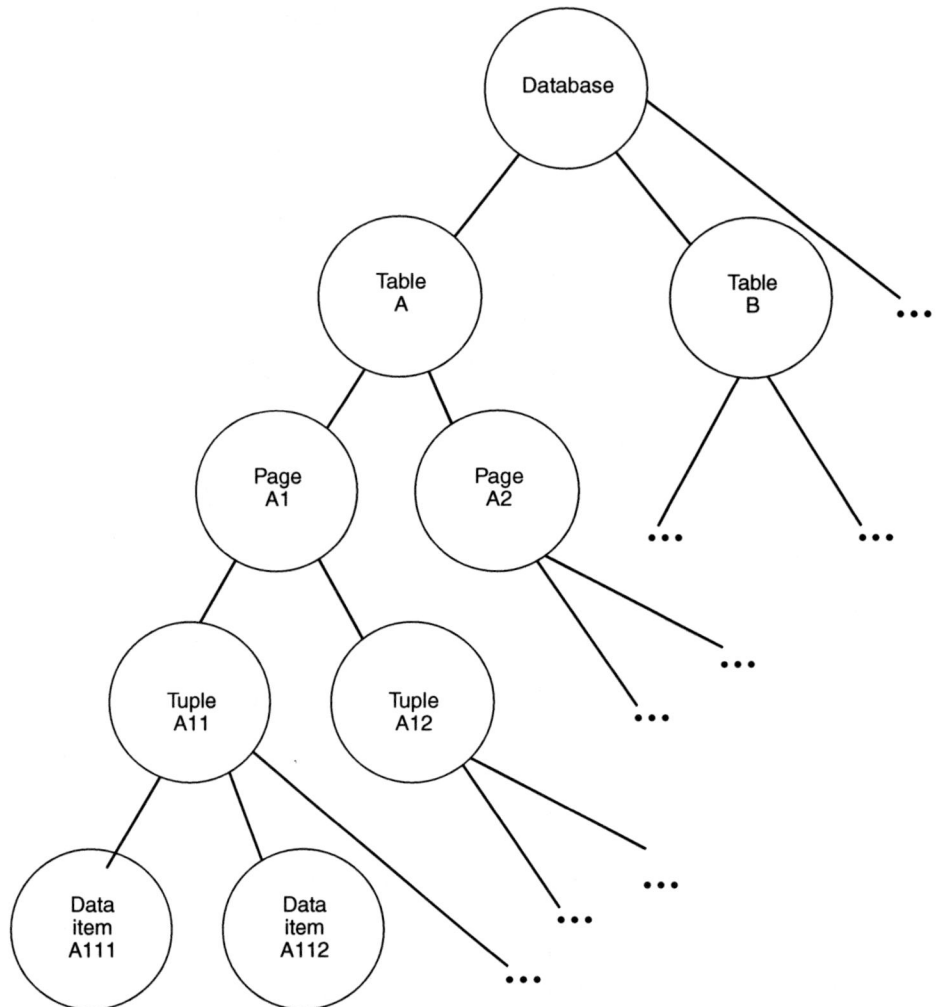

level locks because of the overhead involved. Some lock pages at a time. We could express the fineness or granularity of locks by a hierarchical structure in which nodes represent data objects of different sizes, as shown in Figure 10.14. Here, the root node represents the entire database, the level 1 nodes tables, the level 2 nodes pages of tables, the level 3 nodes records, and the leaves data items. Whenever a node is locked, all its descendants are also locked. For example, locking page A1 of Figure 10.14 locks records A11 and A12 as well as all their data items. If a second transaction requests an incompatible lock on the same node, the system clearly knows that the lock cannot be granted. For example, a request for an exclusive lock on pageA1 will be denied. If the second transaction requests an incompatible lock on any of the descendants of the locked node, the system should check the hierarchical path from the root to the requested node to see if any of its ancestors are locked before deciding whether to grant the lock. Thus if the request is for an exclusive lock on record A11, the system should check its parent, page A1, its grandparent, Table A, and the database itself to see if any of them are locked. When it finds that page A1 is already locked, it denies the request. What happens if a transaction requests a lock on a node when a descendant of a node is already locked? An example is, if a lock is requested on Table A, the system would have to check every page in the table, every record in those pages, and every data item in those records to see if any of them are locked. To reduce the searching involved in locating locks on descendants, the system can use another type of lock called an **intention** lock. When any node is locked, an intention lock is placed on all the ancestors of the node. Thus if some descendant of Table A (e.g., page A1) is locked, and a request is made for a lock on Table A, the presence of an intention lock on Table A would indicate that some descendant of that node is already locked. Intention locks can use either exclusive or shared mode. To ensure serializability with locking levels, a two-phase protocol is used, meaning no lock can be granted once any node has been unlocked, no node can be locked until its parent is locked by an intention lock, and no node can be unlocked until all its descendants are unlocked. The effect of these rules is to apply locking from the root down, using intention locks until the node requiring an actual shared or exclusive lock is reached, and to release locks from leaves up. However, deadlock is still possible, and must be detected and resolved using the methods discussed previously.

10.5   Timestamping

An alternate concurrency control mechanism that eliminates the deadlock problem is **timestamping**. In this scheme, no locks are used, so no deadlocks can occur. A timestamp for a transaction is a unique identifier that indicates the relative starting time of the transaction. It could be the reading on the internal clock at the time the transaction started, or it could be the value of a logical counter that is incremented every time a new transaction starts. In either case, the timestamp value of each transaction T, which we will indicate by $TS(T)$, is unique and indicates how old the transaction is. The effect of timestamping is to assign a serial order to the transactions. The protocol then ensures that the order is met, by not permitting any reads or writes that would violate the order. In addition to transaction timestamps, there are timestamps for data items. Each data item, P, contains two timestamps.

- Read-Timestamp(P), giving the timestamp of the last transaction that read the item. It is updated when a read(P) operation is done by a transaction.

- Write-Timestamp(P), giving the timestamp of the last transaction to write (update) the item. It is updated when a write(P) is done.

10.5.1 Basic Timestamping Protocol

Two problems can arise with timestamping:

1. A transaction, T, asks to read an item that has already been updated by a younger (later) transaction

2. T asks to write an item whose current value has already been read or written by a younger transaction

The first problem is a **late read.** The value that T needs to read is no longer available, since it has already been overwritten, so T must roll back and restart with a later timestamp. The second problem is a **late write,** and a younger transaction has already read the old value or written a new one. Again, the solution is to roll back T and restart it using a later timestamp. The following rules summarize this **basic timestamping protocol.** We always test the timestamp of the transaction, TS(T), against WriteTimestamp(P) and/or ReadTimestamp(P) that identify the transaction(s) that last wrote or read the data item.

1. If T asks to **read** a data item P, compare its TS(T) with WriteTimestamp(P).

   a. If WriteTimestamp(P) <= TS(T) then proceed using the current data value and replace ReadTimestamp(P) with TS(T). However, if ReadTimestamp(P) is already larger than TS(T), just do the read and do not change ReadTimestamp(P).

   b. If WriteTimestamp(P) > TS(T), then T is late doing its read, and the value of P that it needs is already overwritten, so roll back T.

2. If T asks to **write** a data item P, compare TS(T) with both Write-Timestamp(P) and the Read-Timestamp(P).

   a. If Write-Timestamp(P) <= TS(T) and Read-Timestamp(P) <= TS(T) then do the write and replace WriteTimestamp(P) with TS(T).

   b. else roll back T, assign a new timestamp, and restart T.

In the case of a late write, 2(b), the reason why we have to roll back if Read-Timestamp(P) is later than TS(T) is that a younger transaction has already read the current value, and replacing that value now would introduce an error. If Write-Timestamp(P) is later than TS(T), the value T is trying to write is an obsolete value, so it would also introduce an error.

This scheme guarantees that transactions will be serializable and the results will be equivalent to a serial execution schedule in which the transactions are executed in chronological order by the timestamps. Figure 10.15 illustrates what happens when the standard timestamping protocol is applied to the schedule shown in Figure 10.5.

10.5.2 Thomas' Write Rule

A variation of the basic timestamping protocol that allows greater concurrency is one in which some obsolete writes can safely be ignored without rolling back the transaction. It applies in the case where T is trying to do a write to data item P, but a new value has already been written for P by a younger transaction. If a younger transaction has already read P, then it needed the value that T is trying to write, so it is necessary to roll back T and restart it. Otherwise the transaction can proceed, with or without doing a write according to the following write protocol called **Thomas' write rule** that applies to transaction T trying to write P.

1. If Read-timestamp(P) > TS(T), then a younger transaction needed the new value, so T has to be rolled back.

2. If Write-timestamp(P) > TS(T) but Read-timestamp (P) <= TS(T), the write operation can be ignored since it is obsolete, but T can proceed because its write was not needed.

3. else do the write operation and replace Write-timestamp(P) by TS(T).

Time	SUMBAL	TRANSFER	BAL_A,R,W	BAL_B,R,W	BAL_C,R,W	SUM
t1	BEGIN TRANSACTION- Assign timestamp t1		5000,t0,t0	5000,t0,t0	5000,t0,t0	–
t2	SUM = 0;	BEGIN TRANSACTION- Assign timestamp t2	5000,t0,t0	5000,t0,t0	5000,t0,t0	–
t3	read BAL_A *(5000)*	. . .	5000,t1,t0	5000,t0,t0	5000,t0,t0	–
t4	SUM = SUM + BAL_A *(5000)*	read BAL_A *(5000)*	5000,t2,t0	5000,t0,t0	5000,t0,t0	–
t5	read BAL_B *(5000)*	BAL_A = BAL_A – 1000 *(4000)*	5000,t2,t0	5000,t1,t0	5000,t0,t0	–
t6	SUM = SUM + BAL_B *(10000)*	write BAL_A *(4000)*	4000,t2,t2	5000,t1,t0	5000,t0,t0	–
t7		read BAL_C *(5000)*	4000,t2,t2	5000,t1,t0	5000,t2,t0	–
t8		BAL_C = BAL_C +1000 *(6000)*	4000,t2,t2	5000,t1,t0	5000,t2,t0	–
t9		write BAL_C *(6000)*	4000,t2,t2	5000,t1,t0	6000,t2,t2	–
t10	Read BAL_C –*late read* ROLLBACK		4000,t2,t2	5000,t0,t0	6000,t2,t2	–
t11		COMMIT				
t12	restart with timestamp t12					
. . .						

FIGURE 10.15

Timestamping Applied to Figure 10.5

10.5.3 Multiversion Timestamping

The timestamping protocols discussed so far assume that there is only one version of each data item in the database. Concurrency can be increased if we allow multiple versions to be stored, so that transactions can access the version that is consistent for them. Each data item P has a sequence of versions $<P_1, P_2, . . ., P_n>$, each of which has,

- The content field, a value for P_i
- A Write-Timestamp(P_i), which is the timestamp of the transaction that wrote the value

- A Read-Timestamp(P_i), which is the timestamp of the youngest transaction that has read version P_i.

Whenever a write(P) is done, a new version of P is created, with appropriate write-timestamp. When a read(P) is done, the system selects the appropriate version of P. The multiversion timestamp protocol is,

1. When Transaction T does a read(P), the value that is returned is the value of the content field associated with the latest Write-Timestamp that is less than or equal to TS(T). The Read-Timestamp is then set to the later of TS(T) or its current value.

2. When T does a write(P), the version we must use is the one whose write timestamp is the largest one that is less than or equal to TS(T). For that version,

    a. If Read-Timestamp(P) > TS(T), indicating that P has already been read by a younger transaction, roll back T, because it would be a late write.

    b. else create a new version of P, with read and write timestamps equal to TS(T).

For example, in Figure 10.16(a) Transaction 10 requests a data item that has already been updated by Transaction 11. However, an old version of the data item exists with a content value of 100 and a Write-Timestamp of 9. As this is the last Write-Timestamp less than or equal to the transaction's timestamp (10), we use that version for transaction 10. The Read-Timestamp of that version is then changed to 10. The effect of this process is to ensure that the two transactions read data items as if they were actually executed serially. In Figure 10.16(b) transaction 10 is doing a write to an item whose current version was written by a later transaction. However, we examine the version whose Write-Timestamp is less than or equal to 10 (9 in this case). For that version, since the Read-Timestamp is less than or equal to 10, this is not a late write, so we create a new version with both timestamps of 10.

10.6   Validation Techniques

In many environments, conflicts between transactions are relatively rare, and the extra processing required to apply locking schemes is unnecessary for most of the transactions. There is a class of techniques that eliminates this overhead. **Validation** techniques, also called **optimistic** techniques, work under the assumption that conflict will normally not occur. They allow

FIGURE 10.16(a)

Transaction Reads an Item Already Updated by a Younger Transaction

Data Item - VAL			
	Content	Read-Timestamp	Write-Timestamp
(old version)	100	9 (←change to 10)	9
(new version)	150	11	11
Transaction with timestamp 10: read VAL (get 100, using old version, and change its Read Timestamp to 10)			

FIGURE 10.16(b)

Transaction Tries to Write an Item Already Updated by Younger Transaction

Data Item - VAL			
	Value	Read-Timestamp	Write-Timestamp
(old version)	100	10	9
(current version)	150	11	11
Transaction with timestamp 10: read VAL (get 100)			
VAL = VAL −10			
write VAL () (Create a new version of VAL with Value of 90 and Read and Write Timestamps of 10)			
(new version of VAL)	90	10	10

FIGURE 10.16

Multiversion Timestamping Examples

transactions to proceed as if there were no concurrency problems, but just before a transaction commits, a check is performed to determine whether a conflict has occurred. If there is a conflict, the transaction must be rolled back. Since the assumption is that conflict rarely occurs, rollback will be rare. The occasional rollback is the price to be paid for eliminating locks. These techniques allow more concurrency than traditional schemes, because no locking is done.

In optimistic schemes, a transaction goes through two or three phases in order, depending on whether it is a read-only or an updating transaction.

1. A **read** phase that extends from the start of the transaction until just before it commits. During this phase, the transaction reads the values of all the variables it needs, and stores them in local variables. If the transaction does any writes, they are done to a local copy of the data, not to the database itself.

2. A **validation** phase that follows the read phase. During this time, the transaction tests to determine whether there is any interference. For a read-only transaction, this consists of checking to see that there was no error caused by another transaction that was active when the data values were read. If no error occurred, the transaction is committed. If interference occurred, the transaction is aborted and restarted. For a transaction that does updates, validation consists of determining whether the current transaction will leave the database in a consistent state, with serializability maintained. If not, the transaction is aborted. If the update transaction passes the validation test, it goes on to a third phase.

3. A **write** phase that follows the successful validation phase for update transactions. During this phase, the updates made to the local copy are applied to the database itself.

The validation phase is accomplished by examining the reads and writes of transactions that may cause interference. Each transaction, T, is given three timestamps. Start(T) indicates the relative starting time of the transaction. Another timestamp, Validation(T), is given at the end of its read phase as it enters its validation phase. In addition, its finishing time, which is the time it finished (including its write phase, if any), is given a timestamp Finish(T). To pass the validation test, one of the following must be true.

1. All transactions with earlier timestamps must have finished (including their writes) before the current transaction started. Or,

2. If the current transaction starts before an earlier one finishes, then both of the following are true:

    a. the items written by the earlier transaction are not the ones read by the current transaction, and,

    b. the earlier transaction completes its write phase before the current transaction enters its validation phase.

Rule 2 (a) guarantees that the writes of the earlier transaction are not read by the current transaction, while rule 2 (b) guarantees that the writes are done serially.

Although optimistic techniques are very efficient when there are few conflicts, they can result in rollback of individual transactions. Note that the rollback involves only a local copy of the data, so there are no cascading rollbacks, because the writes have not actually reached the database. However, if the aborted transaction is a long one, valuable processing time will be lost, as the transaction must be restarted. If rollback occurs often, it is an indication that the optimistic method is a poor choice for concurrency control in that particular environment.

10.7 Need for Recovery

Recovery after any failure consists of restoring the database to a correct state. There are many different types of failures that can affect database processing. Some failures affect main memory only, while others involve disk storage or backup storage devices. Among the causes of failure are:

- Natural physical disasters such as fires, floods, earthquakes, or power outages

- Sabotage or intentional contamination or destruction of data, hardware, or software facilities

- Carelessness or unintentional destruction or contamination of data or facilities by operators or users

- Disk malfunctions such as head crashes, defective disks, or unreadable tracks, which might result in loss of stored data

- System crashes due to hardware malfunction, resulting in loss of main and cache memory

- System software errors that result in abnormal termination or damage to the database management system

- Applications software errors such as logical errors in the program that is accessing the database

Regardless of the cause of the failure, we need to study the possible effects so that we can protect or limit the damage to the database. The principal effects that concern us are the loss of main memory—including database buffers—and the loss of the disk copy of the database. Fortunately, there are techniques that can minimize these effects.

10.8 Recovery Techniques

Transactions are used as the basic unit for recovery for a database. The DBMS has a **recovery manager** that is responsible for ensuring **atomicity** and **durability** for transactions in the event of failure. Atomicity requires that all of a transaction be performed or none, so the recovery manager has to ensure that all the effects of committed transactions reach the database, and that the effects of any uncommitted transactions be undone as part of recovery. Durability requires that the effects of a committed transaction be permanent, so they must survive both loss of main memory and loss of disk storage.

The possible loss of disk is handled by doing frequent backups, making copies of the database. In the event of a failure, the backup can be brought up to date using a log of transactions, which will be described shortly. If a system failure occurs and the database buffers are lost, the disk copy of the database survives, but it may be incorrect. A transaction can commit once its writes are made to the database buffers, and there might be a delay between the commit and the actual disk writing. Because updates made to buffer blocks are not automatically written to disk, (even for committed transactions), if there is a system failure during this delay, the system must be able to ensure that these updates reach the disk copy of the database. For some protocols, writes made while a transaction is active, even before it commits, can reach the disk copy of the database. If there is a system failure before the transaction completes, these writes need to be undone. To keep track of database transactions, the system maintains a special file called a **log** that contains information about all updates to the database. The log can contain data transactions records, giving the transaction identifier and some information about it. For example, assuming T is the transaction identifier, there is,

- A record of the form <T starts> showing the start of a transaction

- A record of the form <T,X,n> for each write operation showing the transaction identifier, the data item name, and the new value

- A record of the form <T commits> showing the end of the committed transaction **or** a record of the form <T aborts> showing that a transaction has aborted

- Checkpoint records, which we will describe shortly

10.8.1 Deferred Update Protocol

Using the deferred update recovery protocol, the DBMS records all database writes in the log, and does not write to the database until the transaction is ready to commit.

We can use the log to protect against system failures in the following way:

- When a transaction starts, write a record of the form <T starts> to the log.

- When any write operation is performed, do not actually write the update to the database buffers or the database itself. Instead, write a log record of the form <T,X, n>.

- When a transaction is about to commit, write a log record of the form <T commits>, write all the log records for the transaction to disk, and then commit the transaction. Use the log records to perform the actual updates to the database.

- If the transaction aborts, simply ignore the log records for the transaction and do not perform the writes.

Note that we write the log records to disk before the transaction is actually committed, so that if a system failure occurs while the actual database updates are in progress, the log records will survive and the updates can be applied later.

Figure 10.17 illustrates a short transaction, the corresponding log transaction entries, and the database data items involved. Note that the database is not updated until after the commit. In the event of a system failure, we examine the log to identify the transactions that may be affected by the failure. Any transaction with log records <T starts> and <T commits> should be **redone** in the order in which they appear in the log. The transaction itself does not have to be executed again. Instead, the **redo procedure** will perform all the writes to the database, using the write log records for the transactions. Recall all of these will have the form <T,X,n>, which means the procedure will write the value n to the data item X. If this writing has been done already, prior to the failure, the write will have no effect on the data item, so there is no damage done if we write unnecessarily. However, this method guarantees that we will update any data item that was not properly updated prior to the failure. For any transaction with log records <S starts> and <S aborts>, or any transaction with <S starts> but neither a commit nor an abort, we do nothing, as no actual writing was done to the database using the incremental log with deferred updates technique, so these transactions do not have to be undone. This protocol is called a **redo/no undo** method, since we redo committed transactions, and we do not undo any transactions. In the event that a second system crash occurs during recovery, the log records are used again the second

```
T starts;
    read (X);
    X = X + 10;
    write (X);
    read (Y);
    Y = 2 * Y;
    write (Y);
    T commits;
```

FIGURE 10.17(a)

Transaction T

(Assume at the start that X and Y both have value 100.)

Log	Database Data Items	
	X	Y
<T starts>	100	100
<T,X,110>	100	100
<T,Y,200>	100	100
<T commits>	100	100
	110	200

FIGURE 10.17(b)

Log Entries and Database Data Items

FIGURE 10.17

A Transaction and Its Log

time the system is restored. Because of the form of the write log records, it does not matter how many times we redo the writes.

10.8.2 Checkpoints

One difficulty with this scheme is that when a failure occurs, we may not know how far back in the log to search. For example, we might wind up redoing a whole day's transactions, even though most of them have been safely written to the database. To put some limit on the log searching we need to do, we can use a technique called a **checkpoint.** Checkpoints are scheduled at predetermined intervals and involve the following operations:

- Writing the modified blocks in the database buffers out to disk

- Writing all log records now in main memory out to disk

- Writing a checkpoint record to the log. This record contains the names of all transactions that are active at the time of the checkpoint.

Having checkpoints allows us to limit the log search. When a failure occurs, we check the log to find the last transaction that started before the last checkpoint. Assuming that transactions are performed serially, any earlier transaction would have committed previously and would have been written to the database at the checkpoint. Therefore, we need only redo the one that was active at the checkpoint and any subsequent transactions for which both start and commit records appear in the log. If transactions are performed concurrently, the scheme is only slightly more complicated. Recall that the checkpoint record contains the names of all transactions that were active at checkpoint time. Therefore, we redo all those transactions and all subsequent ones.

10.8.3 Immediate Update Protocol

A slightly different recovery technique uses a log with immediate updates. In this scheme, updates are applied to the database buffers as they occur and are written to the database itself when convenient. However, a log record is written first, since this is a **write-ahead log protocol.** The scheme for successful transactions is as follows:

- When a transaction starts, write a record of the form <T starts> to the log.

- When a write operation is performed, write a log record containing the name of the transaction, the field name, the old value, and the new value of the field. This has the form <T,X,o,n>.

- After the log record is written, write the update to the database buffers.

- When convenient, write the log records to disk and then write updates to the database itself.

- When the transaction commits, write a record of the form <T commits> to the log.

If a transaction aborts, the log can be used to undo it, because it contains all the old values for the updated fields. Because a transaction might have performed several changes to an item, the writes are undone in reverse order. Regardless of whether the transaction's writes have been applied to the database itself, writing the old values guarantees that the database will be restored to its state prior to the start of the transaction.

If the system fails, recovery involves using the log to **undo** or **redo** transactions, making this a **redo/undo** protocol. For any transaction, T, for which both <T starts> and <T commits> records appear in the log, we **redo** by using the log records to write the new values of updated fields. Note that if the new values have already been written to the database, these writes, though unnecessary, will have no effect. However, any write that did not actually reach the database will now be performed. For any transaction, S, for which the log contains an <S starts> record, but not an <S commits> record, we will need to **undo** that transaction. This time the log records are used to write the old values of the affected fields and thus restore the database to its state prior to the transaction's start.

10.8.4 Shadow Paging

Shadow paging is an alternative to log-based recovery techniques. The DBMS keeps a **page table** that contains pointers to all current database pages on disk. With shadow paging, two page tables are kept, a **current page table** and a **shadow page table.** Initially these tables are identical. All modifications are made to the current page table, and the shadow table is left unchanged. When a transaction needs to make a change to a database page, the system finds an unused page on disk, copies the old database page to the new one, and makes changes to the new page. It also updates the current page table to point to the new page. If the transaction completes successfully, the current page table becomes the shadow page table. If the transaction fails, the new pages are ignored, and the shadow page table becomes the current page table. The commit operation requires that the system do the following:

- Write all modified pages from the database buffer out to disk

- Copy the current page table to disk

- In the location on disk where the address of the shadow page table is recorded, write the address of the current page table, making it the new shadow page table

10.8.5 Overview of ARIES Recovery Algorithm

The ARIES recovery algorithm is a very flexible and conceptually simple method for database recovery. It uses a log, in which each log record is given a unique **log sequence number** (LSN), which is assigned in increasing order. Each log record records the LSN of the previous log record for the same transaction, forming a linked list. Each database page also has a **pageLSN,** which is the LSN of the last log record that updated the page. The recovery manager keeps a **transaction table** with an entry for each active transaction, giving the transaction identifier, the status (active, committed or aborted), and the **lastLSN,** which is the LSN of the latest log record for the transaction. It also keeps a **dirty page table** with an entry for each page in the buffer that has been updated but not yet written to disk, along with the **recLSN,** the LSN of the oldest log record that represented an update to the buffer page. The protocol uses write-ahead logging, which requires that the log record be written to disk before any database disk update. It also does checkpointing to limit log searching in recovery. Unlike other protocols, ARIES tries to repeat history during recovery, by attempting to repeat all database actions done before the crash, even those of incomplete transactions. It then does redo and undo as needed. Recovery after a crash is done in three phases.

1. **Analysis.** The DBMS begins with the most recent checkpoint record and reads forward in the log to identify which transactions were active at the time of failure. It also uses the transaction table and the dirty page table to determine which buffer pages contain updates that were not yet written to disk. It also determines how far back in the log it needs to go to recover, using the linked lists of LSNs.

2. **Redo.** From the starting point in the log identified during analysis, which is the smallest recLSN found in the dirty page table during the analysis phase, the recovery manager goes forward in the log, and applies all the unapplied updates from the log records.

3. **Undo.** Going backward from the end of the log, the recovery manager undoes updates done by uncommitted transactions, ending at the oldest log record of any transaction that was active at the time of the crash.

This algorithm is more efficient than the ones discussed previously, because it avoids unnecessary redo and undo operations, since it knows which updates have already been performed.

10.9 Transaction Management in Oracle

Oracle uses a multiversion concurrency control mechanism, with no read locks. If a transaction is read-only, it works with a consistent view of the database at the point in time when it began, including only those updates that were committed at that time. The DBMS creates **rollback segments** that contain the older versions of data items and that are used for both read consistency and any undo operations that might be needed. It uses a type of timestamp called a **system change number** (SCN) that is associated with each transaction at its start. The system automatically provides locking at the row-level for SQL statements requiring locks. Several types of locks are available, including both DML and DDL locks, the latter being applied at the table level. Deadlock is handled using a deadlock detection scheme, and rolling back of one of the transactions. Oracle supports two **isolation levels,** which are degrees of protection from other transactions. They are:

- **Read committed.** This is statement-level consistency, guaranteeing that each statement in a transaction reads only data committed before the statement started. However, since data can be changed during the transaction containing the statement, there might be nonrepeatable reads and phantom data. This is the default level.

- **Serializable.** This is transaction-level consistency, ensuring that a transaction sees only data committed before the transaction started.

For recovery, Oracle has a **recovery manager** (RMAN), a GUI tool that the DBA can use to control backup and recovery operations. RMAN can be used to make backups of the database or parts thereof, to make backups of recovery logs, to restore data from backups, and to perform recovery operations including redo and undo operations as needed. It maintains control files, rollback segments, redo logs, and archived redo logs. When a redo log is filled, it can be archived automatically. Oracle also provides a backup feature for environments where high availability is important in the form of a managed standby database. This is a copy of the operational database, usually kept at a separate location, that can take over if the regular database fails. It is kept nearly up to date by shipping the archived redo logs and applying the updates to the standby database.

10.10 Chapter Summary

Database **recovery** is the process of restoring the database to a correct state after a failure. **Concurrency control** is the ability to allow simultaneous use of the database without having users interfere with one another. Both protect the database.

A **transaction** is a logical unit of work that takes the database from one consistent state to another. Transactions can terminate successfully and **commit** or unsuccessfully and be **aborted.** Aborted transactions must be undone or **rolled back.** Committed transactions cannot be rolled back.

Concurrency control is needed when transactions are permitted to process simultaneously. Without it, problems such as the **lost update problem,** the **uncommitted update problem,** and the **inconsistent analysis problem** can arise. **Serial execution** means executing one transaction at a time, with no interleaving of operations. There will be more than one possible serial execution for two or more transactions, and they might not all produce the same results. A **schedule** is used to show the timing of the operations of one or more transactions. A schedule is **serializable** if it produces the same results as if the transactions were performed serially in some order.

Two methods that guarantee serializability are **locking** and **timestamping.** Locks may be **exclusive** or **shared.** Shared locks are sufficient if a transaction needs only read access, but exclusive locks are necessary for write access. A lock compatability matrix shows which type of lock requests can be granted simultaneously. Transactions might be required to wait until locks are released before their lock requests can be granted.

Because transactions can wait for locks, **deadlock** a situation in which two or more transactions wait for locks being held by one another to be released, can occur. Deadlock detection schemes use a **wait-for** graph to identify deadlock. Such a graph depicts transactions as nodes and uses edges to show that one transaction is waiting for another to release a lock. A **cycle** in the graph indicates that deadlock has occurred. The system detects deadlock by periodically checking its wait-for graph for cycles. A deadlock is resolved by choosing a **victim,** a transaction that will be made to fail.

Two-phase locking is a widely used locking protocol. Every transaction acquires all its locks before releasing any. Variations to standard two-phase locking include **strict** and **rigorous.** Another variation allows transactions to begin by acquiring shared locks and to **upgrade** them to exclusive locks just before a write. Upgrading can be done only during the first (growing) phase. In the second (shrinking) phase, a transaction can **downgrade** an exclusive lock to a shared lock. The purpose of this refinement is to maximize concurrent access.

A tree can be used to represent the granularity of locks in a system that allows different sized objects to be locked. When an item is locked, all its descendants in the tree are also locked. When a new transaction requests a lock, it is easy to check all the ancestors of the object to see whether they are already locked. However, it can be time-consuming to check to see whether any of the node's descendants are locked. To reduce the search time, an intention lock is placed on all the ancestors of any node being locked. Therefore, if a node does not have an intention lock, none of its descendants are locked. Serializability is ensured by using a two-phase locking protocol.

In a **timestamping** protocol, each transaction is given a timestamp, a unique identifier that gives the relative order of the transaction, and each data item has a **Read-Timestamp** and a **Write-Timestamp.** Problems arise when a transaction tries to read an item already updated by a younger transaction, or when a transaction tries to write an item whose value has already been updated by a later transaction. The protocol takes care of these problems by rolling back transactions that cannot execute correctly. If multiple versions of data items are kept, late reads can be done.

Validation techniques can be used in situations where conflicts are rare. Each transaction starts with a **read phase,** during which it reads all variables it needs, stores them as local variables, and writes to the local copy only. After the read phase, the transaction moves to a **validation phase,** during which the system determines whether there was any interference. If not, it moves on to a **write phase,** during which the updates to the transaction's local copy are applied to the database. If there was interference, the transaction is aborted instead of moving to the write phase.

To facilitate recovery, the system keeps a **log,** containing transaction records that identify the start of transactions, give information about write operations, and identify the end of transactions. Using an incremental log with **deferred updates,** writes are done initially to the log only, and the log records are used to perform actual updates to the database. If the system fails, it examines the log to determine which transactions it needs to **redo,** namely those that committed but might not have been written to the database. There is no need to undo any writes. At a **checkpoint,** all modified blocks in the database buffers are written to disk, all log records are written to disk, and a checkpoint record identifying all transactions active at that time is written to disk. If a failure occurs, the checkpoint records identify which transactions need to be redone. Using an incremental log with **immediate updates,** updates can be made to the database itself at any time after a log record for the update is written. The log can be used to **undo** as well as to **redo** transactions in the event of failure. **Shadow paging** is a recovery technique that uses no logs. Instead, updates are made to a new copy of each page. A **current page table** points to the new page. A shadow page table continues to point to the old page until the transaction commits, at which time the current page table becomes the shadow page table. The ARIES recovery algorithm is a highly sensitive and flexible algorithm that does recovery by attempting to recreate the exact state the database was in at the time of failure, and then applying redo and undo operations as needed.

Oracle handles concurrency control using a variety of locking and timestamping techniques. It uses rollback segments for both concurrency and recovery. The Oracle recovery manager maintains control files, rollback segments, redo logs and archived redo logs for recovery.

Exercises

10.1   Assume a DBMS that uses immediate updates has the following log entries.

<R starts>

<R,X,1,5>

<R,Y, – 1,0>

<R commits>

<S starts>

<S,Z,8,12>

<checkpoint record>

<S,X,5,10>

<T starts>

<T,Y,0,15>

<S commits>

————————system crash————————

Assuming a system crash occurs as indicated immediately after the <S commits> log record,

a. Which transactions, if any, need to be redone?

b. Which transactions, if any, need to be undone?

c. Which transactions, if any, are not affected by the crash?

10.2   Assume the same transactions and operations as shown in Exercise 10.1 are being done by a system that uses the deferred update protocol.

   a. Rewrite the log entries for the transactions in Exercise 10.1 for this logging method.

   b. Which transactions, if any, need to be redone?

   c. Which transactions, if any, need to be undone?

   d. Which transactions, if any, are not affected by the crash?

10.3   (a) Suppose the log in Exercise 10.1 contained the entry <S aborts> in place of the entry <S commits>.

   a. If the system is using immediate updates and the crash occurred before the rollback took place, what changes, if any, would you make in the recovery process?

   b. If the system were using deferred updates, what changes would you make in the recovery process of Exercise 10.2?

10.4   Assume the following transactions are to be performed.

Transaction S:

read(a);

a = a + 10;

write(a);

read(b);

b=b*5;

write(b);

Transaction T:

read(a);

a = a*2;

write a;

   a. If the initial value of a is 10 and the initial value of b is 20, what are their final values if we perform the transactions serially, using order S,T?

   b. Using the same initial values, what are the final values of a and b if the order of execution is T,S?

10.5 Write a concurrent schedule for transactions S and T in Exercise 10.4 that illustrates the lost update problem.

10.6 Apply the standard two-phase locking protocol to the schedule you devised in Exercise 10.5. Will the protocol allow the execution of that schedule? Does deadlock occur?

10.7 Apply the standard timestamping protocol to the schedule you devised in Exercise 10.5. In the columns for the data items, add read and write timestamps, assuming both were last set by a transaction with timestamp t0, as shown in Figure 10.15. Will the protocol allow the execution of that schedule? Are there any rollbacks?

10.8 Apply the standard timestamping protocol to the schedule shown in Figure 10.3. Will the protocol allow the execution of that schedule? Are there any rollbacks?

10.9 Apply the standard two-phase locking protocol to the schedule shown in Figure 10.4. Does deadlock occur?

10.10 Apply the standard timestamping protocol to the schedule shown in Figure 10.4. Will the protocol allow the execution of that schedule? Are there any rollbacks?

10.11 Apply the standard two-phase locking protocol to the schedule shown in Figure 10.5. Does deadlock occur?

10.12 Apply the standard timestamping protocol to the schedule shown in Figure 10.5. Will the protocol allow the execution of that schedule? Are there any rollbacks?

10.13 Let T_1, T_2, and T_3 be transactions that operate on the same database items, A, B, and C. Let $r_1(A)$ mean that T_1 reads A, $w_1(A)$ mean that T_1 writes A, and so on for T_2 and T_3. Each of the following shows the order of the reads and writes in a schedule for T_1, T_2, and T_3. In each case, draw a precedence graph with nodes for T_1, T_2, and T_3 and draw edges for conflicts. Determine if each schedule is serializable by examining the precedence graph. If it is serializable, give an equivalent serial schedule.

a. $r_1(A)$; $r_2(A)$; $w_1(A)$; $r_3(A)$; $w_3(A)$; $w_2(A)$

b. $r_1(A)$; $r_1(B)$; $r_2(A)$; $r_3(B)$; $r_3(C)$; $w_2(A)$; $w_2(B)$

c. $r_1(A)$; $r_3(C)$; $r_2(C)$; $w_3(A)$; $r_2(B)$; $r_3(B)$; $w_2(B)$; $w_2(A)$

CHAPTER 11

Relational Query Optimization

Chapter Objectives

In this chapter you will learn the following:

- How a relational query is interpreted

- How a query tree represents relational algebra expressions

- Why SELECT operations should be performed early

- How conjunctive conditions can be executed efficiently

- When PROJECT operations should be performed

- Some rules for equivalence of algebraic operations

- Heuristics for query optimization

- Factors that determine the cost of a query

- How to estimate the cost of various methods of performing SELECT operations
- How to estimate the cost of various methods of performing JOIN operations
- Methods of processing PROJECT operations
- Methods of processing set operations
- How pipelining can be used for queries

11.1   Interpretation and Optimization of Queries

In Chapter 6 we saw that some SQL queries could be expressed in different ways. For example, in a SELECT statement involving two or more tables, we could sometimes choose between a join and a subquery. Similarly, in Chapter 4 we considered different sequences of relational algebra commands that produced equivalent results. We noted in passing that certain formulations of these queries were more efficient than others. In this chapter we examine relative efficiency more closely and discuss some techniques for improving the efficiency of queries.

When a relational database management system receives a high-level query in a language such as SQL, it first checks the query syntax to ensure that the language is used correctly. The syntactically correct query is then validated by checking the data dictionary to verify that the attributes, tables, or views referred to are actual database objects and that the operations requested are valid operations on those objects. The query then has to be translated into some form that the system can use. For example, although a query can be expressed in SQL externally, the system must transform it into a lower-level internal representation that it can actually use for processing. Relational algebra can be used for this internal representation, because its operations are easily transformed into system operations. Relational calculus can be used instead, but we will assume relational algebra is used for our examples. The system then examines the internal representation and uses its knowledge of relational algebra operations to determine whether the operations could be rearranged or changed to produce an equivalent, but more efficient, representation. Once the internal representation is as efficient as possible, the system can use its knowledge of table size, indexes, order of tuples, and distribution of values to determine exactly how the query will be processed. In doing so, it estimates the "cost" of alternative execution plans and chooses the plan with the least estimated cost. To estimate cost, it considers the number and type of disk accesses required, the amount of internal and external memory needed, the processing time required, and communication costs, if any. The execution plan is then coded and executed at the appropriate time. Figure 11.1 summarizes this process for an SQL query. Although optimization of this type is time-consuming, the potential savings in query execution time and size of intermediate results can be tremendous, so it is worthwhile to spend the time optimizing before the query is executed. Of course, the optimization itself has a cost associated with it. As we

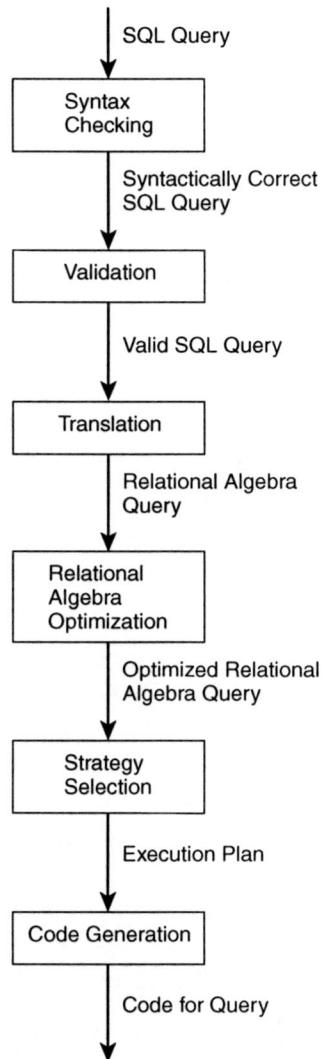

FIGURE 11.1
Interpretation and
Optimization Process

SQL Query

↓

Syntax
Checking

↓ Syntactically Correct
SQL Query

Validation

↓ Valid SQL Query

Translation

↓ Relational Algebra
Query

Relational
Algebra
Optimization

↓ Optimized Relational
Algebra Query

Strategy
Selection

↓ Execution Plan

Code Generation

↓ Code for Query

will see in subsequent sections, to make optimization possible the DBMS must maintain metadata about the database, keeping track of the number of records in tables, the number of values for attributes, the size of indexes, and other statistics to use in its estimates. There is the cost of executing the algorithms used for optimization. Some "smart" optimizers can dynamically change query execution strategies if the chosen strategy is not as efficient as expected when the query is partially executed, a process that incurs additional costs. The trade-off in query efficiency must compensate for these added costs.

11.2   Algebraic Techniques for Query Transformation

We will use the University database schema to illustrate manipulation of relational algebra queries.

```
Student (stuId, lastName, firstName, major, credits)
Class (classNumber, facId, schedule, room)
Faculty (facId, name, department, rank)
Enroll (stuId, classNumber, grade)
```

11.2.1 The Query Tree

A technique that is often used to represent relational algebra expressions is a **query tree** or a **parse tree** for an expression. This kind of a tree is a graphical representation of the operations and operands in a relational algebra expression. Relations are represented by leaf nodes, and unary or binary operations are represented by internal, non-leaf nodes of the tree. In executing a query tree, an internal node can be executed when its operands are available. The node is then replaced by the result of the operation it represents. The root node is the last to be executed, and it is replaced by the result of the entire tree. If relational calculus is used instead, the operations are represented by a **query graph** or **connection hypergraph.** The graph has nodes to represent each constant that appears in a query and each attribute in a relation, allowing repeats for attributes that appear in more than one relation. Edges connecting attribute nodes represent join conditions among tuple variables. Edges connecting constant nodes to attribute nodes represent selection conditions.

11.2.2 An SQL Query and Its Relational Algebra Translation

The query "Find the schedules and rooms of all courses taken by any Math major" could be expressed in SQL as:

```
SELECT    schedule, room
FROM      Class, Enroll, Student
WHERE     major = 'Math' AND Class.classNumber = Enroll.classNumber AND
          Enroll.stuId = Student.stuId;
```

One relational algebra translation for this SQL query is,

```
JOIN Student, Enroll GIVING Temp1
JOIN Temp1, Class GIVING Temp2
SELECT Temp2 WHERE major = 'Math' GIVING Temp3
PROJECT Temp3 OVER schedule, room
```

or symbolically,

$$\Pi_{\text{schedule, room}}(\sigma_{\text{major='Math'}} ((\text{Student} \bowtie \text{Enroll}) \bowtie \text{Class}))$$

The query tree corresponding to this expression is shown in Figure 11.2(a). If we were to execute this relational algebra query as written and as shown in the tree, we would begin by forming the natural join of `Student` and `Enroll` over their common column, stuId. Since this is a key for `Student`, the number of tuples in the join is simply the cardinality of `Enroll`, since there will be exactly one match in `Student` for each stuId in `Enroll`. This operation produces an intermediate table we have called `Temp1`. Now we join this result with `Class`, again producing an intermediate table containing one tuple for each tuple in `Enroll`, since we are joining over classNumber, the key of `Class`. The intermediate table has attributes stuId, lastName, firstName, major, credits, classNumber, grade, facId, schedule, and room. We then perform a selection on the intermediate table, choosing only those rows where the value of major is 'Math'. Finally, we project over two columns, schedule, and room, eliminating duplicates, if any.

11.2.3 Performing SELECT Operations Early

If we assume that `Student` has 10,000 records, `Class` has 2,500 records, and `Enroll` has 50,000 records, the execution just described would involve producing two intermediate tables with 50,000 fairly long records. Note that, for the first join, each `Enroll` record will join with exactly one student record, so there will be 50,000 tuples in `Temp1`. Similarly, each of these records will join with exactly one `Class` record, yielding 50,000 tuples for `Temp2`. Of these, only a small number, those with major = 'Math', are chosen in the SELECT operation. We could easily reduce the size of the intermediate tables by doing the SELECT operation earlier and then considering only those students whose major is mathematics. We could rewrite the query as,

```
SELECT Student WHERE major = 'Math' GIVING T1
JOIN T1, Enroll GIVING T2
JOIN T2, Class GIVING T3
PROJECT T3 OVER schedule, room
```

or symbolically,

$$\Pi_{\text{schedule,room}} (((\sigma_{\text{major = 'Math'}} (\text{Student})) \bowtie \text{Enroll}) \bowtie \text{Class})$$

FIGURE 11.2(a)
Initial Query Tree

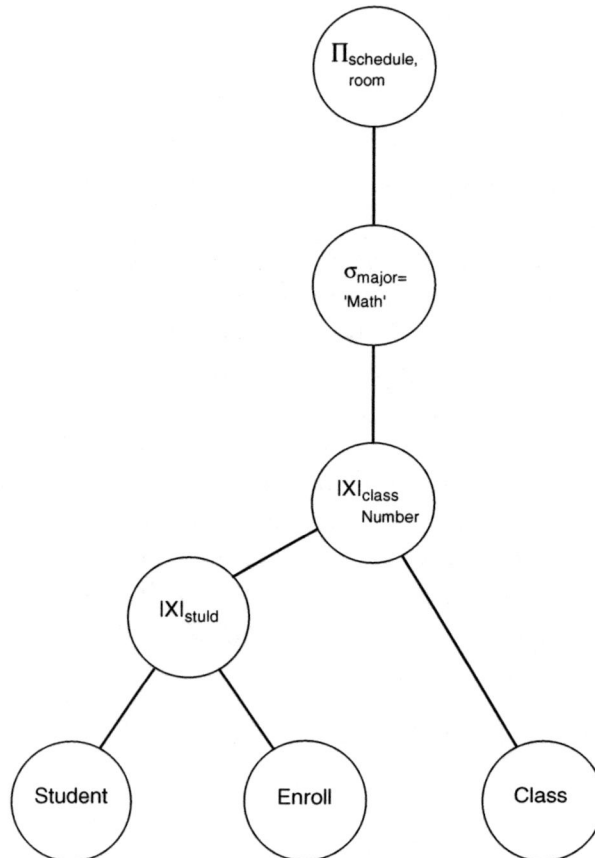

By reordering the operations in this way, we reduce the size of the intermediate tables. If we assume there are 400 mathematics majors, each taking
about five courses, we would expect only about 2000 records to result from
the join, a significant reduction from the 50,000 expected earlier. This
example illustrates the savings possible by performing SELECT operations
early. Figure 11.2(b) shows the query tree for the revised expression. Note
that we have pushed the SELECT down close to a leaf of the tree.

11.2.4 Evaluating Conjunctive Conditions

If the query involves an additional selection criterion, such as finding the
schedules and rooms of courses taken by those mathematics majors who
have more than 100 credits, we would want to apply that criterion as early
as possible, as well. In that case we would have a **conjunctive** condition, so

FIGURE 11.2(b)
Revised Query Tree

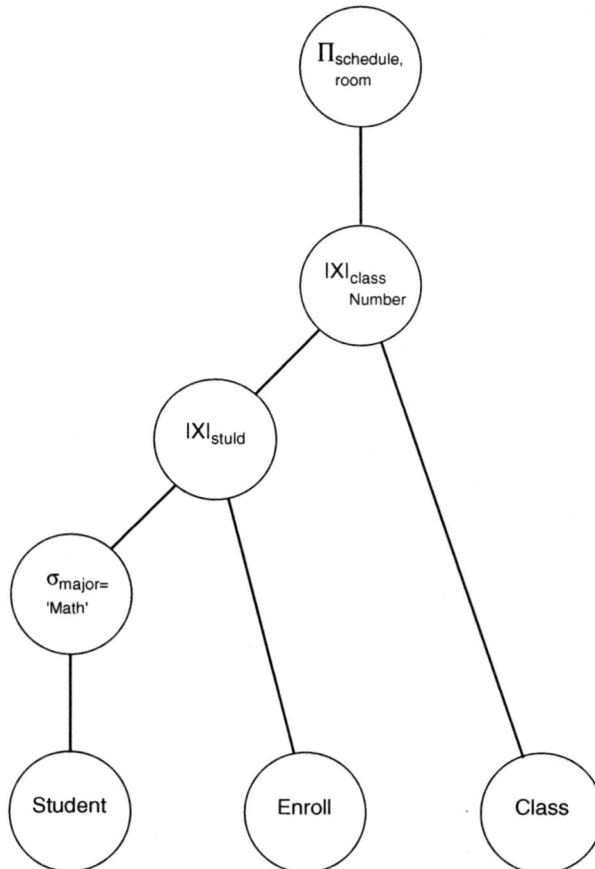

called because it involves a conjunction, an "and" of conditions. The SQL
query is:

```
SELECT schedule, room
FROM Student, Class, Enroll
WHERE major='Math' AND credits >100 AND Class.classNumber = Enroll.classNumber
AND Enroll.stuId = Student.stuId;
```

For the relational algebra expression, we could apply both selection criteria directly to the Student relation before doing the first join,

```
SELECT Student WHERE major = 'Math' AND credits > 100 GIVING T1
JOIN T1, Enroll GIVING T2
JOIN T2, Class GIVING T3
PROJECT T3 OVER schedule, room
```

or symbolically,

$$\Pi_{\text{schedule,room}}(((\sigma_{\text{major='Math' \& credits>100}}(\text{Student})) \; |\times| \; \text{Enroll}) \; |\times| \; \text{Class})$$

This reduces the size of the join still further. The query tree is essentially the one shown in Figure 11.2(b), modified by adding the condition on credits to the predicate for the selection.

Even if the second selection criterion in a conjunctive selection refers to another table, it is best to do it early. For example, if we had been asked to find the schedules and rooms for all mathematics majors who have received a grade of F, we would be unable to apply the conjunction condition,

```
major = 'Math' AND grade = 'F'
```

to the Student table, since the grade appears on the Enroll table. We could form the join first and then apply the conjunctive condition and evaluate the rest of the query,

```
JOIN Student, Enroll GIVING T1
SELECT T1 WHERE major = 'Math' AND grade ='F' GIVING T2
JOIN T2, Class GIVING T3
PROJECT T3 OVER schedule, room
```

which is:

$$\Pi_{\text{schedule,room}} ((\sigma_{\text{major='Math'\&grade='F'}}(\text{Student} \; |\times| \; \text{Enroll})) \; |\times| \; \text{Class})$$

Figure 11.3(a) shows the query tree for this expression. Unfortunately, this brings us back to an intermediate table size of 50,000 records.

However, if we now apply both selections to their corresponding tables before the join, we reduce the size of the intermediate tables,

```
SELECT Student WHERE major = 'Math' GIVING T1
SELECT Enroll WHERE grade = 'F' GIVING T2
JOIN T1, T2 GIVING T3
JOIN T3, Class GIVING T4
PROJECT T4 OVER schedule, room
```

or symbolically,

$$\Pi_{\text{schedule,room}} (((\sigma_{\text{major='Math'}}(\text{Student})) \; |\times| \; (\sigma_{\text{grade='F'}}(\text{Enroll}))) \; |\times| \; \text{Class})$$

Figure 11.3(b) gives the query tree for this version. It is much more efficient than earlier version, since it reduces the chosen tuples of both the Student table and the Enroll table before doing the join, keeping joined tuples to a minimum. Note that when the grade condition is applied to the Enroll table, all Enroll records having a grade of F will be returned, not just the ones belonging to mathematics majors. The natural join of these selected `Enroll` tuples with the selected `Student` tuples eliminates the `Enroll` tuples for other majors.

11.2.5 Performing PROJECT Early

We noted earlier that intermediate tables resulting from two joins consisted of very long records. Regardless of when the selections or joins were performed, the intermediate table always had all of the attributes from the three original tables. We could use projection to reduce the size of the tuples in the intermediate tables. In doing so, we must be careful not to drop any attributes that will be needed later. Taking as our query, "Find the schedule and room of all courses taken by mathematics majors who

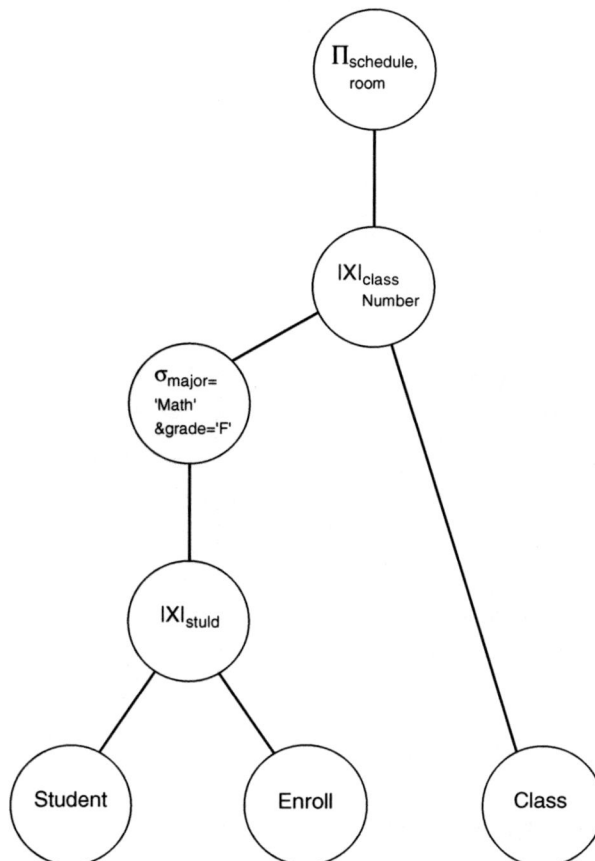

FIGURE 11.3(a)

Initial Query Tree Using Conjunction

FIGURE 11.3(b)
Final Query Tree Using
Conjunction

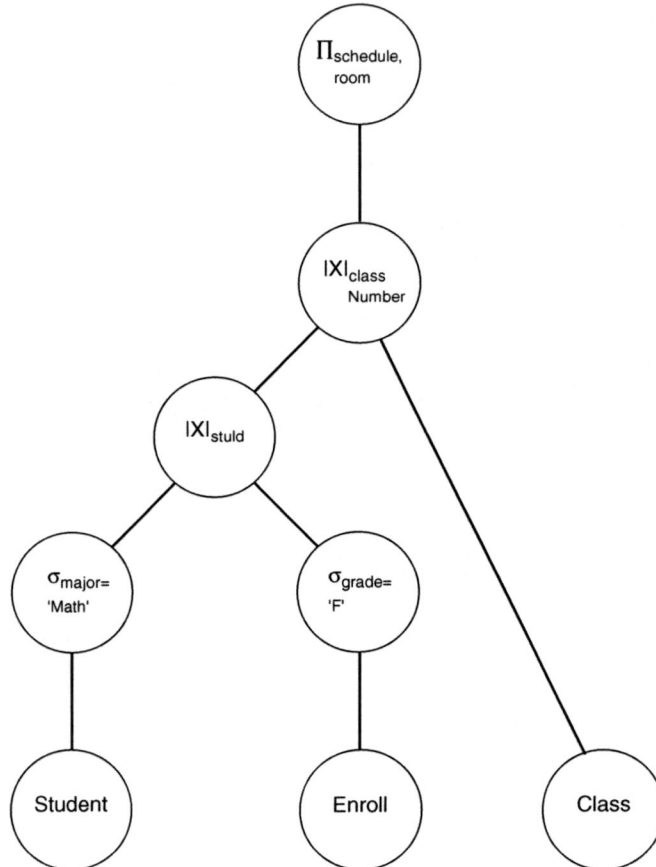

FIGURE 11.3(b)
Final Query Tree Using Conjunction

have an F in any course," we could add projections to reduce the size of intermediate tables,

```
SELECT Student WHERE major = 'Math' GIVING T1
PROJECT T1 OVER stuId GIVING T2
SELECT Enroll WHERE grade = 'F' GIVING T3
JOIN T2,T3 GIVING T4
PROJECT T4 OVER classNumber GIVING T5
JOIN T5, Class GIVING T6
PROJECT T6 OVER schedule, room
```

or symbolically,

$$\Pi_{schedule,room}((\Pi_{classNumber}((\Pi_{stuId}(\sigma_{major='Math'}\ (Student)))\ |\times|$$
$$(\sigma_{grade='F'}\ (Enroll))))\ |\times| Class)$$

The query tree for this expression is shown in Figure 11.4. Whether it is worthwhile performing all the projections depends on the amount of

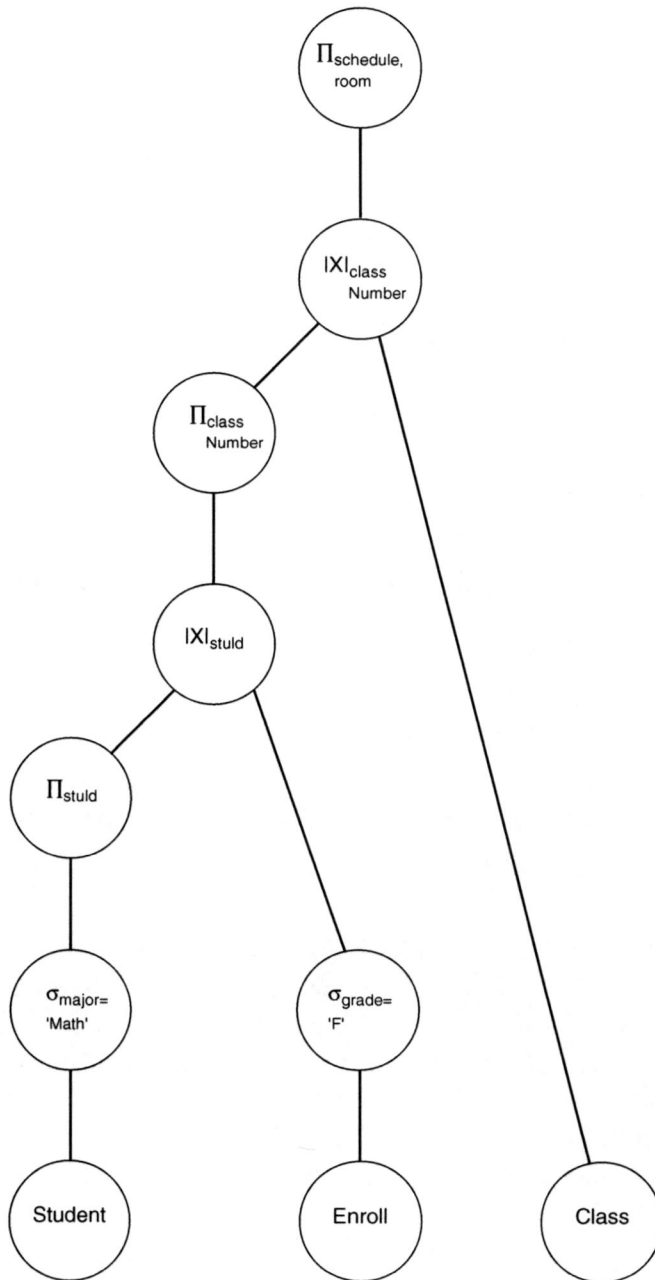

FIGURE 11.4
Query Tree Showing Projection

space saved and the costs involved in processing a projection. In any case, if we decide to do projections, we should do them early, before joins, when possible.

As these examples show, the order in which we perform relational algebra operations in executing a query can greatly affect its efficiency. We need to examine the properties of these operations more closely to determine how they can be reordered.

11.2.6 Properties of the Natural Join

In the example shown in Figure 11.2(a), we found:

(Student $|\times|$ Enroll) $|\times|$ Class)

Natural joins are associative, so we could have processed this expression as,

Student $|\times|$ (Enroll $|\times|$ Class)

Thus we could have found the join of Enroll and Class and formed a large intermediate table which we would have joined with the tuples of Student. This would have been less efficient than the method we chose in Figure 11.2(b). However, there may be instances in which associativity can be used to reduce the size of results.

The natural join is also commutative, if we ignore column order. Therefore, Enroll $|\times|$ Class = Class $|\times|$ Enroll. Using both commutativity and associativity, we could have executed our query as:

(Student $|\times|$ Class) $|\times|$ Enroll

This would have been an inefficient choice for this example, since Student and Class have no common attributes, so their natural join becomes their Cartesian product. If we had 10,000 Student records and 2500 Class records, as we assumed earlier, the intermediate table would have 25,000,000 records. There is obviously no advantage in rearranging the joins for this example. However, if we had started with this expression, we could have used the properties of the natural join to develop the more efficient form seen earlier in Figure 11.2.

11.2.7 Equivalence of Algebraic Operations

Our examples showed some of the ways that relational algebra expressions can be transformed into equivalent ones that are more efficient. We consider two relations to be equivalent if they have the same attributes, even though the attribute order may be different, and if the values associated with those attributes are identical for corresponding tuples of the two relations. The following list presents some laws governing operations in relational algebra, where R, S, and T represent relations or expressions involving relations. It is possible to prove all of the rules listed here, although we will not present the proofs.

1. *Joins and products are commutative.* The commutative law holds for all types of joins and products. Recall we used theta, θ, to stand for any condition for a join. Then we have,

   R × S = S × R and
   R $|\times|_\theta$ S = S $|\times|_\theta$ R and
   R $|\times|$ S = S $|\times|$ R

2. *Joins and products are associative.* Natural joins, theta-joins, and products are all associative.

   (R × S) × T = R × (S × T)
   (R $|\times|_\theta$ S) $|\times|_\theta$ T = R $|\times|_\theta$ (S $|\times|_\theta$ T)
   (R $|\times|$ S) $|\times|$ T = R $|\times|$ (S $|\times|$ T)

3. *Select is commutative.* If p and q are selection conditions, then

   $\sigma_p (\sigma_q (R)) = \sigma_q (\sigma_p (R))$

4. *Conjunctive selects can cascade into individual selects.* If we have a series of select conditions connected by "and," we can break up the conjunction into a sequence of individual selects.

   $\sigma_{p\&q\&...\&z} (R) = (\sigma_p (\sigma_q(...(\sigma_z (R))...)))$

   Obviously, we can use the equivalence in the other direction to combine cascading selects into a conjunctive select, when convenient.

5. *Successive projects can reduced to the final project.* If $list_1, list_2, ...$ $list_n$ are lists of attribute names such that each of each of the $list_i$ contains $list_{i-1}$, then,

   $\Pi_{list1} (\Pi_{list2} (...\Pi_{listn} (R)...) =_{list1}(R)$

   This means that only the last project has to be executed.

6. *Select and project sometimes commute.* If the selection condition involves only the attributes in the projection list, projlist, then select and project commute:

   $\Pi_{projlist} (\sigma_p (R)) = \sigma_p (\Pi_{projlist} (R))$

7. *Select and join (or product) sometimes commute.* If the selection condition involves only attributes of one of the tables being joined, then select and join (or select and product) commute. If we assume the predicate p involves only attributes of R, then the following holds:

$$\sigma_p \ (R \ |\times| \ S) = (\sigma_p \ (R)) \ |\times| \ S$$

This rule also applies to theta-join and product.

8. *Select sometimes distributes over join (or product).* If the selection condition is a conjunctive condition having the form p AND q, where p involves only the attributes of relation R and q involves only the attributes of relation S, then the select distributes over the join:

$$\sigma_{p \ ANDq} \ (R \ |\times| \ S) = (\sigma_p \ (R)) \ |\times| \ (\sigma_q \ (S))$$

Again, the rule applies to theta-join and product.

9. *Project sometimes distributes over join (or product).* If the projection list, projlist, can be split into separate lists, list1 and list2, so that list1 contains only attributes of R and list2 contains only attributes of S, then:

$$\Pi_{projlist} \ (R \ |\times| \ S) = (\Pi_{ist1} \ (R)) \ |\times| \ (\Pi_{ist2} \ (S))$$

For a theta-join, the distributive law holds if the join condition involves only attributes of projlist. If it involves additional attributes, they must first be added to the projection list on the left of the equivalence sign. Then they are placed with either list1 or list2 on the right, depending on which relation or relational expression they are associated with. After the join is performed, a final projection onto the original projection list must be done.

10. *Set operations of union and intersection are commutative.*

$$R \cup S = S \cup R$$
$$R \cap S = S \cap R$$

However, set difference is not commutative.

11. *Set operations of union and intersection are individually associative.*

$$(R \cup S) \cup T = R \cup (S \cup T)$$
$$(R \cap S) \cap T = R \cap (S \cap T)$$

Although union and intersection are associative when used individually, they cannot be mixed in an expression. Set difference is not associative.

12. *Select distributes over set union, set intersection, and set difference.*

$$\sigma_p \ (R \cup S) = \sigma_p \ (R) \cup \sigma_p \ (S)$$
$$\sigma_p \ (R \cap S) = \sigma_p \ (R) \cap \sigma_p \ (S)$$
$$\sigma_p \ (R - S) = \sigma_p \ (R) - \sigma_p \ (S)$$

13. *Project distributes over set union, set intersection, and set difference.*

$$\Pi_{projlist} \ (R \cup S) = (\Pi_{projlist} \ (R)) \cup (\Pi_{projlist} \ (S))$$
$$\Pi_{projlist} \ (R \cap S) = (\Pi_{projlist} \ (R)) \cap (\Pi_{projlist} \ (S))$$
$$\Pi_{projlist} \ (R - S) = (\Pi_{projlist} \ (R)) - (\Pi_{projlist} \ (S))$$

14. *Project is idempotent, meaning repeating it produces the same result.*

$$\Pi_{projlist} \ (\Pi_{projlist} \ (R)) = \Pi_{projlist} \ (R)$$

15. *Select is idempotent.*

$$\sigma_p(\sigma_p \ (R)) = \sigma_p \ (R)$$

This list of transformations is not exhaustive, but it is sufficient to illustrate possible substitutions that the query optimizer could consider for given algebraic expressions.

11.2.8 Heuristics for Query Optimization

Heuristics are "rules of thumb" that can be used to help solve problems. They are not always guaranteed to work in a particular situation, but they are techniques that we can try out to see if they produce a good result. We now examine some heuristics that have been developed for optimizing relational algebra expressions. A cardinal rule is to try to reduce the size of intermediate results by doing selects and projects as early as possible, and to execute first those selects and projects that reduce the table sizes as much as possible. The heuristics are:

1. Do selection as early as possible. If appropriate, use cascading of selects, commutativity of selects with projects, joins and products, and distributivity of select over set union, set intersection, and set difference to move the selection as far down the query tree as possible.

2. Use associativity of join, product, union, and intersection to rearrange relations in the query tree so that the selection operation that will produce the smallest table will be executed first.

3. If a product appears as an argument for a selection, where the selection involves attributes of the tables in the product, transform the product into a join. If the selection involves attributes of

only one of the tables in the product, apply the selection to that table first.

4. Do projection early. If appropriate, use cascading of projects, distributivity of projection over product and set union, intersection, and difference, and commutativity of selection and projection to move the projection as far down the query tree as possible. Examine all projections to see if some are unnecessary.

5. If there is a sequence of selections and/or projections with the same argument, use commutativity or cascading to combine them into one selection, one projection, or a selection followed by a projection.

6. If a subexpression appears more than once in the query tree, and the result it produces is not too large, compute it once and save it. This technique is especially useful when querying on views, since the same subexpression must be used to construct the view each time.

These heuristics can be incorporated into an algorithm that a query optimizer could use to produce the optimized relational algebra query, as shown for the University example queries in Figures 11.2(b), 11.3(b), and 11.4. In fact, we used these rules to optimize the queries for those examples. The next step is for the strategy selector to choose an execution plan.

11.3 Processing Techniques and Cost Estimation

To develop an execution plan, the strategy selector must consider the various ways each of the operations in the query tree could be executed. It "prices" each method by considering the costs of the processes involved.

11.3.1 Cost Factors

The cost of executing a query is determined by the cost of reading files, the processing costs once data is in main memory, the cost of writing and storing any intermediate results, the communication costs, and the cost of writing the final results to storage. Of these, the most significant factor is the number of disk accesses, the read and write costs. In calculating these costs, the system must use statistics stored in the data dictionary and knowledge about the size, structure, and access methods of each file.

A table can be stored in **packed form,** in which blocks contain only tuples from that table, or in **unpacked form,** in which tuples from the table are interspersed with tuples from other tables. If the storage form is unpacked, it is difficult to calculate the number of blocks needed. In the worst case, we would have to assume every tuple of the relation is in a different block. If the storage form is packed, we could estimate the number of blocks needed to hold the table if we knew the tuple size, number of tuples, and capacity of the blocks. We will ordinarily assume all tables are in packed form.

For the University example, if the Student relation is stored in packed form in blocks of 4K bytes, and each of the 10,000 student records is 200 bytes long, then 20 records fit per block (4096/200), ignoring any overhead for block headers and so on. Then, 10000/20 or 500 blocks are needed to hold this file in packed form. The access cost is the number of blocks that must be brought into main memory for reading or that must be written out to secondary storage for writing. The values associated with access cost are:

- $t(R)$, the number of tuples in the relation R

- $b(R)$, the number of blocks needed to store the relation R

- $bf(R)$, the number of tuples of R per block, also called the **blocking factor** of R

If R is packed, then:

- $b(R) = t(R)/bf(R)$

The tuples in the blocks containing R can be arranged in some order, often by increasing value of a primary key, but sometimes by the value of a secondary key. Alternatively, they can be in random order, or hashed on the value of a primary key. The access method used determines the storage structure. The file can be accessed by an index on the primary key, secondary indexes on non-primary key attributes, or a hashing function. For each table, we can have one **clustered index,** which means that tuples with the same value of the index appear in the same block. Other indexes will then be **nonclustered.** An index can be **dense,** having an entry for each tuple of the relation, or **nondense.** The index normally is a multilevel structure such as a **B+ tree** or a similar organization, as described in Appendix A. The purpose of the index is to speed access to the data file, but we must first access the index itself, so the additional overhead of accessing the index must be considered in the access cost. However, it is usually slight compared to the cost of accessing the data records. When using indexes, we will use the following:

- l(*index-name*), the number of levels in a multi-level index or the average number of index accesses needed to find an entry.

The purpose of an index is to tell us which records of the file have a particular value for an attribute. For cost estimation, we often need an estimate of the number of such records. The data dictionary can store this statistic:

- n(A,R), the number of distinct values of attribute A in relation R

From this statistic, we can approximate the number of tuples that have a particular value for A. If we assume that the values of A are **uniformly distributed** in R, then the number of tuples expected to have a particular value, c, for A, which we will call the **selection size** or s(A = c,R), is:

- s(A=c,R) = t(R)/n(A,R)

If the attribute, A, is a candidate key, then each tuple will have a unique value for that attribute, so n(A,R) = t(R) and the selection size is 1.

To illustrate the use of the formula, suppose we try to estimate the number of students in the university with a major of mathematics. We know there are 10,000 students, so t(Student) = 10000. Let us assume there are 25 possible major subjects, so n(major, Student) = 25. Then we can estimate the number of Mathematics majors as:

```
s(major='Math',Student) = t(Student)/n(major,Student) = 10000/25 = 400
```

Notice that we have to assume that majors are uniformly distributed, that the number of students choosing each major is about equal. Some systems store more information about the distribution of values, maintaining **histograms,** which are graphs that display the frequencies of different values of attributes. The histogram would be used to give a more accurate estimate of the selection size for a particular value. Many systems also store the minimum and maximum values for each attribute. In our examples, we will continue to assume uniform distribution.

11.3.2   Cost of Processing Selects

We use these factors to estimate the reading cost of various techniques for performing a selection of the form $\sigma_{A=c}(R)$. Our choice of method depends to a great extent on what access paths exist—whether the file is hashed on the selection attribute(s), whether the file has an index on the attribute(s), and if so, whether the index is clustered, or whether the file is in order by the selection attribute(s).

1. *Using a full table scan.* We begin with the "worst case" method, also called a **full table scan.** This is the method used when there is no access path for the attribute, such as an index, hash key, or ordering on the attribute, and the attribute is not a candidate key. Since this is the default method, we will always compare the cost of other methods with this one, and choose the one with lower cost. The cost is the number of blocks in the table, since we have to examine every tuple in the table to see if it qualifies for the selection, that is:

   ▪ b(R)

   For example, if we want to find all students who have first name of "Tom," we need to access each block of Student. We previously calculated the number of blocks of Student to be 10000/20 or 500, so:

   Reading Cost $(\sigma_{firstName='Tom'}(\text{Student})) = b(\text{Student}) = 500$

2. *Using a hash key to retrieve a single record.* If A is a hash key having unique values, then we apply the hashing algorithm to calculate the target address for the record. If there is no overflow, the expected number of accesses is 1. If there is overflow, we can get an estimate of the average number of accesses required to reach a record, depending on the amount of overflow and the overflow handling method used. This statistic, which we call h, can be available to the optimizer. The cost is:

   ▪ h

   For example, if we are told that the Faculty file is hashed on facId and h=2, then:

   Reading Cost $(\sigma_{facId='F101'}(\text{Faculty})) = 2$

3. *Selection for equality on a key using an index.* When we have an index on a key field, we retrieve whatever index blocks are needed and then go directly to the record from the index. The system may store the number of levels in indexes. Therefore, using l to represent the number of index levels, the cost is:

   ▪ l(index-name) + 1.

Consider the simple selection $\sigma_{stuId = \text{'S1001'}}$ (Student). Since stuId is the primary key, if we have an index on stuId, called Student_stuId_ndx, having 3 levels, we have:

Reading Cost ($\sigma_{stuId=\text{'S1001'}}$(Student)) = l(Student_stuId_ndx) + 1 = 3+1 = 4

4. *Selection for equality on a non-clustering index on a secondary key attribute.* For the predicate A = c with non-clustering index on secondary key A, the number of tuples that satisfy the condition is the selection size of the indexed attribute, s(A=c,R), and we must assume the tuples are on different blocks, which we have to access individually. We will assume that all the tuples having value A=c are pointed to by the index, perhaps using a linked list or an array of pointers. The cost is the number of index accesses plus the number of blocks for the tuples that satisfy the condition, or:

   - l(index-name) + s(A=c,R)

   For example, suppose we have a non-clustering index on major in Student and we wish to do the selection $\sigma_{major=\text{'CSC'}}$ (Student). We would find records having a major value of 'CSC' by reading the index node for 'CSC' and going from there to each tuple it points to. If the index has 2 levels, the cost will be:

   Reading Cost($\sigma_{major=\text{'CSC'}}$ (Student)) = l(Student_major_ndx) + s(major='CSC', Student)= 2 + (10000/25) = 2+400 = 402

   We note that this is only slightly less than the worst case cost, which is 500.

5. *Selection for equality using a clustering index on an attribute.* If our selection involves a secondary key, A, and we have a clustering index on attribute A, we use the selection size for the indexed attribute divided by the blocking factor to estimate the number of blocks we have to retrieve. Note that we assume the tuples of R having value A = c reside on contiguous blocks, so this calculation estimates the number of blocks needed to store these tuples. We add that to the number of index blocks needed. Then the cost is:

   - l(index-name) + (s(A=c,R))/bf(R)

   For example, if the index on major in the Student file were a clustering index, then to select students with a major of CSC, we would assume that the 400 records expected to have this value for major would be stored on contiguous blocks and the index would point to the first block. Then we could simply retrieve the following blocks to find all 400 records. The cost is:

Reading Cost($\sigma_{\text{major}='\text{CSC}'}$ (Student)) = 1(Student_major_ndx) + s(major='CSC', Student)/bf(Student) = 2+(400/20) = 22

6. *Selection on an ordered file.* If the predicate has the form A = c, where A is a key with unique values and records are arranged in order by A, a binary search can be used to access the record with A value of c. Using the cost of the binary search, the cost of this method under these conditions is approximately:

   - $\log_2 b(R)$

   For example, suppose we want to find a class record for a given classNumber, and we are told the Class file is in order by classNumber. We first calculate the number of blocks in the table. If there are 2500 Class records, each 100 bytes long, stored in blocks of size 4K, the blocking factor is 4096/100, or 40, so the number of blocks is 2500/40 or 63. (Note that we round up if part of a block is needed.) Then using the formula, we get the cost estimate:

   $$\sigma_{\text{classNumber}='\text{Eng201A}'} \text{ (Class)} = \log_2(63) \approx 6$$

   If A is not a key attribute, there can be several records with A value of c, and the estimate must be adjusted to consider the selection size, s(A=c,R) divided by the number of records per block. In that case, we get an estimate of:

   - $\log_2 b(R) + s(A=c,R)/bf(R)$

7. *Conjunctive selection with a composite index.* If the predicate is a conjunction and a composite index exists for the attributes in the predicate, this case reduces to one of the previous cases, depending on whether the attributes represent a composite key, and whether the index is clustered or a B+ tree.

8. *Conjunctive selection without a composite index.* If one of the conditions involves an attribute that is used for ordering records in the file, or has an index or a hash key, then we use the appropriate method from those previously described to retrieve records that satisfy that part of the predicate, using the cost estimates given previously. Once we retrieve the records, we check to see if they satisfy the rest of the conditions. If no attribute can be used for efficient retrieval, we use the full table scan and check all the conditions simultaneously for each tuple.

11.3.3 Processing Joins

The join is generally the most expensive operation to perform in a relational system, and since it is often used in queries, it is important to be able to estimate its cost. The access cost depends on the method of processing as well as the size of the results.

11.3.3.1 Estimating the Size of the Result

An important cost factor to consider in processing joins is the size of the result. If R and S are relations of size t(R) and t(S) respectively, then to calculate the size of their join, we need to estimate the number of tuples of R that will match tuples of S on the corresponding attributes. Two special cases exist.

- If the tables have no common attributes, then the join becomes a product, and the number of tuples in the result is **t(R) * t(S).** For example, if we join `Class` and `Student`, which have no common attributes, there are 10,000*2500 tuples in the result.

- If the set of common attributes is a key for one of the relations, the number of tuples in the join can be no larger than the number of tuples in the other relation, since each of these can match no more than one of the key values. For R |×| S, if the common attributes are a key for R, then the size of the join is **less than or equal to t(S).** For example, if we form the natural join of `Student` and `Enroll`, since `stuId` is the primary key of `Student`, the number of tuples in the result will be the same as the number of tuples in `Enroll`, or 50,000, since each `Enroll` tuple has exactly one matching `Student` tuple.

The difficult case is the general one in which the common attributes do not form a key of either relation. We must estimate the number of matches. Let us assume that there is one common attribute, A, and that its values are uniformly distributed in both relations. For a particular value, c, of A in R, we would expect the number of tuples in S having a matching value of c for A to be the selection size of A in S, or s(A=c,S). We saw earlier that an estimate of the selection size is the number of tuples in S divided by the number of different values for A in S, or t(S)/n(A,S). This gives us the number of matches in S for a particular tuple in R. However, since there are t(R) tuples in R, each of which may have this number of matches, the total expected number of matches in the join is given by:

- $t(R \mathbin{|\times|} S) = t(R)*t(S) / n(A,S)$

If we had started by considering tuples in S and looked for matches in R, we would have derived a slightly different formula.

- $t(R \bowtie S) = t(S)*t(R) / n(A,R)$

Normally, we use the formula that gives the smaller result.

The number of blocks needed to write the result of a join depends on the blocking factor. If we know the number of bytes in each of R and S, we can estimate the number of bytes in the joined tuples to be roughly their sum, and divide the block size by that number to get the blocking factor of the result. Then we can find the number of blocks by dividing the expected number of tuples by the blocking factor.

11.3.3.2 Methods of Performing Joins

Now we consider the read costs of different methods of performing a join. The choice of method depends on the size of the files, whether the files are sorted on the join attribute(s), whether indexes or hash keys exist for the join attribute(s).

1. *Nested Loops.* This is the default method, which must be used when no special access paths exist. If we assume both R and S are packed relations, having b(R) and b(S) blocks respectively, and we have two buffers for reading, plus one for writing the result, we can bring the first block of R into the first buffer, and then bring each block of S, in turn, into the second buffer. We compare each tuple of the R block with each tuple of the S block before switching in the next S block. When we have finished all the S blocks, we bring in the next R block into the first buffer, and go through all the S blocks again. We repeat this process until all of R has been compared with all of S. Figure 11.5 illustrates the process. The algorithm is:

```
for each block of R
    for each block of S
        for each tuple in the R block
            for each tuple in the S block
                if the tuples satisfy the condition then add to join
            end
        end
    end
end
```

FIGURE 11.5

**Nested Loop Join with
Two Buffers for Reading**

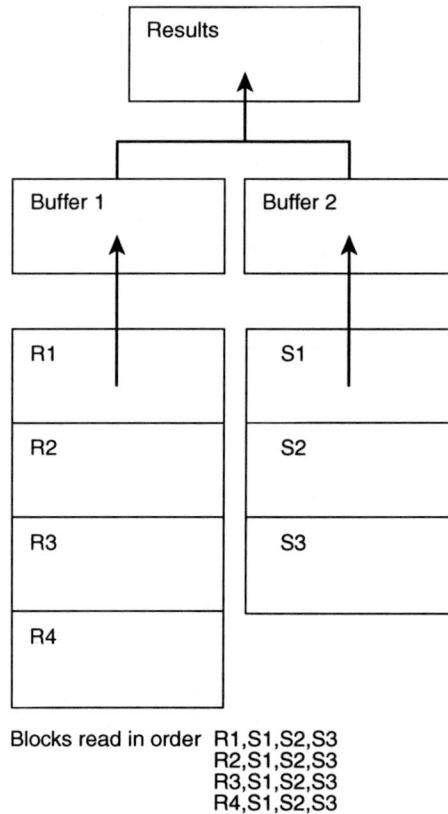

Blocks read in order R1,S1,S2,S3
R2,S1,S2,S3
R3,S1,S2,S3
R4,S1,S2,S3

The number of accesses to read the data for this method is given by,

- Read cost (R $|\times|$ S) = b(R) + (b(R)*b(S))

  since each block of R has to be read, and each block of S has to be read once for each block of R. For the example shown in Figure 11.5, there are 4 blocks of R and 3 blocks of S, giving us 4+4*3 = 16 blocks read. They are read in the order shown below the figure. Note that if R and S were not packed relations, we could not use the block-by-block method, and would have to assume each tuple is on a separate block. The read cost then would have been much larger, namely

- t(R) + (t(R)*t(S))

  We could use the nested loop method to compute the reading cost for performing the join Student $|\times|$ Enroll, assuming both are packed. Let us assume that Student has 10,000 tuples, occupying

500 blocks, and `Enroll` has 50,000 tuples, each 100 bytes. Assuming blocks are 4K as before, the blocking factor is 4096/100, or 40, so the `Enroll` file occupies 50000/40 or 1250 blocks. We assume `Student` has 500 blocks, as calculated previously. Using `Student` for the outside loop, our reading cost for this example is:

$b(Student) + (b(Student) * b(Enroll)) = 500 + (500*1250) = 625,500$

If the files were not packed, then the reading cost for `Student` $|\times|$ `Enroll` would be:

$t(Student) + (t(Student) * t(Enroll))$ or $10000 + (10000*50000) = 500,010,000$.

It is important to note that the size of the file chosen for the outer loop has a significant effect on the reading cost, since the number of tuples (for the unpacked case) or the number of blocks (for the packed case) in the outer loop file must be added to the product of the sizes of the two files. Therefore, we should pick the smaller file for the outside loop. If we had chosen to use `Enroll` for the outer loop, our result for the packed case would have been 626,250 and for the unpacked case 500,050,000.

If the buffer can hold more than three blocks, the best strategy is to read into the buffer as many blocks as possible from the file in the outer loop, and save buffer space for only one block from the file in the inner loop, plus the space for writing the result. For example, if b(B) is the number of blocks the buffer can hold, then, using R as the file for the outer loop and S as the file for the inner loop, we should read b(B)-2 blocks of R into the buffer at a time, and only 1 block of S. The total number of blocks of R accessed is still b(R), but the total number of S blocks that need to be accessed is reduced to approximately $b(S)*(b(R)/(b((B) - 2))$. The cost of accessing the files then becomes:

- $b(R) + ((b(S)*(b(R))/(b((B) - 2))$

However, if there is enough space in the buffer to allow one of the relations to fit with room for one more block from the other file, plus the block for storing the results, then we should choose that one for the inner loop. For example, suppose S fits in main memory. Then S has to be read only once, and we should store it in the buffer while switching in blocks of R one at a time. The cost of reading the two packed files then reduces to the most efficient possible cost, which is:

- $b(R) + b(S)$

2. *Sort-Merge Join.* A very efficient join strategy is achieved when both files are sorted on the attribute(s) to be joined. In this case, the join algorithm is a variation on the algorithm for merging two sorted files. When the files are sorted, we would expect that all tuples having a specific value, say c, for the join attribute, A, would be on a single block in each relation. We begin the join by bringing the first block of each relation into the buffer and finding all the records in R with the first value for A, and then all the records in S with that same value. These are then joined and written to the result file. Then we move on to the next value in each of the files, and so forth. Each block of each file will be read only once, unless there are some records with the same A value in different blocks, which is relatively rare. Therefore the cost for accessing the two files is just:

- $b(R) + b(S)$

Because this join is so efficient, it might be worthwhile to sort the files before a join. In that case, the cost of sorting, which depends on the sorting method used, would have to be added to the cost of accessing the files.

3. *Using an Index or Hash Key.* If one of the files, S, has an index on the common attribute A, or if A is a hash key for S, then each tuple of R would be retrieved in the usual way by reading in the R blocks, and the index or hashing algorithm would be used to find all the matching records of S. The cost of this method depends on the type of index. For example, if A is the primary key of S, we have a primary index on S and the access cost is the cost of accessing all the blocks of R plus the cost of reading the index and accessing one record of S for each of the tuples in R:

- $b(R) + (t(R) * (l(indexname) + 1))$

We could use this to find Student $|\times|$ Enroll if we assume that Student has an index on its primary key stuId. We access each Enroll block in sequence and then, for each Enroll tuple in each block, we use the index on stuId to find each matching Student record. If the index has 2 levels, the read cost is, b(Enroll) +(t(Enroll) *(2+1)) = 1250 + (50000*3) = 151,250

which is about four times as efficient as the nested loop method we priced earlier.

If the index is on an attribute that is not a primary key, we have to consider the number of matches in S per tuple of R, which increases the read cost to:

- b(R) + (t(R) * (l(indexname) + s(A=c,S)))

However, if the index is a clustering index, we can reduce the estimate by dividing by the blocking factor, since several S records on each block will have the same value for A.

- b(R) + (t(R) * (l(indexname) + s(A=c,S)/bf(S)))

If we have a hash function in S instead of an index, then the cost is,

- b(R) + (t(R) * h)

where h is the average number of accesses to get to a block from its key in S.

11.3.4 Processing Other Operations

11.3.4.1 Projection

A projection operation involves finding the values of the attributes on the projection list for each tuple of the relation, and eliminating duplicates, if any exist. If a projection has a projection list containing a key of the relation, then the projection can be performed by reading each tuple of the relation and copying to the results file only the values of the attributes in the projection list. There will be no duplicates, because of the presence of the key. The read cost is the number of blocks in the relation, which is,

- b(R)

and the number of tuples in the result will be the number of tuples in the relation, t(R). However, depending on the size of the projection list, the resulting tuples might be considerably smaller than the tuples of R, so the number of blocks needed to write the result might be much smaller than the blocks needed for R.

If the projection list consists of non-key attributes only, then we must eliminate duplicates. One method is sorting the results so that duplicates will appear next to one another, and then eliminating any tuple that is a duplicate of the previous one until no duplicates remain. To calculate the

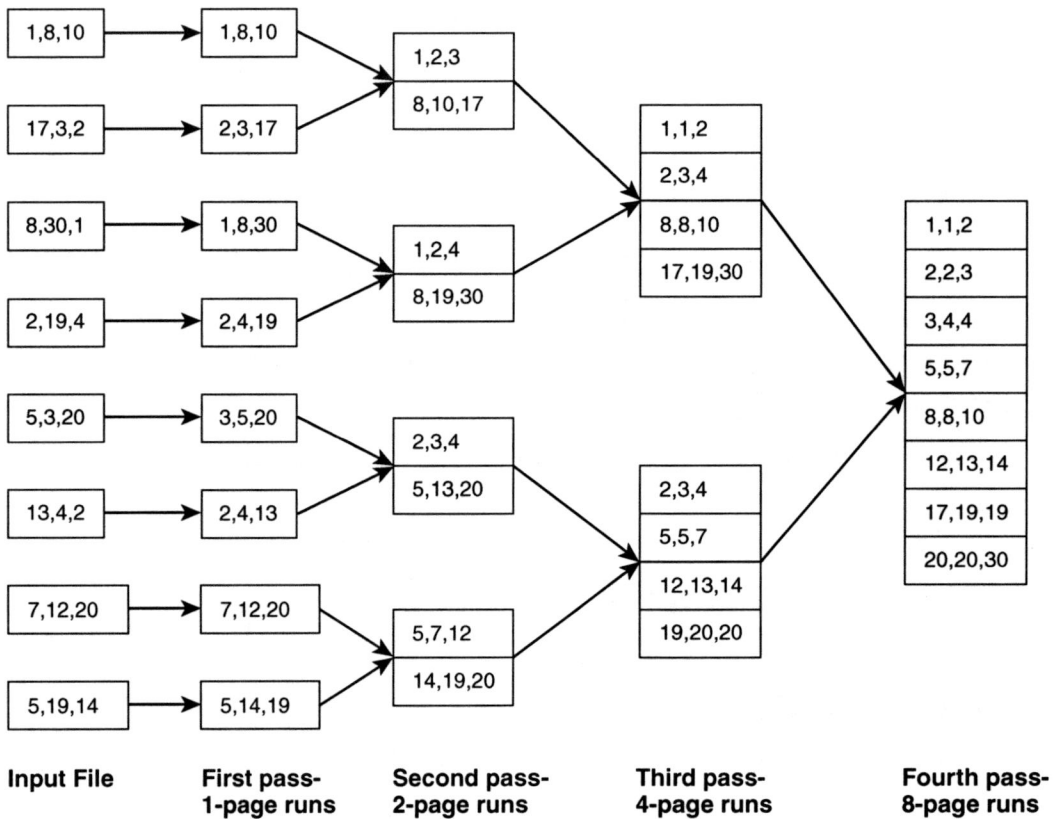

Input File	First pass- 1-page runs	Second pass- 2-page runs	Third pass- 4-page runs	Fourth pass- 8-page runs

FIGURE 11.6(a)

External Two-Way Merge Sort

cost, we find the sum of the cost of accessing all the blocks of the relation to create a temporary file with only attributes on the projection list, plus the cost of writing the temporary file, the cost of sorting the temporary file, the cost of accessing the sorted temporary file from secondary storage to eliminate duplicates, and the cost of writing the final results file. The sorting operation is the most expensive of these steps. In general, external sorting is required in a database environment, since files are too large to fit in main memory. A simple two-way merge sort can be used if there are three buffers available. This sort is illustrated in Figure 11.6. The process involves creating sorted subfiles called **runs** at each step. The runs are then merged at the next step. In the first step shown on the left in Figure 11.6(b), each page of the input file is read in and sorted internally using a standard

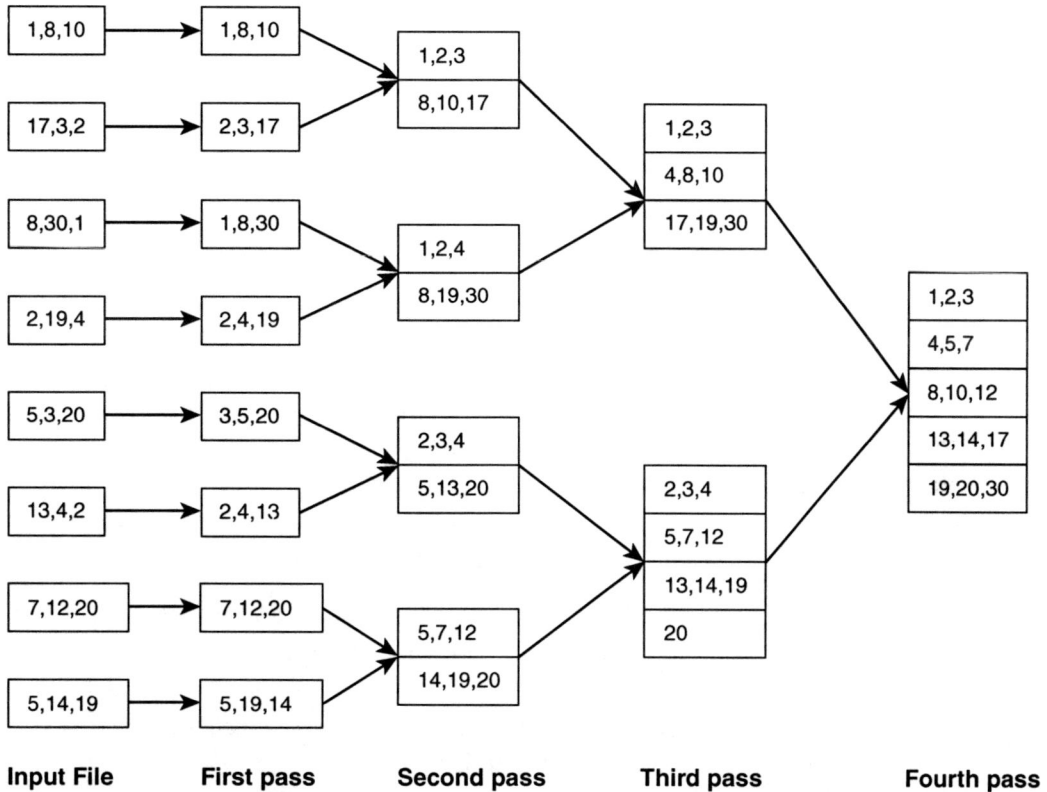

FIGURE 11.6(b)

Revised External Two-Way Merge Sort

in-memory sort algorithm such as Quicksort. The second step is performed by reading in pairs of runs from the previous results, merging them to produce runs of length two pages each. Two pages are read at a time, each in its own buffer. The first value in the first buffer is compared with the first value in the second buffer, and the smaller of the two is written to the output buffer and eliminated from the values to be compared. The larger of the two is then compared with the next value in the buffer from which the first was eliminated. The process continues until all values from both pages have been written to two output pages. Then the next two pages are compared, and so on until all pages have been read. In the third step, the previous runs of length two pages are compared, creating runs of four pages. In the fourth step, a single sorted run is created. The number of disk accesses for this example is 64, because in each step, each of the eight pages must be read and/or written, resulting in 16 input/output operations for each step. For the four steps, 64 operations are needed. In general, if there are n pages in the file, the number of passes needed will be $(\log_2 n)+1$, and the number of disk accesses required just for the sorting phase will be:

- $2n((\log_2 n)+1)$

In our example, we had eight pages, and we needed $(\log_2 8)+1$, which is 3+1, or 4 passes. We needed $2*8((\log_2 8)+1))$, which is 16(4) or 64 disk accesses. The cost can be reduced if more than three buffers are used. The initial cost of reading the entire input file to choose only attributes on the projection list can be eliminated if the first sorting pass is used to drop unwanted attributes, as well as to sort. We can also eliminate duplicates at each merge step, resulting in the improvement shown in Figure 11.6(b) for our example, which requires only 59 disk accesses.

Another method can be used if there are several buffers available. It uses hashing, which requires two phases, a partitioning phase and a duplicate elimination phase. In the partitioning phase, one buffer page is used for reading the table, one page at a time. The remaining buffers form the output pages for the hash partitions. Figure 11.7 shows the partitioning phase. Each tuple in the input page is reduced to its projection list attributes, and then a hashing function is used on the combination of these attributes. The value of the output determines which buffer page the reduced tuple will be placed in, and which partition it will end up in. Since two tuples with the same value on the projection list attributes would hash to the same partition, any duplicates will be placed in the same partition. Therefore, duplicate elimination is performed for each partition. This phase can be accomplished by using a new hashing function on the pages of the partition. Each page of the partition is read in, one at a time, and an in-memory hash table is created. If two tuples hash to the same value, they are compared, and any duplicate is eliminated. When the entire partition has been read, the hash table is written to disk, the buffers are cleared, and the next partition is processed.

11.3.4.2 Set Operations

The set operations of union, intersection, and difference can be done only on files that are union-compatible, having identical structures. If we sort both files on the same attributes, we can then modify the sort-merge algo-

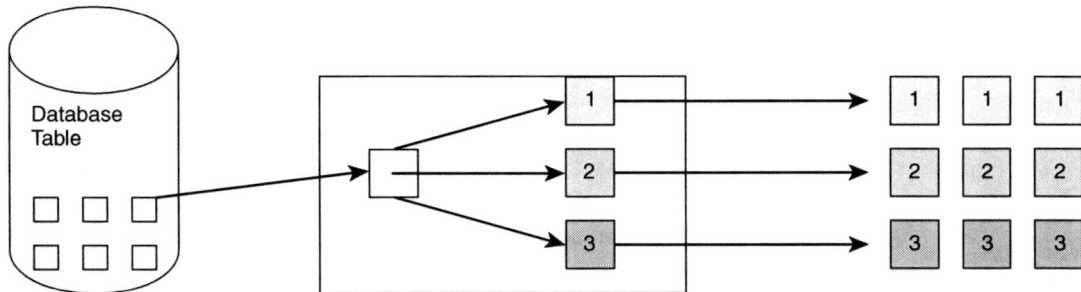

FIGURE 11.7
Projection Using Hashing

rithm to do union, placing in the results file any tuple that appears in either of the original files, but dropping duplicates. To do intersection, we use the same basic algorithm, but place in the results file only the tuples that appear in both of the original files. For set difference, R – S, we examine each tuple of R and place it in the results file if it has no match in S. In each case, the cost is the sum of the cost of accessing all the blocks of both files, sorting both and writing the temporary sorted files, accessing the temporary files to do the merge, and writing the final file.

11.4 Pipelining

In our discussion so far we have assumed that a query involving several relational algebra operations is executed by performing each operation on the relation or relations involved, constructing a temporary results table, and using that table as input for the next operation. This process, known as **materialization,** can be quite expensive, since we have to consider not just the sum of all the costs of the operations, but the cost of writing the intermediate tables. An alternative to materialization is **pipelining,** in which tuples "pass through" from one operation to the next in the pipeline, without creation of a temporary file. For example, if we were to perform the relational algebra operations of join followed by project, as in,

$$\Pi_{\text{firstName,lastName}} (\text{Student} \, |\times| \, \text{Enroll})$$

using pipelining, we would perform the join as one process, and place the joined tuples in a buffer, from which they would be taken as input to the project process, without writing the join out to disk. Although pipelining can be more efficient than materialization, it cannot be used in algorithms that require that the entire relation be available as input, such as the sort-merge join.

11.5   Query Optimization in Oracle

Oracle provides two types of optimization for relational databases—
cost-based, which is the default, and **rule-based.** Its rule-based optimizer
provides efficiency rankings for different types of access paths. The predicate in each SQL statement is examined to determine which of the access
paths apply to the query, and the system chooses the path with the best
score from among those available. For example, the highest ranking (1) is
given to using the primary key to retrieve a single tuple of a table, a middle rank (7) to an indexed cluster key, and the lowest ranking (15) a full
table scan. If the query is,

```
SELECT stuId, firstName, lastName
FROM Student
WHERE major = 'CSC';
```

the optimizer cannot use the primary key rule, since the primary key is
not given in the predicate. If the table has a clustered index on major, the
optimizer will choose that indexed cluster key, which has rank 7, rather
than the full table scan, with rank 15.

Oracle's cost-based optimizer uses statistics to generate estimates of the
cost of various methods of executing queries. The user is responsible for
requesting that the system gather statistics for objects such as specific
columns, tables, or the schema, by executing the package DBMS_STATS.
There is also a COMPUTE STATISTICS command that generates some
statistics. Frequencies of column values are recorded using histograms.
The system prices out various execution plans for a query and chooses the
one that uses minimum resources. However, the user can influence the
choice by providing **hints** in the form of formatted comments in the
query. For example, the user can force the system to use a particular index
by modifying the previous SQL statement to include a commented
+INDEX hint, as in:

```
SELECT /*+ INDEX(Student_major_ndx)*/ stuId, firstName, lastName
FROM Student
WHERE major = 'CSC';
```

Users can examine execution plans for an SQL statement by using the
EXPLAIN PLAN command. Oracle also allows users to extend optimization to user-defined types by using its extensible optimization option,
which gives the user control over many aspects of query plans.

11.6   Chapter Summary

Relational database management systems check each query for syntax errors, translate the query into an internal representation, rearrange or change the operations to produce an efficient order of operations, estimate the cost of executing the query using various plans, and choose the most efficient plan. A **query tree** can be used to represent relational algebra operations. Using properties such as commutativity, associativity, and distributivity, operations can be rearranged to produce an equivalent but more efficient query tree. Heuristics guide in the selection of properties to apply. Simple rules such as, "Do selection early" can result in tremendous cost savings. To choose the actual execution plan, the system considers factors such as file access cost, processing costs, costs of writing and storing intermediate results, communication costs, and the cost of writing final results. The size, structure, and access paths for files must be considered. The system stores statistics such as the number of tuples in each relation, the number of blocks, the blocking factor, the number of levels in each index, and the number of distinct values for each attribute. When choosing a plan involving an index, the type of index is very significant.

There are several methods of processing selects and joins, and the system uses its statistics to estimate the cost of methods before choosing one. Other operations such as projection and set operations have simpler access plans. When a query involves several operations, the cost of materializing the intermediate tables and accessing them must be considered in addition to the cost of the operations. An alternative to materialization is pipelining, in which tuples produced by one operation are passed to the next in a pipeline. Oracle uses both rule-based and cost-based optimizers, with cost-based being the default method. Users are responsible for telling the system to collect appropriate statistics either by running the DBMS_STATS package or using the COMPUTE STATISTICS option.

Exercises

Schema for Exercises **11.1–11.5**

```
Student (stuId, lastName, firstName, major, credits)
Faculty (facId, facName, department, rank)
Class (classNumber, facId, schedule, room)
Enroll (classNumber, stuId, grade)
```

11.1 Write the query tree for the following relational algebra expression:

```
SELECT Class WHERE room = 'A205' GIVING T1
JOIN T1,Faculty GIVING T2
PROJECT T2 OVER facName,dept
```

or symbolically,

$$\Pi_{facName,dept} ((\sigma_{room='A205'} (Class)) \bowtie Faculty)$$

11.2 Consider the following SQL query for the University example:

```
SELECT   facName, schedule
FROM     Faculty, Class, Enroll, Student
WHERE    lastName = 'Burns' AND firstName='Edward'
         AND Class.classNumber =
         Enroll.classNumber AND Faculty.facId = Class.facId AND
         Student.stuId = Enroll.stuId;
```

a. Write an initial relational algebra expression for this query.

b. Using equivalences of relational algebra expressions, rewrite your relational algebra expression in a more efficient form, if possible. Explain why the new expression is efficient.

11.3 Write an efficient relational algebra expression for the following SQL query:

```
SELECT   lastName, firstName, grade
FROM     Student, Enroll, Class, Faculty
WHERE    facName = 'Tanaka' AND schedule= 'MTHF12' AND
         Class.classNumber = Enroll.classNumber AND Faculty.facId =
         Class.facId AND Student.stuId = Enroll.stuId;
```

Explain why your relational algebra expression is efficient.

11.4 Write an initial query tree for the following relational algebra expression:

```
JOIN Class, Enroll GIVING T1
JOIN T1, Student GIVING T2
SELECT T2 WHERE facId = 'F101' GIVING T3
SELECT T3 WHERE major = 'Art' GIVING T4
PROJECT T4 OVER lastName, firstName
```

or symbolically,

$$\Pi_{lastName, firstName}(\sigma_{major='Art'} (\sigma_{facId='F101'} ((Class \bowtie Enroll) \bowtie Student)))$$

Using the heuristics given in Section 11.2.3, optimize the query tree.

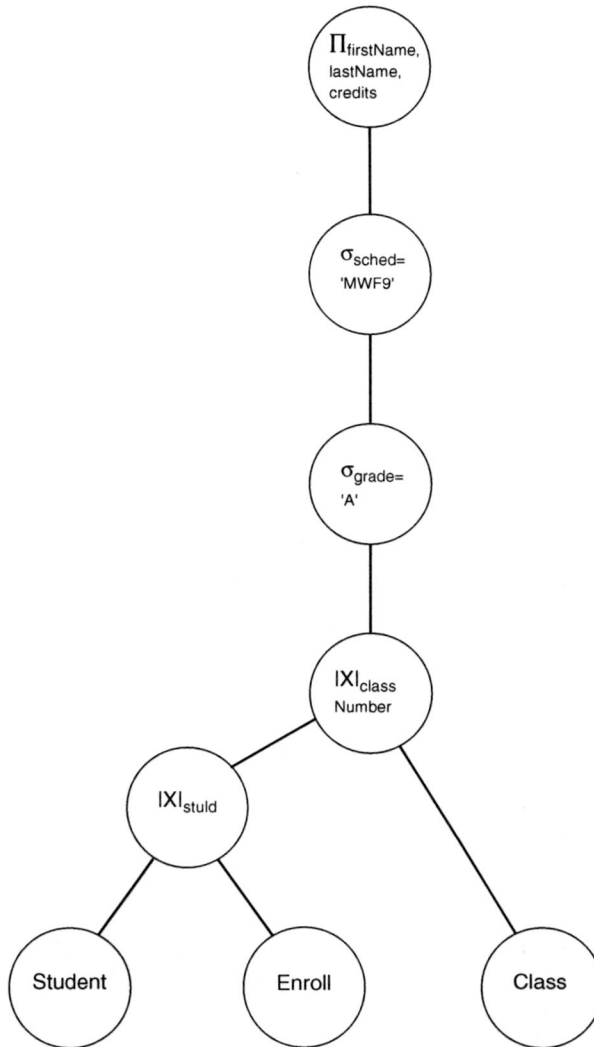

FIGURE 11.8
Query Tree for Exercise 11.5

11.5   Consider the query tree shown in Figure 11.8. Using the heuristics given in Section 11.2.3, write two different optimized query trees for this expression.

Information for Exercises 11.6–11.12: Assume we have the following information about the University database:

All tables are stored in packed form in blocks of length 4096 bytes.

Student has 10,000 tuples, each 200 bytes long. It is hashed on stuId, the primary key, and has a secondary index on lastName, with 3 levels. There are 8,000 values for lastName, 2,000 values for firstName, 25 values for major, and 150 values for credits.

Faculty has 800 tuples of length 100 bytes. It has an index on facId, the primary key, with 2 levels. There is a secondary index on department, with one level. facName has 650 values, department has 25 values, and rank has 4 values.

Class has 2,500 tuples with length of 100 bytes. It is hashed on classNumber, the primary key, and has no secondary indexes. facId has 700 values here, schedule has 35 values, and room has 350 values.

Enroll has 50,000 tuples with length of 100 bytes. It has a composite index on the primary key, {classNumber, stuId}, with 4 levels, and no other index. The attribute grade has 10 values.

11.6   a. Find the blocking factor and total number of blocks needed for each of the four relations. Use this information for the questions that follow.

b. Calculate the following selection sizes:

```
s(major='Art',Student)
s(rank='Professor',Faculty)
s(grade='A',Enroll)
s(room='A205',Class)
```

11.7   a. Estimate the number of tuples in the result of Class $|\times|$ Enroll. Approximately how many blocks are need to store the result?

b. Estimate the number of tuples and the number of blocks in the result of Student $|\times|$ Faculty, where major in Student is compared with department in Faculty.

c. Estimate the number of tuples and blocks for Faculty $|\times|$ Class.

d. Estimate the number of tuples and blocks for Faculty $|\times|$ Enroll.

11.8 Find the read cost only (no writing costs) of Class $\bowtie$ Enroll using nested loops with:

    a. Class as the outside loop and buffer size of only two blocks

    b. Enroll as the outside loop and buffer size of two blocks

    c. Class as the outside loop and buffer size of 10 blocks

    d. Enroll as the outside loop and buffer size of 10 blocks

11.9 Find the total access cost for Faculty $\bowtie$ Student using major and department as the joined fields and assuming that the buffer holds only two blocks, using:

    a. Nested loops, where you choose the best placement of relations in inside and outside loops. Include the cost of writing the results.

    b. The secondary index (a B+ tree having one level) on department in Faculty. Include the cost of writing the results, as found for part (a).

11.10 Find the access cost for performing Enroll $\bowtie$ Student, using the hash key on stuId. Assume the average number of accesses to retrieve a Student record given stuId is 2.

11.11 Give an efficient strategy for each of the following SELECT operations and give the cost of each:

    a. SELECT Student WHERE stuId = 'S1001'

    b. SELECT Student WHERE lastName = 'Smith'

    c. SELECT Student WHERE major = 'Art'

    d. SELECT Student WHERE credits >= 100

    e. SELECT Faculty WHERE department = 'History' and rank = 'Professor'

    f. SELECT Class WHERE facId = 'F101'

    g. SELECT Enroll WHERE grade = 'A'

11.12 Assume we wish to form the three-way join:

Class $\bowtie$ Enroll $\bowtie$ Student

    a. Estimate the cost of (Class $\bowtie$ Enroll) $\bowtie$ Student, using the most efficient strategies for each of the two joins.

b. Estimate the cost of Class $\bowtie$ (Enroll $\bowtie$ Student), using the most efficient strategies for the two joins.

c. Consider the following method:

```
for each block of Enroll
    for each tuple in the Enroll block
        use the value of stuId from the Enroll tuple as the hash
            key for Student and get the matching Student tuple
        use the value of classNumber from the Enroll tuple as the
            hash key for Class and get the matching Class tuple
        write out the join of the three tuples
    end
end
```

Find the estimated cost of this method. Assume the average number of access for a hash key value is 2.

CHAPTER 12

Distributed Databases

Chapter Objectives

In this chapter you will learn the following:

- The definition of a distributed database system

- The advantages of distribution

- The factors to be considered in designing a distributed database system

- Alternative architectures for a distributed system

- The identity and functions of the components of a distributed database system

- Factors in the data placement decision

- Data placement alternatives

- How distributed database system components are placed

- Update synchronization techniques

- How the DDBMS processes requests for data

Exercises

SAMPLE PROJECT: Planning the Distribution of the Relational Database for The Art Gallery

STUDENT PROJECTS: Planning for Distribution

12.1 Rationale for Distribution

A **distributed database system** is one in which multiple database sites are linked by a communications system in such a way that the data at any site is available to users at other sites. Normally, each site or node has a complete information processing system, with its own data administration function, personnel, users, hardware, and software—including a local database, database management system, and communications software. At the very least, a site must have memory and a communications processor. The sites are usually geographically remote and are linked by a telecommunications system, although it is possible to have a distributed system linked by a local area network within a single building or small area. Ideally, users need not be aware of the true location of the data they access, and the system appears to be a local database to them. Depending on the needs of the organization, distributed databases can have the following advantages over a single, centralized system that provides remote access to users.

1. *Local Autonomy.* An important objective of any distributed system is to allow the user to have more direct control over the system he or she uses. If each site has its own system, more of the basic information processing functions such as systems analysis, applications programming, operations, and data entry can be done locally, resulting in greater local control and user satisfaction than if these functions were performed at a central site, remote from user concerns and issues. At the same time, the designers of a distributed system should insist on centralized planning and coordination, so that standards can be developed and enforced, and the individual systems will be compatible.

2. *Improved reliability.* A distributed system is more reliable than a centralized one, because processing is done at several sites, so fail-

ure of a single node does not halt the entire system. Distributed systems can be designed to continue to function despite failure of a node or of a communications link. If a single node fails, users at that site may be unable to use the system, or their requests may be rerouted to another site. Users at other sites are unaffected unless they require data stored only at the failed node, or processing that is performed only at the failed node. If a link fails, the node can be isolated, but the rest of the system can continue to operate. In some systems, the node might have other lines that can be used in place of the failed one.

3. *Better data availability.* Distributed database systems often provide for replication of data. If a node fails, or the only link to a node is down, its data is still available, provided a copy is kept somewhere else in the system.

4. *Increased performance.* As the organizational information processing requirements increase, the existing system may be unable to handle the processing load. In a centralized system, a system upgrade, with accompanying changes in hardware and software, or a change to a new system, with major conversion of software, might be necessary to provide the performance increase required. A distributed system is basically modular, allowing new processors to be added as needed. Depending on the network topology, or physical layout, new sites may be easy to integrate.

5. *Reduced response time.* A distributed system should be designed so that data is stored at the location where it is used most often. This allows faster access to local data than a centralized system serving remote sites. However, in a poorly designed distributed system, the communications system might be heavily used, resulting in greater response time.

6. *Lower communications costs.* If data used locally is stored locally, communications costs will be lower, since the network will not be used for most requests. In a centralized system, the communications network is needed for all remote requests. However, we must consider the additional cost for the database software, additional storage costs for multiple copies of data items and software, higher hardware costs, and higher operating costs that distribution can entail.

12.2   Architectures for a Distributed System

Factors the designer of a distributed database system must consider in choosing an architecture include data placement, type of communications system, data models supported, and types of applications. Data placement alternatives are discussed in detail in section 12.5. They differ in the amount of data replication they permit. Each alternative dictates a different type of system, using different update and request decomposition procedures. If the communications system is slow and expensive to use, this favors local storage and processing. A fast, inexpensive communications system such as a local area network favors centralized storage and processing. Various data models and accompanying manipulation languages are supported in distributed systems, just as they are in centralized systems. In general, a designer should avoid models that use record-at-a-time retrieval, and choose instead those that allow set level operations, because of the number of messages that are required for programmer-navigated retrieval. This is one reason why the relational model is the one most often used for distributed databases. In considering the types of applications to be performed against the chosen database, the designer needs to estimate the size of the database, the number of transactions, the amount of data the transactions require, the complexity of transactions, the number of retrievals relative to the number of updates, and the number of transactions that refer to local data as opposed to remote data. Alternatives include:

12.2.1   Distributed Processing Using a Centralized Database

In this architecture, shown in Figure 12.1, the database itself is not distributed, but users access it over a computer network. Processing can be performed at multiple sites, using data from the central database site. The central site also does processing, often both for its local applications and for some centralized applications. Local sites communicate only with the central site, not with one another, when they access data from the database for processing.

12.2.2   Client-Server Systems

In client-server systems, as shown in Figure 12.2, the database resides on a back-end machine, called a **server,** and users typically access the data through their workstations, which function as **clients.** The database functions are divided between client and server. The client provides the user

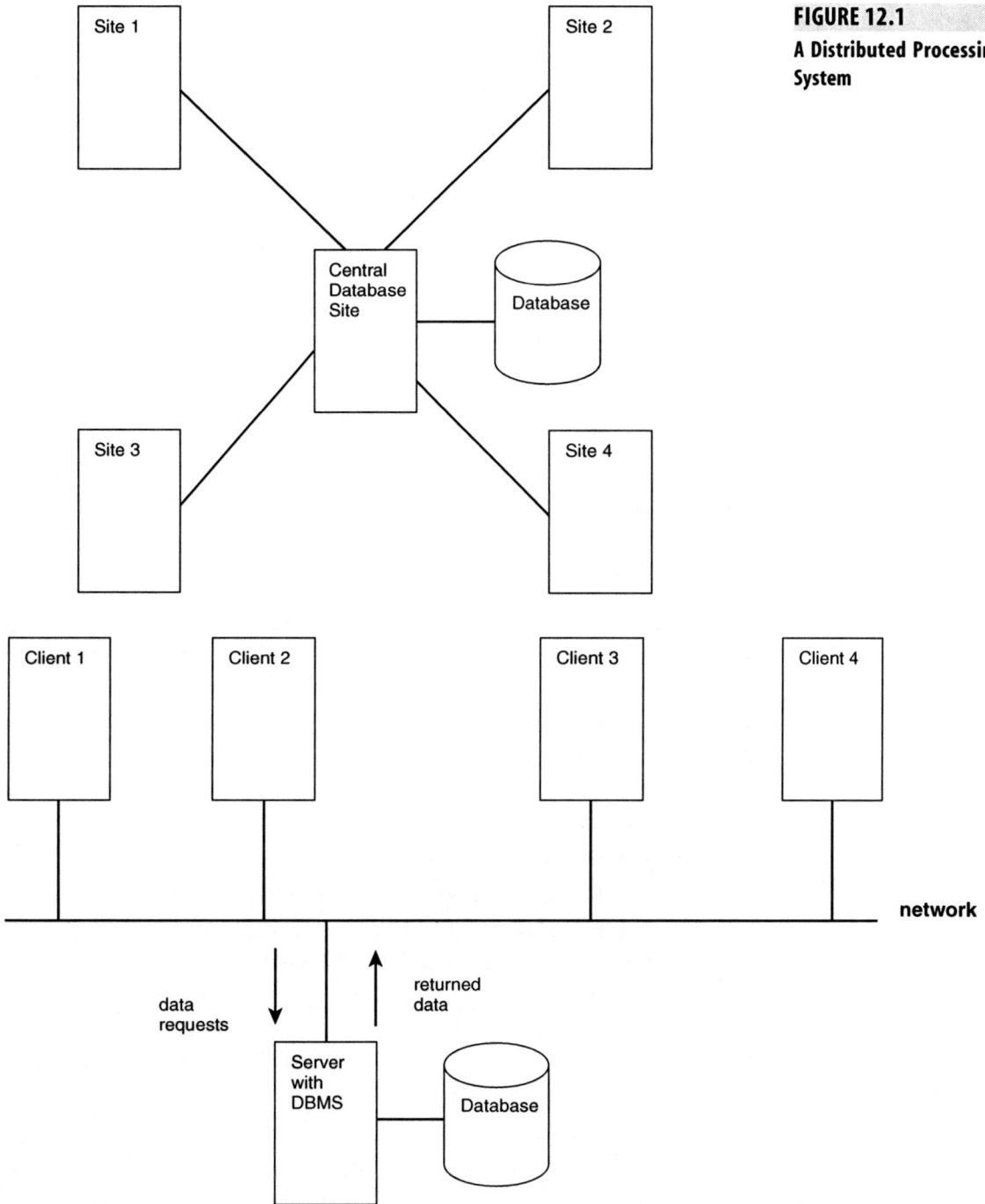

FIGURE 12.1
A Distributed Processing System

FIGURE 12.2
A Client-Server System

interface and runs the application logic, while the server manages the data and processes data requests. In a typical interactive transaction, the user interacts with the client workstation, using a graphical user interface provided either by the database system or by a third-party vendor. Besides handling the application logic, the client performs initial editing of data requests (usually SQL), checks the syntax of the request, and generates a database request, which is sent via the network to the server. The server validates the request by checking the data dictionary, authorization, and integrity constraints; optimizes the query; applies concurrency controls and recovery techniques; retrieves the data; and sends it back to the client. The client presents the data to the user. Application programs also run on the client, passing data requests through an **application program interface** (API) to the server in a similar fashion. If the client adheres to a standard such as ODBC or JDBC, it can communicate with any server that provides a standard interface. Unlike the centralized database environment, the server does not do application processing itself.

12.2.3 Parallel Databases

In parallel database architecture, there are multiple processors that control multiple disk units containing the database. The database may be partitioned on the disks, or possibly replicated. If fault-tolerance is a high priority, the system can be set up so that each component can serve as a backup for the other components of the same type, taking over the functions of any similar component that fails. Parallel database system architectures can be **shared-memory, shared-disk, shared-nothing,** or **hierarchical,** which is also called **cluster.**

- In a **shared-memory** system, all processors have access to the same memory and to shared disks, as shown in Figure 12.3(a). The database resides on the disks, either replicated on them or partitioned across them. When a processor makes a data request, the data can be fetched from any of the disks to memory buffers that are shared by all processors. The DBMS informs the processor what page in memory contains the requested data page.

- In the **shared-disk** design, shown in Figure 12.3(b), each processor has exclusive access to its own memory, but all processors have access to the shared disk units. When a processor requests data, database pages are brought into that processor's memory.

- In **shared-nothing** systems, each processor has exclusive control of its own disk unit or units and its own memory, as shown in Figure 12.3(c), but processors can communicate with one another.

- In **hierarchical** or **cluster** architecture, systems made up of nodes that are shared-memory, are connected by an interconnection network, as seen in Figure 12.3(d). The systems share only communications with one another, making the overall inter-system architecture shared nothing.

The purpose of parallel databases is to improve performance by executing operations in a parallel fashion on the various devices. Careful partitioning of data is essential so that parallel evaluation of queries is possible. Data partitioning can be done by **range partitioning,** which means placing records on designated disks according to a range of values for a certain

FIGURE 12.3
Architectures for Parallel Databases

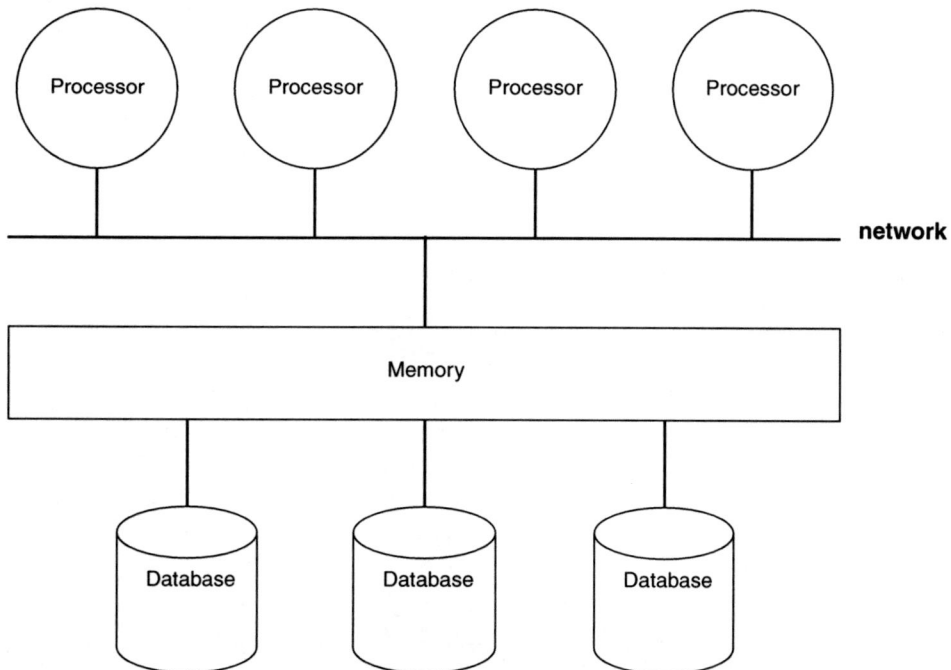

FIGURE 12.3(a)
Shared Memory

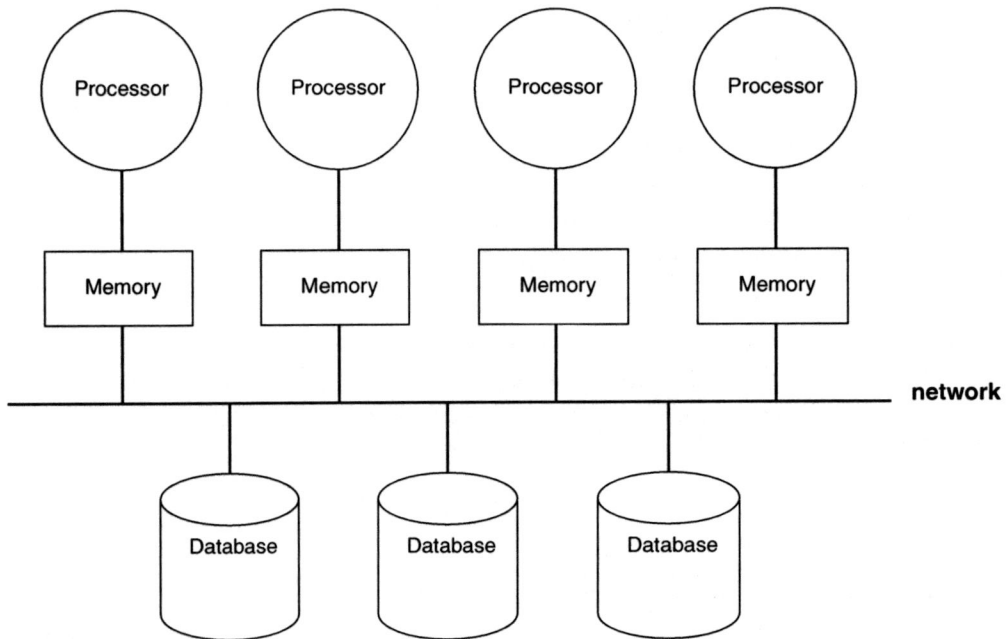

FIGURE 12.3(b)

Shared Disk

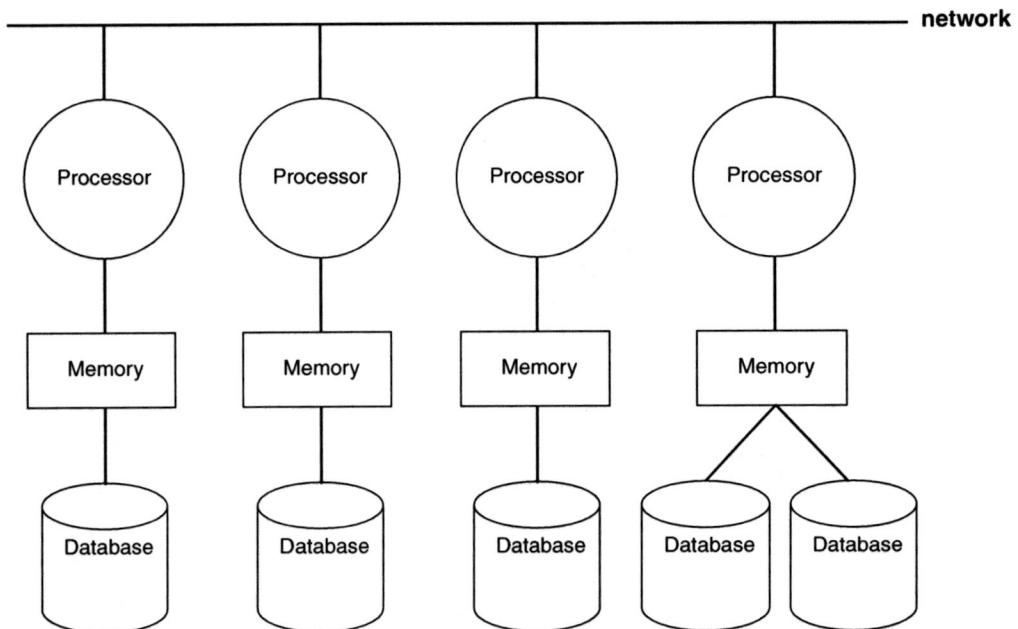

FIGURE 12.3(c)

Shared Nothing

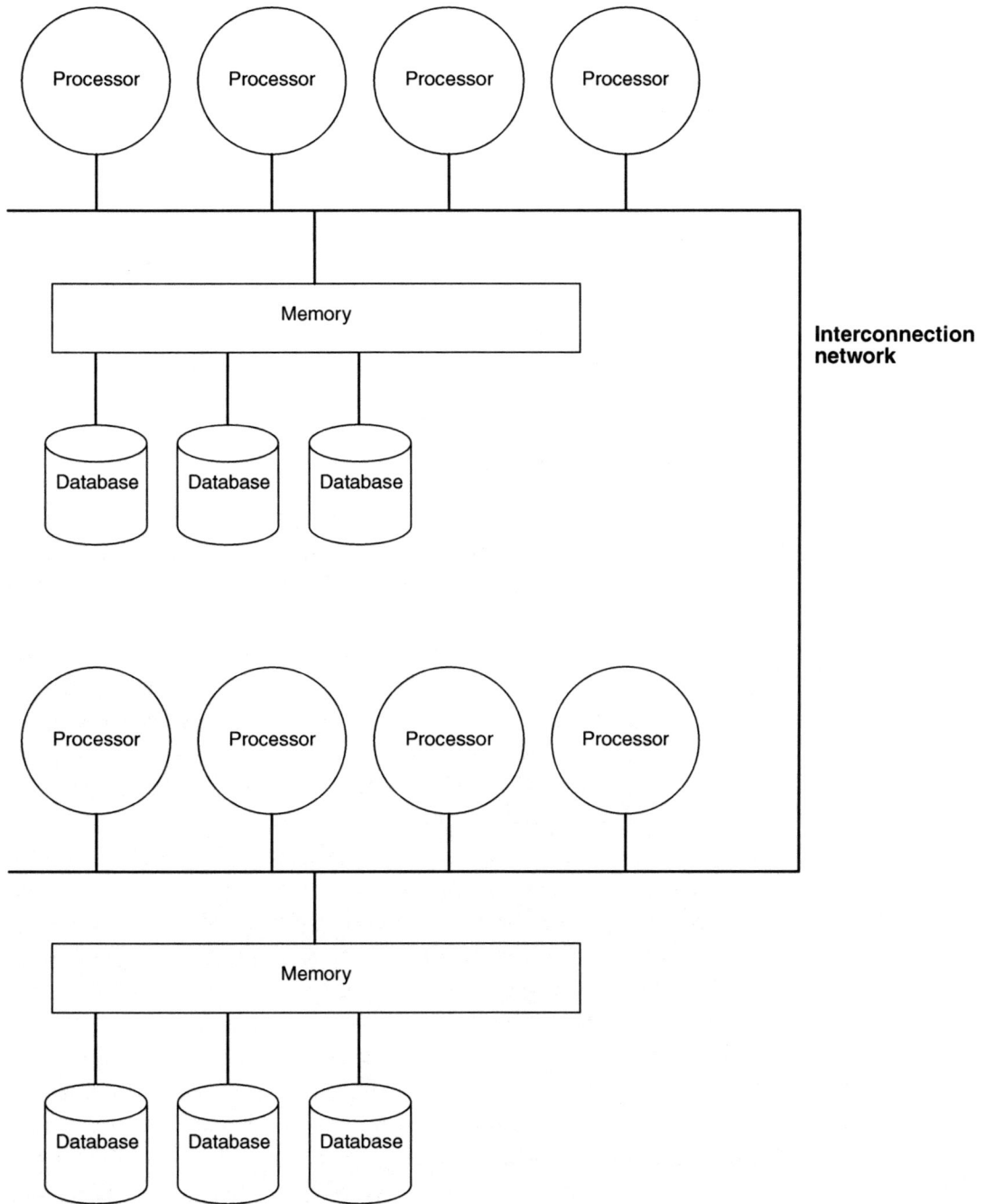

FIGURE 12.3(d)
Hierarchical

attribute. Other methods are by **hashing** on some attribute, or by placing new records on successive disks in **round-robin** fashion. When a query is processed, since the required data may reside on different disks, the query is decomposed into subqueries that are then processed in parallel using the appropriate partition of the database.

Parallel databases using the shared-nothing architecture provide linear **speed-up,** which means that as the number of processors and disks increase, the speed of operations increases in a linear fashion. They also provide linear **scale-up,** which means that they are scalable, so that if more processors and disks are added, the performance level is sustained. This allows us to increase the amount of data stored and processed without sacrificing performance.

12.2.4 Distributed Databases

In this architecture, the database is distributed, possibly with replication, among several relatively autonomous sites. The distribution is transparent to the user, who does not need to specify where the data is located (**location transparency**). A distributed system can be **homogeneous** or **heterogeneous.** In a homogeneous system, all nodes use the same hardware and software for the database system. In a heterogeneous system, nodes can have different hardware and/or software. Since a homogeneous system is much easier to design and manage, a designer would normally choose such a system. Heterogeneous systems usually result when individual sites make their own hardware and software decisions, and communications are added later, which is the norm. The designer then has the task of tying together the disparate systems. In a heterogeneous system, translations are needed to allow the databases to communicate. Since transparency is a major objective, the user at a particular site makes requests in the language of the database management system at that site. The system then has the responsibility of locating the data, which might be at another site that has different hardware and software. The request might even require coordination of data stored at several sites, all using different facilities. If two sites have different hardware but the same database management systems, the translation is not too difficult, consisting mainly of changing codes and word lengths. If they have the same hardware, but different software, the translation is difficult, requiring that the data model and data structures of one system be expressed in terms of the models and structures of another. For example, if one database is relational and the other uses the object-oriented model, objects must be presented in table form to users of the relational database. In addition, the query languages must be translated. The most challenging environment involves different hardware and software. This requires translation of data models, data structures, query language, word lengths, and codes.

12.3 Components of a Distributed Database System

A distributed database system normally has the following software components, as illustrated in Figure 12.4. Note that some sites contain all these components, while others might not.

- **Data communications component (DC).** The data communications component is the software at each node that links it to the network. This DC component includes a complete description of the network's nodes and lines. For each node, it identifies processing performed, storage capacity, processing power, and current state. For each link, it identifies the nodes it connects, type of link, bandwidth, protocols required, and the present state of the link.

- **Local database management component (LDBMS).** The local database management component functions as a standard database management system, responsible for controlling the local data at each site that has a database. It has its own data dictionary for local data, as well as the usual subsystems for concurrency control, recovery, query optimization, and so on.

- **Global data dictionary (GDD).** The global data dictionary is a repository of information about the distributed database. It includes a list of all data items with their location and other information about data stored anywhere in the distributed system.

- **Distributed database management component (DDBMS).** The distributed database component is the management system for the global database. It has many functions, including the following:

  1. *Provides the user interface.* **Location transparency** is one of the major objectives of distributed databases. Ideally, the user need not specify the node at which data is located, but acts as if all data is stored locally and accessed by the local DBMS. The local DBMS, however, is unaware of the distribution, so only requests that can be satisfied locally should be sent to the local

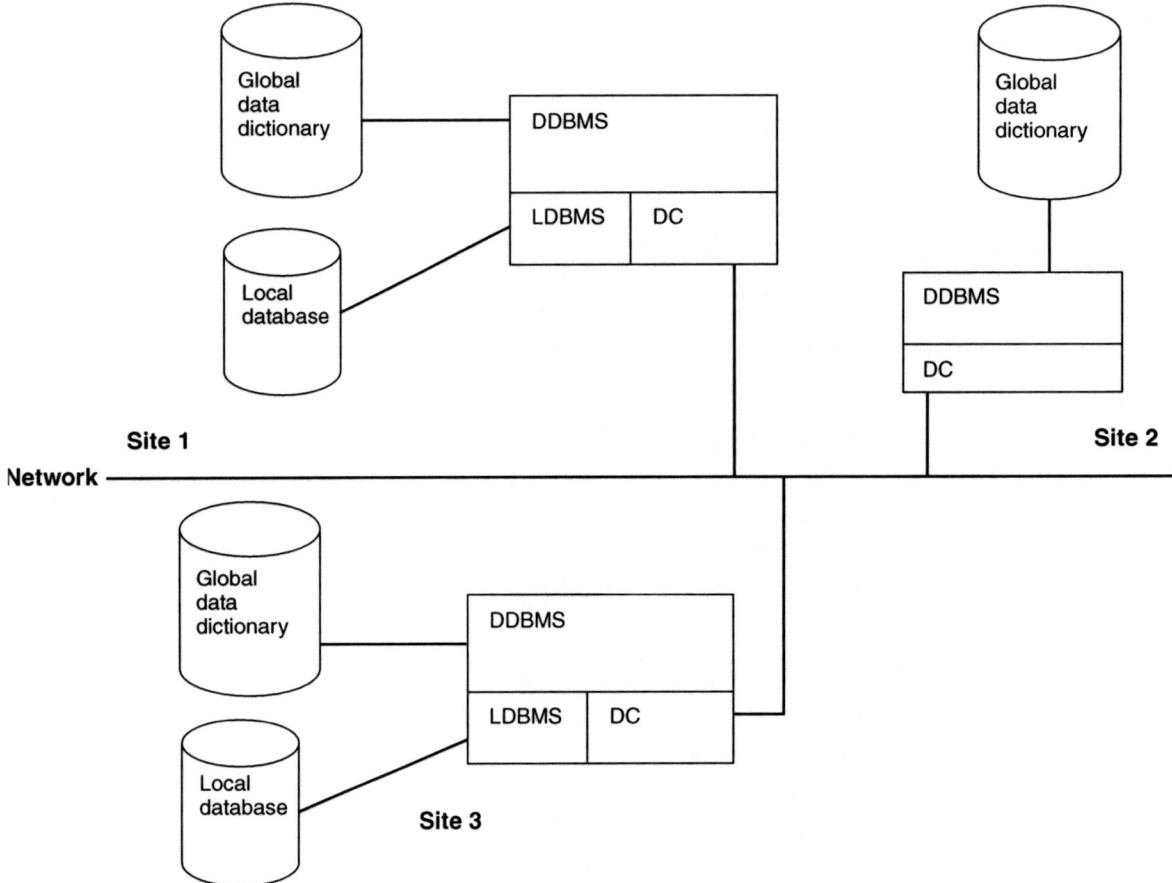

FIGURE 12.4

Components of a Distributed Database System

DBMS. The DDBMS, therefore, intercepts all requests for data and directs them to the proper site(s).

2. *Locates the data.* After receiving a request for data, the DDBMS consults the global data dictionary to find the node or nodes where the data is stored. If the request can be filled entirely at the local node, it passes the query on to the local DBMS, which processes it. Otherwise, it must devise and carry out a plan for getting the data.

3. *Processes queries.* Queries can be categorized as **local, remote,** or **compound.** A local request is one that can be filled by the local DBMS. Local requests are simply handed down to the

local DBMS, which finds the data and passes it back to the DDBMS, which in turn passes it to the user. (Recall the local DBMS has no user interface.) A remote request is one that can be filled completely at another node. In this case, the DDBMS passes the request to the DBMS at that node and waits for the response, which it then presents to the user. A compound request, also called a **global** request, is one that requires information from several nodes. To process a compound request, the DDBMS has to decompose the query into several remote and local requests that together will provide the information needed. It then directs each query to the appropriate DBMS, which processes it and returns the data to the DDBMS. The DDBMS then coordinates the data received to formulate a response for the user.

4. *Provides network-wide concurrency control and recovery procedures.* Although each local DBMS is responsible for handling update and recovery for its own data, only the DDBMS is aware of system-wide problems. Network-wide concurrency control is needed to prevent simultaneous users from interfering with one another. Network-wide recovery procedures are needed because, if a local node fails, although the local DBMS can recover its data to its condition at the time of failure, only the DDBMS can keep track of and apply changes made while the node was inactive.

5. *Provides translation of queries and data in heterogeneous systems.* In heterogeneous systems with different hardware but the same local DBMS, minor translations of codes and word lengths, and slight changes due to differences in implementation are needed. If the local DBMSs are different, major translation is needed. This includes changing from the query language of one DBMS into that of another and changing data models and data structures. If both hardware and DBMSs are different, both types of translation are needed.

12.4 Data Placement

One of the most important decisions a distributed database designer has to make is data placement. Proper data placement is a crucial factor in determining the success of a distributed database system. There are four basic alternatives, namely **centralized, replicated, partitioned,** or **hybrid.** Some of these require additional analysis to fine-tune the placement of data. In deciding among data placement alternatives, the following factors need to be considered.

1. *Locality of data reference.* The data should be placed at the site where it is used most often. The designer studies the applications to identify the sites where they are performed, and attempts to place the data in such a way that most accesses are local.

2. *Reliability of the data.* By storing multiple copies of the data in geographically remote sites, the designer maximizes the probability that the data will be recoverable in case of physical damage to any site.

3. *Data availability.* As with reliability, storing multiple copies assures users that data items will be available to them, even if the site from which the items are normally accessed is unavailable due to failure of the node or its only link.

4. *Storage capacities and costs.* Although the cost of data storage is generally lower than the cost of data transmission, nodes can have different storage capacities and storage costs. These must be considered in deciding where data should be kept. Storage costs are minimized when a single copy of each data item is kept.

5. *Distribution of processing load.* One of the reasons for choosing a distributed system is to distribute the workload so that processing power will be used most effectively. This objective must be balanced against locality of data reference.

6. *Communications costs.* The designer must consider the cost of using the communications network to retrieve data. Retrieval costs and retrieval time are minimized when each site has its own copy of all the data. However, when the data is updated, the changes must then be sent to all sites. If the data is very volatile, this results in high communications costs for update synchronization.

The four placement alternatives, as shown in Figure 12.5, are the following.

1. *Centralized.* This alternative consists of a single database and DBMS stored in one location, with users distributed, as illustrated in Figure 12.1. There is no need for a DDBMS or global data dictionary, because there is no real distribution of data, only of processing.

	Alternative			
Criterion	Centralized	Replicated	Partitioned	Hybrid
LOCALITY OF REFERENCE	lowest	highest	* should be high	*should be high
RELIABILITY	lowest	highest	high for system, low for item	*
AVAILABILITY	lowest	highest	high for system, low for item	*
STORAGE COSTS	lowest	highest	lowest	* should be average
LOAD DISTRIBUTION	poor	best	good	* should be good
COMMUNICATION COSTS	highest	low, except for updates	* should be low	* should be low
* Depends on exact data placement decisions made				

FIGURE 12.5
Evaluation of Data Placement Alternatives

Retrieval costs are high, because all users, except those at the central site, use the network for all accesses. Storage costs are low, since only one copy of each item is kept. There is no need for update synchronization, and the standard concurrency control mechanism is sufficient. Reliability is low and availability is poor, because a failure at the central node results in the loss of the entire system. The workload can be distributed, but remote nodes need to access the database to perform applications, so locality of data reference is low. This alternative is not a true distributed database system.

2. *Replicated.* With this alternative, a complete copy of the database is kept at each node. Advantages are maximum locality of reference, reliability, data availability, and processing load distribution. Storage costs are highest in this alternative. Communications costs for retrievals are low, but cost of updates is high, since every site must receive every update. If updates are very infrequent, this alternative is a good one.

3. *Partitioned.* Here, there is only one copy of each data item, but the data is distributed across nodes. To allow this, the database is split into disjoint **fragments** or parts. If the database is a relational one, fragments can be vertical table subsets (formed by projection) or horizontal subsets (formed by selection) of global relations. In any **horizontal fragmentation scheme,** each tuple of every relation

must be assigned to one or more fragments such that taking the union of the fragments results in the original relation; for the horizontally partitioned case, a tuple is assigned to exactly one fragment. In a **vertical fragmentation scheme,** the projections must be lossless, so that the original relations can be reconstructed by taking the join of the fragments. The easiest method of ensuring that projections are lossless is, of course, to include the key in each fragment; however, this violates the disjointness condition, because key attributes would then be replicated. The designer can choose to accept key replication, or the system can add a tuple ID—a unique identifier for each tuple—invisible to the user. The system would then include the tuple ID in each vertical fragment of the tuple, and would use that identifier to perform joins. Besides vertical and horizontal fragments, there can be **mixed fragments,** obtained by successive applications of select and project operations. This alternative requires careful analysis to ensure that data items are assigned to the appropriate site. Figure 12.6 provides examples of fragmentation. If data items have been assigned to the site where they are used most often, locality of data reference will be high with this alternative. Because only one copy of each item is stored, data reliability and availability for a specific item are low. However, failure of a node results in the loss of only that node's data, so the systemwide reliability and availability are higher than in the centralized case. Storage costs are low, and communications costs of a well-designed system should be low. The processing load should also be well distributed if the data is properly distributed.

4. *Hybrid.* In this alternative, different portions of the database are distributed differently. For example, those records or tables with high locality of reference are partitioned, while those commonly used by all nodes are replicated, if updates are infrequent. Those that are needed by all nodes, but updated so frequently that synchronization would be a problem, might be centralized. This alternative is designed to optimize data placement, so that all the advantages and none of the disadvantages of the other methods are possible. However, very careful analysis of data and processing is required with this plan.

As an example, let us consider how the University database schema might be distributed. We assume that the university has a main campus and four

Student

stuId	lastName	firstName	major	credits
S1001	Smith	Tom	History	90
S1002	Chin	Ann	Math	36
S1005	Lee	Perry	History	3
S1010	Burns	Edward	Art	63
S1013	McCarthy	Owen	Math	0
S1015	Jones	Mary	Math	42
S1020	Rivera	Jane	CSC	15

FIGURE 12.6
Fragmentation

FIGURE 12.6(a)
Horizontal Fragment:
$\sigma_{major='Math'}$ **(Student)**

Student

stuId	lastName	firstName	major	credits
S1001	Smith	Tom	History	90
S1002	Chin	Ann	Math	36
S1005	Lee	Perry	History	3
S1010	Burns	Edward	Art	63
S1013	McCarthy	Owen	Math	0
S1015	Jones	Mary	Math	42
S1020	Rivera	Jane	CSC	15

FIGURE 12.6(b)
Vertical Fragment:
$\Pi_{stuId, major}$ **(Student)**

Student

stuId	lastName	firstName	major	credits
S1001	Smith	Tom	History	90
S1002	Chin	Ann	Math	36
S1005	Lee	Perry	History	3
S1010	Burns	Edward	Art	63
S1013	McCarthy	Owen	Math	0
S1015	Jones	Mary	Math	42
S1020	Rivera	Jane	CSC	15

FIGURE 12.6(c)
Mixed Fragment:
$\Pi_{stuId, major}$ ($\sigma_{major='Math'}$ **(Student))**

branch campuses (North, South, East, and West), and that students have a home campus where they normally register and take classes. However, students can register for any class at any campus. Faculty members teach at a single campus. Each class is offered at a single campus. We will modify the schema slightly to include campus information in our new global schema:

```
Student(stuId, lastName, firstName, major, credits, homecampus)
Faculty(facId, name, department, rank, teachcampus)
Class(classNumber, campusoffered, facId, schedule, room)
Enroll(stuid, className, grade)
```

It is reasonable to assume that `Student` records are used most often at the student's home campus, so we would partition the `Student` relation, placing each student's record at his or her home campus. The same is true for `Faculty` records. The `Class` relation could also be partitioned according to the campus where the class if offered However, this would mean that queries about offerings at other campuses would always require use of the network. If such queries are frequent, an alternative would be to replicate the entire `Class` relation at all sites. Because updates to this table are relatively infrequent, and most accesses are read-only, replication would reduce communication costs, so we will choose this alternative. The `Enroll` table would not be a good candidate for replication, because during registration updates must be done quickly and updating multiple copies is time consuming. It is desirable to have the `Enroll` records at the same site as the `Student` record and as the `Class` record, but these may not be the same site. Therefore we might choose to centralize the `Enroll` records at the main site, possibly with copies at the `Student` site and the `Class` site. We can designate the main site as the primary copy for `Enroll`. The fragmentation scheme would be expressed by specifying the conditions for selecting records, as in:

$$\text{Student}_{\text{Main}} = \sigma_{\text{homecampus='Main'}}(\text{Student})$$
$$\text{Student}_{\text{North}} = \sigma_{\text{homecampus='North'}}(\text{Student})$$
. . . .
$$\text{Faculty}_{\text{Main}} = \sigma_{\text{teachcampus='Main'}}(\text{Faculty})$$
$$\text{Faculty}_{\text{North}} = \sigma_{\text{teachcampus='North'}}(\text{Faculty})$$
. . . .
$$\text{Enroll}_{\text{North}} = \Pi_{\text{stuId,classNumber,grade}}(\sigma_{\text{Student.homecampus='North'}}(\text{Enroll} \mid \times \mid \text{Student})) \cup$$
$$\Pi_{\text{stuId,classNumber,grade}}(\sigma_{\text{Class.campusoffered='North'}}(\text{Enroll} \mid \times \mid \text{Class}))$$

We are not fragmenting the `Class` relation. Because we have made different decisions for different parts of the database, this is a hybrid fragmentation scheme. Figure 12.7 illustrates the data placement decisions for this example.

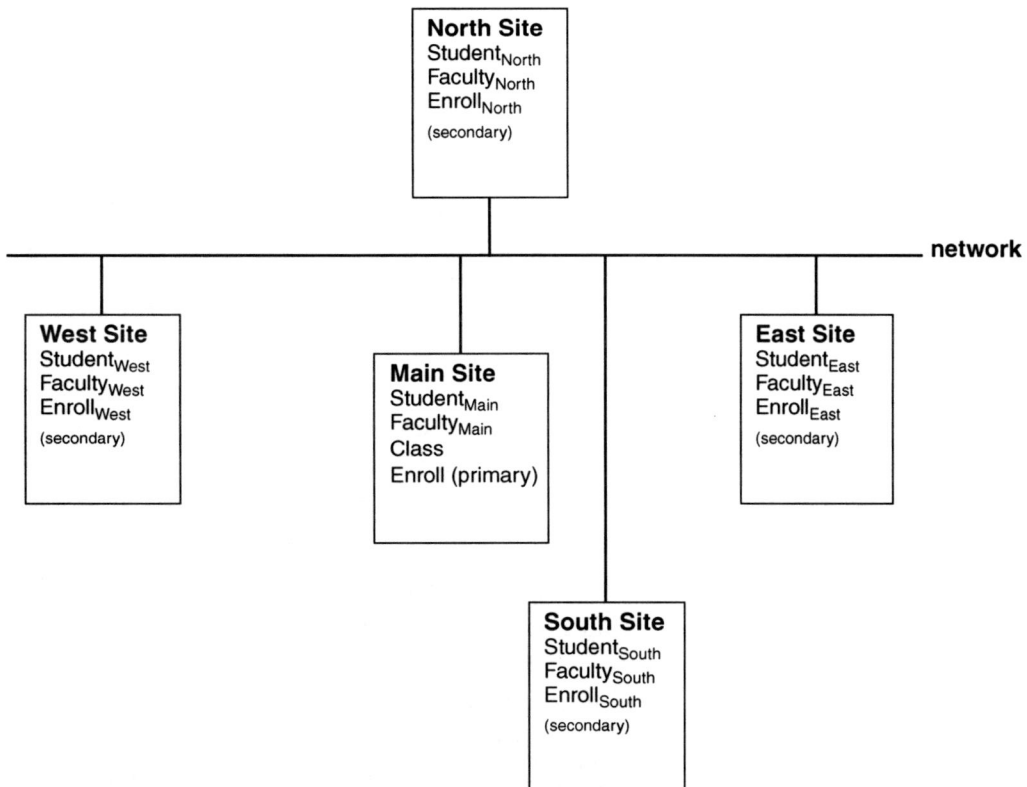

FIGURE 12.7
Data Placement for the Distributed University Schema

12.5 Transparency

Ideally, the distribution in a distributed database system should be transparent to the user, whose interaction with the database should be similar to that provided by a single, centralized database. Forms of transparency that are desirable are as follows:

- **Data distribution transparency.** This type of transparency can take several forms. The user should not have to know how the data is fragmented, a property called **fragmentation transparency.** Users should be unaware of the actual location of the data items they access, a property called **location transparency.** If data is replicated, users should be unaware of the fact that multiple copies exist, a property called **replication transparency.** To support these properties, it is essential that data item names be unique. In a centralized system, it is easy to verify uniqueness. However, in a distributed system, it can be difficult to ensure that no two sites use the same name for different data items. It is possible to guarantee systemwide uniqueness of names if each data item name has a prefix that is the identifier of the site where the item originated, called the **birth site.** Often the Internet address of the site is used. However, this technique compromises location transparency. The problem can be solved by using aliases for data items, which the system can then map to the composite name. Another approach is to have a **name server** where all names are checked for uniqueness and registered. However, the server might become a bottleneck, compromising performance, and if the server fails, the entire system is affected.

- **DBMS heterogeneity transparency.** Users who need to access data from a remote site with a different DBMS from their local one should not be aware of the fact that they are using a different DBMS. Their queries should be submitted in the language that they normally use. For example, if they are Access users, and the remote site uses Oracle, they should be able to use the Access query form to submit queries. The system should take care of any translations needed. The problem of providing such transparency becomes more difficult if the two systems use different data models.

- **Transaction transparency.** The ACID properties of transactions, discussed in Chapter 10 for centralized databases, must also be guaranteed for distributed transactions. The system must therefore guarantee **concurrency transparency,** which ensures that concurrent transactions do not interfere with one another. It must also provide **recovery transparency,** handling systemwide database recovery. These issues will be examined further in Section 12.6.

- **Performance transparency.** A distributed database system should deliver performance that is comparable to one using a centralized architecture. For example, a query optimizer should be used to minimize response time for queries, so that users do not wait too long for results. This issue will be discussed in Section 12.7.

12.6   Transaction Control for Distributed Databases

Each local database management system in a distributed database system has a **transaction manager** including a concurrency controller and a recovery manager that function in the usual manner. Each site that initiates transactions also has a **transaction coordinator** whose function is to manage all transactions—whether local, remote, or global—that originate at that site. For local or remote transactions, the transaction manager at the data site itself takes over. For global transactions, a typical sequence of events when such a transaction is entered at a site requires the transaction coordinator at that particular site to:

- Start executing the transaction

- Consult the global data dictionary to divide the transaction into subtransactions and identify where they will be carried out

- Send the subtransactions to the target sites, using the communications system

- Receive the results of the subtransactions back from the target sites

- Manage the completion of the transaction, which is either a commit at all sites or an abort at all sites

The transaction coordinator is responsible for ensuring distributed concurrency control and distributed recovery. It follows a global concurrency control protocol to ensure serializability of global transactions, and maintains a log for recovery.

12.6.1 Concurrency Control

We have already considered problems of concurrency control in a centralized system in Chapter 10. The **lost update problem,** the **uncommitted update problem,** the **problem of inconsistent analysis,** the **nonrepeatable read problem,** and the **phantom data problem,** which we discussed in that chapter, can all occur in a distributed database as well. We discussed serializability of transactions, and we can now extend that notion for the distributed environment. Locking was the first solution we considered, and we examined the problem of deadlock, the situation in which two transactions each wait for data items being held by the other. We looked at deadlock detection methods, using a wait-for graph. We also examined timestamping as a method for concurrency control. In a distributed database system, if the database is either centralized or partitioned so that there is only one copy of each item, and all requests are either local (can be filled at local site) or remote (can be filled completely at one other site), then the usual locking and timestamping mechanisms are sufficient. More difficult concurrency problems arise when there are multiple copies of data items spread across the system. To solve this **multiple-copy consistency problem,** we must be sure that each location receives and performs the updates to the common data items. We also have to manage compound transactions that require updates to different data items located at different sites. These issues are dealt with using protocols that employ locking or timestamping on a more global level.

12.6.1.1 Locking Protocols

In Chapter 10, we discussed the **two-phase locking protocol,** which guaranteed serializability for transactions in a centralized database. Using this protocol, each transaction acquires all the required locks during its growing phase and releases its locks during its shrinking phase. The transaction cannot acquire any new lock once it releases any lock. We can extend the solution to a distributed environment by managing locks in one of several ways.

- **Single-site lock manager.** In this design, there is a central lock manager site, to which all requests for locks are sent. Regardless of which site originates a transaction, the locking site determines whether the necessary locks can be granted, using the rules of the two-phase locking protocol, as described in Chapter 10. The requesting site can read data from any site that has a replica of an item. However, updates must be performed at all the sites where the item is replicated. This is referred to as **Read-One-Write-All** replica handling. The single-site lock manager scheme is relatively simple and easy to implement. Deadlock detection and recovery are also simple, involving only the techniques discussed in Chapter 10, since only one site manages locking information. However, the site might become a bottleneck, because all lock requests must go through it. Another disadvantage is that the failure of the lock manager site stops all processing. This can be avoided by having a backup site take over lock management in the event of failure.

- **Distributed lock manager.** In this scheme, several sites (possibly all sites) have a local lock manager that handles locks for data items at that site. If a transaction requests a lock on a data item that resides only at a given site, that site's lock manager is sent a request for an appropriate lock, and the lock site proceeds as in standard two-phase locking. The situation is more complicated if the item is replicated, since several sites might have copies. Using the Read-One-Write-All rule, the requesting site requires only a shared lock at one site for reading, but it needs exclusive locks at all sites where a replica is stored for updates. There are several techniques for determining whether the locks have been granted, the simplest being that the requesting site waits for each of the other sites to inform it that the locks have been granted. Another scheme requires that the requesting site wait until a majority of the other sites grant the locks. The distributed manager scheme eliminates the bottleneck problem, but deadlock is more difficult to determine, because it involves multiple sites. If the data item to be updated is heavily replicated, communications costs are higher than for the previous method.

- **Primary copy.** This method can be used with replicated or hybrid data distribution where locality of reference is high, updates are infrequent, and nodes do not always need the very latest version of data. For each replicated data item, one copy is chosen as the **primary copy,** and the node where it is stored is the **dominant node.** Normally, different nodes are dominant for different parts of the data. The global data dictionary must show which copy is the primary copy of each data item. When an update is entered at any node, the DDBMS determines where the primary copy is, and sends the update there first, even before doing any local update. To begin the update, the dominant node locks its local copy of the data item(s), but no other node does so. If the dominant node is unable to obtain a lock, then another transaction has already locked the item, so the update must wait for that transaction to complete. This ensures serializability for each item. Once the lock has been obtained, the dominant node performs its update and then controls updates of all other copies, usually starting at the node where the request was entered. The user at that node can be notified when the local copy is updated, even though there might be some remote nodes where the new values have not yet been entered. Alternatively, the notification might not be done until all copies have been updated. To improve reliability in the event of dominant node failure, a backup node can be chosen for the dominant node. In that case, before the dominant node does an update, it should send a copy of the request to its backup. If the dominant node does not send notification of update completion shortly after this message, the backup node uses a time-out to determine whether the dominant node has failed. If a failure occurs, the backup node then acts as the dominant node. It notifies all other nodes that it is now dominant, sends a copy of the request to its own backup node, locks data and performs its own update, and supervises the updates at the other nodes. It is also responsible for supplying data needed when the original dominant node recovers. If nondominant nodes fail, the system continues to function, and the dominant node is responsible for keeping a log of changes made while the node was down, to be used in recovery. The primary copy approach has lower communications costs and better performance than distributed locking.

- **Majority locking protocol.** In this scheme, lock managers exist at all sites where data items are stored. If a data item is replicated at several sites, a transaction requiring a lock on the item sends its request to at least half of the sites having a replica. Each of these sites grants the local lock if possible, or delays the grant if necessary. When the transaction has received grants from at least half of the replica sites, it can proceed. Note that while several transactions can hold a majority of the shared locks on an item, only one transaction can have the majority of the exclusive locks on a particular item. This protocol is more complex than the previous ones, and requires more messages. Deadlock between sites is also difficult to determine.

Regardless of how the locks are managed, the two-phase locking protocol is applied. The transaction must obtain all of its locks before releasing any lock. Once it releases any lock, no further locks can be obtained.

12.6.1.2 Global Deadlock Detection

Locking mechanisms can result in deadlock, a situation in which transactions wait for each other, as discussed in Chapter 10. Deadlock detection in a centralized database involves constructing a **wait-for** graph, with transactions represented by nodes, and an edge from node T1 to node T2 indicating that transaction T1 is waiting for a resource held by transaction

T2. A **cycle** in the graph indicates that deadlock has occurred. In a distributed environment, each site can construct its **local wait-for graph.** Nodes on the graph can represent both local transactions using local data and non-local transactions that are using the data at that site. Any transaction that is using a site's data is therefore represented by a node on the graph, even if the transaction itself is executing at another site. If a cycle occurs on a local wait-for graph, deadlock has occurred at that site, and it is detected and broken in the usual way: by choosing a victim and rolling it back. However, **distributed deadlock** can occur without showing up as a cycle in any local wait-for graph. Figure 12.8(a) shows a global schedule with four sites executing transactions concurrently. At site 1, transaction T2 is waiting for a shared lock on data item a, currently locked exclusively by T1. In Figure 12.8(b), the local wait-for graph for site 1 shows an edge from T2 to T1, but no cycle. Similarly, sites 2 through 4 have wait-for graphs, each of which has no cycle, indicating no deadlock at that site.

FIGURE 12.8

Wait-for Graphs for Deadlock Detection

Time	Site1	Site2	Site3	Site4
t1	T1: Xlock a	T2: Slock g	T3: Slock m	T4: Xlock q
t2	T1: Xlock b	T2: Xlock h	T3: Xlock n	T4: Slock r
t3	T2: request Slock a	T3: request Xlock g	T4: request Slock n	T1: request Slock q
t4	. . . T2wait . . .	. . . T3wait . . .	. . . T4wait . . .	. . . T1wait . . .

FIGURE 12.8(a)

Global Schedule of Transactions T1, T2, T3, T4

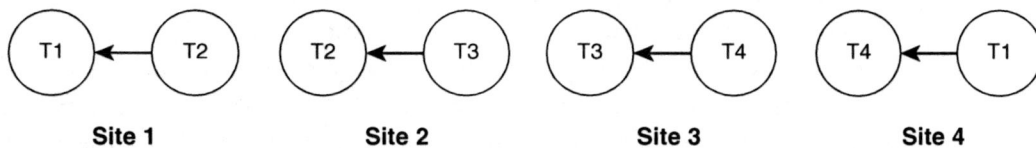

Site 1   Site 2   Site 3   Site 4

FIGURE 12.8(b)

Local Wait-for Graphs with No Cycle

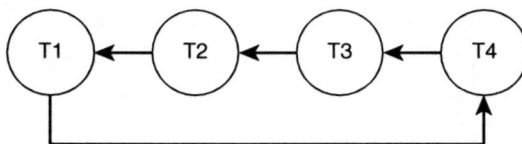

FIGURE 12.8(c)

Global Wait-for Graph with Cycle

However, when we take the union of the graphs, Figure 12.8(c), we see that the global wait-for graph has a cycle. At Site 4, T1 is waiting for T4, which is waiting at Site 3 for T3, which is waiting at Site 2 for T2, which is waiting at site 1 for T1. Therefore we have a cycle indicating distributed deadlock. No single site could detect that deadlock by using its local graph alone. Therefore the system needs to maintain a **global wait-for graph** as well as the local ones. There can be a single site identified as the **deadlock detection coordinator** that maintains the graph, or the responsibility could be shared by several sites, to avoid bottlenecks and improve reliability.

The deadlock detection coordinator is responsible for constructing a global graph using information from the lock managers at all sites. These managers transmit messages informing the coordinator whenever an edge is added to or deleted from their local graphs. The coordinator continuously checks for cycles in the global graph and, if one is detected, the coordinator is responsible for selecting a victim and informing all participating sites that they must roll back that transaction.

12.6.1.3 Timestamping Protocols

In Chapter 10, we discussed timestamping in a centralized system, and examined protocols that guaranteed that transactions were executed as if in timestamp order. We can apply essentially the same protocols to distributed systems, if we can guarantee unique timestamps. This can be done either by issuing timestamps from only one site, or by specifying that timestamps will have two parts. The first is the usual timestamp generated by the local clock or logical counter, and the second part is the node identifier. Since the clock or counter is advanced at each node for each transaction, this guarantees that every transaction will have a unique timestamp, although two transaction timestamps can have the same first part. It would be desirable to have some type of global clock, so we could determine which of two transactions entered at different sites was actually first, but it is virtually impossible to fully synchronize all the local clocks involved. Instead, there is usually a scheme to prevent local timestamps from diverging too much. For example, there can be a rule that if a node receives a timestamp with first part, t, greater than its current clock reading, it automatically advances its clock to $t + 1$. This prevents nodes that have frequent transactions from getting too far ahead of less active nodes. As in the centralized case, the protocol includes resolution procedures to follow in the case of conflicting transactions. The basic timestamping protocol, Thomas' Write Rule, and multiversion timestamping can all be applied directly to the distributed environment using the unique timestamps.

12.6.2 Recovery

As with a centralized database, a distributed database management system must ensure that its transactions are atomic and durable, despite system failures. If the transaction aborts, its effects must be completely undone throughout all the sites it affected. If it commits, its effects must persist at all the sites where they should.

12.6.2.1 Failures and Recovery

In addition to the types of failures that can occur in a centralized database, such as disk crashes or system failures, distributed databases can suffer from failures due to loss of messages, failure of a site, or failure of a communications line. They must also be able to deal with a situation called **network partitioning.** This occurs when failure of a line or node that had provided a link between parts of the network fails, resulting in splitting the network into groups of nodes so that nodes within a group can communicate, but there is no communication between the groups.

It is difficult to tell whether one of the nodes or links has failed. If a site is unable to communicate with a node, it may be due to the fact that the node is busy, that the node itself has failed, that the communications link has failed, or that the network is partitioned due to the failure of a different node or another link. In the case of a link failure, rerouting may be used, and the system could continue as before. If no other link exists, the node is isolated, and the link failure is treated as a node failure. The system can recognize a node failure either by self-reporting of the failed node or, if that is not possible, by a time-out method. In that case, if a node fails to respond to a message within a prespecified time, it is assumed to have failed, and recovery procedures are started. It is essential that the timeout be sufficiently long that recovery procedures are not triggered unnecessarily. The following steps are used to allow the system to continue following the failure of a node.

1. The system should flag the node or link as failed, to prevent any other node from trying to use it and thus generating a second recovery procedure.

2. The system should abort and roll back any transactions affected by the failure.

3. The system should check periodically to see if the node has recovered or, alternatively, the node should report when it has recovered.

4. Once restarted, the failed node must do local recovery, rolling back any partial transactions which were active at the time of failure.

5. After local recovery, the failed node must update its copy of the data, so that it matches the current state of the database. The system keeps a log of changes made during the node's failure for this purpose.

12.6.2.2 Commit Protocols

The transaction coordinator is responsible for determining whether a transaction commits or aborts. If the transaction involves several sites as participants, it must commit at all of them or abort at all of them. The coordinator must use a protocol to determine the outcome of a transaction and to handle any failure. The simplest protocol is the two-phase commit protocol. The three-phase commit protocol in an enhanced version that addresses some additional problems.

1. **Two-Phase Commit Protocol.** This relatively simple protocol consists of a **voting phase** and a **resolution phase.** At the end of a transaction's execution, the transaction coordinator asks the participant sites whether they can commit the transaction T. If all agree to commit, the coordinator commits; otherwise it aborts the transaction. The phases consist of the following activities.

    - **Phase 1-Voting Phase.** The coordinator writes a <begin commit T> record to its log, and force-writes the log to write to disk. The coordinator sends a <prepare T> message to all participant sites. Each site determines whether it can commit its portion of T. If it can, it adds a <ready T> message to its own log, force-writes the log to disk, and returns a <ready T> message to the coordinator. If a site cannot commit, it adds an <abort T> to its log, force-writes the log, and returns an <abort T> vote to the coordinator.

    - **Phase 2-Resolution Phase.** The coordinator resolves the fate of the transaction according to the responses it receives.

        a. If the coordinator receives an <abort T> message from any site, it writes an <abort T> message to its log and force-writes the log. It sends an <abort T> message to all participant sites. Each site records the message in its own log and aborts the transaction.

b. If a site fails to vote within a specified time (the timeout period), the coordinator assumes a vote of <abort T> from that site and proceeds to abort as specified above.

c. If the coordinator receives <ready T> messages from all participating sites, it writes a <commit T> record to its log, force-writes the log, and sends a <commit T> message to all participants. Each site records the message in its own log and responds to the coordinator. When all acknowledgments are received, the coordinator writes an <end T> message to its log. If any acknowledgment is not received during the timeout, the coordinator assumes that the site has failed. In the event of failure of either the coordinator or a participating site, the protocol determines the actions to be taken.

(1) *Failure of a participating site.* As described above, if the coordinator does not receive a vote from a site within the timeout, it assumes an <abort T> vote and aborts the transaction. If the site votes to accept the commit and fails afterward, the coordinator continues executing the protocol for the other sites. When the failed site recovers, the site consults its log to determine what it should do for each transaction that was active at the time of failure.

i. If the log has a <commit T> record, it does a redo(T).

ii. If the log has an <abort T> record, it does an undo(T).

iii. If the log does not have ready, abort, or commit records for T, then it must have failed before responding with a vote, so it knows the coordinator had to abort the transaction. Therefore it does an undo(T).

iv. If the log has a <ready T> record, the site tries to determine the fate of the transaction. It consults the coordinator, and if the coordinator responds that the transaction committed, the site does a redo(T). If the coordinator responds that the transaction was aborted, the site does an undo(T). If the coordinator does not respond, the site assumes the coordinator has failed, and the site may attempt to determine the transaction's fate by consulting other participant sites. If it cannot determine the fate, the site is **blocked** and must wait until the coordinator has recovered.

(2) *Failure of the coordinator.* If the coordinator fails during the commit protocol, the participating sites try to determine the fate of the transaction. Several possibilities exist:

   i. If one of the sites has an <abort T> in its log, T is aborted.

   ii. If one of the sites has a <commit T> in its log, T is committed.

   iii. If a site exists without a <ready T> in its log, that site cannot have voted to commit T, so the coordinator cannot have decided to do a commit. Therefore, T can now be aborted.

   iv. In all other cases (all active sites have a <ready T> but no site has either <abort T> or <commit T>), it is impossible to tell whether the coordinator has made a decision about the fate of T. T is **blocked** until the coordinator recovers.

2. **Three-Phase Commit Protocol.** As discussed, the two-phase commit protocol can result in blocking under certain conditions. The three-phase commit protocol is a non-blocking protocol, unless all of the sites fail. Conditions for the protocol to work are:

   - At least one site has not failed

   - There is no network partitioning

   - For some predetermined number k, no more than k sites can fail simultaneously

The protocol adds a third phase after the voting phase but before the resolution phase. The coordinator first notifies at least k other sites that it intends to commit, even before it force-writes its own commit log record. If the coordinator fails before issuing the global commit, the remaining sites elect a new coordinator, which checks with the other sites to determine the status of T. Since no more than k sites can fail, and k sites have the "intend to commit" message, those sites can ensure that T commits. Therefore blocking does not occur unless k sites fail. However, network partitioning can make it appear that more than k sites have failed, and unless the protocol is carefully managed, it is possible that the transaction will appear to be committed in one partition and aborted in another.

12.7   Distributed Query Processing

In Chapter 11 we discussed techniques for transforming SQL queries into a low-level representation such as relational algebra, and methods of transforming relational algebra expressions into equivalent but more efficient ones. We also presented various methods for estimating the cost of processing queries for various relational algebra operations. The dominant factor in the cost estimates was the number of disk accesses required. A distributed environment requires that we also consider the cost of transmitting data over the network. If the network is relatively slow, this factor can become the dominant cost factor. If the data is replicated, we have to consider the issue of choosing the best of several possible sites for performing all or part of a query. Partitioning of data complicates queries that require the use of more than one of the partitions. Therefore, in a distributed database system, we must consider additional query optimization procedures.

As described earlier, database queries can be categorized as **local, remote,** or **compound** (also called **global**). A local request is one that can be satisfied at the node where it is entered. A remote request can be satisfied at a single, remote node. A compound request is one that requires access to more than one node. In satisfying a compound request, the DDBMS is responsible for breaking down the query into several subqueries, each of which is directed to a specific node for processing. The DDBMS must then collect and coordinate the responses to obtain an overall result. Ideally, the user should not be aware of the distribution of data, and should not need to specify where the data items are located.

12.7.1 Steps in Distributed Query Processing

Some or all of the following steps must be performed by the DDBMS in answering a query.

1. *Accept the user's request.* The user interface is the responsibility of the DDBMS, rather than the local DBMS at each node. Because the local DBMS is not aware of the distribution, it is unable to handle queries about data items not stored locally.

2. *Check the validity of the request.* This requires checking that the correct query language syntax is used, and that the data items referred to actually exist. This is external level validity checking, which requires that the DDBMS have access to the user's sub-schema.

3. *Check authorization.* Access control information must be available to the DDBMS, so that it can check whether the user is authorized to perform the operations requested on the data items specified. This checking should be done both at the user's node and at every node where the request is processed. This is logical level checking, and requires that the schema be available to the DDBMS.

4. *Map external to logical level.* The DDBMS maps the user's data names and views to the corresponding logical level objects.

5. *Determine a request processing strategy.* The DDBMS must consult the global data dictionary to determine the location of the data items requested. If the request is local, it forwards it to the local DBMS for processing. If the request is remote, it goes on to the next step. If the request is compound, it must break it into sub-queries and direct each to a node. There may be several ways of breaking up the query, so the DDBMS normally uses some form of optimization to determine which decomposition to use. Optimization in a centralized system involves several techniques. For example, if there are multiple conditions, testing can be done first on the condition that eliminates the largest number of records, or the one that requires the fewest I/O operations. In accessing records, the shortest access paths are chosen. In a distributed system, the optimization also includes the use of the communications system. An objective of optimization might be to minimize response time, which would dictate decomposing the request in

such a manner that parallel processing could be performed at several nodes, especially if the communications system is fast and the processing load is light. Sometimes several nodes perform the same process, and results are obtained from the one that finishes first. If the system is heavily used, other objectives might be more appropriate. These include minimizing total processing time, which consists of the sum of the (possibly simultaneous) processing times of the nodes and the time used for executing communications software and consolidating the results. In selecting an algorithm, true optimization requires that the DDBMS find all the ways of processing the query and then "cost out" each one, by using mathematical formulas that include processing costs, communications costs, and storage costs. Because of the difficulty of finding all possible processing methods, a "hill climbing" method is often used. This consists of finding an initial solution and costing it out, then evaluating a slightly different alternative, choosing the better of the two. The better one then becomes the basis for a comparison with another alternative, and the process continues until no other method can be found or a certain number of iterations fail to produce substantial improvement.

6. *If the system is heterogeneous, translate each query into the DML of the data node.* In remote or compound requests, the node where the data is located may use a different DBMS from the user's node. Therefore, the DDBMS must provide translation due to hardware and software differences. In the worst case, different data models and data structures as well as different codes and word lengths might be involved.

7. *Encrypt the request.* Security is improved if every request and every response is encrypted before being passed to the communications system. The receiving node must then decrypt the message before processing.

8. *Depending on the system, the local data communications component may determine the routing.* The requesting node must provide logical identifiers for each node that is to receive a subrequest. The function of translating a logical identifier to a physical identifier and choosing a path requires a network description, which is available to the DC component. Routing may be direct or indirect,

requiring that the message pass through intermediate nodes. If indirect, the routing may be determined by the originating node in advance, or may be dynamically determined by the intermediate nodes.

9. *The DC component transmits the message through the communications system.* Since communications between databases are process-to-process communications, the message must pass down through all the data communication layers at the source node, be transmitted to the destination, and pass back up through all the communication layers at the destination node.

10. *Decrypt the request.* If the message was encrypted at the source, it must now be decrypted at the destination node before processing can begin.

11. *Perform update synchronization, if needed.* If the request is an update, the DDBMS at the receiving node must go through synchronization procedures, as described in Section 12.6.

12. *Local DBMS does its processing.* The local DBMS at the data node performs logical and physical binding, determines local processing strategy, and retrieves the data requested of it.

13. *If the system is heterogeneous, translate the data.* The requesting node, data node, or some intermediate node can perform any necessary translation.

14. *Send the results to the destination node.* Normally, query results are returned to the requesting node, but other nodes might also be specified as destinations. The results might be encrypted before they are returned.

15. *Consolidate the results, edit, and format the response for the user.* The requesting node usually coordinates the entire query decomposition process, and it is normally the site where final consolidation of partial results is performed. In addition, the DDBMS at that node consults the user's external model to present data in the form the user expects. However, other nodes may perform some of these functions.

16. *Return the results to the user.* Since the user interface is provided by the DDBMS, it is responsible for displaying the results.

12.7.2 Estimating Data Communications Cost

We will assume we have the schema discussed in Section 12.4, with the number of bytes for each attribute indicated as follows.

```
Student(stuId(5), lastName(15), firstName(15), major(12), credits(4),
homecampus(10))
Faculty(facId(5), name(15), department(15), rank(20), teachcampus(10))
Class(classNumber(10), campusoffered(10), facId(5), schedule(10), room(5))
Enroll(stuId(5), classNumber(10), grade(3))
```

Example 1

We wish to find class schedule information for all CSC majors, using the data distribution shown in Figure 12.7. The query is: Find the stuId, lastName, firstName, classNumber, campusoffered, schedule, and room of all CSC majors, regardless of campus. In SQL, we write:

```
SELECT stuId, lastName, firstName, classNumber, campusoffered, schedule, room
FROM Student, Enroll, Class
WHERE major='CSC' AND Student.stuId = Enroll.stuId AND
Enroll.classNumber=Class.classNumber;
```

Strategy 1.

1. At each site, select the CSC majors, $(\sigma_{major='CSC'}(\text{Student}))$.

2. At each site, join those tables with Enroll over the stuId.
    $(\sigma_{major='CSC'}(\text{Student}))|\times|\text{Enroll}$

3. Project results onto classNumber, stuId, firstName, lastName at each site.
    $\Pi_{classNumber, stuId, firstName, lastName}((\sigma_{major='CSC'}(\text{Student}))|\times|\text{Enroll})$

4. Ship the results from the 4 remote sites to Main.

5. At Main, join with Class.
    $(\Pi_{classNumber, stuId, firstName, lastName}((\sigma_{major='CSC'}(\text{Student}))|\times| \text{Enroll}))|\times|\text{Class}$

6. At Main, project onto stuId, lastName, firstName, classNumber, campusoffered, schedule, room.

In step 4, we need to determine the cost of shipping the results from each of the remote sites. Assume there are 25 major fields available at all five campuses, and each campus has 2000 students. There should be 2000/25 or 80 CSC majors at each campus. When we join these with `Enroll`, assuming students take an average of five classes each, we get 5*80 or 400 records. We project onto the desired attributes, which total 45 bytes, for a total of 45*400 or 18,000 bytes from each of the 4 sites, or **72,000** bytes. The rest of the query is executed at the Main site, as indicted in Steps 5 and 6. The cost is determined by the methods discussed in Chapter 11. If the query is entered at the Main site, there are no additional shipping costs. However, if it is entered at another site, we would have to add the costs of shipping the results back to that site.

Strategy 2.

1. At each site, select the CSC majors and project the results onto `stuId`, `lastName`, `firstName`. The relational algebra operations are:

    $\Pi_{stuId,lastName,firstName}$ ($\sigma_{major='CSC'}$ (Student))

2. Ship the four intermediate tables from North, South, East, and West to the Main site.

3. Join all five intermediate tables with `Enroll` at Main.

    ($\Pi_{stuId,lastName,firstName}$ ($\sigma_{major='CSC'}$ (Student))) $|\times|$ Enroll

4. Join the resulting table with `Class` at Main.

    (($\Pi_{classNumber,stuId,firstName,\,lastName}$($\sigma_{major='CSC'}$ (Student))) $|\times|$ Enroll) $|\times|$ Class

5. Still at Main, project the results onto `stuId`, `lastName`, `firstName`, `classNumber`, `campusoffered`, `schedule`, `room`.

The only shipping costs are the costs of sending each of the four intermediate tables (from North, South, East, and West) to Main. The result of the SELECT has 80 records, each 61 bytes. When the project is performed, the size is 35 bytes, so we need to ship 80*35 or 2800 bytes from each of the four sites, for a total of **11,200** bytes shipped. The rest of the query is executed at the Main site, as indicted in steps 3, 4 and 5.

Comparing the two strategies, the shipping costs for the first are about six times those of the second.

Example 2

For each faculty member from all campuses, find the faculty `name` and the `classNumber`, `campus`, and `schedule` of all courses that the faculty member teaches. We assume there are 2500 `Class` tuples and 800 `Faculty` tuples. The query is entered at the West campus. In SQL, it is:

```
SELECT name, classNumber, campusoffered, schedule
FROM Faculty, Class
WHERE Faculty.facId = Class.facId;
```

Strategy 1. Send the entire `Class` file to the West campus. Also send `Faculty` subtables from the other campuses to the West campus. Complete the entire query at the West campus. The communications costs are:

`Class` file: 2500 tuples, each with 40 bytes, for a total of 100,000 bytes shipped.

Four `Faculty` subtables: 640 tuples total, each with 65 bytes, for a total of 41,600 bytes shipped.

Grand total of **141,600** bytes shipped.

Strategy 2. Send each `Faculty` subtable to the Main site, and join with `Class` there. Project onto `name`, `classNumber`, `campusoffered`, `schedule` and send the results to the West campus.

`Faculty` subtables: 640 tuples total, each with 65 bytes, for a total of 41,600 bytes shipped.

`Results` subtable: 2500 tuples, each 45 bytes, for a total of 112,500 bytes shipped.

Grand total of **154,100** bytes shipped.

For this example, the first strategy is more efficient because there is no need to ship the results file. Note that if the query were entered at the Main campus, the second strategy would have been more efficient.

12.7.3 The Semijoin Operation

For many distributed databases, an operation called a **semijoin,** which we described in Chapter 4, can be very cost effective. If A and B are tables, then the left-semijoin A ⋉ B, is found by taking the natural join of A and B and then projecting the result onto the attributes of A. The result will be just those tuples of A that participate in the join. We defined the right-semijoin in a similar fashion. As an example of the use of the semijoin in a distributed environment, we will use the following simple schema.

Department(<u>deptCode(5)</u>, deptName(20), *chairpersonId(5)*, telephone(10), office(5)

stored at site A. Assume there are 100 records, 45 bytes each.

Faculty(<u>facId(5)</u>, *deptCode (5)*, firstName(15), lastName(15), birthDate(12), rank(10), socialSecurityNumber(9))

stored at site B. Assume there are 1000 records, 71 bytes each.

Consider the query "Find the name of each department, and the name of the chairperson of that department," entered at site A. In SQL, we write:

```
SELECT firstName, lastName, deptName
FROM Faculty, Department
WHERE Department.chairpersonId = Faculty.facId;
```

Strategy 1

Ship the entire `Faculty` file to site A and do the join there. Shipping cost is 1000*71 or **71,000** bytes. Then project the results onto `firstName`, `lastName`, `deptName` and present the results to the user at site A, with no further shipping.

Strategy 2

Ship the entire `Department` file to site B and do the join there. Shipping cost is 100*45 or 4500 bytes. Then ship the results to site A. Shipping cost is 50*1000 or 50,000 bytes, for a total of **54,500** bytes.

Strategy 3

Project `Department` onto `chairpersonId` and ship only `chairpersonId` to site B. Since Id is 5 bytes, we ship 5*100 or 500 bytes so far.

At site B, join with `Faculty` over `facId`. Project the result and transfer only `firstName`, `lastName` and `deptCode` back to site A. Cost is 35*100 or 3500 bytes.

At site A, join the result with `Department` on `DeptCode`, and project the result onto `firstName`, `lastName`, and `departmentName`. No further shipping costs are involved.

Total shipping cost is **4,000** bytes.

As you can see, the initial projection identified only the Ids of chairpersons, substantially reducing the amount of data to be shipped. The semijoin was done at site B, where we did a join and then projected the results onto the attributes of `Faculty` (`firstName`, `lastName`, and `deptCode`) that were in the join.

The semijoin is often used this way in distributed systems, especially in queries where few tuples will participate in the join. The optimizer considers a semijoin in place of a join when the tables to be joined reside at different sites.

12.8 Chapter Summary

A **distributed database system** has multiple sites connected by a communications system, so that data at any site is available to users at other sites. The system can consist of sites that are geographically far apart but linked by telecommunications, or the sites can be close together, and linked by a **local area network.** Advantages of distribution may include **local autonomy, improved reliability, better data availability, increased performance, reduced response time,** and **lower communications costs.**

The designer of a distributed database system must consider the **type of communications system, data models supported, types of applications,** and **data placement alternatives.** Final design choices include **distributed processing using a centralized database, client-server systems, parallel databases,** or **true distributed databases.** A distributed database can be **homogeneous,** where all nodes use the same hardware and software, or **heterogeneous,** where nodes have different hardware or software. Heterogeneous systems require translations of codes and word lengths due to hardware differences, or of data models and data structures due to software differences.

A distributed database system has the following software components: **data communications component (DC), local database management system (DBMS), global data dictionary (GDD),** and **distributed database management system component (DDBMS).** The responsibilities of the distributed database management system include providing the user interface, locating the data, processing queries, providing network-wide concurrency control and recovery procedures, and providing translation in heterogeneous systems. **Data placement alternatives** are **centralized,**

replicated, partitioned, and **hybrid.** Factors to be considered in making the data placement decision are locality of reference, reliability of data, availability of data, storage capacities and costs, distribution of processing load, and communications costs. The other components of a distributed database system may be placed using any of the four alternatives.

Forms of transparency that are desirable in a distributed database include **data distribution transparency,** (which includes **fragmentation transparency, location transparency,** and **replication transparency**), DBMS **heterogeneity transparency, transaction transparency,** (which includes **concurrency transparency** and **recovery transparency**), and **performance transparency.**

One of the most difficult tasks of a distributed database management system is **transaction management.** Each site that initiates transactions also has a **transaction coordinator** whose function it is to manage all transactions, whether local, remote, or global, that originate at that site. **Concurrency control** problems that can arise include the **lost update problem,** the **uncommitted update problem,** the **problem of inconsistent analysis,** the **nonrepeatable read problem** and the **phantom data problem,** as well as the **multiple-copy inconsistency** problem, which is unique to distributed databases. As for the centralized case, solutions for the distributed case include techniques such as **locking** and **timestamping.** The two-phase locking protocol has variations in the distributed environment that include **single-site lock manager, distributed lock managers, primary copy,** or **majority locking.** The **Read-One-Write-All** rule is often used for replicated data. Distributed deadlock is detected using a **global wait-for graph.** Timestamping can also be used to guarantee serializability. Timestamps may include two parts—a normal timestamp and a node identifier. To prevent timestamps from different sites from diverging too much, each site can automatically advance its timestamps whenever it receives a later timestamp than its current time. Recovery protocols include the **two-phase commit** and the **three-phase commit** protocols.

Another important task of the distributed database management system is **distributed query processing,** which includes several steps, the most difficult of which is to **determine a request processing strategy** and supervise its execution. Standard query optimization techniques must be extended to consider the cost of transferring data between sites. The semijoin operation is sometimes used when a join of data stored at different sites is required. It can result in substantial savings when a join is required.

Exercises

12.1   Using the data distribution scheme shown in Figure 12.7 for the distributed University example, describe at least two strategies for each of the following queries. Estimate the data transfer cost for each strategy.

a. Find the `className` and the `names` of all students enrolled in all classes with schedule 'MWF9'.

b. Find the `className`, `facId` of the teacher, and the campus of all classes being taken by Rosemary Hughes, who is a student at the North campus.

12.2   Consider the query "Find the `className`, `schedule` and `lastName` of all enrolled students for all classes being taught by Professor Smith of the North campus." The query is entered at the North campus.

a. Describe a strategy that does not use the semijoin and estimate the data transfer cost of that strategy.

b. Describe a semijoin strategy for the same query and estimate the data transfer cost.

12.3   For the distributed `Department, Faculty` schema described in Section 12.7.3:

a. Consider the query "For each faculty member, print the `first name`, `last name` and `department name`."

i. Give two different strategies for processing this query without using a semijoin and the communications cost of each.

ii. Give a strategy using a semijoin and the cost of this strategy.

b. Consider the query "For each faculty member, print the `first name`, `last name`, `department name` and `chairperson name`."

i. Explain why this query is more complex than the previous one.

ii. Devise an efficient strategy for executing this query and give the communications cost for it.

12.4   A database is to store listing information for a residential real estate agency that uses a multiple listing service. A multiple listing service is a cooperative service in which different real estate agencies agree to list and show one another's properties for sale, dividing the sales commission. People who wish to sell homes contact one of the agencies and register with only that agency. Properties to be offered for sale are visited by an agent (the listing agent) who collects information. Once listed, the property can be sold by any agent in any agency (the selling agent). However, when a binder (a declaration of a buyer's intention to purchase) and a deposit are placed on the property, no agent can show the property to another prospective buyer. If no contract follows within a month, or if the buyer retracts the bid, the property becomes available again. If the sale goes through and a contract is signed by all parties, the binder status and the listing status are marked as sold, and the contract date is recorded in the binder table. At the end of each month, the listing and binder information for all houses sold that month (i.e., for which contracts have been signed) are removed from their corresponding tables, and the information is put in the `Sold` table. Prospective buyers can register with only one agent. When the property is sold, the commission is divided between the listing agent and the selling agent, who can be the same person. The commission is always 10% of the selling price. Assume the following schema is used:

```
AgencySalesOffice(name, address, numberOfAgents, generalTelephone)
Agent(agentName, salesOfficeName, agentTelephone)
ActiveListing(address, type, style, size, askingPrice, dateListed,
ownerName, ownerTelephone, lotSize, houseSize, numBedrooms, numBaths,
numFloors, features, status, listingAgent)
Sold(address, type, style, size, askingPrice, dateListed, ownerName,
ownerTelephone, lotSize, houseSize, numBedrooms, numBaths, numFloors,
features, status, listingAgent, sellingAgent, buyerName, sellingPrice,
dateOfContract)
ProspectiveBuyer(name, address, telephone, typeWanted, styleWanted,
sizeWanted, bedroomsWanted, highestPrice, dateRegistered,
specialRequests, agentName)
Binder(buyerName, listingAddress, sellingPrice, dateBid, dateAccepted,
amountDeposit, status, dateCancelled, dateOfContract)
```

For simplicity, assume all names are unique. The attribute `features` in `Listing` is a description of the property containing at most 100 characters. The `specialRequests` attribute in `ProspectiveBuyer` lists any special needs of the client.

a. Chose a data distribution plan for this data and justify your choice, using the criteria listed in Section 12.5.

b. Write a fragmentation schema as follows: Decide how the data should be fragmented to fit the distribution plan. Use relational algebra or SQL commands to create the fragments. For each fragment, identify the location(s) where it will be stored.

c. Explain how the following query would be answered: Find the names and addresses of all prospective buyers and their agents for a new listing. It is a residence (i.e., `type` = 'residence') colonial style, with four bedrooms and asking price of $800,000.

d. Explain how the following query would be answered: Find all the houses that are suitable to show a prospective buyer who is interested in a two-story residence with three bedrooms and two baths that cost under $500,000. For each house, show all the listing information, plus the name and telephone number of the listing agent.

e. Explain how the following query would be answered: For all houses sold last month for which Jane Hayward was the listing agent, find the name of the selling agent.

12.5   Assume a chain of computer stores that sells computers, components, and parts uses the following global schema for a relational database that keeps information about items at each store:

```
Item(itemNo, itemName, supplier, unitCost)
Store (storeName, address, manager, telephone)
Stock (itemNo, store, qtyOnHand, qtyOnOrder, reorderPoint)
```

The company has 20 stores that stock about 15,000 different items. Each item comes from only one supplier, but there are different suppliers for different items. The database keeps track of what items are in what store, what items have been reordered at each store, and the reorder point, which is the number of items that is the minimum each store wishes to keep in stock. When the quantity on hand falls to the reorder point, a new order is placed, unless the item has already been reordered. Each store serves customers in its own geographical area, but if an item is out of stock, the manager can obtain the item from another store. All information is currently stored in a central database. We wish to design a distributed system to make operations more efficient.

a. Choose a data distribution plan and justify your choice.

b. Write a fragmentation scheme, using relational algebra or SQL to create the fragments. For each fragment, identify the location(s) where it will be stored.

c. Explain how the following query would be answered: Find the total quantity of item number 1001 on hand in all stores.

d. If the number of bytes in each data item is 10, find the communications cost involved in the strategy you used for the query in (c).

e. Assume a customer at store A has requested a large quantity of an item that is out of stock in store A. Explain how the database will enable the manager of that store to locate stores that would provide enough items to fill the order, assuming no single store would have sufficient quantities to fill the entire order. Write the SQL or relational algebra query for the request.

f. Assuming each data item occupies 10 bytes, estimate the communications cost involved in the strategy you used for the query in (e), making assumptions as needed.

SAMPLE PROJECT: PLANNING THE DISTRIBUTION OF THE RELATIONAL DATABASE FOR THE ART GALLERY

We will assume The Art Gallery has expanded to three locations, Midtown, which is the original gallery, plus Uptown and Downtown. We wish to distribute the database among the three locations. We will use the set of relations developed in Chapter 6 as the global schema. The schema is:

```
(1) Artist (artistId, firstName, lastName, interviewDate, interviewerName,
areaCode, telephoneNumber, street, zip, salesLastYear, salesYearToDate,
socialSecurityNumber, usualMedium, usualStyle, usualType)
(2) Zips (zip, city, state)
(3) PotentialCustomer (potentialCustomerId, firstName, lastName, areaCode,
telephoneNumber, street, zip, dateFilledIn, preferredArtistId,
preferredMedium, preferredStyle, preferredType)
```

(4) Artwork (<u>artworkId</u>, *artistId,* workTitle, askingPrice, dateListed, dateReturned, dateShown, status, workMedium, workSize, workStyle, workType, workYearCompleted, *collectorSocialSecurityNumber*)

(5) ShownIn (<u>*artworkId,showTitle*</u>)

(6) Collector (<u>socialSecurityNumber</u>, firstName, lastName, street, *zip,* interviewDate, interviewerName, areaCode, telephonenumber, salesLastYear, salesYearToDate, *collectionArtistId,* collectionMedium, collectionStyle, collectionType, SalesLastYear, SalesYearToDate)

(7) Show (<u>showTitle</u>, *showFeaturedArtistId,* showClosingDate, showTheme, showOpeningDate)

(8) Buyer (<u>buyerId</u>, firstName, lastName, street, *zip,* areaCode, telephoneNumber, purchasesLastYear, purchasesYearToDate)

(9) Sale (<u>*InvoiceNumber, artworkId,*</u> amountRemittedToOwner, saleDate, salePrice, saleTax, *buyerId, salespersonSocialSecurityNumber*)

(10) Salesperson (<u>socialSecurityNumber</u>, firstName, lastName, street, *zip*)

- Step 12.1. Write out a set of end user locations and the applications performed at each. The three locations are Midtown (the main site), Uptown, and Downtown. The applications performed at each branch for that branch's own data are:

  1. Maintaining artwork records

  2. Producing sales invoice

  3. Maintaining sales records

  4. Maintaining the potential customer records

  5. Producing the Works for Sale report

  6. Producing the Sales This Week report

  7. Producing the Buyer Sales Report

  8. Producing the Preferred Customer Report

  9. Producing the Salesperson Performance Report

  10. Producing the Aged Artworks Report

  11. Producing the Owner Payment Stub

  12. Producing the Art Show Details report

In addition, the following applications are performed at Midtown only.

13. Maintaining artist records

14. Maintaining collector records

15. Producing the Active Artists Summary report

16. Producing the Individual Artist Sales report

17. Producing the Collectors Summary report

18. Producing the Individual Collector Sales report

- Step 12.2. For each application, decide what tables are required.

  1. Maintaining artwork records—`Artwork`, `Artist`, and `Collector` tables

  2. Producing sales invoice—`Sale`, `Buyer`, `Salesperson`, `Artist`, `Collector`, and `Zip` tables

  3. Maintaining sales records—`Sale`, `Buyer`, `Salesperson`, `Zip`, and `Artwork` tables

  4. Maintaining the potential customer records—`PotentialCustomer`, `Zip`, and `Artist` tables

  5. Producing the Works for Sale report—`Artwork`, `Artist`, and `Collector` tables

  6. Producing the Sales This Week report—`Sale`, `Salesperson`, `Buyer`, `Artist`, `Artwork`, `Zip`, and `Collector` tables

  7. Producing the Buyers Sales Report—`Buyer`, `Zip`, `Sale`, `Artwork`, and `Artist` tables

  8. Producing the Preferred Customer Report—`PotentialCustomer`, `Zip`, `Buyer`, `Artwork`, and `Artist` tables

  9. Producing the Salesperson Performance Report—`Sale`, `Artwork`, `Artist`, `Salesperson` and `Zip` tables

  10. Producing the Aged Artworks Report—`Artwork`, `Collector`, and `Artist` tables

  11. Producing the Owner Payment Stub—`Sale`, `Collector`, `Zip`, and `Artist` tables

  12. Producing the Art Show Details report—`Show`, `ShownIn`, `Artwork`, and `Artist` tables

13. Maintaining artist records—`Artist` and `Zip` tables

14. Maintaining collector records—`Collector`, `Zip`, and `Artist` tables

15. Producing the Active Artists Summary report—`Artist`, `Zip`, `Sale`, and `Artwork` tables

16. Producing the Individual Artist Sales report—`Artist`, `Zip`, `Sale`, and `Artwork` tables

17. Producing the Collectors Summary report—`Collector`, `Artist`, `Zip`, `Sale`, and `Artwork` tables

18. Producing the Individual Collector Sales report—`Collector`, `Artist`, `Zip`, `Sale`, and `Artwork` tables

- Step 12.3. Using the normalized relations, perform selection and projection operations, to create the set of vertical, horizontal, and mixed data fragments needed for each application.

Artist.   Parts of this table are used at all sites for all their applications (1 through 12). Only the `artistId` is needed for most of these, but the `name` is needed for a few. The required data could be produced by projecting the `Artist` table onto the required columns, creating a fragment we will call `ArtistFragment1`.

$$\text{ArtistFragment1} = \Pi_{\text{artistId, firstName, lastName}} (\text{Artist})$$

At each branch, the Owner Payment Stub also requires the artist's name, address, and social security number, if the artist is the owner. We form another fragment for this projection.

$$\text{ArtistFragment2} = \Pi_{\text{artistId, firstName, lastName, street, zip, socialSecurityNumber}} (\text{Artist})$$

Midtown needs the entire table to maintain the artist records (13), and the collector records (14), and for all its reports, 15 through 18.

Zips.   Since the table is rarely updated and is needed at every location, we will replicate the entire table at each branch.

PotentialCustomer. Each branch will have its own potential customer records. The ID will begin with a code indicating the branch.

```
PotentialCustomerDowntown=σID LIKE 'D%' (PotentialCustomer)
PotentialCustomerMidtown=σID LIKE 'M%' (PotentialCustomer)
PotentialCustomerUptown=σID LIKE "U%" (PotentialCustomer)
```

Artwork.   Each branch needs this table to maintain records of artworks at that branch (1), and sales records (3). We can form fragments using a selection operation, if we assume the `artworkId` contains a code indicating the branch, as we did for `PotentialCustomer`. The fragments are identified using:

ArtworkDowntown=$\sigma_{ID\ LIKE\ 'D\%'}$(Artwork)
ArtworkMidtown=$\sigma_{ID\ LIKE\ 'M\%'}$(Artwork)
ArtworkUptown=$\sigma_{ID\ LIKE\ 'U\%'}$(Artwork)

The branch also uses these same table fragments to produce its own Works for Sale report (5), Buyer Sales report (7), Salesperson Performance report (9), Aged Artworks report (10), and Art Show Details report (12).

Midtown also uses the entire table for reports 15, 16, 17, and 18.

ShownIn.   Each branch uses this table for its Art Show Details report (12). However, it needs only the horizontal fragment for its own works and shows. We will add an attribute, `branch`, to the `Show` table, identifying the branch each show is in. The `ShownIn` table can then be fragmented horizontally, using an SQL subquery to identify the appropriate branch. For example, for the downtown branch, we create the horizontal fragment, `ShownInDowntown`, as

```
SELECT *
FROM ShownIn
WHERE showTitle IN (SELECT showTitle
                    FROM Show
                    WHERE branch='Downtown');
```

Similarly we form `ShownInMidtown`, and `ShownInUptown`.

Collector.   Each branch uses this table for maintaining artwork records (1), producing the sales invoice (2), and for reports 5, 6, 10 and 11. For some of these, the `collectorId` and `name` are needed. We can fragment this table by using projection as we did for the `Artist` table.

CollectorFragment1 = $\Pi_{collectorId,\ firstName,\ lastName}$(Collector)

The Owner Payment Stub requires the collector's name, address, and social security number, if a collector is the owner. We form another Fragment for this projection.

CollectorFragment2 = $\Pi_{collectorId,firstName,lastName,street,zip,socialSecurityNumber}$(Collector)

Midtown uses the entire table for maintaining collector records (14) and for reports 17 and 18.

Show.   Each branch uses this table for its Art Show Details report (12). We will add an attribute, branch, to the Show table, and create fragments as follows:

ShowDowntown=$\sigma_{\text{branch='Downtown'}}$(Show)
ShowMidtown=$\sigma_{\text{branch='Midtown'}}$(Show)
ShowUptown=$\sigma_{\text{branch='Uptown'}}$(Show)

Buyer.   Each branch uses this table for producing sales invoices (2), maintaining sales records (3) and for reports 6, 7, and 8. Assuming the buyerId is a string containing a code for the branch where the buyer makes a purchase, we can use selection to form horizontal fragments.

BuyerDowntown=$\sigma_{\text{ID LIKE 'D%'}}$(Buyer)
BuyerMidtown=$\sigma_{\text{ID LIKE 'M%'}}$(Buyer)
BuyerUptown=$\sigma_{\text{ID LIKE 'U%'}}$(Buyer)

Sale.   Each branch uses this table for producing sales invoices (2), maintaining its sales records (3), and for reports 6, 7, 9, and 11. Each branch can use its own set of invoice numbers, whose initial digit identifies the branch. We can create horizontal fragments to identify the branch for each sale, using:

SaleDowntown=$\sigma_{\text{invoiceNumber>=0 and invoiceNumer<20000}}$(Sale)
SaleMidtown=$\sigma_{\text{invoiceNumber>=20000 and invoiceNumer<40000}}$(Sale)
SaleUptown=$\sigma_{\text{invoiceNumber>=40000 and invoiceNumer<60000}}$(Sale)

Midtown also uses the entire table for reports 15, 16, 17, and 18.

Salesperson.   Each branch uses this table for producing sales invoices (2), maintaining sales records (3), and for reports 6 and 9. We will add an attribute, branch, to the table to identify the branch a salesperson belongs to. Using selection, we form the horizontal subsets:

SalespersonDowntown=$\sigma_{\text{branch='Downtown'}}$(Salesperson)
SalespersonMidtown=$\sigma_{\text{branch='Midtown'}}$(Salesperson)
SalespersonUptown=$\sigma_{\text{branch='Uptown'}}$(Salesperson)

- Step 12.4. Map the fragments to the applications and locations. For each fragment that is required at more than one application location, decide whether the fragment can be replicated, by considering frequency of use and of update.

Artist. The `Artist` table will be updated very infrequently, and `artist ID` and name appear in many applications at all branches. Therefore, we will choose to replicate the fragment `ArtistFragment1` at all branches. Midtown needs the entire table for its applications, so we will store the entire table there. We note that `ArtistFragment2` ($\Pi_{\text{artistId, firstName, lastName, street, zip, socialSecurityNumber}}$(`Artist`)) contains sensitive data—the artist's address and social security number—and is needed at branches only for the owner payment stub when the artist is the owner. Therefore, we would choose to keep this fragment only at the Midtown branch, and allow other branches to access it as needed. However, since Midtown already has the entire `Artist` table, we will create a view to replace `ArtistFragment2`, which allows branches to access the view when payments are made to artists, and not create the fragment.

Zips. This table is needed at every location, is rarely updated, and does not contain any sensitive date, so we replicate it everywhere.

PotentialCustomer. Each branch stores data about its own potential customers, using the fragments, `PotentialCustomerDowntown`, `PotentialCustomerMidtown`, and `PotentialCustomerUptown`.

Artwork. Each branch stores records about is own artworks, using fragments `ArtworkDowntown`, `ArtworkMidtown`, and `ArtworkUptown`. Midtown stores a copy of the the entire table.

ShownIn. Each branch uses the fragment of this table for its own shows, namely `ShownInDowntown`, `ShownInMidtown`, and `ShownInUptown`.

Collector. Each branch stores a copy of `CollectorFragment1`, which has Id and name. Midtown stores the entire table and provides access to `CollectorFragment2` as a view on that table.

Show. Each branch stores the records of its own shows, namely `ShowDowntown`, `ShowMidtown`, and `ShowUptown`.

Buyer. Each branch stores the records of its own buyers, namely `BuyerDowntown`, `BuyerMidtown`, and `BuyerUptown`.

Sale.　Each branch has its own sales records, identified by invoice number as `SaleDowntown`, `SaleMidtown`, and `SaleUptown`. Midtown also keeps a copy of the entire table.

Salesperson.　Each branch keeps records of its own salespersons, namely `SalespersonDowntown`, `SalespersonMidtown`, and `SalespersonUptown`.

- Step 12.5. Make a table showing a geographical network, listing nodes and applications and showing the data fragments at each node.

  The table is shown in Figure 12.9.

- Step 12.6. For each application in the geographical network, determine whether access will be local, remote, or compound. Make up a table showing each site, and the applications requiring local access, remote access, and compound access.

  The table is shown in Figure 12.10.

- Step 12.7. For each of the non-local accesses, identify the application and the location of the data. Estimate the number of accesses required per day. If it is high, justify your choice of non-local storage.

  The only applications requiring remote access are the sales invoice and the owner payment stub applications, which require that the branches access the midtown location to determine the name, address, and social security number of the owner of the artwork. We have decided to maintain these in only one site for privacy reasons. The volume will correspond to the number of sales in each site. For original artwork of the type offered at The Art Gallery, the number of transactions per day will not be large.

- Step 12.8. Make any adjustments indicated by your analysis of applications and traffic, and plan a final geographical network.

  Since most accesses are local, there is no need to adjust the geographical network shown in Figure 12.10.

STUDENT PROJECTS: PLANNING FOR DISTRIBUTION

For the project you have chosen, assume the processing is to be distributed to at least four locations. Identify the applications that will be performed at each of the locations, and then follow the steps shown in the case study to plan the distribution of your database.

Application	Downtown	Midtown	Uptown
1 Maintaining Artwork Records	ArtworkDowntown ArtistFragment1 CollectorFragment1	Artwork Artist Collector	ArtworkUptown ArtistFragment1 CollectorFragment1
2 Producing Sales Invoice	SaleDowntown BuyerDowntown SalespersonDowntown ArtistFragment1 CollectorFragment1 Zip	Sale BuyerMidtown SalespersonMidtown Artist Collector Zip	SaleUptown BuyerUptown SalespersonUptown ArtistFragment1 CollectorFragment1 Zip
3 Maintaining Sales Records	Sale Downtown BuyerDowntown SalespersonDowntown ArtworkDowntown Zip	Sale BuyerMidtown SalespersonMidtown Artwork Zip	SaleUptown BuyerUptown SalespersonUptown ArtworkUptown Zip
4 Maintaining Potential Customer Record	PotentialCustomerDowntown ArtistFragment1 Zip	PotentialCustomerMidtown Artist Zip	PotentialCustomerUptown ArtistFragment1 Zip
5 Works for Sale Report	ArtworkDowntown ArtistFragment1 CollectorFragment1	Artwork Artist Collector	ArtworkUptown ArtistFragment1 CollectorFragment1
6 Sales This Week	SaleDowntown BuyerDowntown SalespersonDowntown ArtworkDowntown ArtistFragment1 CollectorFragment1 Zip	Sale BuyerMidtown SalespersonMidtown ArtworkMidtown Artist Collector Zip	SaleUptown BuyerUptown SalespersonUptown ArtworkUptown ArtistFragment1 CollectorFragment1 Zip
7 Buyers Sales Report	BuyerDowntown Zip SaleDowntown ArtworkDowntown ArtistFragment1	BuyerMidtown Zip SaleMidtown ArtworkMidtown Artist	BuyerUptown Zip SaleUptown ArtworkUpown ArtistFragment1
8 Preferred Customer Report	Potential CustomerDowntown Zip BuyerDowntown ArtworkDowntown ArtistFragment1	PotentialCustomerMidtown Zip BuyerMidtown ArtworkMidtown Artist	PotentialCustomerUptown Zip BuyerUptown ArtworkUptown ArtistFragment

Application	Downtown	Midtown	Uptown
9 Salesperson Performance Report	SalespersonDowntown SaleDowntown ArtworkDowntown ArtistFragment1 Zip	SalespersonMidtown SaleMidtown ArtworkMidtown Artist Zip	SalespersonUptown SaleUptown ArtworkUptown ArtistFragment1 Zip
10 Aged Artworks Report	ArtworkDowntown CollectorFragment1 ArtistFragment1	ArtworkMidtown Collector Artist	ArtworkUptown CollectorFragment1 ArtistFragment1
11 Owner Payment Stub	SaleDowntown CollectorFragment1 Zip ArtistFragment1	SaleMidtown Collector Zip Artist	SaleUptown CollectorFragment1 Zip ArtistFragment1
12 Art Show Details Report	ShowDowntown ShownInDowntown ArtworkDowntown ArtistFragment1	ShowMidtown ShownInMidtown ArtworkMidtown Artist	ShowUptown ShownInUptown ArtworkUptown ArtistFragment1
13 Maintaining Artist Records		Artist, Zip	
14 Maintaining Collector Records		Collector, Zip, Artist	
15 Active Artists Summary Report		Artist, Zip, Sale, Artwork	
16 Individual Artist Sales Report		Artist, Zip, Sale, Artwork	
17 Collectors Summary Report		Collector, Artist, Zip, Sale, Artwork	
18 Individual Collector Sales		Collector, Artist, Zip, Sale, Artwork	

FIGURE 12.9

Geographical Network for The Art Gallery

Application	Downtown	Midtown	Uptown
1 Maintaining Artwork Records-all local access	local	local	local
2 Producing Sales Invoice-remote access from branches for owner address, phone, and social security number	remote	local	remote
3 Maintaining Sales Records-all local access	local	local	local
4 Maintaining Potential Customer Records-all local access	local	local	local
5 Works for Sale Report-all local access	local	local	local
6 Sales This Week-all local access	local	local	local
7 Buyers Sales Report-all local access	local	local	local
8 Preferred Customer Report-all local access	local	local	local
9 Salesperson Performance Report-all local access	local	local	local
10 Aged Artworks Report-all local access	local	local	local
11 Owner Payment Stub-remote access from branches for owner address, phone, and social security number	remote	local	remote
12 Art Show Details Report-all local access	local	local	local

Application	Downtown	Midtown	Uptown
13 Maintaining Artist Records-local access	local	local	local
14 Maintaining Collector Records-local access	local	local	local
15 Active Artists Summary Report-local access	local	local	local
16 Individual Artist Sales Report-local access	local	local	local
17 Collectors Summary Report-local access	local	local	local
18 Individual Collector Sales-local access	local	local	local

FIGURE 12.10

Applications with Local, Remote, and Compound Access

13 CHAPTER

Databases and the Internet

Chapter Objectives

In this chapter you will learn the following:

- Why organizations provide Internet access to their databases

- Terminology and concepts fundamental to an understanding of the World Wide Web

- The origins of the Internet and the World Wide Web

- Characteristics of http

- Fundamentals of HTML and XML

- Characteristics of XML documents

- The structure of a DTD

- The structure of an XML Schema

- What makes an XML instance document valid
- The characteristics of tiered architecture
- The functions and technologies used in the presentation layer
- The functions and technologies used in the middle tier
- The functions of the data layer
- The characteristics and graphical representation of the semi-structured data model
- Some fundamental XML query operations
- Some methods used to convert between XML and relational database formats

13.1 Introduction

The widespread use of the World Wide Web presents new opportunities for organizations to capture and use data in innovative ways, and provides significant challenges for database designers and database administrators. The Web can be viewed as a huge, loosely organized information resource whose potential is enormous. Many websites currently store resources in separate static linked HTML (or other format) files. Management of the files and links can become a problem if they are created and updated by different authors. If they contain data taken from a database, the static HTML files may become inconsistent when the database is updated. Therefore many organizations are choosing to provide dynamic access to databases directly from the Web.

E-commerce is revolutionizing the way businesses interact with their customers, suppliers, and contractors. Organizations are developing Web-based applications to create worldwide markets for their products, to deliver information, to provide cheaper and better customer service, to communicate with their suppliers, to provide training for employees, to expand the workplace, and to implement many other innovative activities.

To cultivate and manage this resource requires a combination of communications technology, information retrieval technology, and database technology. There has been a rush to develop standards, and many competing models have been proposed. At the present time, XML has emerged as a promising standard for document storage, exchange, and retrieval that may lead to the integration of competing technologies. The XML standard for describing the content of documents facilitates the development of online applications, including e-commerce applications.

13.2   Fundamental Concepts of the Internet and World Wide Web

In order to understand the technologies and standards used on the World Wide Web, some background information about the Internet is needed.

13.2.1 Origins of the Web

The terms **Internet** and **World Wide Web** are sometimes used interchangeably, but they actually have different meanings. The Internet predates the Web by a few decades. The Internet is a large network composed of smaller networks (internetwork). It developed from **Arpanet,** a communications network that was created in the 1960s using funds from the U.S. Department of Defense Advanced Research Project Agency (DARPA) for the purpose of linking government and academic research institutions. The network used a common protocol, **TCP/IP** (Transmission Control Protocol/Internet Protocol), to facilitate communications between sites. Later, the National Science Foundation took over the responsibility for managing the network, which was now referred to as the Internet. Although the Internet allowed access to resources at distant sites, it required considerable sophistication on the part of the user, who had to find the resources of interest, log on to the remote system containing them, navigate the directories of that system to find the desired files, copy the files to a local directory, and then display them correctly.

In 1989 Tim Berners-Lee proposed a method of simplifying access to resources that led to the development of the World Wide Web. His proposal included:

- A method to identify the location of resources, called a **Uniform Resource Locator (URL)**

- A standard protocol, Hypertext Transfer Protocol **(HTTP),** for transferring documents over the Internet

- A language called Hypertext Markup Language (**HTML**) that integrated instructions for displaying documents into the documents themselves

- **Hypertext,** a technique for using embedded links in documents to reference other resources

- A **graphical browser** that displayed content in a window, which could contain embedded links

Berners-Lee's proposal made it possible to automate the complicated process of finding, downloading, and displaying files on the Internet.

13.2.2 Browsers, Links, and URIs

Users access the Web using a Web browser such as Microsoft Explorer or Netscape. As they use the browser to visit a site, they may type in the URL that identifies the site's Web server. The site may have a number of Web pages, each of which has a corresponding root document that tells how the page is to be displayed. The pages may have links that contain the URLs of other resources. Clicking on links allows the user to visit the sites that contain those resources and display the information from them without typing in their URL.

A URL is a specific type of **Uniform Resource Identifier (URI),** which is a string that identifies the location of any type of resource on the Internet, including Web pages, mailboxes, downloadable files, and so on. An example of a URI is *http://www.iona.edu/about.htm*. The first part identifies the protocol, http, that is to be used for accessing the resource. The next part, www.iona.edu, identifies the server where the resource is located. The last part, the path name, identifies the document, about.htm, to be accessed.

13.2.3 HTTP

The Hypertext Transfer Protocol (HTTP) is the most widely used protocol on the Internet. A **communications protocol** is a set of standards for the structure of messages between parties. Using this protocol, a Web browser, functioning as an HTTP client, first sends a request to an HTTP server. An HTTP request has a few lines of text, with an empty line at the end. An example is:

```
GET about.htm HTTP/1.1
User-agent: Mozilla/4.0
Accept: text/html, image/gif, image/jpeg
```

The first line, the request line, has three fields.

- The HTTP method field, which can be GET or POST; here it is GET
- The URI field, which gives the name of the object to get or post; here it is `about.htm`
- The HTTP version field, which tells what version of the protocol the client is using; here it is 1.1

The second line, the user agent line, shows the type of the client. The third line tells the types of files the client will accept.

After receiving such a request message, the server sends back an HTTP response message. The server retrieves the object requested (`about.htm` in this example), uses the page or resource to assemble the HTTP response message, and sends the message back to the client. It has several lines, including a status line, some header lines, and the body of message, which usually contains the requested object. The status line is the first line. It gives the HTTP version, a status code, and a server message. For example, a status line such as,

```
HTTP/1.1 200 OK
```

means that the request was successful, (indicated by the status code of 200 and the message OK), and the requested object is in the body of message which follows. Other status code values and corresponding messages indicate that the resource was not found, or that an error occurred. Header lines can include information about the date and time of the response, the date the object was modified, the number of bytes in the content of the object, and the type of the content. The body of the message, which contains the actual object, follows the header lines. It usually contains HTML formatting information as well as the content.

When the client browser gets the response message containing the requested object, it uses the HTML in the file to display the object properly. If the object contains links, it uses the HTTP protocol and the URIs to establish a connection with each resource to retrieve the associated objects.

HTTP is a **stateless** protocol. Each request message and its response are self-contained, with no facility for remembering previous interactions. This creates a problem in the context of e-commerce, which requires a continuous session with the user. The application must encode any state information either in the client or the server, not in the protocol.

13.2.4 HTML

HTML, Hypertext Markup Language, is a data format used for presenting content on the Internet. It is a **markup** language, so called because HTML documents contain marks or tags that provide formatting information for the text. Markup languages have been used for many years to specify the format of documents; for example, they specify what part of a document should be underlined, where to insert spaces, where a new paragraph should start, and so on. HTML tags are enclosed in angled brackets, < >. Most of the tags occur in pairs, having the form *<tag>* and *</tag>*. The first of the pair specifies where the special formatting is to start, and the second where it is to end. For example, **<B>** means bold, so that in,

```
The last word in this sentence is in <B> boldface</B>.
```

we can interpret the <B> to mean "turn on bolding" and </B> to mean "turn off bolding." An HTML document starts with the tag **<HTML>** and ends with **</HTML>**. The heading of a document can be enclosed in tags **<HEAD>** and **</HEAD>**, and the body can be enclosed in tags **<BODY>** and **</BODY>**. There are many other tags, but some of the most useful ones are:

- <UL> for unordered list, used to identify a list of items to follow
- <LI> for list item, used for each item on the list
- <H1> for Heading 1, which specifies that the usual format for a level-1 heading should be used
- <H2> through <H6>, for level 2 through level 6 headings
- <I> for italics
- <U> for underline

These tags all require an ending tag, but some tags, such as the one for a new paragraph, <P>, do not always require an ending tag.

Besides text, an HTML document can contain a wide variety of objects such as Java applets, audio files, images, video files, and others. When the document is retrieved by the user's browser, the text is displayed in accordance with the formatting commands, the applets are executed, the audio files play, the video is displayed, and so on, at the user's workstation. Figure 13.1 shows a sample HTML document.

FIGURE 13.1

HTML Document Showing a Customer List

```
<HTML>
<HEAD>
<TITLE>Customer List</TITLE>
</HEAD>
<BODY>
<H2>Corporate Customer List</H2>
<UL>
        <LI> WorldWide Travel Agency</LI>
        <LI> 10 Main Street, New York, NY 10001</LI>
        <LI> 212 123 4567</LI>
</UL>
<H2>Individual Customer List</H2>
<UL>
        <LI> Mary Jones</LI>
        <LI> 25 Spruce Street, San Diego, CA 92101</LI>
        <LI> 619 555 6789</LI>
</UL>
<UL>
        <LI> Alice Adams</LI>
        <LI> 25 Orange Blossom Street, Miami, FL 60601</LI>
        <LI> 305 987 6543</LI>
</UL>
</BODY>
</HTML>
```

13.2.5 XML

Although HTML works well for displaying text, it uses a limited set of tags with fixed meanings, making it relatively inflexible. In the example shown in Figure 13.1, we can infer the meanings of the items, but the document does not describe them. HTML is an application of a more powerful and general language, Standard Generalized Markup Language (**SGML**). SGML is actually a meta-language that allows users to define their own markup languages. However, SGML is quite complex. A simpler language based on SGML and HTML, called **XML** (Extensible Markup Language), was created in 1996 by the World Wide Web Consortium XML Special

Interest Group. The objective was to retain the flexibility of SGML and the simplicity of HTML. XML also allows users to define their own markup language. For example, users can create tags that describe the data items in a document. The database community has a great interest in XML as a means of describing documents of all types, including databases. Using XML, it is possible to define the structure of heterogeneous databases, facilitating translation of data between different databases.

13.2.5.1 Standalone XML Documents

Figure 13.2 shows an example of an XML document. An XML document usually begins with an optional **declaration** which identifies the XML version used for the document, and, optionally, the coding system used, and/or whether the document has an external document type definition (DTD) or not. The most common coding system for XML documents is Unicode, identified by UTF-8. A document without an external DTD is described as "standalone." An example of a declaration is:

```
<?xml version="1.0" encoding="UTF-8" standalone="yes"?>
```

If there is an external DTD, the name of the file containing the DTD appears on the second line, as in:

```
<?xml version="1.0" encoding="UTF-8"?>
<!DOCTYPE CUSTOMERLIST SYSTEM "C:\BOOK\EXAMPLES\CUSTOMERLIST.DTD">
```

The declaration is followed by one or more XML **elements,** each of which has a **start tag** showing the name of the element, some **character data,** and an **end tag**. XML is case-sensitive. An element is the basic component of an XML document. Elements can be subelements of other elements. Elements must be properly nested, so that if an element's start tag appears inside the body of another element, its end tag must also appear before the end tag of the enclosing element. The first element in the DTD must be a single root element, in which every other element is nested. Figure 13.2 shows the root element CUSTOMERLIST, which contains all the information about customers. Within this element, the element CUSTOMER gives all the information about one customer. An element can also be empty, which can be indicated using the self-terminating tag:

```
<EMPTYELEMENT/>.
```

Elements can have **attributes** whose names and values are shown inside the element's start tag. Note that CUSTOMER has an attribute named

FIGURE 13.2
XML Instance Document
Showing Customer List

```xml
<?xml version="1.0" encoding="UTF-8" standalone="yes"?>
<CUSTOMERLIST>
<CUSTOMER type="Corporate" status="Active">
        <NAME>WorldWide Travel Agency</NAME>
        <STREET>10 Main Street</STREET>
        <CITY>New York</CITY>
        <STATE>NY</STATE>
        <ZIP>10001</ZIP>
        <AREACODE>212</AREACODE>
        <PHONE>123 4567</PHONE>
</CUSTOMER>
<CUSTOMER type="Individual"> <!--start of individual customers-->
        <NAME>Mary Jones</NAME>
        <STREET>25 Spruce Street</STREET>
        <CITY>San Diego</CITY>
        <STATE>CA</STATE>
        <ZIP>92101</ZIP>
        <AREACODE>619</AREACODE>
        <PHONE>555 6789</PHONE>
</CUSTOMER>
<CUSTOMER type="Individual" status="Inactive">
        <NAME>Alice Adams</NAME>
        <STREET>25 Orange Blossom Street</STREET>
        <CITY>Miami</CITY>
        <STATE>FL</STATE>
        <ZIP>60601</ZIP>
        <AREACODE>305</AREACODE>
        <PHONE>987 6543</PHONE>
</CUSTOMER>
</CUSTOMERLIST>
```

type whose values appear as either "Corporate" or "Individual," and an attribute named status whose values appear as "Active" or "Inactive." The attribute values are shown in quotes. The designer has a choice of whether to represent data using an element or an attribute. Attributes occur only once within each element, while subelements can occur any number of times.

We can insert **comments** wherever we wish in the document. A comment starts with <!-- and ends with -->, and can contain any explanatory text, except the string --, as shown in Figure 13.2 for the second customer.

We can refer to external files, common text, Unicode characters, or some reserved symbols by using an **entity reference.** The reference begins with the ampersand character, **&,** and ends with a semicolon, ;. When the document is displayed in a browser, the reference will be replaced by its content. If you wish to include reserved symbols that have special meaning in XML, it is necessary to use the **&. . .;** as an escape sequence. These predefined entities are &, <, >, ' and ", which we refer to by their mnemonic names amp, lt, gt, apos, and quot. For example, to indicate the string,

```
value>'a'&value<'z'
```

we would write:

```
value&gt;&apos;a&apos;&amp;value&lt;&apos;z&apos;
```

References are also used to insert Unicode characters in the text. For example, to insert the symbol © we write &00A9; since the Unicode character for © is 00A9.

An XML document, such as the one shown in Figure 13.2, is said to be **well formed** if it obeys the rules of XML. It must conform to the following guidelines:

- It starts with an XML declaration like the one shown in the first line of Figure 13.2

- It has a root element that contains all the other elements, such as the element CUSTOMERLIST in Figure 13.2.

- All elements are properly nested. If the start tag of an element occurs within another element, the end tag occurs within the element as well. For example, each NAME element is nested within CUSTOMER element.

13.2.5.2 DTDs

Users can define their own markup language by writing a **Document Type Declaration (DTD)** or by writing an **XML Schema.** A DTD is a specification for a set of rules for the elements, attributes, and entities of a document. A document, which we will now refer to as an instance document as opposed to a DTD, that obeys the rules of its associated DTD is said to be **type-valid.** Processors can validate XML instance documents by checking their DTDs. Several instance documents can share the same DTD. Figure 13.3 shows a sample DTD that describes the structure of the instance document CUSTOMERLIST. A DTD must obey these rules:

- The DTD is enclosed in <!DOCTYPE *name*[*DTDdeclaration*]>

- *name* is the name of the outermost enclosing tag, which is CUSTOMERLIST in our example

- The *DTDdeclaration*, which is enclosed in square brackets, gives the rules for documents that use this DTD

FIGURE 13.3

Possible DTD for CUSTOMERLIST Document

```
<!DOCTYPE CUSTOMERLIST[
<!ELEMENT CUSTLIST (CUSTOMER)*>
<!ELEMENT CUSTOMER (NAME,ADDRESS+,TELEPHONE?)>
     <!ELEMENT NAME (#PCDATA)>
     <!ELEMENT ADDRESS (STREET,CITY,STATE,ZIP)>
          <!ELEMENT STREET (#PCDATA)>
          <!ELEMENT CITY (#PCDATA)>
          <!ELEMENT STATE (#PCDATA)>
          <!ELEMENT ZIP (#PCDATA)>
     <!ELEMENT TELEPHONE (AREACODE,PHONE)>
          <!ELEMENT AREACODE (#PCDATA)>
          <!ELEMENT PHONE (#PCDATA)>
<!ATTLIST CUSTOMER TYPE (Corporate|Individual) #REQUIRED>
<!ATTLIST CUSTOMER STATUS (Active|Inactive) "Active">
]>
```

- Each **element** is declared using a type declaration with the structure <!ELEMENT *(content type)*> where the content type can be

  - Other elements that are subelements of the declared element. In Figure 13.3 the element CUSTLIST has subelement CUSTOMER, the element CUSTOMER has subelements NAME, ADDRESS, and TELEPHONE, and both ADDRESS and TELEPHONE in turn have subelements.

  - #PCDATA, which means the element value consists of parsed character data. In Figure 13.3, the element NAME has this content type, as do STREET, CITY, STATE, ZIP, AREACODE, and PHONE.

  - The empty element, indicated by <EMPTYELEMENT/>.

  - The symbol ANY, which means any content is permitted.

  - A regular expression that is constructed from these four choices.

- In an element declaration, the name of any subelement can optionally be followed by one of the symbols *, + or ?, to indicate the number of times the subelement occurs within its enclosing element. The meanings are:

  * The element occurs zero or more times. In Figure 13.3, CUSTOMER elements can occur zero or more times, indicating that a CUSTOMERLIST could have no customers, or many.

  + The element occurs one or more times. In Figure 13.3, ADDRESS can occur one or more times for each customer.

  ? The element occurs zero or one times. In Figure 13.3, TELEPHONE occurs zero or one time for each customer.

- **Attribute** list declarations for elements are declared outside the element. They specify which elements have attributes, the name of each attribute, the data type, possible values (optional), whether the attribute is required, and default value, if any. They have the form <!ATTLIST elementName attName (attType)default>. Several attribute types exist, including string types and enumerated types. String type is declared as **CDATA.** An enumerated type is shown by listing all its possible values. An attribute declaration can also have a default specification. A required attribute is identified by writing #REQUIRED. If the attribute is not required, a default value may appear. The default value will be provided when no other value is specified for the attribute. In Figure 13.3, the CUSTOMER element has two attributes, TYPE and STATUS. The TYPE attribute is an enumerated type having possible values Corporate and Individual. It is a required attribute. The STATUS attribute has possible values Active and Inactive, with Active being the default. It is not required.

Domain-specific DTDs have been developed for a number of fields, and more are likely to be developed in the future. They will allow seamless data exchange between documents with the same DTD. For example MathML, Mathematics Markup Language, is a widely used DTD for documents in mathematics.

13.2.5.3 XML Schemas

XML Schema is a new, more powerful way to describe the structure of documents than DTDs. It permits more complex structure, additional fundamental data types, user-defined data types, user-created domain vocabulary (namespaces), and also supports uniqueness and foreign key constraints. An XML schema defines the organization and data types of an XML structure. An instance document that obeys XML rules is said to be **well-formed** and a **type-valid** instance document is one that conforms to a DTD. If an instance document conforms to an XML schema, it is called **schema-valid.** XML schemas are themselves XML documents, and can be schema-validated against the standards provided by the World Wide Web Consortium, W3C, as specified at `www.w3.org`. This site contains an XML standard schema document for all user-defined XML schema documents, as well as links to schema validators, which can be found at `http://www.w3.org/XML/Schema`. XML Schema is a very large topic, and a comprehensive treatment of it is beyond the scope of this book, but a brief introduction to provide the basic flavor of it follows.

A simple XML schema is shown in Figure 13.4. Like a DTD, an XML schema lists elements and attributes. Elements may be complex, which means they have subelements, or simple. In Figure 13.4 the element `Customer List` is of complex type, consisting of any number of `Customer` elements. `Customer` is also a complex type element, consisting of `Name`, `Address`, and `Telephone`. `Name` is a simple element of string type. `Address` is a complex type consisting of the simple string-type elements `Street`, `City`, `State`, and `Zip`. `Telephone` is a complex type consisting of the simple

```
<xsd:schema xmlns:xsd="http://www.w3.org/2001/XMLSchema">
 <xsd:element name ="CustomerList">
  <xsd:sequence>
    <xsd:element name="Customer" minoccurs="0" maxoccurs="unbounded">
      <xsd:complexType>
        <xsd:sequence>
          <xsd:element name="Name" type="xsd:string"/>
          <xsd:element name="Address" minoccurs="1" maxoccurs="unbounded">
            <xsd:complexType>
              <xsd:sequence>
                <xsd:element name="Street" type="xsd:string"/>
                <xsd:element name="City" type="xsd:string"/>
                <xsd:element name="State" type="xsd:string"/>
                <xsd:element name="Zip" type="xsd:string"/>
              </xsd:sequence>
            </xsd:complexType>
          </xsd:element>
          <xsd:element name="Telephone" minoccurs="0" maxoccurs="unbounded">
            <xsd:complexType>
              <xsd:sequence>
                <xsd:element name="AreaCode" type="xsd:string"/>
                <xsd:element name="Phone" type="xsd:string"/>
              </xsd:sequence>
            </xsd:complexType>
          </xsd:element>
        </xsd:sequence>
        <xsd:attribute name="Type" use="required">
          <xsd:simpleType>
            <xsd:restriction base="xsd:string">
              <xsd:enumeration value="Corporate"/>
              <xsd:enumeration value="Individual"/>
            </xsd:restriction>
          </xsd:simpleType>
        </xsd:attribute>
        <xsd:attribute name="Status" type="xsd:string" default="Active"/>
      </xsd:complexType>
    </xsd:element>
  </xsd:sequence>
 </xsd:element>
</xsd:schema>
```

FIGURE 13.4
Possible XML Schema for CustomerList

string type elements `AreaCode` and `Phone`. `Customer` has two attributes, `Type` and `Status`. `Type` is a required attribute that is an enumerated type. Its base type is string and its possible values are "Corporate" or "Individual." `Status` is a string type with default value of "Active."

Attributes or elements can be used to store data values. Attributes can be used for simple values that are not repeated, such as Type and Status. Elements can be complex or simple, and can occur multiple times. Type and Status could be represented as elements instead of attributes, as shown in Figure 13.5.

13.3 Tiered Architectures

For data-intensive applications, we can identify three major functions that are required in an Internet environment: presentation, application logic, and data management. The placement of these functions depends on the architecture of the system.

13.3.1 Single-tier Architecture

Initially, databases were created in a centralized mainframe environment, accessed by batch processes by dumb terminals. The database itself resided on secondary storage, and the database management system, the application, and the user interface all resided on a single computer, as illustrated in Figure 13.6(a)

13.3.2 Two-tier Architecture

As PCs became cheaper and more widely used, two-tier architecture developed. In this architecture, the user's workstation or other device functions as a client, and the database management system resides on a server. The two systems interact using a networking protocol. If the client provides only the user interface, and the server runs the application as well as handling data access, the client functions as a **thin client.** This architecture, which is illustrated in Figure 13.6(b), is typical when simple devices such as PDAs or cell phones are used as clients.

If the client takes on some of the application processing as well as handling the user interface, it functions as a **thick** or **fat client,** as shown in Figure 13.(c). PCs and workstations can function as thick clients in two-tier architecture, because they provide the needed processing power and storage. The server handles tasks such as validation as well as data access.

```
<xsd:schema xmlns:xsd="http://www.w3.org/2001/XMLSchema">
  <xsd:element name ="CustomerList">
    <xsd:sequence>
      <xsd:element name="Customer" minoccurs="0" maxoccurs="unbounded">
        <xsd:complexType>
          <xsd:sequence>
            <xsd:element name="Name" type="xsd:string"/>
            <xsd:element name="Address" minoccurs="1" maxoccurs="unbounded">
              <xsd:complexType>
                <xsd:sequence>
                  <xsd:element name="Street" type="xsd:string"/>
                  <xsd:element name="City" type="xsd:string"/>
                  <xsd:element name="State" type="xsd:string"/>
                  <xsd:element name="Zip" type="xsd:string"/>
                </xsd:sequence>
              </xsd:complexType>
            </xsd:element>
            <xsd:element name="Telephone" minoccurs="0" maxoccurs="unbounded">
              <xsd:complexType>
                <xsd:sequence>
                  <xsd:element name="AreaCode" type="xsd:string"/>
                  <xsd:element name="Phone" type="xsd:string"/>
                </xsd:sequence>
              </xsd:complexType>
            </xsd:element>
            <xsd:element name="Type" type="xsd:string"/>
            <xsd:element name="Status" type="xsd:string"/>
          </xsd:sequence>
        </xsd:complexType>
      </xsd:element>
    </xsd:sequence>
  </xsd:element>
</xsd:schema>
```

FIGURE 13.5

Another XML Schema for CustomerList

FIGURE 13.6(a)
Single-tier Architecture

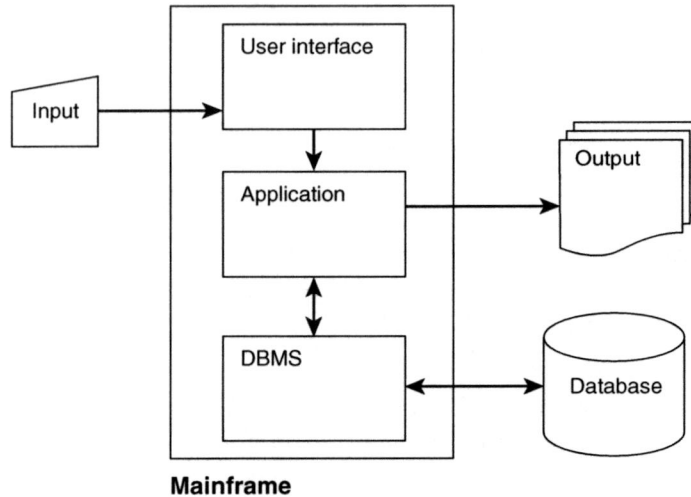

Mainframe

FIGURE 13.6(b)
Two-tier Architecture for Thin Clients

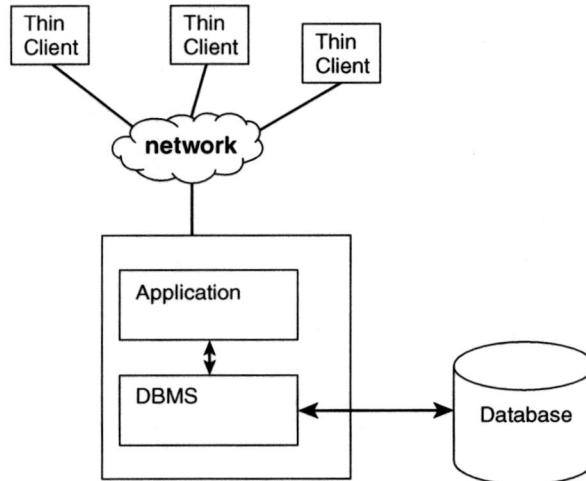

Several problems arise in this environment. The first is a problem of scalability, because the server is unable to handle a large number of clients simultaneously. The number of independent connections to the database is limited. Second, since the application logic is handled primarily by the client, the server has to trust that the application code will not damage the database. The applications themselves have to include transaction management routines, including exception handling and rollback if needed. The trust problem can be addressed by requiring registration of programs with the server. The server will then reject any unregistered applications.

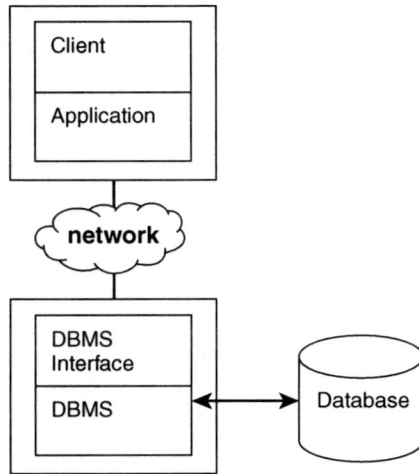

FIGURE 13.6(c)
Two-tier Architecture for Thick Clients

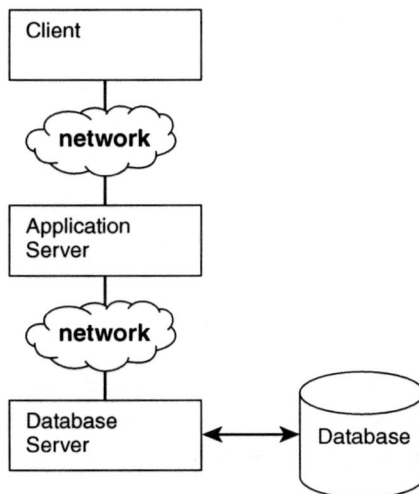

FIGURE 13.6(d)
Three-tier Architecture

The third problem is that there may be a large number of clients running applications, and there is no central place to maintain business logic.

13.3.3 Three-tier Architecture

Three-tier architectures completely separate application logic from data management. The client handles the user interface, which is called the **presentation layer** or the first tier. The interface can be Web-based. A separate **application server** executes the application logic and forms the **middle**

tier. The database server, which runs the DBMS and handles the data access, forms the third tier. The communications network connects each tier to the next one. This layered architecture is similar to the layering found in communications protocols and other fields, and its purpose is to support standardization among vendors and provide flexibility. The three-tier architecture allows:

- Support for thin clients, because clients need only handle the presentation layer

- Independence of tiers. Each tier can use whatever platform or software is best suited to its environment. Well-defined APIs can be used to standardize and control the interactions between layers. Code at any tier can be modified independently without affecting the other tiers.

- Easier application maintenance, because the application server is a central location where most business logic is stored

- Integrated data access, because data from several heterogeneous databases can be handled by the middle layer in a fashion that is transparent to the client

- Scalability, because the middle tier can share database connections with many clients simultaneously

13.3.3.1 The Presentation Layer

At the first tier, a user-friendly interface that is suitable for the device must be presented. At this layer, the user typically sees forms through which he or she issues requests and sees responses to those requests. HTML forms are often used for this purpose. Script code in Perl, JavaScript, JScript, VBScript, and similar scripting languages can be embedded in the HTML to provide some simple client-side processing. Style sheets that specify how data is presented on specific devices may also be used.

HTML forms can be used to pass input values from the client to the middle tier. The user's browser displays a Web page containing a form with input fields, text areas, drop-down lists, and other objects in which the user can enter input data. An HTML document can contain multiple forms. Each form can have any HTML tags except another FORM tag. The

HTML code for a simple sign-on form is shown in Figure 13.7. The HTML for a form begins with a FORM tag, and has the general format

```
<FORM ACTION="applicationURL" METHOD="GET" NAME="formName">
<INPUT TYPE="inputType" SIZE=size NAME="name" VALUE="value">
. . .
</FORM>
```

A FORM tag has the following fields:

- ACTION—gives the URI of the application that will process the input provided on the form. It is a relative reference that specifies the directory and the program to be executed. If no directory is specified, it uses the URI of current page.

- METHOD—specifies the method used to submit input from the filled-in form to the server. Possible values are GET or POST. A GET method sends the program name and the input information from the form in a single step. With a POST method the program name is part of the URL, and the input information is transmitted in a separate message.

- NAME—optionally allows the form to be given a name, so that programs can refer to the form and its fields by name.

  Forms can include INPUT, SELECT, and TEXTAREA tags that specify user input objects. The INPUT tag has no terminating tag. Input tag attributes include TYPE, SIZE, NAME, and VALUE. TYPE specifies the type of the input field. If the type is

```
<FORM ACTION="/cgi-bin/signon.cgi" METHOD="GET" NAME="UserLogin"
    <P>
    User ID:<INPUT TYPE="text" SIZE=20 NAME="userID">
    <P>
    Password:<INPUT TYPE="password" SIZE=20 NAME="password">
    <P>
    <INPUT TYPE="submit" VALUE="Log on">
    <INPUT TYPE="reset" VALUE="Clear">
<FORM>
```

FIGURE 13.7
A Simple HTML Form

text, the input box appears as a blank rectangle of the size specified in SIZE where the user can type in text. If the type is password, the characters entered will display as stars to protect the password. If the type is reset, a labeled button will appear. If the user presses that button, all input fields in form will be reset to their defaults. If the type is submit, a labeled button appears that sends values of all input fields to the server when the user presses it. The NAME provides a name for the field to identify the field contents to the server. The name must be provided for all input types except submit and reset. VALUE is an optional field that can be used to specify the default value of an input field. It is also used to provide a label for the button for submit or reset.

User input can also come from TEXTAREA and SELECT tags in a manner similar to INPUT tags.

The URI that appears in the ACTION attribute of the FORM tag must be that of an application, page, or script. If the method is GET, the action and each input area name and value are concatenated into a request URI having the form:

action?inputName1=inputValue1&inputName2=inputValue2&inputName3=inputValue3

For example, for the form shown in Figure 13.7, if the user entered the name Adam Adams and the password sesame, the request URI would be:

`http://localhost/cgi-bin/signon.cgi?userID=Adam+Adams&password=sesame`

Note that blanks are replaced by + and names are connected to their values by =. Any special characters are encoded using the form %xxx, where xxx is the ASCII value for the character.

Scripting Languages Scripting languages including Perl, JavaScript, JScript, and VBScript can be used to add simple programs that run at the client tier. Scripts are identified by a SCRIPT tag embedded in an HTML document. Its form is:

`<SCRIPT LANGUAGE="`*scriptLanguageName*`" SRC="`*externalFileName*`"></SCRIPT>`

The LANGUAGE attribute gives the name of the scripting language, such as "JavaScript." The SCR attribute gives the name of the external file with the script code, such as "checkForm.js." The code is automatically embedded in the HTML document. Scripts are used at the client for processes such as checking the validity of data that the user has entered in the form, identifying the type of browser the client is running, and controlling some browser functions.

Style Sheets: CSS and XSL Style sheets contain instructions that tell a Web browser or other display controller how to present data in a manner that is suitable for the client's display. For example, the same Web page can be rendered slightly different by Netscape and Explorer, and considerably different by a cellphone or PDA display. The style sheet dictates how fonts, colors, margins, and placement of windows are tailored for the specific device.

Cascading Style Sheets (CSS) can be used with HTML documents. The same style sheet can be used for many documents, allowing Web designers to apply a design template to all the pages at a given site, if the organization wishes to have a uniform look to the pages. A link to the style sheet can be included in the HTML document by writing a link tag having the form:

```
<LINK REL="StyleSheet" HREF="nameOfStyleSheet">
```

The style sheet itself consists of a set of specifications for properties of the document, such as colors, fonts, spacing, and so on. Each specification is given by a line of the style sheet having the form:

```
Attribute {property: value}
```

> For example, to set a font size and color for the level-one headings, we would write in CSS:

```
H1 {FONT-SIZE: 24pt; COLOR: blue}
```

Then an HTML document that uses the style sheet would replace any H1 tags with the specifications given in the style sheet.

The Extensible Stylesheet Language (XSL) is a language for writing style sheets for XML files. XSL files contain specifications of attributes that control the display of XML documents in a manner similar to the way CSS controls HTML displays. It is a much more powerful language than CSS, allowing the structure of documents to be changed using XSL Transformation Language (XSLT), allowing parts of the documents to be referenced using XML Path Language (XPath), and formatting objects for display.

13.3.3.2 The Middle Tier

The application server at the middle tier is responsible for executing applications. This tier determines the flow of control, acquires input data from the presentation layer, makes data requests to the database server, accepts query results from the database layer, and uses them to assemble dynamically generated HTML pages. Server-side processing can involve many different technologies such as Java Servlets, Java Server pages, and others.

CGI (Common Gateway Interface) can be used to connect HTML forms with application programs. This protocol defines how inputs from forms are passed to programs executing at the middle tier. Programs that use this protocol are called **CGI scripts,** and are often written in Perl. A typical Perl script extracts the input arguments from the HTML form, and constructs as output from the program a dynamically constructed Web page that it sends to the browser.

It is possible for each page request to start up a new process on the server, but this limits the number of simultaneous requests that can be handled. Instead, an application server maintains a pool of threads or processes and uses these to execute requests, avoiding the overhead of creating a new process for each request. They allow concurrent access to several data sources. The application server also manages sessions, detecting when a session starts, identifying which sessions belong to which users, and detecting when a session ends. To identify a session, the server can use cookies, hidden fields in HTML forms, and URI extensions. A cookie is a small text string that the server sends to the user's browser when the browser connects to it. It is essentially a session identifier that is stored in the memory of the browser and remains stored after the connection ends. Whenever the user reconnects to the server, the browser returns a copy of the cookie to the server, thereby establishing that the user is the same as for the previous session. Cookies are therefore used to store user information between sessions.

A major job of the application server is to **maintain state,** since HTTP is a stateless protocol. Any multi-step transaction that requires several interactions with a user requires that the state of the transaction be maintained. In a typical e-commerce transaction, the user will sign in, view products recommended for purchase based on his or her interests, browse through the site's offerings, place items in a shopping basket, modify the shopping basket several times, and then move on to the purchase. At that time, the shopper has to enter the shipping name and address, enter or confirm his or her own name and address, provide a credit card number and expiration date, and request any special services such as gift wrapping, express shipping, and so on. The final total, including any tax and extra charges, must be calculated and displayed, and the shopper must agree to the amount before the purchase is complete. A confirmation message is then sent back to the shopper. These steps require that the state of the transaction be maintained. Since HTTP is a stateless protocol, either the client or the server must be able to maintain state. On the client side, cookies are used for this purpose. Cookies are easily generated at the middle tier using Java's Cookie class and sent to the client, where they can be stored in the browser cache. The client's browser sends the cookie to the server with each request. A problem with this solution is that users might refuse to accept cookies, or might clean up the browser cache before the cookie expires, erasing the cookie. State could also be maintained in the database itself, but all queries or updates to the state, such as signing in or modifying the shopping basket, would require a database access. This solution is best used for relatively permanent information such as past orders, customer name and address, customer preferences, and so on. It is also possible to maintain state at the middle tier, using local files at that level.

Server-side processing can use Java servlets, JavaServer pages, or several other technologies. Java servlets are Java programs that implement the Servlet interface. They can use the HttpServlet class, which provides methods for receiving input from HTML forms and for constructing dynamic Web pages from the program results. Both the request and the response are passed as servlet parameters. Servlets have all the functionality of standard Java programs, allowing them to implement complicated transactions involving the database. Because they are Java programs, they are platform independent, and they run in containers. They can access all APIs including JDBC. They run on the middle tier, either in a Web server or an application server.

JavaServer pages are written in HTML but contain special tags that allow some servlet-type code, using JavaScript. JavaScript is a full featured programming language that can be embedded in HTML. JavaServer pages do not usually support complex applications, but are used for building user interfaces. However, they are executed like servlets.

13.4   The Semi-structured Data Model

The Web can be viewed as a massive collection of documents that include links and multimedia content such as sound, images, or video as well as text. Techniques for searching text documents were originally developed in the field of information retrieval, which was the domain of librarians rather than the public or database managers. However, with the development of the Web, the creation of collections of documents and the searching of those documents became an activity that was done primarily by ordinary computer users rather than by librarians. Because of the availability of the rich information resources the Web provides, the fields of information retrieval and database management have converged. In the database field, the documents on the Web are viewed as data sources similar to other databases, and the process of searching them can be seen as akin to querying a database. XML provides a bridge between the disciplines of information retrieval, which has traditionally included markup languages, and database management, which has relied on structured data models. XML allows documents to be marked up with meta-data, and can include tags that give some structure to documents. The semi-structured data model is a method of describing such partial structure. A semi-structured model contains a collection of nodes, each containing data, possibly with different schemas. The node itself contains information about the structure of its contents.

13.4.1   Graphical Representation

The semi-structured data model can be represented using a graph consisting of nodes and edges. Each document can be represented as a **tree,** having a single **root** node and a sequence of **child** nodes. Each child node can itself have child nodes, which in turn can have child nodes, and so on. A strict rule for trees is that every node, except the root, has exactly one parent node, which is at the level above it in the tree. The nodes can represent either complex objects or atomic values. An edge can represent either the relationship between an object and its sub-object, or the relationship between an object and its value. Leaf nodes, which have no sub-objects, represent values. There is no separate schema, since the graph is self-describing. For example, Figure 13.8

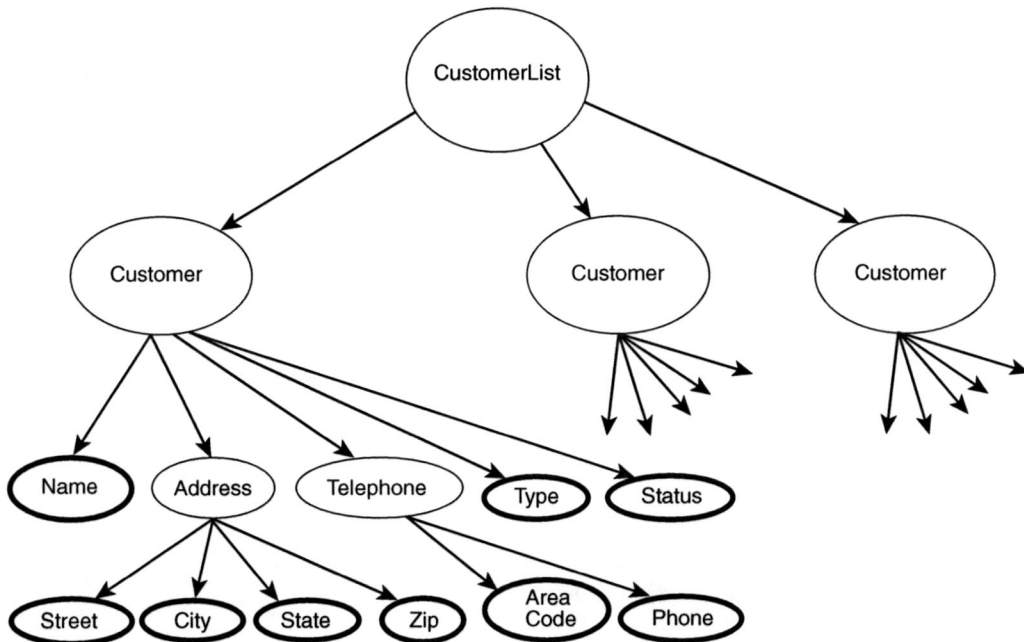

FIGURE 13.8
Hierarchical Representation of CustomerList

shows a hierarchical representation for the Customer List data that corresponds to the XML schema of Figure 13.5. The entire document, CustomerList, becomes the root of the tree. Each Customer element is represented as a child of the root. The sub-elements of Customer, namely Name, Address, Telephone, Type, and Status, are represented as children of Customer. The sub-elements of Address and Telephone are represented as their children. An instance document for this schema is shown in Figure 13.9. The instance document mirrors the structure of the XML schema (or of a DTD, if applicable), and shows the values provided for leaf nodes of the tree. All data resides in leaf nodes. If any attributes are present, they also become leaf nodes.

13.4.2 XML Data Manipulation

XQuery is the current W3C standard query language for XML data. It uses the abstract logical structure of a document as it is encoded in XML, possibly in a DTD or an XML Schema definition.

FIGURE 13.9

**Instance Document
for CustomerList Schema
of Figure 13.5**

```
<CustomerList xmlns:xsi="http://www.w3.org/2001/XMLSchema-instance"
        xsi:noNamespaceSchemaLocation="C:\XML\XMLExample1">
 <Customer>
  <Name>WorldWide Travel Agency</Name>
  <Address>
     <Street> 10 Main Street </Street>
     <City> New York </City>
     <State> NY </State>
     <Zip> 10001 </Zip>
  </Address>
  <Telephone>
     <AreaCode> 212 </AreaCode>
     <Phone> 123 4567 </Phone>
  </Telephone>
  <Type>Corporate</Type>
  <Status>Active</Status>
 </Customer>
 <Customer>
  <Name>Mary Jones</Name>
  <Address>
     <Street> 25 Spruce Street </Street>
     <City> San Diego </City>
     <State> CA </State>
     <Zip> 92101 </Zip>
  </Address>
  <Telephone>
     <AreaCode> 619 </AreaCode>
     <Phone> 555 6789 </Phone>
  </Telephone>
  <Type>Individual</Type>
  <Status>Active</Status>
 </Customer>
```

```
<Customer>
   <Name>Alice Adams</Name>
   <Address>
      <Street> 25 Orange Blossom Street </Street>
      <City> Miami </City>
      <State> FL </State>
      <Zip> 60601 </Zip>
   </Address>
   <Telephone>
      <AreaCode> 305 </AreaCode>
      <Phone> 987 6543 </Phone>
   </Telephone>
   <Type>Individual</Type>
   <Status>Inactive</Status>
  </Customer>
</CustomerList>
```

FIGURE 13.9
Continued

13.4.2.1 XPath Expressions

Queries make use of the notion of a **path expression**, which comes from an earlier language, **XPath**. A path expression usually consists of the name of the document and a specification of the elements to be retrieved, using a path relationship. An example is:

```
Document(''CustomerList.xml'')//Customer/Name
```

The expression specifies the name of the document that is to be searched and one or more steps specified by / or //. The separator // means the next element can be nested anywhere within the preceding one (i.e., any descendant of the preceding node), while the separator / means the next element named must be nested immediately under the preceding one (i.e., in the graph it must be a child node of the preceding one). The steps in the path expression cause reading to advance through the document. The nodes of the graph for a structured XML document are ordered using pre-order traversal, which is a depth-first, left-to-right order. For an XML document, the entire document is the root node, which is followed by element nodes, other node types that we have not discussed here, and attribute nodes. Each element precedes its children, and all children of an element node precede the node's siblings. The nodes of the entire document are seen to be totally ordered by the language processor. In Figure 13.10, the numbers in the nodes show the order in which each node is encountered using normal (forward) traversal. Each node is given an object identifier based on this order. In the instance document in Figure 13.9 the nodes are listed in the same order. The path expression is normally evaluated by reading forward in the document until a node of the specified type is encountered. For the path expression in this example, the first customer node is found and the name of that customer, WorldWide Travel Agency, is targeted. We can add conditions to any nodes in a path expression. For example, if we write,

```
doc(''CustomerList.xml'')//Customer/Address[State=''CA'']
```

the first node that satisfies this condition is the Address node of the second customer. The condition forces the reading to advance through the nodes of the document until it finds one that satisfies the condition. XQuery allows both forward and backward directions for reading. The user can specify an axis or direction for searching. A forward axis allows a search for a child,

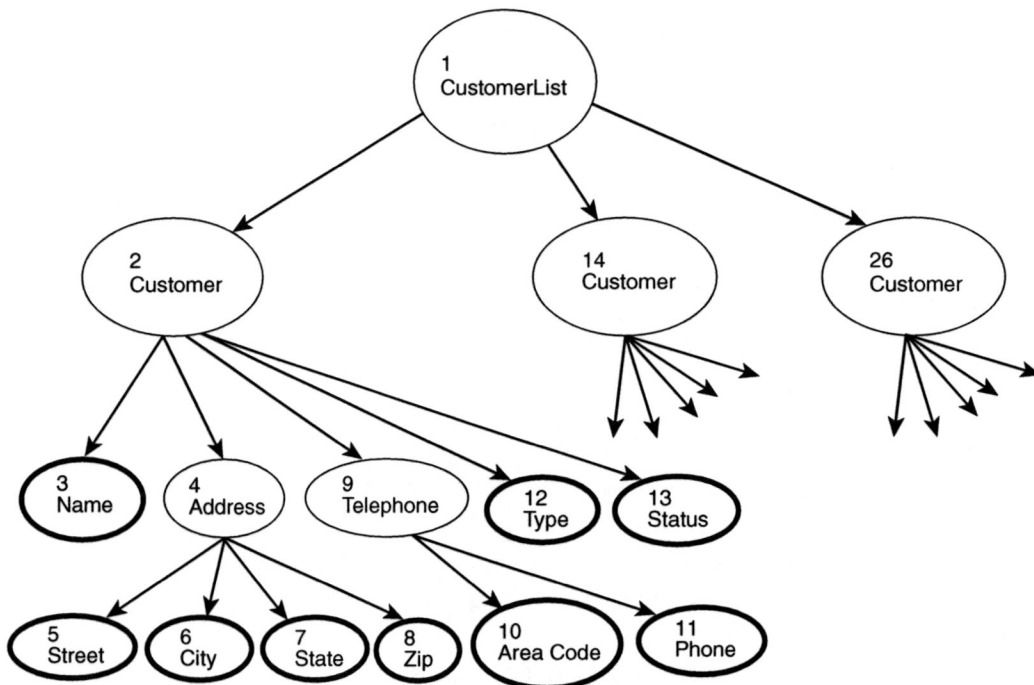

FIGURE 13.10

Pre-order Traversal of Graph

descendant, self, attribute, following sibling, and so on. A reverse axis allows a search for a parent, ancestor, self, preceding sibling, and so on.

13.4.2.2 XQuery Expressions

A simple query using a path expression usually returns a set of nodes that qualify for the expression. For example, for the query,

```
FOR
    $N IN doc(''CustomerList.xml'')//Customer/Name
RETURN <Result> $N </Result>
```

the variable $N is bound to each `Name` node in turn. Query evaluation begins by reading the root node, then advancing to the first `Customer` node, then to the `Name` node that is a child of the customer. This node becomes the **context node**, also called the current node, which is bound to the variable. From this position, reading advances to the next node that satisfies, i.e., the next `Name` node, which becomes the new context node, and so on. The query constructs a list of names and the RETURN clause generates an XML document containing the list of values to which $N is bound in turn. The `Result` tag is applied to each of the `Name` nodes found by the query. The result of this query is this XML document:

```
<Result><Name> WorldWide Travel Agency </Name></Result>
<Result><Name> Mary Jones </Name></Result>
<Result><Name> Alice Adams </Name></Result>
```

13.4.2.3 FLWOR Expressions

XQuery uses a general form called a FLWOR expression. FLWOR, pronounced "flower" stands for FOR, LET, WHERE, ORDER BY, and RETURN, which are the clauses found in such expressions. Not all of these clauses are required. The expressions allow for binding of variables to results, and also for iterating through the nodes of a document. They also allow joins to be performed, and data to be restructured. An example is,

```
FOR $C IN
    doc(''CustomerList.xml'')//Customer)
WHERE $C/Type=''Individual''
ORDER BY Name
RETURN <Result> $C/Name, $C/Status </Result>
```

which produces the following XML document:

```
<Result><Name>Alice Adams</Name><Status>Inactive</Status></Result>
<Result><Name>Mary Jones</Name><Status>Active</Status></Result>
```

The results are ordered by Name, as specified in the query. If no order is specified, results appear in the order in which they are encountered in the document.

XQuery also allows nodes to be constructed, and joins to be performed. For example, let the schema shown in Figure 13.11 describe a second XML document that represents orders placed by customers. An instance document is shown in Figure 13.12. We can use XQuery to form a join of the CustomerList document with the OrdersList document. For exam-

FIGURE 13.11

XML Schema for OrdersList

```
<xsd:schema xmlns:xsd="http://www.w3.org/2001/XMLSchema">
 <xsd:element name ="OrdersList">
  <xsd:sequence>
   <xsd:element name="Order" minoccurs="0" maxoccurs="unbounded">
    <xsd:complexType>
     <xsd:sequence>
      <xsd:element name="OrderNumber" type="xsd:integer"/>
      <xsd:element name="Customer" type="xsd:string" minoccurs="1"/>
      <xsd:element name="OrderDate" type="xsd:date" minoccurs="1"/>
      <xsd:element name="Item" minoccurs="1" maxoccurs="unbounded">
      <xsd:complexType>
        <xsd:sequence>
         <xsd:element name="ItemName" type="xsd:string"/>
         <xsd:element name="Price" type="xsd:decimal"/>
         <xsd:element name="Quantity" type="xsd:integer"/>
        </xsd:sequence>
       </xsd:complexType>
      </xsd:element>
     </xsd:sequence>
    </xsd:complexType>
   </xsd:element>
  </xsd:sequence>
 </xsd:element>
</xsd:schema>
```

```
<OrdersList xmlns:xsi="http://www.w3.org/2001/XMLSchema-instance"
        xsi:noNamespaceSchemaLocation="C:\XML\XMLExample2">
  <Order>
    <OrderNumber>1001</OrderNumber>
    <Customer>Mary Jones</Customer>
    <OrderDate>08-Feb-2004</OrderDate>
    <Item>
       <ItemName>pen</ItemName>
       <Price>15.99</Price>
       <Quantity>1</Quantity>
    </Item>
    <Item>
       <ItemName>desk lamp</ItemName>
       <Price>34.98</Price>
       <Quantity>1</Quantity>
    </Item>
  </Order>
<Order>
    <OrderNumber>1002</OrderNumber>
    <Customer>WorldWide Travel Agency</Customer>
    <OrderDate>8-Feb-2004</OrderDate>
    <Item>
       <ItemName>folder</ItemName>
       <Price>1.59</Price>
       <Quantity>12</Quantity>
    </Item>
    <Item>
       <ItemName>printer</ItemName>
       <Price>336.49</Price>
       <Quantity>1</Quantity>
    </Item>
    <Item>
       <ItemName>telephone</ItemName>
       <Price>95.00</Price>
       <Quantity>1</Quantity>
    </Item>
</Order>
```

FIGURE 13.12

Instance Document OrdersList

FIGURE 13.12

Continued

```
<Order>
   <OrderNumber>1003</OrderNumber>
   <Customer>Mary Jones</Customer>
   <OrderDate>10-Feb-2004</OrderDate>
   <Item>
      <ItemName>filing cabinet</ItemName>
      <Price>45.00</Price>
      <Quantity>1</Quantity>
   </Item>
</Order>
</OrdersList>
```

ple, the query "Find the name and address of the customer for each order" requires a join of these documents. The query can be expressed as,

```
<Result>
{ FOR $0 IN doc(''OrdersList.xml'')/Order,
    $C IN doc(''CustomerList.xml'')/Customer[Name=$0/Customer]
ORDER BY Customer
RETURN
   <OrderCust>
       {$0/OrderNumber, $0/Customer, $C/Address}
   </OrderCust>
</Result>
```

This expression constructs an XML document consisting of OrderCust elements, each of which has an order number, customer name, and customer address, arranged in order by the customer name. The condition [Name=$0/Customer] specifies that the Name node of the Customer element in the CustomerList document matches the Customer element in the Orders document, which is a join condition.

XQuery provides many predefined functions, including count, avg, max, min, and sum, which can be used in FLOWR expressions. For example, the following example lists customers who have more two or more orders:

```
<RepeatList>
FOR $C IN DISTINCT(doc(''CustomerList.xml''))
LET $0 := doc(''OrderList.xml'')/Customer[Customer=$C.Name]
WHERE count($0)>1
RETURN
```

```
<RepeatCustomer>
{$C/Name,$C/Address}
</RepeatCustomer>
<RepeatList>
```

For the data shown in the instance documents in Figures 13.9 and 13.12, the `RepeatList` xml document will be:

```
<RepeatCustomer>
<Name>Mary Jones</Name>
<Address>
<Street>25 Spruce Street</Street>
<City>San Diego</City>
<State>CA</State>
<Zip>92101</Zip>
</Address>
</RepeatCustomer>
```

XQuery is a very powerful language with many additional features that are beyond the scope of this book. Complete details of the current specifications for the language can be found at the W3C Web site.

13.5 XML and Relational Databases

It is sometimes desirable to store XML data in a relational database in a manner that allows retrieval and update of the data. The basic issue is how to map the hierarchical structure of XML documents into a relational model. A simple but not very flexible solution is to let the entire document be represented as a single attribute. A more satisfactory solution is to "shred" the document into parts that are represented as attributes. However, this requires an intelligent mapping algorithm. The XML Schema can be used to facilitate this mapping. We might also wish to be able to transform relational data into XML form and to publish it in that form.

13.5.1 Representing XML Data in a Relational Database

Many vendors of relational database management systems have extended their native data types to allow storage of XML documents. For example, Oracle provides the data type XMLType. One method of handling XML documents is to create a table in which each document is a single tuple. For example, the statement,

```
CREATE TABLE xml_Customer of XMLTYPE;
```

creates a table with a single column that can contain documents. The column is actually a pseudocolumn, XMLDATA, for which the underlying type is CLOB. The usual CLOB operations can be used to store and retrieve the column. An INSERT statement can be used to populate the table, as follows:

```
INSERT INTO xml_Customer VALUES
(xmltype('<?xml version=''1.0''?>
<Customer><Name>WorldWide Travel Agency</Name><Address><Street>
10 Main Street </Street><City> New York </City><State> NY </State><Zip> 10001
</Zip></Address><Telephone><AreaCode> 212 </AreaCode><Phone> 123 4567
</Phone></Telephone><Type>Corporate</Type><Status>Active</Status>
</Customer>
<Customer><Name>Mary Jones</Name><Address><Street> 25 Spruce Street
</Street><City> San Diego </City><State> CA </State><Zip> 92101 </Zip>
</Address><Telephone><AreaCode> 619 </AreaCode><Phone> 555 6789</Phone>
</Telephone><Type>Individual</Type><Status>Active</Status>
</Customer> <Customer><Name>Alice Adams</Name><Address><Street>
25 Orange Blossom Street </Street><City> Miami </City><State>
FL </State><Zip> 60601 </Zip></Address><Telephone><AreaCode>
305 </AreaCode><Phone> 987 6543 </Phone></Telephone><Type>
Individual</Type><Status>Inactive</Status></Customer>'));
```

This insertion process can obviously take data directly from an XML instance document, even without an XML Schema. You can query the table using SQL Select statements, such as:

```
SELECT c.getClobVal() FROM xml_Customer c;
```

Although treating a document as a single attribute is simple and is possible without an XML Schema, it is limited because of the limitations on CLOB operators. If we wish to access individual elements of the documents, we have to resort to XPath or XQuery operators.

An alternative is to use an XML Schema and to create a table in which the XML elements are mapped to objects in an object-relational database. For example, if we have a schema such as the one shown in Figure 13.5, we can create a table in which each Customer element is a tuple, by writing:

```
CREATE SCHEMA xml_Orders OF XMLTYPE
XMLSCHEMA ''schema location''
ELEMENT ''Order'';
```

The columns of the table correspond to the elements of Order in the XML document. We can insert records as before, but now we can also refer to the individual elements by using the XMLDATA pseudocolumn. For example, we can impose a uniqueness constraint on `OrderNumber` by writing:

```
ALTER TABLE xml_Orders ADD (UNIQUE(XMLDATA.''OrderNumber''));
```

It is possible to use SQL with XPath expressions to retrieve values from the database. The EXTRACTVALUE function is used with an XMLType instance and uses an XPath expression to return a scalar value of type VARCHAR2. For example, the SQL query,

```
SELECT EXTRACTVALUE('/Customer/Name') AS ''Customer Name''
FROM xml_Customers;
```

produces a table having customer names.

Customer Name
WorldWide Travel Agency
Mary Jones
Alice Adams

Since we created the `xml_Customer` table with a single CLOB column, without using an XML Schema, we are limited to a VARCHAR2 return. However, if the database was created from a document using its XML schema, as we did for `xml_Orders`, additional scalar types can be returned, based on the types of the instance nodes. For the SQL query,

```
SELECT EXTRACTVALUE('/Order/Customer') AS ''Customer Name'',
EXTRACTVALUE('Order/OrderDate') as ''Date'',
FROM xml_Orders;
```

the resulting table has a VARCHAR2 column for `Customer Name`, and a DATE column for the order date based on the types of the underlying XML data.

The EXTRACT function works in a similar fashion, except that it returns an XML type. For example,

```
SELECT EXTRACT ('/Customer/Name') AS ''Customer Name''
FROM xml_Customers;
```

produces a table with XML data.

Customer Name
<Name>WorldWide Travel Agency</Name>
<Name>Mary Jones</Name>
<Name>Alice Adams</Name>

13.5.2   Publishing Relational Database Data in XML Format

Existing heterogeneous databases can be queried using standard languages such as SQL, and the query results can be placed into an XML instance document. The query language has to have facilities that can tag and structure relational data into XML format. The existing relational database schema can be used to determine the XML elements and/or attributes. For example, using Microsoft SQL Server, if we wish to extract data from the Student table of the University relational database, we can write this SQL statement:

```
SELECT *
FROM Student
    FOR XML RAW;
```

The resulting XML document appears as shown in Figure 13.13.

The FOR XML RAW clause causes each column of the relational table to become an attribute of the XML document. (Note: XML attributes differ from XML elements and can have only single values.) If we wish to map to elements instead of attributes, we can write,

```
SELECT *
FROM Student
FOR XML AUTO, ELEMENTS;
```

which produces a document like the one shown in Figure 13.14. It is also possible to map some columns to elements and others to attributes, using FOR XML EXPLICIT.

```
<Student stuId="S1001"lastName="Smith     "firstname="Tom      "major="History"credits=90/>
<Student stuId="S1002"lastName="Chin      "firstname="Ann      "major="Math   "credits=36/>
<Student stuId="S1005"lastName="Lee       "firstname="Perry    "major="History"credits=3/>
<Student stuId="S1010"lastName="Burns     "firstname="Edward"major="Art        "credits=63/>
<Student stuId="S1013"lastName="McCarthy"firstname="Owen   "major="Math   "credits=0/>
<Student stuId="S1015"lastName="Jones     "firstname="Mary     "major="Math   "credits=42/>
<Student stuId="S1020"lastName="Rivera    "firstname="Jane     "major="CSC    "credits=15/>
```

FIGURE 13.13
Result of SQL Query SELECT * FROM Student FOR XML RAW;

```
<Student><stuId>S1001</stuId><lastName>Smith</lastName><firstName>Tom</firstName>
<major>History</major><credits>90</credits></Student>
<Student><stuId>S1002</stuId><lastName>Chin</lastName><firstName>Ann</firstName>
<major>Math</major><credits>36</credits></Student>
<Student><stuId>S1005/stuId><lastName>Lee</lastName><firstName>Perry</firstName>
<major>History</major><credits>3</credits></Student>
<Student><stuId>S1010</stuId><lastName>Burns</lastName><firstName>Edward</firstName>
<major>Art</major><credits>63</credits></Student>
<Student><stuId>S1013</stuId><lastName>McCarthy</lastName><firstName>Owen</firstName>
<major>Math</major><credits>0</credits></Student>
<Student><stuId>S1015</stuId><lastName>Jones</lastName><firstName>Mary</firstName>
<major>Math</major><credits>42</credits></Student>
<Student><stuId>S1020</stuId><lastName>Rivera</lastName><firstName>Jane</firstName>
<major>CSC</major><credits>15</credits></Student>
```

FIGURE 13.14
Result of SQL Query SELECT * FROM Student FOR XML AUTO, ELEMENTS;

13.6   Chapter Summary

The World Wide Web can be viewed as a loosely organized information
resource. Many Web sites have static linked HTML files, which can easily
become inconsistent and outdated. Some organizations allow dynamic access
to their databases directly from the Web. The emergence of e-commerce has
pushed organizations to develop Web-based database applications
to create worldwide markets, to deliver information, to provide better

customer service, to communicate with their suppliers, to provide training for employees, to expand the workplace, and many other innovative activities. XML is a promising standard for document storage, exchange, and retrieval that integrates competing technologies.

The Internet developed from **Arpanet,** a communications network created in the 1960s using funds from a US agency, DARPA, for the purpose of linking government and academic research institutions. It used a common protocol, **TCP/IP,** to facilitate communications between sites. The US National Science Foundation took over the management of the network, which was then referred to as the **Internet.** Navigating and using the Internet required considerable sophistication on the part of the user. In 1989 Tim Berners-Lee proposed a method of simplifying access to Internet resources that led to the development of the **World Wide Web.** His proposal included the notions of **URL, HTTP, HTML, hypertext,** and **graphical browsers** with embedded **links.** Berners-Lee's proposal made it possible to automate the complicated process of finding, downloading, and displaying files on the Internet.

HTTP is a **stateless** protocol with no facility for remembering previous interactions. This creates a problem for e-commerce, which requires a continuous session with the user.

HTML is a data format used for presenting content on the Internet. It is called a **markup** language because HTML documents contain marks or tags that provide formatting information for the text. An HTML document can contain Java applets, audio files, images, video files, and content. When the document in retrieved by the user's browser, the text is displayed according to the formatting commands, the applets are executed, the audio files play, the video is displayed, and so on, at the user's workstation. **XML** or Extensible Markup Language was created in 1996 by the World Wide Web Consortium (W3) XML Special Interest Group. XML allows users to define their own markup language, including their own tags that describe the data items in documents, including databases. Using XML, it is possible to define the structure of heterogeneous databases and support translation of data between different databases.

An **element** is the basic component of an XML document. A document contains one or more XML elements, each of which has a **start tag** showing the name of the element, some **character data,** and an **end tag.** Elements can be **sub-elements** of other elements. Sub-elements must be properly nested. Elements can have **attributes** whose names and values are shown inside the element's start tag. Attributes occur only once within each element, while sub-elements can occur any number of times. A document can contain **entity references** to refer to external files, common text, Unicode characters, or some reserved symbols. An XML document is said to be **well formed** if it obeys the rules of XML. Users can define their own markup language by writing a **Document Type Declaration** (DTD) or by writing an **XML Schema.** A DTD is a specification for a set of rules for the elements, attributes, and entities of a document. An instance document that obeys the rules of its associated DTD is said to be **type-valid.** Domain-specific DTDs have been developed for a number of fields, and more are likely to be developed in the future. **XML Schema** is a new, more powerful way to describe the structure of documents than DTDs. It permits more complex structure, additional fundamental data types, user-defined data types, user-created domain vocabulary (namespaces), and it also supports uniqueness and foreign key constraints. An XML schema defines the organization and data types of an XML structure. If an instance document conforms to an XML schema, it is called **schema-valid.** An XML schema lists elements and attributes. Elements may be complex, which means they have sub-elements, or simple. Attributes or elements can be used to store data values. Attributes can be used for simple values that are not repeated while elements can be complex or simple, and can occur multiple times.

Three major functions required in an Internet environment are presentation, application logic, and data management. The placement of these functions depends on the architecture of the system. **Three-tier architectures** completely separate application logic from data management. The client handles the user interface, which is called the **presentation layer** or the first tier. A separate **application server** executes the application logic and forms the **middle tier.** The **database server** forms the third tier. The communications network connects each tier to the next one. The three-tier architecture allows support for **thin clients** that need only handle the presentation layer, independence of tiers that can use different platforms, easier application maintenance on the application server, integrated transparent data access to heterogeneous data sources, and scalability.

HTML forms are often used at the presentation layer. Code in Perl, JavaScript, JScript, VBScript, and similar scripting languages can be embedded in the HTML to provide some client-side processing. **Style sheets** specify how data is presented on specific devices. The application server at the middle tier is responsible for executing applications. It determines the flow of control, acquires input data from the presentation layer, makes data requests to the database server, accepts query results from the database layer, and uses them to assemble dynamically generated HTML pages. Server-side processing can involve many different technologies such as Java Servlets, Java Server pages, and others. **CGI,** Common Gateway Interface, can be used to connect HTML forms with application programs. To maintain state during a session, servers may use cookies, hidden fields in HTML forms, and URI extensions. Cookies are easily generated at the middle tier using Java's Cookie class and sent to the client, where they can be stored in the browser cache.

XML allows documents to be marked up with meta-data, and can include tags that give some structure to documents. The **semi-structured data model** is a method of describing such partial structure. A semi-structured model contains a collection of nodes, each containing data, possibly with different schemas. The model uses a graph consisting of nodes and edges. Each document can be represented as a **tree,** having a single **root** node and a sequence of **child** nodes. Each child node can itself have child nodes, which in turn can have child nodes, and so on. A strict rule for trees is that every node, except the root, has exactly one **parent** node, which is at the level above it in the tree. The nodes can represent either **complex objects** or **atomic values.** An **edge** can represent either the relationship between an object and its sub-object, or the relationship between an object and its value. **Leaf** nodes, which have no sub-objects, represent values. The nodes of the graph for a structured XML document are ordered using **pre-order traversal,** which is a depth-first, left-to-right order. There is no separate schema, since the graph is self-describing.

XQuery is the current W3C standard query language for XML data. It uses the abstract logical structure of a document as it is encoded in XML, possibly in a DTD or an XML Schema definition. Queries make use of the notion of a **path expression**, which comes from an earlier language, **XPath.** A path expression usually consists of the name of the document and a specification of the elements to be retrieved, using a path relationship. We can add conditions to any nodes in a path expression. The path expression is normally evaluated by reading forward in the document until a node of the specified type and condition is encountered. The user can specify an axis or direction for searching. XQuery uses a general form called a **FLWOR** expression, for FOR, LET, WHERE, ORDER BY, and RETURN clauses. The expressions allow for binding of variables to results, and also for iterating through the nodes of a document. They also allow joins to be performed, and data to be restructured. XQuery provides many predefined functions, including count, avg, max, min, and sum, which can be used in FLOWR expressions.

Many vendors of relational database management systems have extended their native data types to allow storage of XML documents. It is also possible to use SQL with XPath expressions to retrieve values from the database. Existing heterogeneous databases can be queried using standard languages such as SQL, and the query results can be placed into an XML instance document. The query language has to have facilities that can tag and structure relational data into XML format.

Exercises

13.1 Define the following terms.

a. e-commerce

b. World Wide Web

c. DARPA

d. hypertext

e. Arpanet

f. TCP/IP

g. HTML

h. HTTP

i. URI

j. browser

k. stateless protocol

l. SGML

m. XML

n. markup language

o. entity reference

p. well-formed document

q. type-valid document

r. schema-valid document

s. W3C

t. thin client

u. presentation layer

        v. style sheet

        w. cookie

        x. semi-structured model

        y. XQuery

        z. XPath

13.2   Explain what is meant by the convergence of database processing and document processing.

13.3   If a Web site uses static linked HTML files for displaying data, what problems can arise?

13.4   What are HTML forms used for in e-commerce?

13.5   How is state maintained during a long e-commerce transaction?

13.6   How are HTML, SGML, and XML related?

13.7   What is the purpose of style sheets?

13.8   What makes an XML document well-formed?

13.9   When is an XML document type-valid?

13.10   What makes an XML document schema-valid?

13.11   How can you determine whether an XML schema document is schema-valid?

13.12   Explain the difference between an element and an attribute in an XML document.

13.13   Create an HTML document similar to the one shown in Figure 13.1 for a list of products, and test it using a browser.

13.14   For the list of products in Exercise 13.16, create a well-formed XML document, similar to the one shown in Figure 13.2.

13.15   Write a DTD for the list of products in Exercise 13.16, making sure the instance document is type-valid for the DTD.

13.16   Write an XML schema for the same list of products.

13.17   Write a new instance document listing products, making sure the new list is schema-valid.

13.18   Draw a hierarchical diagram for the data in Figure 13.12.

13.19   Using XQuery, write two queries for the data in Figure 13.12.

Lab Exercises

Lab Exercise 13.1: Browsing an E-Commerce Website That Uses a Database

Browse the website of a large bookstore. Observe the features of the homepage and the linked pages, making note of forms as you go along. Search for books on a subject of interest to you. Choose a book that you might want to order and place it in your shopping basket. Go back to browse other books. Choose another to add to the shopping basket, and observe how the basket is updated. Begin the ordering process, being careful not to finalize the order. Observe the number of interactions required for the order process. Cancel the order before completing it.

Lab Exercise 13.2: Creating Web Pages Using Access

This lab will provide practice in creating web pages and a home page for the University database using Access. (Note: If you have not already done so, crop the University database from the website for this book, or create it in Access.)

1. To create a web page for the `Class` table in Access, follow these steps:

   a. Open the University database and choose the *Pages* object in the left panel, then *Create data access page by using wizard.*

   b. Choose the `Class` table, and select all its fields, then *Next.*

   c. Do not use grouping levels (If a field for grouping shows, double click on its name header to get rid of the grouping.), then *Next.*

   d. Do not choose sorting; just click *Next.*

   e. Type in a name for your page—`Class`.

   f. Choose *Modify the page's design,* and choose to apply a theme. Click *Finish.*

   g. Look at the themes and choose one such as *Blends.*

   h. A form appears, and you should enter a title, `Class Form`, at the top. You should see each field and its label in the body of the form.

   i. Examine each text box to make sure it is associated with the correct data source. Select the text box (**not** the label), right click, choose *Element Properties,* click the *Data* tab, click on *Control Source,* and make sure the correct attribute name is chosen from the drop-down list. This connects the page to the correct attribute in the correct table. Close the pop-up window.

j. If your web page is to be used for input, you want to use drop-down lists for any fields that have a known list of possible values, to prevent users from making data entry errors. For the `Class` table this includes `facId`.

   i. Click on the text box for `facId`, and press the *Delete* key to remove it from the form. If the toolbox is not already displayed, choose *View, Toolbox* from the menu.

   ii. Single-click on the *Dropdown List* tool from the Toolbox and scroll it out on the form where you deleted the field. This places the box and a default label on the form and starts a new wizard.

   iii. Choose *I want the combo box to look up the values from a table or query.* Click *Next.* Choose the `Faculty` table, *Next,* then select the `facid` field, then *Next.* You will see the `facId` values from the `Faculty` table. Click *Next.* For the label, which users will see later, enter `Faculty ID`. Click *Finish.*

   iv. Now you have to associate this box with the correct data source in the `Class` table, so each record will have the correct `facId`. Select the drop-down box, right click, choose *Element Properties,* click the *Data* tab, highlight *Control Source,* and make sure the `facId` attribute name is chosen from the drop-down list. Close the pop-up window.

k. Save the page—click on the web page icon in the upper left corner, *Close,* and enter the name `Class`. Leave the absolute reference when prompted, and choose *OK.*

l. When the page is saved, choose *Pages* and look at the `Class` page. Notice that the controls allow you to browse through the records, add new records, modify records, or delete records on the page. Add a new class record, making up a class number, choosing a `facId` from the drop-down list, and making up a schedule, and a room. Save the `Class` page and close it. Open the `Class` table and see that the new record is inserted.

m. Test the `Class` page using a browser. Open Explorer, choose *File, Open, Browse,* find the `Class` page in the directory where you saved it, and click *OK* to open it. Browse through the records. Add another new class through the browser and save it. Go back to Access, look at the table, and see that the new record is there.

2. Create a `Student` web page, following steps a–i, this time using the `Student` table. To make the `major` field a drop-down list by entering your own values:

    i. Click on the `major` text box and press the *Delete* key. From the toolbox, choose a drop-down box and scroll it out.

    ii. Single-click on the dropdown list box from the Toolbox and scroll it out on the form where you deleted the field.

    iii. Choose *I will type in the values that I want,* then *Next.* Type in the valid values for major-`History`, `Math`, `Art`, `CSC`. Click *Next.* For the label (which users will see later) enter `major`. Click *Finish.*

    iv. Now you have to associate this box with the correct data source in the `Student` table. Select the drop-down box, right click, choose *Element Properties,* click the *Data* tab, click on *Control Source,* and make sure the `major` attribute name is chosen from the drop-down list.

    v. Save the page—click on the web page icon, *Close, Save Changes,* and enter the name `Student`, keeping the absolute reference.

3. Create the `Faculty` web page in the same way, creating a drop-down list for department in which you enter values as you did for the `Student` `major` attribute. Be sure to connect the combo box with the data source department in the `Faculty` table before you save the page.

4. Create the `Enroll` web page, this time having the combo box pick up values for `stuId` from the `Student` table and values for `classNumber` from the `Class` table. Connect each combo box with the corresponding attribute in the `Enroll` table before you save it. (Select the drop-down box, right click, choose *Element Properties,* click the *Data* tab, click on *Control Source,* and choose the correct attribute name.)

5. Create a home page to link to the pages you created. You will find a sample home page for these files in the Notepad file called `Home.txt` on the website for this book. Copy and save the file as `Home.htm`, to create your own home page in the same directory as your Access pages. If you used different names for your pages, modify the file to refer to those names.

6. To test the system, open Explorer, choose *File, Open, Browse,* find the Home page in the directory where you saved it, and open it. Click on each button to test the connections. Browse through the records and add new records to each table to test the forms.

SAMPLE PROJECT: CREATING A WEBSITE FOR THE ART GALLERY USING ACCESS

- Step 13.1. For each of the tables designed for the relational model, we created an Access table by executing the SQL DDL statements. We entered the data using the SQL INSERT commands. We created a web page for each table, using drop-down lists where appropriate, following the step illustrated in Laboratory Exercise 2. We designed a simple homepage that links to each of these pages. The website for this book contains the files for this project.

STUDENT PROJECTS: CREATING A WEBSITE FOR THE STUDENT PROJECTS

- Step 13.1. If you have not already done so, create an Access database for your project, by executing the SQL DDL commands to create the tables, or by using the Access user interface to create tables in design view, as demonstrated in Laboratory Exercise 1.2 in Chapter 1. Insert records using either the SQL Insert commands or the spreadsheet form in Access. Create a web page for each of the tables you have created, as demonstrated in Laboratory Exercise 13.2. Create a homepage to link to each of these pages by modifying the Notepad file Home.txt provided on the website for this book. Test out your design by displaying and updating the pages in a browser.

CHAPTER 14

Social and Ethical Issues

Chapter Objectives

In this chapter you will learn the following:

- The meaning of intellectual property

- What forms of protection exist for intellectual property

- The meaning of copyright and how it works

- The history of copyright laws

- How US and international copyright laws differ

- How patents are issued

- How patents are used internationally

- What constitutes a trade secret

- How trade secrets are protected

- What constitutes a trademark or service mark

14.1   Computerization and Ethical Issues

The effect of computerization on society is often described as a revolution that surpasses the industrial revolution. Like other emerging technologies, computerization has created new situations and possibilities that challenge society's moral codes. It takes time and reflection for society to develop values, moral principles, and codes to deal with the issues created by any new technology. Since computer technology advances so quickly, products come into the market before society has had a chance to consider the moral issues they raise and to formulate the values and moral principles to guide their use. Given the vacuum created by this lag, individuals formulate their own rules for behavior, often without adequate consideration of the implications of their actions. Computer technology provides new temptations because of seven factors, according to Richard Rubin ("Moral Distancing and the Use of Information Technology: The Seven Temptations." In Kizza, J. M. *Ethical and Social Issues in the Information Age 2nd ed.* New York: Springer 2003, pp 58–59). The seven factors are:

1. **Speed.** Since actions can be carried out so quickly, people think their chances of being caught are slim, and they can get away with unethical actions.

2. **Privacy and anonymity.** Having computers in less publicly visible places such as homes, and software that guarantees anonymity, creates a tempting environment for unethical actions.

3. **Nature of medium.** Being able to copy data without affecting the original arouses little or no suspicion and encourages unethical actions.

4. **Aesthetic attraction.** New technology offers challenges that provide a sense of achievement to the person who overcomes them. The feelings of success and accomplishment are incentives to those who intrude into a computer system.

5. **Increased availability of potential victims.** Computer networks make it possible for a perpetrator to reach an unprecedented number of people.

6. **International scope.** The Internet makes it possible for people to try to circumvent the laws of their own country by committing illegal acts in another country.

7. **The power to destroy.** Computers appear to give enormous invisible power to users, which can be a temptation to people to see how much damage they can do.

The rule of law that is recognized in well-ordered societies is challenged by the Internet. Since it is a global entity, no single country can apply its laws to the entire Internet. In cyberspace, individuality is highly prized, and the Internet community is very resistant to attempts by governments to control it. Society must come to some agreement about the balance of control between states and individuals. The Internet provides a forum for all people to express themselves freely to a vast audience, exercising their fundamental human right to freedom of speech. Without some controls on content, however, abuses such as pornography and hate rhetoric can become rampant. Another area of disagreement is how intellectual property laws and protections such as copyrights, patents, trade secrets, and trademarks can be adapted to the changing environment of the digital age. On one hand there are those who believe that every use of copyrighted works, including transmission of them to personal computers for personal use and storage of them in temporary Internet files, is subject to copyright restrictions. On the other hand there are those who believe that all information should be free and that intellectual property laws do not apply to cyberspace. The issue of linking to other Web sites can also be controversial. For example, if a link brings a browser to a Web page with copyrighted material, does it violate the copyright? If a link bypasses the home page of another site to bring the user to an internal page, thereby avoiding the advertisements that may appear on the home page, does that violate the rights of the site owner, since it diminishes the value of the advertising space?

The issue of intellectual property protection for software is also hotly debated. Commercial software is usually protected by copyright and other means. The justification for such protection is based on notions of justice and the desire to foster enterprise. On the other side, there is a strong "free software" movement that supports the notion that all software should be free and freely copied. The Free Software Foundation and the Open

Source movements challenge the protection of software on philosophical and practical grounds. Richard Stallman, president of the Free Software Foundation, has written and spoken extensively about the reasons why software should not be compared to property, and why ownership of programs is unethical. Eric Raymond's book (*The Cathedral and the Bazaar.* Sebastopol, CA: O'Reilly & Associates 2001) provides an analogy used by open source advocates. He explains that when the source code for software is made available, the independent programmers and hackers who work on it can develop better software than a select group of highly paid programmers at a software company. The "cathedral" represents a software company such as Microsoft that employs the professional team, while the "bazaar" represents the loosely affiliated group of independent programmers. The argument is that the bazaar approach is better because the collective intelligence of the independents can be used to fix bugs and improve the software more rapidly. Privacy is another issue that is controversial. Most countries have laws that protect the privacy of individuals from intrusion by the government and private businesses, on the grounds that privacy is a fundamental human right. Individual privacy is challenged by the widespread use of computer technology to share personal information that is stored in databases.

Opponents of privacy legislation claim that the sharing of customer data among businesses is a form of free speech that should be protected. They compare it with the traditional sharing of information among businesses in communities. This sharing, which existed before computerization, they characterize as gossip. Since database data is more accurate and less personal than gossip, which is unregulated, they claim that restricting sharing of database data by businesses is not justified. The responsibilities that computer professionals have to make their products easier and safer for users, and the best ways to do that are also debated.

14.2   Intellectual Property

The question of who owns intellectual property and what rights the owners have to that property, including software and databases, is complex and controversial. The rights and obligations of creators or owners of intellectual products are the subject of debate in public forums, especially on the Internet. Legislation exists in most countries to protect intellectual property rights, and international agreements have been signed to attempt to guarantee these rights throughout the world.

14.2.1 Definition of Intellectual Property

Property ownership is a fundamental concept in most well-ordered societies. Legal systems devote considerable attention to rights and obligations of property owners. However, a simple definition of property is elusive. The notion of ownership is closely related to the notion of property. Sir William Blackstone described the origins and nature of the rights of property owners in the eighteenth century. He wrote:

> There is nothing which so generally strikes the imagination, and engages the affections of mankind, as the right of property; or that sole and despotic dominion which one man claims and exercises over the external things of the world, in total exclusion of the right of any other individual in the universe (*Commentaries on the Laws of England,* 1765–1769).

Property originally referred to land. Blackstone listed among the rights of an owner of a piece of land as the right to use it as he sees fit, to receive income from it, to transfer ownership, and to exclude others from it. The collection of property rights forms what came to be known as the **Blackstonian bundle.** The notion of property was extended to mean "tangible assets over which someone has or claims control" (McFarland, Michael. "Intellectual Property, Information and the Common Good," in *Proceedings of the Fourth Annual Ethics and Technology Conference,* 1999, pp. 88–95). A person who owns a piece of land, a bank account, a piece of jewelry, or a car can use it, can control who else can use it, and can transfer ownership of it, as long as it does not interfere with the safety or property of other people.

Compared with tangible property, intellectual property is harder to define and the rights associated with it are more difficult to identify. Unlike land, intellectual property is usually intangible. Intellectual property refers to products of the mind—such as literature, music, art, architecture, inventions, formulas for products, and software. A broad definition is, "the legal rights which result from intellectual activity in the industrial, scientific, literary, and artistic fields" (World Intellectual Property Organization, *WIPO Intellectual Property Handbook: Policy, Law and Use,* p. 3).

In the case of tangible property such as a piece of land or a car, use of it is exclusive, since only one person can use it at a time. Intellectual property differs because it is non-exclusive in that many people can use it at the same time, and their simultaneous use of it does not diminish its value. The cost of providing additional access to it is usually low, even though the cost of producing it originally might have been high. The notion of justice is at the foundation of intellectual property rights. Since the creator or inventor of an original work has invested his or her time and resources in its creation, he or she is entitled to reap the rewards. By guaranteeing a return for his or her work, society encourages authors and other creative people to continue to develop new works. In the case of a software writer, a database designer, or a database developer, the individual has spent time, effort, and money in both acquiring the knowledge to be able to do those tasks and in creating the product. The individual is entitled to some return. If the person is an employee who created the work for hire, the employer is entitled to a return.

14.2.2 Legal Protections for Intellectual Property

The rights of owners of intellectual property are protected by a variety of mechanisms, including by copyright, patent, trade secret, trademarks, and service marks.

14.2.2.1 Meaning of Copyright

Copyright is a right given to the creator of a literary or artistic work. The copyright is given by the government of the country of origin for a limited period of time. During that time, the author of the work has sole, exclusive rights to make copies, publish, and sell the work. According to the World Intellectual Property Organization (WIPO), the following kinds of works can be covered by copyright:

> . . . literary works such as novels, plays, poems, reference works, newspapers, and computer programs; databases; films, musical compositions, and choreography; artistic works such as paintings, drawings, photographs and sculpture; architecture; and advertisements, maps, and technical drawings (WIPO, http://www.wipo.org/about-ip/en/).

To be eligible for copyright protection, the work must be original, it must have a tangible form, and it must be fixed in a medium, conditions generally referred to as **originality, expression,** and **fixation.** Anyone who creates a work that could be copyrighted automatically owns the copyright. It is not necessary to publish the work, to use the copyright symbol, ©, on it, or to make a formal application for a copyright. It is automatic. Therefore every Web page, software program, database, term paper, and so on that is original and fixed in a medium (e.g., a paper, a disk, a server) is automatically copyrighted. Copyright protects the owner's right to make copies of the work, to use it as the basis of a new work (called a **derivative** work), to distribute or publish it, to publicly display the work, and to publicly perform the work. Publishing the work includes posting it on the Internet. Distributing the work includes electronic distribution. Publicly displaying the work can include displaying it on a computer screen. Publicly performing the work includes publicly playing a recording of it. The owner has exclusive rights in these areas, with limited exceptions that are in a category called **fair use,** such as in reviews of the work. Anyone who wants to use the copyrighted work must obtain permission from the owner of the copyright, and possibly pay a fee, unless the use is fair use.

Works protected by copyright can always be used freely for personal use, such as reading. Fair use of a copyrighted work also allows limited nonpersonal use of copyrighted materials without the author's permission. This area includes using a small amount of the material for educational purposes, quotation in reviews, parody, or other limited uses. It is often difficult to determine whether the use of a work falls under the category of fair use. There are four factors to be considered when making such a decision. The judgment requires that all four factors lean in the direction of fair use. They are:

1. **The character of the use.** If the use is for review, parody, commentary, reporting, or similar purposes, and it is personal, educational, or nonprofit, it is more likely to be considered fair use. If the use is commercial, it is likely not fair use.

2. **The nature of the work to be used.** If the work is factual and published, the use is more likely to be fair use, while if it is imaginative and unpublished, it is less likely to be fair use.

3. **The amount of the work to be used.** A small amount is likely to be fair use, while a significant portion of the work is not fair use.

4. **The effect it would have on the market for the original work or for permissions, if the kind of use were widespread.** This factor should be considered only after evaluating the first three factors. If the use takes away from sales of the original work, or avoids paying royalties on the original work, it is not fair use. However, if the original is not available for purchase, or if the owner of the copyright cannot be identified, it is more likely to be fair use.

Some intellectual works are not protected by copyright, and can be used freely. The following list includes works that are considered utilitarian or trivial.

- Titles, names, short phrases, and slogans; familiar symbols or designs; mere variations of typographic ornamentation, lettering, or coloring; mere listings of ingredients or contents

- Ideas, procedures, methods, systems, processes, concepts, principles, discoveries, or devices—as distinguished from a description, explanation, or illustration

- Works consisting entirely of information that is common property and containing no original authorship (for example: standard calendars, height and weight charts, tape measures and rulers, and lists or tables taken from public documents or other common sources) (U.S. Copyright Office, *Copyright Basics, Circular 1*)

Facts are always in the public domain, but a specific arrangement and expression of them, such as that found in a database, can be copyrighted. Ideas are also in the public domain, but a particular explanation of them, such as an essay, can be copyrighted. Mathematical and chemical formulas are in the public domain, but product formulas can be copyrighted. Some of the other exceptions, such as symbols, are eligible for protection under trademark laws, and others, such as processes, are eligible for patents or trade secret protection.

Other works in the public domain include works on which the copyright has expired and has not been renewed, those on which the copyright has been lost, and those that the author has intentionally put in the public domain. Works in the public domain can be used freely by anyone, without permission.

14.2.2.2 International Copyright Laws and US Copyright Laws

Copyrights are recognized internationally, but each country makes its own laws concerning them. The United States, England, and France originally had copyright laws dating back to the eighteenth century. Most copyright laws are based on the **Berne Convention** for the protection of Literary and Artistic Works, which first convened in 1886 at the instigation of Victor Hugo. Revisions to the Berne Convention were made in 1896, 1908, 1914, 1928, 1967, 1971, and 1979. The purpose of the convention was to ensure that each country recognized copyrights of works published in other member countries. The convention did not require that the work be registered or that it display the copyright symbol. It set the duration of copyright as the lifetime of the author plus 50 years. Although the Berne Convention set guidelines, each member country made its own laws to adhere to the guidelines. The Berne Convention is administered by the World Intellectual Property Organization (**WIPO**), which was founded in 1967.

Because US copyright laws differed from the guidelines, the United States did not originally sign the Berne Convention. In 1952, UNESCO founded the Universal Copyright Convention (UCC), which was signed in Geneva by countries that did not subscribe to the Berne Convention, including the United States, the Soviet Union, and most Latin American countries. Under the less strict UCC standard, copyright was not automatic, and member countries such as the United States could require that the work be published, have a copyright symbol, and be registered in order to be copyrighted. However, the United States changed its copyright laws in 1978 to a form that adheres to the stricter standard, and it signed the Berne Convention in 1989. Most other UCC member countries have also signed the Berne Convention, making the UCC less important.

The World Trade Organization (WTO) was established at Geneva in 1995 to administer the TRIPPS (Trade Related Aspects of Intellectual Property Rights) agreement that was reached under the Uruguay Round GATT (General Agreement on Tariffs and Trade) Protocol of 1994. It has 146 member countries. The summary of the TRIPPS Agreement states:

> With respect to copyright, parties are required to comply with the substantive provisions of the Berne Convention for the protection of literary and artistic works, in its latest version (Paris 1971), . . . It ensures that computer programs will be protected as literary works under the Berne Convention and lays down on what basis databases should be protected by copyright. Important additions to existing international rules in the area of copyright and related rights are the provisions on rental rights. The draft requires authors of computer programmes and producers of sound recordings to be given the right to authorize or prohibit the commercial rental of their works to the public. (World Trade Organization. *A Summary of the Final Act of the Uruguay Round*).

In Article 10, the agreement specifically deals with computer programs and databases.

1. Computer programs, whether in source or object code, shall be protected as literary works under the Berne Convention (1971).

2. Compilations of data or other material, whether in machine readable or other form, which by reason of the selection or arrangement of their contents constitute intellectual creations shall be protected as such. Such protection, which shall not extend to the data or material itself, shall be without prejudice to any copyright subsisting in the data or material itself (World Trade Organization, *Uruguay Round Agreement: TRIPS Part II—Standards concerning the availability, scope and use of Intellectual Property Rights*, Article 10).

Copyright protection in the United States has its origins in the Constitution. Article 1, Section 8 of the Constitution of the United States gives Congress the power,

> To promote the progress of science and useful arts, by securing for limited times to authors and inventors the exclusive right to their respective writings and discoveries, . . .

The first US copyright law, designed by Congress to protect those rights, was passed in 1790. The law was amended in 1831 and 1870. The Copyright Act was adopted in 1909 and remained in effect, with slight modifications, until 1978. That law required publication of the work and the use of the copyright symbol on it in order to claim copyright protection. In 1976 a new Copyright Act was passed by Congress, and it went into effect in 1978.

The US Copyright Office lists the type of works that can be protected by copyright under the current Act:

> Copyright protects "original works of authorship" that are fixed in a tangible form of expression. The fixation need not be directly perceptible so long as it may be communicated with the aid of a machine or device. Copyrightable works include the following categories:

1. literary works

2. musical works, including any accompanying words

3. dramatic works, including any accompanying music

4.   pantomimes and choreographic works

5.   pictorial, graphic, and sculptural works

6.   motion pictures and other audiovisual works

7.   sound recordings

8.   architectural works

These categories should be viewed broadly. For example, computer programs and most "compilations" may be registered as "literary works"; maps and architectural plans may be registered as "pictorial, graphic, and sculptural works" (US Copyright Office. *Copyright Basics Circular1,* http://www.copyright.gov/circs/circ1.html#wwp).

This law requires originality, fixation, expression, but it does not require publication, use of the copyright symbol, or registration of the work with the Copyright Office. These changes brought the US law into compliance with the Berne Convention, which was signed by the United States in 1989. However, for the purpose of protecting the copyright and determining the dates of protection, the Copyright Office advises authors to register the work, and to affix the claim of copyright, which should include the copyright symbol or word, the author's name, and the date of publication. To complete the registration process, the author must fill out a registration form, pay a fee, and send two copies of the published work to the Copyright Office for deposit in the Library of Congress. Registration allows the author to claim copyright protection in a court of law in the case of infringement. The US Copyright Office offers guidelines for copyright registration.

In general, copyright registration is a legal formality intended to make a public record of the basic facts of a particular copyright. However, registration is not a condition of copyright protection. Even though registration is not a requirement for protection, the copyright law provides several inducements or advantages to encourage copyright owners to make registration. Among these advantages are the following:

* Registration establishes a public record of the copyright claim.

* Before an infringement suit can be filed in court, registration is necessary for works of US origin.

* If made before or within five years of publication, registration will establish *prima facie* evidence in court of the validity of the copyright and of the facts stated in the certificate.

- If registration is made within three months after publication of the work or prior to an infringement of the work, statutory damages and attorney's fees will be available to the copyright owner in court actions. Otherwise, only an award of actual damages and profits is available to the copyright owner.

- Registration allows the owner of the copyright to record the registration with the US Customs Service for protection against the importation of infringing copies (US Copyright Office, *Copyright Basics, Circular 1*).

The published work must be deposited with the Library of Congress. In fact, the law required that any work published in the US be deposited with the Library of Congress within three months of publication, regardless of whether it is registered. The 1976 Copyright Act specified the duration of copyright. For works published before 1978, the copyright was to expire 75 years after the date the copyright was issued. For copyrights received after 1978, the copyright was to remain in effect for the lifetime of author plus 50 years. Works for hire were to be protected for 75 years from date of first publication of the work or 100 years from date of creation of the work. The Act was amended several times. One important change was the Sonny Bono Copyright Term Extension Act, which extended the duration of all copyrights by 20 years, so that for works created before 1978 copyrights are for 95 years, copyrights for post-1978 works are for the lifetime of the author plus 70 years, and works for hire 95 or 120 years. A 1980 amendment was made to cover software, both source code and object code.

In 1998, The **Digital Millennium Copyright Act** was enacted by Congress. This law implements the TRIPPS agreement concluded under GATT, as well as two WIPO agreements, the WIPO Copyright Treaty and the WIPO Performances and Phonograms Treaty, under which each member country must provide protection for works from other member countries in the same way that they protect the works of their own citizens. However, it has some controversial provisions relating to tools designed to circumvent protection or encryption systems, making it a crime to use such a tool.

No person shall circumvent a technological measure that effectively controls access to a work protected under this title (Digital Millennium Copyright Act, Sect 1201,1a).

It is also a crime to manufacture or offer a tool that is designed primarily for the purpose of circumventing protection technologies, has limited use other than such circumvention, or is marketed for the purpose of circumventing protection.

No person shall manufacture, import, offer to the public, provide, or otherwise traffic in any technology, product, service, device, component, or part thereof, that:

A. Is primarily designed or produced for the purpose of circumventing a technological measure that effectively controls access to a work protected under this title;

B. Has only limited commercially significant purpose or use other than to circumvent a technological measure that effectively controls access to a work protected under this title; or

C. Is marketed by that person or another acting in concert with that person with that person's knowledge for use in circumventing a technological measure that effectively controls access to a work protected under this title (Digital Millennium Copyright Act, Sect 1201,2a).

Specific exceptions are made for libraries, archives, and educational institutions, but only for the purpose of evaluating the work to determine whether to acquire a copy of it. Exceptions are also made for law enforcement agencies, and under limited circumstances, for reverse engineering to allow interoperability of products, for encryption research, for computer repairs, and similar uses. The law also limits the liability of Internet service providers for online copyright infringement by subscribers to the Internet service.

Copyright **infringement** means that a person uses or sells an item protected by copyright, or intentionally supports others in doing so, violating the owner's property rights. The owner of the copyright has to prove that the person did not make fair use of the item. Courts usually want the copyright owner to prove that he or she owns the work, that the violator had knowledge of the work, and that the new work produced is not substantially different from the copyrighted one. The penalty is a heavy fine.

14.2.2.3 Patents

Another form of protection for intellectual property is a patent, which is designed to protect an invention or discovery. A patent is the grant of a property right to the inventor. Patents are issued by the governments of individual countries, although there are some international treaties concerning them. In the United States, patents are issued by the Patent and Trademark Office, which is an agency of the Department of Commerce. A patent gives the inventor the right to prevent others from making, using, offering to sell, or selling the invention in the United States or its territories or possessions, or from importing the invention into the United States. It is up to the inventor to enforce his or her right to exclude these activities. The term of the patent is generally 20 years from the time of the filing of the application, or from the date an earlier related application was filed, but it can be extended in special cases. During this time, the inventor has the opportunity to recover the costs of creating the invention.

United States patent laws, like copyright laws, have their origins in Article 2, Section 8 of the Constitution. Congress enacted the first US patent law in 1790, and revised it in 1952. In 1999, Congress enacted the American Inventors Protection Act (AIPA). According to the law,

> . . . any person who invents or discovers any new and useful process, machine, manufacture, or composition of matter, or any new and useful improvement thereof, may obtain a patent, subject to the conditions and requirements of the law. The word "process" is defined by law as a process, act or method, and primarily includes industrial or technical processes (United States Patent and Trademark Office, *General Information Concerning Patents*).

The invention must be **useful,** which means that it has a useful purpose and can actually work. An idea or suggestion for a useful device is not sufficient. It must be demonstrated that the creation works. The invention must be **new,** which means it must not have been known, published, or used previously. It must be **non-obvious** to a person who has ordinary skill in the area. The inventor must file an application that includes a specification, describing the invention in detail:

> The specification must include a written description of the invention and of the manner and process of making and using it, and is required to be in such full, clear, concise, and exact terms as to enable any person skilled in the technological area to which the invention pertains, or with which it is most nearly connected, to make and use the same (United States Patent and Trademark Office, *General Information Concerning Patents*).

Drawings may also be required to further describe the invention. The Patent Office reviews the application and sends it to one of its technology centers to determine whether the invention is new, useful, and non-obvious. If the patent is granted, it remains in effect for 20 years. During that time, others can use the ideas but not the process of the patent. After the patent expires, anyone can examine the disclosures and use the invention.

Patents given in one country have no automatic legal basis in another. However, under the **Paris Convention** for the Protection of Industrial Property, of which the United States is a member, a treaty was signed that provides that each of the 140 member countries guarantees to give citizens of the other countries the right to patent (and trademark) that it offers its own citizens. In addition, if an inventor files a regular first patent application in one of the member countries, he or she can, within a specified period, file for patent protection in all the member countries. Even if this filing was made later, it will be considered to have been filed on the same date as the first regular application, for purposes of determining right of priority if another person should file for the same invention. The Patent Cooperation Treaty of 1970 creates a standard application format and a centralized filing procedure for the filing of patents in all the member countries.

Owners of patented inventions normally display the patent number on the product. People who have applied for a patent for an invention are permitted to display the words "Patent Pending" or "Patent Applied For" on the product while the patent application is being reviewed. Both of these practices are methods of warning the public that a patent exists or may exist, and to help the inventor to identify violations by having the public report any suspected infringement. It is up to the patent owner to identify and investigate any infringement, and it can be costly and time-consuming to do so. If the patent owner can prove infringement, the penalties are heavy.

14.2.2.4 Trade Secrets

Trade secrets provide another way to protect intellectual property. A trade secret is any information that is used in the operation of a business that is kept secret and that gives it a competitive edge. It can be a formula, process, pattern, compilation, program, method, technique, device, or any other information. The formula for a soft drink, the secret ingredients of a cosmetic, and the process for manufacturing a distinctive product are all examples of trade secrets. Unlike copyrights and patents, there is no way to register a trade secret under any national or international law. In the United States, trade secrets are protected by states, most of which have adopted laws based on the work of the National Conference of Commissioners of Uniform State Laws, which drafted the Uniform Trade Secrets Act in 1970 and amended it in 1985. These laws protect the company from misappropriation of the secret, making it a crime to improperly acquire a trade secret. The protection remains as long as the information is kept secret. The biggest threat to a trade secret usually comes from within the company itself. Current employees may reveal the secret accidentally in casual discussions at business meetings, at professional conferences, or in personal conversations, or they may be bribed by business competitors to reveal it. Former employees bring with them knowledge of the business processes of a company and other proprietary information, and they may reveal this information to their new employers. Companies usually protect trade secrets by limiting the number of employees who have access to them, by guarding the documents containing them carefully, and by requiring employees who have access to them to sign non-disclosure agreements.

Litigation often results when a trade secret is revealed. The courts must determine whether the information constitutes a trade secret. According to R. Mark Halligan ("The Sorry State of Trade Secret Protection" http://www.rmarkhalligan2.com/trade/default.asp), there are six factors that courts use in determining whether something is a trade secret.

1. How widely the information is known outside the company. If the information is widely known outside the company, it is less likely that it is a protectable trade secret.

2. How widely the information is known by employees and others in the company. The more employees who know the information, the less likely that it is a trade secret.

3. The extent of measures taken to guard the secrecy of the information. The more carefully the information is guarded, the more likely that it is a trade secret.

4. How valuable the information is to the owner and the competitors. Unless both the company and its competitors consider the information valuable, it cannot be a trade secret.

5. How much time, effort, and money was spent in developing the information. The more spent by the company in developing the information, the more likely that it is a trade secret.

6. How difficult it would be for others to acquire or duplicate the information properly. If it is easy to duplicate the information, it is less likely to be a trade secret.

Misappropriation of trade secrets is often traced to employees or former employees who had access to the secret and who revealed it. If the owner can establish that it was a trade secret using the factors previously described, and that the secret was obtained by improper means such as bribery, the owner can receive compensation. There are heavy fines for violating trade secret laws.

Since protection under patent laws requires full disclosure and protection under trade secret laws requires that the secret never be disclosed, a company cannot claim a trade secret and also apply for a patent for the same information.

14.2.2.5 Trademarks and Service Marks

Trademarks and service marks are also eligible for protection under intellectual protection laws. Marks can include one or more letters, numbers, or words. They can also be drawings, symbols, colors, sounds, fragrances, or the shape or packaging of goods that are distinctive. According to the United States Patent and Trademark Office,

- A **trademark** is a word, phrase, symbol, or design, or a combination of words, phrases, symbols, or designs, that identifies and distinguishes the source of the goods of one party from those of others.

- A **service mark** is the same as a trademark, except that it identifies and distinguishes the source of a service rather than a product (US Patent and Trademark Office, *What Are Patents, Trademarks, Servicemarks, and Copyrights?*).

In the United States trademarks are protected by both federal law under the **Lanham Act** (Trademark Law of 1936) and by state laws. Registration of them is not required. A company can establish its right to a mark simply by using it, and can designate it as a trademark using the TM symbol, or as a service mark using the SM symbol. However, marks used in interstate or foreign commerce can be protected by registering them with the Patent and Trademark Office. Registration requires a clear reproduction of the mark, including any three-dimensional aspects, a sample of it in use, a list of goods and services for which the mark will be used, as well as other requirements. A search is then conducted to ensure that the mark is appropriate and distinctive and does not infringe upon any other registered mark. Once registered, owners can use the federal registration symbol ® to designate the mark. Registering the mark allows the owner to notify the public of ownership of the mark, establishes the legal right to ownership and exclusive right to use it, allows the owner to bring a court action concerning infringement of the mark, allows him or her to use it as a basis of registration of the mark in foreign countries, and allows the owner to file the registration with the US Custom Service to prevent infringing foreign goods from being imported.

To prove infringement, an owner must show that consumers are likely to be misled by the use of the infringing mark. Registration is valid for 10 years, but it can be renewed. Many countries have adopted either the **Madrid Protocol** or the Madrid Agreement Concerning the International Registration of Marks. WIPO administers a system of international registration of marks based on these two treaties. More than 60 countries form the Madrid Union, and have signed one or both of these agreements. To register the mark, the owner must first file an application with the trademark office of one of the member countries. Once the mark has been registered in a member country, the owner can use that as the basis for getting an international registration that is valid in the member countries of the Madrid Union. Although the United States is not currently a member of the Madrid Union, registration of a mark in the US Patent and Trademark Office can also be used as the basis for international registration.

14.2.3   Intellectual Property Protection for Software

Software and its packaging can be protected by copyright, by patent or trade secret laws, by trademark, or by some combination of these devices. Although the algorithms that are used to create software cannot be copyrighted because they are ideas, software programs themselves can be copyrighted because they are classified as expressions. Both US copyright laws and the Berne Convention specifically mention software as subject to copyright. Software does not have to be published in order to be copyrighted. As soon as it is created, the program is copyrighted and all rights belong to the owner, who can be the programmer or an employer, in the case of a work for hire. Therefore it is illegal for anyone to make a copy of any program, unless the owner gives permission to do so, except for the limited fair use described earlier. The documentation that accompanies software, including all the manuals, is also protected by copyright, regardless of whether it displays a copyright symbol. Except for fair use, it is also illegal to copy manuals unless permission to do so has been given. Often, there is also a trademark associated with software. It is illegal to market competing software using a mark that is so similar to the trademark that customers might be misled into thinking it is the original product. Sometimes the software contains a technical protection device to prevent copying. Tampering with that device or creating technology to facilitate tampering in order to circumvent the protection violates the DMCA in the United States, and violates the Berne Convention standards.

A customer who buys software is actually buying a **license to use** the software, not the software itself, which remains the property of the owner. The customer is leasing the software. The terms of the lease are often displayed on an opening screen when the software is installed, and the customer signifies agreement to the terms before installing the product. The usual terms are that the customer has a right to use the software, and to make a backup copy, but only one copy of the program can be used at a time. In that case, it is illegal for the customer to run the backup on a second computer at the same time the original is being used. It is certainly illegal, and constitutes software piracy, for the customer to give a copy of the software to another person to use. Often, product registration using a unique license number is required by the vendor, but the protection applies even if registration is not required. A business or other organization may purchase a license to use a certain number of copies of software at a time. If more than the licensed number of copies is ever used simultaneously, the organization is committing software piracy. The organization should use some mechanism to count the number of copies being used simultaneously to prevent abuse of the license. Some organizations purchase site licenses that allow an unlimited number of copies of software to be used only at a certain site. It would then be software piracy to allow the software to be used at a second location, such as a branch office.

Some software, referred to as **open source,** is free and available for copying. This type of software may have enhancements, manuals, or trademarks that are protected by intellectual property rules. Although copying the open source software is legal, copying any related product that is protected is clearly not.

Another category of software is **shareware,** which allows people to download and use the software in order to evaluate it. If they wish to continue to use the software after the trial period, they are asked to pay for its use. In some cases, the vendor states that although the trial software can be downloaded free, the customer is required to register. Then it is illegal for the customer to give a copy to another person, since that person should also register. Some products have protective devices that disable the software after the trial period or after a certain number of uses. However, even if the software continues to function after the trial period, any further use violates the agreement the user makes in downloading the product, and is illegal.

Commercial database management system software, such as that from major vendors, is usually protected using the same intellectual property protection methods as other software. The custom applications that may have been written by a company for a database, such as a customized user interface or customized reports, also qualify for the software protections mentioned. The same rules that apply to other software apply to this software. Some major DBMS vendors allow customers to download a free personal edition of their database software, for their own use. Others offer the personal edition only for a limited trial period. Editions for an enterprise are usually not available free.

Databases themselves are also qualified for different kinds of intellectual property protection. For example, the database can be copyrighted, because it is an expression, even though the facts contained in the database cannot be copyrighted. This protection applies even if the owner has published the data on the Web. Since all expressions are automatically copyrighted, even if they are published without a copyright symbol, users should assume that all data on the Web is copyrighted, unless otherwise stated. Therefore, except for fair use, making copies of data on the Web is illegal, unless the data is clearly identified as copyright-free. The information in a database can also be treated as a trade secret, since it can be used to provide a competitive advantage. In that case, of course, the data is not published. However, if a person gains access to this proprietary information, he or she is not free to use it because of trade secret laws. Sensitive data or data that should be kept secure under privacy laws should be protected using the security subsystem of the database management system and possibly other security safeguards, and should be stored in encrypted form, as well as being encrypted whenever it is transmitted. Bypassing the security devices to gain unauthorized access to the data is then illegal.

14.3 Privacy Issues

Much of the data that people provide about themselves in the regular course of their lives ends up in databases. School records, which contain personal information such as name, address, date of birth, and details about performance in school, are often kept in a database. When people apply for employment, information about their goals, their job history, their educational background, and their references may be stored in a database long after they have completed the application process. When people file their income tax returns, they provide detailed information about the sources and amounts of their income, as well as name, address, and social security number. Sometimes people unwittingly provide information about their buying habits. Whenever a consumer makes a purchase and pays by personal check, credit card, debit card, or uses a "preferred customer" card with an identifying number, that purchase can be linked with the buyer. If the purchase is made via a Web site, by telephone, or by mail order, or if the customer registers for a warrantee or service agreement, the same link can be made. In the registration process, customers might unknowingly provide personal information such as education level, family income, hobbies, and other data unrelated to the purchase. People provide similar background information in the process of filling out survey forms, or when they enter sweepstakes or other contests. When they apply for a loan or a credit card, they authorize companies to check their credit records.

Database technology makes it possible to store massive amounts of data about individuals. Data matching software could be used to match records obtained from databases developed by different companies or government agencies. Communication technology makes it possible to transfer all kinds of data to third parties, who could compile their databases containing profiles of individuals. All of these technologies could potentially be used to compile information about individuals without their knowledge or consent. The issues of whether it is ethical to collect certain data about an individual, to use it without the consent of the individual, and to share it with third parties are the subject of much debate. There is a conflict between the individual's right to privacy and the desire of governments and businesses to have information that would be useful to them.

14.3.1 Privacy and Security

In Chapter 9, we loosely defined **privacy** as the right of individuals to have some control over information about themselves. Personal data that is collected and stored in databases forms the bulk of the information that individuals might be concerned about. In general, people provide this information willingly, often without realizing that it can be stored and possibly misused. By providing or allowing access to personal information, consumers surrender what they consider to be a small amount of privacy for real or perceived benefits. However, if the organizations or people who initially collect the data pass on or sell the information to a third party without the consumer's consent, the consumer's privacy might be violated. There is disagreement about how much privacy people are entitled to, and what constitutes a violation of privacy.

Database security means protecting the database from unauthorized access, modification, or destruction. Chapter 9 dealt with database security from a technical standpoint. In addition to the need to preserve and protect data for the smooth functioning of the organization, database designers have a responsibility to protect the privacy of individuals about whom data is kept. Database designers and database administrators should be aware of applicable privacy legislation and should be able to set and to implement corporate policies that respect the privacy rights of people. The security mechanisms discussed in Chapter 9 should be used in implementing these policies.

14.3.2 Privacy as a Human Right

In an 1890 article, Justice Louis Brandeis and Samuel Warren defined privacy as the "right to be left alone" ("The Right to Privacy," *Harvard Law Review* 4, 1890 pp. 193–220). Justice Brandeis wrote that modern devices (faster photographic equipment, in that case) allow violations of privacy to be committed against a person without his or her knowledge, and argued that the law needed to be extended to cover such circumstances. The collection and dissemination of massive amounts of personal information made possible by databases and communications technology certainly fall into the category of potential violations of privacy under this definition.

Recent scholars have defined privacy in more complete terms and provided a philosophical basis for privacy. Alan Westin, author of the seminal 1967 work *Privacy and Freedom,* defined privacy as "the desire of people to choose freely under what circumstances and to what extent they will expose themselves, their attitude and their behavior to others" (*Privacy and Freedom,* New York: Atheneum, 1967, p. 7). In 1990, the Calcutt Committee stated, "Nowhere have we found a wholly satisfactory statutory definition of privacy," but it provided its own definition in its first report on privacy: "The right of the individual to be protected against intrusion into his personal life or affairs, or those of his family, by direct physical means or by publication of information" (**Report of the Committee on Privacy and Related Matters,** Chairman David Calcutt QC, 1990, Cmnd. 1102, London: HMSO, 1990, p. 7). Deborah Johnson, in her book on computer ethics (*Computer Ethics 3rd ed.,* Prentice Hall, 2001) argued that privacy has intrinsic value because it is "an essential aspect of autonomy," and autonomy is an intrinsic good. James Moor, in his 1997 article, "Towards a Theory of Privacy for the Information Age" (*Computers and Society* (27)3, pp. 27–32), argued that privacy is not a core value, which he defined as a value found in all human cultures. He asserted that the core values are life, happiness, freedom, knowledge, ability, resources, and security. He said privacy itself is not a core value, because it is possible that in some societies it is not valued, but it is an expression of the core value of security in our society. He stated that, "As societies become larger and highly interactive, but less intimate, privacy becomes a natural expression of the need for security." Richard Spinello identified "information privacy" in his book *Cyber Ethics* as "the right to control the disclosure of and access to one's personal information" (*Cyber Ethics,* Sudbury, MA: Jones and Bartlett 2000 p. 103).

Privacy is recognized as a fundamental human right enshrined in the constitutions of many countries, in a declaration of human rights by the United Nations, in conventions adopted by the European Council, and in laws enacted both in the United States and throughout the world. In the Universal Declaration of Human Rights adopted in 1948, the General Assembly of the United Nations proclaimed in Article 12,

> No one shall be subjected to arbitrary interference with his privacy, family, home, or correspondence, nor to attacks upon his honour and reputation. Everyone has the right to the protection of the law against such interference or attacks.

Despite the adoption of this declaration by the United Nations, privacy is not universally protected, even among the member nations. Among countries where privacy legislation exists, there is considerable variation in the definition of privacy and the degree to which privacy is protected.

14.3.2.1 Privacy Legislation in the United States

The Constitution of the United States does not address individual privacy directly, but the Fourth Amendment to the Constitution protects people against unreasonable searches, by guaranteeing that,

> The right of the people to be secure in their persons, houses, papers, and effects, against unreasonable searches and seizures, shall not be violated, and no warrants shall issue, but upon probable cause, supported by oath or affirmation, and particularly describing the place to be searched, and the persons or things to be seized.

The history of privacy legislation and attempts at legislation in the United States demonstrates a growing awareness on the part of the public and legislators of the value of privacy. An early set of principles governing private information was the Code of Fair Information Practices, which were part of a 1972 report prepared for the US Department of Health, Education, and Welfare (HEW). The Fair Information practices included these principles:

1. There must be no personal data record keeping systems whose very existence is secret.

2. There must be a way for a person to find out what information about the person is in a record and how it is used.

3. There must be a way for a person to prevent information about the person that was obtained for one purpose from being used or made available for other purposes without the person's consent.

4. There must be a way for a person to correct or amend a record of identifiable information about the person.

5. Any organization creating, maintaining, using, or disseminating records of identifiable personal data must assure the reliability of the data for their intended use and must take precautions to prevent misuses of the data.

(U.S. Department of Health, Education, and Welfare, Secretary's Advisory Committee on Automated Personal Data Systems, Records, computers, and the Rights of Citizens viii (1973).)

These principles can be considered the basis for many of the privacy laws that have been enacted in the United States. United States privacy laws are divided into two categories—those that provide protection from government interference and those that provide protection from interference by others, including businesses.

US Privacy Laws Concerning Government Agencies The Freedom of Information Act of 1966 requires that agencies of the executive branch of the federal government, including cabinet and military departments, government corporations, regulatory agencies and others, provide access to their records. With certain exceptions defined in the law, these agencies must provide copies of agency rules, opinions, orders, records, and proceedings to individuals who request them. The subject of the records need not be the person making the request. Amendments were enacted in 1974, 1986, and 1996.

The Privacy Act of 1974 was an important step in protecting the privacy rights of individuals from government interference. It allows individuals access to government records about themselves. Its stated purpose was,

> . . . to balance the government's need to maintain information about individuals with the rights of individuals to be protected against unwarranted invasions of their privacy stemming from federal agencies' collection, maintenance, use, and disclosure of personal information about them.

A component of this legislation was an attempt to prevent the government from using social security numbers as "universal identifiers" that could possibly be used to link information from different sources. The overview states that,

> [Congress was] . . . concerned with potential abuses presented by the government's increasing use of computers to store and retrieve personal data by means of a universal identifier—such as an individual's social security number.

There were four basic policy objectives on which the Act focused:

1. To restrict *disclosure* of personally identifiable records maintained by agencies.

2. To grant individuals increased rights of *access* to agency records maintained on themselves.

3. To grant individuals the right to seek *amendment* of agency records maintained on themselves upon a showing that the records are not accurate, relevant, timely, or complete.

4. To establish a code of *"fair information practices,"* which requires agencies to comply with statutory norms for collection, maintenance, and dissemination of records.

In 1988, Congress enacted the Computer Matching and Privacy Protection Act to protect individuals from certain computer matching activities by government agencies. It states,

> These provisions add procedural requirements for agencies to follow when engaging in computer-matching activities; provide matching subjects with opportunities to receive notice and to refute adverse information before having a benefit denied or terminated; and require that agencies engaged in matching activities establish Data Protection Boards to oversee those activities.

The Computer Matching and Privacy Protection Amendments of 1990 added to the due process provisions of the Act.

The Patriot Act of 2002, signed into law in October 2001, has weakened the provisions of some of the privacy laws, in the interests of national security. The purpose of the law is to combat terrorism by allowing law enforcement agencies more access to information about potential terrorist plans. The law relaxes restrictions on information sharing among federal agencies, allows law enforcement officials to obtain "roving wiretaps" to monitor cellular telephone conversations of suspected terrorists, provides greater subpoena power to obtain e-mail records of terror suspects, and gives law enforcement agencies easier access to banking records to prevent money laundering. This law is highly controversial and a number of challenges to it have been filed.

United States Privacy Laws Concerning Private Businesses The laws discussed above restricted the government's use of personal data, but did not apply to private businesses, in general, except for government contractors. Instead, individual laws were passed to deal with practices in various business sectors. These include:

- Fair Credit Reporting Act of 1970
- Family Educational Rights and Privacy Act of 1974
- Right to Financial Privacy Act of 1978

- Federal Managers Financial Integrity Act of 1982
- Cable Privacy Protection Act of 1984
- Cable Communications Policy Act of 1984
- Electronic Communication Privacy Act of 1986
- Computer Security Act of 1987
- Video Privacy Protection Act of 1988
- Telephone Consumer Protection Act of 1991
- Driver's Privacy Protection Act of 1994
- Health Insurance Portability and Accountability Act of 1996
- Children's Online Privacy Protection Act of 1998
- Gramm Leach Bliley Financial Services Modernization Act of 1999

In general, privacy laws in the United States attempted to apply the principles of the HEW Code of Fair Information Practices Act to the industry to which they apply. Except for instances explicitly covered by privacy legislation, they do not prevent businesses from collecting information about their customers and sharing that information with third parties. Even in instances where the sharing of customer information is restricted, such as in the Gramm Leach Bliley Financial Services Modernization Act of 1999, Congress has chosen to apply the restrictions using an "opt-out" rather than an "opt-in" mechanism. With "opt-in," an organization cannot share customer information unless the customer specifically agrees to the sharing, while with "opt-out" the data can be shared unless the customer requests that it not be shared. Organizations are required to notify customers of their right to opt-out of data sharing, but if a customer fails to respond, the organization can assume that permission has been granted. It is generally agreed that it is more restrictive to require opt-in than opt-out, and many privacy advocates in the United States were disappointed by the approval of the opt-out provisions.

14.3.2.2 Privacy Legislation in Europe

In Europe, a different standard exists, and that difference has some important implications for US firms doing business in the European market, since it limits the flow of data across borders. While US laws have historically restricted government activities and handled business activities only on a sector-by-sector basis, European laws are more restrictive of business activities. They also require opt-in rather than opt-out as the mechanism for obtaining customer approval of data sharing. The European community based its directives on principles developed by the Organization of Economic Cooperation and Development (OECD), an international organization with 30 member countries and cooperative relationships with 70 others. In 1980, the organization developed standards called the Fair Information Practices, including these eight principles taken from the OECD Guidelines on the Protection of Privacy and Transborder Flows of Personal Data (OECD, Paris, 1981):

- **Collection Limitation Principle.**
  - There should be limits to the collection of personal data
  - The data should be obtained by lawful and fair means
  - Data should be collected with the knowledge or consent of the subject, where possible and appropriate.

- **Data Quality Principle.** Personal data should be:
  - Relevant to the purposes for which they are to be used
  - Collected only to the extent necessary for those purposes
  - Accurate, complete and up-to-date.

- **Purpose Specification Principle.**
  - The purposes for which personal data are collected should be specified in advance of data collection
  - Data should not used again except for fulfilling those purposes

- **Use Limitation Principle.** Personal data should not be shared or used for purposes other than those stated in the Purpose Specification principle except with the consent of the subject or by the authority of law.

- **Security Safeguards Principle.** Reasonable security measures should be used to protect personal data against unauthorized access, use, disclosure, modification, destruction, and loss.

- **Openness Principle.** There should be a general policy of openness about practices concerning personal data. It should be easily possible to know about its existence, nature, purpose of use, and the name and contact information of the person who controls it (called the **data controller**).

- **Individual Participation Principle.** An individual should be able to:

  - Find out whether the data controller has data relating to him or her

  - Find out what that data is within a reasonable time, at a reasonable charge (if any), and in a form that is understandable

  - Challenge the denial of any such request and to challenge data related to him or her. If the challenge is successful, the individual has the right to have the data corrected or erased.

- **Accountability Principle.** A data controller should be accountable for complying with the principles

In the Convention for the Protection of Individuals with regard to Automatic Processing of Personal Data, which was proposed in 1981 and adopted in 1985, the Council of Europe set policy for its member countries regarding processing of personal information. The summary of the convention states:

> This Convention is the first binding international instrument which protects the individual against abuses which may accompany the collection and processing of personal data and which seeks to regulate at the same time the transfrontier flow of personal data.

> In addition to providing guarantees in relation to the collection and processing of personal data, it outlaws the processing of "sensitive" data such as a person's race, politics, health, religion, sexual life, or criminal record, in the absence of proper legal safeguards. The Convention also enshrines the individual's right to know that information is stored on him or her and, if necessary, to have it corrected.

> Restriction on the rights laid down in the Convention are only possible when overriding interests (e.g., State security, defence, etc.) are at stake.

> The Convention also imposes some restrictions on transborder flows of personal data to States where legal regulation does not provide equivalent protection. (Council of Europe. Strasbourg, 1981)

Both the OECD principles and the Council of Europe's Convention, which is similar, have been used as the basis of privacy laws in dozens of countries. The exact provisions and phrasing varies by country, but in general they require that personal information must be obtained fairly, be used only for the purpose originally specified, be relevant and adequate for the purpose, not be excessive for the purpose, be accurate, and that it be destroyed after its purpose is completed.

In 1995, the European Union adopted the European Data Protection Directive, "Protection of Individuals with regard to the processing of personal data and on the free movement of such data," which required all of its member countries to adopt legislation by 1998 that enforced the same privacy protection standards, which are essentially those of the OECD and COE. The directive included a provision that data about citizens of European Union countries must be afforded the same level of protection when it leaves the country. Other countries have ensured that they can safely receive such data by adopting laws using the same standards, but the United States has not. Therefore, US companies doing business in or having business partners in the European Union and countries having EU-type privacy laws had problems obtaining the data needed for their business, since they could not legally obtain customer information from those countries. A partial solution was worked out in 2000 between the European Union and the US Federal Trade Commission using the **Safe Harbor** mechanism. United States companies can certify that they follow the rules of the safe harbor agreement, which means that they comply with the EU rules in the way they treat data. The companies must annually certify to the US Department of Commerce that they meet the standards, and state in their public privacy policy statements that they do so. Certification requires that a company either subscribe to a self-regulatory monitoring agency (such as TRUSTe) or develop its own self-regulatory policy. The list of companies that belong to the safe harbor program is published by the Department of Commerce. Enforcement is the responsibility of the Federal Trade Commission or other federal or state agencies. Punishment is by severe fines and by expulsion of the offending company from the safe harbor program.

14.4   Human Factors

14.4.1 Human Factors in Software Development

Human factors in software development refer to factors that promote or facilitate optimal performance on the part of the user. These factors include both physical characteristics of the user and psychological factors. Human factors are vitally import in critical software such as that used in life-support systems, nuclear power plants, medical treatment devices, airplanes, and many other areas where error or failure can have life-threatening consequences. In business, design for human factors can reduce errors and increase productivity, especially in repetitive tasks such as order entry. Good design resulting from consideration of human factors promotes user acceptance and satisfaction. By careful design for human factors, physical problems such as fatigue and psychological problems such as stress can be reduced. The result of user-centered design is an increase in user comfort and user safety, greater productivity, increased user satisfaction, and a reduction in errors. It also reduces training costs, as well as the costs of dealing with and recovering from errors.

A human factors system engineering approach includes consideration of the user at every stage of the system project. A typical system project can include these stages:

- **Conceptualization.** Designers identify the objectives of the system and define specifications for it.

- **Definition.** Designers define the system, including any subsystems. They describe the environment in which it will be used and the way it will be used.

- **Overall design.** Designers identify all system components and their functions. Components include hardware, software, and human components. They analyze tasks and requirements.

- **Interface design.** Designers use appropriate design standards to create user interfaces. They apply design principles, statistical data, mathematical modeling, results of empirical studies, and experience.

- **Development.** Developers implement the system, test it, and modify it if indicated by the testing.

- **Deployment.** When the system is deployed, developers evaluate its use and make modifications as needed.

- **Maintenance.** Once the system is operational, procedures for continued evaluation, system evolution, and improvement are put in place.

At every stage, the designers and developers benefit by considering human factors. Including users in discussions during the conceptualization, definition, and design stages to capture their input about the proposed system at these early points helps to ensure that the system design is user-centered. Human factors specialists who are employed by the enterprise or who work as consultants can be valuable members of the design team. At the interface design stage, designers should incorporate interface design principles that have been developed by experts in the field. IEEE and other organizations publish software engineering standards that can be used. Books and articles on systems design can be used. Other sources for design principles include a number of excellent research institutes, such as the University of Maryland Human-Computer Interaction Lab, the Human-Computer Interaction Institute at Carnegie-Mellon University, the Media Lab at the Massachusetts Institute of Technology, and the Stanford University Program in Human-Computer Interaction. Usability testing should continue during development, deployment, and maintenance phases, because even slight changes that seem insignificant to the developers can have a large impact on usability.

14.4.2   The Human-Database Interface

The ultimate measure of the success of a database project is the extent to which the users actually use it to obtain the information they need. A database designer normally spends a considerable amount of time making sure that the database is useful, that it actually satisfies the information needs of the enterprise. As explained in Chapter 2 and illustrated throughout later chapters, the designer interviews users to determine their data needs, designs the conceptual model, applies techniques such as normalization to ensure the quality of the model, chooses the most appropriate database management system, does the logical mapping, designs the internal model, creates the system, and develops the database. The designer can be satisfied if the database itself is well designed and highly efficient. However, if it is not usable because of a poor user interface, end users will not be satisfied and will be disinclined to use the database. Usability is an aspect of quality that merits the same kind of careful attention that the rest of database design does.

Jakob Nielsen, an expert in usability, distinguishes between **utility,** which means the functionality of the design, and **usability.** Both are attributes of quality, and both are essential to the success of a database project. Without utility, the database does not provide what users need, and without usability, users cannot get what they need because the user interface is too difficult. Both utility and usability can be measured by user research methods.

The International Standards Organization (ISO), publishes a standards document on usability in which usability is defined as, "The extent to which a product can be used by specified users to achieve specified goals with effectiveness, efficiency and satisfaction in a specified context of use." (ISO, *Ergonomic requirements for office work with visual display terminals (VDTs)—Part 11: Guidance on usability*)

Nielsen describes usability as "a quality attribute that assesses how easy user interfaces are to use" (Jakob Nielsen. "Usability 101" http://www.useit.com/alertbox/20030825.html). He lists five components of usability.

1. **Learnability** refers to the ease with which users can accomplish tasks the first time they see the design.

2. **Efficiency** refers to how quickly users can accomplish tasks once they have mastered the design.

3. **Memorability** refers to how easily users can reestablish proficiency in using the design after a period of not using it.

4. **Errors** refers to the number and severity of errors that users make, and how easily they can recover from them.

5. **Satisfaction** refers to how pleasant it is to use the design.

For end users, usability is closely tied to productivity. Nielsen suggests that about 10 percent of a project's budget should be spent on usability. He claims that such an investment will substantially improve software, will double a Web site's quality metrics, and will improve an intranet's quality metrics almost as much. In gross measures, such improvements mean cutting training costs in half and doubling the number of transactions that can be performed by employees or customers.

14.4.3 Usability Testing for Database Applications

When designing for interactive users, database designers should consider the elements of interactive design, which include use of metaphors (e.g., desktop look and feel), quality and consistency of navigational cues, quality of error messages, effective feedback, and visual components such as layout, fonts, and color. The layout should be consistent from screen to screen, the screen should not be too crowded, the colors and fonts should enhance readability, and the language should be unambiguous, simple, clear, and appropriate for the users. Care should be taken to use language and symbols that do not offend any group or subgroup. Illustrations and examples that demonstrate and enhance diversity should be chosen.

Some basic techniques can be used for studying usability. Nielsen suggests repeated user-testing. The process consists of finding some representative users, having them perform representative tasks, and observing their actions, noting where they succeed and where they have problems with the interface. As few as five users can provide valuable information. Nielsen suggests conducting many small tests as the design progresses, revising the design in an iterative fashion between tests. Using the elements of interactive design mentioned above, it is straightforward to create test designs using various components and layouts and to conduct small studies to see the effect of changes. Small studies can be done as case studies. It is possible to perform formal hypothesis testing using a limited number of subjects, provided appropriate statistical distributions such as the Student's t distribution are used. However, before deployment of the final system, formal hypothesis testing should be done using statistically robust methods on a larger sample.

14.4.4   Ethical Standards for Computer and Software Professionals

In their work, professionals encounter situations that require moral judgments. Many professions have codes of ethics that guide their members' actions in such situations. Professional organizations in computing have developed codes of conduct that provide guidance for computing and software professionals. The first, reproduced here in its entirety, is the Code of Ethics and Professional Conduct adopted by the Association for Computing Machinery.

ACM Code of Ethics and Professional Conduct

Adopted by ACM Council 10/16/92.

Preamble

Commitment to ethical professional conduct is expected of every member (voting members, associate members, and student members) of the Association for Computing Machinery (ACM).

This Code, consisting of 24 imperatives formulated as statements of personal responsibility, identifies the elements of such a commitment. It contains many, but not all, issues professionals are likely to face. Section 1 outlines fundamental ethical considerations, while Section 2 addresses additional, more specific considerations of professional conduct. Statements in Section 3 pertain more specifically to individuals who have a leadership role, whether in the workplace or in a volunteer capacity such as with organizations like ACM. Principles involving compliance with this Code are given in Section 4.

The Code shall be supplemented by a set of Guidelines, which provide explanation to assist members in dealing with the various issues contained in the Code. It is expected that the Guidelines will be changed more frequently than the Code.

The Code and its supplemented Guidelines are intended to serve as a basis for ethical decision making in the conduct of professional work. Secondarily, they may serve as a basis for judging the merit of a formal complaint pertaining to violation of professional ethical standards.

It should be noted that although computing is not mentioned in the imperatives of Section 1, the Code is concerned with how these fundamental imperatives apply to one's conduct as a computing professional. These imperatives are expressed in a general form to emphasize that ethical principles which apply to computer ethics are derived from more general ethical principles.

It is understood that some words and phrases in a code of ethics are subject to varying interpretations, and that any ethical principle may conflict with other ethical principles in specific situations. Questions related to ethical conflicts can best be answered by thoughtful consideration of fundamental principles, rather than reliance on detailed regulations.

1. GENERAL MORAL IMPERATIVES.

As an ACM member I will . . . .

1.1 Contribute to society and human well-being.

This principle concerning the quality of life of all people affirms an obligation to protect fundamental human rights and to respect the diversity of all cultures. An essential aim of computing professionals is to minimize negative consequences of computing systems, including threats to health and safety. When designing or implementing systems, computing professionals must attempt to ensure that the products of their efforts will be used in socially responsible ways, will meet social needs, and will avoid harmful effects to health and welfare.

In addition to a safe social environment, human well-being includes a safe natural environment. Therefore, computing professionals who design and develop systems must be alert to, and make others aware of, any potential damage to the local or global environment.

1.2 Avoid harm to others.

"Harm" means injury or negative consequences, such as undesirable loss of information, loss of property, property damage, or unwanted environmental impacts. This principle prohibits use of computing technology in ways that result in harm to any of the following: users, the general public, employees, employers. Harmful actions include intentional destruction or modification of files and programs leading to serious loss of resources or unnecessary expenditure of human resources such as the time and effort required to purge systems of "computer viruses."

Well-intended actions, including those that accomplish assigned duties, may lead to harm unexpectedly. In such an event the responsible person or persons are obligated to undo or mitigate the negative consequences as much as possible. One way to avoid unintentional harm is to carefully consider potential impacts on all those affected by decisions made during design and implementation.

To minimize the possibility of indirectly harming others, computing professionals must minimize malfunctions by following generally accepted standards for system design and testing. Furthermore, it is often necessary to assess the social consequences of systems to project the likelihood of any serious harm to others. If system features are misrepresented to users, coworkers, or supervisors, the individual computing professional is responsible for any resulting injury.

In the work environment the computing professional has the additional obligation to report any signs of system dangers that might result in serious personal or social damage. If one's superiors do not act to curtail or mitigate such dangers, it may be necessary to "blow the whistle" to help correct the problem or reduce the risk. However, capricious or misguided reporting of violations can, itself, be harmful. Before reporting violations, all relevant aspects of the incident must be thoroughly assessed. In particular, the assessment of risk and responsibility must be credible. It is suggested that advice be sought from other computing professionals. See principle 2.5 regarding thorough evaluations.

1.3 Be honest and trustworthy.

Honesty is an essential component of trust. Without trust an organization cannot function effectively. The honest computing professional will not make deliberately false or deceptive claims about a system or system design, but will instead provide full disclosure of all pertinent system limitations and problems.

A computer professional has a duty to be honest about his or her own qualifications, and about any circumstances that might lead to conflicts of interest.

Membership in volunteer organizations such as ACM may at times place individuals in situations where their statements or actions could be interpreted as carrying the "weight" of a larger group of professionals. An ACM member will exercise care to not misrepresent ACM or positions and policies of ACM or any ACM units.

1.4 Be fair and take action not to discriminate.

The values of equality, tolerance, respect for others, and the principles of equal justice govern this imperative. Discrimination on the basis of race, sex, religion, age, disability, national origin, or other such factors is an explicit violation of ACM policy and will not be tolerated.

Inequities between different groups of people may result from the use or misuse of information and technology. In a fair society, all individuals would have equal opportunity to participate in, or benefit from, the use of computer resources regardless of race, sex, religion, age, disability, national origin or other such similar factors. However, these ideals do not justify unauthorized use of computer resources nor do they provide an adequate basis for violation of any other ethical imperatives of this code.

1.5 Honor property rights including copyrights and patent.

Violation of copyrights, patents, trade secrets and the terms of license agreements is prohibited by law in most circumstances. Even when software is not so protected, such violations are contrary to professional behavior. Copies of software should be made only with proper authorization. Unauthorized duplication of materials must not be condoned.

1.6 Give proper credit for intellectual property.

Computing professionals are obligated to protect the integrity of intellectual property. Specifically, one must not take credit for other's ideas or work, even in cases where the work has not been explicitly protected by copyright, patent, etc.

1.7 Respect the privacy of others.

Computing and communication technology enables the collection and exchange of personal information on a scale unprecedented in the history of civilization. Thus there is increased potential for violating the privacy of individuals and groups. It is the responsibility of professionals to maintain the privacy and integrity of data describing individuals. This includes taking precautions to ensure the accuracy of data, as well as protecting it from unauthorized access or accidental disclosure to inappropriate individuals. Furthermore, procedures must be established to allow individuals to review their records and correct inaccuracies.

This imperative implies that only the necessary amount of personal information be collected in a system, that retention and disposal periods for that information be clearly defined and enforced, and that personal information gathered for a specific purpose not be used for other purposes without consent of the individual(s). These principles apply to electronic communications, including electronic mail, and prohibit procedures that capture or monitor electronic user data, including messages, without the permission of users or bona fide authorization related to system operation and maintenance. User data observed during the normal duties of system operation and maintenance must be treated with strictest confidentiality, except in cases where it is evidence for the violation of law, organizational regulations, or this Code. In these cases, the nature or contents of that information must be disclosed only to proper authorities.

1.8 Honor confidentiality.

The principle of honesty extends to issues of confidentiality of information whenever one has made an explicit promise to honor confidentiality or, implicitly, when private information not directly related to the performance of one's duties becomes available. The ethical concern is to respect all obligations of confidentiality to employers, clients, and users unless discharged from such obligations by requirements of the law or other principles of this Code.

2. *MORE SPECIFIC PROFESSIONAL RESPONSIBILITIES.*

As an ACM computing professional I will . . . .

2.1 Strive to achieve the highest quality, effectiveness and dignity in both the process and products of professional work.

Excellence is perhaps the most important obligation of a professional. The computing professional must strive to achieve quality and to be cognizant of the serious negative consequences that may result from poor quality in a system.

2.2 Acquire and maintain professional competence.

Excellence depends on individuals who take responsibility for acquiring and maintaining professional competence. A professional must participate in setting standards for appropriate levels of competence, and strive to achieve those standards. Upgrading technical knowledge and competence can be achieved in several ways: doing independent study; attending seminars, conferences, or courses; and being involved in professional organizations.

2.3 Know and respect existing laws pertaining to professional work.

ACM members must obey existing local, state, province, national, and international laws unless there is a compelling ethical basis not to do so. Policies and procedures of the organizations in which one participates must also be obeyed. But compliance must be balanced with the recognition that sometimes existing laws and rules may be immoral or inappropriate and, therefore, must be challenged. Violation of a law or regulation may be ethical when that law or rule has inadequate moral basis or when it conflicts with another law judged to be more important. If one decides to violate a law or rule because it is viewed as unethical, or for any other reason, one must fully accept responsibility for one's actions and for the consequences.

2.4 Accept and provide appropriate professional review.

Quality professional work, especially in the computing profession, depends on professional reviewing and critiquing. Whenever appropriate, individual members should seek and utilize peer review as well as provide critical review of the work of others.

2.5   Give comprehensive and thorough evaluations of computer systems and their impacts, including analysis of possible risks.

Computer professionals must strive to be perceptive, thorough, and objective when evaluating, recommending, and presenting system descriptions and alternatives. Computer professionals are in a position of special trust, and therefore have a special responsibility to provide objective, credible evaluations to employers, clients, users, and the public. When providing evaluations the professional must also identify any relevant conflicts of interest, as stated in <u>imperative 1.3</u>.

As noted in the discussion of <u>principle 1.2</u> on avoiding harm, any signs of danger from systems must be reported to those who have opportunity and/or responsibility to resolve them. See the guidelines for <u>imperative 1.2</u> for more details concerning harm, including the reporting of professional violations.

2.6   Honor contracts, agreements, and assigned responsibilities.

Honoring one's commitments is a matter of integrity and honesty. For the computer professional this includes ensuring that system elements perform as intended. Also, when one contracts for work with another party, one has an obligation to keep that party properly informed about progress toward completing that work.

A computing professional has a responsibility to request a change in any assignment that he or she feels cannot be completed as defined. Only after serious consideration and with full disclosure of risks and concerns to the employer or client, should one accept the assignment. The major underlying principle here is the obligation to accept personal accountability for professional work. On some occasions other ethical principles may take greater priority.

A judgment that a specific assignment should not be performed may not be accepted. Having clearly identified one's concerns and reasons for that judgment, but failing to procure a change in that assignment, one may yet be obligated, by contract or by law, to proceed as directed. The computing professional's ethical judgment should be the final guide in deciding whether or not to proceed. Regardless of the decision, one must accept the responsibility for the consequences.

However, performing assignments "against one's own judgment" does not relieve the professional of responsibility for any negative consequences.

2.7 Improve public understanding of computing and its consequences.

Computing professionals have a responsibility to share technical knowledge with the public by encouraging understanding of computing, including the impacts of computer systems and their limitations. This imperative implies an obligation to counter any false views related to computing.

2.8 Access computing and communication resources only when authorized to do so.

Theft or destruction of tangible and electronic property is prohibited by imperative 1.2 - "Avoid harm to others." Trespassing and unauthorized use of a computer or communication system is addressed by this imperative. Trespassing includes accessing communication networks and computer systems, or accounts and/or files associated with those systems, without explicit authorization to do so. Individuals and organizations have the right to restrict access to their systems so long as they do not violate the discrimination principle (*see* 1.4). No one should enter or use another's computer system, software, or data files without permission. One must always have appropriate approval before using system resources, including communication ports, file space, other system peripherals, and computer time.

3. *ORGANIZATIONAL LEADERSHIP IMPERATIVES.*

As an ACM member and an organizational leader, I will . . . .

BACKGROUND NOTE: This section draws extensively from the draft IFIP Code of Ethics, especially its sections on organizational ethics and international concerns. The ethical obligations of organizations tend to be neglected in most codes of professional conduct, perhaps because these codes are written from the perspective of the individual member. This dilemma is addressed by stating these imperatives from the perspective of the organizational leader. In this context "leader" is viewed as any organizational member who has leadership or educational responsibilities. These imperatives generally may apply to organizations as well as their leaders. In this context "organizations" are corporations, government agencies, and other "employers," as well as volunteer professional organizations.

3.1 Articulate social responsibilities of members of an organizational unit and encourage full acceptance of those responsibilities.

Because organizations of all kinds have impacts on the public, they must accept responsibilities to society. Organizational procedures and attitudes oriented toward quality and the welfare of society will reduce harm to members of the public, thereby serving public interest and fulfilling social responsibility. Therefore, organizational leaders must encourage full participation in meeting social responsibilities as well as quality performance.

3.2 Manage personnel and resources to design and build information systems that enhance the quality of working life.

Organizational leaders are responsible for ensuring that computer systems enhance, not degrade, the quality of working life. When implementing a computer system, organizations must consider the personal and professional development, physical safety, and human dignity of all workers. Appropriate human-computer ergonomic standards should be considered in system design and in the workplace.

3.3 Acknowledge and support proper and authorized uses of an organization's computing and communication resources.

Because computer systems can become tools to harm as well as to benefit an organization, the leadership has the responsibility to clearly define appropriate and inappropriate uses of organizational computing resources. While the number and scope of such rules should be minimal, they should be fully enforced when established.

3.4 Ensure that users and those who will be affected by a system have their needs clearly articulated during the assessment and design of requirements; later the system must be validated to meet requirements.

Current system users, potential users and other persons whose lives may be affected by a system must have their needs assessed and incorporated in the statement of requirements. System validation should ensure compliance with those requirements.

3.5 Articulate and support policies that protect the dignity of users and others affected by a computing system.

Designing or implementing systems that deliberately or inadvertently demean individuals or groups is ethically unacceptable. Computer professionals who are in decision making positions should verify that systems are designed and implemented to protect personal privacy and enhance personal dignity.

3.6 Create opportunities for members of the organization to learn the principles and limitations of computer systems.

This complements the imperative on public understanding (2.7). Educational opportunities are essential to facilitate optimal participation of all organizational members. Opportunities must be available to all members to help them improve their knowledge and skills in computing, including courses that familiarize them with the consequences and limitations of particular types of systems. In particular, professionals must be made aware of the dangers of building systems around oversimplified models, the improbability of anticipating and designing for every possible operating condition, and other issues related to the complexity of this profession.

4. COMPLIANCE WITH THE CODE.

As an ACM member I will . . . .

4.1 Uphold and promote the principles of this Code.

The future of the computing profession depends on both technical and ethical excellence. Not only is it important for ACM computing professionals to adhere to the principles expressed in this Code, each member should encourage and support adherence by other members.

4.2 Treat violations of this code as inconsistent with membership in the ACM.

Adherence of professionals to a code of ethics is largely a voluntary matter. However, if a member does not follow this code by engaging in gross misconduct, membership in ACM may be terminated.

This Code and the supplemental Guidelines were developed by the Task Force for the Revision of the ACM Code of Ethics and Professional Conduct: Ronald E. Anderson, Chair, Gerald Engel, Donald Gotterbarn, Grace C. Hertlein, Alex Hoffman, Bruce Jawer, Deborah G. Johnson, Doris K. Lidtke, Joyce Currie Little, Dianne Martin, Donn B. Parker, Judith A. Perrolle, and Richard S. Rosenberg. The Task Force was organized by ACM/SIG-CAS and funding was provided by the ACM SIG Discretionary Fund. This Code and the supplemental Guidelines were adopted by the ACM Council on October 16, 1992.

In addition to the ACM Code of Ethics and Professional Practice, which describes practices for all computing professionals, ACM and IEEE have jointly created a code of ethics and professional practice to guide software engineers. These guidelines apply to professionals who design any software, including database management systems, software that enhances the capabilities of database management systems, or database applications developed for a client.

Software Engineering Code of Ethics and Professional Practice (Version 5.2) as recommended by the ACM/IEEE-CS Joint Task Force on Software Engineering Ethics and Professional Practices and jointly approved by the ACM and the IEEE-CS as the standard for teaching and practicing software engineering.

PREAMBLE

Computers have a central and growing role in commerce, industry, government, medicine, education, entertainment and society at large. Software engineers are those who contribute by direct participation or by teaching, to the analysis, specification, design, development, certification, maintenance and testing of software systems. Because of their roles in developing software systems, software engineers have significant opportunities to do good or cause harm, to enable others to do good or cause harm, or to influence others to do good or cause harm. To ensure, as much as possible, that their efforts will be used for good, software engineers must commit themselves to making software engineering a beneficial and respected profession. In accordance with that commitment, software engineers shall adhere to the following Code of Ethics and Professional Practice.

The Code contains eight Principles related to the behavior of and decisions made by professional software engineers, including practitioners, educators, managers, supervisors and policy makers, as well as trainees and students of the profession. The Principles identify the ethically responsible relationships in which individuals, groups, and organizations participate and the primary obligations within these relationships. The Clauses of each Principle are illustrations of some of the obligations included in these relationships. These obligations are founded in the software engineer's humanity, in special care owed to people affected by the work of software engineers, and the unique elements of the practice of software engineering. The Code prescribes these as obligations of anyone claiming to be or aspiring to be a software engineer.

It is not intended that the individual parts of the Code be used in isolation to justify errors of omission or commission. The list of Principles and Clauses is not exhaustive. The Clauses should not be read as separating the acceptable from the unacceptable in professional conduct in all practical situations. The Code is not a simple ethical algorithm that generates ethical decisions. In some situations standards may be in tension with each other or with standards from other sources. These situations require the software engineer to use ethical judgment to act in a manner which is most consistent with the spirit of the Code of Ethics and Professional Practice, given the circumstances.

Ethical tensions can best be addressed by thoughtful consideration of fundamental principles, rather than blind reliance on detailed regulations. These Principles should influence software engineers to consider broadly who is affected by their work; to examine if they and their colleagues are treating other human beings with due respect; to consider how the public, if reasonably well informed, would view their decisions; to analyze how the least empowered will be affected by their decisions; and to consider whether their acts would be judged worthy of the ideal professional working as a software engineer. In all these judgments concern for the health, safety and welfare of the public is primary; that is, the "Public Interest" is central to this Code.

The dynamic and demanding context of software engineering requires a code that is adaptable and relevant to new situations as they occur. However, even in this generality, the Code provides support for software engineers and managers of software engineers who need to take positive action in a specific case by documenting the ethical stance of the profession. The Code provides an ethical foundation to which individuals within teams and the team as a whole can appeal. The Code helps to define those actions that are ethically improper to request of a software engineer or teams of software engineers.

The Code is not simply for adjudicating the nature of questionable acts; it also has an important educational function. As this Code expresses the consensus of the profession on ethical issues, it is a means to educate both the public and aspiring professionals about the ethical obligations of all software engineers.

PRINCIPLES

Principle 1: PUBLIC

Software engineers shall act consistently with the public interest. In particular, software engineers shall, as appropriate:

1.01. Accept full responsibility for their own work.

1.02. Moderate the interests of the software engineer, the employer, the client and the users with the public good.

1.03. Approve software only if they have a well-founded belief that it is safe, meets specifications, passes appropriate tests, and does not diminish quality of life, diminish privacy or harm the environment. The ultimate effect of the work should be to the public good.

1.04. Disclose to appropriate persons or authorities any actual or potential danger to the user, the public, or the environment, that they reasonably believe to be associated with software or related documents.

1.05. Cooperate in efforts to address matters of grave public concern caused by software, its installation, maintenance, support or documentation.

1.06. Be fair and avoid deception in all statements, particularly public ones, concerning software or related documents, methods and tools.

1.07. Consider issues of physical disabilities, allocation of resources, economic disadvantage and other factors that can diminish access to the benefits of software.

1.08. Be encouraged to volunteer professional skills to good causes and contribute to public education concerning the discipline.

Principle 2: CLIENT AND EMPLOYER

Software engineers shall act in a manner that is in the best interests of their client and employer, consistent with the public interest. In particular, software engineers shall, as appropriate:

2.01. Provide service in their areas of competence, being honest and forthright about any limitations of their experience and education.

2.02. Not knowingly use software that is obtained or retained either illegally or unethically.

2.03. Use the property of a client or employer only in ways properly authorized, and with the client's or employer's knowledge and consent.

2.04. Ensure that any document upon which they rely has been approved, when required, by someone authorized to approve it.

2.05. Keep private any confidential information gained in their professional work, where such confidentiality is consistent with the public interest and consistent with the law.

2.06. Identify, document, collect evidence and report to the client or the employer promptly if, in their opinion, a project is likely to fail, to prove too expensive, to violate intellectual property law, or otherwise to be problematic.

2.07. Identify, document, and report significant issues of social concern, of which they are aware, in software or related documents, to the employer or the client.

2.08. Accept no outside work detrimental to the work they perform for their primary employer.

2.09. Promote no interest adverse to their employer or client, unless a higher ethical concern is being compromised; in that case, inform the employer or another appropriate authority of the ethical concern.

Principle 3: PRODUCT

Software engineers shall ensure that their products and related modifications meet the highest professional standards possible. In particular, software engineers shall, as appropriate:

3.01. Strive for high quality, acceptable cost and a reasonable schedule, ensuring significant tradeoffs are clear to and accepted by the employer and the client, and are available for consideration by the user and the public.

3.02. Ensure proper and achievable goals and objectives for any project on which they work or propose.

3.03. Identify, define and address ethical, economic, cultural, legal and environmental issues related to work projects.

3.04. Ensure that they are qualified for any project on which they work or propose to work by an appropriate combination of education and training, and experience.

3.05. Ensure an appropriate method is used for any project on which they work or propose to work.

3.06. Work to follow professional standards, when available, that are most appropriate for the task at hand, departing from these only when ethically or technically justified.

3.07. Strive to fully understand the specifications for software on which they work.

3.08. Ensure that specifications for software on which they work have been well documented, satisfy the users' requirements and have the appropriate approvals.

3.09. Ensure realistic quantitative estimates of cost, scheduling, personnel, quality and outcomes on any project on which they work or propose to work and provide an uncertainty assessment of these estimates.

3.10. Ensure adequate testing, debugging, and review of software and related documents on which they work.

3.11. Ensure adequate documentation, including significant problems discovered and solutions adopted, for any project on which they work.

3.12. Work to develop software and related documents that respect the privacy of those who will be affected by that software.

3.13. Be careful to use only accurate data derived by ethical and lawful means, and use it only in ways properly authorized.

3.14. Maintain the integrity of data, being sensitive to outdated or flawed occurrences.

3.15. Treat all forms of software maintenance with the same professionalism as new development.

Principle 4: JUDGMENT

Software engineers shall maintain integrity and independence in their professional judgment. In particular, software engineers shall, as appropriate:

4.01. Temper all technical judgments by the need to support and maintain human values.

4.02. Only endorse documents either prepared under their supervision or within their areas of competence and with which they are in agreement.

4.03. Maintain professional objectivity with respect to any software or related documents they are asked to evaluate.

4.04. Not engage in deceptive financial practices such as bribery, double billing, or other improper financial practices.

4.05. Disclose to all concerned parties those conflicts of interest that cannot reasonably be avoided or escaped.

4.06. Refuse to participate, as members or advisors, in a private, governmental or professional body concerned with software related issues, in which they, their employers or their clients have undisclosed potential conflicts of interest.

Principle 5: MANAGEMENT

Software engineering managers and leaders shall subscribe to and promote an ethical approach to the management of software development and maintenance. In particular, those managing or leading software engineers shall, as appropriate:

5.01 Ensure good management for any project on which they work, including effective procedures for promotion of quality and reduction of risk.

5.02. Ensure that software engineers are informed of standards before being held to them.

5.03. Ensure that software engineers know the employer's policies and procedures for protecting passwords, files and information that is confidential to the employer or confidential to others.

5.04. Assign work only after taking into account appropriate contributions of education and experience tempered with a desire to further that education and experience.

5.05. Ensure realistic quantitative estimates of cost, scheduling, personnel, quality and outcomes on any project on which they work or propose to work, and provide an uncertainty assessment of these estimates.

5.06. Attract potential software engineers only by full and accurate description of the conditions of employment.

5.07. Offer fair and just remuneration.

5.08. Not unjustly prevent someone from taking a position for which that person is suitably qualified.

5.09. Ensure that there is a fair agreement concerning ownership of any software, processes, research, writing, or other intellectual property to which a software engineer has contributed.

5.10. Provide for due process in hearing charges of violation of an employer's policy or of this Code.

5.11. Not ask a software engineer to do anything inconsistent with this Code.

5.12. Not punish anyone for expressing ethical concerns about a project.

Principle 6: PROFESSION

Software engineers shall advance the integrity and reputation of the profession consistent with the public interest. In particular, software engineers shall, as appropriate:

6.01. Help develop an organizational environment favorable to acting ethically.

6.02. Promote public knowledge of software engineering.

6.03. Extend software engineering knowledge by appropriate participation in professional organizations, meetings and publications.

6.04. Support, as members of a profession, other software engineers striving to follow this Code.

6.05. Not promote their own interest at the expense of the profession, client or employer.

6.06. Obey all laws governing their work, unless, in exceptional circumstances, such compliance is inconsistent with the public interest.

6.07. Be accurate in stating the characteristics of software on which they work, avoiding not only false claims but also claims that might reasonably be supposed to be speculative, vacuous, deceptive, misleading, or doubtful.

6.08. Take responsibility for detecting, correcting, and reporting errors in software and associated documents on which they work.

6.09. Ensure that clients, employers, and supervisors know of the software engineer's commitment to this Code of ethics, and the subsequent ramifications of such commitment.

6.10. Avoid associations with businesses and organizations which are in conflict with this code.

6.11. Recognize that violations of this Code are inconsistent with being a professional software engineer.

6.12. Express concerns to the people involved when significant violations of this Code are detected unless this is impossible, counter-productive, or dangerous.

6.13. Report significant violations of this Code to appropriate authorities when it is clear that consultation with people involved in these significant violations is impossible, counter-productive or dangerous.

Principle 7: COLLEAGUES

Software engineers shall be fair to and supportive of their colleagues. In particular, software engineers shall, as appropriate:

7.01. Encourage colleagues to adhere to this Code.

7.02. Assist colleagues in professional development.

7.03. Credit fully the work of others and refrain from taking undue credit.

7.04. Review the work of others in an objective, candid, and properly-documented way.

7.05. Give a fair hearing to the opinions, concerns, or complaints of a colleague.

7.06. Assist colleagues in being fully aware of current standard work practices including policies and procedures for protecting passwords, files and other confidential information, and security measures in general.

7.07. Not unfairly intervene in the career of any colleague; however, concern for the employer, the client or public interest may compel software engineers, in good faith, to question the competence of a colleague.

7.08. In situations outside of their own areas of competence, call upon the opinions of other professionals who have competence in that area.

Principle 8: SELF

Software engineers shall participate in lifelong learning regarding the practice of their profession and shall promote an ethical approach to the practice of the profession. In particular, software engineers shall continually endeavor to:

8.01. Further their knowledge of developments in the analysis, specification, design, development, maintenance and testing of software and related documents, together with the management of the development process.

8.02. Improve their ability to create safe, reliable, and useful quality software at reasonable cost and within a reasonable time.

8.03. Improve their ability to produce accurate, informative, and well-written documentation.

8.04. Improve their understanding of the software and related documents on which they work and of the environment in which they will be used.

8.05. Improve their knowledge of relevant standards and the law governing the software and related documents on which they work.

8.06 Improve their knowledge of this Code, its interpretation, and its application to their work.

8.07. Not give unfair treatment to anyone because of any irrelevant prejudices.

8.08. Not influence others to undertake any action that involves a breach of this Code.

8.09. Recognize that personal violations of this Code are inconsistent with being a professional software engineer.

14.5 Chapter Summary

Computerization has created new situations that challenge society's moral codes. Computer technology provides temptations due to factors such as speed, privacy, anonymity, ease of copying, aesthetic attraction, availability of potential victims, international scope, and the power to destroy. The Internet is largely unregulated because it is not subject to the rules of any single country, and because of its culture. It provides a forum for free speech, but abuses such as pornography and hate rhetoric can become rampant. Another issue is intellectual property protection both for Internet and database content and for software. The Free Software movement challenges the notion of software as property. Individual privacy is compromised by the widespread use of computer technology to share personal information stored in databases. Opponents of privacy legislation claim that the sharing of customer data among businesses is a form of free speech. Responsibilities of computer professionals to make their products easier and safer for users, and the best ways to do that are also debated.

Intellectual property refers to products of the mind, such as literature, music, art, architecture, inventions, formulas for products, and software. The foundation of intellectual property rights is that since the creator of an original work has invested time and resources, he or she is entitled to a just return, which in turn encourages creative people to develop new works. Intellectual property is protected by a variety of mechanisms, including by copyright, patent, trade secret, trademarks, and service marks.

A **copyright** is given by the government of the country of origin of a work for a limited period of time. During that time, the author has exclusive rights to make copies, publish, distribute, publicly display, or publicly perform the work or to use it as the basis of a derivative work. The work must be original, have a tangible form, and be fixed in a medium. Anyone who creates a work that could be copyrighted automatically owns the copyright, even without publication, copyright symbol, or formal registration. Anyone who wants to use the copyrighted work must obtain permission from the owner of the copyright, and possibly pay a fee, unless the use is **fair use.** Fair use allows limited nonpersonal use of copyrighted materials, including using a small amount for educational purposes, and similar uses. Four factors to be considered are the character of the use, the nature of the work, the amount of the work to be used, and the effect it would have on the market for the original work. Facts, ideas, and formulas are always in the public domain, but a specific arrangement and expression of them, such as that found in a database, can be copyrighted. Copyrights are recognized internationally, but each country makes its own laws concerning them. Most copyright laws are based on the **Berne Convention.** In the United States, for works created before 1978, copyrights are for 95 years, while copyrights for post-1978 works are for the lifetime of the author plus 70 years, and works for hire are covered for 95 or 120 years. The copyright law covers software, both source code and object code. The 1998 **Digital Millennium Copyright Act** has some controversial provisions relating to tools designed to circumvent protection or encryption systems, making it a crime to use, manufacture, or offer such a tool. Exceptions are made for libraries, archives, and educational institutions, for the purpose of evaluating the work to determine whether to acquire a copy of it. Exceptions are also made for law enforcement agencies, for reverse engineering to allow interoperability of products, for encryption research, for computer repairs, and similar uses. The law also limits the liability of Internet service providers for online copyright infringement by subscribers.

Another form of protection for intellectual property is a **patent,** which grants the property right to an inventor. Patents are issued by the governments of individual countries. A patent gives the inventor the right to prevent others from making, using, offering to sell, selling, or importing the invention. The term of the patent is generally 20 years, during which time the inventor has the opportunity to recover the costs of creating the invention. The invention must be useful, new, and non-obvious. The inventor must file an application that includes a specification, describing the invention in detail.

A **trade secret** is any information that is used in the operation of a business that is kept secret and that gives it a competitive edge. In the United States, trade secrets are protected by states. These laws protect the company from misappropriation of the secret, making it a crime to improperly acquire a trade secret. The protection remains as long as the information is kept secret. Factors that courts use in determining whether something is a trade secret are how widely the information is known both outside and inside the company, the extent of measures taken to guard its secrecy, the value of the information to the owner and the competitors, the amount of time, effort, and money spent in developing it, and how difficult it would be for others to duplicate it exactly.

Trademarks and **service marks** are also eligible for protection under intellectual protection laws. Marks can include letters, numbers, words, drawings, symbols, colors, sounds, fragrances, or shape or packaging of goods that are distinctive.

Software and its packaging can be protected by copyright, by patent or trade secret laws, by trademark, or by some combination of these devices. A customer who buys software is actually buying a **license to use** the software, not the software itself, which remains the property of the owner. **Open source** software is free and available for copying. Another category of software is **shareware,** which allows people to download and use the software for an evaluation period, after which they pay for its continued use. Commercial database management system software is usually protected using the same intellectual property protection methods as other software. The custom applications written for a database also qualify for the software protections mentioned. Databases themselves are also qualified for different kinds of intellectual property protection. For example, the database can be copyrighted, because it is an expression, even though the facts contained in the database cannot be copyrighted. The information in a database can also be treated as a trade secret, since it can be used to provide a competitive advantage.

Database technology makes it possible to store massive amounts of data about individuals. Data matching and communication technologies could be used to compile and share information about individuals without their knowledge or consent. The issues of whether it is ethical to collect certain data about an individual, to use it without the consent of the individual, and to share it with third parties are the subject of much debate, and practices in the United States and the European Union differ significantly. There is a conflict between the individual's right to privacy and the desire of governments and businesses to have information that would be useful to them. Privacy is recognized as a fundamental human right enshrined in the constitutions of many countries, in a declaration of human rights by the United Nations, in conventions adopted by the European Council, and in laws enacted both in the United States and throughout the world. Laws regulating government activities in the United States include the Freedom of Information Act, the Privacy Act of 1974, and the Computer Matching and Privacy Protection Act. The Patriot Act of 2002 has weakened the provisions of some of the privacy laws, in the interests of national security. Individual laws were passed to deal with practices in various business sectors. Examples are the Fair Credit Reporting Act of 1970, the Right to Financial Privacy Act of 1978, the Cable Privacy Protection Act of 1984, the Electronic Communication Privacy Act of 1986, the Video Privacy Protection Act of 1988, the Telephone Consumer Protection Act of 1991, the Health Insurance Portability and Accountability Act of 1996, and the Gramm Leach Bliley Financial Services Modernization Act of 1999. Generally, they require that consumers have to **opt-out** to prevent their information from being shared. European laws are more restrictive of business activities. They also require **opt-in** rather than opt-out as the mechanism for obtaining customer approval of data sharing. They are based on principles developed by the Organization of Economic Cooperation and Development (OECD), which include the principles of collection limitation, data quality, purpose specification, use limitation, security safeguards, openness, individual participation, and accountability. Data about EU citizens must be afforded the same level of protection when it leaves the country. Therefore, US companies doing business in EU countries had problems obtaining the data needed for their business, because they could not legally obtain customer information from those countries. However, US companies can certify that they follow the rules of the **Safe Harbor** agreement, which means that they comply with the EU rules in the way they treat data, and can receive such data.

Human factors in software development refer to physical and psychological factors that promote or facilitate optimal performance on the part of the user. User-centered design increases user comfort, safety, productivity, and satisfaction, and reduces training costs and errors. A human factors system engineering approach includes consideration of the user at every stage of the system project. Five components of **usability** are learnability, efficiency, memorability, error reduction, and satisfaction.

Professional organizations in computing have developed codes of conduct that provide guidance for computing and software professionals. The ACM Code of Ethics and Professional Practice describes practices for all computing professionals, and ACM and IEEE have jointly created a code of ethics and professional practice to guide software engineers.

Exercises

14.1   Define the following terms.

    a. intellectual property

    b. copyright

    c. patent

    d. trade secret

    e. trademark

    f. service mark

    g. infringement

    h. open source

    i. freeware

    j. Blackstonian bundle

    k. fair use

    l. public domain

    m. Berne Convention

    n. WIPO

    o. TRIPPS

    p. Digital Millennium Copyright Act

    q. Freedom of Information Act

    r. Privacy Act of 1974

    s. universal identifier

    t. Patriot Act of 2002

    u. Gramm Leach Bliley Financial Services Modernization Act of 1999

    v. opt-out

    w. OECD

    x. data controller

    y. Safe Harbor

    z. usability

14.2 Choose one of the US laws mentioned in this chapter and research its origins, its provisions, and its legislative history. Summarize the arguments in favor of the law and against the law. Prepare a presentation describing your findings.

14.3 Choose one of the international conventions or agreements mentioned in this chapter and research its history, its provisions, the countries that participate in it, and its relationship to US law in the same area. Summarize the arguments in favor of the agreement and against it. If you were the president of the United States, would you subscribe to the agreement? Prepare a presentation describing your findings.

14.4 Research the open source software movement and read about its philosophical basis. Write an essay defending your position on this issue.

14.5 Assume you and a group of friends have developed an innovative piece of software for which you wish to protect your intellectual property rights. Identify the mechanism you would choose, and describe what you would need to do (if anything) to establish your ownership and to enforce your ownership of the software.

Would your rights be recognized in other countries? If not, is there any mechanism you can use to enforce them overseas?

14.6   Assume you have a position as database administrator in a large corporation. The company has been collecting data about employees, including monitoring their working habits by recording their keystrokes, timing their telephone interactions with clients, and scanning their e-mail for personal correspondence. As DBA, you are asked to help set up a recordkeeping system to store such data. Does the company have a legal right to perform this kind of monitoring? What is your professional responsibility in this situation? Do the ACM and IEEE Codes of Ethics have any provisions to guide you?

15 CHAPTER

Data Warehouses and Data Mining

Chapter Objectives

In this chapter you will learn the following:

- How data warehouses originated

- How data warehouses differ from operational databases

- What types of processing data warehouses support

- How OLAP differs from OLTP

- The basic architecture of a data warehouse

- What data models are used for data warehouses

- The meaning of the terms rollup, drill-down, cross-tabulation, and slice and dice

15.1   Origins of Data Warehouses

Many organizations that use standard database technology to collect, store, and process massive amounts of their operational data have begun to look closely at their current and historical data stores as information sources to help them make better business decisions. They have developed data warehouses for **decision support systems (DSS)** and similar applications. Decisions such as where to open a new store, what audience to target for an advertising campaign, which customers to approve loans for, and when to order additional stock can be made with more confidence when they are based on a careful examination of patterns found in existing data. Vendors of DBMSs including Oracle and IBM have been quick to add features to their product line to allow warehousing of the data from their standard database systems. New and powerful analytic tools have been developed to draw more information from data stored in such warehouses. SQL:1999 contains extensions that support the functions required by data warehouses. The data in a data warehouse is often collected from various departments or sites belonging to a large enterprise. The term was coined by W. H. Inmon, who described a data warehouse as, "a subject-oriented, integrated, nonvolatile, time-varying collection of data that is used primarily in organizational decision making" (Inmon, 2002). A data warehouse is intended for decision-support applications rather than for processing of ordinary transactions. It is optimized for data retrieval, as opposed to processing transactions.

15.2   Operational Databases and Data Warehouses

Traditional operational databases support **online transaction processing (OLTP),** which characteristically involves a limited number of repetitive transactions, each of which affects a few tuples at a time in a relational database. A database such as this is developed to serve the information needs of end users, and is designed to support their day-to-day business operations. High availability and efficient performance are critical factors in the success of an operational database. It must provide support for a large volume of transactions, and it must deliver responses to user queries or other online operations in a short time frame. An operational database is updated in real-time, as business transactions occur. Updates, insertions, and deletions must be done quickly to keep the database in a state that reflects the current environment of the enterprise.

- How data warehouse queries are expressed in SQL
- How bitmap indexes and join indexes can be used
- How view materialization and view maintenance are handled
- The purpose of data mining
- The types of knowledge data mining can produce
- How decision trees, regression, neural networks, and clustering are used
- Some application areas for data mining

By contrast, data warehouses support **OLAP** (On-Line Analytical Processing) as well as decision making. The data in a data warehouse can be taken directly from multiple operational databases, at different periods of time (historical data), and may also include data from other sources, summarized data, and metadata. The sources may have different models or standards, but the data warehouse integrates the data so that users see a consistent model. The data warehouse typically contains a very large amount of data, and it is optimized for efficient query processing and presentation of results for decision support. Updates are not as frequent as they are in the operational database, but are done periodically. OLAP applications typically must go through large amounts of data in order to produce results. Analysts examine the data stored in the warehouse using complex queries, generally involving group-by and aggregation operators. They may do time-series analysis using the historical data. **Data mining** is the process of discovering new information by searching large amounts of data. The purpose is to discover patterns or trends in the data that will be useful to the organization.

15.3   Architecture of a Data Warehouse

Unlike an operational database, for which requirements can be specified in advance, a data warehouse must be designed to support *ad hoc* queries and new and unanticipated types of analysis. A typical architecture is shown in Figure 15.1. Data is taken from data sources, which may include multiple operational databases, other inputs such as independent files, and environmental data such as geographic information or financial data. The data must be extracted from the sources using back-end system tools that can accommodate the differences among the heterogeneous sources. The data is reformatted into a consistent form. The data can also be checked for integrity and validity, a process called **data cleaning,** to ensure its quality prior to loading it into the warehouse. Data is then put into the data model for the warehouse and loaded. The loading process is a long transaction, since a large volume of data is typically involved, so the system must use transaction management tools to ensure proper recovery in the event of failure during the loading transaction. The database management system that supports the data warehouse has a system catalog that stores metadata, as well as other database system components. The data warehouse is then used to support queries for OLAP, to provide information for decision support systems that are used by management for making strategic decisions, and to provide the data for data mining tools that dis-

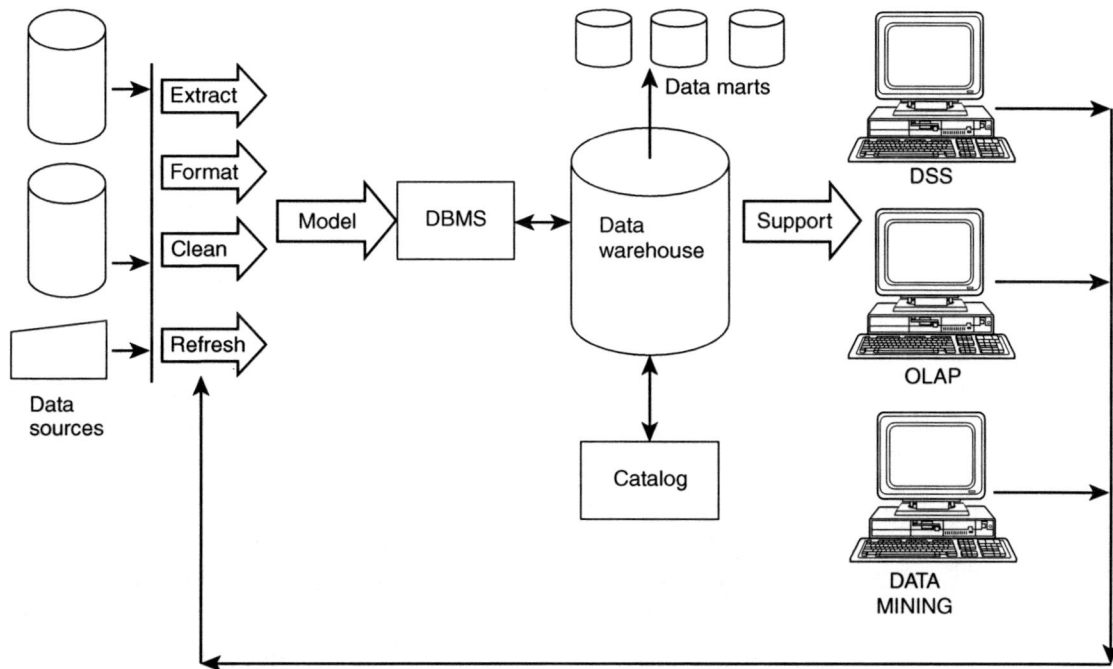

FIGURE 15.1
Data Warehouse Architecture

cover new information about patterns in the data. Certain segments of the data are organized into subsets called **data marts,** which focus on specific subjects. For example, a data mart could contain specialized information about a single department within the organization. All of these uses can result in new knowledge, which can then be used as a data source from which data can be formatted and put into the warehouse. Data from all data sources must be periodically refreshed. If there is sufficient storage space, the new data is simply added to the existing warehouse, and the old data is kept as long as it is useful. Otherwise, data that is no longer used is purged periodically, and new data is added. The frequency and scope of the updates depend on the environment. Factors that must be considered in deciding the update policy include how much storage is available, whether the warehouse needs recent data, whether it can be off-line during refresh, and how long the process for transmitting the data, cleaning, formatting, loading, and building indexes will take. The usual policy is to do a partial refresh periodically.

15.4   Data Models for Data Warehouses

Although the models in the data sources may vary, the data warehouse itself must use a single consistent model that accommodates the needs of users. Data warehouses generally use a multidimensional model. Data can be thought of as residing in a multidimensional matrix called a **data cube.** Figure 15.2(a) shows a three-dimensional data cube called Sales. On the front, visible face of the cube, we see sales figures for the month of June for four departments (dairy, grocery, produce, pharmacy) in three supermarkets (store 1, store 2, store 3). Note that all stores have these same four departments, which correspond to categories of products sold in supermarkets. The figures might represent sales in thousands of dollars. The sales data for each month appears in spreadsheet form, which is a presentation style that would be familiar to many users. The third dimension in this example is time, as indicated by the labels for the months of June, July, August, September, and October. Each month's sales figures for each department in each supermarket appear in a cell in the three-dimensional matrix. Users can view the data by whatever dimension is of interest to them. For example, if a user wishes to see data about sales for each department, the cube can be **pivoted,** or rotated to display a different dimension of interest, as shown in Figure 15.2(b). Here, the visible face of the cube shows the dairy department sales for the months of June through October for each of the three supermarkets. If we rotated on another axis, we could examine data for each store. The front face of the cube would show, for a single store, the sales for each department during each month.

In a multidimensional model, a coarser level of data granularity can be created by combining or aggregating data, a process called **rollup.** For example, using the data cube shown in Figure 15.2(a) we could roll up on department, combining data from all departments of each store, to give the total sales for each store for each month, as shown in Figure 15.3(a). We could have rolled up on stores, giving the data for each department, regardless of store, for each month. Similarly, we could have rolled up on the month. A different granularity of rollup would be generated by combining the months into seasons, showing summer season sales by department and store on one spreadsheet display, and similarly for fall, winter, and spring.

The inverse process is **drill-down.** In this process, we provide more detail on some dimension, using finer granularity for the data. For example, we

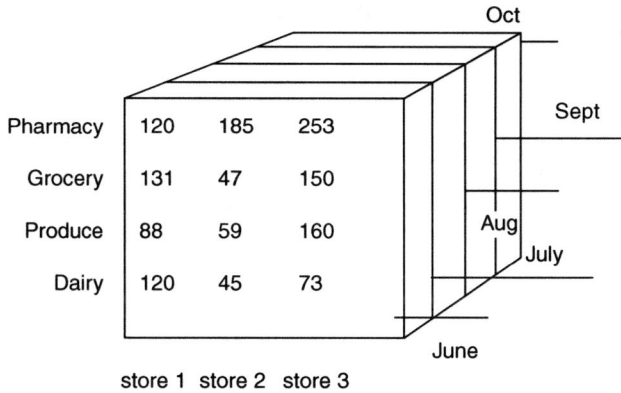

FIGURE 15.2(a)
Sales Data Cube

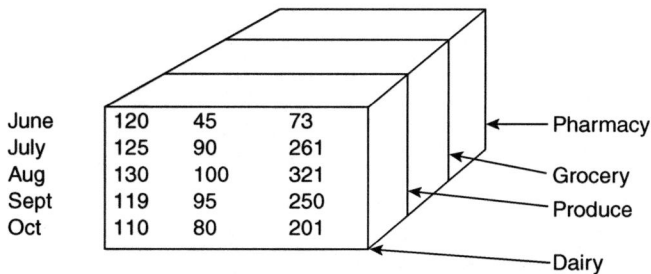

FIGURE 15.2(b)
Pivoted Sales Data Cube

might drill down on department, showing the sub-departments or categories in each of the departments. Figure 15.3(b) provides an example in which departments are broken down into categories for the month of June. The remainder of the cube would show the same breakdown for the other months. This data could not be obtained from the data cube shown in Figure 15.2(a), but requires that the more detailed data be stored, or that it be possible to obtain it from data stored in the data warehouse.

When pivoting and/or rollup of a data cube results in a two-dimensional spreadsheet-style display, it is natural to add totals for the rows and columns, forming a **cross-tabulation,** as illustrated in Figure 15.3(c). This example shows a cross-tabulation of the sales figures by store and month, showing totals for each store, totals for each month, and the total for both. Using pivoting, we could get cross-tabulations by department and store, or by department and month.

If we examine a portion of the data cube by using a selection where we specify equality conditions for one or more dimensions, this type of operation is also called **slicing** the data cube, because it appears as if the user

FIGURE 15.3(a)
**Rollup of Sales
on Department**

	June	July	Aug	Sept	Oct
Store1	459	351	340	345	360
Store2	336	340	334	330	370
Store3	636	650	645	599	700

FIGURE 15.3(b)
**Drill-Down of Sales on
Department Showing
Month of June**

Pharmacy		Store 1	Store 2	Store 3
	Vitamins	25	85	53
	Skin care	20	25	75
	Hair care	50	40	25
	Stomach remedies	15	20	50
	Cold remedies	5	8	25
	First aid	5	7	25
Grocery				
	Canned goods	20	20	50
	Baked goods	40	20	50
	Paper goods	30	4	30
	Cleaning supplies	25	1	10
	Detergents	5	1	5
	Housewares	11	1	5
Produce				
	Vegetables	40	30	100
	Fruits	48	29	60
Dairy				
	Milk	90	40	65
	Butter	10	2	4
	Cheese	5	1	1
	Yogurt	5	1	1
	Ice cream	10	1	2

FIGURE 15.3(c)
**Cross-Tabulation of Sales
by Store and Month**

	June	July	Aug	Sept	Oct	Total
Store1	459	351	340	345	360	**1855**
Store2	336	340	334	330	370	**1710**
Store3	636	650	645	599	570	**3100**
Total	**1431**	**1341**	**1319**	**1274**	**1300**	*6665*

has cut through the cube in the selected direction(s). For example, for the data cube shown in Figure 15.2(a), if we specify the condition WHERE month = 'July', we would get the spreadsheet for that month, taking a slice of the cube. For the rotated cube in Figure 15.2(b), if we write WHERE department = 'grocery' we get a similar slice of the cube. An additional operation, called **dicing,** is performed if we specify a range of values in a selection. For example, if we sliced the data cube in Figure 15.2(a) by specifying the month of July, we can dice further by specifying WHERE store = 'store2' OR store ='store 3'.

There is no reason to limit the data in a data cube to two or three dimensions. Designers can store date using as many dimensions as they wish, if those dimensions are of interest to them. However, beyond the third dimension, we cannot draw a physical representation of the data cubes. The cubes of these higher dimensions are referred to as **hypercubes.** It is still possible to apply the processes of pivoting, rollup, and drilling down to hypercubes.

Early data warehouses stored data using multidimensional arrays, creating **multidimensional OLAP (MOLAP)** systems. If a relational model is used instead, we describe the system as a **relational OLAP (ROLAP)** system. A ROLAP warehouse consists of multiple relational tables.

A widely used schema for data warehouses is a **star schema.** There is a central table of raw data, called the **fact table,** that stores unaggregated, observed data. The fact table has some attributes that represent dimensions and other, dependent attributes that are of interest. Each dimension is represented by its own table, and the **dimension tables** can be thought of as the points of a star whose center is the fact table. For example, in Figure 15.4(a) the fact table, ORDER, is shown in the center. Each tuple of the fact table provides information about one order, which involves the sale of one product to one customer on a particular day. For each order, the fact table records the orderNumber, productNumber, customerId, salespersonId, date, unitPrice, and numberOrdered. There are dimension tables for the product, customer, salesperson, and date. Each of these could be used as a dimension in a hypercube, allowing us to ask queries about the sales of a particular product, the sales to a particular customer, the sales made by a specific salesperson, or the sales made on a specific date. The dimension tables—Product, Customer, Salesperson, and Date—are shown relating to their corresponding dimension attributes of the fact table. Normally those attributes are foreign keys in the fact

FIGURE 15.4(a)

A Star Schema

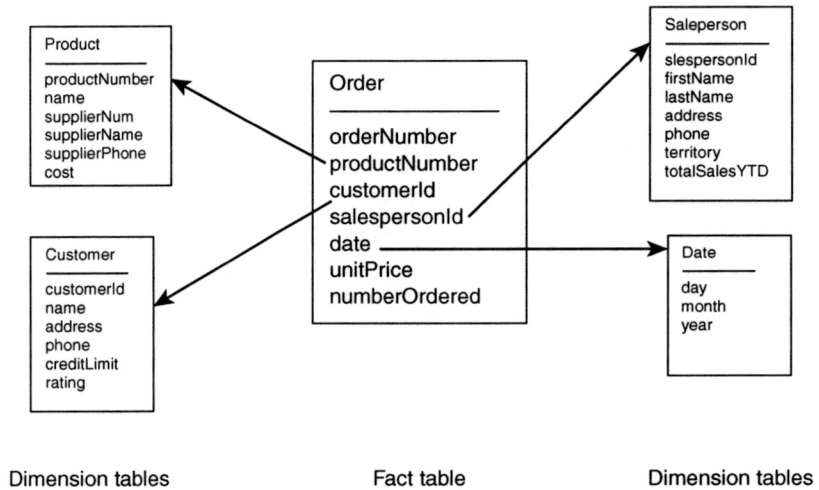

| Dimension tables | Fact table | Dimension tables |

FIGURE 15.4(b)

A Snowflake Schema

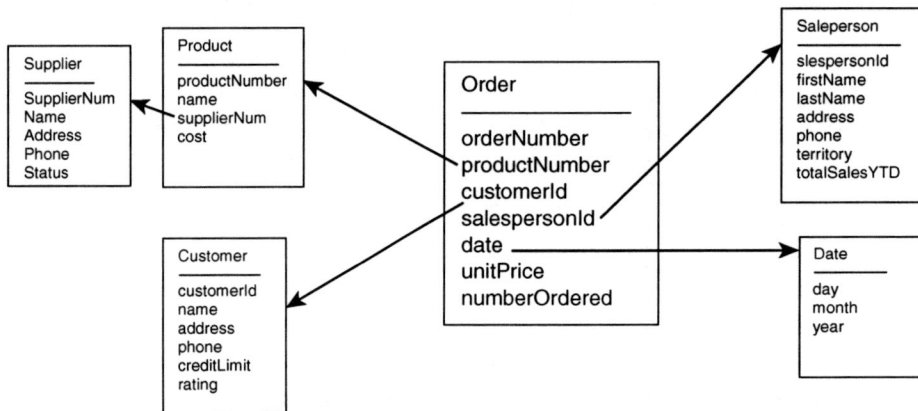

table. The dimension tables provide additional information about each dimension. For example, the `Salesperson` dimension table provides more details about the salesperson who took the order. The remaining attributes of the fact table, `orderNumber`, `unitPrice`, and `numberOrdered`, are dependent attributes. A variation of the star schema is the **snowflake schema,** in which the dimension tables themselves have dimensions, because they are normalized. For example, in Figure 15.4(b) we show the `Product` dimension having a `Supplier` dimension table. We removed from the `Product` table all the supplier attributes except supplierNum, as those attributes are functionally dependent on supplierNum, and placed them in a separate Supplier table. If any of the other dimension tables were not normalized, we would have done the same for them, creating a snowflake with the fact table as the center.

15.5 Data Warehouse Queries and SQL:1999 OLAP Extension

The aggregate functions of SUM, COUNT, MAX, MIN, and AVG are part of the SQL92 standard. These functions can be used in some limited slicing and dicing queries for a data warehouse. The general form of such a query is:

```
SELECT <grouping attributes> <aggregation fuction>
FROM <fact table>, <dimension table(s)>
WHERE <attribute = constant> . . . <attribute = constant>
GROUP BY <grouping attributes>;
```

For example, for the fact table Order shown in Figure 15.4(a) with schema,

```
Order (orderNumber, productNumber, customerId, salespersonId, date, unitPrice,
numberOrdered)
```

and the dimension table Product with schema,

```
Product (productNumber, name, supplierNum, supplierName, supplierPhone, cost)
```

we could write,

```
SELECT productNumber, SUM(numberOrdered)
FROM Order O, Product P
WHERE O.productNumber = P.productNumber AND
        P.supplierNum = 'S101'
GROUP BY P.productNumber;
```

which gives us a list of the products supplied by S101 and the total number of each. Note that we sliced on Product and diced on supplierNum for this query.

Typical queries for data warehouses require additional aggregate functions. SQL:1999 includes the functions **stddev** (standard deviation), and **variance** for single attributes. These are standard statistical measures that indicate how "spread out" a set of data values are from the mean. For example, a high standard deviation for total monthly sales in the dairy department would mean that the amount of sales fluctuates widely from month to month, while a low standard deviation would indicate that sales remain fairly constant throughout the period. Additional statistical functions are **correlation** and **regression,** which apply to pairs of attributes.

SQL:1999 also has functions to calculate **rank** for data values. For example, if the `Salesperson` table has schema,

```
Salesperson(salespersonId, firstName, lastName, address, phone, territory,
totalSalesYTD)
```

we might want to be able to find the rank of salespeople according to their `totalSalesYTD`. The command,

```
SELECT salespersonId, rank( ) over(order by (totalSalesYTD) desc)
FROM Salesperson
WHERE lastName = 'Jackson';
```

will display the `salespersonId` and the `rank` of salesperson Jackson. If two people have the same sales amount, they are given the same rank, but the next rank value is skipped. For example, if two salespeople are tied for the highest sales, they are both ranked number 1, but the next person is ranked number 3. If we do not wish to skip numbers, we can use the dense_rank( ) option in place of the rank( ) option. Note that the "order by" phrase in the SELECT line simply tells what attribute to use for the ranking. It does not display the tuples in the order of the ranking. If we wish to have the results for all salespeople displayed with the highest ranking first rather than the order of existing tuples, we must add an ORDER BY line, as in:

```
SELECT salespersonId, rank( ) over(order by (totalSalesYTD) desc) as salesRank
FROM Salesperson
ORDER BY salesRank;
```

The GROUP BY clause has also been extended in SQL:1999 with special **CUBE** and **ROLLUP** options for data cubes. For example, if we have a fact table `Sales` with schema,

```
Sales(storeNumber, departmentName, month, amount)
```

and dimension tables for store, department, and month for the supermarket data represented by the data cube in Figure 15.2, the query,

```
SELECT departmentName, storeNumber, month, sum(amount)
FROM Sales
GROUP BY CUBE(departmentName, storeNumber, month);
```

produces all eight possible GROUP BY combinations for the three attributes department, store, and month. The grouping will be done by department alone, by store alone, by month alone, by the combination of store and month, the combination of store and department, the combination of month and department, the combination of all three, and of none. In contrast to the cube, which gives grouping on all possible combinations of attributes named, the ROLLUP option allows users to specify what attributes are to be used for aggregation. If we write,

```
SELECT departmentName, storeNumber, month, sum(amount)
FROM Sales
GROUP BY ROLLUP(departmentName, storeNumber);
```

we aggregate on all pairs of departmentName and storeNumber values, and also on departmentName alone, but not on storeNumber alone.

15.6   Index Techniques

The amount of data in a warehouse can be so large that efficient indexes are important so that queries can be executed in a reasonable amount of time. Since the data in a data warehouse is not updated by ordinary transactions, it is relatively static. Therefore once indexes are created for the data, the cost of maintaining them is not a factor. Special indexing techniques, including bitmap indexing and join indexing, that are efficient for a large amount of static data are applied to the data warehouse environment.

Bitmap indexes can be constructed for any attributes that have a limited number of distinct possible values. They are especially appropriate if the domain is small. For each value in the domain, a bit vector is constructed to represent that value, by placing a 1 in the position for that value. For example, Figure 15.5 shows the Faculty table with a bitmap index for rank and another one for department. Because the first Faculty record has a rank of Professor, the first row of the rank index has a 1 in the Professor column. Because the department of the first Faculty record is Art, there is a 1 in the Art column of the first row department index. Bitmap indexes take much less space than standard indexes, and they allow efficient processing of some queries directly from the index. For example, for the SQL query,

```
SELECT COUNT(*)
FROM Faculty
WHERE rank = 'Professor' AND department = 'Art';
```

the two indexes can be compared by constructing a new bit vector by using a bitwise AND, comparing the fourth bit of the rank vector with the first bit of the department vector. The number of 1s in the new bit vector

FIGURE 15.5(a)

The Faculty Table

facId	name	department	rank
		Faculty	
F101	Adams	Art	Professor
F105	Tanaka	CSC	Instructor
F110	Byrne	Math	Assistant
F115	Smith	History	Associate
F221	Smith	CSC	Professor

FIGURE 15.5(b)

A Bitmap Index for Rank

Instructor	Assistant	Associate	Professor
0	0	0	1
1	0	0	0
0	1	0	0
0	0	1	0
0	0	0	1

FIGURE 15.5(c)

A Bitmap Index for Department

Art	CSC	History	Math
1	0	0	0
0	1	0	0
0	0	0	1
0	0	1	0
0	1	0	0

is the number of Professors in the Art department. Similar procedures can be used to speed up other operations, including the join.

Because the join is difficult when tables are large, data warehouses can use join indexes to speed up join queries. Most join operations are done on foreign keys. In a data warehouse using a star schema, the join operation often involves comparing the fact table with dimension tables. A **join index** relates the values of a dimension table to the rows of the fact table. For each value of the indexed attribute in the dimension table, the index stores the tuple IDs of all the tuples in the fact table having that value.

15.7 Views and View Materialization

Views play an important role in data warehouses, as they do in operational databases, in customizing the user's environment. SQL operators, including the OLAP extension operators of CUBE and ROLLUP, can be performed on views as well as on base tables. The SQL CREATE VIEW command simply defines the view, and does not create any new tables. When a query is written on a view, one way it can be executed is through **query modification,** which replaces the reference in the WHERE line by the view definition. For example, we can have a view, `BestSalespeople` defined by,

```
CREATE VIEW BestSalespeople
AS SELECT S.salespersonId, S.lastName, S.firstName, S.phone, S.salesYTD
FROM Salesperson S
WHERE S.salesYTD > (SELECT AVG(salesYTD)
                    FROM Salesperson);
```

If we write a query using the view such as,

```
SELECT SUM (B.salesYTD)
FROM BestSalespeople B;
```

then if query modification is used, the reference in the FROM line is replaced by the view definition, resulting in:

```
SELECT SUM (B.salesYTD)
FROM (SELECT S.salespersonId, S.lastName, S.firstName, S.phone, S.salesYTD
   FROM Salesperson S
   WHERE S.salesYTD > (SELECT AVG(salesYTD)
                       FROM Salesperson) )AS B;
```

In a data warehouse environment, where queries and views are very complex and where analysts use the system in an interactive environment, query modification might result in unacceptable delays in response time. Therefore, an alternative method of handling views is to **materialize** them, pre-computing them from the definition and storing them for later use. To further speed up processing, indexes can be created for the materialized views.

The data warehouse designer must consider which views should be materialized, weighing the storage constraints against the possible benefits of speeding up the most important queries. The designer must also decide on a maintenance policy for materialized views. When the underlying base tables change, the view should also be updated. This can be done as part of the update transaction for the base tables, a policy called **immediate view maintenance,** which slows down the refresh transaction for the data warehouse. An alternative is to use **deferred view maintenance.** Several policies are possible, including:

- **Lazy refresh,** which updates the view when a query using the view is executed and the current materialized version is obsolete

- **Periodic refresh,** which updates the view at regular intervals of time

- **Forced refresh,** which updates the view after a specified number of updates have been made to the underlying base tables

The refresh process can be done by re-computing the entire materialized view. However, for complex views, especially those with joins or aggregations, this can be too expensive. Instead, the refreshing can be done incrementally, incorporating only the changes made to the underlying tables.

15.8   Data Mining

Data mining means discovering new information from very large data sets. Usually, the knowledge discovered is in the form of patterns or rules. In addition to database technology, data mining uses techniques from the fields of statistics and artificial intelligence, especially machine learning. Because it involves large amounts of data, it is necessary to have a large database or a data warehouse. Data mining can be used with an operational database, provided it is large enough. We previously described data mining as one of the primary applications for a data warehouse, along with OLAP and decision support systems. A data warehouse that is used as a source for data mining should include summarized data as well as raw data taken from original data sources such as operational databases. Since the types of operations used in data mining differ from the analytic ones for OLAP and decision support systems, the data mining application should be considered in the original design of the warehouse. Data mining generally requires knowledge of the domain (e.g., the environment of the business being studied) as well as knowledge of the data mining process. The data format required most often is a "flat file" in which all the data for each case of observed values appears as a single record, rather than relational or object-oriented. If data is not represented as individual cases, or if joins are needed in order to place all data for a case together, considerable effort must be expended in preparing the data and reformatting it. Therefore, the warehouse design should be created with data mining in mind.

15.9   Purpose of Data Mining

For most businesses, the ultimate purpose of data mining is to provide knowledge that will give the company a competitive advantage, enabling it to earn a greater profit. Companies use data mining in the hope that they will be able to accomplish the following:

- Predict the future behavior of attributes. For example, by studying the data from the three supermarkets in the earlier example, we are probably able to predict sales figures for the same period next year. If we have a public health database that contains data about the spread of influenza for the past five winters, we are probably able to predict the number of such infections for the coming winter.

- Classify items by placing them in the correct categories. For example, given data about the credit worthiness of customers in the past, we can classify a new customer as credit worthy or not credit worthy. Classification is also used in medicine, to determine which of several possible diagnoses is the appropriate one for a patient, based on past data about other patients and symptoms.

- Identify the existence of an activity or an event. For example, if we know the typical patterns of stock sales that were present in previous cases of insider trading, and we see the same pattern occurring again, we might be able to identify a current case of insider trading. Insurance companies study patterns and characteristics of prior claims known to be fraudulent to determine which new claims might be fraudulent.

- Optimize the use of the organization's resources. Data mining can model scenarios to help determine the best placement of equipment, the most lucrative way to invest money or the most efficient way to use available time in order to maximize productivity or reach some other goal.

15.10 Types of Knowledge Discovered

In expert systems, knowledge is obtained by the use of logical deduction. An expert system's inference engine is used to apply the laws of logic to facts stored in a database to deduce new facts in a mechanical fashion. Data mining uses **induction** rather than deduction. It examines a large number of cases and concludes that a pattern or a rule exists. The knowledge can be represented in a variety of ways, including as rules, decision trees, neural networks, or frames.

Outputs can include:

- **Association rules,** which have the form {x} $\Rightarrow$ {y}, where x and y are events that occur at the same time. A typical example involves pairs of products that customers often purchase together, using market basket data, which shows what items were purchased for a transaction. For example, if a customer buys bread, he or she is likely to buy butter at the same time. The rule can be expressed as an implication:

    {bread} $\Rightarrow$ {butter}

    Note that both the left-hand side (bread in this example) and the right-hand side (here, butter) can be sets of items rather than individual items. Two important measures connected with association rules are **support** and **confidence.** For a set of items, the support is the percentage of transactions in the data set that contain all these items included in both left- and right-hand sides. Note that the transaction can include additional items that are not part of the association. For example, if we have one million sales records, and 100,000 of them include both bread and butter, the support for the rule bread $\Rightarrow$ butter is 10%. Confidence is a measure of how often the rule proves to be true; that is, for the cases where the left-hand side of the implication is present, confidence is the percentage of those in which the right-hand side is present as well. For one million sales records, perhaps 500,000 include bread, but only 100,000 of the ones that include bread also include butter, so the confidence in this rule is 20%.

- **Classification rules.** Classification is the problem of placing instances into the correct one of several possible categories. The system is developed by providing a set of past instances for which the correct classification is known, called a **training set.** Using these examples, the system develops a method for correctly classifying a new item whose class is currently unknown. A classical example of a classification rule is the problem of deciding which customers should be granted credit, based on factors such as income, home ownership, and such.

- **Sequential patterns.** A typical application of sequential patterns is the prediction that a customer who buys a particular product in one transaction will follow up with the purchase of a related product in another transaction. For example, a person who buys a printer in a computer supply store will probably buy paper on a subsequent visit. Such patterns are represented as sequences. The sequence {printer}{paper} represents two visits by the same customer in which the sequential pattern is observed, that is, the customer purchased a printer on the first visit and paper on a subsequent visit. The percentage of times such a sequence occurs in the entire set of sales transactions is the support for the pattern. We refer to the first subsequence, {printer}, as a **predictor** of the second subsequence {paper}. The confidence for this prediction is the probability that when {printer} occurs on a visit, {paper} will occur on a subsequent visit. This probability can be calculated by examining the raw data from observed sales transactions. Sequential patterns might involve more than one item in each subsequence, and more than one subsequence. In general terms, if the sequence $S_1, S_2, \ldots S_n$, where each S_i is a set of items, has been found to be valid, then S_1 is a predictor of S_2 through S_n.

- **Time series patterns.** A **time series** is a sequence of events that are all the same type. For example, if the sales total for a supermarket is calculated and recorded at the end of each month over a long period of time, these measures constitute a time series. Time series data can be studied to discover patterns and sequences. For example, we can look at the data and find the longest period when the sales figures continue to rise each month, or find the steepest decline from one month to the next. Stock prices, interest rates, inflation rates, and many other quantities can be analyzed using time series.

15.11 Methods Used

15.11.1 Decision Trees

One method of developing classification rules is to develop a **decision tree,** an example of which is shown in Figure 15.6. This tree is used to make decisions about whether to accept a student at a university, based on a prediction of whether the student will be a poor, average, good, or excellent student. It considers the student's high school average and total SAT score. If the average is below 70% and the SAT is below 1000, the prediction is that the applicant will be a poor student in college. At the other extreme, if the average is above 90 and the SAT is above 1400, the system predicts that the student will be excellent. The tree would be constructed initially by examining the records of past students, considering their entering characteristics of HSAver and SAT. These attributes are called **partitioning attributes,** because they allow the set of training instances to be broken up or partitioned into disjoint classes. The **partitioning conditions** are shown on the branches. Note that the conditions do not have to be identical for all branches. For example, if the high school average is above 90, we consider only SAT scores of above or below 1400, and do not use the value 1000, as we did for the other branches.

FIGURE 15.6

A Decision Tree

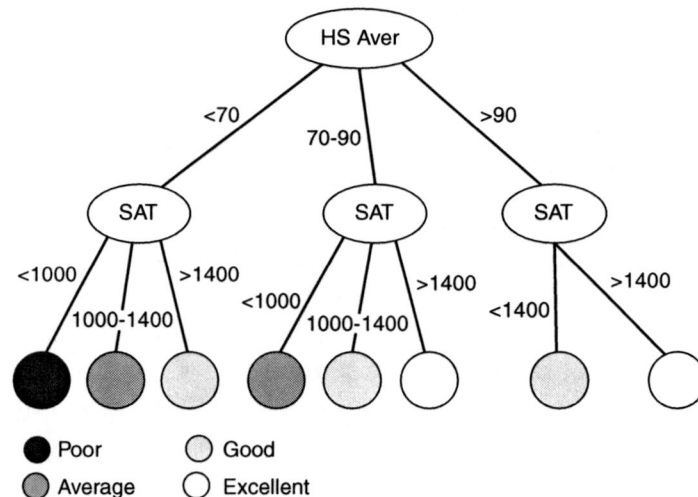

15.11.2 Regression

Regression is a statistical method for predicting the value of an attribute, Y, (called the dependent variable), given the values of attributes X_1, X_2, . . ., X_n (called the independent variables). An example is using student's SAT scores and high school average as independent variables to predict his or her cumulative grade-point average at the end of four years of college, which is the dependent variable. Many statistical software packages allow users to identify the potential factors that are useful for predicting the value of the dependent variable. Using **linear regression,** the package then finds the contribution or weight of each independent variable for the prediction, in the form of the coefficients, a_0, a_1, . . ., a_n for a linear function having the form:

$$Y = a_0 + a_1 X_1 + a_2 X_2 + . . . + a_n X_n$$

The formula derived represents a curve that fits the observed values as closely as possible.

In data mining, the system itself can be asked to identify the independent variables, as well as to find the regression function. Data mining systems can also use non-linear regression, using a curve-fitting approach, finding the equation of the curve that fits the observed values as closely as possible. They can also deal with non-numerical data.

15.11.3 Neural Networks

This technique includes a variety of methods using a set of samples for all variables to find the strongest relationships between variables and observations. The methods originated in the field of artificial intelligence. They use a generalized form of regression, using a curve-fitting technique to find a function from the set of samples. Neural networks use a learning method, adapting as they learn new information by examining additional samples. Figure 15.7 shows a very simple model of a neural network that represents purchases from websites. The aim of the system is to predict which potential customers will order from specific websites. Several input variables involving age, education, and income are used in the prediction. The sample shows that high school graduates over age 21 with income greater than 50,000 are most likely to order from a camera equipment

FIGURE 15.7

Simple Model of a Neural Network

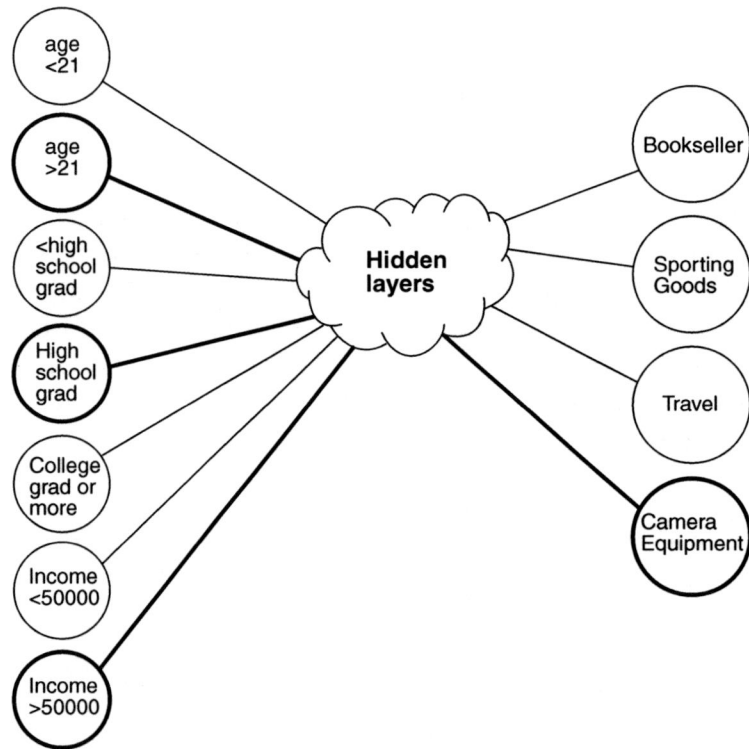

website. In the learning stage, the network is provided with a training set of cases that provide facts about these input values for a sample of customers, and also the websites that the customers ordered from. The hidden layers are developed by the system as it examines these cases, using generalized regression techniques. As additional cases are provided, the system refines its hidden layers until it has learned to predict correctly a certain percentage of the time. Then test cases are provided to evaluate the system. If it performs well on the test cases, the system can be used on new data where the outcome is unknown.

Neural networks have several drawbacks that make them difficult to work with. A major problem is **overfitting** the curve. The training set data, like any real raw data, always has a certain amount of "noise," inconsistencies or variations that are not actually significant and that should be ignored. Instead, the network can accommodate its prediction function to account for these values, producing a curve that fits the training set data perfectly. The prediction function will then perform poorly on new data. A second problem is that the knowledge of how the system makes its predictions is

Clustering

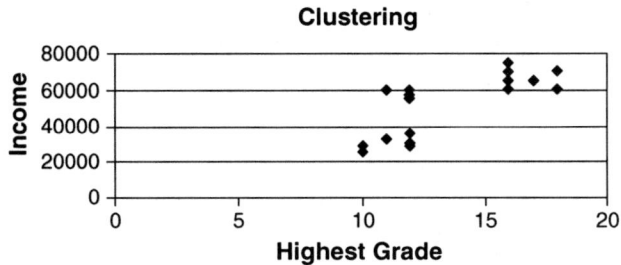

FIGURE 15.8

Clustering

in the hidden layers, so users do not have a good view of the reasoning used. Unlike the regression model, where the co-efficients show the contribution of each attribute, the weights assigned to the factors in the model cannot be interpreted in a natural way by users. Although the model might work well, the output can be difficult to understand and interpret.

15.11.4 Clustering

Clustering or segmentation refers to methods used to place tuples into clusters or groups that can be disjoint or overlapping. Using a training set of data, the system identifies a finite set of clusters into which the tuples of the database can be grouped. The tuples in each cluster are similar, sharing some properties, and they are dissimilar to the tuples in other clusters. Similarity is measured by using some type of **distance function** that is defined for the data. For example, if age is an attribute, the difference in people's ages could be used as the distance function. In some problems, the categories can be organized hierarchically. Figure 15.8 shows an example in which people are clustered by education and income levels. It shows the highest grade completed by each person on the x-axis and the annual income of each on the y-axis. From the data, it appears that there are three clusters. There are people with lower education level who have low income, people with low education level with moderately high income, and people with high education level with high income.

15.12 Applications of Data Mining

Data mining has been used in a wide variety of applications. Among the most successful are the following:

- **Retailing**
  - **Customer relations management (CRM)** is an emerging application of data mining. CRM allows a retailer to provide a

personalized shopping experience to customers in order to build customer loyalty. Data mining is used to identify and anticipate customer needs, so that the retailer will have the items they request and will be able to suggest related items that the customer will buy. For example, Internet booksellers often analyze the customer's stated preferences and previous purchase history to suggest new purchases, or to suggest purchases related to the current one.

- **Advertising campaign management** uses data mining to identify the customers who will be most likely to make purchases in response to advertising. For mail-order firms, it is used to identify the households that will respond positively to catalogs. Data can come from responses to previous direct mail items or to test items. Data mining identifies the factors that are associated with a positive response to build a model. That model, which includes demographic and geographic data, is used to identify the people most likely to respond positively to new campaigns, based on their demographic and other attributes.

- **Banking and Finance**

  - **Credit scoring.** Retailers, banks, and others who extend credit to customers can use a variety of data mining techniques to build a model to determine whether to extend credit to new applicants.

  - **Fraud detection and prevention.** Data mining has been used successfully to detect fraudulent credit card transactions, either after the fact or in real-time, to deny the potential transaction. Insurance companies have also used data mining to determine whether claims are fraudulent. Stock trades are routinely investigated to identify possible cases of insider trading or other illegal activity. The telecommunications industry also uses data mining to detect fraudulent use of telephone systems.

- **Manufacturing**

  - **Optimizing use of resources.** Data mining models can be used to determine the best deployment of equipment, human resources, and materials.

  - **Manufacturing process optimization.** The manufacturing process itself can be analyzed to determine the most cost-effective and/or efficient way to produce products.

- **Product design.** By examining data about product defects and repairs, manufacturers can eliminate parts that are likely to be defective, improving the design. Results of market research can also be used to design products that consumers would prefer.

- **Medicine**

  - **Determining effectiveness of treatments.** Patients, health-care providers, and health insurers all benefit from being able to determine which courses of treatment are most effective. Data mining not only provides the basis for sound statistical results of studies of various treatments, but it can reveal hidden factors that influence the treatment outcome.

  - **Analyzing effects of drugs.** Both before and after new drugs come to market, a vast amount of data must be collected and provided about the drugs effects. Large scale drug studies, involving huge amounts of data, play a vital role in the health-care industry.

  - **Finding relationships.** Patterns among patient care and the outcome of treatments can be determined. In addition to the obvious relationships between course of treatment or drugs and patient outcomes, hidden relationships among other factors, such as the setting where care is provided, and outcomes can be discovered using data mining.

15.13 Chapter Summary

Data warehouses store massive amounts of data taken from the operational databases used by an enterprise, as well as from other data sources. They are used for **decision support systems (DSS), online analytical processing (OLAP),** and **data mining.** Data is taken from data sources using back-end system tools. The extracted data is reformatted, cleaned, put into the proper model, and loaded into the warehouse. **Data marts** containing specialized data can also be created. Warehouses often use a **multidimensional model.** Data can be represented using multidimensional **data cubes,** which can be **pivoted** or rotated to display a different dimension. If the dimension is more than three, we use the term **hypercube. Rollup** is a process of aggregating data along dimensions, while its inverse, **drill-down,** is a process of providing more detail for some dimension. A **cross-tabulation** is a spreadsheet-like display with totals added to the data.

Slicing a data cube is equivalent to performing a selection with equality condition for one or more dimensions, while **dicing** is equivalent to a range selection.

Early multidimensional OLAP systems stored data as multidimensional arrays, called **MOLAP** systems. Relational OLAP, called **ROLAP** systems, use multiple relational tables. A **star schema** uses a central table of data values called the **fact table,** with attributes that represent dimensions. Each dimension has its own **dimension table** that is connected to the fact table. In a variation called a **snowflake schema,** the dimension tables themselves have dimension tables because they are normalized.

Queries for a data warehouse can use the standard aggregate functions from SQL, usually with GROUP BY options. SQL:1999 provides additional functions for the statistical measures of **standard deviation, variance, correlation,** and **regression.** There is also a **rank** function that returns the rank of a tuple with respect to some attribute. The GROUP BY clause can include the option **GROUP BY CUBE** and **GROUP BY ROLLUP** for data cubes.

Special index techniques can be used in a data warehouse environment to speed up queries. **Bitmap indexes** are useful if the domain of values for an attribute is small. A bit vector is constructed for each tuple, showing which of the values the tuple has by placing a 1 in the appropriate position of the vector. It is possible to answer some queries directly from the index, without accessing the data records. A **join index** is constructed by storing, for each value of the indexed attribute in a dimension table, the tuple Ids of all tuples in the fact table having that value for the attribute.

For the sake of efficiency, views are often created by **view materialization,** pre-computing them and storing them for future use. Indexes can also be created for materialized views. A view maintenance policy is needed for materialized views. It can be immediate or deferred. If deferred, the refresh policy can be lazy, periodic, or forced.

Data mining means discovering new information from very large data sets. The purpose is to gain a competitive advantage by being able to predict behavior, classify items, identify an activity or event, or optimize the use of resources. Knowledge discovered can be **association rules,** which have measures of support and confidence. Knowledge can also be expressed as **classification rules,** sequential patterns, or **time series patterns.** The data set that is used to teach the system is called the **training set.** Data mining methods include **decision trees, regression, neural net-**

works, and **clustering.** Application areas include retailing, banking and finance, manufacturing, and medicine.

Exercises

15.1 Define the following terms:

a. data warehouse

b. decision support system

c. OLAP

d. OLTP

e. data mining

f. data mart

g. data cleaning

h. data cube

i. rollup

j. drill-down

k. pivoting

l. slice and dice

m. bitmap index

n. join index

o. view materialization

p. star schema

q. regression

r. neural network

s. clustering

t. decision tree

u. association rule support and confidence

v. training set

w. time series

x. overfitting

y. customer relations management

15.2 Let the following relations represent a fact table, Orders, and associated dimension tables Customers, Salespeople, and Products.

Orders			
CustId	**prodId**	**salesPersonId**	**Quantity**
101	1	10	20
101	2	11	8
101	3	10	15
102	1	11	10
102	2	10	12
102	3	10	15
103	1	11	9
103	2	10	40
103	3	10	12

Customers		
custId	**name**	**creditRating**
101	Adams	10
102	Burke	12
103	Collins	15

Products		
prodId	**name**	**Price**
1	Widget	3
2	Bolt	1
3	Drill	10

Salespeople		
salesPersonId	**lastName**	**firstName**
10	Yates	Tom
11	Zorn	Steve

a. Draw a star schema for this data.

b. Draw a data cube similar to the one shown in Figure 15.2, showing the quantity of orders placed by customers for products through salesperson 10 as the visible face. Let customer be the x axis and product be the y axis on this face. Salespeople should be the z-axis for the third dimension. If no order has been placed by a customer for a product through salesperson 10, place a 0 in the cell.

c. Pivot the cube to show orders placed by customers and salesperson, with product as the third dimension. The visible face should be for product 1.

d. Pivot the cube to show orders placed by salesperson and product. The visible face should be for customer 101. Add totals to make this a cross tabulation.

15.3   a. For the data cube for Exercise 15.2(b) show the rollup on salesperson.

b. Assume there are two types of widgets, bolts, and drills—small and large. Show a drill-down on product for the data cube in Exercise 15.2(b).

c. For the data cube for Exercise 15.2(b) show the slice that corresponds to the selection WHERE salesPersonId = 2.

d. For the slice in Exercise 15.3(c) dice for the range prodId < 2.

15.4   a. For the data in the Orders table in Exercise 15.2, write out bitmap indexes on custId, prodId, and salesPersonId.

b. Devise a query that can be answered by using the indexes alone.

c. Write out join indexes for customers, products, and salespeople.

15.5 The following transactions were observed at a supermarket.

TransNo	CustId	Date	Time	Market Basket
1	10	Jun 06	10:00	{bread, milk, juice}
2	11	Jun 06	10:10	{coffee, milk}
3	12	Jun 06	10:20	{bread, butter, milk}
4	13	Jun 06	10:25	{bread, eggs}
5	14	Jun 06	10:30	{milk, juice}
6	10	Jun 07	10:00	{butter, meat}
7	11	Jun 07	10:05	{paper towels, juice}
8	13	Jun 07	10:30	{butter, paper towels}
9	14	Jun 07	10:45	{milk, bread}

a. What is the support for the association rule bread $\Rightarrow$ milk? What is the confidence for this rule?

b. What is the support for the sequential pattern {bread}{butter}? What is the confidence for this pattern?

c. Can you find any other associations or sequential patterns of interest in this data? If so, give the support and confidence for them.

d. Add some items or transactions that will yield a new association rule with both support and confidence of at least 50%.

e. Add some transactions that will yield a new sequential pattern with both support and confidence of at least 50%.

Bibliography

Abiteboul, S., R. Hull, and V. Vianu. *Foundations of Databases.* Addison-Wesley, 1995.

Abiteboul, S. and P. Kanellakis. "Object Identity as a Query Language Primitive," SIGMOD Conference, 1989: 159–173.

ACM/IEEE-CS Joint Task Force on Software Engineering Ethics and Professional Practices. *Software Engineering Code of Ethics and Professional Practice.* ACM,1999.

Agrawal, R., T. Imielinski, and A. Swami. "Mining Association Rules between Sets of Items in Large Databases," SIGMOD Conference, 1993: 207–216.

Agrawal, R. and R. Srikant. "Fast Algorithms for Mining Association Rules in Large Databases," VLDB Conference, 1994: 487–499.

Aho, A., C. Beeri, and J. Ullman. "The Theory of Joins in Relational Databases," ACM Transactions on Database Systems 4(3): 297–314 (1979).

Aho, A. and J. Ullman. "The Universality of Data Retrieval Languages," POPL Conference, 1979: 110–120.

Albano, A., L. Cardelli, and R. Orsini. "Galileo: A Strongly-Typed, Interactive Conceptual Language," ACM Transactions on Database Systems 10(2): 230–260 (1985).

Association for Computing Machinery. *ACM Code of Ethics and Professional Conduct.* ACM, 1992.

Armstrong, W. "Dependency Structures of Data Base Relationships," IFIP Congress, 1974: 580–583.

Atzeni, P. and V. De Antonellis. *Relational Database Theory.* Benjamin/Cummings, 1993.

Bancilhon, F. and R. Ramakrishnan. "An Amateur's Introduction to Recursive Query Processing Strategies," SIGMOD Conference, 1986: 16–52.

Bancilhon, F., D. Maier, Y. Sagiv, and J. Ullman. "Magic Sets and Other Strange Ways to Implement Logic Programs," Symposium on Principles of Data Systems, 1986: 1–16.

Banerjee, J., H. Chou, J. Garza, W. Kim, D. Woelk, N. Ballou, and H. Kim. "Data Model Issues for Object-Oriented Applications," ACM Transactions on Information Systems 5(1): 3–26 (1987).

Banerjee, J., W. Kim, H. Kim, and H. Korth. "Semantics and Implementation of Schema Evolution in Object-Oriented Databases," SIGMOD Conference, 1987: 311–322.

Batini, C., S. Ceri, and S. Navathe. *Conceptual Database Design: An Entity-Relationship Approach.* Benjamin/Cummings, 1992.

Batini, C., M. Lenzerini, and S. Navathe. "A Comparative Analysis of Methodologies for Database Schema Integration," ACM Computing Surveys 18(4): 323–364 (1986).

Bayer, R. and E. McCreight. "Organization and Maintenance of Large Ordered Indices," Acta Informatica 1(3): 173–189 (1972).

Beeri, C. and R. Ramakrishnan. "On the Power of Magic," Symposium on Principles of Data Systems, 1987: 269–283.

Berners-Lee, T., R. Caillian, A. Lautonen, H. Nielsen, and A. Secret. "The World Wide Web," Communications of the ACM 13(2): August, 1994.

Bernstein, P. "Synthesizing Third Normal Form Relations from Functional Dependencies," ACM Transactions on Database Systems 1(4): 277–298 (1976).

Bernstein, P. and N. Goodman. "Concurrency Control in Distributed Database Systems," ACM Computing Surveys 13(2): 185–221 (1981).

Bernstein, P., V. Hadzilacos, and N. Goodman. *Concurrency Control and Recovery in Database Systems.* Addison-Wesley, 1987.

Bischoff, J., and T. Alexander (eds.). *Data Warehouse: Practical Advice from the Experts.* Prentice-Hall, 1997.

Blackstone, W. *Commentaries on the Laws of England.* Clarendon Press, 1765-1769.

Carey, M., D. DeWitt, and S. Vandenberg. "A Data Model and Query Language for EXODUS," SIGMOD Conference, 1988: 413–423.

Cattell, R., *The Object Database Standard: ODMG-93.* Morgan Kaufmann, 1993.

Ceri, S. and G. Pelagatti. *Distributed Databases: Principles and Systems.* McGraw-Hill Book Company, 1984.

Ceri, S., G. Gottlob, and L. Tanca. *Logic Programming and Databases.* Springer-Verlag, 1990.

Chen, P. "The Entity-Relationship Model—Toward a Unified View of Data," ACM Transactions on Database Systems 1(1): 9–36 (1976).

CODASYL. *CODASYL Data Base Task Group April 71 Report,* ACM, 1971.

Codd, E. "A Relational Model of Data for Large Shared Data Banks," Communications of the ACM 13(6): 377–387 (1970).

Codd, E. "Further Normalization of the Data Base Relational Model," IBM Research Report, San Jose, California RJ909 (1971).

Codd, E. "Relational Completeness of Data Base Sublanguages," IBM Research Report, San Jose, California RJ987 (1972).

Codd, E. "Extending the Database Relational Model to Capture More Meaning," ACM Transactions on Database Systems 4(4): 397–434 (1979).

Codd, E. "Is Your DBMS Really Relational?" *Computerworld.* October 14, 1985.

Codd, E. "Does Your DBMS Run By the Rules?" *Computerworld.* October 21, 1985.

Comer, D. "The Ubiquitous B-Tree," ACM Computing Surveys 11(2): 121–137 (1979).

Das, S. *Deductive Databases and Logic Programming.* Addison-Wesley, 1992.

Date, C. *An Introduction to Database Systems* (8th Ed.). Addison-Wesley, 2004.

DeWitt, D., S. Ghandeharizadeh, D. Schneider, A. Bricker, H. Hsiao, and R. Rasmussen. "The Gamma Database Machine Project," IEEE Transactions on Knowledge and Data Engineering. 2(1): 44–62 (1990).

DeWitt, D., R. Katz, F. Olken, L. Shapiro, M. Stonebraker, and D. Wood. "Implementation Techniques for Main Memory Database Systems," SIGMOD Conference, 1984: 1–8.

Elmasri, R. and S. Navathe. *Fundamentals of Database Systems* (4th ed.). Addison-Wesley, 2004.

Eswaran, K., J. Gray, R. Lorie, and I. Traiger. "The Notions of Consistency and Predicate Locks in a Database System," Communications of the ACM 19(11): 624–633 (1976).

Fagin, R. "Multivalued Dependencies and a New Normal Form for Relational Databases," ACM Transactions on Database Systems 2(3): 262–278 (1977).

Fagin, R., J. Nievergelt, N. Pippenger, and H. Strong. "Extendible Hashing—A Fast Access Method for Dynamic Files," ACM Transactions on Database Systems 4(3): 315–344 (1979).

Fishman, D., D. Beech, H. Cate, E. Chow, T. Connors, J. Davis, N. Derrett, C. Hoch, W. Kent, P. Lyngbæk, B. Mahbod, M. Neimat, T. Ryan, and M. Shan. "Iris: An Object-Oriented Database Management System," ACM Transactions on Information Systems 5(1): 48–69 (1987).

Gallaire, H., J. Minker, and J. Nicolas. "Logic and Databases: A Deductive Approach," ACM Computing Surveys 16(2): 153–185 (1984).

Garcia-Molina, H., J. Ullman, and J. Widom. *Database Systems: The Complete Book.* Prentice Hall, 2002.

Gifford, D. "Weighted Voting for Replicated Data," SOSP Proceedings, 1979: 150–162.

Goldberg, A. and D. Robson. *Smalltalk-80: The Language and Its Implementation.* Addison-Wesley, 1983.

Graefe, G. "Query Evaluation Techniques for Large Databases," ACM Computing Surveys 25(2): 73–170 (1993).

Graefe, G. and D. DeWitt. "The EXODUS Optimizer Generator," SIGMOD Conference, 1987: 160–172.

Gray, J. "Notes on Data Base Operating Systems" in Bayer, R., M. Graham, and G. Seegmuller. (eds.). *Operating Systems: An Advanced Course* Springer-Verlag, 1978: 393–481.

Gray, J., A. Bosworth, A. Layman, and H. Pirahesh. "Data Cube: A Relational Aggregation Operator Generalizing Group-By, Cross-Tab, and Sub-Total," International Conference on Database Engineering, 1996: 152–159.

Gray, J., P. McJones, M. Blasgen, B. Lindsay, R. Lorie, T. Price, G. Putzolu, and I. Traiger. "The Recovery Manager of the System R Database Manager," ACM Computing Surveys 13(2): 223–243 (1981).

Gray, J. and A. Reuter. *Transaction Processing: Concepts and Techniques.* Morgan Kaufmann, 1993.

Guttman, A. "R-Trees: A Dynamic Index Structure for Spatial Searching," SIGMOD Conference, 1984: 47–57.

Halligan, R. and & R. Weyand. "The Sorry State of Trade Secret Protection," *Corporate Counsellor* August 2001.

Hammer, M. and D. McLeod. "Database Description with SDM: A Semantic Database Model," ACM Transactions on Database Systems 6(3): 351–386 (1981).

Haskin, R. and R. Lorie. "On Extending the Functions of a Relational Database System," SIGMOD Conference, 1982: 207–212.

Henschen, L. and S. Naqvi. "On compiling queries in recursive first-order databases," Journal of the ACM 31(1): 47–85 (1984).

House of Commons Committee on Privacy and Related Matters. *Report of the Committee on Privacy and Related Matters, Chairman David Calcutt QC,* (XLVII) Cm. 1102, HMSO, 1990.

Hull, R. and R. King. "Semantic Database Modeling: Survey, Applications, and Research Issues," ACM Computing Surveys 19(3): 201–260 (1987).

Inmon, W. *Building the Data Warehouse* (3rd ed.) John Wiley & Sons, 2002.

International Standards Organization. *Ergonomic requirements for office work with visual display terminals (VDTs)—Part 11: Guidance on usability* ISO9241-1:1997.

Jarke, M. and J. Koch. "Query Optimization in Database Systems," ACM Computing Surveys 16(2): 111–152 (1984).

Johnson, D. *Computer Ethics* (3rd ed.). Prentice Hall, 2001.

Kent, W. *Data and Reality,* North-Holland, 1978.

Kim, W. "On Optimizing an SQL-like Nested Query," ACM Transactions on Database Systems 7(3): 443–469 (1982).

Kizza, J. *Ethical and Social Issues in the Information Age* (2nd ed.). Springer, 2003.

Klug, A. "Equivalence of Relational Algebra and Relational Calculus Query Languages Having Aggregate Functions," Journal of the ACM 29(3): 699–717 (1982).

Knuth, D. *The Art of Computer Programming, Volume III: Sorting and Searching.* Addison-Wesley, 1973.

Lamport, L. "Time, Clocks, and the Ordering of Events in a Distributed System," Communications of the ACM 21(7): 558–565 (1978).

Litwin, W. "Linear Hashing: A New Tool for File and Table Addressing," VLDB Conference, 1980: 212–223.

Loney, K. and G. Koch. *Oracle9i: The Complete Reference.* Oracle Press, 2002.

Loomis, M. *Object Databases: The Essentials.* Addison-Wesley, 1995.

Maier, D. *The Theory of Relational Databases.* Computer Science Press, 1983.

Maier, D., J. Stein, A. Otis, and A. Purdy. "Development of an Object-Oriented DBMS," OOPSLA Conference, 1986: 472–482.

McFarland, Michael. "Intellectual Property, Information and the Common Good," Ethics and Technology Conference 1999: 88-95.

Melton, J. and A. Simon. *Understanding the New SQL: A Complete Guide.* Morgan Kaufmann, 1993.

Mohan, C., D. Haderle, B. Lindsay, H. Pirahesh, and P. Schwarz. "ARIES: A Transaction Recovery Method Supporting Fine-Granularity Locking and Partial Rollbacks Using Write-Ahead Logging," ACM Transactions on Database Systems 17(1): 94–162 (1992).

Moor, J. "Towards a Theory of Privacy for the Information Age," Computers and Society (27)3: 27-32(1997).

Mylopoulos, J., P. Bernstein, and H. Wong. "A Language Facility for Designing Database-Intensive Applications," ACM Transactions on Database Systems 5(2): 185–207 (1980).

Nielsen, J. *Designing Web Usability: The Practice of Simplicity.* New Riders Publishing, 2000.

Nievergelt, J., H. Hinterberger, K. Sevcik. "The Grid File: An Adaptable, Symmetric Multikey File Structure," ACM Transactions on Database Systems 9(1): 38–71 (1984).

O'Neil, P. and E. O'Neil. *Database Principles, Programming, Performance* (2nd ed.). Morgan Kaufmann, 2003.

Organisation for Economic Co-operation and Development. *OECD Guidelines on the Protection of Privacy and Transborder Flows of Personal Data.* OECD, 1981.

Ozsu, M. T., and Valduriez, P. *Principles of Distributed Database Systems* (2nd ed.). Prentice-Hall, 1999.

Papadimitriou, C. "The serializability of concurrent database updates," Journal of the ACM 26(4): 631–653 (1979).

Ramakrishnan, R. and J. Gehrke. *Database Management Systems* (3rd ed.). McGraw-Hill, 2003.

Ricardo, C. *Database Systems: Principles, Design and Implementation.* Macmillan, 1990.

Salzberg, B. *File Structures, An Analytic Approach.* Prentice-Hall, 1988.

Samet, H. *The Design and Analysis of Spatial Data Structures.* Addison-Wesley, 1990.

Schek, H. and M. Scholl. "The relational model with relation-valued attributes," Information Systems 11(2): 137–147 (1986).

Selinger, P., M. Astrahan, D. Chamberlin, R. Lorie, and T. Price. "Access Path Selection in a Relational Database Management System," SIGMOD Conference, 1979: 23–34.

Shapiro, L. "Join Processing in Database Systems with Large Main Memories," ACM Transactions on Database Systems 11(3): 239–264 (1986).

Shasha, D. *Database Tuning—A Principled Approach.* Prentice-Hall, 1992.

Sheth, A. and J. Larson. "Federated Database Systems for Managing Distributed, Heterogeneous, and Autonomous Databases," ACM Computing Surveys 22(3): 183–236 (1990).

Shipman, D. "The Functional Data Model and the Data Language DAPLEX," ACM Transactions on Database Systems 6(1): 140–173 (1981).

Silberschatz, A., H. Korth, and S. Sudarshan. *Database System Concepts* (4th ed.). McGraw-Hill, 2002.

Simon, A. *Strategic Database Technology: Management for the Year 2000.* Morgan Kaufmann, 1995.

Smith, J. and D. Smith. "Database Abstractions: Aggregation and Generalization," ACM Transactions on Database Systems 2(2): 105–133 (1977).

Snodgrass, R. "The Temporal Query Language TQuel," ACM Transactions on Database Systems 12(2): 247–298 (1987).

Spinello,R. *Cyber Ethics: Morality and Law in Cyberspace.* Jones and Bartlett, 2000.

Stonebraker, M. "Implementation of Integrity Constraints and Views by Query Modification," SIGMOD Conference, 1975: 65–78.

Stonebraker, M., Ed. *Readings in Database Systems* (2nd ed.). Morgan Kaufmann, 1994.

Stonebraker, M. and L. Rowe. "The Design of Postgres," SIGMOD Conference, 1986: 340–355.

Stonebraker, M., E. Wong, P. Kreps, and G. Held. "The Design and Implementation of INGRES," ACM Transactions on Database Systems 1(3): 189–222 (1976).

Teorey, T., D. Yang, and J. Fry. "A Logical Design Methodology for Relational Databases Using the Extended Entity-Relationship Model," ACM Computing Surveys 18(2): 197–222 (1986).

Thomas, R. "A Majority Consensus Approach to Concurrency Control for Multiple Copy Databases," ACM Transactions on Database Systems 4(2): 180–209 (1979).

Ullman, J. "Implementation of Logical Query Languages for Databases," ACM Transactions on Database Systems 10(3): 289–321 (1985).

Ullman, J. *Principles of Database and Knowledge-Base Systems, Volume I.* Computer Science Press, 1988.

Ullman, J. *Principles of Database and Knowledge-Base Systems, Volume II.* Computer Science Press, 1989.

United States Congress. *Digital Millennium Copyright Act.* Public Law 105-304 (1998).

United States Copyright Office, Library of Congress. *Copyright Basics (Circular 1).* 2004.

United States Department of Health, Education and Welfare, Secretary's Advisory Committee on Automated Personal Data Systems. *Records, computers, and the Rights of Citizens.* 1973.

United States Patent and Trademark Office. *General Information Concerning Patents.* 2003.

Valduriez, P. "Join Indices," ACM Transactions on Database Systems 12(2): 218–246 (1987).

Warren S. and L. Brandeis. "The right to privacy," *Harvard Law Review* 4:193–220 (1890).

Westin, A. *Privacy and Freedom.* Atheneum, 1967.

Wiederhold, G. *Database Design* (2nd ed.). McGraw Hill, 1983.

Wong, E. and K. Youssefi. "Decomposition—A Strategy for Query Processing," ACM Transactions on Database Systems 1(3): 223–241 (1976).

World Intellectual Property Organization. *WIPO Intellectual Property Handbook: Policy, Law and Use.* WIPO, 2001.

World Trade Organization. *A Summary of the Final Act of the Uruguay Round.* 1994.

World Trade Organization, *Uruguay Round Agreement: TRIPS Part II—Standards concerning the availability, scope and use of Intellectual Property Rights.* 1994

Zaniolo, C. S. Ceri, C. Faloutsos, R. Snodgrass, V. Subrahmanian, and R. Zicari. *Advanced Database Systems.* Morgan Kaufmann, 1997.

Index

(*Note:* Page numbers in *italics* indicate tables and figures.)

Outstanding New Titles:

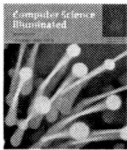

Computer Science Illuminated, Second Edition
Nell Dale and John Lewis
ISBN: 0-7637-0799-6
©2004

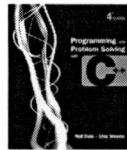

Programming and Problem Solving with Java
Nell Dale, Chip Weems,
and Mark R. Headington
ISBN: 0-7637-0490-3
©2003

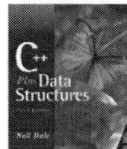

Databases Illuminated
Catherine Ricardo
ISBN: 0-7637-3314-8
©2004

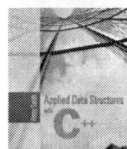

Foundations of Algorithms Using Java Pseudocode
Richard Neapolitan and Kumarss Naimipour
ISBN: 0-7637-2129-8
©2004

Artificial Intelligence Illuminated
Ben Coppin
ISBN: 0-7637-3230-3
©2004

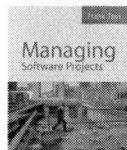

The Essentials of Computer Organization and Architecture
Linda Null and Julia Lobur
ISBN: 0-7637-0444-X
©2003

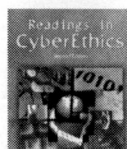

A Complete Guide to C#
David Bishop
ISBN: 0-7637-2249-9
©2004

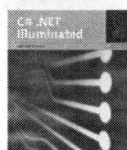

A First Course in Complex Analysis with Applications
Dennis G. Zill and Patrick Shanahan
ISBN: 0-7637-1437-2
©2003

Programming and Problem Solving with C++, Fourth Edition
Nell Dale and Chip Weems
ISBN: 0-7637-0798-8
©2004

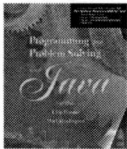

C++ Plus Data Structures, Third Edition
Nell Dale
ISBN: 0-7637-0481-4
©2003

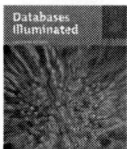

Applied Data Structures with C++
Peter Smith
ISBN: 0-7637-2562-5
©2004

Foundations of Algorithms Using C++ Pseudocode, Third Edition
Richard Neapolitan and Kumarss Naimipour
ISBN: 0-7637-2387-8
©2004

Managing Software Projects
Frank Tsui
ISBN: 0-7637-2546-3
©2004

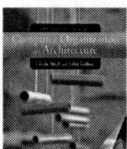

Readings in CyberEthics, Second Edition
Richard Spinello and Herman Tavani
ISBN: 0-7637-2410-6
©2004

C#.NET Illuminated
Art Gittleman
ISBN: 0-7637-2593-5
©2004

Discrete Mathematics, Second Edition
James L. Hein
ISBN: 0-7637-2210-3
©2003

Take Your Courses to the Next Level

Turn the page to preview new and forthcoming titles in Computer Science and Math from Jones and Bartlett…

Providing solutions for students and educators in the following disciplines:

- Introductory Computer Science
- Java
- C++
- Databases
- C#
- Data Structures

- Algorithms
- Network Security
- Software Engineering
- Discrete Mathematics
- Engineering Mathematics
- Complex Analysis

Please visit http://computerscience.jbpub.com/ and http://math.jbpub.com/ to learn more about our exciting publishing programs in these disciplines.

LaVergne, TN USA
09 November 2009
163490LV00003B/64/P